KU-166-562

JOHNSON AT 10

Sir Anthony Seldon is an educator, historian, writer and commentator. He's a govenor of the Royal Shakespeare Company and Chair of the National Archives Trust. A former headmaster and vice chancellor, he is author or editor of over forty books on contemporary history, politics and education, including *The Impossible Office?: The History of the British Prime Minister*, *May at 10: The Verdict* and *The Path of Peace: Walking the Western Front Way*.

Raymond Newell is a contemporary historian and researcher, holding masters' degrees in Political Economy and Data Science from King's College London and the University of Oxford. He has previously collaborated with Anthony Seldon as co-author on *May at 10: The Verdict*, and currently works in Public Affairs and Communications at Hanbury Strategy.

JOHNSON AT 10

THE INSIDE STORY

ANTHONY SELDON
AND RAYMOND NEWELL

Atlantic Books
London

First published in hardback in Great Britain in 2023 by Atlantic Books, an imprint of Atlantic Books Ltd.

10 9 8 7 6 5 4

A CIP catalogue record for this book is available from the British Library.

Hardback ISBN: 978 1 83895 802 2
Trade paperback ISBN: 978 1 80546 095 4
E-book ISBN: 978 1 83895 803 9

Printed and bound by CPI (UK) Ltd, Croydon CR0 4YY

Atlantic Books
An imprint of Atlantic Books Ltd
Ormond House
26–27 Boswell Street
London
WC1N 3JZ

www.atlantic-books.co.uk

To Sarah and Jessie

CONTENTS

Liz Truss's eagerness to succeed Johnson was clear to him from early on

DRAMATIS PERSONAE

Boris Johnson: Mayor of London (2008–16), Foreign Secretary (2016–18), Prime Minister (2019–22)

Carrie Johnson (née Symonds): Partner of Boris Johnson (2018–21), thence wife (2021–)

Cabinet

Steve Barclay: Downing Street Chief of Staff (2022), Chancellor of the Duchy of Lancaster (2021–22), Brexit Secretary (2018–20), Health Secretary (2022)

Michael Gove: Chancellor of the Duchy of Lancaster (2019–21), Levelling Up, Housing and Communities Secretary (2021–)

Matt Hancock: Health Secretary (2018–21)

Chris Heaton-Harris: Chief Whip (2022)

Sajid Javid: Chancellor of the Exchequer (2019–20), Health Secretary (2021–22)

Robert Jenrick: Housing Secretary (2019–21)

Kit Malthouse: Chancellor of the Duchy of Lancaster (2022)

Priti Patel: Home Secretary (2019–22)

Dominic Raab: Foreign Secretary (2019–21), Deputy Prime Minister (2021–22), Lord Chancellor (2021–22), First Secretary of State (2019–21)

Jacob Rees-Mogg: Leader of the House of Commons (2019–22), Brexit Opportunities Minister (2022), Chair of the European Research Group (2018–19)

Grant Shapps: Transport Secretary (2019–22)

Alok Sharma: International Development Secretary (2019–20), Business Secretary (2020–21), President of COP26 (2021–22)

Mark Spencer: Chief Whip (2019–22), Leader of the Commons (2022)

Rishi Sunak: Chancellor of the Exchequer (2020–22)
Liz Truss: Foreign Secretary (2021–22) , Secretary of State for International trade (2019–21)
Ben Wallace: Defence Secretary (2019–)
Gavin Williamson: Education Secretary (2019–21)
Nadhim Zahawi: Education Secretary (2021–22), Chancellor of the Exchequer (2022)

Advisers

John Bew: Foreign Affairs Adviser to the Prime Minister (2019–22)
Liam Booth-Smith: Economic Adviser to the Prime Minister (2019–20), Special Adviser to the Chancellor (2020–22)
Michael Brooks: Deputy Campaign Director (2019)
Lee Cain: Director of Communications (2019–20)
David Canzini: Deputy Chief of Staff (2022)
Dominic Cummings: Chief Adviser to the Prime Minister (2019–20)
Nikki da Costa: Director of Legislative Affairs (2019–21)
Jack Doyle: Director of Communications (2021–22)
Simone Finn: Deputy Chief of Staff (2021–22)
David Frost: Chief Brexit Negotiator (2020–21)
Ben Gascoigne: Political Secretary (2019–21), Deputy Chief of Staff (2021–22)
Andrew Griffith: Director of No. 10 Policy Unit (2022)
Guto Harri: Director of Communications (2022)
Ross Kempsell: Political Adviser in the Policy Unit (2019–20), Political Director of Conservative Campaign Headquarters (2021–22)
Isaac Levido: Conservative Electoral Campaign Manager (2019), Adviser to the Prime Minister (2019–22)
Oliver Lewis: Brexit Adviser to the Prime Minister (2019–21)
Eddie Lister: Chief Strategic Adviser (2019–20), Acting Downing Street Chief of Staff (2020–21)
Munira Mirza: Director of No. 10 Policy Unit (2019–22)
Dan Rosenfield: Downing Street Chief of Staff (2021–22)
James Slack: Director of Communications (2020–21)
Dougie Smith: Aide to the Prime Minister (2019–22)
Will Walden: Mayor of London's Director of Communications and External Affairs (2012–2016), Adviser to Boris Johnson (2019)
Cleo Watson: Deputy Chief of Staff, Head of Priorities and Campaigning (2019–2020)

Members of Parliament

Steve Baker: MP for Wycombe (Conservative 2010–), Chair of the ERG (2019–20)

Graham Brady: Chair of the 1922 Committee (2019–), MP for Altrincham and Sale West (Conservative 1997–)

Mark Francois: MP for Rayleigh and Wickford (Conservative 2010–, as MP for Rayleigh 2001–), Chair of the ERG (2020–)

Mark Harper: MP for Forest of Dean (Conservative 2005–), Chair of the COVID Recovery Group (CRG) (2020–22)

Jeremy Hunt: MP for South West Surrey (Conservative 2005–)

Owen Paterson: MP for North Shropshire (Conservative 1997–2021)

Chris Pincher: MP for Tamworth (Conservative, 2010–22, Independent 2022–), Deputy Chief Whip (2022)

Officials

Simon Case: Cabinet Secretary (2020–)

Stuart Glassborow: Deputy Principal Private Secretary (2019–22)

Sue Gray: Cabinet Office Second Permanent Secretary (2021–)

Samantha Jones: Permanent Secretary to the Office of Prime Minister (2022)

Emily Lawson: Covid-19 Vaccine and Booster rollout and Head of Delivery Unit (2021–)

Helen MacNamara (Towers): Deputy Cabinet Secretary (2020–21), Director General for Propriety and Ethics in the Cabinet Office (2018–20)

Martin Reynolds: Principal Private Secretary (PPS) to the Prime Minister (2019–22)

Tom Scholar: Permanent Secretary to the Treasury (2016–22)

Mark Sedwill: Cabinet Secretary (2018–2020)

Mark Sweeney: Director General, Domestic and Economic Affairs, Cabinet Secretariat (2019–22)

Patrick Vallance: Chief Scientific Adviser (2018–23)

Chris Whitty: Chief Medical Officer for England (2019–)

Johnson leaves No. 10 for the House of Commons Liaison Committee as his premiership crumbles around him, 6 July 2022

INTRODUCTION

Boris Johnson was Britain's most iconoclastic and outlandish Prime Minister since David Lloyd George a hundred years before. Johnson saw the country through one of the most historic resets in Britain's relationship with continental Europe, the worst health epidemic and the severest challenge to Northern Ireland's continuation in the United Kingdom since Lloyd George was at No. 10. Both succeeded failing Prime Ministers of the same party with one great objective to fulfil. Having achieved that, both won landslides in the month of December after leading unstable parliamentary majorities. Both saw themselves akin to the US President, with a direct mandate from the people, and had little love for their party or Parliament. Both were captivated by international affairs abroad and building infrastructure at home. Both tried to use the power of the state to spread opportunity more equally across the country, the attempts of both to 'level up' faltering. The vaulting ambitions of both were thwarted by lack of money, with cost of living crises overshadowing their end. Russia dominated their latter premierships. Both fell because they lost trust and credibility with the public, amid accusations that they had tarnished the office and public life.

Lloyd George nearly died of the Spanish flu in September 1918; Johnson came equally close to death from Covid in April 2020 at the very same age, fifty-five. Both men cast caution aside to travel to see war zones at first hand: Lloyd George to the Western Front, Johnson to Ukraine.

Both fell in similar ways, having lost the trust of the parliamentary Conservative Party. While the Cabinet remained mostly loyal to both, it was the desertion of junior ministers that built momentum, with the ultimate fall in both cases triggered by the decisive actions of key figures – in Lloyd George's case, the former Conservative leader, Andrew Bonar Law; in Johnson's, the Chancellor of the Exchequer, Rishi Sunak.

Their characters were strikingly similar too. They lit up the room, were beguiling orators and giants among their peers. They injected raw adrenalin into the political system and, for a while, made the weather. Lloyd George's character was captured by his friend the newspaper owner Lord Riddell, but he could have been talking about Johnson:

> His energy… and power of recuperation are remarkable… He has no respect for tradition or convention. He is always ready to examine, scrap or revise established theories and practices… He is one of the craftiest of men [with] extraordinary charm of manner. He is full of humour and a born actor… He has an instinctive power of divining the thoughts and intentions of people with whom he is conversing… His chief defects are: Lack of appreciation of existing institutions, organisations, and stolid, dull people…; Fondness for a grandiose scheme in preference to an attempt to improve existing machinery; Disregard of difficulties in carrying out big projects… he is not a man of detail.[1]

They shared a willingness to take enormous risks with the constitution, as with their casual relationship with the truth and malleable principles. Their ferocious sexual and financial appetites led them into deep and repetitive trouble. Both thought nothing of using powers of patronage to make outrageous appointments which were nakedly to their own benefit. Both indeed rather enjoyed being outrageous.

Johnson wrote a book about Winston Churchill. But it was Lloyd George who he resembled far more. The title of Lloyd George's book, *Where Are We Going?*, could have been Johnson's leitmotif.

The comparisons are not endless; as with mere mortals, no two premiers are exactly alike. Lloyd George was much better at appointing close advisers, choosing Maurice Hankey as his Cabinet Secretary, Philip Kerr (later Lord Lothian) as his private secretary and W. G. S. Adams as his chief aide. A Prime Minister is only as good as their personal team: Lloyd George knew that, Johnson didn't. Lloyd George created the Cabinet Office and post of Cabinet Secretary; Johnson all but eviscerated it and his Cabinet Secretaries. Lloyd George chose a broad-based, accomplished Cabinet and let them achieve extraordinary success; Johnson went narrow and weak, and never trusted or used them. Lloyd George was an outsider desperate to be regarded as an insider; Johnson, an insider wanting to be seen as an outsider. Above all, Lloyd George held to a seriousness in his objectives, a trait absent in Johnson.

The similarities, though, provide a helpful framing for the examination of power and success in British politics. Why did Lloyd George achieve more in his premiership? How did Johnson squander a great landslide election victory within little more than two years? Was his premiership destined to splatter to an early end overtaken by events? These are the questions we address in this book.

Johnson was an unusual leader, governing at an extraordinary time in British history. Unlike other Prime Ministers, he was not underpinned by religious faith or ideology or a fixed set of party beliefs. Nor was his premiership bolstered by strong, loyal relationships with colleagues in Cabinet throughout his time in No. 10. A close relationship with their spouse has supported every great Prime Minister in history; Johnson's wife Carrie was a source of both great joy and great conflict for him. Johnson was the most isolated premier for fifty years since Ted Heath, the Prime Minister who took Britain into the EU; nor did Johnson have close relationships with the leaders of France, Germany or the United States, which have affirmed other PMs. Though constantly surrounded by people, he remained a deeply lonely figure: seeking affection yet despising his own vulnerabilities, demanding complete trust from others yet drawing them into his web, leaving many feeling compromised and used.

He was no ordinary Prime Minister.

Prime Ministers generally have one defining event landing on their time in office. Johnson had three: resolving Brexit, the Covid pandemic and the war in Ukraine. He governed at a time when the Conservative Party lost its way, the public discourse was in turmoil over culture wars, when Britain's place in the world was insecure, and the cohesion of the United Kingdom was in doubt.

His was no ordinary premiership.

Johnson tried to bounce the monarchy, had his actions judged unlawful by the Supreme Court and knowingly put forward proposals to break international law. He was the first Prime Minister to have been found by the police to have broken the law. Johnson was not alone in his chaos: had he lost the 2019 general election, Jeremy Corbyn as Prime Minister would have been differently destabilizing and unconventional. Abroad, the global figure to which Johnson had been compared the most, US President Trump, denied the legitimacy of the electoral process and the constitution for the first time since 1787.

These were no ordinary times.

The Johnson premiership poses a challenge to contemporary historians. Even more so than his immediate predecessors, many decisions around which history turned with this anarchic Prime Minister did not take place in minuted meetings or round the Cabinet table, but through WhatsApp messages and private discussions. Where memories of crucial witnesses are still fresh and moments remembered in context, contemporary history has a particular role to provide a meaningful contribution.

Contemporary history is important so we can learn from the recent past while memories are fresh, recapture the truth of events and hold governments to account. This book is in part a cautionary tale which highlights individual and institutional failure. Our hope – naïve maybe – is that the conclusions within might be drawn on to prevent them from recurring.

The course of a premiership is always skewed by the noisy and powerful when they are in office, who further compound the distortion by publishing their memoirs or diaries in which their own role is magnified and personalized. This book draws rather from the testimony of over 200 witnesses, the great majority of whom are silent, merely referenced as 'an official' or 'an aide'. Few, if any, will write their memoirs or publish their diaries. Sometimes we refer to interviewees by name, but for serving officials, by far the greatest majority, going on the record is not an option. The occasion on which we may depart from verbatim accuracy is in the quotations liberally deployed in the text emphasizing how much of importance to this administration took place outside recorded meetings. The quotations, which were always related to us by interviewees, aim nevertheless to capture the *spirit* of the conversations. As always with historians, we are only as accurate as our sources. To enhance the book's accuracy and fairness, we have sent individual sections to witnesses who saw the particular stories at close hand.

We have sought to break new ground. Where others have written books, such as about the crises and scandals that led to Johnson's resignation, or the politics and personalities of Brexit, we avoid covering these areas in detail. We have equally weighted the book towards the accounts we have been told afresh in interviews or have otherwise discovered for ourselves, rather than recounting secondary sources. For the purpose of clarity where surnames overlap, just three people in this account will be referred to on occasion on a first name basis – Boris Johnson, Carrie Symonds/ Johnson and Marina Wheeler.

Longer books than ours will be written on Johnson and, given his unconventional life, further revelations will emerge. In due time inquiries will report, not least on Covid. Twenty-five years after the events of this book the National Archives will begin to publish the Prime Minister's ('PREM') files, another invaluable source of material. But our study of Johnson and its conclusions on his character, style and record we believe will fundamentally stand the test of time and reveal the truth of his premiership.

Churchill returned to No. 10 in October 1951 after six years in opposition. Lloyd George tried to do so, but failed. Readers of the book must decide whether Johnson's career in the future will follow the trajectory of his hero or his doppelgänger.

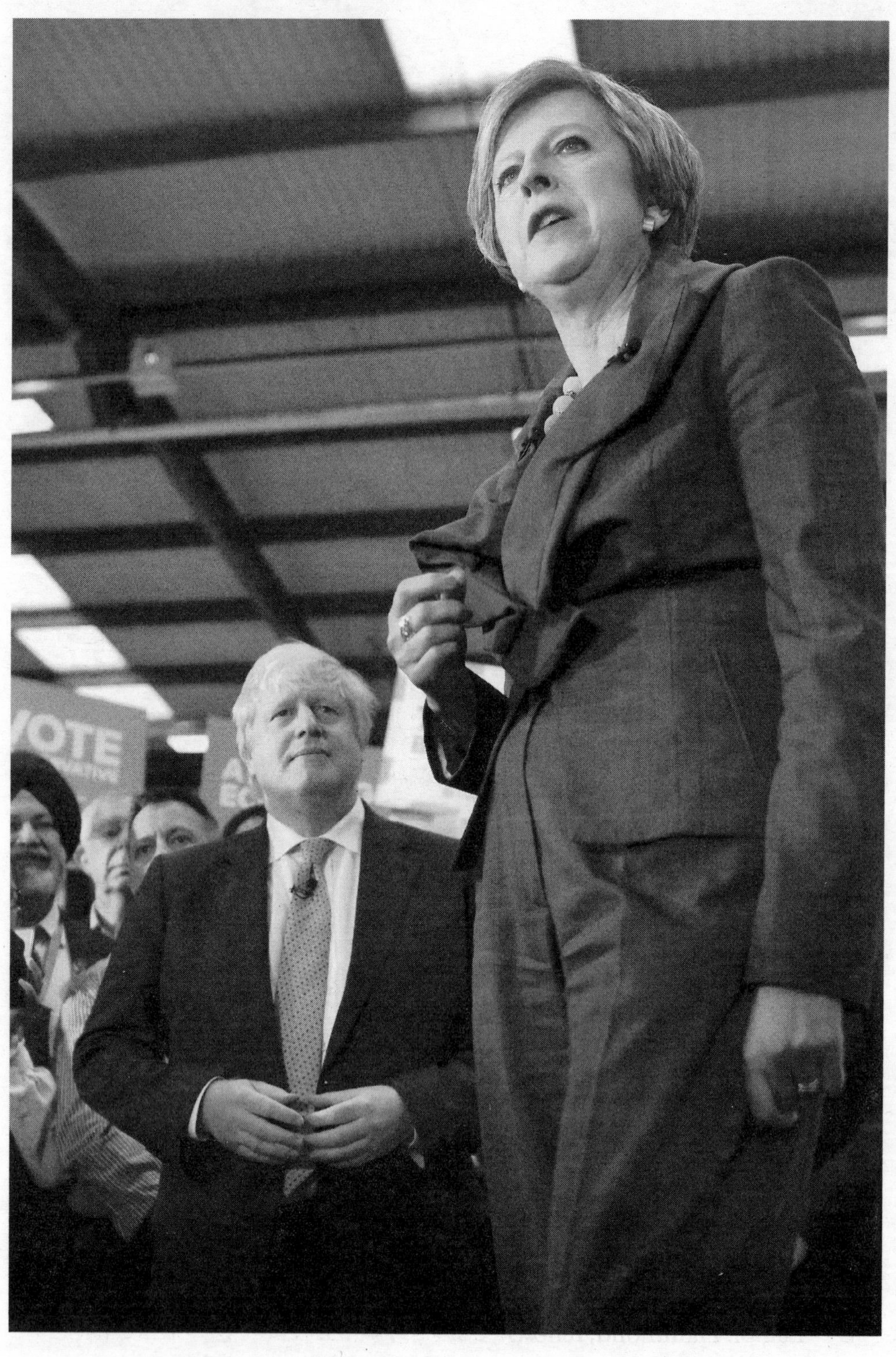

Johnson always believed that he should have become Prime Minister in 2016, not Theresa May

1

RISE

In my beginning is my end.

By the time Boris Johnson graduated from Balliol College, Oxford at the age of twenty-three, his irrepressible and lawless character had been largely forged, a character that would propel him to the very top of British politics. Once at the pinnacle, the seeds of his inevitable decline and fall began to flower.

Alcibiades more than Pericles, certainly not Cincinnatus, the Roman statesman he likened himself to when finally departing Downing Street.

Falstaff, a would-be Prospero perhaps, more than a Henry V.

Robert Walpole, Britain's defiant first Prime Minister, or transgressing David Lloyd George indeed who established the modern office, far more than Winston Churchill or Margaret Thatcher.

A figure not entirely of this century. Nor indeed of the last. The gilded, anything-goes world of court politics and shifting factions before the 1832 Reform Act when neither Cabinet, Whitehall nor the Conservative Party had fully formed would have been a more natural milieu.

Martin Hammond, Johnson's housemaster at Eton, captured him in his written reports with greater insight than any of his tutors at Balliol. Hammond, renowned as a schoolmaster of rare intellectual depth and judgement, wrote in a collection of reports:

> Boris really has adopted a disgracefully cavalier attitude to his classical studies… sometimes seems affronted when criticised for what amounts to a gross failure of responsibility… I think he honestly believes that it is churlish of us not to regard him as an exception, one who should be free of the network of obligation which binds everyone else… he doesn't have the instincts of a real scholar, and tends to 'sell himself short' when an exercise requires intellectual preparation. He is, in fact, pretty idle about it all… Efficiency and organisation have been constant problems.[1]

Thousands of words have been penned about the formative years of Boris Johnson.[2] Thousands more will be written. No need here in a book about his time at No. 10 to dilate further on his rootless childhood in the US, in England and Brussels, his free-spirited father and his troubled yet remarkable mother, his rumbustious schooling and time at Oxford, his charm, kindnesses and eloquence, his lies, evasions and equivocations in his early career before 1999.

His three core character traits were evident from early on. What were they?

- A skill exceptionally rare among political leaders to communicate using charisma and humour with the public far and wide, to read the mood and currents of politics, and to inject his inimitable energy into the system to change thinking about what could be achieved. Very few politicians in the last century could match his larger-than-life persona. At his best, he could be extraordinarily kind, agreeable and thoughtful about individuals and people at large, lovable even, with a more inclusive vision of contemporary society than many in the Conservative Party.

- An all-consuming self-absorption and self-belief that impelled him to be the most important and visible person, and to be impatient of any person, precedent or procedure getting in the way. He had no interest or understanding of how organizations work or the jobs people need to perform within them, nor any interest in finding out. He hated taking decisions if it risked becoming unpopular, offending influential people (hence 'cakeism') or delaying gratification: 'I want it all and I want it now' was an impulse in his political as well as in his personal life that he found difficult to overcome.
- A lack of moral seriousness not mitigated by his razor-sharp intellect and beguiling rhetorical skills. Causes, commitments, colleagues as well as pledges, policies and partners were regarded as merely transitory and transactional. Any could be picked up only to be jettisoned when they no longer served his interests or pleasure. With few enduring bonds and relationships with friends or colleagues, his trust in others was always conditional and relating to a particular crisis or need: when his need or crisis passed, or a more exciting offer hoved into view, they would be blithely dropped.

These added up to three flaws that, unaddressed, would prove fatal: an inability to value truth and to set or pronounce on moral boundaries; to recognize merit, appoint the best people and trust them to do their jobs; and to stick by any decision or person without changing his mind.

In my beginning is my end.

Many leaders have had similar traits, but they learned to temper them on the way to the top. Would Johnson double down on his best qualities? Up, up and up he ascended, dispensing charm and banter liberally, drawing into his web writers, aides and politicians who were transfixed, all hoping to benefit from his aura and infectious optimism, unique apart from Tony Blair in the relatively lacklustre world of early twenty-first-century British politics. None of the other three big beasts who dominated the 2010s – David Cameron, George Osborne and Michael Gove – came close to matching Johnson's magnetism and popular appeal.

To serve as Prime Minister is a serious business and requires total dedication from an incumbent operating at their very peak. Service first to country, not just self-interest, has been at the heart of most of Britain's successful premierships, and certainly in the last hundred years. Johnson had a burning desire to be Prime Minister. Was he prepared to put in the requisite hard work in the jobs to prepare for it, and to learn the right lessons from them?

Every would-be leader faces a Manichean struggle between their higher and lower natures. The characters of Prime Ministers might be formed early on, as was Johnson's, but refining and shaping them in posts on the road to Downing Street makes the difference. Every single aspect of a leader's character will be tested to the ultimate degree in the intense heat of No. 10, and they will be cruelly exposed if they are not prepared. Johnson's hero and biography subject Winston Churchill was shaped as a minister in ten departments, including Chancellor of the Exchequer and Home Secretary. Painful and chastening experiences on the way up included the failure of the Dardanelles campaign in 1915 while he was First Lord of the Admiralty, prompting his decision to resign and join the army, facing mortal danger on the Western Front many times. Churchill's period in the wilderness in the 1930s, rejected and depressed, caused him to reflect how he might make the most of his opportunity at the top, were it to come. Did Johnson reflect on his reversals, even as his pen was flicking over the surface of his manuscript on the great man? Margaret Thatcher was forged and shaped in two Whitehall departments and in the critical role of Leader of the Opposition over four years till 1979. A figure of moral and intellectual depth, she was preparing herself intentionally throughout her journey to the top.

Would the three principal jobs that Johnson was to hold before 2019 encourage his better nature to blossom? Or would they confirm him in his sense that he could behave as he wanted, provided no harm to his prospects seemed to flow from it? Might his chorus of admirers indeed celebrate him even more enthusiastically when he did behave poorly? All Prime Ministers had mentors to guide and shape their behaviour. Who were Johnson's, and would they warn him if he risked stepping over a line? Would he listen to them if they did? Each of Britain's nine most successful Prime Ministers enjoyed stable and dependable relationships, eight with spouses, one (William Pitt the Younger) with his mother, which helped anchor them throughout the almost impossible office of Prime Minister.[3] Would Johnson find the same?

The *Spectator*

Johnson was appointed editor of the *Spectator* in 1999 by proprietor Conrad Black after the lacklustre editorship of Frank Johnson (no relation). It was hoped that Boris's stardust would make up for his evident lack of managerial acumen. As a condition of the role, Johnson promised 'in a hilarious sequence of oaths and affirmations that he wouldn't dream of standing as a candidate [for Parliament]', according to Black.[4] In this first leadership position, in the words of successor but one Fraser Nelson, he proved a 'brilliant editor' who boosted sales, but delegated to others with abandon, 'rarely came into the office', and was 'a very secretive character' whose great gift was 'picking the right people' (a quality he was to repeat as London Mayor if not always in Downing Street).[5] 'Totally unmanageable, frequently absent and famously late' is the verdict of *Spectator* colleague Martin Vander Weyer.[6] His celebrity status, boosted by his appearances on the BBC's satirical news quiz *Have I Got News For You*, and his penchant for risky and provocative journalism, helped the popularity of the weekly magazine to soar. Savvy eggheads were the common stock of *Spectator* editors, not rock stars like Johnson.

Salaried staff in the office adored him, though the magazine's commercial managers led by the publisher Kimberly Quinn (previously Fortier) were in despair at his total lack of interest in or willingness to help in their side of the operation. Freelance writers dependent on one-off fees likewise tired of him. 'Yes, yes, tremendous idea,' he would bluster when they suggested a feature topic. 'When can I have it, I need it now.' So they would rush off and submit on time, only to hear nothing. When they asked for feedback, he would say, 'Yes, marvellous marvellous piece.' But then they would find that their articles never appeared, with no explanation, nor fee for their efforts. On Thursdays, Johnson would preside over gossipy and irreverent editorial meetings, hugely entertaining but with little reference to what topics might be covered in the next issue. Senior staff, notably long-suffering deputy editor Stuart Reid, then had to scramble frantically around commissioning articles to fill gaps in the magazine.

In June 2001, in contravention of his promises, Johnson sought a parliamentary seat and was elected MP for Henley, putting still further pressure on his time as editor. Further squeeze came when, in 2003, Conservative leader Michael Howard appointed him vice-chairman of the party, and in May 2004, shadow Arts Minister.

In 1993, Johnson had divorced his first wife Allegra Mostyn-Owen and married barrister and childhood friend Marina Wheeler. By 1999, they had produced four children together. Johnson had a happy home: he and Marina were soulmates, intellectual equals and appeared ideally suited. But Johnson's eye was still prone to wander after he became editor, alighting on many women. When the press was sniffing around about alleged affairs, he told a colleague, 'It's none of their business, I don't ever comment, and no one cares.' He developed a soft spot for his editorial assistant Mary Wakefield. Soon the talk in the office was that he was infatuated with her, staff noticing that he left Post-it notes openly on her computer screen: 'See you in the pub in 10 minutes.' She resolutely denied anything ever happened between them, issuing a statement following *Sunday Times* journalist Charlotte Edwardes' allegations of Johnson's sexual misbehaviour,[7] clarifying that 'Boris was a good boss and nothing like this ever happened to me.'[8] In 2011, she married Dominic Cummings.

Johnson's blithe dismissal of allegations in November 2004 that he was having an affair with columnist Petronella Wyatt, 'an inverted pyramid of piffle' in his words, was shown to be a blatant lie. Staff recalled him coming into the *Spectator* office, seeing the lurid headlines on the newspapers ranged out on the table, and rocking with rueful laughter. Howard took a dim view of Johnson's lying and dismissed him from the shadow Cabinet.

But just when Johnson appeared down, his fortunes changed. Turning a blind eye to his infidelities, incoming Conservative leader David Cameron invited him back into the shadow Cabinet to become shadow Higher Education Minister. The new *Spectator* chair Andrew Neil, finding him totally unmanageable as well as untrustworthy, insisted that he now stand down as editor in 2005.[9]

Johnson had in many ways been a stunning editor, substantially boosting *Spectator* sales to a peak circulation of 70,000, a record for the magazine.[10] His may have been a chaotic regime, but despite the scandals and equivocations that characterized it, he emerged triumphant into Cameron's shadow Cabinet. The lesson he had been absorbing since adolescence, that people cared much more about his persona, patronage and popularity than his conduct, was reinforced.

London Mayor: 2008–16

'The *Spectator* didn't count,' says Eddie Lister, who in 2011 became his right-hand man as Mayor. 'London was the first time in his life that Boris had *real* leadership responsibility.' Becoming Mayor of London in 2008 proved the making of Johnson in establishing him as a national figure; in other ways, it was his unmaking. 'He learned a lot and changed a lot – maturing isn't quite the right word, but he… grew into it,' Lister believes.[11]

'Boris thought David and I were trying to trick him when we proposed he stand for Mayor: he thought it was a plot to try to get rid of him,' says George Osborne.[12] Johnson had entered Parliament in 2001 with Cameron and Osborne, clearly the standout candidates of the small intake of twenty-six new Conservative MPs. They were friendly rivals, but by 2007 Johnson's career was languishing compared to theirs as Leader of the Opposition and shadow Chancellor. 'I want you to promise me I can hang onto my seat if I lose in London,' he told them. They gave him that assurance, expecting him probably to lose, but knowing that if he won, he'd have to resign as an MP and he would be out of their hair. Local government they all knew was not a promising route for an aspirant to No. 10. Not since Neville Chamberlain in Birmingham ninety years before had a Prime Minister been mayor of a major city. Chamberlain subsequently had six years as Chancellor of the Exchequer to acclimatize to national politics. Johnson's campaign was helped by the enthusiastic support of the *Evening Standard*, the daily London newspaper, which lauded him while pummelling the incumbent Ken Livingstone. In 2009, Evgeny Lebedev and his Russian oligarch and former intelligence agent father had bought a controlling share in the paper. Anxious to make his way in the British establishment independently of his father, Evgeny alighted on Johnson as just the man to help. Their relationship drew unfavourable comment and speculation up to and beyond Johnson's attempt to appoint him to the House of Lords in 2020. Johnson made up his mind he would enjoy being Mayor to the hilt helped by discovering he could take the role comfortably in his stride. No. 10 was to prove a different planet, and not one to which he ever fully adapted. At City Hall, though, the decisions were immeasurably fewer; stakes, much lower; scrutiny and accountability, far less; Conservative MPs and the need to build coalitions and win friends, absent; opposition, non-existent; and a seemingly endless stream of pleasant things to announce without constant hard choices and trade-offs to be made. Tedious matters, Johnson realized to his utter delight, could simply be delegated to others, while much of the time he could do what he loved best: saying yes, dreaming dreams, swanning around in the public eye and trying to make people feel good. A far cry from the demands of Downing Street.

Johnson was above all a showman as Mayor, receiving his highest ratings from the public when he was stuck on a zip wire during the 2012 Olympic Games. 'He loved the adulation of the crowds during the Olympics. He developed an almost god-like aura during them,' said his City Hall communications director Will Walden, who recalls Johnson saying, 'It just doesn't get better than this.' The Olympics were to be the centrepiece of his mayoralty: his first term was devoted to preparing for them, his second, to reaping the harvest. But in Downing Street, there was to be no equivalent to the Olympics, nor anything that came near to giving him the same buzz, however hard he looked, and he looked hard.[13] He was a buzz addict.

The hard-working and capable grafters he so evidently needed at City Hall plonked into his lap: Simon Milton then Lister (policy and planning), Neale Coleman (Olympics), Roisha Hughes (de facto chief of staff), Peter Hendy and Isabel Dedring (transport) and Munira Mirza (education). Reuniting the 'dream team' for No. 10, however, was a non-starter. Milton had died in 2011, Johnson was unable to persuade Hughes or Dedring, who understood him best, to come in with him, and others like Walden refused. Lister and Mirza did go into No. 10 and, while among his most effective lieutenants there early on, neither found they could dominate the Whitehall landscape as they had at City Hall. Simply replicating the personnel would not have been a guarantee of success, especially if Johnson failed to empower them, as he did Lister and Mirza.

It was also easier for Johnson's flaws to be mitigated as Mayor, and his strengths emphasized than at No. 10. 'Johnson was good company, fun to be around, lifted spirits, injected purpose,' recalls the man he dubbed 'Comrade Coleman'.[14] 'But he was very poor on detail, hopeless on numbers and money, obsessed with grand projects and totally ill-focused.' 'Comrade Coleman' showed the inclusive side of Johnson: a lifelong Old Labourite, he (unlike Johnson) took a brilliant First in Classics at Balliol, and Johnson relied heavily on him. Johnson's tendency to draw advice from any individual he liked, regardless of background, status or political affiliation, would follow in several of his No. 10 appointments including Dominic Cummings.

Johnson's re-election as Mayor in 2012, masterminded as in 2008 by campaign supremo and his political rock Lynton Crosby, bolstered his confidence and ambition massively. Unlike his first victory in 2008 when the electorate voted against Labour's tired regime, this was London voting for him personally and for his record. He was enjoying himself. The success of the Olympics confirmed him as the most popular and recognizable politician in Britain, to the evident discomfort of Cameron and Osborne, and evident delight of Johnson. 'He was really intrigued by them,' recalls Lister. 'He wanted to understand exactly how they operated, particularly George as Chancellor.' Few aspects of his job were sweeter for Johnson than extracting money out of the Treasury, at which he was adept. They worked together closely on the redevelopment of Battersea Power Station and bringing life to East London after the Olympics were over. 'High on vision and enthusiasm, but terrible on money: he had no idea if something was going to cost £1 million, £10 million or £1 billion,' says Osborne.[15]

He was skilful at obtaining money from the private sector too, such as for 'Boris Bikes', the public cycle hire scheme he rejoiced in. With established routines and the high-quality team guiding him, his avoidance of own goals and reversals added to his credibility as a national politician. He took particular pride in representing London as a leading global city: 'I truly think that the state of

London today is as good if not better than at any time in its history,' he said in May 2016, the month he stood down as Mayor at the conclusion of his second term.[16]

Johnson had defied the low expectations of him as a fun but essentially flippant figure when first elected. The global financial crisis, driving the City towards banking meltdown, helped him to come across as more than an amiable buffoon. He revelled in his self-styled role as global salesman for the capital. London gradually acquired a more 'benign and affable' reputation, open for business to all-comers, in contrast to the more provincial aspirations of his Labour predecessor Ken Livingstone. Headline-grabbing failures such as the cancelled Garden Bridge, impractical Cable Car and unused water cannons did not dent Johnson's confidence. No matter that 'a lot of London's success has not been because of Boris Johnson' but down to 'luck', while upon leaving office 54 per cent of Londoners believed that he had been 'successful'.[17] His legacy since has been hotly contested.[18]

Johnson naturally didn't attribute any success in London to luck, but to his unique qualities and judgement. What did he learn? How to campaign and win elections, and how to be a popular and effective Mayor of a global city. But without his strong team, what price his considerable gifts? He learned little about the craft of leadership, how to head the nation as a whole, how to pick, motivate and lead a Downing Street team, how to drive change through a system, or how to formulate decisions independently of decisive voices around him. Nor did he learn about moral authority.

Nor how to behave.

2016 Referendum and First Attempt at the Premiership

If Johnson was to be better prepared for the giant step up to Downing Street, though, at the very least he needed to cut the mustard in a top Cabinet post. That opportunity was to come, but first, he had a tilt for the leadership after the fall of David Cameron in July 2016, a fall in which he played a critical role.

Britain's continued membership of the European Union, an issue that Cameron hoped he could ignore as Prime Minister, was threatening to tear the Conservatives apart. So in January 2013, he had pledged to hold a national referendum after renegotiating Britain's terms of membership, if the Conservatives won the next general election, on whether Britain should remain within the EU. Cameron hoped that his gamble would close down the debate for a generation. If anyone had been in doubt about the strength of anti-EU feeling in the country, the European Parliament elections in May 2014 disabused them, with an insurgent party, UKIP, winning more seats than the Conservative or Labour parties. Cameron and Osborne now knew that they had a very difficult fight on their hands, and that it would only be won by a close margin.

The Conservatives, to the surprise of many, won the 2015 general election outright, ending the Tory–Lib Dem coalition that had run the country since 2010. The in-out referendum was duly announced for 23 June 2016, with all eyes on whether the renegotiation in Brussels would win over the undecided. The key influencer on voters, as No. 10 was all too aware, would be Johnson. Charismatic, huge name recognition, and capable of reaching the non-voters who would turnout for the referendum, he was a massive electoral asset. He knew it too, and loved the power it gave him. He had one overriding question in his mind: would his chances of making it to No. 10 be improved by voting Remain or voting Brexit?

'Boris had decided he wanted to become Prime Minister long before he went to London. We didn't really talk about it: it was just a kind of unspoken assumption,' says Lister. Johnson, though, was talking openly to others about it, if not to Lister. The Olympics over, his gaze had focused less and less inwards to City Hall and more across the Thames to Downing Street.[19] 'He was absolutely determined to become Prime Minister,' says election strategist Mark Fullbrook.[20] Johnson would say, 'I've watched Dave doing it and I've seen George wanting to do it. Why can't I do it? If they can, I can.' No doubt about it, Osborne, preening himself to succeed, now viewed the Mayor as his number one rival. Johnson watched anxiously as Osborne artfully deployed his patronage powers as Chancellor of the Exchequer to build up a coterie of supporters among MPs, replicating precisely what Gordon Brown had done a decade before to prepare the ground for his own takeover at the top.

Ambitious MPs realized what was happening, given Cameron's announcement he wouldn't fight another general election, and were weighing up which way to jump in the likely leadership barney in 2018–19.[21] Without any clear Johnson platform to attract supporters, judgements were particularly influenced by whether an MP had an in with Osborne or not. Ben Wallace didn't; 'Boris, unlike George, cared about real people,' he says. 'I think you should be the next leader of the party. I'd like to help you,' Wallace, then a junior whip, told Johnson when he visited him at City Hall in 2012.[22] Johnson was very conscious he knew little about Conservative MPs: 'Will you help me test the water?' he asked. Walden was recruited to handle communications for Johnson's as yet undeclared leadership campaign. 'We organized dinners in London's Barbican,' he says, 'in which Boris tried out his ideas on us, including not being a Thatcherite, saying, some would always need a safety net, and wanting to extend devolution and opportunity across the whole country.'

First, having resigned as MP for Henley in June 2008 when he became Mayor, his team helped him find a seat in Parliament. A constituency that ringed London would be ideal so he could visit without spending too much time travelling. He duly won the nomination in the safe perch of Uxbridge and South Ruislip in West London in September 2014. Suburbia was never exactly Johnson's scene, least of all compared to the bucolic delights of rural Henley, but he accepted the beat as necessary for a greater end. Timing was tight.

Tension built month on month after Cameron's election victory in May 2015. Osborne had been Cameron's loyal ally for ten years and the Prime Minister didn't want to do anything to damage the prospects of his chosen successor, least of all to benefit their joint rival, Johnson. So in the post-election reshuffle, Cameron offered him 'only' the post of Culture Secretary, arguing that the post's oversight of sports and the arts would give him, after the Olympic Games, the ideal platform. Osborne, meanwhile, was to be left at the all-mighty Treasury.

Johnson smelt a rat, as he always did around those two, foreshadowing his suspicions of all and sundry when he became Prime Minister, and thought he was being sidelined. Johnson and Cameron had first met at Eton, where Cameron was two years his junior, then again at Oxford. Despite their shared membership of the elite, all-male Bullingdon Club, the two were not personally close, and Johnson considered himself the far more talented of the two; Cameron beating him to a First (Johnson receiving a 2:1) then his meteoric rise as the star of the 2001 intake ahead of Johnson himself was the source of some bewilderment. Financial worries were also to the fore. Johnson's complicated family arrangements and lavish lifestyle cost money, an estimated £500,000 per annum, vastly more than his ministerial salary, but exactly the advance he was offered in mid-2015 to write his biography of Shakespeare (his biography of Churchill had been published in 2014).[23] Now Cabinet Secretary Jeremy Heywood stepped in and refused to allow him to be Culture Secretary and write the book at the same time as being London Mayor. So by mutual agreement Johnson agreed to step back until his mayoralty finished a year later.

The job he had really wanted was to be Cabinet minister responsible for infrastructure, industry, transport and the regions, to do to the UK, he grandly believed, what he had done to London. But he now found himself on the backbenches, where he was given clear instructions by Wallace to keep a low profile and build support by befriending MPs. To play Osborne at his own game. So Johnson endured a series of curry evenings with potential supporters among MPs, his parliamentary team slowly gathering strength around Wallace, Jake Berry, Nigel Adams and Amanda Milling.

Johnson's voting intentions in the EU referendum had, by the autumn of 2015, moved to the forefront of Cameron's and Osborne's minds. How would he jump? The Prime Minister moved unashamedly onto a charm offensive. At the party conference that October, he said, 'I want to single someone out. He's served this country. He's served the party. And there's a huge amount more to come. So let's hear it for the man who for two terms has been Mayor of the greatest capital city on earth: Boris Johnson.'[24] Word was put out that, once Johnson ceased to be Mayor in a few months, a 'big' Cabinet position would be coming his way, the Foreign and

Commonwealth Office indeed, a platform to prove his worthiness for the top job.

Johnson saw through their game. According to advisers, 'They brought him under huge pressure, constant phone calls, texting, nudges. It made him think, "They're desperate, but equally, they don't really respect me".' The story of how and why he decided to commit to Vote Leave is aired fully in the next chapter. It will be clear by now, though, that Johnson's decision on whether to back Remain or not was going to be guided predominantly by his personal calculus. At this time, like most people, he assumed Cameron would win the referendum, if closely, and Britain would remain in the EU. Should he be a loyal lieutenant to Cameron and Osborne, or be leader of the side that lost? 'One thousand per cent cynical', was the judgement of Osborne.[25] 'I think it was a straight calculation,' says Oliver Lewis who became his Brexit right-hand.[26] He reckoned it was win-win. 'If I come out for Brexit and we lose, I position myself as a hero Eurosceptic, from which I can win the leadership at the next contest. If we win, then I'll be clear favourite for Prime Minister.' And so it proved.

Fast forward to June 2016. Most of the running on Vote Leave had been down to campaign director Dominic Cummings, who imparted messianic passion and energy to the cause. Johnson's value, as it was to prove again in the general election three years later, was as a figurehead, an orator and booster of morale. The ideal partner, Vote Leave believed, for Michael Gove, who was seen as bringing intellectual gravitas and credibility to the Brexit cause, in contrast to the populism of Nigel Farage. Until he gave up London in May, Johnson was only able to devote Fridays and weekends to the campaign. Even then he was not singularly focused, penning his book on Shakespeare as he travelled around the country and performing excerpts from the Bard's plays to amused staff in a voice of mock pomposity. So Cummings deployed him like a battering ram in the areas which research told him could be won. Johnson was mostly happy to delegate to Cummings, in awe of his bravura, not least the slogan 'We send the EU £350 million a week – let's fund our NHS instead'. But he became anxious when the words unleashed fury, and was straight on the phone to Cummings about it. 'Don't worry, Boris,' he replied. 'Everyone knows the real figure is not 350 million after rebates, but every time a journalist tells you that it's only 170 million, everyone thinks 170 million is a f**k of a lot of money. The more they ask, the better. It's great for Vote Leave.'[27]

Johnson's worst clash with Cummings was over another Vote Leave slogan on a poster suggesting that Turkish accession to the EU would put Britain at risk of being swamped. 'He was incandescent when he saw it and wanted to have it out immediately with Cummings,' recalls Walden.[28] 'It was the closest I saw him to quitting. He wanted to come down to London and apparently punch Cummings.' 'It wouldn't look good. It'll seep out,' the adviser told him. Johnson, who had been a liberal Mayor and had championed inclusivity, was selectively uncomfortable about anything that smacked of racism or xenophobia. But there were to be no fisticuffs, nor row, nor slogan change, despite Johnson's sound and fury.

The referendum result was declared at 7.20 a.m. on 24 June after all 382 voting areas and twelve UK regions had declared their results, with 51.9 per cent voting to leave the EU. Cameron and

Osborne had been right to see Johnson as the trump card. With the margins so tight, they believed 'without question' that his backing carried Vote Leave over the line because, says Osborne, 'Boris made it respectable for middle of the road people to vote Brexit.' Most in the UK and across the world were shocked by the result. Cameron's team had expected Remain to win, if narrowly. Theresa May and her team had expected Remain to win, so some took themselves off on pre-arranged holidays. Boris Johnson had expected Remain to win: 'Holy s**t, f**k, what have we done?' he uttered under his breath on hearing the result.

Just after 8 a.m. that Friday, Cameron, with his wife Samantha by his side, announced on the steps of Downing Street, 'I do not think it would be right for me to be the captain that steers our country to its next destination', finishing, 'I love this country'.[29] May was in shock and in tears at the result: 'the ones who voted for Brexit will be the ones who suffer the most,' she told her closest aide, thinking of those in the left-behind areas.[30] 'Oh my God, oh my God, what have we done?' was Johnson's response listening to Cameron. An exit so long yearned for, yet now it had come, lacking all sweetness and light.

Johnson was finding it hard to think straight. He had been up all night watching the coverage on television at his Islington home. Only towards dawn did he realize that Vote Leave would actually win. He disappeared to bed for twenty minutes but came back and paced around in a Brazilian football shirt and bottom-hugging shorts looking ashen-faced and distraught. 'What the hell is happening?' he kept saying. The impact on the markets suddenly became his concern. Then a pang of guilt struck him when he saw pictures of Samantha Cameron on the television looking utterly distraught. 'Oh my God. Look at Sam. God. Poor Sam.' Soon after, stopping in his tracks, a new thought struck him: 'Oh s**t, we've got no plan. We haven't thought about it. I didn't think it would happen. Holy crap, what will we do?' Still muttering, he went off to write the speech he knew he would in no time have to deliver.

Cameron had previously expressly ruled out quitting as PM if he lost.[31] Johnson thought, in as far as he had given it any, that if Vote Leave won Cameron would bring in a team including Gove and Gisela Stuart (the Labour politician who co-fronted Vote Leave) to negotiate Brexit with the EU. Those who knew Johnson intimately say they had never seen him more frightened and dismayed than at this moment of triumph. Crowds were shouting angrily outside his house: 'People who had patted him on the back when he had been Mayor were now screaming at him,' recalls an adviser. He made it out to the car and his driver shot off down the road but had to stop at a red traffic light at the end. Aides by his side screamed for the driver to shoot straight through the lights, but he refused. 'The crowds began banging angrily on the windows and roof. Boris looked terrified. He stared dead ahead, sensing that from this moment on, everything in his life would change.'

It was to change quicker than he thought. Within just hours of the result being declared, cracks began to appear between the two front runners to succeed Cameron – Johnson and Gove. The pirouettes and waltz of the four politicians who dominated Westminster in the 2010s – Cameron, Osborne, Johnson and Gove – defined how political history was shaped. At the start, Cameron, Osborne and Gove were a triumvirate. By mid-decade, the former two had lined up against the latter two. Now, Johnson and Gove began to split. The power behind their throne, Cummings, decided that Johnson stood the better chance of beating Labour leader Jeremy Corbyn, with Gove doing the hard yards as Chancellor. The calculus was a mirror image of Tony Blair versus Gordon Brown in 1994 after the death of Labour leader John Smith. Then as now, one had the popular appeal, the charisma and the ability to put across the big picture, the other the superior intellect and command of detail. The choice was a no-brainer for the master strategist. Johnson had already sounded him out: 'Do you think I might win? Do you think Michael will run? Would you talk to him? What do you think?' Cummings and Vote Leave media deputy Lee Cain felt 'Boris would be the better front man, and Michael would be better running the show from the Treasury,' according to one Vote Leave and Boris campaign alum.

Johnson was no Blair, however, except in one respect: his astonishing public reach. His key claim over Gove and any other candidate was his appeal to both Tories and non-Tories. 'That was his USP – he really was the Heineken politician – able to reach and attract support that no other Conservative could dream of,' says Mark Fullbrook, who ran the leadership campaign polling in 2016 and whose research showed Johnson was better placed to take on Corbyn than his peers.[32] The research further showed that none of the voters' reservations about him were fatal. Worries about his colourful private life were tempered by no one being able to claim he was a hypocrite (while some positively liked him for it). His undeniable upper-class and South-East background? The referendum campaign had shown that when he went to the North and working-class towns, more than any other, he was mobbed. His known ineptitude at running organizations? It could be countered by his appointing people around him who were capable of compensating. The clincher to Fullbrook, who had worked with right-of-centre leaders for forty years, was Johnson offered 'the two things voters want from politicians'. Namely, he makes people smile and lights up the room when he enters, and his optimism makes them believe their families' lives will be better tomorrow than they are today.

Gove read the runes. He fancied himself as Prime Minister, but didn't want to take on Johnson and be marginalized if, as looked likely, he lost. On Saturday 25 June he convened his senior lieutenants at Cummings' Islington home. They accepted, reluctantly, that Gove wouldn't stand himself, but they wanted to row back from the unconditional promise of support that Gove had offered Johnson shortly after Cameron's surprise resignation. An aide recalls that Cummings was clear: 'You are going to be Chancellor, Michael, run the Brexit negotiations with the EU, and run the civil service.'

'But I don't think any one person can run all three,' Gove protested.

'You don't have to – others will look after the rest: you do the Treasury.'

'But I can't be Chancellor.'

'Why not?'

'Because I can't add up.'

'Others will do the numbers.'

'That wouldn't work.'

'Look, Osborne couldn't do the numbers either and was a figurehead. We will get a team of ninjas for you to do the negotiations. Don't worry. You'll be the top man.'

Gove was becoming visibly flustered about the whole prospect, but to Cummings, the success of the post-referendum project hinged on Johnson and Gove continuing to work in tandem, as they had during the campaign. Holding the team together was an article of faith for him. 'Dom was a total force of nature,' says

Vote Leave press chief Paul Stephenson.[33] 'He had brought these guys together, he held them together. But the second he was out, it began to fall apart.'

At some point over the next few days (accounts vary), Gove had second thoughts, while Johnson's team dug in, with Wallace, Crosby and Walden deeply suspicious of Gove and the arrival of Cummings. United during Brexit, now, on the verge of the ultimate prize in politics, Downing Street, the teams around the principals fumbled the keys over who would step through the door. Both wanted to maximize their own futures in the Brave New World they had unleashed. Like Johnson, Gove liked to listen to the views of his court of trusted advisers around him, weighing up their differing advice. Aides Simone Finn, Henry Cook and Henry Newman, as well as his then wife Sarah Vine, argued robustly for him to stand against Johnson, arguing that they had seen he was simply not up to the top job. 'That may be true,' Stephenson and fellow aide Henry de Zoete said, but he shouldn't run now, arguing that it would be political suicide for his senior lieutenant to turn on him: 'You'll never recover.' Gove listened and weighed up the arguments before deciding to take Johnson head-on. In his mind, he felt he himself could have made the major impact on the referendum, he'd been in the front line, given the cause the intellectual weight that Johnson hadn't, and that he now had a much better organized and better prepared campaign to pitch than Johnson. Particularly disconcerting for him was Johnson offering him the post of his campaign manager, and then blithely saying that he should share it with one of his own team. 'It was all so lackadaisical. I just didn't think his heart was really in being Prime Minister,' says an aide on the campaign.

'I'm running for this,' Gove reportedly phoned Crosby to say.

'You mean the campaign? I don't understand,' he replied.

'No, I'm going to run to be Prime Minister.'

'What? Have you told Boris?'

'Not yet.'

'Don't you think you better, mate?' the Australian replied, failing to conceal his anger.

Johnson's team had been worried. They had been hearing concerning reports throughout the day. Key members of the team had gone missing. They couldn't understand what was happening. Crosby decided to leave it ten to fifteen minutes before talking it over with Johnson, to allow Gove to break the news to him over the phone.

'Good day, matey,' Crosby said nervously on arrival.

'I've just got out of the shower,' said a relaxed Boris Johnson.

'Has Michael phoned?'

'No, why?'

'Because he's running for the leadership.'

There followed a very long silence.

'I guess it's all over then.'

'Don't take any rash decisions,' Crosby advised (as relayed to the authors by a third party).

Johnson was absolutely stunned by the news. 'Boris cannot provide the leadership or build and unite the team in order to take this country forward,' Gove announced to a dumbfounded public. Never before had a colleague turned against Johnson like that. His trust in others, never in great supply before, would not recover; it scarred him. 'It was one of the very few times I saw him in tears,' says one of his colleagues. 'He didn't trust anyone again,' says a family member. 'I don't know if he ever quite trusted his old friends or even his family in the same way.'

Johnson quickly assembled his close team at his temporary campaign headquarters. Should he continue without Gove? The switching to Gove of former party leader Michael Howard was viewed as an ominous sign. 'We spent a long time talking it through,' says Crosby. 'It has to be a decision for both of you,' he told Johnson and Marina. Johnson pressed his master election strategist for an opinion. 'It will be tight.' Crosby's worry was that if he continued in the race, Gove would maintain his damaging line of attack. Indications of support given by some one hundred MPs had fallen to an estimated forty on Gove's news. 'We might no longer win,' Fulbrook said. Johnson went upstairs with his wife: neither have spoken in public about what passed between them, but when they came down again, their decision was clear cut. 'I'm not going ahead. I can't win this time.' Those present detected a look of resignation, even relief on his face. Case closed? Not quite.

'I'm not sure I made the right decision,' he said twice in his car as he was driven away. 'Typical Boris,' says an aide who was with him in the car. 'He has never quite known what he should do.' 'The lesson he absorbed,' says a close confidant, who believes Johnson should never have listened to the advice to quit, 'was don't ever resign again. I think that explains why he clung on for so long as Prime Minister in 2022.'

Gove, who was knocked out shortly after and whose standing with Conservative MPs never recovered, was disturbed at the seismic events he had unleashed. He later told Osborne that he had saved the country from the 'sheer horror' of a Johnson premiership in 2016 (as he said he tried to by standing again in 2019). But equally, Gove realized he was isolated in a dangerous no man's land, and he set out trying to rebuild bridges quickly. So, just days after turning on him, he decided to write Johnson a letter saying that 'your place in history will be guaranteed' because he had been the leader of Vote Leave. When no word came back, and with Gove now sacked by the new Conservative PM Theresa May and jobless, he pitched up unannounced at 10.30 p.m. to Johnson's office in the House of Commons. Walden, realizing it was going to be extremely awkward, motioned silently to leave. Johnson shot back a look and stayed rooted to the spot. 'My intuition was he wanted me there because it would restrain him from socking Michael. When I was sure that he wouldn't strike him, I left them alone to argue it out.' Returning home in the car to Islington later that evening Johnson intoned several times 'what the f**k', totally confused about what Gove had been trying to say.

Had Gove not struck out, had Johnson not stood down, had he won the crown there and then, the next few years would have been very different. Theresa May would never have become Prime Minister: for all her dedication and hard work over her three years, she was unable to secure a deal on Britain's exit from the EU. Johnson could have been a totally different Prime Minister to her in 2016, driving a harder bargain with the EU and perhaps securing an earlier and a better deal than the one he eventually achieved four years later. Marina Wheeler too would have been by his side in No. 10, a mature woman and a strong restraining hand on her husband, ready to rein him in when needed. His former wife might not have been physically present throughout his premiership, but she is one (of two) ghostly presences to hover over it. Ambitious Brexiteer Gove rather than the frugal and pro-Remain Philip Hammond would have become Chancellor, and the momentum and verve of Vote Leave would have remained unbroken.

Critically, more of Johnson's City Hall team would have transferred straight across, even if they were not the total solution.

But by 2019, several had moved on. Without the three years of bitterness that ensued, tearing the party apart, Johnson would have had the chance in July 2016 to pick a much stronger and more broad-based Cabinet team. Many who knew Johnson best believe he would have been a much better Prime Minister three years earlier. Gove's decision to take him out is thus one of the most momentous in the political history of the century so far.

Most likely, Johnson would have been even more exposed than he was in 2019. His tendencies towards chaos, grandstanding and inability to govern consistently on a day-to-day basis may have been containable when Mayor – not so when Prime Minister. The lack of experience at the top level in his City Hall team would quickly have been exposed, Johnson's difficulty in either grasping the levers of government or entrusting power to those around him who could being no less evident than in 2019–22. Factionalization within No. 10 would have erupted still, Cummings' coarseness and centralization of power making infighting an inevitability. There is little in the pages that follow to suggest Johnson's fatal flaws could have been mitigated if only the timing were different.

Foreign Secretary, 2016–18

Not becoming Prime Minister in July 2016 did, in fact, have a potential silver lining for Johnson: it gave him the chance to prove his mettle and learn the trade in a top Cabinet post. How was he to fare? With almost unseemly haste, May moved into Downing Street on 13 July. 'I bet it's the Ministry of Paperclips,' he confided gloomily to aides when she invited him into No. 10 to discuss jobs. A Cabinet reflecting all shades in the party was her aim, and she could hardly ignore her biggest beast. 'I'm going to be the effing bloody Foreign Secretary!' he texted friends when he came out, inwardly thrilled, outwardly making light of it. His eyes had watered when she offered him the job, recalls Fiona Hill, who was with May in the Cabinet Room. 'Blown away, gobsmacked,' recalls Nick Timothy, May's other top aide. 'This is a great honour,' Johnson told the new PM. 'Having played a part in making Brexit happen, I feel real responsibility for making sure that it works out.' Timothy, a passionate Brexiteer, was not entirely sure if Johnson believed, as he uttered the words, it would work out. May left him with this message: 'You and I have had a patchy history, but I know there are two Borises. One deadly serious, intellectual, capable and a very effective person; the other, playing-around Boris. I want this to be your opportunity to show you can be the former.'[34] Rarely did she utter a more perceptive personal observation.

'He expected and hoped for a job,' says Lister, 'but he hadn't expected anything as big as Foreign Secretary.'[35] He was now, after May herself and Hammond as the new Chancellor, the third most senior figure in the government. He achieved the job that Cameron and Osborne had dangled in front of him earlier in the year, the ideal platform for him to develop his experience as a Cabinet minister at the national level. He was captivated by foreign policy too, while knowing little about the issues when he arrived at the Foreign Office. He had loved his trip in 2008 to the Beijing Olympics and discovering that his magic and personal idiosyncrasies could translate abroad, and a trip in 2014 to Erbil in Iraq with Nadhim Zahawi, organized by Lister, had also been a highlight. 'That visit gave him a real taste for foreign travel,' Lister recalls, 'but he didn't enjoy being Foreign Secretary nearly as much as he had London Mayor.'

One reason was Johnson's freedom had been constrained from the very outset. The creation of the new Department for Exiting the European Union (DExEU; under David Davis) took away from the Foreign Secretary the single most important objective of the government, a Brexit deal, while the creation of the Department for International Trade (under Liam Fox) prised away from the Foreign and Commonwealth Office (FCO) its high-profile work on securing post-Brexit trade deals. He nevertheless began with high hopes, as his new department had of him after diligent but dour Hammond. Officials liked working for him. 'He was a breath of fresh air. He was nice to everyone. He cracked jokes. He said "thank you". Basic stuff, but it had been missing,' says a senior diplomat. Simon McDonald, the permanent under-secretary, was all too aware that his department had a pro-Remain reputation, and strove to assure the new boss of their loyalty. 'The office was intrigued and excited to have, just three weeks after the referendum, the one-man embodiment of Vote Leave, the biggest personality in government,' he says.[36]

But within very few months, Johnson had become disillusioned. He found May impossible, evasive and even rude. 'He'd always be wanting to have meetings with her and she'd say, "No, sorry, I'm too busy." She never wanted his input, on Brexit, or on any other matter. In Cabinet, she could be uncharacteristically cutting. A regular phrase, which made some Cabinet colleagues wince, was "no, Boris, it's not that simple".'[37] May herself finally lost patience with him after only nine months over a leak to the *Sun* about her refusal to back air strikes in Syria. From then on, they were at war.

Desperate to make a mark on the historic office, Johnson's attention turned to exploring whether a new relationship could be built with Russia, against strong resistance from No. 10, and building up personal relationships, including with Mohammed bin Salman, Crown Prince of Saudi Arabia, Khalifa bin Zayed, President of the United Arab Emirates, and Abdel Fattah el-Sisi, President of Egypt, none of them committed to democracy or human rights. But with Chrystia Freeland, his opposite number in Canada, also a former journalist, he most certainly was interested in building a strong bond. 'He would have their mobile numbers on speed dial and drive the civil service crazy, because he just phoned them up,' says an official. While some diplomats delighted in his gift for striking relations with foreign ministers, others, he realized to his annoyance, didn't have a high opinion of him: 'He suddenly found himself Foreign Secretary without a clue how to do it,' says one of that persuasion. He felt patronized by some officials, whose hopes of a big-hitter turned to disillusion with his lack of seriousness. He has an acute nose for when people don't rate him, and they had a scarring effect on him, shaping his jaundiced attitude to the civil service as an institution once he became Prime Minister; inevitable, given it was the only Whitehall department he worked in. But equally, he was over-ready to see offence when none was intended, especially if egged on by partisan aides.

Because the Prime Minister had appointed a known political enemy as Foreign Secretary, it made it harder for him to be taken seriously at home and abroad. 'Within the EU, leaders held him personally responsible for Brexit,' says his most senior official, Simon McDonald, who was to play a significant part in his downfall.[38] He trusted McDonald to get on and run the service, but was close to a small group of officials, notably Philip Barton, whose work on the Salisbury poisonings in 2018 he admired for his hands-on style, and whom he appointed as McDonald's successor in 2020: 'The most effective public servant I have ever seen,' he said of him. Permanent Representatives to the EU Tim Barrow and to the UN Karen Pierce along with Martin Reynolds, his principal private secretary (PPS), were others with whom he chimed (all of whom he promoted once Prime Minister). But on Europe, in as far as his opinions counted with May, he ceded total control to former diplomat David Frost: 'He became his EU brain: he knew the detail, he knew all the arguments, he wrote his minutes on the EU to Cabinet – and he knew that Johnson was very happy to be guided by him,' says a senior observer. 'We just both hit it off. He wanted an expert to help navigate him on the EU,' says Frost. 'He knew I knew the ropes a lot better and could explain to him in detail what was happening. His political team recognized there weren't many people who understood the wiring, how to get decisions through the system and get things to land. That was my value to them.'[39]

The novelty of being Foreign Secretary soon wore off. His mind turned increasingly to other matters, including his hopes of the top job. Gaining supportive coverage in the Tory press was essential. But he knew *Times* and *Sun* owner Rupert Murdoch, and Paul Dacre, editor-in-chief of the *Daily Mail*, had less use for him now that he had served his purpose and the referendum had been won. They thought he was a dilettante, a philanderer, lacking seriousness. While working out how to win them round, he tried a parallel track of phoning *Evening Standard* owner Alexander Lebedev after the announcement that Sarah Sands was standing down as editor in January 2017 and suggesting he succeed her. Arch-rival Osborne was preferred. Johnson extracted part revenge when, in October 2022, after he ceased to be Prime Minister, he turned down the offer to edit the paper.

By mid-2017 he was growing despondent, still more so when May, then at the height of her power, called a surprise early general election which she looked destined to win, leaving him out in the cold for years. Cabinet colleagues remember him looking totally black and thunderous when she sprung the news on them. 'He knew he was f**ked, totally despondent', is how a Cabinet witness describes his reaction. But the deplorable election result for the Conservatives, with a chastened May barely clinging on to power thanks to a deal with Northern Ireland's Democratic Unionist Party (DUP), cheered him greatly and gave him fresh hope. So weak was she, he toyed with the idea of striking against her there and then. Chief Whip Gavin Williamson went across to the Foreign Office to disabuse him of the notion: 'You're not going to be moving against her, are you, Boris?' Johnson considered whether Williamson meant it as a question or a threat.[40] Williamson, the holder of many secrets, could be very intimidating when he thought the occasion demanded. Which he thought it did now. 'If you move against her, our pact with the DUP will crumble, we will have a general election, and Corbyn will be Prime Minister,' he told Johnson slowly and deliberately, never once taking his eyes off him. 'Absolutely not,' Johnson stuttered out, assuring him, 'I won't do anything to undermine her. I will be completely supportive.' The meeting lasted just twenty minutes, but it gave May's team the answer they needed.

Indicative of her perilous state is what May said to the 1922 Committee of Tory backbenchers days later when she admitted that the general election result was her fault alone. 'I will serve only as long as you want me to serve,' she said. This was a clear signal to Johnson, David Davis and other would-be challengers that she wouldn't fight another general election. 'Back off for now: your moment will come', was her message.

From the New Year, a small group of Cummings, Frost and Cain (now Johnson's media adviser) began to meet on Friday afternoons to plot Johnson's way forward. The crunch point came at the Brexit summit at Chequers in July 2018, when May tried to corral her Cabinet into agreeing her plan. At first, Johnson lent support, leading a toast to her plan at the dinner at the elegant country house following their discussions. But when whispers of Davis's resignation as Brexit Secretary reached him, he agonized during the weekend over whether to resign himself, petrified that he might be jumping prematurely. He was due to appear at the NATO summit in Brussels the following week, and he didn't want to miss US President Trump's imminent visit to the UK.

News of Davis's resignation over May's deal brought matters to a crisis point. Frost, Cain and Ben Gascoigne, whom he had brought over from City Hall, were convinced he should go. 'If you don't resign now, No. 10 will try to bind you into her Chequers deal forever, and you will lose your moral authority,' Cain told him. A tortured Monday morning of talks at his official residence in Carlton Gardens followed. It meant he missed his leading role hosting a summit on the Western Balkans that day: 'His antics', according to *The Economist*, rendered the summit 'like a scene from one of the *Carry On* films'.[41]

May repeatedly tried to call him, and when she eventually got through Johnson was all over the place. 'What are you planning to do, Boris?' she asked pointedly. He dithered, prevaricated and talked in circles until finally he blurted out that he would step down.[42] He could not stay any longer in the 'gilded cage' of the Foreign Office, as his staff described it, and duly wrote his resignation letter declaring that the 'dream' of Brexit was being 'suffocated by needless self-doubt'.[43]

'While David Davis left over a genuine difference to be respected,' says May's Chief of Staff Gavin Barwell, 'Johnson resigned thinking not about the country but about his own narrow position.'[44] His prospects of becoming Prime Minister, not the precise merits of her deal, certainly weighed most heavily with Johnson, if not with Frost. If he could secure a better post-Brexit settlement for the country once in Downing Street, all would be forgiven, he reasoned.

Johnson had showed periodically, as in his leadership of his opposite numbers abroad after the Salisbury poisonings, the kind of Foreign Secretary he could have been. But overall, he fell short. As May feared, the 'bad Johnson' eventually came out on top. The best Foreign Secretaries prevailed against the difficulties they faced, and Johnson certainly had many. He had the opportunity to be a star on the international stage, for all the scepticism about him, setting out clearly what 'Global Britain' meant after Brexit. Frost and Cummings on one side, and his officials on the other, were equally disappointed by his dearth of strategic thought, notwithstanding his periodic stands such as championing women's education. His political team noted with alarm how easily he could be pushed around in his thinking by his officials when bored or unsure of his ground, especially on issues where Frost and Gascoigne opposed conventional thinking, such as on Johnson's support of the Iran nuclear deal. They were happy enough to influence Johnson themselves, but unhappy when officials did so.

He confirmed the scepticism about him at home and abroad with a series of gaffes, including attempted jokes about dead bodies in Libya, reciting colonial-era verses in Myanmar by the unfashionable Rudyard Kipling, but none more egregious than his inept comments about British Iranian national Nazanin Zaghari-Ratcliffe, who had been imprisoned in Iran while visiting her family on charges of spying. Johnson wrongly claimed that she was 'simply teaching people journalism', which was seized upon by Iran as proof she was spreading 'propaganda against the regime' and resulted in her continued incarceration in Iran until March 2022. Damage at home to his credibility was exacerbated by his disingenuously flying to Kabul in June 2018 to avoid having to vote against the government in the Commons on Heathrow Airport's expansion which he vigorously opposed.

'Johnson's job as Foreign Secretary was to convince the world that Brexit did not mean Britain's withdrawal from global affairs. The question remains: what is British foreign policy? It is a question that Boris Johnson's successor will have to answer', was the verdict of the BBC's James Landale.[45] Few argued with that judgement.

Nor did his two years at the FCO see him grow in understanding about the seriousness of such a senior post. There was little sense that he understood, as he had told May on appointment, the 'honour' element of the role. Frivolity and an evasion of responsibility were never far away. His 'f**k business' comment, made to an ambassador regarding the fears of industry leaders over Brexit in June 2018,[46] might have been mitigated if his remorse had been convincing. But he didn't feel remorse: he was livid with business for its negativity towards Brexit. He took attacks on Brexit as a vendetta against himself and his role in bringing it about. His easy-going attitude and liberal openness to the views of others was being gradually supplanted by a vindictive dismissiveness, always lurking below the surface, of those who criticized him or failed to take him seriously. Searching questions about his personal morals and affairs continued to plague him too, detracting from his stature, not least after Marina had finally left him in the spring (the news becoming public in September). Questions were asked about his new partner, Carrie Symonds, after he tried to bring her in as chief of staff at the FCO, and was found with her in his office in a compromising position. Moral issues of fidelity to his wife and honour aside, it raised concerns about how far he could be trusted with – or even grasped – sensitive state intelligence.

Johnson had forged some important personal relationships that were to bear fruit later, but had learned little of value as Foreign Secretary about leadership to take forward with him into Downing Street, least of all about the kind of people on whom he would have to rely, and about how to define strategy then deliver it. 'I didn't see any great imprint on him from his time as Foreign Secretary. He was much more a Mayor of London PM than a Foreign Secretary PM', is the verdict of a senior official. A squandered opportunity that was to cost him dear.

Wilderness Months and the Leadership Contest: 2018–19

Johnson was out in the cold, like his great hero Churchill had been in the 1930s. Like Churchill in his wilderness years, Johnson stared into the abyss of political and career annihilation, with no way back, just as Churchill had feared. Gove had returned to Cabinet, still unreconciled with Johnson and eager for a second tilt at the big prize, while stars from the Eurosceptic 2010 Conservative parliamentary intake were emerging on the right including Dominic Raab, Jacob Rees-Mogg and Liz Truss, threatening to block off his 'mount the attack from the right' strategy. 'He went through two or three months of feeling pretty downbeat' following his resignation, says Frost.[47] 'Did I do the right thing, do you think, by resigning?' he would repeatedly ask close advisers, who bore the brunt of nursing a dejected Johnson through this dark period, 'sitting together in what we called his punishment room in Parliament. It reminded us of *Porridge* [the 1970s television series set in a prison],' recalls one aide. But light was beginning to shine from the North. Cummings, after prolonged hibernation, was beginning to stir his limbs: 'unbeknown to absolutely anybody', he began to be influential on Johnson's mind again. Frost too, though no longer officially on his team, was a regular prison visitor, shaping and emboldening the jail bird.

With the annual party conference in Birmingham looming, Nigel Farage raised adrenaline levels by announcing his return to front line politics to 'fight back' against May's 'fraudulent' Chequers deal. Johnson had to break free, seizing the initiative to burst back on the scene on 9 September, describing her deal as a 'suicide vest… We look like a seven-stone weakling being comically bent out of shape by a 500lb gorilla.' FCO Minister Alan Duncan attacked his former boss's comments on suicide vests as 'one of the most disgusting moments in modern British politics'. Unbowed, Johnson forged ahead, using his reborn weekly column in the *Telegraph* to ascend to new levels of historical hyperbole to tear into the 'constitutional abomination' with a stretched comparison. May's Chequers deal would mean that 'for the first time since 1066 our leaders [would be] deliberately acquiescing in foreign rule'.[48] Days later, he was describing her deal as 'deranged'. Big beasts on the right vied shamelessly to outdo each other in the strength of their condemnation of the Prime Minister's proposal. It was an unedifying spectacle.

Deeply happy to be back among adoring crowds at the party conference for the first time since his resignation, he told delegates at a fringe event that May's deal was 'dangerous and unstable, politically and economically… This is not what we voted for… locked in the tractor beam of Brussels.' The audience loved it. Johnson was on top of the world again as he strutted along the corridors being slapped on the back. May would not let his taunting go unanswered. In a speech described by ITV's political editor Robert Peston as 'arguably her most important',[49] she gave a ringing put-down to Johnson for his earlier business expletive, saying the

Tories' job was to 'back business'. His popularity with the general public plummeted after the conference, a YouGov poll showing his net favourability declined from minus 28 before the conference to minus 35 after it.[50]

Depression, never very far away, descended again on Johnson. But not for long this time. As May's star waned again that autumn, Johnson's spirits rose. He found happiness too in his blossoming relationship with Carrie Symonds, and was able to draw on her experience as a media adviser who had worked at Conservative headquarters. After all the anguish of separating from Marina, Carrie gave him newfound levels of contentment and confidence for the ultimate challenge ahead. While some colleagues were happy for them, her arrival on the scene caused divisions too, and sparked cynicism from some: 'She was simply the girl of the moment when the music stopped. Hardly made for stability around him.' Unfavourable comparisons were soon being made with Marina for her measured and moderating influence. Aides became disconcerted then jealous at the constant stream of WhatsApp messages Carrie was sending him as a switched-on figure highly engaged in day-to-day politics.

The hope was that, with Carrie Symonds, Johnson would put his 'trouser problem', as a friend described it, behind him and finally turn over a new leaf. He had ground to make up. A dossier about his private life and foibles was passed to the *Sunday Times* at the time of the party conference, containing 'a catalogue of lurid allegations… and damning assessments of his character', which further ruffled the atmosphere.[51] Jennifer Arcuri, the American technology entrepreneur with whom it was said he had an affair from 2012, formed part of the tawdry background. No. 10 flatly denied responsibility for circulating the document, though it emerged that it had been produced originally by May's team during the Conservative leadership election in 2016, but not released. Such, even then, was the depth of the May–Johnson animosity.

The May premiership's protracted and painful death throughout the first half of 2019, and Johnson's ascent to be crowned Prime Minister on 24 July that year, has been told in our previous volume, *May at 10*. We highlight here merely features which foreshadow his behaviour once in Downing Street. Long before May announced on 24 May she would resign as Prime Minister, Johnson's team had been stealthily at work, orchestrated initially from his Commons office by Cain. The contest, according to rules introduced in 1998 by then Tory leader William Hague, had two parts: whittling candidates down to a final two during 13–20 June in the race for support among Conservative MPs, and then a vote by Conservative members in the country on those two. The outcome of the latter contest was considered a foregone conclusion – given his stellar national profile and popularity, Johnson would win hands down against all-comers. The beef was thus on getting him into the final two in the first leg, and that outcome was far from certain.

In 2016, Johnson had been coming at the leadership fresh off his success as London Mayor and leader of Vote Leave. In the following three years, he had not covered himself in glory. The Nazanin Zaghari-Ratcliffe controversy and the trip to Afghanistan during the Heathrow vote were standout black marks with MPs. After the latter, arch-supporter Nigel Adams had remarked, 'We are totally f**ked now. He'll never come back from that.'

'The task of making Boris Johnson Prime Minister was far harder in 2019 than it would have been in 2016,' his team believed, in the words of one member. Raab, Davis and Gove had emerged as far more convincing flag wavers for the Brexit cause since 2016. The European Research Group (ERG), a group of hardline Eurosceptics within the parliamentary Conservative Party, was far from persuaded that he was a true hard Brexit believer, the knowledge of which made him tack more and more in their direction. Steely Raab, talked of as the coming man, went further and said he would be willing to countenance 'no deal' and to do whatever it took to secure Brexit, music to the ears of many on the right of the party after three years of failure to agree under May. 'Raab was the person we needed to eliminate as he was splitting Boris's vote. He was our first target,' says one of Johnson's team. Throughout the campaign, as at No. 10, Johnson was far more wary of the right than centre-ground MPs. Some of Johnson's mainstream supporters from 2016 too were certainly not back in the fold. Wallace for one made it clear he had no confidence in his new campaign, while others were angry that he had caved in so quickly in 2016, leaving them high and dry.

The civil wars that characterized Johnson's time in Downing Street, his verbal incontinence, inability to provide strategic leadership and his domination by powerful aides were all foreshadowed in the campaign. His two principal lieutenants, ex-MP James Wharton and May's hatchet-man Williamson, had a dim view of the rabble of MPs which Johnson had assembled around him. One adviser described them as like the Addams Family or the Munsters. 'When I joined, the momentum was with Raab; Boris was seen as a spent force. That all changed when James and I started knocking it into shape,' says Williamson.[52] Iron discipline was instituted, as they tried against the odds to whip the unruly Johnson into some kind of shape. He was given strict instructions on which MPs to see, had a timekeeper to hold him to twenty-minute slots and was told to read just half a page of information on each MP to pretend he knew something about them. It became embarrassingly obvious early on that he knew precious few Conservative MPs.

Johnson's willingness to say anything to anyone to gain their backing became a nightmare for his minders. Wild promises were made about seats in the House of Lords, public offices, ambassadorships, posts in No. 10 and more. 'So we drafted in Grant Shapps to sit in the room and make a careful note of what on earth Boris was promising,' says Williamson.

His team were savvy, knowing exactly which MPs to publicize had joined the bandwagon. A decisive coup was the headline article in *The Times* on 5 June that three 'future talents' and established careerists, Rishi Sunak, Oliver Dowden and Robert Jenrick, were to back Johnson – 'We hit Gove hard: he thought that all three were his people and in the bag,' says one Johnson campaigner. More than that, it showed that Johnson could attract serious centrists. They proved vital, tipping the balance in his favour. On that very day, the bookies declared Johnson the front runner.

Sunak had been key to persuading Dowden and Jenrick. Carrie Symonds was key to persuading Sunak. She was worried that Johnson's 'Brexity' image was out of touch with young media-savvy technocrats in the party. So she engineered the evening that took place on Bank Holiday Monday, 27 May, at Jenrick's Westminster home in Vincent Square. 'I want to recapture the spirit of my mayoralty, bring the team into Downing Street, and run the country in the same inclusive spirit,' Johnson told them, using the phrase 'levelling up', the first time any of them had heard it. 'I want to raise living standards across the whole country,' he announced with growing confidence. None were sure he could win and that he wouldn't do a runner, as in 2016. But they listened to his eloquent flow attentively. 'I hope I've passed my viva,' said a departing Johnson as he and Carrie left them alone to discuss his audition. Sunak said he thought Jeremy Hunt would be a much better administrator as PM from his chair in the Cabinet Room, but that he didn't think he had it in him to win a general election. They concluded that, for all their reservations, only Johnson had any chance of beating Corbyn and ending the prolonged Brexit impasse. The other candidates would either get outmanoeuvred by an impossible Parliament when playing within the rules (as May experienced), or lack the necessary popularity to take on Corbyn at an election, or both. That was the Faustian pact (one of several to feature in our story) they and many others knowingly entered into.

Keeping Johnson focused once the novelty of the campaign wore off remained a challenge. 'He was so totally disorganized. We had to keep the pressure on him to give MPs a call. He remained evasive and we kept the heat on him till he proved he had called them,' a campaigner says. Johnson had learned it was very easy to pass vivas when you told the examiners exactly what they wanted to hear. It raised a question that no one at the time wanted to address: if Johnson would say anything to win people over now, and if he was so open to being manipulated as he had been during the leadership contest, how would he fare in the infinitely more complex world of being Prime Minister?

Once his team had seen off Raab, Johnson's never-far-away suspicions of Gove screeched back to the surface. The folklore among his team was that, 'after knifing him in 2016, Gove had taken off with all the data on MPs' voting intentions'. As a result, his team decided that no one else but themselves should have access to the data in 2019, which is why it ended up in the hands of Shapps.

When all other candidates were eliminated bar Johnson, Gove and Hunt, the team pounced. 'Boris was worried about Gove throughout, the concern being that 2016 might be repeated somehow. None of us wanted Michael in the final, who we thought was dangerous and clever, whereas we felt Jeremy Hunt was much more manageable and less likely to cause lasting damage. It seemed clear Boris also wanted rid of Michael because he wanted to get his own back for what had gone on the last time,' says Wharton.[53] Williamson now brought his dark arts into play. He broached Cameron's Chief Whip, Patrick McLoughlin, who was running Hunt's campaign, with a kill-Gove offer he couldn't refuse. 'They were very reluctant at first, but then relented. They agreed to some of our own secure votes being transferred to Jeremy as the way to dump Michael into third place. It worked. Beating Jeremy was then dead easy.'

His team's 'shock and awe' tactics proved successful. In the fifth and final ballot on 20 June, Johnson secured 51 per cent of the votes from MPs, Hunt 24.6 per cent and Gove, with just two fewer MPs in support, 24 per cent. Little noticed by his team at the time was that MPs had not voted for him because of any inchoate ideas he might have advanced, but because he was the man to get Brexit done and to beat Corbyn. It was a contract, transactional merely, not bonded by love. The second stage, with grassroots party members casting their vote, proved uneventful. With Johnson so clearly the front runner, his team saw no advantage in launching their unguided missile on TV debates, turning down ones planned by Sky News and the BBC, agreeing only to an ITV debate hosted by Julie Etchingham on 9 July. In the end, Johnson cruised home on 23 July with 66.4 per cent of the members' votes to Hunt's 33.6 per cent.

Carrie Symonds' desperation to avoid a repetition of 2016, her pronounced opinions about the campaign and the personnel running it had made for a stormy time, not least when she wanted Wharton and Williamson, as well as Fullbrook, running the contest in the country sacked and her own (younger) people and (more progressive) priorities inserted. Insiders were at a loss to know how far Johnson's views were his own and how far they were hers. They were to encounter the same conundrum in Downing Street.

Seeing how deeply committed Johnson was to Carrie, and sensing her suspicions about his old City Hall team, his team trod on eggshells, trying to accommodate her on the campaign trail and head off the inevitably intense media interest. 'No one is showing her love or respect,' Johnson would complain to his team after flare-ups such as when he ignored their advice to stay overnight in Manchester rather than return to London after the solitary ITV debate. The most serious clash came after a complaint was made about the couple rowing at her South London flat in the early hours of Friday 21 June, when the police were called. 'He didn't tell us until thirty minutes before the story broke,' says one of his team. 'It was so typically Boris, so self-centred, thoughtless, unnecessary.' The instant fear on the campaign was that the story of the two shouting at each other, followed by 'slamming and banging',[54] would derail Johnson's bid and remind MPs that his proclivity for attracting scandals may have been entertaining as Mayor, but could be damaging for a Prime Minister. In fact, it proved nothing more than a minor blip, fizzling out over that weekend.

The legitimate future role of the partner of the Prime Minister, especially one experienced in politics and anxious to be politically active, needed to have been defined and ground rules agreed before the couple entered Downing Street. But they weren't, in part because of uncertainty about whether he would be bringing Carrie in with him: he was very tight about his intentions, perhaps, some close to him thought, because he didn't know whether she would join him in Downing Street. So only the most perfunctory of conversations took place about her duties and responsibilities, with inevitable consequences.

Johnson was about to be crowned king. His lifelong ambition was achieved. But how long before those three untempered character traits, outlined above, bubbled up to the surface once in No. 10? For how long would he be there?

Not long, Johnson feared. Immediate concerns were securing a Brexit deal, discussed in the next chapter, and winning a general election to secure his own mandate, discussed in Chapter 3. In the crucial days leading up to his entering No. 10 on 24 July, once the outcome of the run-off against Hunt was clear, decisions were made that shaped his premiership – and consequently the nation – from top to bottom. Johnson found trusting anyone extremely difficult at the best of times. But, fatefully, 'he felt the whole establishment was against him. He didn't trust anyone other than his tight circle,' says Lister.[55] 'The civil service is out to destroy me,' he confided in his close colleague. Brexit tribalism had seeped deep into his veins. He was never an ERG-style true believer in Brexit, but he knew that his future, and avoiding being the shortest-serving Prime Minister in history, depended on him getting a deal through, even threatening no deal to secure it, upending the constitution, and giving undertakings which he knew were not watertight. He was the master now, and an article of faith among Team Johnson was that Whitehall and Westminster could not be trusted, even if he and they had only the haziest experience of both.

A fateful meeting with Peter Hill, May's PPS, and James Slack, official spokesman at No. 10, intended to establish Johnson's broad plans for government in the weeks leading up to him entering Downing Street, had gone badly. Hill was a high-grade, proven civil servant, but Johnson had taken a dislike to him when he had been

May's top official. Nor had his working before that for Remainer high priest Peter Mandelson in the EU helped Hill's cause. Had Johnson rushed to judgement prematurely? 'They thought it was a total shambles. They didn't think we knew what we were talking about when we discussed how to operationalize our plan for the first thirty days. Boris looked confused throughout the meeting,' says one present. Hill and Slack were right. Johnson and his team were totally at sea, not least in contrast to Blair and Cameron who had spent months planning their No. 10 operations. On the cusp of Rome, Johnson had begun panicking. 'He was worried that we would start in No. 10 without the team to deliver the plan. In 2008 he had arrived at City Hall without one and Conservative Central Office had foisted people onto him,' says Lister. Every new Prime Minister and their team arrive in Downing Street with a deep suspicion of their predecessors; but never like this.[56]

After the meeting Cain grabbed Johnson and told him that he needed some serious, on-message figures in his No. 10 team or he would be out by Christmas. 'I don't care if it's Lynton [Crosby] or if it's Dom running it as chief of staff, but we need somebody incredibly serious and capable to run this,' Cain was heard to say. Crosby was not interested in the job and, besides, was in bad odour with Symonds after his concerns over the reported shouting incident with Johnson at her flat the previous month. Cummings, though, she backed strongly: 'They will make mincemeat of Boris unless you are there with him,' she said. Cain too, to whom Johnson was wedded, enthusiastically agreed; so did others in the core Vote Leave team, who were beginning to gravitate in these final days around Johnson. This included Mirza's husband, the mysterious Dougie Smith, who had established himself as a fixer for the Conservative Party in the 2000s. Despite his prominence as a power-broker for over two decades, including working with party leaders, he maintained an all but invisible digital footprint.[57] His exact role when entering No. 10 was so uncertain, having a desk in the Downing Street political office yet not being employed as a special adviser, that the *Telegraph* claimed it was 'as though he does not exist'.[58]

Worried about the gulf between the incoming Prime Minister's increasingly polarized team and the civil service, Lister arranged a private dinner at the discreet Alfred's Club in Mayfair, just Johnson, Lister, Cabinet Secretary Mark Sedwill and his deputy Helen MacNamara. 'Look, Boris,' Lister told him, 'you might not trust them, but you're going to need to work with them.' 'Boris was on best behaviour,' one recalls. 'We will help you all the way with whatever you want to do', was the message the two officials gave. They talked over his team and the strategy, Johnson outlined his ambitions for office with huge gusto if little precision, and the officials left thinking that all had been agreed. After many months of uncertainty and near-anarchy since 2016, it seemed to them that order would be re-established at the heart of government.

In the days before preparing to enter No. 10, with officials arranging the transition in nearby Admiralty House, Johnson took them to one side. 'I want to bring in Dominic Cummings,' he announced. He looked at them and waited for them to respond. The officials sensed his disappointment when they didn't react as he expected. 'It's a decision I might live to regret,' he said as he swept away.

Johnson signing the trade deal with the EU, David Frost looking sternly on

2

BREXIT

To Boris Johnson, there existed a cause more important than Britain's economic interest. Something more compelling than the stability of Britain's relationship with the United States and Europe, which had twice ripped itself apart in the last century in the bloodiest wars in history. Something of higher purpose than the stability of the United Kingdom indeed, with its delicate relationship with Northern Ireland and its contested bond with Scotland.

What could that be?

His own career and prospects of reaching and remaining in Downing Street.

It does not mean that Johnson lacked profound reservations and misgivings about the European Union, not least its vaulting and growing political ambitions, its byzantine bureaucracy and above all its constant gnawing away at the sovereignty of the United Kingdom. Rather that these were all secondary to a greater concern, of self and desire for the premiership.

In fifty years' time, we will look back at the Johnson premiership and remember it for one overwhelming fact: Brexit. It was one of those rare decisions which reverberates through history, its importance enduring to the history of the United Kingdom. It was Lloyd George's solution of Northern Ireland remaining in the Union with its own devolved government which created the political minefield that

Johnson had to navigate when he sought a workable agreement for leaving the EU. Ted Heath's government (1970–74) is remembered not for the myriad of organizational and economic reforms and attendant crises, but for taking Britain into the European Economic Community. The Johnson imprint on history will be judged in large part on the two foremost events which he shaped: Britain's exit from the European Union, and the deal reached on the future relationship.

Without his knife-edge decision to lead Vote Leave, given the closeness of the result that followed, Britain would have remained in the European Union, for better or worse. Without his role in torpedoing Theresa May's deal, Britain might have left on very different terms, again for better or worse. The future relationship reached on Christmas Eve 2020, for all the heavy footprints of those who shaped it, was the responsibility of Johnson, who told his negotiating team, 'I want you to make it the best Brexit possible.' The ambiguity as to what would constitute the 'best' Brexit was, in typical Johnsonian style, entirely deliberate.

Was he acting in a principled manner, torn to the core over Britain's continued relations with the EU before reaching an agonizingly difficult decision? Was he a master healer, steering the country confidently after the three-year impasse following the referendum vote which threatened to spark the gravest political crisis and social unrest since 1945? How far did his gung-ho approach shape the Brexit process and impose his vision on the deal to leave the European Union? If he was the convinced Brexiteer some believe, why did he not want to be remembered in history for Brexit, but for his legacy to lie elsewhere, as he told aides?[1] And why was he to prove so half-hearted about driving through the opportunities Brexit provided? These are the questions this chapter will explore, detailing how Johnson resolved the 2019 Brexit crisis.[2]

Instinct and Opportunism: 1973–2016

In April 1973, Stanley Johnson took his family to Brussels, including eight-year-old Alexander, as his eldest son was still known. Fresh career opportunities had come from Heath's accession to the European Economic Community (EEC) earlier that year, and Stanley was to become the head of the aptly named 'Prevention of Pollution and Nuisance Division', a European environmental taskforce. The young Johnson was no stranger to the upheaval of his father's career moves, and attended the European School in Uccle to the south of Brussels provided for the children of EEC officials.[3] His stay was not lengthy, returning to England to attend Ashdown House prep school in East Sussex after two years.[4]

Johnson returned to the EEC aged twenty-five in 1989, now stylized as Boris, working as Brussels correspondent for the *Telegraph*. It was here he made his name in journalism, finding, like his father, European employment at an opportune time when the Conservatives were slowly transitioning away from the party of Europe under Heath. The nascent Euroscepticism exploded into the open after Thatcher's celebrated Bruges speech in September 1988 protesting against further encroachments on national sovereignty. The Maastricht Treaty negotiated by John Major in 1993 under which the EEC became the European Union proved too great a lurch to federalism for many Conservatives, leaving a gap for a talented comic writer to turn the dry bureaucracy of European politics into an enrapturing political narrative for the *Telegraph*-reading classes.

Johnson was perfectly placed to be the outsider's insider. He relished 'buck[ing] the conventional opinion' with his writing, as he would later put it, taking a story with a kernel of truth and comically spinning it into a grand Eurosceptic narrative.[5] Favoured themes were of cunning European administrators outwitting the hapless Brits, and the plots of the satanic Jacques Delors, President of the European Commission, to bring about a federal European superstate. Johnson treated issues with a uniform mockery, whether tackling serious matters of Europe's changing political economy or supposed EU proposals to regulate the curvature of bananas, condom dimensions or banning prawn cocktail crisps. The veracity of many stories was questionable, but that wasn't the point.

Johnson relished the confusion his half-truths had caused back home and how his writing propelled him from a relative unknown to 'Thatcher's favourite journalist'.[6] On BBC Radio 4's *Desert Island Discs* in 2005, he described writing the columns as 'chucking these rocks over the garden wall, and I listened to this amazing crash from the greenhouse next door over in England as everything I wrote from Brussels was having this amazing, explosive effect on the Tory Party'.[7] The one consistent theme in his fulminating was his dislike of faceless Eurocrats regulating the lives of others. David Frost describes the articles as 'a reaction against the bureaucratization of Europe, the homogenization, the loss of colour and experimentation'.[8]

Johnson was not a little Englander or a xenophobic nationalist, like some of those conspiring to make Major's life hell as Prime Minister between 1990 and 1997. He savoured the continent's diverse culture, its languages and the long view of history it provided. As he wrote in his first book, about his constituency at Henley, *Friends, Voters, Countrymen* (2001), what initially convinced him to support remaining in the EU is that outside 'we would lose influence in the designing of the continent. And it has been the object of 500 years of British diplomacy to ensure that continental Europe is not united against our interests.'[9] But while he cheered on Britain's continuing membership, at a time when many Conservative MPs were having doubts, he most certainly didn't cheer the EU's structured, opaque and self-serious identity.

After he moved on from the Brussels beat to the *Spectator* in 1999 his public displays of Euroscepticism waxed and waned, alternating between his cultural pro-Europeanism and his scepticism of a European superstate, even employing both where the occasion called for it.[10] Had he been an unashamed Eurosceptic, as upwardly ambitious Conservatives and the Tory press increasingly were, he had ample reason to declare his identity. But fence-sitting and periodic rock-chucking as his mood took him were his preferred *modus operandi*.

Frankly, few truly cared what Boris Johnson thought about the EU until he became a prominent national politician as Mayor of London, a city which was prospering within the European Union. Cameron's pledge to hold a referendum after his renegotiation, based on his false belief that, post-Eurozone crisis, the EU would be up for significant structural changes, lit the touchpaper. Total transformation. Shares in Boris Johnson's thinking went up astronomically. Both sides in the referendum battle realized that this political rock star was the key to them winning. No other politician in Britain could get anywhere close to his appeal in those areas of the country which would swing the election where traditional politicians couldn't reach. Both sides from now on had just one principal aim. Bag Boris. He loved it.

Cameron took it on himself to 'fix Boris', reassuring Osborne that he would come down on their side. Osborne too was convinced that Johnson was a Remainer: 'I told him loads of times you are on our side,' he recalls.[11] Ominously, though, Osborne believed that

Johnson wouldn't hesitate to jump ship if he perceived there would be a significant boost to his leadership prospects by doing so.

Gove and Cummings were equally determined to get Johnson playing on their side, and drew on every ounce of their considerable intellects and persuasive skills to sign him up. Both had animus against Cameron, Cummings for the way he had been disparaged and trashed by No. 10 as a special adviser at Education, and Gove because of his demotion from the department in July 2014 to a more junior job (Chief Whip) on less pay. It terminated what had once been a close personal friendship: Cameron and Gove would go on holiday together with their families, and Gove's wife, the journalist Sarah Vine, was godmother to the Camerons' youngest daughter Florence. This was personal as well as political.

Cameron's belief that Gove would not back Brexit rested in part on bonds of friendship being all-important. Then, in a bolt from the blue, on 20 February 2016 Gove announced, in a 1,500-word essay, that he would be backing Brexit.[12] Cameron thought Gove promised him that if he did come out for Brexit, he would 'take a back seat'.[13] But when Gove criticized his renegotiation, Cameron was shocked by his 'ferocity and mendacity'.[14] Osborne wanted Cameron to attack Gove's continuing claims head-on, but Cameron was reluctant, though he thought Gove's infamous comment in June that 'people in this country have had enough of experts' made him 'an ambassador for the post-truth age'.[15] Cameron in short felt totally betrayed by Gove. As Johnson himself was to feel, not once, but twice. From now on, the famed political quartet would be dancing to a different tune.

With no such emotional ties to either Cameron or Osborne, Johnson was always going to be much more of a freestyle dancing partner, more Samba Axé than a European waltzer. He offered advice to Cameron ahead of the pivotal renegotiation of Britain's status in the EU in February 2016, but claimed to be unimpressed by both the style and content of his efforts when the Prime Minister reported back to Parliament on Monday 22 February. Johnson told his aides that Cameron had lacked the boldness and bravura necessary and failed to make the EU realize that the UK might leave if only a lacklustre deal was offered. Indicatively and crucially, he believed that he himself would have done a better job of negotiating. Cameron was becoming desperate and cranked up the pressure further on Johnson to back the deal. But Johnson's text messages became less and less reassuring, and Cameron felt he was 'revolving like a hotel lobby door'.[16]

Johnson's final decision was taken over the weekend of 20–21 February immediately before the statement to Parliament, against a backdrop of scathing press commentary about Cameron's renegotiation. 'David Cameron is mounting a last-ditch effort to woo London mayor Boris Johnson to back his campaign to stay in the European Union, by drawing up plans for a new constitutional settlement that puts the sovereignty of British institutions beyond doubt,' said the *Guardian* on Saturday morning.[17] Basking in the attention, Johnson penned the most famous paired articles in modern British history. Even his closest friends, allies and family were unsure that weekend whether he'd press send to the editor on the Remain or the Leave columns. Over the previous few months he had told various family, friends and colleagues that he held a range of positions on Brexit, attuned of course to the particular predilections of the listener. To City Hall staff he said categorically in late 2015 he would be coming out for Remain.[18] He was still Mayor of London, a city whose electorate and influential voices were strongly pro-EU. Will Walden felt that Johnson had made his mind up for Remain when at dinner with him as late as the start of the week before he wrote the articles.[19] Even in the very act of writing them, a close family member watched him 'agonize' over the decision, uncertain how he would land.

The two articles, both their existence and content, have since been used to advance almost every interpretation of Johnson's decision to back Leave, and attributed with various levels of strength dependent on the beholder. To the pro-EU diplomat turned Eurosceptic Frost, 'This thing about never being sure which side to go on was bollocks. No doubt he thought hard about it, but the Brexit article is written from the heart and the other merely an intellectual case.'[20] But to Frost's right-hand man Lewis, it was pure 'win-win' opportunism. For Johnson's pro-EU confidants, 'The Remain column was completely conclusive. The Leave piece was all about regulation, and how Britain could plough its own furrow in pettifogging negotiations.'

While his father and siblings were urging him in one direction, one other key person in his life was tipping him in the other: his wife Marina Wheeler. She had outlined her long and deeply held thinking most recently in the *Spectator* the previous week, critical of the trajectory of the European courts and their impact on the constitutional coherence of the UK.[21] Unsure of himself and his position, his closest source of advice was gently encouraging him not to cave in to the pressures of No. 10 and to think independently of the duelling arguments in his own mind.

'Sovereignty,' as Ben Wallace says, 'was huge for him in his decision.' Ultimately, though, the factor that weighed most heavily in his mind was not in doubt: the interest of Boris Johnson, and his desire to rule.

Three Years of Failure: 2016–19

Once he made his decision, Johnson felt liberated and became hugely energized by the Vote Leave campaign to an extent that surprised and delighted him, basking in his popularity across the country. But Gove's post-victory betrayal at the end of June left Johnson exhausted and in a state of despair. He felt he had thrown away his chances of the premiership, perhaps even his entire political career, and for what? Forever being associated with a cause he didn't wholeheartedly believe in, and which might turn out overhyped? But at his lowest ebb – as proved so often in his case – fortune was smiling at Johnson.

His sense of shock and alienation at finding himself in such an unfamiliar habitat as the Foreign Office prompted him, on the recommendation of Gisela Stuart, to appoint former diplomat David Frost to help him shape (in as far as May would listen to him) what Brexit might look like in practice. His encounters with the pro-EU diplomatic service rapidly drove him, as was his wont, in the other direction. 'When I came in he was probably more a proponent of a hard Brexit than me. There wasn't an evolution in his views as Foreign Secretary, but he did get to understand the problems *better*,' says Frost.[22] Johnson, guided by instinct, didn't exactly know what he thought beyond seeing Brexit as a means to an end. In this clouded pond, technocrat Frost helped turn Johnson's broad and amorphous desires for sovereignty and independence into more precise plans for what an actual Brexit outcome would look like.

The 2017 general election brought a new team into the heart of No. 10, with May's fervently pro-Brexit aide Nick Timothy replaced by a team that Frost and Johnson thought irredeemably hostile to it: new Chief of Staff Gavin Barwell and a coterie of Cabinet colleagues Philip Hammond, David Gauke and Julian Smith in the ascendant. Presiding over the Brexit negotiations was official Oliver Robbins, hand-picked by Cabinet Secretary Heywood and deeply and viscerally mistrusted by the Brexiteers.

As the issue of Northern Ireland came to dominate negotiations in late 2017, Frost and Johnson pushed the arguments of being completely out and independent of the Customs Union. The 'Irish Trilemma' had grown to define the Brexit process with regards to Northern Ireland, presenting the choice that the UK could only obtain *two* of the following in any negotiations: a Single Market and Customs Union exit; a whole UK exit; or no border on the island of Ireland. Frost and Johnson were frustrated with May's commitment to regulatory alignment in the Joint Report, the document summarizing EU and UK negotiating agreements, at the end of 2017. 'Johnson never really accepted – and in my view he was right not to – the arguments that said if the border was going to be open then Northern Ireland needs to be in the Single Market. He was convinced that he could do it another way,' says Frost.[23]

Johnson toyed with resigning at that point, but he and his team deemed the issue too niche, and he might have found the technicalities difficult to explain under fire. In all likelihood, it was hardly a serious proposition. Opinion on the backbenches had not yet swayed against May's approach to negotiations, some still continuing to believe in her commitment to the strong Lancaster House pledges she had made early that year, including exit from the Single Market and Customs Union, ending all European Court of Justice (ECJ) interference in the UK and, if necessary, walking away from the negotiating table if the deal was poor. 'No deal for

Britain is better than a bad deal for Britain,' she proclaimed, to the enthusiastic approval of her Brexiteer MPs.

It was not until the notorious Chequers away day in July 2018 that his position of 'wait and see' began to unravel. 'It gradually dawned on us that there wasn't ever going to be a Brexit under May we wanted,' says Frost.[24] May was pushing for Cabinet to back her vision for the future relationship in which the UK would be committed to harmonization with the EU rulebook on some goods to ensure a completely frictionless land border between the UK and Ireland. Johnson initially espoused a Frost-prepared speech encouraging a change of negotiating strategy to break with the accords reached by the Joint Report. But as fellow Vote Leave champion Gove fell into line at Chequers behind May's proposals, Johnson, without Frost by his side putting lead in his pencil, grew more moderate in his criticism. By dinner he was gaily toasting May's skills and discussing writing a joint op-ed with Chancellor Hammond (claiming he initially agreed to this in the hopes he could later wriggle out of the commitment).

As Johnson recovered his mobile phone (confiscated, like those of other attendees, at the door of Chequers and not returned until 10 p.m.) it lit up with angry texts from Brexit true-bloods following the news online. They were shocked both at the outcome and the reports that Johnson had toasted it. 'I hope to God that what's been reported isn't what you've actually agreed to,' messaged pro-Brexit MP and committed Johnsonite Conor Burns. With David Davis's weekend resignation as Brexit Secretary forcing his hand, Johnson had little choice but to step down or lose all credibility. He no doubt disliked elements of May's Chequers plan, but it was considerations of his own career prospects which proved decisive in his resignation, which effectively sabotaged May's strategy.

Free to roam in the wilderness again, Johnson grasped the need to push ahead with insurgent ruthlessness. Vote Leave allies Cummings and Oliver Lewis joining the camp of Frost, Cain and Gascoigne added political savvy and communications verve to the cause. When Johnson was the major attraction at the fringes of the party conference in Birmingham at the start of October 2018, his excoriating speech and whipping up of anti-Chequers sentiment among the party base was a source of major consternation for May. His harder Brexit line registered with the party, and he even began to attend ERG meetings to line them up in support of his inevitable leadership bid.[25]

Having catapulted himself into the leading voice among the crowd of critics, he continued to bash away at May's agreement: 'woeful', full of 'appalling defects' and set to turn the EU into 'our colonial masters'.[26] He, along with 114 other Conservative MPs, voted No in the first of two 'meaningful votes' on her deal on 15 January 2019. It was the biggest government defeat in parliamentary history, losing by a margin of 230 votes, eclipsing the previous high water marks of 166 and 161 suffered by Ramsay MacDonald's minority Labour government in 1924. May's second bite of the cherry proved scarcely more fruitful, recording the fourth largest defeat (a margin of 149) on 12 March 2019. Johnson once again voted against the deal, now with a diminished group of seventy-four Conservative comrades alongside him. Johnson did not revel in the company of his new Brothers in Arms; rather, he kept his distance. They were comrades of convenience, not his ideological soulmates – and they knew it.

May felt she had little choice but to delay Brexit beyond the deadline of 29 March in the hopes of securing a deal, setting a new short extension until 22 May and, if the deadlock had not been resolved by then, a longer extension until 31 October. In a foreshadowing of Johnson's rhetoric to come, May responded by publicly denigrating disputatious MPs as she addressed the nation on 20 March: 'This delay is a matter of great personal regret for me. And of this I am absolutely sure: you the public have had enough. You are tired of the infighting. You are tired of the political games and the arcane procedural rows. Tired of MPs talking about nothing else but Brexit when you have real concerns about our children's schools, our National Health Service, and knife crime. You want this stage of the Brexit process to be over and done with. I agree. I am on your side.'[27]

Conventions tumbled as the deadlock appeared irresolvable. Collective Cabinet responsibility was contravened, and three Cabinet ministers (Greg Clark, Gauke and Amber Rudd) defied a three-line whip after abstaining from a vote which would have demanded to block no deal Brexit, rather than voting against it as the whips demanded. Government control of the order paper was usurped, as Speaker John Bercow allowed backbench MPs to use Standing Orders for emergency debates to take control and initiate legislation (an innovation which would later prove a thorn in Johnson's side). The Prime Minister had lost control of the party, the Parliament and even the Cabinet. Merely the attempt to get her deal back in front of the House proved challenging, as Bercow drew on a convention stretching back to 1604 that the same question may not be brought forward again that same session after being rejected twice.[28] To resolve the Speaker's intervention she split the confirmatory votes on the deal in two, asking MPs to approve just the Withdrawal Agreement at first, leaving the Future Relationship until later.

As May pressed the question to the House a third time, Johnson began to wobble. It was not just the position of May that looked perilous, but of Brexit, the Conservative Party and, most significantly, Johnson's very career. His team were deeply concerned by the measures May might entertain if she failed on a third occasion, including a second referendum which could even undo Brexit. 'I said vote for the third time and we'll sort it out later,' recalls Frost, 'which was the wrong decision, but it's what I said. As we've seen subsequently, sorting stuff out later is not as easy as people say.'[29]

Johnson was one of forty-one Conservative MPs to switch their vote and back the deal, but it would not be enough: the government was still defeated 286 votes to 344 on 29 March, doomed by the DUP and ERG 'Spartans' who held steadfast against the deal. Johnson's blushes and leadership aspirations were spared, rendering his vote but an embarrassing aside which the true Brexit believers were content – for the time being – to forget. As May's leadership collapsed following failed talks with Labour and the historically disastrous performance in the 2019 European elections, Johnson positioned himself as the only credible candidate who could deliver Brexit and defeat Jeremy Corbyn. He had spent a career on the sidelines throwing rocks. Now it was time to deliver.

By Any Means Necessary: July–August 2019

Johnson entered No. 10 on 24 July under no illusions as to the fragility of his position. May had secured an extension of the Brexit deal deadline to 31 October, giving him just three months to obtain a deal capable of gaining the consent of Parliament. It had been over three years since the referendum, with progress as deadlocked as ever. Having trampled repeatedly all over May's own attempts to make Brexit happen, he could not now fail to deliver himself.

He had promised in the leadership campaign to leave the EU by

31 October, deal or no deal, no more delay, do or die. To convey his seriousness to prospective backers, a whiteboard had been placed conspicuously in his Westminster office to give the sense he had a clear strategy.[30] 'BREXIT PLAN DELAY IS DEFEAT', it read in his handwriting, with five objectives listed below:

- Leave October 31 deal or no deal
- Come out of Customs Union & Single Market
- Ensure flexibility for next phase
- End controversy
- Unite party

If he failed, it would be curtains for his premiership: he had been elected as May's successor with a very specific mandate. 'He was consumed with the idea that it could all be over very quickly unless he did absolutely everything he could and took the necessary risks,' reflects Gove.[31] Johnson's sense of peril sharpened his mind as he stood on the threshold of Downing Street. He was acutely aware of his personal shortcomings and weaknesses: indecision, lack of detailed grasp, disorganization and, above all else, a tendency to avoid difficult decisions and conversations. To help compensate and achieve the five objectives, he needed a crack Brexit team which could be trusted, a team sufficiently radical and steadfast in the face of criticism. Where he as principal lacked resolve and grip, they would inject it.

There was no question as to who would lead for him in Brussels. 'He never actually asked me,' says Frost, 'there was just an assumption. I messaged him asking if I was the right kind of person a week before he was to become PM, and he replied saying, "Don't be ridiculous!", so my name was just added to the list of people who came in on 24 July.'[32] Johnson trusted Frost to negotiate with minimal input – he was the only person the PM intellectually deferred to in the team. With Cummings Johnson would spar; never with Frost. Wherever disagreements arose or he was confused, Johnson asked Frost to explain his reasoning and he accepted it.

Likewise, Frost's deputy Oliver Lewis was a revered ally, a super brain who had stuck with Johnson during his wilderness months. A Vote Leave member and former Gove adviser, Lewis was of a similar political extraction to and close ally of Cummings, sharing a hardline attitude towards the EU and scepticism of the ERG's ability to achieve anything. A still young and polite man, he differed in style from Cummings in preferring to build bridges with those deemed of 'lesser intellect' rather than shun them.

Cummings' infamous ability to make enemies was only matched by his ability to command devotion from those in whom he placed his faith. The eleventh hour addition of the former Vote Leave director was intended as both complement and compensation for the Prime Minister's unique political profile. Unlike the 'shopping trolley' Prime Minister that Cummings described in his 2021 testimony to a Commons inquiry hearing,[33] Cummings would not be blown around by events or sway with the emotions of Westminster. He had a far acuter organizational and strategic mind, able to add coherence and planning – two words he believed absent from Johnson's vocabulary. Above all, Cummings was willing to operate outside of the conventional rules of politics and cross the lines Johnson's aides wouldn't. 'I couldn't make Brexit happen, nor could Lynton Crosby. It required an approach to ignoring the rules neither of us would have been prepared to accept,' comments Johnson's campaign director Mark Fullbrook.[34] Johnson had signed a Faustian pact with the only man he believed could deliver for him, and his team were about to discover the implications. 'We needed a political terrorist to do Brexit, and that was what Dom provided.'

They were bolstered by another strong figure, Director of Legislative Affairs Nikki da Costa. She had crossed from Raab's team at the behest of Oliver Dowden and Eddie Lister, but unlike the rest of the team had no close working relationship with Johnson and was sceptical as to how hard a stance he would be willing to take. 'I went with Dom [Raab] because I knew he was willing to countenance no deal and do what it takes to get us out. Having seen Boris in action previously, including at the Foreign Office where he was persuaded by others to give ground, I didn't know if he had it in him,' says da Costa.[35] She soon found that any misgivings around Johnson's toughness were alleviated by the attitude of his empowered team. 'That first day in No. 10 I was told that Dom [Cummings] wanted to chat. He said he was happy to have me on board, but wanted to convey that Brexit was to be achieved "by any means necessary". We totally shared that viewpoint – that the referendum had to be honoured.'[36]

Cummings hit the ground running. On Thursday 25 July, the day after Johnson became Prime Minister, he convened a meeting for political staff in the upstairs Pillared Drawing Room in Downing Street. 'Brexit is the government's sole objective for the ninety-five days till the deadline on 31 October,' he announced. Six times he told them, 'We are leaving by any means necessary,' lest they had failed to grasp it. Holidays were to be cancelled for everyone, with intense hard work the new norm, and an emergency Budget due in October. 'We were given the firm sense that we had wasted the last three years, and poor performance wouldn't be tolerated,' says one present. 'Anyone leaking Cabinet papers will be fired in a new one strike policy,' he told startled attenders. 'And if any of you try taking me to an employment tribunal, you will be dead to me.' The warning could hardly have been starker. 'From now on, No. 10 will be run like NASA', was the leitmotif, with Cummings in charge at mission control. He was totally in his element: here he was ruling the roost in No. 10, as if 'all his past life had been but a preparation for this hour and for this trial', as Churchill had said. Those present were intimidated, intrigued and riveted.

Cummings gripped hold of the No. 10 timetable. His first meeting for senior staff in the Cabinet Room was at 8 a.m. 'All his meetings were focused on the task at hand, no fluff, all about getting Brexit done, exclusively on theme. He was phenomenal, the messaging, slogans, coherence, all perfect,' says a senior adviser. Johnson himself then chaired a meeting at 8.30 a.m. in his study next door – Cummings thought he was a terrible chair, and would send messages by WhatsApp to staff such as 'What the f**k is he saying?' To Cummings, the PM's meetings achieved nothing. Cummings then drove business throughout the day until, at 7 p.m., he chaired the final meeting of the evening.

To deliver on Brexit, Johnson and his team had no choice but to work with the civil service they distrusted to the core. 'Because Boris was leading the Brexit charge and felt the establishment was against him, he didn't trust anyone other than those who he knew,' says Lister.[37] Vote Leave had a particular paranoia about how the 'deep state', a group of officials they believed treated Vote Leave as dangerous radicals acting to foment no deal, might behave. The civil service was about to encounter the most sceptical incoming administration in history. By the account of one No. 10 official, 'Civil servants hadn't a clue what they were up against. The PM's team had a very strong conviction that Whitehall was imbued with people sceptical of Brexit, or sceptical of Boris. Or both.'

Whitehall was in a state of disquiet about what havoc Cummings might create. But in his first few months he proved oddly amenable. As a senior official says, 'Dom was complimentary and respectful to the civil service. He went out of his way to reassure us that the stalling on Brexit was a failure of politicians, not officials. There was blame for sure aimed at the late Jeremy Heywood and at Olly Robbins, and a belief the Treasury was not on board in planning for Brexit, but he was very respectful on a personal level in that early period.' Even then, they sensed the 'phoney war' phase would not last any longer than it had in 1939–40.

Praise for Cummings' leadership at No. 10 during the first six months was widespread among both political and civil service staff.[38] 'A total force of nature in that period, he put us on a war footing. The whole system changed around him in No. 10 and he gave the machine the impetus it had lacked before,' says one long-serving official. Another had 'never seen Downing Street so clearly focused, ever'. They were less enthused by his disregard for constitutional norms, the damage of no deal and implications for Northern Ireland, 'but for people who worked directly with the Prime Minister and Cummings, it was clear that being tough on Brexit in a Trumpian sense was just part of their negotiating tactic, and most of us understood that.'

Who was the monkey and who was the organ grinder? It was not Johnson providing the strategic vision, but his team to whom he gave the authority to undertake the high-stakes, high-risk work in his name. A No. 10 official confirms that 'this strategy was notionally set by the PM but really it was Cummings driving it, who had the PM's complete confidence at this stage'. Lewis concurs:

'Dom was leading, but Boris got the idea. He bought the basic logic that Parliament had created this whole horror, and Dom's line that it was the MPs who had forced us into this position, and our job was forcing them out of a horror they created.'[39] Johnson 'got the idea': there's a lot in those words.

Three years of stasis and multiple failed attempts to pass the Withdrawal Agreement meant the Johnson team was having to play chess in an end-game with drastically diminished pieces. 'After May we were left with just a pawn and a king, so it was getting the team to understand we were working within huge constraints,' says da Costa.[40]

Johnson was desperate to dump his predecessor's 'backstop', an attempted solution to the problem Brexit threw up in Northern Ireland that had proved unpopular among his backbench support. If prices were to be paid elsewhere in the deal, so be it. Maximum freedom for the future, minimum alignment. It was a deal Frost believed they could obtain (with difficulty) from the EU, and crucially it was a deal Johnson's strategists believed could be sold to the electorate if necessary.

But the ultimate weapon in the government's arsenal in securing Brexit was to be willing to leave the EU without a deal on 31 October. Cummings took it on himself to raise the temperature in No. 10 and beyond: 'No deal is real. It's a real thing. The country is not ready. The government is not ready. If no deal happens, we have to make certain the lights stay on, medical supplies are available,' he told shocked staff regularly.

Johnson, long a proponent of leveraging the *threat* of no deal, was eager for Cummings to make it credible through intensifying the contingency planning.[41] The preparation for no deal (hitherto stymied by Chancellor Hammond's refusal to fund it) would require a Herculean effort of administrative skill to achieve in just three months, and had to be driven by a Cabinet minister. Organization and financial acumen being at the bottom of Johnson's strengths, he was talked into assigning the task to Gove. The Prime Minister's still live animosity was countered by Cummings vigorously extolling his former boss's undoubted virtues. Despite Gove's backing of May's Chequers proposal, they still thought him the best candidate, the only candidate indeed on a notably lacklustre frontbench, capable of gripping the machine with the intensity and vigour that would be needed. Gove was distinctly apprehensive about pursuing no deal, and the lengths Johnson might go to in resolving Brexit. But any uneasiness he felt about the methods were outweighed by his fear of a complete collapse of the Conservative Party if the government once again failed to deliver Brexit.[42]

To tackle the upheaval across government and country no deal would cause, No. 10 implemented an innovative Cabinet committee structure. Chaired by Gove, the EU Exit Operations Committee brought together Cabinet ministers, senior officials and No. 10 advisers in a daily COBRA meeting, working through item by item the list of preparations needed before 31 October and troubleshooting problems in delivery to an extraordinary level of detail for a Cabinet committee. The sprint to prepare enforced a gruelling rhythm, with senior civil servants working overnight on their 6 p.m. papers to have them ready for 10 a.m. meetings the following day.[43] 'Gove pushed everything at a furious pace from July to October. It was all massively centralized,' recalls one permanent secretary.

The preparations included a 'Get Ready for Brexit' publicity campaign, conveying that 31 October would mean a definitive break from the EU, deal or no deal. The communication was not just aimed at companies that needed to prepare – it was to communicate to voters at large how far the government was going in its pursuit of Brexit.

Would Johnson really go through on the threat if pushed to it? In contrast to his public declarations, he held his cards close to his chest about how serious he was. 'He was smart enough not to let anyone know, not even David Frost, what he really thought,' explains one official who worked closely with the Prime Minister on the issue. 'How far he actually was willing to go, I don't know. Maybe he doesn't himself. There is a bit of him who would have been happy to stick up two fingers to prove that it was not as bad as everyone thought it would be.'

The counter-factual is unknowable, but faced with the cliff edge it is unlikely Johnson would have pursued no deal for the very same reason he appointed hardliners to front the process: he lacked the bravery to take decisions which would make him unpopular. Even with planning, a no deal Brexit would plunge the country into chaos for which Johnson would be blamed. 'Better to retain my popularity than my promises,' he thought. In the end, Parliament ensured he would not have the choice.

No. 10 vs the State: August–September 2019

For the next few weeks, the focus shifted to a protracted, and perhaps arcane debate over the parliamentary timetable. During the wilderness months after Johnson left the Foreign Office, Cummings and Lewis had been working together to explore tactical and legal options open to them to break through those forces in Parliament trying to resist Brexit. Shortly after the Chequers summit, ERG 'Spartan' Jacob Rees-Mogg had raised with Lewis the option of 'prorogation', the formal ending of a parliamentary session to circumvent opposition in Parliament by limiting the time available, an expedient which hadn't been used since 1948. But the idea did not progress beyond the early planning stages within the team. Simultaneously, da Costa was doing research of her own. 'I later learned that Theresa May had looked at prorogation as a possibility to create the space for her to get to the European Council before MPs moved against her, but found it too unpalatable.'[44] It was after publishing a leadership contest piece in *The Times*' 'Red Box' blog on how the Conservative PM should be strategizing, that Raab's team took notice and she was approached by them to work on a package of measures to get them to the October European Council meeting with minimal disruption from turbulent parliamentarians.

Every trick in the book was considered to keep the parliamentary timetable in government control and stop Remainers in their tracks: a Queen's Speech, a Budget and prorogation. The last, a royal prerogative, came out top of the list. It would end the parliamentary session, wiping unfinished business off the table and preventing the introduction of new anti-Brexit legislation during the period before Parliament reconvened. Raab's pushing publicly for prorogation during the leadership contest had worried and annoyed Johnson's team. 'It became an issue which we didn't want. I said to Boris, "Don't lie and say you won't do it, but suggest that you're not attracted to the idea," as obviously in an ideal world we wouldn't have to,' recalls Lewis.[45] After Raab's campaign sank, da Costa transferred the prorogation playbook over to Johnson, very much aware he was not in an ideal world.

At a Chequers strategy meeting on 9 August, she took the Brexit team and those working on the election campaign through her rationale. The parliamentary session had dragged on too long, and prorogation for a Queen's Speech was needed and justifiable, giving them cover for what Cummings really wanted: to minimize the number of days spent in Parliament where the government could be defeated and anti-Brexit legislation introduced. Johnson's team believed that with prorogation in place the Remainers wouldn't have the legislative time or judicial ability to block no deal, keeping the threat in play. Cummings addressed the team: 'They will have to be very well organized. If they get the best lawyers and luck they might be able to mount a defence,' adding, 'But I don't think they will.'

This was the plan. Prorogation was to last five weeks, to commence between 9 and 12 September before Parliament reconvened on 14 October. The Queen's Speech upon MPs' return would give the government control for several days of debate, taking them up until the crucial European Council meeting beginning on 17 October. This was feasibly the last date on which a deal could be agreed with the EU, after which no deal would cease to have value as a credible threat and instead be an inevitability for both sets of negotiators. Parliament had five working days between 3 and 9 September to prevent Johnson from pursuing a no deal Brexit before the crucial showdown with the EU.

In the weeks before prorogation was actioned Johnson had nervously discussed the legality of the measure with Attorney General Geoffrey Cox, the figure who pronounces on the legality of government action. Cox's provisional view was that the prorogation as proposed should and would probably be found a 'non-justiciable' issue and the courts would therefore not touch it. Nevertheless, he was concerned that the Supreme Court showed worrying signs of an appetite for expanding its constitutional role, and he texted Johnson to caution that 'we can never be confident that it will not interfere'.[46] In an email, and in a subsequent meeting between the two in the

Downing Street flat in early August, Cox recommended that the Prime Minister secure his advice in writing before pressing ahead.

Da Costa wrote her fateful memo on prorogation to the Prime Minister on 15 August, with a recommendation of the timetable and emphasizing that MPs would need to return by the time of the EU October Council in order to pass a deal. Johnson's response in the margin: '✓ YES'.[47] He was not 100 per cent enthused.

One of the very few copied into the memo, Cabinet Secretary Mark Sedwill, was caught out by the move, as were most of his senior civil service. He told the Wednesday morning meeting of permanent secretaries on 19 August that he hadn't been consulted on the decision, and that they had taken advantage of his absence on holiday to push it through. His expressed concern was not at the prorogation itself, but that the timetable might deny Parliament an opportunity to debate, and that a no deal Brexit might happen by default. More constitutionally perilous still, that it would be perceived as an abuse and misuse of prerogative power, thereby politicizing the Crown. 'Buckingham Palace was very unsettled by the Queen being dragged in,' says an official privy to the discussions. 'They hadn't been properly prepared and warned when on holiday in August, and the Palace felt they would have been in a stronger position had they been contacted earlier and had a chance to think it through.' Decoding the language, they were mightily pissed off.

For the trio at the helm of the 'deep state', the so-called magic circle of Cabinet Secretary Sedwill, the Queen's private secretary Edward Young and No. 10's Peter Hill (in his final weeks as PPS), it was an incredibly delicate issue, sparking tension between Buckingham Palace and No. 10 unseen in recent years. 'There was a serious risk at the imminent Privy Council that the Queen wasn't going to have been informed of what was going on,' says one Cabinet Office source. 'There's no doubt it caused a lot of consternation,' says a close source, a masterly understatement. Palace legal advice suggested the issue was likely non-justiciable, but nevertheless placed the Queen in a highly difficult position in forcing her to act, by convention, on prime ministerial advice which may not have been beyond reproach.

Also caught unawares was Cox. Despite asking to deliver his written advice before any decision was taken, he was not aware of the move until five days *after* Johnson had ticked the memo, only later informed by da Costa of the change in position. Now Johnson was wanting him to 'sell' the plan to Cabinet. Ten minutes before Cabinet and Cox spoke (via telephone) on 28 August to discuss it, Cox received a call from the Prime Minister. He told him that the Queen had already consented to the prorogation over the phone the day before, and went on, 'Geoffrey, we're about to have this ministerial call and some of our friends are very jumpy.' Alluding to their previous informal discussions, he said, 'Please don't spook the Cabinet by talking about litigation risk.'[48] Cox accordingly gave his professional view that the prorogation was indeed lawful and within the constitution, downplaying accusations of unlawfulness as 'politically motivated', according to minutes later leaked to Sky News.[49]

As the small Privy Council met with the Queen for her to consent to the prorogation on 28 August, a tidal wave of fury from MPs swept over Westminster. Parliament was not set to return until 3 September, but Tory MPs Dominic Grieve and Cameron's confidant Oliver Letwin, together with pro-EU Labour frontbenchers including Hilary Benn, had already begun plotting their own next steps. First was to take control of the order paper governing the timetable upon Parliament's return. Speaker John Bercow had shown considerable appetite for enabling Parliament to take control over the legislative timetable during May's downfall, and the reaction to prorogation and the sidelining of Parliament only strengthened support for the Grieve group. Using the six-day period before prorogation, they would seek to push through legislation preventing the Prime Minister from pursuing no deal.[50] Known as the Benn Act, after Hilary Benn who introduced it, the bill proposed that if the House of Commons had not consented to either a Withdrawal Agreement or no deal by 19 October, the Prime Minister would be compelled to seek an extension of the withdrawal date to 31 January 2021.

As planned, the order paper was seized to allow for the debating of the bill. Twenty-one Conservative MPs voted to allow for it, including Ken Clarke, Philip Hammond, Rory Stewart and David Gauke. No. 10 was furious, but not surprised. The team already had their strategy planned for this very eventuality. 'We'd discussed in 2018 the idea of expelling any rebels,' recounts Lewis. 'We told Boris that you now have to demonstrate that you mean it. Honouring the election and referendum results is more important than keeping the peace.'[51] Cummings and Lewis were enthusiasts for tough action, and saw it as the way of reasserting No. 10's hold over the party – Lister, who lacked their revolutionary spirit, was sceptical, as was Johnson himself. For the first time since arriving in office, he began to question the extreme strategy. Stories started emerging that he was 'not in a good place. He's telling friendly Cabinet ministers that he is concerned it has got out of control and is asking what he should do.'[52] Delivering bad news was an activity Johnson detested to his core. Until now he had delegated decisions he knew would cause him pain; removal of the whip rested with him alone.

Chief Whip Mark Spencer pressed Johnson to come to a verdict on the rebels' fates: 'If this has to happen, then it has to happen now.' After rounds of discussion in the team, Cummings turned to Lister and asked him again for his view. 'I don't like it, but I just don't know what else we can do.' The nod from his loyal lieutenant was enough for Johnson. The whip was withdrawn from twenty-one Conservatives, with two more – Amber Rudd and the Prime Minister's brother Jo Johnson – resigning from Cabinet and leaving voluntarily in the following days. The two had spoken about their predicament before making the decision, worried they would end up 'like frogs being boiled' if they failed to take a stand.[53] His brother's resignation hit Johnson hard. Not only siblings, Jo's wife was close friends with Marina, and Johnson was struggling to come to terms with the upheavals in his personal life, exacerbated by the bombshell news of Carrie discovering she was pregnant. The pent-up frustration unbottled itself as he addressed his aides, as one recalls. 'Those perfidious f**kers,' he told them. 'I'll deal with anyone who goes against me.'

Having inherited a fragile minority government with a majority of 317, Johnson was now attempting to rule with fewer than 300 MPs. In the words of da Costa, 'We had made the calculation that it really didn't matter whether we lost by seven votes or by forty. They're no different, it's still a defeat.'[54] Leading a near-decimated Conservative Party, Johnson doubly believed the only way through was to change the numbers, and set about calling for a general election to little avail – he was many votes short of the two-thirds required by the Fixed-term Parliaments Act.[55]

While Spencer set out the following day offering a short ladder back to the party for any penitent rebels who regretted their vote, Johnson chaired a stunned Cabinet. Many present had friends among those summarily booted out from the party but only Northern Ireland Secretary Julian Smith, used to being forthright in his previous tenure as Chief Whip, spoke up in opposition and insisted the whip should be restored. Cabinet was cowed and, whatever its members' private reservations, leaned towards accepting the decision. At its conclusion, the Prime Minister pulled aside one hesitant minister: 'You have to understand why we've done this. These people are c**ts, utter c**ts.' The Cabinet minister was shocked, but not for the reason that Johnson intended. The Prime Minister had failed to appreciate that not just his actions, but also his language, were grossly offensive.

Later that afternoon, Benn presented his bill to Parliament for second and third readings. No longer possessing a majority, the government was helpless to resist. The hope in No. 10 remained that proceedings could be sufficiently slowed down in the House of Lords that even if it passed both Houses, it would be snuffed out by the closure of Parliament. 'A major miscalculation,' admits a No. 10 adviser. 'Nobody had picked up that all bills flagged for Royal Assent get it automatically in prorogation.' The Chief Whip's senior civil servant might have pointed it out had they not been on holiday, as might government lawyers, had No. 10 not been reluctant to discuss the political motivations for prorogation with them. The bill duly received Royal Assent on 9 September, the first major blow for No. 10's strategy.

The reaction in Downing Street was vitriolic. This was war. Johnson felt that Parliament had forced him into a position where he had little opportunity to pursue a deal now that the no deal cliff edge was taken away. But Cummings, sitting in the Prime Minister's chair at the 8 a.m. meetings in the following days, came up with an audacious fight-back plan to counter the 'Surrender Act' as he began to refer to it. To beat those who were thwarting them, they needed to use their secret weapon: Brexit had become an impasse that necessitated a general election to fix it. A clip from the 1970 film *Cromwell* circulated on their WhatsApp groups, actor Richard Harris uttering the famous words to dissolve Parliament: 'In the name of God, go!'

The stakes were rising ever higher. 'Enemies' such as Grieve baulked at the use of 'Surrender Act', but their demands for Johnson to recant his words after using the phrase fifteen times in the Chamber on the day Parliament reconvened served only to goad on No. 10.[56] 'It just made Dom, Boris and I refer to it as "surrender" even more. We were now into complete trench warfare,' says da Costa.[57]

In reaction to the legislation Cummings' methods grew even more extreme, advising that the Prime Minister should break the law if he had to. Officials were horrified as they were told to produce written text warning of a no deal exit on 31 October, telling the public the UK was leaving the EU 'come what may'. They knew the warnings to be untrue in light of the Benn Act, but were pushed to produce them regardless. When senior officials attempted to stand up for their colleagues, insisting that any breach of the civil service code in their advice was unacceptable, Johnson's team harangued them as obstructionists. 'We had made it clear that we were not granted the right to speak something that we knew was not true. It was very unpleasant to have Cummings shouting at us over it,' recalls one. Some who raised concerns found their careers subsequently blighted: briefed against in the press, pushed to resign, or their contracts not renewed.

No. 10's problems did not end with the Benn Act. Contingency planning for no deal, nicknamed 'Operation Yellowhammer', had partially leaked in August. Warning of food and medicine shortages in a reasonable worst case scenario made for grim reading. Still in control of the order paper, Grieve pressed the government with a motion to publish the full documents, as well as disclose communications relating to the suspension of Parliament. A defeat on 9 September was Johnson's sixth loss in six days; he had lost total control of the House of Commons.

The flurry of legislative action from the anti-no deal MPs had rendered prorogation unsuccessful, failing in its core objective. Parliament had successfully tied No. 10's hands within the six days afforded to them, not only preventing no deal but embarrassing the government and forcing Johnson to remain in government rather than call an election for good measure. When Parliament's overseer Black Rod entered the Chamber shortly before 2 a.m. on 10 September to mark the commencement of the prorogation ceremony, Johnson survived the ordeal, but nothing more. Having faced down the legislature, up next was the judiciary. Challenges to prorogation had been making their way through the courts that month. The High Court in England had rejected Remain campaigner Gina Miller's case against the Prime Minister, on the basis that prorogation was inherently a political act, and that it could not be judged legitimate or illegitimate by legal standards. Joanna Cherry of the Scottish National Party (SNP) found greater success in Scotland, with the Inner House of the Court of Session ruling prorogation unlawful due to the Prime Minister's attempt to use the measure as a tool to avoid parliamentary scrutiny. The cases went jointly to the Supreme Court.

Inside No. 10, there was panic among officials as they saw Cummings blocking notes on the Cherry case from going to the Prime Minister to keep him in the dark and thus to underplay the emerging risk of prorogation, according to senior civil servants. 'Cummings didn't care if decisions were not taken by the Prime

Minister. He tried to take them himself, as if he *was* the Prime Minister,' alleges one, a harbinger of what was to come. Cummings believed the greatest threat to the Prime Minister's position was the Prime Minister himself and would do whatever it took to keep him on track, constitutionality be damned. Senior advisers necessarily shape and influence the information flow the Prime Minister receives, but not deliberately to circumvent him. Even when the Prime Minister did receive guidance he was left frustrated; one official watched him physically rip up a piece of prorogation advice from the Cummings team on account of it being so poorly argued and written.

In its 24 September ruling the Supreme Court unexpectedly saw the issue as justiciable, and thereafter savaged the government's position in its ruling, finding unanimously for Miller and Cherry.[58] 'It is impossible for us to conclude, on the evidence which has been put before us, that there was any reason – let alone a good reason – to advise Her Majesty to prorogue Parliament for five weeks... It follows that the decision was unlawful.'[59] The government had failed to put forward a cogent argument for prorogation, the Court finding that the Prime Minister had advised the Queen to act unlawfully. The decision had profound constitutional significance, a major landmark in the debate over prerogative powers and principles, but Johnson cared little about that. What mattered to him was the severe personal embarrassment of the Supreme Court undoing his advice, necessitating a grovelling apology to the Queen.

In New York for the annual trip to the United Nations General Assembly Johnson erupted in anger at the news, cursing Supreme Court President Lady Hale herself for the ruling, then extending his fury to those he felt had failed to warn him of the risks. 'What the f**k am I reading? You all told me this would be fine.' He had embarrassed himself in front of the Queen and the establishment whose approval he sought, all for nothing. A mixture of the team's devotion to Cummings and Johnson's lack of trust towards outsiders meant there were no dissenting voices within the political team reminding the Prime Minister of the risks. But the blame ultimately lay at the judgement of the Prime Minister: he had appointed the singular team for the very reason that he would waver over such decisions if given the opportunity. Likewise he had disregarded the caveats to Cox's legal advice, focusing instead on the 'yes' he sought to hear. Johnson's inability to recognize inconvenient truths had brought him to this point.

The Benn Act had already killed the prospect of pursuing no deal; the Supreme Court verdict merely put the nail in the coffin. Prorogation undone, Parliament now had ample time to legislate as they saw fit, allowing for the closing any potential loopholes Johnson and Cummings may have found. The strategy of prorogation had backfired totally and completely, galvanizing the rebels and failing to achieve any of No. 10's strategic objectives.

The Compromise: October 2019

Negotiations directly with the EU were back on, which had been a long time coming. Johnson's mid-August dinners with Chancellor Angela Merkel in Berlin and President Emmanuel Macron in Paris had paved the way, but were the subject of heated debate in No. 10. 'It would be ridiculous to go to them, we'd look just like May, chasing them all around Europe,' Cummings told the Prime Minister. 'That's not right. You have to engage, to create a process with the Europeans so that you can negotiate with them later,' the officials rebutted. Johnson for once sided with the mandarins, and earned from Merkel the opportunity to find an alternative solution to the backstop 'in the next thirty days'. With her nod, the Withdrawal Agreement had been reopened.

Only on 8 September was it clear to the civil servants working on Brexit that Johnson would eventually pursue a deal with Europe. Johnson, a far from happy Cummings, Frost and officials met for a strategy session at the government's country house Chevening in Kent, holding a lengthy discussion about the shape Brexit needed to take now. Johnson, as ever, was considering his career as he led them to his conclusion: 'Chaps, it's clear we need a deal to secure a majority at the election. So we go for a deal.' Officials had been nervy as to what he truly wanted before, but now there was no doubt: a deal it was.

By the end of September, options for No. 10 were beginning to look slim. Failure to prevent the Prime Minister being restrained at the October European Council meeting and the humiliating ruling on prorogation had very significantly diminished his stature. The dual defeats of the Benn Act and the Supreme Court verdict led to open speculation about Johnson's imminent fall. Even Cummings was advocating for a more conciliatory approach with the EU.

Reopening negotiations would not be easy despite Merkel's signal. EU leaders had not warmed to the UK approach under Johnson; indeed, animosity from other EU leaders was palpable in their discussions in early October, seeing their new interlocutor as lacking seriousness and credibility. As the government attempted to re-establish negotiations with the EU, Merkel, despite her earlier encouragement, tore Johnson to shreds in a phone call on 8 October, insisting that Northern Ireland would remain bound to EU rules in perpetuity. Two days earlier Macron had similarly eviscerated the Prime Minister over both the fact and execution of

Brexit, in what had become a routine occurrence for Johnson since the vote. Cummings believed the haranguings would play well for No. 10 domestically, and briefed an edited version of the Merkel conversation to journalists.[60] But any gain from such positive headlines was just a distraction. What Johnson needed was an EU decision-maker with whom he could draw up a compromise, given Europe's two most influential leaders appeared unwilling to provide a resolution to the major stumbling block of Northern Ireland.

Backchannels had been established by both the civil service and political teams, to mixed effectiveness. John Bew, Johnson's foreign affairs adviser and historian drafted in from academia, had been working on one. Bew was neither a Tory nor a Brexiteer, and had become nervous at the rhetoric used by No. 10 over the previous months. He found common ground with fellow historian in the Irish Taoiseach's office Patrick Geoghegan, in wanting to avoid a no deal outcome. Along with Frost, he visited Dublin during September. Officials, however, contest the importance of their role in the process. 'We had to send Bew and Lister to Dublin with the team to make it look like there was some involvement on the political side, but it was the relationship between Sedwill and [his opposite in the Taoiseach's office] Martin Fraser which got the conversations going,' says one. Along with Sedwill, the Cabinet Office's Brendan Threlfall and No. 10's Jonno Evans had been leading talks between the UK and Irish civil servants, in which the bulk of the preparation for a potential deal was being done. 'It's hard to overstate how little the political team engaged with Dublin; it was all the official side making this happen behind the scenes,' says one observer.

After Taoiseach Leo Varadkar and Johnson had hit it off at September meetings in Dublin and at the UN in New York, that relationship became the Prime Minister's strongest within the EU, and the best way to a deal. Northern Ireland continued to be the major stumbling block in negotiations, and if Johnson could find a solution with which Ireland agreed, the rest of the EU was likely to fall in behind it. Varadkar had not found May's cold awkwardness easy to engage with, so her successor's upbeat exuberance was a breath of fresh air. The idea to approach the EU through Varadkar had been bolstered during Johnson's early September visit to Balmoral: after a private walk with the Queen he suggested to officials that she had delicately planted, without saying so explicitly, the idea of talking to Varadkar to solve the impasse. Johnson and Varadkar held a critical phone call in the early days of October, when the Prime Minister talked about his desire to perform a 'backstopectomy' but still avoid a hard border.[61] The Taoiseach was willing to hear what Johnson had to offer, and agreed to a summit on 10 October.

Officials were bemused by the selection of Thornton Manor in the Wirral as the setting. 'It was all rather weird, a hotel of the kind Premier League footballers use for their weddings,' recalls an official present. The choice was intentionally atypical from the usual diplomatic haunts, set somewhere Johnson's advisers thought could encourage a break from the entrenched mindsets and positions which had dogged negotiations. Civil servants' expectations for the meeting were accordingly low, despite officials from each premier's team working closely towards an agreement in the run-up. 'We'd constructed the shared group carefully before the meeting, but only once they are in the room together do you know if the principals can find the words to do a deal,' says one.

On the journey up from London, Frost and Johnson discussed the Battle of Brunanburh, supposed to have taken place near to the location of the venue. In 937 Anglo-Saxon King Athelstan scored a great victory over the King of Dublin, preventing a break-up of his kingdom and providing the inception of English nationalism. The parallels were too tempting for Johnson to miss.

After a nervous introduction between the two camps, Tuesday's phone call still fresh in the mind, the principals were put in a room alone, the idea being a short bilateral meeting to ease tension and lay the groundwork for an area of agreement. Staff awkwardly waited outside, while Johnson and Varadkar were locked in conversation for ninety minutes, until finally Johnson emerged. 'Mark and David, could you come in?' he gestured to his Cabinet Secretary and chief negotiator.

They entered, along with two of Varadkar's aides. 'We've agreed!' proclaimed Johnson. The two recounted the meeting, and the advisers felt a spurt of optimism that, for the first time since Johnson became Prime Minister, the issue was likely to be unlocked.

Until this point, Johnson had left the strategizing and negotiating to his team, abrogating the lead role in the formulation of Brexit. The compromise had been orchestrated between Johnson's and Varadkar's teams, but in those crucial ninety minutes he had channelled his strength of charisma to mend a gap of his own creation. 'There's an open question about how much he contributed to the substance of Brexit,' considers a senior official, 'but with Varadkar he personally played a dynamic role in landing a deal. There's strong evidence that the Prime Minister was important in getting us there.'

There were two vital differences between Johnson and Varadkar's agreement and May's Brexit deal for the Northern Ireland Protocol. The first was Varadkar's agreement to 'a consent mechanism', through which the Northern Ireland Legislature would have to vote on renewing the Protocol after four years. 'It allowed us to accept a lot of things which would otherwise be unacceptable, so the scope of it spread and spread,' recalls Frost.[62]

The second was moving the de facto border for goods to the Irish Sea. For Irish Unionists this was a deeply uncomfortable notion, and May had fought the EU hard to procure the backstop and ensure Northern Ireland would remain aligned with the rest of the UK. 'No UK Prime Minister could ever agree to [a border in the Irish Sea],' she told the House of Commons in February 2018.[63] Johnson, speaking at the Democratic Unionist Party conference in November 2018, echoed his predecessor. 'We would be damaging the fabric of the Union with regulatory checks and even customs controls… no British Conservative government could or should sign up to any such arrangement,' he told the crowd, receiving raucous applause.[64] He was burning that promise, and burning the DUP, less than a year later.

'Johnson believed the EU would take a generous view of the Protocol and that they would make concessions. I don't think he ever admitted to us that he had made concessions,' says a senior official. This view was not universal within No. 10, and some recall Johnson displaying discomfort with the outcome of negotiations when the implications were described. Even as he secured a premiership-saving agreement, the Prime Minister's swerving between his choices persisted.

The deal itself was imperfect for No. 10, but a border down the Irish Sea was the only way to achieve an immediate resolution allowing for the level of regulatory divergence Johnson and his team sought. His hope was that he could shake hands with the EU now and simply change the parts he disliked later. One No. 10 aide says, 'He always felt that the Northern Ireland agreement would never hold. It's typical of him, because he'll agree to something today even if it means a bigger problem tomorrow. He always meant to tear the Protocol up.'

Johnson also knew he could not publicly utter the truth of the matter, that he was creating divergence between Great Britain and Northern Ireland. 'There's no question of there being checks on goods going NI/GB or GB/NI,' he told Sky's Sophy Ridge, in denial of leaked Treasury analysis.[65] Johnson was not naïve about the implications of the deal, nor had he misunderstood what was agreed as Cummings later claimed.[66] Instead he believed he could get around the issue, and if he couldn't then at least he would have told the people what they wished to hear. 'People saying now he didn't know what he signed up for, it's completely wrong,' argues one senior political adviser. 'He was desperate to move the country on, and signed thinking he could change it later. It was best in his mind to get the deal and fight the election with it.' Johnson's comments in August 2020 that there would be a trade border in the Irish Sea 'over my dead body' were not borne of ignorance as to the deal he had signed up for, but of a brazen disregard for honesty.[67]

Frost now defends Johnson's Unionism as similar to May's, but their choices both in the deal and how they pursued it reveal a gulf in priorities between the premiers. 'May was, in the end, willing to subordinate a clean Brexit to keeping Northern Ireland in alignment with Great Britain, and if the price was Britain remaining aligned with the EU forever then she was willing to pay that. We weren't.'[68] The strategy Johnson empowered Cummings to pursue had little time for questions of the Union or the peace process. The chief adviser was eager to weaponize the issue wherever it might apply pressure on the EU, including the threat of withdrawing security cooperation in the region. 'I don't give a f**k if Northern Ireland falls into the sea,' he exclaimed in a meeting where it was suggested that Parliament would need to vote on legislation to protect Northern Ireland in the event of no deal.[69] Johnson placed his political survival ahead of the integrity of the United Kingdom, the very thing his predecessor had refused to do.

The constructive ambiguity in the deal between Varadkar and Johnson held. On Johnson's return to Downing Street, the team finally felt there was momentum behind a deal. Official Jonno Evans was tasked with piecing together the details of a deal from the bilateral meeting's rough outline. Brexit Secretary Stephen Barclay, who had been peripheral to Frost in the negotiating process, met with the EU's chief negotiator Michel Barnier to advance the paperwork. By the European Council meeting on 17 October the deal had been wrapped up and unanimously endorsed, in part due to the skilful work of Permanent Representative to the EU Tim Barrow in keeping channels of communication on the continent open and receptive.

Not content with success in Europe, Cummings was adamant to vanquish their adversaries at home. The Benn Act required the Prime Minister to send a letter extending the withdrawal date on 19 October only in the event of no deal. With a deal in hand, the Prime Minister could keep his promise to leave the EU by 31 October if Parliament could be convinced. As Johnson held a special Saturday sitting of Parliament, moving to pass the new Withdrawal Agreement, Oliver Letwin sprang his trap – an amendment delaying Parliament's approval of the deal until all legislation had been passed, removing the one chance the Prime Minister had to not send the letter. Cummings had joked with the team about how to frustrate the Benn Act before, with suggestions such as sending it by carrier pigeon, or getting a staff member to walk it from Downing Street to Brussels and 'hoping' it arrived by

31 October, but he was deadly serious about finding any available loophole to get around it. As was Johnson, recalling his incendiary statement in September that he would rather be 'dead in a ditch' than accept an extension from the 'Surrender Act'.[70]

Cummings continued to push Sedwill, Cox and Advocate General for Scotland Richard Keen for a way to circumvent the requirement of an extension. They were aghast at Cummings' behaviour in meetings with the Prime Minister. Cox and Keen had repeatedly to explain that it would be appalling for the Prime Minister to act as Cummings wished and break the law. Cummings stood up, screamed words to the effect of 'you f**king idiots' and left the room in frustration, only for Johnson to 'run after him like an anxious husband would to his wife', as one witness describes. Cummings was not just of the opinion that signing the letter could be avoided, but that if proceedings were brought it could be beneficial for the Prime Minister, the ultimate demonstration to the electorate that they had put everything on the line to achieve Brexit and were being hamstrung by the establishment. Johnson caught his chief adviser outside the room, and they came back in with an agreement that they would send the letter with caveats: the Prime Minister would not personally sign it, and there would be a second accompanying letter stating that the extension was not his personal view.

No. 10 pressed on with passing the deal through Parliament, undeterred and determined. The ERG had been wined and dined from July, with Johnson eager to get them on board. Lewis and Danny Kruger, No. 10 political secretary, were charged with converting hardliners to the view that the deal would be an acceptable compromise. Key ERG figures including Steve Baker, Bill Cash and Iain Duncan Smith gave their fundamental demands to No. 10.[71] These were then fed to Frost and accommodated by the negotiation team, yet the ERG were still hesitant to get on board. 'What do you want us to do?' Lewis finally exclaimed to them. 'We prorogued Parliament, we've pushed as far as we can. If we go any further then Parliament will replace us. This is the limit.'[72] Begrudgingly they accepted his argument, and their integration into the deal-making process ensured they were tethered to the agreement for the eventual vote.

The ERG had been allied with the DUP throughout the Brexit process. Now faced with a border down the Irish Sea (despite Johnson's denials), the DUP could follow them no further. Meetings between Johnson, Bew and DUP leader Arlene Foster proved unfruitful. Discussions between Lewis and the DUP's key figures were no more successful. The price of the Northern Ireland Protocol had been the loss of the Unionists.

The Conservative whips launched a 'charm and harm' offensive on a third faction, the MPs who had lost the whip. 'Vote for the deal now, and there's a future for you in the party. Vote against, and your career is over', was the message.[73] Exhausted by nearly a year of ferment in Parliament, cognizant that the agreement would end the uncertainty of no deal which had been their red line, all but three MPs fell into place.

The loss of the DUP meant that even with independents back on board, Conservative votes would not be enough. Kruger was leading negotiations with a group of MPs, led by pro-Brexit Labour MP Caroline Flint. He believed there was potential for the bill to be passed before 31 October, but Cummings was sceptical. 'Even if they say they'll vote for it, you can't trust them. The only way out of this is with a general election.'

At second reading on 22 October the Withdrawal Agreement passed by 329 votes to 299, nineteen Labour rebels and the bulk of the ex-Conservative independents voting in favour of the deal. After four votes on the Withdrawal Agreement, two rounds of indicative votes on eight different propositions and eleven months since Theresa May had first brought her deal back from Brussels, Parliament had at last passed a vote intended to resolve the question of Brexit.

To keep Johnson's promise to leave and pass the all-important third reading before 31 October the government would need to act with rapidity. A programme motion was tabled, but the government soon found that the Labour MPs who had voted for the bill at second reading had no interest in supporting the breakneck pace of proceedings. Cummings was proven correct in his estimation of the Labour rebels – all but five of the nineteen would switch their vote against the government. Seven independent MPs switched too, and the government was defeated 308 votes to 322.

The Prime Minister had finally reconciled to his adviser's view that this Parliament was utterly, fundamentally, irreparably broken. The deal ready but timetable shot down, Johnson knew there was just one lever remaining to secure control: a general election.

Brexit, Done?

Johnson and Brexit are two rare phenomena inextricably intertwined in history. Without Johnson, no Brexit; without Brexit, Johnson may never have become Prime Minister. Brexit made Johnson: the cause galvanized Conservative MPs to gather around the flag of a politician whose time at the top was languishing. In return Johnson made Brexit happen, aided by Cummings' single-minded determination, though both, curiously, were detached from proving Brexit a success. Their methods were transgressive, but the result was undeniable. Why then was he so bashful about his legacy being Brexit?

Despite this co-dependence with it, Johnson was never a true believer nor lover of his bedfellow. Brexit was never the love of his life: he was always searching for something more meaningful to him, if amorphous, like levelling up. The necessary instincts were present in him throughout, but at each juncture it was the prospect of career advancement that was his primary spur: in his decision to campaign for Leave, his resignation from the Foreign Office, even the deal he reached, he was motivated by the belief that any damage to the Union and institutions was secondary to his winning the general election and securing his place in No. 10. Johnson did what was best for himself; if Britain benefited in the process, well, it was a fortunate occurrence.

Though he would campaign on 'getting Brexit done' in the general election to come through his exit deal, Johnson knew the issue was far from resolved. Brexit may have withdrawn from the immediate public consciousness and disappeared from the front pages of the papers, but the forces Johnson unleashed in 2016 were not a moment; they were a process. The exit deal was merely the first step. Johnson's task now was not to break a deadlock, but to craft an enduring vision of Britain's place in the world. How seriously he took that quest, and with what effect, will be revealed later in our story.

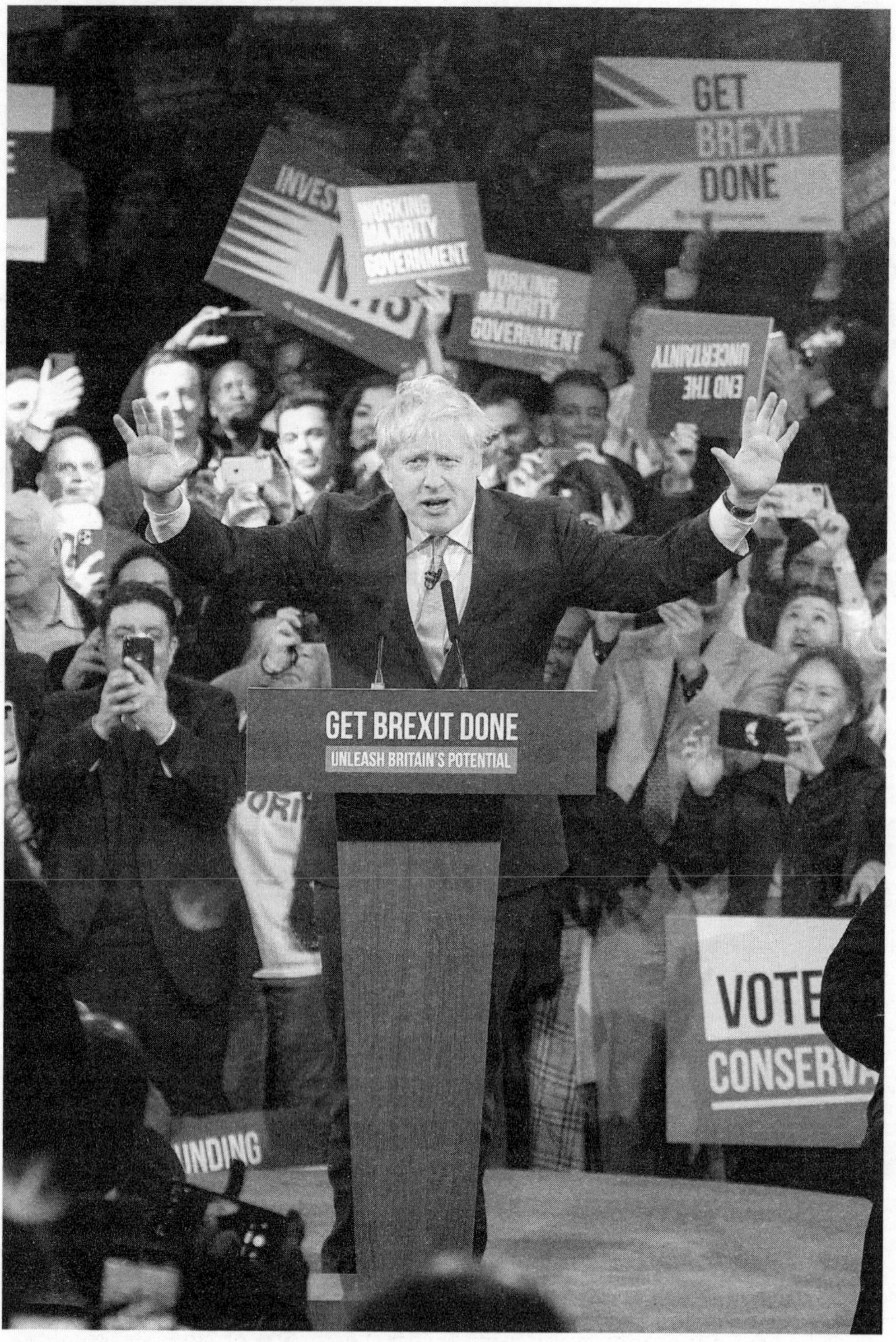

Johnson rallies the crowd the day before his general election victory

3

ELECTION

'Remind me, how long was the shortest tenure of a Prime Minister?' Johnson is barely two months into his premiership, and he's worried.

'One hundred and nineteen days, Prime Minister. George Canning,' replies an aide.

'Ah yes,' Johnson replies apprehensively. He is dreading being defeated in a general election and becoming the briefest Prime Minister in British history.

Just months before, in the summer of 2019, the electoral landscape could hardly have been more dire for a Conservative Party wondering if its entitlement to govern could endure much longer. The diabolical result in May 2019, just 8.8 per cent of votes in the European parliamentary election, its worst result ever in a national poll, showed just how grim things could be. Fear of the abyss might have driven Tory MPs lemming-like to back Johnson, despite their qualms over his integrity, methods and lack of policy. But was even his legendary appeal enough for victory nationally? Labour leader Jeremy Corbyn, a reduced figure since 2017, was a huge asset as a motivator for Conservative MPs and voters alike to unite against Labour. What else could Johnson magic up, given he had no philosophy to offer, and with the party rent from top to bottom on policy? The next general election was not due until the summer of 2022. What if he failed to finesse a general election being called before: might the party become bored with him by 2020 or 2021? Worse, what happened if one did take place – and he lost? The idea of being leader in opposition had as much attraction to him as, to use one of his favourite expressions, polishing a turd.

Worryingly, the change in leadership had provided only the slightest uptick for the Conservatives. In July, as he came to power, government approval lay at a mere 14 per cent.[1] Westminster voting intentions were scarcely better, 25 per cent of voters saying they would back the party, down from the 42 per cent May had acquired in 2017. One reason for optimism at least was that the Conservative Party led the Liberal Democrats by two points, Labour by six, and Farage's revitalized Brexit Party by eight.[2]

What followed over the next few months was the biggest electoral turnaround in modern political history, with a continuation of the 'shock and awe' tactics No. 10 had deployed, if not always successfully, to blast their way through the Brexit impasse. Just six months after coming into office in July, without a majority in Parliament, Johnson found himself with the greatest of electoral records, burnishing his brand as the most successful political campaigner in Conservative history since Margaret Thatcher. With their most decisive win since 1987, the party received 42.4 per cent of the vote and nearly 14 million ballots cast. The precipitous and miraculous turnaround in the fortune of the party was comparable indeed to Thatcher's greatest election victory in 1983, all the more remarkable because Johnson didn't have a Falklands War to boost his authority.

The eighty-seat majority in December 2019 marked the pinnacle of Johnson's entire period in office. John Major was the only other Conservative leader since 1945 to have won a fourth consecutive general election victory for the party, in April 1992, and that was with a measly majority of twenty-one, down from Thatcher's 101 landslide nearly five years before. Johnson was intent on avoiding the nonsense government he thought Major then presided over for five miserable years. No, he seized on the victory as a personal vindication from voters, an endorsement of himself rather than of the party he led to victory. As if he had been elected president with a direct mandate from the people, like his political hero Ronald Reagan, rather than as head of a party for which he had little affection. He had no more respect for the leadership of Cameron or May than he had for Major. All he considered were second-raters, lacklustre. Now, he was going to show the country what real leadership was about, to do to Britain what he had done to London. To be the twenty-first-century Churchill or Thatcher.

How did this bolt from the electoral blue come to be? And was he justified in thinking that his leadership and his brand had personally secured the victory?

Setting the Strategy

The power to call a general election before the Fixed-term Parliaments Act of 2011 (another Cameron mistake, Johnson mused) had been one of the greatest weapons in the Prime Minister's arsenal. No longer. The road to the Early Parliamentary General Election Act passing through the Commons on the evening of 29 October 2019 was a long and winding one.

Johnson entered No. 10 with few illusions as to the difficulty of the parliamentary situation and the problems a lack of a majority would pose a Prime Minister. Johnson, the master of pandering to his flock, was anxious to reassure his nervous MPs gathered for an all-too-rare summer garden party at No. 10 that 'the last thing

I want to do is call another election',[3] while at the same time his team was planning for just that. 'He said exactly what he thought his audience wanted to hear. It was typical Boris,' laughs Graham Brady, chair of the 1922 Committee.[4]

Behind the scenes, his team were frantically plotting how to engineer an election being called, given the decision no longer rested with the Prime Minister but with MPs following the 2011 Act. In weekend meetings at Chevening over that summer, Johnson brought together in strictest secrecy the key players on Brexit and election strategy. Time was running out. Nikki da Costa recounts that 'Dom and I came to the view early on that a general election was both necessary and unavoidable, so a lot of the strategy for 2019 was how we would reach that point.'[5]

Most prominent in election planning were Cummings and Isaac Levido, the Australian election strategist and protégé of Johnson ally Lynton Crosby. Levido had an impressive record for someone still in their mid-thirties. His stellar rise within Crosby's political consultancy had encompassed work on the 2015 and 2017 Conservative campaigns, as well as the successful 2019 Liberal Party campaign in Australia. One assignment he hadn't enjoyed was Johnson's 2016 leadership bid, any more than Crosby himself. Johnson's amateurish team, still fatigued from the referendum campaign, had not impressed him. Neither did the man himself, whom he thought unprepared for the premiership, still in shock at the events he had put into motion, and listless. He needed to be impressed that, three years on, Johnson was the real deal.

So Levido was relieved to find that Johnson's leadership team in 2019 was a camp gaining momentum, energy and belief – in stark contrast, he thought, 'to most others in SW1'. The political weather had begun to shift decisively in Johnson's favour. Conservative MPs no longer sought a figure like May to heal a divided party; they were desperate for a lion to gnaw through the Gordian knot of Brexit, defeat Corbyn and come to their rescue. 'For better or worse, you needed those three years of Theresa to create the conditions for Boris to present himself as the answer; why he was right to take over and solve the problem,' believes Levido.[6]

Johnson's bumbling appointments habit almost lost him Levido. As the leadership contest reached the play-off stage between Johnson and Hunt he had held conversations with Johnson about a future role in Downing Street. A very smart cookie, the PM-in-waiting wanted him inside the building. Johnson ran him through his latest thinking: he was to be director of strategy, which would've been a tantalizing prospect, Cain director of communications and Lister de facto chief of staff. But Cummings' late insertion into the team effectively rendered Levido's job at No. 10 redundant. Cummings had plans for him, as Levido recalls. 'On the morning Johnson was to become Prime Minister Dom and I sat down very early at Patisserie Valerie in Marylebone. He asked me to run the campaign. I made sure to discuss it with Boris after I spoke to Dom, to check he was happy. I needed to be sure we were all on the same page.'[7]

Despite Johnson's fulsome assurances that of course they were, his doubts about Levido remained. One trait Johnson did share with Churchill was extreme distrust of new faces. With the election massively in his mind, with the possibility of catastrophe and his own political demise never far away, he hankered for the known and proven comfort blanket of Crosby, the genius behind his two mayoral elections, as well as Cameron's victory in 2015. But he knew this to be impossible. 'Look, he asked me to run both his leadership election and general election, but I said I wasn't going anywhere near them, though I told him I thought he'd win,' Crosby says (as relayed to the authors by a third party). His clash with Carrie Symonds had led Johnson's election Svengali to formally distance himself from the campaign.

With Crosby ruling himself out, and the stakes so high, Johnson yearned for the other figure who had delivered him victory at the ballot box – Cummings. 'OK, I get Isaac is leading, but Dom will be *really* in charge, right?' he half-asked, half-implored his senior team. 'Isaac is leading, he's great. You'll be fine,' Johnson's advisers reiterated to the jittery Prime Minister. Johnson nodded, but warily as ever consulted Crosby on the direction the campaign took. 'Much like his love life, Boris doesn't tend to be monogamous in his advice. He's always had multiple advisers on the side as well as his "main man",' jokes one senior campaign figure.

His minders were equally clear that the great Lothario was going to do exactly as he was told for the duration, and not set up ad hoc structures at whim. Crosby attributed primary blame for the disastrous 2017 general election result to blurred lines of authority between campaign staff and No. 10. So too did his senior aides, a bitter experience which further pointed to Levido being the undisputed boss. Cummings, who was quite happy to delegate to individuals he trusted, readily agreed that he would distance himself from the campaign regardless of Johnson's nerves. 'Effectively,' says Levido, 'I ended up doing the supremo job that Lynton had done in 2015.'[8]

Rarely has a general election campaign been so brutally dissected as that in 2017. The lack of a clear message was a key lesson. May had no convincing explanation about why she was asking the country for a larger majority to implement Brexit so soon after a general election just two years before.[9] A compelling case needed to be built to explain why an election was the only way out of the

Brexit deadlock in 2019, and why granting the Conservatives a fresh mandate was needed to drag Westminster back from the mire in which it had been stuck.[10]

The general election and Brexit resolution were therefore inextricably linked in the minds of both Cummings and Johnson. As Cummings informed staff, 'We go in as hard as we must to get out, whatever it takes. And in order to stop us, the opposition are going to have to do something really unreasonable, something that will be very, very unpopular in the country. And if they do that, we'll smash them in the election.'[11] No. 10 was determined to push the opposition all the way screaming and howling to breaking point, and justify the decision to call an election in doing so.

Levido wasted no time getting down to business, briefing No. 10 staff about the strategy while recruiting a team of his own: pollster Michael Brooks, former Vote Leave communications director Paul Stephenson and Conservative Party campaigner Ben Mascall.

Brooks, like Levido, was an alumnus of Crosby's consultancy and had worked with him on the 2019 Australian campaign. Attempting to replicate their antipodean successes too would be left-field communications agency Topham Guerin. It had pioneered a digital messaging strategy which drew on a mixture of memes, slogans and a signature style of 'professional amateurism' – content which intentionally looked error-strewn so that it would receive mocking shares and retweets, thereby boosting engagement and spreading the reach of core messaging.

Levido's election team had distinct qualms about no deal being aired as leverage to obtain the best possible exit offer from the EU. In the bowels of No. 10, the expectation might have been an eventual pivot towards an agreement, but the gung-ho no deal strategy stunk to Levido. He was acutely aware that, tired of Brexit and desperate for a resolution though voters were, they were nervous of the uncertainty and economic damage that could be caused by a no deal exit. While Cummings had assured him at their Patisserie Valerie meeting that only a Brexit strategy acceptable to the public would be pursued, Levido's campaign team were acutely aware of the considerable uncertainty remaining about the divide with the EU.

Levido's team were right to be worried. While voters who had abandoned the Conservatives for UKIP in the 2014 European parliamentary elections might have preferred no deal, Conservative defectors to the Lib Dems detested it. Brooks' research further indicated that both sets of voters would be content with a deal, 60 per cent of Brexit Party and 70 per cent of Lib Dem switchers finding it an acceptable outcome. 'The only route to winning an election was to reunite those two distinct groups of defectors… getting a deal was the most critical aspect that enabled the political success of that campaign,' he says.[12]

Johnson needed little encouragement. He was, in the words of a senior comms adviser, 'desperate to move the country on. Let's get a deal and fight the election with it rather than try and outflank Farage on no deal.' So no deal was to remain on the table but only as a bargaining chip, and Johnson and Cummings were united in their belief they could make it appear a genuine threat, gaining sufficient leverage to get more out of negotiations than May.[13] Parliament needed to be perceived as the block, and a Johnson-led majority the remedy.

The general election had to be framed about much more than just Brexit, though. Voters may have wanted the issue resolved, but the campaign team's polling and research in August and September indicated strongly that it was not an end in itself. 'Brexit as a political issue was seen as the roadblock to politicians addressing the policy areas they were supposed to be addressing, the tangible issues that make a difference in people's everyday lives. Brexit was the hinge which enabled access to another brighter, more optimistic future where politicians could focus on these tangible issues, rather than more arguing about Brexit for years,' says Brooks.[14] It suited Johnson fine. Campaigning on broad issues was where he felt most comfortable, free to orate bounteously about the sunlit uplands and great future that lay ahead for the nation, spreading around cash like confetti.

Unleashing Britain's Potential

Thus was hatched the strategy of Johnson-max and a bonanza of spending announcements. Johnson was rolled out left, right and centre to front up a photo-op blitz, maximizing his association with the public's policy priorities and emphasizing what could be achieved if only the Brexit deadlock was broken. 'The strategy was clear. Get Boris into as many hospitals, schools and police stations to have his picture taken as was possible. While the public was being fed pictures of MPs shouting at each other in Parliament, Boris was out there in the community. It conveyed the message that once we got Brexit done then we were going to do the things that people wanted us to do,' says a media aide.

One of the earliest coups, announced at the very end of August, was a massive boost to school funding, £14 billion spread over several years. 'Dom was clear from what they'd been hearing on the doorsteps that this was something that needed to be fixed now, way before any general election,' says an aide. Because May had been trying for several months against resistance from Hammond to do exactly this, 'it required only a couple of tweaks' to get it through the system. The announcement was duly made of an extra £14 billion at the end of August. No. 10 felt very pleased with themselves. The sheer speed with which it was done was not without hazard, as highlighted by one observer: 'This was still a campaigning, not a governing premiership: the ease with which they sorted out school funding made them think that governing was going to be a whole lot easier than it was to prove.'

A torrent of policy change was promised once a re-elected Johnson was safely back in No. 10. 'It seemed dynamic and wild, but in hindsight it was a pretty good bundle of rolling announcements for an election campaign,' recalls one senior civil servant. 'Treasury mandarins, though, were horrified, and Sajid Javid [Chancellor of the Exchequer] and his team were completely wrongfooted by it', a warning of what was to come.

The 2019 Spending Review unveiled in September was the culmination of these announcements. It read (unsurprisingly) like a focus group's wish list. On crime No. 10 announced 20,000 new police officers by 2023, reversing the Cameron–Osborne cuts to the force. Ten thousand additional prison places and an urgent sentencing review to look at harsher punishments for violent and sexual offenders was red meat for the right. On education came a commitment to 'level up' through further increasing per-pupil spending, pay increases for teachers and additional funding for special educational needs. The spree continued with a reaffirmation of the commitment to May's NHS spending increases announced by Hunt in 2018 when Health Secretary, with a pledge to build forty new hospitals and a funding increase for recruitment. 'They were keen to show the public we were undoing the worst aspects of austerity,' says an official.[15] Some claims were of deliberately dubious veracity, such as the '40 new hospitals'.[16] But the reasoning was, the more the media debated their accuracy, the more the discussion gravitated to the campaign's commitment to spending.

A portmanteau slogan was still needed to bring it all together. Brooks was busy conducting focus groups in the Bury area in Lancashire in early September, testing various taglines to little success. Traditional buzzwords such as 'delivering', 'strong' and 'forward' failed to capture the energy the Johnson campaign thought to project. More importantly, they failed to resonate with voters, who associated them with the same old politics the novel campaign sought to subvert. So Brooks asked the moderator to pitch a different slogan: 'Get Brexit done and focus on the real issues.'

The first half of the slogan instantly lit up those present, capturing the weariness of the electorate over the protracted issue. It would take a further two months to finalize the sub-strap, the campaign team deliberating between 'Unlock Britain's Potential' and 'Unleash Britain's Potential'. Johnson was to be the adjudicator, as Brooks recalls. 'He wanted to interrogate the words, and started playing around with "unleash" as if he was swilling wine, tasting it and sensing it: "unleash, unlock, undo, unzip", working through every "un"-word he could conceive of.'[17] Suddenly, he alighted upon the slogan 'Get Brexit Done, Unleash Britain's Potential'. They had it. Hurriedly, they all committed to it before he had a chance to change his mind. But for their shining new slogan's aspiration to be realized, Johnson needed to unleash an election.

Triggering the Election

When MPs returned to Westminster after the summer on 3 September, as we have seen, they immediately seized the parliamentary timetable, incensed by prorogation. The furious Johnson team met that day to decide how to respond: the vote had made clear that any progress within this Parliament was unfeasible, and the only way out would be 'to change the numbers', that is, somehow to build up a majority of MPs on their side. Cummings' ploy was for Johnson to ask for a general election, believing that voters would reward him for fighting against an establishment thwarting Brexit, while simultaneously looking like he wasn't asking for one – that he'd been driven to this point against his will.

Knowing that the Benn Act would likely pass the following day, it was decided that Johnson should deliver a defiant address outside No. 10 that very evening. Against the backdrop of protestors chanting 'stop the coup' he was addressing both Parliament and the nation, urging them to avoid any delay beyond 31 October, and to resolve Brexit 'without an election. I don't want an election, you don't want an election.' The words were spoken in full knowledge that the scale of the ensuing rebellion would render an election necessary if Johnson were to maintain control of Parliament.

No. 10 may have been ready, eager indeed, for an election, but they hadn't prepared for the scenario that played out. 'Nobody in the political team had really thought that the opposition, against such a divided Conservative Party, would oppose the election,' says an adviser in the deliberations. 'When we had the meeting before calling for it, Peter Hill pointed out, "This is not my lane, but have you thought what happens if Labour say no?" Nobody took it seriously, and then it happened.'

The 2011 Act required a two-thirds majority of all MPs to trigger an early election. After Johnson's expulsion of twenty-one MPs from what was already a minority government the whips could muster up a mere 298 votes in support on 4 September, and 293 at the second attempt on 9 September. With a general election not required till 2022, the likelihood of triggering it any time soon seemed remote. Corbyn railed against an early election on the grounds it could bring about no deal if Johnson were to declare the date near to or past 31 October – an idea not considered appealing by the Tory strategists as it would require campaigning on an unpopular platform. Cummings was livid. 'We will talk about the election every f**king day. Every f**king day,' he told No. 10 staff. 'They won't be able to resist the pressure, we will go on about it until they [Labour] cave or make a mistake.'

With leading Conservatives such as Grieve and Letwin working overtime to frustrate no deal, No. 10 was desperate to find a way out of the impasse, portraying the Benn Act as a deliberate frustration of democratic will – even briefing to journalists that they would take the bill to the Supreme Court to show the nation how far its institutions were frustrating them.[18]

When Johnson's team debated how their strategy was being perceived by the electorate, the evidence was inconsistent. While their belligerent strategy such as on prorogation hurt their popularity in isolation,[19] Cummings was certain that the polling was missing something. He argued that the overall effect – even of the 24 September Supreme Court ruling – was positive as it burned into the electorate's mind that Johnson would stop at nothing to deliver Brexit. Brooks agreed that it showed them willing 'to put the interests of the public ahead of politicians and institutions'.[20] Johnson listened, but remained uneasy and spoke to staff of his discomfort at the torrent of abuse directed at him by figures across the establishment. In the last resort, though, critically aware of his own political mortality, he felt he had no alternative but to put his career in the hands of his chief aide, possessing an unshakeable faith in Cummings as a man of preternatural campaigning ability, for all his disquiet at his methods.

Cummings' take-no-prisoners strategy served too to highlight the decisiveness of Johnson against the shilly-shallying of Corbyn. Upon Parliament's return from prorogation on 25 September Johnson unleashed both barrels of his mockery at the Labour leader's ambivalence about an election:

> The Leader of the Opposition changes his mind so often, I wonder whether he supports an election today, or whether the shadow Chancellor, or the shadow Attorney General, have overruled him again… Is he actually going to vote no confidence in this Government? Is he going to dodge a vote of no confidence in me as Prime Minister, in order to escape the verdict of the voters? I wonder, does he in his heart even want to be Prime Minister any more?[21]

Johnson's team were now ready to play their ace, most riskily, a vote of no confidence in the government, brought by itself, leading to a general election. No. 10 was reasonably confident that no alternative Prime Minister to Johnson would be found in time, as the rules made possible within a two-week frame, Corbyn being far too divisive a figure for the Lib Dems and whipless ex-Tories to select in his place. But the move could look weak and backfire altogether.

An alternative was a short bill, a one-line piece of legislation which could bypass the Fixed-term Parliaments Act and enable an election; the problem was the government would still require a majority to pass it. Corbyn was still loath to give Johnson what he wanted. Fortunately for No. 10, they wouldn't need Labour votes to secure an election if they could convince the SNP, Lib Dems and independent MPs to back the government.

Thus began the 'divide and conquer' black arts campaign to get this fractured Parliament behind the call for a general election. No. 10 aides privately sowed suspicion when talking with their opposition counterparts, highlighting each party's incentives and weaknesses: the SNP's desire for an election before former leader Alex Salmond's sexual assault trial began in January 2020, the Lib Dems' interest in capitalizing upon their status as *the* party of Remain, and opportunities for independent MPs to either rejoin the Conservative Party or depart altogether from Westminster politics having enabled a deal and avoided the no deal outcome they feared most.

Thus it was supreme irony that the pro-EU opposition finally granted Johnson his wish for a general election. The Lib Dems and the SNP, fearing that they were running out of time to stop Johnson's Withdrawal Bill and force an election centred around Brexit, conspired to put forward a motion to circumvent the Fixed-term Parliaments Act. The proposal was conveniently leaked to the papers before it made its way to Parliament, and all hell broke loose among the opposition parties, each blaming the other for the leak. No. 10 seized upon the opportunity of the disunited opposition to put forward their own short bill on 29 October proposing an early general election.

Labour realized the game was up. With the withdrawal date extended to 31 January 2020 as a result of the Benn Act, it became evident to Corbyn that continuing to resist an election without the excuse of preventing no deal could only worsen his party's position. Cummings had been proved absolutely right – Labour could stand the pressure no longer and caved, abstaining from the vote. The Early Parliamentary General Election Bill passed by 299 votes to 70, setting the date for polling day: 12 December. The first December election, deemed to be unpopular with voters and therefore bad for turnout, since 1923. The mood had been bleak in the Johnson camp in the weeks leading up to this. 'We had been through some desperate times thinking that we would never trigger an election,' says Conservative Campaign Headquarters (CCHQ) electioneer David Canzini. 'Then, suddenly, it happened. It was as if Boris shed a skin. He became like a Marvel character.'[22]

The Red Wall

With the passing of the Early Parliamentary General Election Act on Thursday 31 October, and the final date for nomination of candidates on 14 November, a four-week campaign was automatically triggered before polling day on Thursday 12 December. The planning, long in the preparation, now stepped up several gears. 'Isaac and I sat down with the PM and Dom and asked, "What is the margin we need for a parliamentary working majority?"' recalls Brooks, 'and we decided on the figure of 350 seats as the buffer which would enable the PM to deliver his agenda.'[23]

Levido continued to draw heavily on his memories of 2017. The May campaign, emboldened by early polling and the size of the projected majority, overcommitted resources into the 'stretch' seats they would need to win for a large victory. As the swing moved against the Conservatives, it became clear they had been hubristic, but were slow to adjust. In aspiring to win a landslide in 2017, the planners had under-allocated time, energy and resources to the mainstream seats vital to win to give them the majority necessary to secure a Brexit deal.

Johnson's constant anxiety, that the election would be lost, or that, like Theresa May, he would become a lame duck with no working majority, never fully abated. But as polling from the start of the campaign suggested a Conservative victory, and with a Brexit agreement to put to the electorate, even with their cautious approach, it looked as if the Remain-leaning seats in the South were safe for the Conservatives.

The focus for gains was to be primarily in the newly minted 'Red Wall'. First identified by Tory strategist James Kanagasooriam, he found that the 2017 Conservative Party vote was lower than expected, given demographics and their EU referendum vote, in an entire stretch of sixty-three Labour-held constituencies starting from North-East Wales, across the Midlands and up to the North of England.[24] These seats were historically working-class Labour voters, dominated by heavy industry and coal mining until their decline in the 1980s. As the economic and political landscape of the UK morphed in the post-Thatcher years so too had the seats, creeping towards the Conservative Party during the Blair years and even in 2017, despite the poor Tory performance nationally.[25]

Brexit had severed historical ties between these communities and Labour, leaving the older, socially conservative voters without a natural political home. Labour for many years had tended to favour the progressive social politics of its wealthier, younger, highly educated voters as opposed to the preferences of its poorer, older, less-educated ones. The Conservatives sensed the time was ripe to realign themselves along socially conservative yet fiscally interventionist lines, initially in their 'left behind' agenda of the 2017 campaign then in the 2019 campaign's promise of levelling up, hoovering up new voters in a period of low party loyalty and high levels of vote-switching.[26]

Johnson did not understand the models, regressions or underlying analysis. What did resonate most powerfully with him was the story of the disenfranchised, bitter towards a Westminster and political class that had failed them. These were precisely the voters he first met in the 2016 referendum, touring disaffected ex-industrial seats, and he marvelled that they liked him back. Unlike stuffy SW1, they loved him for saying whatever he wanted, that he wasn't remotely like May, Cameron or Blair; they were entranced by his character, the entertaining and upbeat persona. He wasn't working-class like them, true; but unlike other politicians he didn't patronize them by pretending to be.

Johnson didn't walk in this territory alone. A potential wrecking force they had now to reckon with seriously was Farage and the Brexit Party, capable of splitting their vote right down the middle and risking Corbyn winning. Farage, like Johnson, appealed to those who felt Westminster had nothing to offer them, and that the solution was a politician who defied convention – a charismatic *caudillo* who could fix a broken system by breaking it some more. No. 10 were only too aware that Brexit Party candidates were alarmingly well placed to appeal to disillusioned Labour supporters who had voted Leave in 2016.

Brexit had created a significant overlap too in Conservative and Farageist donors, and Johnson's success in charming those with open wallets was not a given. Killing off the Farage challenge stone dead was the ideal. But could they achieve this? Johnson and his heavyweight friends swung into action to urge him to clear the way for the Conservatives, with Chairman Ben Elliot and Dougie Smith holding private discussions with Brexit Party supremos in a bid to convince their candidates to stand down. The early signs were promising when Farage's long-time ally, businessman Arron Banks, went public to get Farage to withdraw Brexit Party candidates from Labour marginals.[27] Farage, ever a proud man, agreed to stand his troops down – but only from the 317 existing Conservative-held seats: he would continue to contest the Red Wall. 'They tried to bribe me with offers of peerages and influential positions on committees,' Farage says. 'Go to hell, I told them. I took the decision because I feared that from the South-East to Penzance would go Liberal Democrat and risk having a Corbyn/Lib Dem coalition, followed by a second referendum, with all the Götterdämmerung that would unleash.'[28]

The move eased some pressure on Remain-voting seats where the Lib Dems were looking to gain from a split vote. But these seats were relatively few and far less impacted by the presence of the Brexit Party than Red Wall targets. Internal Conservative analysis showed that Labour Leave voters within Red Wall target seats would have split 70–30 for the Tories in the absence of a Brexit Party candidate, with Farage's supporters switching to Johnson to help secure Brexit.[29] In the reckoning on polling day, Farage failed to gain any seats, but his party cost the Conservatives an estimated twenty-five MPs, with the net impact of his withdrawal of Brexit Party candidates estimated to be just two seats possibly gained.[30] Unsurprisingly, relations with Farage during the campaign, and still more after, were icy.

New thinking in the 2019 election included the type of candidate selected, with more state-school educated, more women and more LGBT people.[31] One qualification for selection stood out above all others. Candidates were to be uniformly and fervently anti-EU. No. 10 fixer Dougie Smith led the process of slotting candidates into seats, his chief criterion being above all else the status of 'true Brexit believers'. Did the mass adoption of economically left and socially right Labour Leave voters into its ranks see the Conservative Party reinventing itself to accommodate a new electoral coalition, as it had done so many times throughout history? It had been the party of protectionism and of free trade, of Empire and decolonization, of *laissez-faire* and the welfare state. Now the party that had brought the United Kingdom into Europe was attempting to build a new coalition as the party campaigning to take the nation out. The election strategists might have been successful in avoiding the hubris of 2017, but were they inventing a new form of hubris?

Johnson's Campaign

Johnson had won the leadership contest in July in the belief that, compared to his final contender Hunt, he possessed a unique electoral appeal to save MPs' seats and to reach parts of the country beyond the reach of any other candidate. Crosby had struggled in 2017 to find a signature theme for May: 'strong and stable' was the best he could do; rarely has such an unfortunate label been articulated. No such head-scratching in 2019. Central to the Johnson magic was the persona he had projected since Eton – an affected scruffiness, bombastic attitude, risqué humour and openly loose relationship with the truth. Crucially, unlike May in 2017, his long exposure and familiarity with public and media meant his strengths and weaknesses were battle-tested.

The image was one he had consciously cultivated, drawing on his two greatest PR victories: succeeding as London Mayor, and winning the EU referendum as the respectable face of Brexit. Neither saw him come across as a strong 'Conservative'. The irony of the general election was that he both entered and left it less personally popular than May had been in 2017, and was saved by the public dislike of Corbyn which had developed in the two intervening years.[32]

Conservative governments had struggled since Thatcher to regain her popularity, while the legacy of austerity and Budget cuts after 2010 had done nothing to recover it among the electorate. The public viewed Johnson as a break with the Conservative governments since 2010, a remarkable status for a politician who had carried the Conservative label for close to two decades.[33] The cumulative effect of his mayoralty, the Brexit referendum campaign and vocal opposition to Cameron and May meant the campaign was able to position Johnson in 2019 as a 'change' candidate, offering a break with governments of the past rather than a continuation of Conservative rule. Thus did it capitalize on Johnson's difference with the previous fourth-election-winning Conservative leader in 1992, John Major, who had been unable to distance himself from his predecessor, who was still deeply loved and revered, whereas the party was ambivalent at best about its five leaders since Major stood down in 1997.

The cause was helped by Labour failing to estimate the threat Johnson posed to them. 'We were surprised: even John McDonnell [Shadow Chancellor], who we rated, continued to regard Boris as a buffoon, rather than as a serious threat,' says David Canzini. 'They were locked into the mentality of this is a rerun of 2017, with a different leader: one more swing of the axe, and the deed will be done.'

In tailoring the campaign around the strengths of its champion, it demanded an equally disruptive approach and willingness to step outside traditional structures. Johnson's reputation for unconventional and eye-catching set-pieces enabled the campaign to plan moments which would have rebounded against a traditional candidate, but played to the Johnson brand. Never more so than in the final days of the campaign on 10 December when he famously broke through a polystyrene wall of 'gridlock' driving a JCB digger equipped with a bucket emblazoned with the campaign slogan of 'Get Brexit Done'.

The relentless focus on the messaging of 'Get Brexit Done' and 'Unleash Britain's Potential' was punctuated by other injections of Johnson's japes and flourishes, introducing vintage 'Boris-isms' to maintain press and public attention. The Brexit deal was 'oven-ready', in contrast to Labour's 'dither and delay' over the issue, and Britain would be made 'Corbyn-neutral by 2020'.

Travelling in tandem was Topham Guerin's digital campaign with a Johnson-led *Love Actually* parody and an hour-long mix of music set to Johnson's election stump speech titled '*lo fi boriswave beats to relax/get brexit done to*' among the highlights. Both featured a smiling if awkward Johnson playing along and racked up millions of views on social media (1.3 million on YouTube for the latter), possessing an undeniably memetic quality. More dishonestly, the digital campaign included rebranding the CCHQ Twitter page as 'factcheckUK' during the leadership debate and editing an interview to make it appear that Keir Starmer, then shadow Brexit Secretary, had struggled to answer a basic question on Labour's Brexit strategy, when in actuality he had instantly responded.[34]

No. 10 and CCHQ found it hard to manage the always delicate balance in a general election campaign for a PM between campaigning and ongoing government roles. Yorkshire and the Midlands had experienced severe flooding in mid-November, and Johnson was eager to be seen addressing the matter, not least with Corbyn visiting flood-stricken areas. Propriety and Ethics rules, governing the extent of civil service support during the period of restricted pre-election government activity, slowed the process severely. By the time Johnson finally arrived, Corbyn had long disappeared, leaving him having to answer the angry locals in appalling weather and unable to assert his campaign message. For once, Johnson was only too happy to return to Westminster from the Red Wall, grateful that the miserable experience had not seemingly affected his popularity.

A different challenge was presented by the habitual television debates. To Levido and Cummings, they were potential perils, where just one Johnson gaffe – moments he was no stranger to – could undermine the campaign and swing momentum towards Labour. They let Johnson attend two low-risk head-to-heads with Corbyn, which proved damp squibs: the Labour leader was never going to present the same level of threat as a trained television interviewer. Johnson landed some punches on Labour's unclear Brexit policy, Corbyn on the potential of NHS privatization in a US trade deal. Neither performed so well or badly as to alter the trajectory of the election.

The Manifesto

The manifesto was another case where lessons had been learned from 2017. May, under the influence of her own version of Cummings, Nick Timothy, had opted for a daring slate, a direct repudiation of 'untrammelled free markets'. But controversy focused rather on her manifesto, specifically the proposal to resolve the long-standing social care crisis: charging users through their assets (including homes) until they hit a £100,000 'floor'.

Within days it was being savaged as a 'dementia tax' and an undignified U-turn resulted, made worse by May refusing to acknowledge that she had been forced into such a move. Her statement to a bewildered press pack that 'nothing had changed' fatally undermined her credibility and the core 'strong and stable' image.

No. 10 policy chief Munira Mirza asked Rachel Wolf to write the manifesto with her, a respected policy adviser who had previously worked on Johnson's first mayoral campaign. 'Very early on the decision was taken that what mattered most was a manifesto that didn't lose the election. Everyone agreed it was much better for the document to be criticized by the media for being boring than risk it being interesting for the wrong reasons,' says Wolf.[35] The 2017 manifesto had been a closed affair. Driven by fear of leaks from May's passionately disloyal Cabinet and the risk they would destabilize the launch, the manifesto was drafted in great secrecy, with Cabinet ministers consulted only on their own departmental areas, if that.

'In direct and deliberate contrast to that experience, there were lots of different inputs,' Wolf recalls of the changes for 2019. 'Every Cabinet minister meticulously saw the relevant passage and was allowed to give commentary. First, individual Cabinet ministers with their thoughts, second, we gathered together ideas from MPs and constituency parties, third, think tanks were asked for submissions, and, finally, the Policy Unit had its own contributions.'[36] Brooks and Levido's aspiration to win over aspirant and would-be Tory voters meant a particular drive to incorporate ideas of what focus groups were saying they wanted after the delivery of Brexit. The various inputs were fed into a Google spreadsheet, with a ministerial committee of James Cleverly, Gove, Raab and Liz Truss overseeing the process before Mirza, Wolf and the Policy Unit finalized the decisions. Social care, the potentially nuclear issue, merited just one bland paragraph.

All policies were intensively polled and focus-grouped, with unpopular proposals summarily binned. Cummings' wry verdict was 'like Blairism but without caring about the causes of crime'.

The bullet point list of six policies on the cover page was as uncontroversial as any Conservative manifesto in recent memory: 'extra funding for the NHS', '20,000 more police', 'we will not raise the rate of income tax', an 'Australian-style points-based system to control immigration', investment 'every week' in schools and science, and 'reaching Net Zero by 2050'. The output from the elongated consultation did indeed give it a whiff of Blairite blandness. The resemblance to New Labour's 1997 manifesto and pledge card was unmistakable and deliberate too, even down to the inclusion of the party leader's signature 'My Guarantee' imitating Blair's contract with the electorate. No one dared whisper it, but the unspoken hope too was for Johnson to lead a ten-year government that would redefine British politics.

On reading the draft, Johnson's reaction to staff out on the campaign trail was not the ringing endorsement for which its authors had been hoping. 'It doesn't say *anything*. It doesn't capture my vision.' What they dared not reply was that he didn't have a vision; or not one which could be readily translated into informing a coherent policy document. The detail-shy document was to store up problems further down the line. It was hardly a roadmap for government, nor did it often provide the opportunity down the line for reference to be made to mandates and manifesto pledges. The seeds of Johnson's future troubles can be traced back to the manifesto: once Brexit had been completed, what then? Johnson insisted personally on writing his own Foreword, a thirty-seven-paragraph splurge of pure Johnsonism. He flatly denied that he was without his own distinctive mission and ideology for power. His Foreword opened with characteristic swagger: 'For the last three and a half years, this country has felt trapped, like a lion in a cage. We have all shared the same frustration – like some super-green supercar blocked in the traffic. We can see the way ahead. We know where we want to go – and we know why we are stuck.'

Robert Colvile, head of the Centre for Policy Studies think tank, had been brought in to finesse the final drafts, but found it quite impossible to replicate Johnson's language and phraseology in the rest of the document. Johnson insisted too on use of his phrase 'levelling up'. The manifesto writers struggled with the phrase, specifically pinning it down into coherent policy proposals within the manifesto, despite Johnson's pushing. 'It was an insight, not an agenda,' as Wolf puts it with pinpoint accuracy.[37] Where the manifesto did contain precise policies, they were rarely a product of the levelling-up vision as imagined by Johnson: small but tangential improvements to high streets, towns, safety and crime certainly were there; but not the repivoting of the UK economy away from its South-East axis, nor the grand infrastructure projects Johnson felt so passionately about.

Launching three days after Labour, the Conservative Party's manifesto 'Get Brexit Done. Unleash Britain's Potential' would provoke the first, and only, major wobble of the campaign. Like Johnson, the public was underwhelmed. 'Safety first' had been the chosen general election theme in 1929 of Conservative Prime Minister Stanley Baldwin. Ninety years later, it most definitely wasn't Johnson's theme, and with some justification he thought the manifesto appeared weak contrasted to Labour's offering of expansive spending and radical reform.[38] 'Because we'd set out our stall as a campaign with Boris being an agent of change, the manifesto ended up looking too safe. It was probably an overreaction from 2017,' admits Brooks.[39]

Indeed, the 'safety first' lesson of 2017 had been so thoroughly dominant that there was little new or interesting for the press to sink their teeth into. 'I went to the papers to give them the Sunday reveal, and all we really had were things like a pothole fund. We'd dropped most of the good stuff before, and the genuinely radical policy of getting Brexit done people were bored with,' recalls Paul Stephenson. 'There wasn't a great central message of "this is what Boris is about" there.'[40]

To Levido's horror, the party's ratings dipped and the polling tracks narrowed with Labour. Brooks reiterated the need to get the campaign back to the message of Brexit and the electorate's priorities. Johnson thus fronted a press conference with the old Vote Leave team of Gisela Stuart (shortly to become a non-affiliated peer) and Michael Gove on the morning of 29 November, with two weeks to polling day, to assert the benefits of Brexit and overhauling state aid rules.

Campaign Helter-Skelter

Plans to regain the initiative appeared at first threatened by the terror attack on 29 November at London Bridge in which two people were fatally stabbed and the perpetrator, out on early release after a 2012 terrorism offence, was shot dead.

The attack had come eerily close to the point in the campaign, a fortnight from election day, where the Manchester Arena bombing (which left twenty-seven dead) derailed May's 2017 campaign. Lessons were applied. 'Corbyn was allowed to portray Manchester as the result of cuts and austerity,' says a senior adviser. 'Theresa was reluctant to come out and be tough. So we gave Boris some strong lines about the need for a firm response and a review of early release schemes.'

Advice from Stephenson was that halting the campaign for as long as possible would be the right response. The conventional wisdom is that doing so benefits the party leading the race (as they were) by icing the ability of either campaign to make ground. The lessons of 2017, however, weighed heavily on Levido's mind and he favoured a shorter pause for a day or two. What if the bumpy manifesto launch was the start of a lurch downwards in the polls, and freezing proceedings only reinforced the momentum?

Ultimately the decision rested not with CCHQ but within No. 10, and for the first time since the campaign began, Cummings broke his self-denying ordinance. He believed critical advantage would be gained, not by pausing the campaign, but by being strong in taking a popular and hardline stance. Here, he sensed, was the chance to hold Corbyn's feet to the fire. The Labour leader's equivocal reaction to the 2018 Novichok poisonings in Salisbury had been considered borderline unpatriotic, while claims of his being 'present but not involved' at a wreath-laying for Palestinians responsible for the 1972 Munich Olympics massacre made him vulnerable to attacks of being a terrorist sympathizer. Cummings got his way, with Johnson and Corbyn agreeing jointly not to suspend campaigning as they had in 2017.[41] To order, Corbyn was soon being grilled on his position on early prisoner release schemes, an issue highlighted by the murders, and, unlike in 2017, could not reframe the issue around austerity and cuts – in part due to Johnson's announcements since becoming PM on expanding the police force.

The tragedy put Johnson and Cummings back in lockstep, their instincts perfectly aligned. It proved a stabilizing influence for the campaign, allowing them to exploit the divide between the liberal and authoritarian ranks among Labour voters. The latter perfectly fitted the profile of the new voters the team wanted to win over to the Conservative cause. After the brief manifesto wobble, the Conservative Party was back out in front.

With the London Bridge attack still playing out in the media, the team's focus switched to the BBC which had approached them on three events: a *Question Time* debate, a leadership head-to-head against Corbyn, and an interview with the formidable interrogator Andrew Neil. While consenting, albeit apprehensively, to the first two, the team agonized over letting Johnson face a grilling from the man who had dismissed him from the *Spectator*. During the leadership contest in July, moreover, Neil had humiliated him over his claim that he had driven down crime in London quicker than elsewhere. Johnson recoiled at the memory, and his response was emphatic. 'No f**king way am I doing that, I don't want to,' one aide recalls him saying. The BBC were palmed off with a non-committal response from the campaign team.

The BBC had been delighted by the high profile given to Neil's probing of Corbyn on 26 November (which led to front page stories across the press about Corbyn refusing to apologize for antisemitism). But it made them all the more concerned to land the Neil–Johnson interview. Would it not undermine their requirement for balance if Neil did not interview Johnson, they asked? Greeted by a brick wall, the BBC pumped out stories that the Prime Minister was running scared. Carrie Symonds was a solitary voice persuading him to do the interview, arguing that it was expected of a Prime Minister, and dodging it made him look weak. Ranged against her was the formidable trio of Levido, Cain and Cummings, back on their theme of the palpable risk of Johnson slipping up against an interviewer who knew all his weak spots, political and personal. As the clear front runner, what could he possibly gain from the exposure?

Their internal discussion went on all that long week which began on Monday 25 November. Their 7.30 a.m. meetings were feisty, with Cummings holding nothing back. 'Andrew Neil knows all about you, Boris, he's going to bring up your love life and humiliate you.' Johnson was in a funk. He always abominated it when he had Carrie whispering one thing in one ear, and his chief adviser the opposite in the other. Some thought Cummings was being perverse, enjoying his discomfort, milking it. 'In classic Dom fashion, just because there was a rule saying you should do the interview, he didn't want to,' says one adviser present.

Cain and Cummings, like boxing promoter Don King flaunting Muhammad Ali, enjoyed teasing the big beasts in the television jungle. This might not have quite been the 'Rumble in the Jungle', but they had the rights over a superstar who the media were desperate to interview. So they approached the BBC's Andrew Marr and insisted he conduct the interview instead of Neil. The BBC initially refused a Marr interview until Johnson had appeared with Neil, only to cave within days. Marr went hard on Johnson on 1 December – he had much to prove, not least that he wasn't the soft touch interviewer the row might have implied him to be. But in the end, Marr was unable to land many punches, to the glee of Johnson's team and CCHQ.

Pressure to accept the Neil interview did not abate with his Marr appearance, Carrie in particular continuing to press Johnson to do it. Attendees of the strategy meeting observed that Johnson agreed with his partner when she was in the room – 'I must do it, I must. We simply have to' – only to phone Cain and Cummings a few minutes later, Carrie no longer in earshot, and admit, 'You guys are completely correct, just proceed as you are.' 'In his heart he knew that we were the team who would let him win, and he had faith in our judgement,' says an aide. Johnson walked away having convinced both camps that he was on their side, and that he couldn't possibly be held responsible for the view the other camp had forced upon him. For now, Johnson's inability to decide between warring factions was a distraction; later, it would prove fatal.

The controversy around Johnson's decision only intensified, and Neil's response with a short video in which he laid out his proposed line of questioning – probing why Johnson 'so often in his career politically and in journalism has had people deeming him to be untrustworthy' – received massive attention. But to the Johnson campaign, the furore on social media and 'within SW1', as they often said, was immaterial. What mattered was any impact of the dispute on polling: and their evidence was telling them that it was not having any negative impact, and may even be having a positive effect among some targeted groups of potential Tory voters who disliked the BBC's approach. The probing interview did not take place. But for the team, the furore was another nail in the coffin of the Remain-loving BBC.

The last week of the campaign was plush with non-stories. Trump visiting for the NATO summit on 2–4 December was a matter of potential anxiety. Given many voters' detestation of the American President, and comments that he would favour privatizing the NHS, it was a moment of high peril. But it proved uneventful – in part due to Trump's interview with Piers Morgan being cancelled thanks to the timely intervention of Rupert Murdoch on behalf of a nervous No. 10. 'We were lucky that we got away just with the President's comment on the NHS possibly being in a trade deal, which wasn't helpful, but it could've been so much worse,' says Levido.[42]

In the final days of the campaign, the team battled to restrict Johnson's media appearances to minimize risk, but seasoned Johnson-minders though they had become, they could not altogether prevent gaffes, such as Johnson pocketing a TV journalist's phone mid-interview after being shown a picture of a four-year-old with suspected pneumonia asleep on the floor of an overcrowded A&E unit, or ducking into a fridge to avoid a live interview with ITV's *Good Morning Britain*. The polling did not move, though, and the Conservatives remained ahead in even the most pessimistic of their models.

The Reckoning

Johnson and his close colleagues gathered in No. 10 at 10 p.m. on 12 December as the last votes were cast. They were very tired and sleep-deprived, with many, like Cummings and Cain, having had no respite since July. Earlier that day, together with Brooks and Levido they had visited No. 10 to give their model's final numbers to Johnson: 350 to 370 seats for the Conservatives. Johnson was surprised at the swing, and doubtful. Like Blair in 1997, he still harboured the fears which had driven him through the campaign, that it would all end up badly – even in a hung Parliament.

In step with the rest of the country, they listened intently as the exit poll compiled by Ipsos MORI for the BBC, Sky News and ITV suggested the Conservatives were set to secure 368 seats with Labour on course for 191. The pent-up pressure of half a year without a break suddenly released. Johnson feared no more. Sitting with Carrie and the coterie of campaign staff in the Thatcher Room, he leaped from his chair as the numbers left newsreader Huw Edwards' lips, a moment of wild jubilation before the few lingering nerves caught up. 'It's only the exit poll,' he reminded the team.[43]

After results in the constituencies began to flow in in the early hours, and the victory became indisputable, bottles were opened and chants of Levido's name rang round CCHQ. 'Everybody was becoming cock-a-hoop, swelled with the power and possibility of government,' describes one present at the celebrations. The Prime Minister and his aides made their way over from No. 10. Cummings was experiencing mixed emotions. One moment he was giddy about his plans coming to fruition, his second victory in a national poll of historic consequence. He had spent much of the last few weeks planning for power – radical government reforms punctuated by a series of dismissals at the top of the civil service. He was at last in a position to realize his life's ambition, to make the changes he had spent years advancing.[44] The next moment he had a premonition of his disillusioned self, leaving Downing Street less than a year later dejected and rejected. 'The PM won't need us any more, now we've won. Carrie will try and push us out,' he confided to a close ally.

No such agonies for the victorious Prime Minister. Johnson was consumed by writing his speech as they sat in the CCHQ chairman's room at 3 a.m. As they struggled to stay awake, he was in his element, deciding how his speech would highlight what he could now deliver for a country eager to move away from the divisive politics and dramas of the last three and a half years.

His caffeine-rich words delivered at the lectern outside the front door of Downing Street constituted the most personal public statement he gave of why he wanted to be Prime Minister. Gracious in victory, he was conscious of holding together the broad coalition that had secured the win. 'To all those who voted for us, for the first time, all those whose pencils may have wavered over the ballot, and who heard the voices of their parents and their grandparents whispering anxiously in their ears, I say thank you for the trust you have placed in us and in me.'[45] As a non-ideological Brexiteer, it was no doubt easier for him to reach out across the nation at this extraordinary moment. But then, the other, more cynical Boris Johnson kicked in. As he walked back inside No. 10, he turned to his team and said, 'All that about lending us their vote, let's try not to refer to that again. If we keep saying it, people might start to believe it.'

A lot of votes had indeed been lent – 13,966,454 to be precise, translating into 365 seats and a majority of 80. The first landslide since Blair, it was the Conservatives' largest majority since 1987, their highest share of the vote since 1979.

Red Wall seats accounted for over two-thirds of Labour's sixty-seat loss, including Sedgefield – the County Durham constituency which had once belonged to Blair himself. Johnson pointedly held a victory rally at Sedgefield Cricket Club on 14 December, addressing the adulatory crowd. 'You have changed the political landscape. You've changed the Conservative Party, for the better. And you have changed the future of our country.'[46] It was a new electoral coalition for the party, new voters, new MPs, new promises. 'I know people will have been breaking the voting habits of generations to vote for us. Everything I do as Prime Minister will be devoted to repaying that trust.'

Prime Ministers are all inclined to speak hyperbolic words in their moment of victory, and perhaps we shouldn't hold them to the letter of what they said. But equally, Johnson did utter the words, and they bear repeating: 'Everything I do as Prime Minister will be devoted to repaying that trust.' Ultimately, it was because that trust to voters was not repaid, or honoured, that he could do nothing more as Prime Minister, and had to resign.

Was Johnson right to see it less as an achievement for the party than for its leader? Less than three years later, as the government fell apart around him, Johnson claimed at the despatch box that he personally had been handed a 'colossal mandate' in December 2019, an idea in conflict with the principle of parliamentary democracy within which all Prime Ministers serve. True believers would again brandish the victory as a personal mandate when calling for his return to No. 10. Why were they wrong to do so?

Johnson was never the popular politician he and his followers imagined. At no point during the 2019 campaign was he more popular with the general public than Theresa May in 2017.[47] Her U-turn, denials and hapless style did not render her as divisive to voters as Johnson's gung-ho buffoonery and rule-breaking. For all the hype, the Conservatives under Johnson had gained just 300,000 more votes than the party had under May (and 130,000 fewer than they achieved under Major, with a smaller electorate, in 1992). The difference with 2017 was in the perception of the Labour leader. In 2017, Corbyn was fresh and still credible, not yet damaged by a series of errors of judgement. By 2019, Corbyn had become an electoral fiasco for Labour. He pushed wavering Labour voters with socially conservative views away from the party, and he pushed those considering voting Lib Dem to the Conservatives in fear of letting in a Corbyn government, bolstering the Tory Party on both fronts. Many other Corbyn-sceptic Labour voters did not switch directly to other parties: rather, they didn't vote at all, the Labour vote falling by a catastrophic 2.6 million from 2017.

Corbyn and Brexit were thus central to understanding the result. 'The PM was the third most important factor after them in the election campaign,' opines Brooks. 'But his contribution cannot be dismissed. The campaign was built for him, around his strengths.'[48] His major contribution had nothing to do with his brand, bombast or boldness. It was principally in seeking and accepting a deal with the European Union sufficient for Middle England ex-Labour

Leavers and southern Conservative-voting Remainers to bite their tongue and vote for the offered resolution. Given his inheritance, this was still a considerable feat.

The 2019 general election result created or blurred more problems than it solved. The influx of 106 new Conservative MPs, mostly Brexiteers with aspirations for Brexit-dividend spending in their constituencies, had little emotional commitment to their fellow MPs or their leader. It allowed Johnson to think that the victory was his own, and that, as when he was London Mayor, he could run the government much as he wished, without reference to his Cabinet, to ministers at large or MPs. To achieve that would have required a superb team of aides around him, as he had at City Hall and during the general election. But his aptitude for picking the right people when not in a crisis position, and, increasingly, the field willing to put themselves forward to work with him, was problematic.

Another fiction about the election was that it cemented a durable realignment of voters in British politics, as the Conservatives established at the beginning of periods of hegemony throughout their history, as in 1924 under Baldwin, 1951 under Churchill or 1979 under Thatcher. But if this was an electoral coalition of working-class social conservatives bolted onto the Cameron-era gains of upper-middle class liberals, it was one of convenience, contingent upon Brexit not yet being completed, Labour continuing to put up unelectable leaders and the incoming government being able to satisfy the aspirations they had aroused in the Red Wall. Even less durable than the electoral coalition was the fragile parliamentary coalition of Conservative MPs at Westminster, united on almost nothing bar self-interest in retaining their seats. A majority of eighty would typically have been considered sizable. In an era of rampant parliamentary dissent, the highest since 1945, it was no longer as solid as it seemed, quicksand beneath the Prime Minister's feet when called to back him on any issue of controversy. How could he possibly admonish the dissidents for replicating the very behaviour which had won him the premiership?

Some have seen the fall of Boris Johnson as originating in events in late 2021. But the origins can be traced to this election, and back to the three character flaws evident from his early years as a young man, as outlined at the opening of the book.

For now, these worries seemed far away. With the security of tenure he had sought and a party apparently united behind him, Johnson had the greatest policy freedom of any Prime Minister for years. He had ceased to dwell on the sad fate of George Canning with his meagre 119 days and had his eyes now fixed on emulating Margaret Thatcher or Tony Blair's ten years.

Only one question remained. What did he want to do with his power?

Johnson's vision to transform Britain's infrastructure was one of his animating spirits

4

DREAMS

A year has passed since the general election was called. It is early November 2020. The frenetic and intoxicating certainty in No. 10 of the year before has long since evaporated. Two weary figures, prematurely aged, sit opposite each other in the Prime Minister's study.

'You don't have any clear priorities, Prime Minister, you don't know what you want to do,' says one.

'Well, that's simply nonsense,' replies the other.

'Is it?'

'Yes, it is. I've got thirty different priorities.'

'That's ridiculous. You can't have thirty priorities!'

'Why not?'

'Because it doesn't work like that.'

'Don't tell me I don't know what to do!'

'You don't know how to be Prime Minister either.'

'Yes I bloody well do. I did Brexit. I'm going to rebuild Britain.'

'But what are your top three priorities now?'

'It's obvious.'

'Is it? What are they?'

'Ahm, ahm, ahm.'

Thus went a conversation between a friend who had stuck with Johnson through thick and thin, and, like many who had believed in him, had grown weary of his indecision and lack of strategy.

Henry VIII, after engineering the breach with Rome, passed the first Act of Supremacy in 1534, declaring him to be 'the only supreme head on Earth of the Church of England'. Sovereignty was repatriated to the country. The break from Europe with Brexit was similarly designed to repatriate sovereignty to Britain. Its return to these lands, we have agreed, is what most attracted Johnson to Brexit outside of his own thirst for recognition. How would Johnson, the man who wanted to be king, seize the opportunity to use repatriated powers to restructure Britain internally, and re-establish its position in the world? His starring role in making Brexit happen earned him that entitlement, necessity indeed, to justify what he had done, to reward those who voted for it, to gain respect from the establishment and prove the naysayers wrong.

Johnson believed that his irrepressible character and his unique, inclusive vision justified his ambition to gain the keys of Downing Street – and to retain the keys. This chapter explores his self-belief and vision, and what really mattered to him on his peregrinations below all the confusion on the surface. Some saw in him a figure of destiny and greatness; others suspected he wanted the job merely for its own sake. To prove that he could do it. To prove he was the best.

'Boris absolutely *loved* being Prime Minister, its prestige and the trappings. He revelled in it even more than Cameron did and wasn't so troubled by it. His philosophy on the way up had been to do, pledge, say anything to get over the firing line because I'm the best, I deserve it, I'm the king. Now I'm here in No. 10 without any core political beliefs, I can say and do whatever I need to remain here.' Thus spoke one of his Cabinet ministers, a friend, a view shared by several ministerial colleagues.

'You could read Boris Johnson on any issue, he'd be the champion of the underdog, the voice of the silent, always incredibly kind,' says a top aide who worked for him in Downing Street day after day.

Utterly shallow and devoid of original ideas, thought Dominic Cummings, the most powerful of all his policy advisers.

Which is the true Johnson? The egotist, the altruist dreamer or the 'shopping trolley'? The answer, as we will see, is he aspired to altruism, but circumstances and his ineptitude at knowing how to deliver it through the system propelled him into egotism and mayhem.

Prime Ministers can be divided into dogmatists like Ted Heath (1970–74) or Liz Truss (2022) who arrive at Downing Street with a clear ideology and sense of what they want to do, and pragmatists, like Harold Macmillan (1957–63) or James Callaghan (1976–79) who have broad principles but who determine issues very much on their merits.

Johnson was a blend of both outlooks. He arrived resolved to get Brexit done and to win a general election. But then, after the first six months, his pragmatic instincts rose to the top. The exclusive club of great Prime Ministers to which he aspired, containing just nine by our reckoning, were a mixture of dogmatists like William Gladstone (1868–74, 1880–85, 1886, 1892–94) and Clement Attlee (1945–51), and pragmatists like Robert Walpole (1721–42) and David Lloyd George (1916–22).[1]

Pre-echoes of Johnson among Conservative premiers have been traced to the muscular Unionism of Lord Salisbury in the 1880s and 1890s; to Churchill's 'setting the people free' in the early 1950s; to Macmillan's repositioning of the Tory Party after his own equivalent of Brexit, the Suez Crisis; and to Thatcher's battle with 'loony' Labour under Michael Foot's leadership (1980–83).[2] But searching history for exact precedents is ultimately a fool's game. Resemblances can certainly be found in the past – but they weren't *inspirations* for what Johnson did. He loved British political history, but knew surprisingly little about it, and philosophy, but his philosophy equally did not draw from the greats, modern *or* classical. His most surprising choice of Prime Minister he would most like to meet, when asked for a programme celebrating the 300 years of the office in April 2021, was William Gladstone. Either he was not taking the question seriously, or didn't know his Gladstone.[3] Among Conservative Prime Ministers, Benjamin Disraeli (1868, 1874–80) provides some illuminating parallels. Both flamboyant showmen with a love of the grand statement, a loose philosophy, a looser relationship with the truth, and with a natural literary talent drawn out by worries of financial insecurity. They were classicists, dreamers, lovers of their Queen and with romantic notions of their place in history. Both took relish in the controversy and chaos surrounding their public life, and both took a similar view on leadership and hierarchy – a curious mix of elitism and equality. Both sought to help the worst-off: Disraeli promised an 'equality that elevates and creates', Johnson a 'levelling up' of those left behind.[4] Both were fascinated by global politics, Disraeli the first Prime Minister to travel abroad, in 1878 to the Congress of Berlin; Johnson never more truly himself at No. 10 than when standing up for Ukraine against the Russian bear.

Johnson's name could happily be substituted for Disraeli's in what Douglas Hurd and fellow biographer Edward Young write below about his great and only election victory:

> There was no detailed manifesto, no blueprint of policies, no agenda for reform ready to be unveiled [after the election] – only the sentiment implied by his speeches of a… government, committed to improving the living standards of the people and

> protecting British interests… The secret here was that there was no secret. To be prime minister had always been Disraeli's ambition.[5]

But the Disraeli analogy breaks down because of many glaring dissimilarities. Johnson happily challenged and attacked the status quo, Parliament, the judiciary, the civil service and the fourth estate; to Disraeli, the defence of the institutions of the country was his core responsibility. Where Johnson was apt to be frivolous, Disraeli was serious-minded, a thoughtful and profound writer of speeches and books (including seventeen novels); it is hard to recall many phrases from a Johnson speech which managed to be both memorable and substantive, and his books to date will not endure. Disraeli was a conservative who was the undisputed master of the office; Johnson was a liberal who let the servants run riot in the citadel.

Lloyd George's personality and premiership, though, remains by a distance the closest match, to an almost uncanny extent. Not that Johnson ever consciously sought to emulate the Welsh Wizard. He just did it without thinking, or even knowing.

The Road to No. 10

Central to Johnson's success throughout his ascent was the constructive ambiguity he would employ to gain popularity. There he stood on platform after platform, all things to all people – or at least to a sufficient number required to succeed. At Oxford, when he failed to secure the Union presidency standing as an old-school Tory dependent on the Old Etonian network, he rebranded himself as a Social Democrat, a stance more attuned to the anti-Thatcherism of the 1980s. Success!

Johnson then as now was an avid reader, with at least one book on the go, and often several. He relished quoting from Greek or Latin literature as a flourish of his effortless intellect, and could recite large chunks of the *Iliad* from memory; but there is no evidence that any of his voluminous reading made a great impact on him philosophically. He loved classical Greece and Roman history, and would regularly refer to them, but did not have any hero he tried to emulate – he would confess his admiration of Pericles,[6] or declare Emperor Augustus as his favourite (and history's most successful) politician,[7] but never engaged with their leaderships at a deeper level. He loved Shakespeare, quoting him occasionally if far less regularly than was later depicted in the TV dramatization about Covid entitled *This England*. But the plays left little imprint on his actions. He loved global history, gaining a reputation among his fellow G7 leaders for peppering their conversations with historical analogies: in one gathering, Justin Trudeau of Canada announced he himself was going to 'do a Boris' before launching into his own historical analogy. But for all that, it's hard to see history shaping his thinking beyond inspiration from his biography subject Churchill over Ukraine.

He selectively loved theatre and films, and in the latter we would see periodic inspirations, as to Mayor Vaughn in Spielberg's *Jaws*, who tried to keep the beach open when presented with evidence of a man-eating shark, a stance in Johnson's mind as he battled to keep the country open during Covid. Or the final scene in *Butch Cassidy and the Sundance Kid* in which the characters of Paul Newman and Robert Redford quit a building straight into a hail of gunfire, a scene in his mind in the final days before his resignation.[8]

Not in his youth, nor indeed subsequently, did Johnson try to set out his political credo in any form longer than an article. No thinker or indeed mentor shaped him. Neither in No. 10 nor in Cabinet did he ever find an intellectual soulmate, the equivalent of Neale Coleman at City Hall, a formidable brain with whom he would joust for hours.[9] Tony Blair had come under the influence at Oxford of the charismatic Geoff Gallop who infused him with the ideals of the social mission he sought to enact once in power. Blair, Brown and May were deeply influenced by their Christian faith. Yet neither religion, nor ideology, nor causes, nor teachers, nor friends, nor foes made any deep mark on Johnson.

More than any Prime Minister in this series of books starting with John Major in 1990, he arrived at Downing Street lacking specific policy plans. Major, Brown, Cameron and May were deeply imbued in their party's policy debates. Blair was most like Johnson in that his political views were fluid early on: but they were beginning to clarify by his late twenties, and by the time he arrived at No. 10 he had locked in both policies and an accomplished team (one that Johnson was to belatedly try to emulate in No. 10). Johnson's views too began to crystallize if sketchily in his weekly *Telegraph* columns and on the broader canvas of the *Spectator* of which he became editor aged thirty-five, which gave him unrivalled platforms to espouse his iconoclastic thoughts. At the latter, he was seen as liberal by colleagues, even 'liberal libertarian' by Stuart Reid. Johnson told his right-hand man that he was opposed to any sanctimony about sex, favoured legalizing drugs and was pro-enjoyment of life, wanting the magazine to be a haven for uncensored entertainers with a firm ban on 'preachers'.[10] Such freedoms did not always extend to those he saw as unlike himself. His tenure as Mayor began by banning drinking on Transport for London services: neither alcohol nor public transport were particular indulgences of the relatively sober cyclist. Freedoms for me, not for thee, cynics mouthed. But he confounded them all by proving liberal on immigration and campaigning for the introduction of a living wage.

Arnold Schwarzenegger, as governor of California, became intrigued by Johnson and came to visit him in London to learn from him as a right-wing leader espousing liberal causes and green politics: the relationship remained to the end of his premiership, Johnson quoting one of the actor's catchphrases, 'Hasta la vista, baby' as a farewell in his final Prime Minister's Questions.[11] No doubt another iconic Schwarzenegger quote from the *Terminator* film series was playing on Johnson's mind as he departed: 'I'll be back.' His parting words to Britain's democratic chamber – neither Socrates, Sophocles, nor Cicero, but Schwarzenegger.

American politicians, perhaps in part because of his country of birth, had a greater hold on his imagination than British counterparts. Reagan, the President when he came of political age in the 1980s, was his greatest inspiration, because he focused on the big picture including the end of the Cold War, and had a phenomenal ability to connect with people far and wide. He was in awe of Bill Clinton's magnetism and easy charm, but was less persuaded by George W. Bush. As a young MP, he had voted for the Iraq War in 2003, but had regretted it deeply thereafter.[12] His style as Prime Minister was much better attuned to the US President, ruling without having to attend the legislature, or worry too much about party or Cabinet, underpinned by a direct connection to the electorate. There he suspected power really lay, rather than in Parliament.

His lack of seriousness about what he was in politics to do came back to bite him when he could no longer get away with jokes and pirouettes. The first time his personal manifesto had to be unveiled and assessed on a national platform was when he stood for election to succeed Cameron in 2016. What now? Gove and his team were frustrated by his unwillingness to commit his personal credo to paper. 'We were desperately trying to get him to write his launch speech setting out his vision. Here was the man who had always wanted to be world king. And it became brutally, shockingly clear to us he didn't have any vision,' says one of Gove's team. This evasiveness, vacuum indeed, is given as one reason why Gove wielded the knife. The speech on 30 June was to be the most important he had given in his life, laying out his vision for the country. Dreams would no longer suffice. Rambling and lacking coherence, though, were the hallmarks of the concoction he delivered. 'I am no communist… But I want a capitalism that is fairer,' citing FTSE 100 chief executives earning 150 times more than the average pay in their companies. Instead of a statement of beliefs and policies, he digressed at length about his achievements in London, but spoke little about the benefits of Brexit, beyond the opportunities for deals with growth economies such as India and the US. Then at the peroration, in a moment of intended high theatre, he announced that this uniquely and eminently qualified candidate for PM would not be running. Smarting at the injustice of it all, he was intent on creating problems for whoever was to pick up his crown. In that at least, he succeeded.

Even as a Cabinet minister under May with continuing aspirations on the top job, he didn't work at developing a coherent set of beliefs across domestic policy. Nor did he forge close links to any think tank, party faction or thinkers beyond Brexit specialists. When the opportunity came again to stand in 2019, he showed the ERG a bit of his right leg, but its true believers knew he was never one of them. The One Nation caucus on the other wing remained suspicious, not least because of his Brexit lunge and despite his proclaiming his politics as 'One Nation' and folk memories of his voting for Ken Clarke to succeed William Hague in the 2001 Conservative leadership election. 'At heart, he was always a One Nation Conservative', was Gove's verdict. 'He courted figures like John Redwood and Mark Francois for political purposes, but he was never one of them.'[13] All sides sooner or later found him dissembling, only ever willing to commit to a position if he wanted something, or if his hand was forced: so they ensured his hand was regularly forced. Some questioned if he was even a Conservative at all. Was it all just a game to him, they wondered?

Johnson's utterances during the leadership campaign in 2019 were carefully monitored and controlled by his team, ensuring he said just what he needed to say to the various audiences, mission heavy and belief light. So no clues can be found then to his aspirations for power. The closest we can get to seeing inside his soul came after he won the leadership, at the small dinner in a private room at Alfred's Club in Mayfair, organized by Lister in July on the very eve of his coronation. 'He was in full flow, on fire with grand visions about levelling up, how money could be invested in major infrastructure projects to heal the damage caused by Thatcher's policies in the 1980s when large parts of the country were lost to industrial decline,' says one source. 'It was all Ozymandias [Shelley's great sonnet about the vain dreams of rulers], full of purpose, energy and belief,' says another. Those present were surprised and excited even by how inspirational he appeared. An official present thought, 'Here is a Prime Minister who actually wants to lead, to provide a strong sense of direction, to underpin the Union and make government more effective.'

After three years of May's inconclusive leadership, it struck them all as a breath of fresh air. 'He imagined a brave new shining world as soon as Brexit could be out of the way, mistakes and errors of the past addressed and corrected, with talk about a "great leap forward" [an unwitting reference to Mao's brutal transformation of China after 1949].' The Treasury came under fire for not doing more to allow investment in infrastructure as he told his rapt dinner guests how he would address slow growth and productivity (not natural Johnsonian habitats). By all accounts, it was a *tour de force*.

So, what happened to this vision?

The Three Impulses

The answer takes up the rest of this book, but the Alfred's dinner shows conclusively and beyond any doubt that he had a zeal to do specific things as Prime Minister after Brexit, even if his objectives were amorphous, uncosted and would have required at least a full five-year term of focused work in a favourable economic and political environment to have had any prospect of success.

We can catch a glimpse of that passion too in his speech on the steps of Downing Street on 24 July when he spoke at length about the opportunities of levelling up to produce a fairer country. Opportunities aplenty he said would arise from Brexit, including freeports, improved welfare of animals and blight-resistant crops. Restoring trust in government by exiting the European Union on 31 October would be *sine qua non*. Fixing social care 'once and for all' was a rare precise pledge: aides and officials were baffled to hear him say that a 'clear plan' for government had been 'prepared'. It hadn't. Nothing spoke more clearly of his nascent thinking, his total ignorance of government and his good intentions than this unheralded announcement.

As soon as he was inside the door, he would be gobbled up for the next six months by the two all-consuming objectives of making Brexit happen and winning the general election. In both, pragmatism was to the fore. Keeping the centre on side and maximizing the appeal across classes meant largesse in the September Spending Review on hospitals, schools, police and buses. Keeping his right-wing on side entailed throwing them red meat with the Northern Ireland Protocol and tacking further towards a hard Brexit than he would have wanted in the economic interests of the country. In the general election, his passions were equally cast to one side, sometimes forcefully by his minders. The manifesto, as we have seen, was the child of focus groups dictating what needed to be included to secure victory. More of his personal credo can be seen in his very personal introduction to the manifesto. Releasing a Britain 'trapped like a lion in a cage' dominates his text, to be achieved principally by 'getting Brexit done', mentioned six times in his opening paragraphs. Once achieved, he wanted to accomplish his 'fantastic programme' of levelling up because 'talent and genius are uniformly distributed throughout the country. Opportunity is not.' 'An infrastructure revolution' would help realize this, as would 'world-class public services' to be paid for by 'the millions of British businesses' which the government would 'foster and encourage'. His words are full of energy and naïveté: 'We don't want to waste 2020', but for it to be 'a year of hope, of prosperity and growth'.[14]

Only once he had won the general election in December 2019 and gained a personal and large mandate did he at last have the opportunity to build the Britain he wanted.

The problem was that he hadn't reckoned on other people having their own ideas which clashed with his own, or Covid intervening which ate up time, goodwill, energy and money, or the landslide majority of eighty turning into muddy land sliding under his very feet. Neither did he understand that a Prime Minister can only make their fine dreams happen by working through a team, all the more vital for a person 'whose eyes go straight to the end, without any clear idea of how to get there', in the words of David Frost.[15]

The task was made no easier by divisions in a Conservative Party deep into its tenth year in office, split from head to foot over Brexit, the economy and whether it wanted to be a free-market small-state Thatcherite party, or an interventionist large-state one. Instinctively, Johnson inclined to the latter, but did not hesitate to attack the sacred Thatcher head-on: 'there really is such a thing as society', he told a nation locking down as Covid was surging in March 2020.[16] He was not so imprudent as to denigrate Thatcher's legacy in front of his MPs, and paid due obeisance to the Conservative playlist classics of a 'dynamic free market' and their birthright to be the 'party of capitalism' in speeches. Indicatively, 'the one achievement he really admired her for was getting the Channel Tunnel built, bashing it through a system that repeatedly said it could not be done', says Guto Harri, his former comms director.[17] He was never an adherent to the 'Singapore-on-Thames' model of hyper-capitalist deregulation like Frost. To those who persist in believing that Johnson was a true Brexit believer is the irrefutable evidence that, unlike those who deeply believed in it, he gave so little time and energy to drive policy to show how it would benefit Britain.

It took many months, once he was through the door of No. 10, for the different factions to realize that he was not one of them. He continued to string them along for as long as he could, as an insider says: 'The premiership had no ideological consistency whatsoever. Everybody wanted different things, so what the Prime Minister did was to indulge them all.' So if he wasn't a Thatcherite, a free-marketeer, a One Nation Tory, an ideological Brexiteer, what on earth was he?

The answer is that slowly emerging from the primordial swamp were 'three impulses' which shaped his entire premiership. Infrastructure first, a passion for long-term projects which he believed the political cycle neglected to the long-term loss of the economy. Levelling up second, so that those disadvantaged by geography, class and age would have better opportunities. Patriotism third, very different to the right-wing nationalism of some Conservatives and UKIP, which he despised. Part of the problem for his team, as it is for historians, is that he never articulated these three impulses consistently. But when, after the excoriating year following the general election, his incoming Chief of Staff Dan Rosenfield asked him in December 2020 'what do you really want to do as Prime Minister?', these are the three ideas he produced. The three-part categorization is the closest we will ever get to defining 'Johnsonism', to bringing the dreams into the clear light of day.

Cabinet Making

Johnson became Prime Minister without any understanding of what Cabinet was for, what domestic departmental ministers did, who his talent to draw on was or what skills they would require in office. It was as if a gifted visionary on the staff was suddenly appointed to run a multinational company. Officials wondered how long he could possibly last. 'Are you really sure you are making the right appointment here, Prime Minister?' they nervously enquired as he trotted out name after name given to him on a list. 'Oh, this is only temporary,' he replied, dodging the question. 'As soon as we get Brexit out of the way, I'll do it properly. And I'll have a much smaller Cabinet too.' The wish for a small Cabinet, officials noted, was another giveaway sign of jejune incomers.

With a Prime Minister as inexperienced as Johnson, a high quality Cabinet running the main departments, and a Rolls-Royce system at the Cabinet Office in the centre making it all run on time, was a prerequisite for a successful administration.

Just days before entering No. 10, he gathered his team around him. 'We spent hours in front of the whiteboard in Andrew Griffith's Westminster house,' recalls Lister, who was joined by Cain, Walden, Gascoigne, Smith and incoming Chief Whip Mark Spencer. Johnson had some one hundred ministerial posts in his gift – the problem was he had told dozens more that they would get a job if they gave him their support. With absolutely no rationale for government in his mind, a starting point at least was jobs for the (mostly) boys in his leadership team. Conor Burns, Jake Berry and Amanda Milling were all thus very early entries on the whiteboard. So too were the Young Turks, Oliver Dowden, Robert Jenrick and Rishi Sunak, similarly deemed to have been helpful in the campaign. Rewards were needed too for his campaign managers. James Wharton was put in the House of Lords a year later, but Gavin Williamson proved more problematic. Cabinet Secretary Mark Sedwill made it clear that the security services refused to let him go anywhere near sensitive intelligence following his dismissal as Defence Secretary after a leak that May, which rendered him unsuitable for transfer to the Duchy of Lancaster, so he was given Education. Grant Shapps was rewarded for his service in the leadership campaign with Transport: indicatively, he provides the only tangible evidence of Johnson appointing a Cabinet minister with a brief to advance two of his three impulses in infrastructure and levelling up.

Was Johnson's desire to show the Conservative Party as open and liberal part of his motivation? Apparently not. Dougie Smith pushed Kemi Badenoch as Education Secretary, not for her minority ethnic background but for her reputation as an 'anti-woke warrior' (others at the whiteboard argued she was not ready for it).

His Cabinet might have been the most minority-friendly in history, but 'Boris was not consciously or deliberately doing it to promote diversity: he was colour-blind and just saw talent (and loyalty),' as one present emphasizes.[18] Sajid Javid (Chancellor of the Exchequer) was thus appointed because 'he'd been very helpful in the campaign' but also because Carrie Symonds 'loved him'. Sunak (Chief Secretary to the Treasury) was given the nod for no other reason than 'to keep an eye on Saj', as Smith never fully trusted him to deliver. The Prime Minister admired Kwasi Kwarteng (Business Minister) for his 'upfront decisiveness' but dithered over his appointment due to his status as a loose cannon. Alok Sharma (International Development Secretary) got the job because Johnson had rated him as a junior minister at the FCO when he had been Foreign Secretary. Priti Patel (Home Secretary) was seen as a capable and strong presenter, and Johnson wanted to have a forthright Brexiteer in a top job to give a strong signal to business and the party. He came later to think her better at holding the status of a hardline politician than delivering the policies of one, and agonized about retaining her at every subsequent reshuffle over possible replacements such as Kit Malthouse.

'This was a Cabinet with one principal end in mind: to get Brexit done,' says an official. Having some who voted Remain in Cabinet was deemed politic, including choosing Spencer as Chief Whip, a strong Johnson loyalist. He pushed hard to include other Remainers such as Brandon Lewis (Security Minister). The post was originally earmarked for Ben Wallace, who had been eager for a Cabinet job, but their once-seminal relationship never fully recovered from the furore over who had leaked Johnson's twin *Telegraph* articles to Tim Shipman at the *Sunday Times* in February 2016: Wallace strenuously denies that it was him. Johnson needed 'a lot of persuasion' to make Wallace Defence Secretary, who was told on appointment that any leak on security matters would result in his automatic dismissal.

'Cabinet reshuffles start with just one principal figure,' the officials carefully explained to Johnson. In this case, that figure was Jeremy Hunt, pencilled in for Defence. Johnson was hopeful his rival in the final leadership round would accept. He tried hard to persuade him, but Hunt said he would like to stay as Foreign Secretary. 'That ship had sailed,' one present recalls him replying, reserved for Dominic Raab, loyal and able to shore up the right behind Johnson. Conscious of the need to stamp his authority on the appointments and not give jobs to those who asked for them as he felt that May had done, he politely declined the suggestion. So Wallace, a name pushed by Walden, became Defence Secretary, remained throughout, and came into his own in 2022 over Ukraine. The job of Prime Minister is so all-encompassing that its holders need an effective and loyal Deputy Prime Minister (DPM) at their side overseeing huge swathes of domestic policy. Thatcher had Willie Whitelaw, and after he withdrew through ill health in January 1988, her effectiveness declined. Major found life much easier when Michael Heseltine became his DPM in 1995. Blair had John Prescott as de jure as well as Gordon Brown as de facto DPM. All three Prime Ministers were vastly better administrators than Johnson. Despite this, he didn't believe he needed a deputy, until he appointed Raab as a sop in 2021 but without giving him the authority of the office. Till then Raab had been given the title of First Secretary. Why didn't Johnson have a proper DPM, beyond not realizing he needed one? Trust – he never would have trusted anyone else to do it.

The standout figure best suited to the role, the most effective departmental minister under Johnson's two predecessors, was the fourth big beast. Vote Leave alumni were keen for the capable Gove to be handed a big task and lobbied heavily for giving him the key role in Brexit delivery. Johnson acquiesced but, simmering still with anger and distrust, was never going to give him anything more than Chancellor of the Duchy of Lancaster charged with preparing for no deal. It was a long way short of Chancellor of the Exchequer with oversight over domestic policy, the job he would have had if Johnson had become PM in 2016.

There were several odd-ones-out in the Cabinet who did not fit the Brexiteers-mainly mould. Carrie Symonds pushed for more female representation, including the retention of Amber Rudd at the Department for Work and Pensions (DWP) and the appointment of Nicky Morgan to the Department for Digital, Culture, Media and Sport (DCMS). Chief Whip Julian Smith was moved to Northern Ireland despite his association with May's failed Withdrawal Agreement, a decision taken in recognition of his relationship with the DUP, well-tested ability to navigate tense negotiations, and the damage former whips can inflict on an incoming administration if left unsatisfied. Left-field discussions took place over offering Theresa May a role in the Cabinet and promoting Labour's (and ex-Vote Leave) Gisela Stuart to the House of Lords with a ministerial job. Both were ruled out, judged 'too difficult'.

Cummings had joined too late to have had influence on the appointments, and was as generally dismissive of the importance of Cabinet as Johnson. 'He thought you could run government around rather than through [Cabinet],' says an official. Johnson's decision to have a weak Cabinet suited Cummings to a T. He did, though, indirectly influence the appointment of ERG 'Spartan' Steve Baker, marked down on the whiteboard as going back to DExEU as Minister of State – a promotion. He was duly called to No. 10. But Johnson was sidetracked with two difficult appointments: Conor Burns and Jake Berry (both were chafing at their posts). It meant that Baker had to wait in No. 10 becoming more and more agitated, and began to imagine (without grounds) that known ERG-hater Cummings had invited him in deliberately to play games and embarrass him. When Johnson eventually got to see him, Baker said, 'Stop dicking around with me. I want the room. I want the room.' 'Boris looked at us despairingly,' one present recalls, 'and we left the room for five minutes, which turned into fifteen minutes, but Boris was still unable to persuade Baker to do the job.' To provide ballast from the ERG side, Johnson appointed Jacob Rees-Mogg, at one time fancifully mentioned as Chancellor, who proved loyal, though not close to Johnson personally. Baker went on to become a sworn enemy, a champion of the Covid Recovery Group, formed to campaign against lockdown.

Over the next three years, Johnson was never to initiate his root-and-branch reshuffle, as initially foreshadowed. He hated the very idea of reshuffles and was content to leave tame loyalists in post. The lower the risk of an up-and-comer challenging him for the throne, the better. 'We don't want young, hungry lions,' an aide recalls him saying disapprovingly in reaction to Sunak's meteoric rise after introducing the furlough scheme, 'we want old, tired lions.' So the Lion King spent the next three years presiding over weekly meetings of his generally lacklustre pride, making them feel he had little time or use for them – until the end, when some rose up to tear him limb from limb.

Grand Projects and Infrastructure

Grand projects and infrastructure in the style of US President F. D. Roosevelt (1933–45) or France's President Mitterrand (1981–95) seized Johnson's imagination. These are what excited him about being at No. 10, and it was the very lack of such projects that had frustrated him at the Foreign Office. It's what had enthralled him as Mayor, where aspirational ideas were not penalized or patronized as they would be in No. 10.

With the general election secured, the talk was of ten years of Johnson at 10. The ideals he articulated in private during the leadership campaign and at Alfred's Club, on ice for six long months, could now come out freely into the open without his minders telling him to bottle them. Cummings was irritated that he hadn't immediately seized the day after 12 December, but took time off to recuperate on the exclusive private island of Mustique in the Caribbean. But in January, the long-awaited away day took place at Chequers to map out the next decade, a forum for the Prime Minister to set out his priorities. 'The election had solved the puzzle of how to renew the base of the Conservative Party, and now we needed to move on and deliver,' says Ross Kempsell, a party insider present.[19] The atmosphere was giddy, attenders felt, sensing the political team's triumphalism. 'All were convinced that there would be ten years of Boris Johnson,' says an official.

Johnson set enormous store by his former City Hall adviser Munira Mirza, head of the No. 10 Policy Unit, to outline just what that creative thinking should be. The daughter of Pakistani immigrants, a former member of the Revolutionary Communist Party with a sociology PhD, Mirza's background was suitably unconventional for the Prime Minister. She had joined City Hall in 2008, working first as culture adviser then as deputy mayor for education and culture since 2012, and was one of the five women Johnson named as the most influential on his life (his list, including Boudicca and Kate Bush, was frivolous to form; a genuine roll would have included Mirza, his mother Charlotte, sister Rachel, Marina and Carrie).[20] Mirza was for his first year and more in No. 10 the closest thing Johnson had to a friend in the world of politics. 'Munira was one of the very, very few people in the building who were willing to tell the Prime Minister the truth,' a No. 10 official reflects. 'Most people just told him what they thought he wanted to hear, she told him what he needed to hear' (until he was no longer listening). Mirza was more than inspiration and check: building on her long knowledge of his mind, she was the best at picking out his embryonic instincts and weaving them into something coherent, shaping a policy programme to fit.

Indicatively, Chancellor Javid had not been invited to Chequers. It was not an oversight. He and Johnson had already clashed badly on spending: his card was marked. Johnson never had any time for the Treasury view of spending, which he considered irredeemably short-termist, unwaveringly pro-London and utterly unimaginative. As Mayor he had driven ambitious projects with strong iconography, believing that history remembers the builders of enduring landmarks and monuments, not those who fretted about the pennies. His *grands projets* Mitterrand-style had not always been successful. 'Boris Island', his proposal for a new London airport in the Thames estuary, was deemed too expensive and environmentally harmful in 2014, while his aborted Garden Bridge over the Thames was another high-profile failure. But its £43 million of wasted public funds had not dampened Johnson's enthusiasm for building.[21] Not a bit: 'grand projects' were at the centre of his ideas of levelling up.

Officials came to Chequers intent on pinning down what he really cared about. Deliberately verbatim notes were recorded so these words would resound across Whitehall: 'the Prime Minister wants'. Already, because of his frequent changes of mind, his instructions had acquired a reputation for slipperiness. But on the substance of what he said at Chequers, those present were most struck by his lucid flow of words about the grand projects to be spread across the entire country. 'Tunnels, trains, bridges, freeports, the green economy. He was in his element on all of these,' says one.

Mirza had deftly woven his own passions into her presentation, the most important of the day after his, about enhancing economic prospects and giving people better opportunities, with constant reference to the Prime Minister's aspirations. Meanwhile, the third big beast at Chequers, Cummings, was, everyone noticed, remaining ostentatiously quiet – an early signal that he and Johnson's agendas were no longer aligned.[22]

Officials hoped that at last they had their direction; but before the day was over, they realized it was not going to be that easy. 'The second we started to talk about implementation it was clear he found it all so boring,' says one. Back in Downing Street in follow-up meetings, they found that projects that Johnson had spoken about with great gusto at Chequers he quickly found tiresome after practicalities were raised, while those he did maintain enthusiasm for tended to be of minor importance, utterly unworkable, or both. 'To keep him engaged we would manage his timetable to ensure he did the serious stuff a Prime Minister has got to get through, then allow him some slots for "fun" like the bridge to Northern Ireland, zero-emission buses and the "Festival of Brexit",' says aide Cleo Watson.[23]

The idea of a rail crossing from Scotland to Northern Ireland was emblematic of Johnson's passion projects: spectacularly ambitious, crushingly expensive and fatally unrealistic. Johnson's commissioned report had deemed the costs 'impossible to justify'. Talking with ally Lord Bamford shortly after his resignation, he still ached for the bridge as a part of his legacy. 'I'm just so upset we didn't push it forwards. Someone told me the other day that it could have been done. Why didn't we?' The Prime Minister's great legacy for office proved to be a breeder of white elephants. Time was not on his side: he'd had eight years as Mayor, while Roosevelt had thirteen, Mitterrand fourteen and Mao twenty-seven years in power. As PM, Johnson's own 'great leap forward' had to be contained within just three years. All the more can we understand his frustration not to have had his ten years.

One piece of infrastructure which Johnson did succeed in pushing through was HS2, the plan for a high speed railway connecting London to Birmingham and Manchester (HS1, from London to the continent, travelled through the Channel Tunnel agreed by Thatcher and Mitterrand in 1987). Ironically, HS2 was the plan almost everyone was against. 'It was the first big decision for us after the general election,' says an official. 'The Prime Minister thought it embodied levelling up while delivering a grand project of the kind he's naturally attracted to.' In October 2013, he had visited China on a mayoral trip and was 'utterly mesmerized' by the bullet train between Beijing and Shanghai travelling at 220 miles per hour. HS2 had been a thorny issue for the Conservatives, not least on grounds of environmental damage and sheer cost since it opened to consultation in 2010, but time was running out to scrap the initial leg with £11 billion of funding already spent. The Department for Transport had ordered a review in August 2019, and with the findings arriving in early 2020, the government had a stark choice: commit or cancel. 'The Treasury hated it, Dom hated it, Andrew Gilligan [No. 10 transport adviser] hated it. Nobody was emboldening the Prime Minister in-house, everybody was against it, but the debate went on for weeks and he stood his ground,' says the official. Gilligan, a former journalist who had advised him on cycling as Mayor, called it 'the greatest infrastructure mistake in fifty years'.[24] Johnson's only real ally was Transport Secretary Grant Shapps, who received frequent calls from Cummings, saying, 'Can you just tell your officials that HS2 is dead? It just isn't going to happen. Dump it and spend the money elsewhere.' Shapps had the sense that Cummings wasn't asking.[25]

When forces were ranged against Johnson, he could be at his most effective and switched on, devouring his briefs and mastering the detail. Officials in Downing Street had never seen him so engaged. As he pushed back against his aides' advice, tempers began to fray. 'I want to do it, it's symbolic of the country I want us to be.'

'But it's 1980s technology for the 2030s, by the time it opens it will be utterly obsolete,' Gilligan flashed back.

'People don't want this s**t, they don't like it,' added Cummings.

'Don't you tell me what the people want, I've just won a landslide,' snapped Johnson.

The final showdown took place in Johnson's office in early February. Javid at least, if not with whole-hearted Treasury support, was not against. With his acquiescence, it became clear to the room that the decision would only go one way: HS2 would proceed. 'As a nation we have to commit, undertake transformative change. We cannot chop and change our way to success. We must be bold,' a charged and victorious Johnson told the room, one present recalls. The megaproject Prime Minister had at last got his way.

Levelling Up

Johnson's personal passion for levelling up was honed as Mayor. 'He believed strongly that London was an incubator for businesses across the country – and that the regions where they were based could become more prosperous because of it,' says Will Walden.[26] Transport for London's supply chains, Johnson had boasted, supported thousands of jobs outside London, as did Wrightbus's 'New Routemaster' buses made in Ballymena in Northern Ireland, or bricks constructed in Newcastle-under-Lyme, a sample of which he famously brandished to cooing delegates at the annual party conference in September 2014. Putting the heat on Cameron and Osborne by reminding them (and voters) that his reach from London extended all over the country was part of the mischief, but it went beyond that. 'While he primarily wanted London and London business to thrive, he saw small and medium-sized enterprises outside London as vital to that success, to regional successes and by extension UK plc,' says an aide.

His final period as Mayor saw him exploring ideas for the Northern Ireland bridge, and reimagining Crossrail (the East–West line across London partially built in his time as Mayor) across the Pennines, reopening lines closed by Beeching in the early 1960s in the process. This thinking lay behind his hopes for Cameron to create an amalgamated department for him – covering business, the regions, housing, communities and transport, a revealing illumination of his interests in politics.

When Cameron wouldn't oblige, and Johnson spun off to head Vote Leave, the referendum campaign proved a revelation to him, the closest in his life to a Road to Damascus experience. The searcher, at a critical juncture in his life, had found the cause for which he had been seeking. Here he encountered a new swathe of voters with impassioned stories of neglect by Westminster, the disillusioned in left-behind post-industrial towns who no longer felt they could trust Labour, nor indeed the political system at large. He came to believe he could uniquely appeal to them with his personal charm and charisma. 'Touring the North he heard story after story on the doorstep of how successive governments since Thatcher had failed to counteract the slow decline of British industry within the region,' recalls Walden. 'He heard how the buses and trains were inadequate, that the country revolved around London.'[27] Johnson sensed an opportunity to widen his base in his claim for the crown, a mixture of self-advancement and genuine empathetic indignation.

Thus was born 'levelling up', foreshadowed by Johnson during the general election campaign in his 5 November article in the *Telegraph* when he spoke about his ambition for 'this One Nation Conservative government'[28] and first officially rolled out in the 2019 manifesto. The impulse was not of course unique. Britain's chronic ill-balance between a prosperous South-East and the rest of the country had been exacerbated by international competition from the 1920s undermining its staple industries, textiles, iron and steel, shipbuilding and coal, and depressing the areas in which they were based. Governments from the 1930s onwards had tried to address the issue, without success. Most recently had come Osborne and Cameron's 'Northern Powerhouse' and Theresa May's attempt to tackle the 'burning injustices' across the regions. What separated levelling up from these was the level and clarity of electoral commitment imparted directly by the Prime Minister. 'Johnson saw the North-East leaning more Tory than it had twenty-five years before, and levelling up was the opportunity to bag them. To him it was a political no-brainer,' says an official. This was a specific bid to win marginal seats in the Red Wall. He and his team believed that to retain them without Corbyn or Brexit would require delivering on commitments – by, as they unceremoniously put it to their fellow strategists, 'building a load of stuff in the North'. But with expectations in these constituencies soaring impossibly high, and the Brexit dividend yet to bolster the left-behind areas, it was going to require more than just a load of stuff. There needed to be an intellectual underpinning to structure the ambition: 'Compared to Northern Powerhouse, which had its own theory and empirical framework about how to create prosperity behind it, it was just aspiration,' says George Osborne.[29] Osborne may have had his own vested interest in arguing this, but he wasn't the only figure to believe it.

In No. 10, Johnson would remonstrate with officials, 'Why can't we have regional cities like Munich, Lyon, Barcelona? All these places left behind, we need to fix them.' When Johnson referred to himself as a One Nation Conservative, or a 'Brexity Hezza' [after Michael Heseltine] as he once told his Cabinet, it was this enthusiasm he had in mind. But what exactly did levelling up mean? When the phrase was first uttered in Parliament in 1868 by an Irish MP, Disraeli (no less) swung round on him and said, 'I'd very much like to have the [opponents'] views as to the distinct meaning they attribute to the phrase'.[30]

Senior civil servants scratched their heads in the run-up to the general election as they struggled to find anybody in the No. 10 team able to delineate for them what exactly levelling up meant. 'There was the assumption it involved infrastructure and investment, but no one had actual detail. There was a belief that there would be time to sort it all out after the election. To be honest, we thought for Boris it was a concept, not a programme,' says a Cabinet Office official. Johnson's vague cakeist notion was not necessarily considered a handicap, though, by those charged with developing the policy. 'He understood that levelling up wasn't taking from London to give to Liverpool, it was about increasing the size of the pie. He even referenced "Pareto efficiency" – the intellectual explanation of cakeism,' says Andy Haldane, brought in to co-author the Levelling Up White Paper.[31] Johnson knew Pareto's first name (Vilfredo); it's unclear, however, how much of the economic theory he understood beyond the metaphors of pies and cakes.

As Johnson was to discover, levelling-up policies, if they were to be successful, required money, and throwing money at them was not a prescription the Treasury shared. Before long, as we will see later, he was to encounter not a Red Wall but a brick wall in the form of the mighty Treasury. As one of its officials makes clear, 'The Treasury is largely sceptical of spending, and the economics literature largely sceptical of levelling up. We never bought that you could level up like Boris wanted through infrastructure spending.'

Johnson was to turn his energies increasingly to levelling up in other areas he cared about, notably the disadvantaged young in education and for the elderly with social care. As with HS2, social care had dogged the Conservative Party since coming into government in 2010, with the Dilnot Commission on Funding of Care and Support proposing funding reforms in 2011, accepted by Cameron in 2013, but postponed by him in 2015. The Dilnot plan was then mothballed by May, who commissioned a Green Paper and proposed in 2017 a less regressive system in the general election, only to have it dubbed the 'dementia tax' with devastating impact on Tory seats. Succeeding in resolving an issue that had eluded his two predecessors was a prime motivation for Johnson. Behind the black door of No. 10 after his initial statement as Prime Minister, officials and aides alike were in a panic at his off-the-cuff pledge to resolve the thorny issue of social care. 'What plan? We don't have a plan.' Upon questioning as to what exactly the plan was that he had just told the world he had, Johnson responded, 'Well, we'll have to decide which option we go for, won't we?'

'Boris just thought it was one of the big issues he would sort out,' says a policy official. 'He didn't particularly understand it initially, but got that several PMs had ducked the issue, and he had a personal commitment to resolving it.' He had been greatly affected by his elderly mother Charlotte's experience of living with early onset Parkinson's disease. When the going was tough, it pushed him to solve the issue. 'He was always asking, "Where are we on social care? I want to be making progress",' recalls the official. It helped him bond with others, including actress Dame Barbara Windsor who visited with representatives from the Alzheimer's Society for tea in September 2019.[32] He regaled her with tales of his mother, and as she gave him a kiss and clung onto his arm while walking to the door he told her, 'We're going to reform this. But because it's so expensive we'll have to create a new tax to solve it.' As the guests departed, aides scrambled to tell Barbara Windsor and her party before they could leave, 'Thank you for coming, and please don't tell *anybody* Boris said anything about a tax.'

As with infrastructure, on levelling up Johnson ran headlong into the Treasury. For a man so determined to make things happen, and with so little understanding of the economy and finance, friction was inevitable. His battle to make social care a reality, his first commitment as Prime Minister, was to set in motion a series of disagreements leading to the resignation which precipitated his downfall.

Patriotism

Johnson was a patriot more than a nationalist, though some of his dog-whistle utterances placed him perilously close to the uber-nationalists like Farage whom he despised. You glimpse his romantic patriotism in his attempt to build the Northern Ireland bridge to unify the country physically, his love of British writers and history, and his backing for a post-Brexit 'Festival of Brexit'. Making Britain a sovereign country again we know was at the top of his list of reasons for choosing Brexit. He had an instinctive liking for patriotic leaders wanting to put their country first, and, like Ukraine's Volodymyr Zelenskyy, defending it from invasion.

Surprising then that, having very deliberately announced he would be 'Minister for the Union' during the leadership campaign, he gave so little thought to how to make the Union stronger, and was less concerned by it than any Prime Minister of this century. The new post was formally announced on 26 July 2019, but there was to be no department, no junior ministers nor strategic plan. 'Cynical rebranding' was how the SNP dismissed the appointment. Johnson had little inclination to build bridges with Remain-voting Scotland where he was unpopular (he was never good with those who didn't buy into his aura), nor was he notably mindful of Northern Ireland's position in the Union with his Brexit settlement. Instead, he delegated thinking to Luke Graham, a Conservative Scottish MP defeated in the 2019 general election, whom he invited to head up a 'Union unit' within No. 10. But the team was small, and Johnson never very engaged with its work: 'The Union was a second-order priority for him,' says an official.

Less surprisingly, given his experience as Foreign Secretary, he had little idea in his first year about Britain's place in the world. The party at No. 10 to celebrate the UK formally leaving the EU on 31 January 2020 saw him in a euphoric mood. The throng of jubilant supporters counted down to the moment at which the UK left, marked by Johnson himself thwacking a tiny gong with sufficient brio to knock it clean off its stand, and nearly toppling a tipsy Johnson too. It was 'Boris' unbound, Johnson at his most crowd-pleasing. His speech was greeted by extravagant whoops and cheers, but Cummings and his supporters heard less the gong being sounded than alarm bells. 'It was the big moment for him to give a sense of what the country could do and be. But he just waffled on with the same old rubbish about French knickers and cider,' says one.

This was his Henry VIII moment, if it was to happen. Brexit was the political project that had defined his career and propelled him into No. 10. Yet Johnson's vision as to Britain's place in the world was no less vague and cliché-ridden than his views on other policy areas. 'We never got him interested in the hard choices involved in a genuine geopolitical view of the world. He always liked being friends with everybody, as far as he could, including Russia and China,' says Frost.[33] International cakeism was no more a strategy for Britain's future foreign policy than cakeism, domestic-style.

Remodelling the State to Deliver the Revolution

Leaving the EU ushered in an extraordinary moment of possibility for British politics, with the potential for a revolution in the structure of the state.

Johnson the iconoclast, most definitely not a conservative on the constitution, was the ideal Prime Minister to pull this off. But he had no vision for it, none at all. In its place he had a long list of dislikes for elements of the constitution. Whitehall, headed by the Treasury, was top of the list. Scarred by what he considered were patronizing attitudes by diplomats when he was Foreign Secretary, he entered No. 10 believing the civil service saw him as a virus and wished only to see him off as speedily as possible (as indeed his successor Liz Truss believes it successfully did to her premiership). He loathed the civil service, considering it Blairite, irredeemably pro-Remain and dominated by the 'blob', that body of officials over-concerned with process who didn't want anything to get done which he felt had grown to monstrous proportions under his predecessors. But recognizing he was no good at systems thinking, he was content enough to let Cummings lead the charge, as Thomas Cromwell did for Henry.

A massive restructuring of the machinery of government was the Cummings-led plan. A post-election reshuffle was delayed until after it could be discussed at the January away day at Chequers. Sedwill was eager to fulfil what Cummings/Johnson wanted, to prove that Whitehall wasn't the den of doomsayers they imagined. The centre of government was to be brought under the closer control of the Prime Minister, and the key No. 10 functions were to be transferred into a new 'command centre' in the Cabinet Office. The FCO and Department for International Development were to merge as the Foreign, Commonwealth and Development Office (FCDO), helping to align aid with foreign policy goals. A 'Department of Infrastructure' was to be established, locating Johnson's passions in one place while removing the remits of energy from the Department for Business, Energy and Industrial Strategy

(BEIS) and housing from the Ministry of Housing, Communities and Local Government (MHCLG), seen to have failed in handling them. The Home Office was to split into a 'Department of Homeland Security' and a 'Police and Justice Department', easing the tension which had plagued successive Home Secretaries of being privy to threats to national security but having little or no power to act. Finally, if only briefly, the Treasury was to be split into finance and economics ministries as a way of diminishing its leverage over departments, thereby realigning Whitehall incentives away from parsimonious policy-making intended to balance the books in the short term, and towards cost-effective investment which could sustain long-term growth. Sedwill and his team baulked only at this final suggestion. Even for a freshly elected, landslide-winning, chest-thumping Prime Minister at the height of his powers, taking on the Treasury would, they worried, end in Pyrrhic victory at best. The Treasury was not for turning, as it had shown most recently in 1969, when such a plan was reversed after just five years.

Johnson intended to run the country with a small loyal team around him, as he had done at City Hall. The last-minute addition of Cummings showed he had given his team's composition little thought. He had found Cabinet purgatory in his two years under May and he had no intention of using it or its committees more than a bare minimum. After his spate of initial appointments in July 2019 he insisted the high headcount would only be temporary, and that in the long term he would be moving to a Cabinet consisting of ministers from just a dozen departments, once Brexit was out of the way. At the January 2020 away day, senior officials suddenly found that Johnson was no longer so keen on minimalism: 'We heard them talking about limiting numbers a thousand times, but when it came down to making the change, it was never going to happen.

There were too many people to whom they had made promises to or needed to buy off.' The departments in the firing line such as BEIS and DCMS were too useful for the purposes of patronage. Here was the volatility at the heart of Johnsonism: when balancing stated reform against placating allies, Johnson chose the latter.

Parliament was another part of the constitution for which he would have little time, now that he had a majority of eighty. Nor would he have space for the Conservative Party, for convention, or ethics advisers. He was about to show the country how to be a twenty-first-century Prime Minister.

Culture, Immigration, Education and Environment

Lacking ideology or set Conservative beliefs, it is no surprise that on broad swathes of issues Johnson had no preconceived position. Notably absent from discussion at the January 2020 away day were any issues of culture. 'Boris had no interest in this,' Cummings wrote later on his blog.[34] This is partially true. While Johnson was reluctant to express views on most cultural issues, he remained receptive to the aides around him who held strong beliefs and to the mores of the Conservative press, notably the *Telegraph* and *Daily Mail* titles. The 'war on woke' within No. 10 emanated primarily from Smith, Mirza and Policy Unit wonk Elena Narozanski. To Johnson's intense irritation, his three years coincided with a peak in culture wars, from Black Lives Matter to gender identity and free speech. Try as he might, as we will see, he was unable to remain totally above the fray.

On other issues too, he could not be placed on a left/right barometer. The environment for one. 'The first time I spoke to him as an undergrad I asked him his views and he said to me he was a "green Tory",' says fellow Oxford graduate Gove.[35] Although he had wavered on occasion over the years, dismissing wind turbines as unable to 'pull the skin off a rice pudding', he was becoming a true believer by the time he had secured the premiership.[36] Significant influences on him were father Stanley and brother Leo, both lifelong environmentalists, Carrie Symonds, a devoted animal lover, as well as her former boss and close friend Zac Goldsmith. Johnson's was a bucolic and eclectic environmentalism, rolled up with an admiration for technological solutions that he shared with Cummings (albeit without his grasp of the science). All these turned the generally winsome Johnson into a green warrior challenging head-on the scepticism of the Conservative right and hostility from the Treasury. But typically on housing, an area he considered he knew about from his mayoralty, he adopted a contradictory position: Housing Secretary Robert Jenrick was excited to have a hawk on new homebuilding, until Johnson's MPs got at him, and he backed down.

Johnson's views on immigration placed him on the left of the party. As Mayor he was the self-described 'only politician… who is actually willing to stand up and say that he's pro-immigration' and publicly extolled its virtues.[37] Immigration's salience peaked during the Brexit referendum campaign with many voters demanding a firmer approach, so he clarified his position: 'I'm pro-immigration, but above all I'm pro *controlled* immigration.'[38] But a firm hand on immigration was never Johnson's view even if he would tease the electorate with his position, and he saw it as subordinate as an issue to the principle of democratic control. 'It is said that those who voted Leave were mainly driven by anxieties about immigration,' he wrote in his regular Monday *Telegraph* column just after the referendum result. 'I do not believe that is so. After meeting thousands of people in the course of the campaign, I can tell you that the number one issue was control – a sense that British democracy was being undermined by the EU system'.[39]

But the difficulty for Johnson was that many Conservative voters *did* believe, for all his protestations to the contrary, that it was a major issue. Cummings would frequently look at the data and urge him to take a harder tack, particularly in the run-up to the election. At the party conference in September 2019, a row erupted between the two, Cummings of one mind with Levido and Cain in utilizing stronger rhetoric, Johnson squeamish about going in harder on the issue, conscious that his careless comments about veiled Muslim women looking like 'letter boxes' could come back and bite him. As in the referendum campaign in 2016, Cain and the team would try to jink a strong line past him, using Home Secretary Priti Patel to announce that the government would lower overall immigration. 'Boris was furious,' says one campaign staffer. 'He gave the team a talking to. "I said we're not going to campaign on migration, so why am I seeing this?"' As during the referendum, Johnson was offended that his team placed winning above respecting his delicate position.

The manifesto spoke of 'firmer and fairer Australian-style' points-based immigration, tying in rhetoric the idea of worthiness to employability, an ability to speak English and lack of a criminal record – yet it also committed to the overhaul being 'more fair and compassionate' to avoid a repeat of the Windrush scandal that came to light in 2018 casting a long shadow over May's premiership. Johnson had a difficult juggling act: putting in Patel at the Home Office as a sop to the right, while trying a more liberal approach than her or his predecessor, one which cohered with both the general decline in the salience of immigration following the referendum and a growing public acceptance of the positive impact of immigration on Britain's economy and culture.[40]

No area saw a more dramatic change in acceptance of right-wing tropes to a position far to the left of the party than education. The manifesto had been flimsy on the subject beyond repeating the additional funding announced in the summer of 2019, while saying little about school reform. So in January 2020, realizing that a Prime Minister ought to have views on the subject, Johnson summoned the Department for Education (DfE) high command to the Cabinet Room for an hour-long meeting, intended to set the direction of policy for the coming years. Education Secretary Williamson sat with his permanent secretary Jonathan Slater by his side, across the table from Johnson flanked by Mirza and Sedwill. Cummings ambled into the meeting wheeling the scribbled-upon whiteboard he had been using to brief Johnson in his preparatory tutorial in his office, and sat at the far end of the Cabinet table, projecting his authority over proceedings, and expecting the PM to parrot what he had been told.

Moments into the discussion, it became clear to the DfE team that Johnson's view was not aligned with what was written on the whiteboard. Cummings' suggestion of a rebalancing of teacher pay to bring London and regional rates to a similar level was batted away by Johnson, who interjected that 'as the MP for Uxbridge this isn't a policy I would implement'. As Williamson and Slater tried to redirect the conversation towards the technical issue of building capacity for multi-academy trusts, it all became too much for Johnson whose impatience snapped at the profusion of technical terms and acronyms. 'When I was at school,' he said, defaulting as he often would to his time at Eton, 'we were all ranked from one to two hundred, and it injected this competitive spirit in us. We need something like that in our schools now.' Cummings failed to suppress a laugh, while Williamson and Slater tried hard to suppress their shock.

The meeting was indicative of Johnson's position on much of policy, and the inability to place an effective process around him in No. 10 to help delineate his views. 'His thinking was very shallow, there was nothing substantial at all there,' says one senior official. 'He hadn't thought about education beyond his own school experience: all his ideas were related to what he had known.' Instead of turning up to the meeting with an agreed position cooked up in a series of pre-meets, Johnson and his political team arrived disorganized and divided, arguing against each other rather than directing ministers and their departments.

Therefore, Johnson's passion, in as far as it was present, was to replicate the best parts of his own schooling. 'His regular contribution was that we needed to get Classics in the curriculum more. He came up to me about once every three months saying he wanted it to be funded better, to be in state schools,' says Williamson.[41] Sport – as long as it was competitive sport – was another Johnson passion. He'd enjoyed his sport at school. Johnson's two principal interventions on education – on skills and adult entitlement – and his attempt to inject a vast amount of spending into education catch-up post-Covid both came to him late in the day.

The post-general election period should have seen No. 10 ablaze with energy, ideas and strategy pinging off the walls as the direction was set until 2024, and even 2029. It was one of those moments, Macmillan after 1957, Thatcher after 1983 or Blair after 1997, when the Prime Minister had the chance to embed a fresh political agenda for the country. As Johnson himself wrote in the 2019 manifesto, 'We don't want to waste 2020'.

Johnson was adamant he wanted to be remembered for so much more than Brexit. Once Covid, to which we now turn, was substantially over by the end of 2020, how would he turn his three broad impulses into solid policy achievements?

An exhausted Johnson addresses the nation from Downing Street

5

COVID

By January 2020, Johnson believed that with the crises of Brexit and the snap election behind him it would be relatively plain sailing for the next five and more years. Instead, he ran headlong into the worst health crisis since the Spanish flu epidemic of 1918–19. Johnson proved to be completely unsuited to the challenges that now lay ahead. Few predecessors since Lloyd George would not have handled it better.[1] Johnson's defective and indecisive leadership, desperation to please all the wrong people and failure to oversee a calm and unified response team contributed to government failures dealing with the crisis in 2020.

Most Prime Ministers are faced with a predominant crisis, the handling of which defines their premiership and place in public memory. For Cameron and May, it had been the EU referendum and subsequent attempt to leave the EU; for Brown, it had been the global financial crisis; for Blair, the Iraq War; for Major, Black Wednesday and the UK's departure from the European Exchange Rate Mechanism. Some crises are already in full flow when the incumbent steps into No. 10; others develop when the premiership is in full flow. Some are of the Prime Minister's own making; others are forced upon them. Some are handled by the premier with skill, instinct and experience; others, as happened with Covid, sniff out a leader not up to the task, and a system that buckled.

Over the New Year holiday, Johnson had been fretting about HS2, whether Big Ben would bong for Brexit on the day of the UK's departure from the EU (Elizabeth Tower was undergoing repairs), and whether to jilt Javid in his reshuffle. As he did so, a new virus was emerging on the other side of the globe. Originating in Wuhan, China, and dubbed Covid-19, it provided the most extensive peacetime challenge to the British state for a hundred years, drawing the government into unprecedented levels of intervention in the social and economic lives of its citizens.

Inquiries have been and will be set up, reports published, memoirs flaunted and academic texts written about the handling of the epidemic and how the government fared in its response. It was a rare moment in history where days happened in minutes, months in hours, and years in mere weeks. The full truth may never be fully known, but the period will be dissected with forensic scrutiny, drawing on a wealth of accounts and archival material to provide lessons of systemic failure in crises, policymaking under pressure when faced with extreme uncertainty. Some analyses will be years in the composition. This chapter, drawing heavily on the silent voices of those who will never publish memoirs and diaries, focuses on the Prime Minister and No. 10: how did they fare, and what lessons can be learned?

Mitigation: 7 January–7 March 2020

It was 7 January 2020 when Johnson first picked up on Covid-19, in discussion with Health Secretary Matt Hancock, who himself had learned of the virus spreading in Wuhan the week before. Johnson was relaxed. The British system had been lauded for its pandemic preparedness, regarded by the Global Health Security Index as the second best prepared country, narrowly behind the US. The 2011 influenza preparedness strategy laid the foundation for the UK's response, the plans then trialled in the 2016 'Exercise Cygnus' in which the ability of Whitehall departments to coordinate across government was stress-tested in a fictitious flu, wiping out 200,000–400,000 people if the government didn't step in.[2] Within weeks, it became clear the UK's supposed pre-eminence in pandemic preparedness was a dangerous mirage.

In a brief window of transparency in January before the shutters descended again, China had published the virus's genome. The UK's planning had been for an influenza mutation, but the genomic data showed that this was no flu. It was in fact a coronavirus, a variant of Severe Acute Respiratory Syndrome (SARS), and flu-specific preparations would be of limited use.

As reports of cases in China mounted, yet little tangible or published data was available, the Scientific Advisory Group for Emergencies (SAGE) held its first meeting on 22 January to discuss the unfolding situation and map out the UK's potential response. A specialist crisis body drawing together scientific experts to act as its senior advisory body, SAGE had previously convened on the H1N1 swine flu (2009), Ebola outbreaks (2013–16) and the Salisbury poisonings (2018); it was to have over one hundred meetings on Covid, eclipsing the fifty-two across previous crises.

Leading it were Chief Medical Officer Chris Whitty and Government Chief Scientific Adviser Patrick Vallance. Through them, SAGE fed advice to the Civil Contingencies Committee, more commonly known as COBRA. From COBRA, government departments were coordinated, ministers informed and decisions taken.

The thinking through January and February was dominated by Whitty, Vallance and the Department for Health and Social Care

(DHSC). DHSC Permanent Secretary Chris Wormald commented to the team that 'We're so lucky to have exactly the right people in the room here.' And on the face of it, he was right. Whitty fortuitously had been a researcher of infectious diseases, Vallance an expert in medicines development and discovery for emerging diseases, and Wormald himself an expert in crisis management with the necessary departmental grip after four years helming the DHSC. Discussions at the time had an unreality to them. According to one observer, 'The atmosphere was weird in that period before mid-March. There was an intensity, but the penny hadn't dropped about all the implications of the challenge in front of us. There was a sense among the medics that finally we were getting to the real issues, that epidemics were huge existential issues, and that meant having the right people in charge.'

The 'right people' did not include the Prime Minister. No. 10 was not even a spectator, absent from SAGE. 'Initially there were no No. 10 representatives at our meetings, until eventually one began to attend, and even then Downing Street wasn't really engaging with it,' recalls an influential SAGE member.

Likewise, Johnson was absent from COBRA for the first five meetings of the pandemic in January, leaving Hancock to chair them. Within No. 10 and the Cabinet Office, Covid in its early stages was seen more as a foreign policy challenge, the initial operational response focused on chartering flights to get British citizens out of Wuhan. Only in February did it move to a health issue, with early thinking about testing and hospital visits. But, 'Even in February, the government's health policy focus wasn't Covid. It was finding a way to deliver the forty hospitals, 50,000 nurses, reducing GP waiting times as promised during the election,' according to a No. 10 source.

The failure to attend SAGE and COBRA was not the neglect of duty it seemed. SAGE was a largely technical health forum, of the type that would typically have its advice digested and interrogated by the Cabinet Office before being integrated with policy considerations from economic experts. Senior politicians, officials and aides alike across No. 10, the Cabinet Office, DHSC and Public Health England (PHE) questioned whether COBRA was the right forum for making the necessary policy decisions. Opportunism was one of the concerns. 'Every time we had a discussion, Nicola Sturgeon would disappear as soon as the meeting was over and brief. It couldn't be a high-trust forum when she was taking the piss like that,' says an official. The SNP leader was not alone. As Johnson began to lead COBRA from February little changed in the advice and decisions taken. 'It was ill-designed for the pandemic,' says another attendee. Where crucial decisions needed to be made, they were debated upon outside of the meetings, with COBRA treated as a rubber-stamping exercise. Rather like Johnson's full Cabinet, in fact.

No. 10's relatively late attention to the virus did not doom the UK's response. Ben Warner, a Downing Street data scientist brought in by Cummings, attended his first meeting on 20 February, the ninth SAGE meeting on Covid, and briefing of Johnson began by Whitty at the Prime Minister's request. 'Whitty was always very measured and hedging on the progress of the virus when talking to him. It wasn't presented as serious then. Yes, it could threaten the country perhaps in March, but the virus didn't demand imminent action from Boris from the way Chris spoke about it,' says an aide present.

Johnson, distracted by the February reshuffle and upcoming Budget, had latched onto Whitty as his guru to guide him through a crisis he found hard to grasp. 'He liked Patrick [Vallance], but he was absolutely *captivated* by what Whitty said. He was hugely influential, and tailored his advice to Boris's mindset,' says a No. 10 staffer. Johnson committed early on to a position of 'follow the science'. For him this meant registering the conclusions of Whitehall scientists – but certainly not tracking wider debates within the scientific and international community, or delving into the data, as a more activist Prime Minister might have done on the cusp of a crisis.

Whitty remained cautious, hesitant to advise radical action too early or to present too extreme a view. He and Vallance preferred to present SAGE's view as a single position to COBRA and the Prime Minister, rather than a spectrum with greater complexity. 'There's always a large amount of uncertainty around things like the fatality rate, but what Chris adopted as the reasonable worst case presented [to COBRA and the Prime Minister] was effectively a compromise between [modeller] Neil Ferguson pushing hard and Chris raising the many uncertainties,' says a more hawkish SAGE attendee. The 'wait and see' approach favoured by Johnson was led by SAGE's initial modelling, which suggested a large gap between where the UK and Italy (then the worst affected country in Europe) were in the progression of the pandemic. 'There was this impression that we had more time at that stage [before 13 March],' says a No. 10 aide.

Whitty was not alone. The hesitancy to react within the scientific community in part stemmed from the belief that the lesson learned from SARS in the early 2000s was that Asian countries had intervened too hard, too early, and caused a huge amount of economic damage in doing so. The lack of coordination between specialists within the system in the early period of the pandemic meant SAGE felt pressured to internalize economic arguments it was not equipped to handle. Only at the very end of February did the scale of the British problem become apparent: Covid was spreading more widely than first thought.

The sense within SAGE suddenly morphed from confidence that the virus could be controlled to a certainty that it was an oncoming wave that could not be stopped – only contained, delayed and mitigated. This thinking was reflected in a 3 March government strategy document.[3] Coupled with the consensus that no vaccine could be produced in the short term, and certainly not within a year, the best available option was to 'flatten the curve' and minimize the burden on the NHS while ramping up healthcare capacity. The elderly and vulnerable could be protected; the rest of the population would catch it and build antibodies until a sufficient percentage had gained immunity and the disease could spread no further. Implicitly this was a plan of 'herd immunity', though SAGE stopped short of using the emotive phrase in documentation.

As the virus intensified in late February, No. 10 began to pivot towards tackling it head-on. The UK had its first detected case of internal transmission on 28 February, while data from Northern Italy suggested the burden on the NHS would be double the early assumptions. Johnson chaired his first COBRA on 2 March, and in the following days perceptions shifted at an alarming speed. A pandemic with severe health impacts was no longer avoidable.

Within No. 10 a handful of Policy Unit and Private Office staff were working on Covid, but the sense was growing that leadership was lacking, above all to elevate Covid to being *the* singular priority for the government, and to structure a whole-government response to the emerging pandemic. Within the Cabinet Office there was recognition that Covid required elevating as an issue too, with senior officials urging Sedwill to broaden the scope of the government's response. This switch was too little too late, and the Cabinet Office had not stepped up to provide the necessary interface between the Prime Minister and health advice which would have allowed him to receive a range of opinions on the evidence and take informed decisions.

No. 10, in the absence of a Prime Minister rising to the occasion, needed a figure with the intellectual capacity and influence to grasp the scale of the problem and focus activity. Step up Dominic Cummings. He too had pivoted towards the issue at the end of February and began attending SAGE meetings from 5 March. 'He was the one person who began to fill the leadership vacuum,' confirms a senior policy adviser. Cummings had emailed an ally in the science community in early February asking him how worried he was about the virus. The recipient, James Phillips, a young neuroscientist who had been studying the preliminary data from China and would be brought into No. 10 shortly after, was baffled that Cummings even needed to ask – any set of parameters around the estimated ranges for infectiousness and fatality rate would be disastrous. Cummings stayed close to the scientists, in particular Vallance, sending out questions to the system in the hope that it would return advice to the Prime Minister.

Although he would soon shift to a position of hardline suppression, Cummings was not at this time pushing back against the implied strategy of herd immunity put forward by the scientists. 'He wasn't fully convinced [of the need to lock down]. He took his time in finding the hardline stance,' says a No. 10 official. Cummings helped drive the system's attention towards the issue but had yet to be convinced that decisive action was required, and was happy to accept the assumption that the UK needed to ride out a one-wave virus – or else there would be a second, even worse, peak in winter.

Praise for Cummings' seizing the reins must be balanced by criticism of the institutional failure which required his intervention. His leadership style was also to cause harm and problems, officials believe: 'It's mad that Dom was the driver for the first lockdown. It's not an effective way of organizing government to have scientists reporting through a maverick with disregard for any process.' 'Dom was making time for Covid, but his grip was on policy detail, it wasn't... managerial.' For the time being, his destructive method was seen as necessary: 'His repeatedly saying "it's f**ked, it's not working" about everything with vehemence could be effective for making progress.'

But a more measured approach was required, in the form of strong managerial leadership. Did it transpire? One official believes not: 'There just weren't that many forces holding the system together in March. The top of the civil service didn't rise, the Cabinet committee structures didn't endure. The model of Jeremy Heywood [the powerful Cabinet Secretary who died of cancer in 2018] appointing the best person to lead in a crisis didn't happen.' Not for the first time, the late civil service chief was sorely missed. Where the Cabinet Office machinery didn't turn, the No. 10 Private Office was left to pick up the slack – consisting of just a handful of officials in early March.

The result was that the scientific advice and the shortcomings of health bodies were left unchecked and unchallenged. An early example came at the 5 March meeting. Whitty raised concerns about so-called compliance fatigue in the event of lockdowns, the idea that the public would not tolerate a lockdown for long, and that their compliance – and therefore the reduction in the rate of transmission – would wane the longer the lockdown went on. The view was largely borne of intuition, with thin evidence of compliance fatigue in historical pandemics including the 1918–19 Spanish flu. It was one of many factors which influenced SAGE erroneously into delaying the recommendation of greater lockdown restrictions as the virus spread throughout the UK.

Another crucial error No. 10 struggled to correct was testing. The lack of tests was a product of insufficient coordination across the system. PHE had the responsibility for developing tests and authorizing labs to perform them – NHS England had the responsibility for carrying out tests, but the body in charge of NHS procurement lay within DHSC, creating a chaotic back and forth between the three offices. Nobody knew who was responsible for expanding test capacity; it was all of them and none of them. Likewise for personal protective equipment (PPE), responsibilities were split between DHSC and NHS England, creating yet more confusion. The complex systems built up around healthcare in times of normality, geared towards providing value for money, were exposed as woefully inadequate when put under pressure.

By the time Johnson appreciated how inadequate testing was, it was already too late. Vital days and weeks were lost because of the lack of grip. Without an accurate picture of how far and fast and where Covid was spreading, the right decisions could never be taken. Officials were infuriated at the attempts of the health bodies to absolve themselves of blame, mindful, as many were during the epidemic, of how they would be seen in the inevitable inquiry, rather than resolve the problems of testing and PPE. The late arrival of the virus in the UK could have been exploited, with opportunities to learn from other countries. Instead, the UK was scrambling to accumulate medical supplies after other countries had already bought out the markets.

'We were flying blind,' says a senior health official. 'Without testing, NHS England had to use a vague definition of what counted as a Covid case, which included symptoms and a travel history from Wuhan or South-East Asia. But it turned out that a lot of infections in late February and early March came from those returning from Italy, France and Spain.' Yet testing was not being done on those returning from abroad, nor monitoring at the key rail and air travel pinch points where there was maximum transmission, nor was there randomized community testing. The UK's best measure of the spread was hospitalizations, a figure which proved inadequate at giving an accurate picture of the rapidly changing situation: numbers lagged around eight days behind infection, hospitalization rates were unknown and the demographic spread uncertain.[4]

Duncan Selbie, chief executive of PHE, posted at the end of February that there had been no positive Covid cases that week, a 'testament to the... diagnostic and testing work' in the UK. Reuters estimates that, based on current assessments of the fatality rate, the real figure at the time was between 1,500 and 5,000 infections.[5] Johnson was following the science, but the science was based on fantastical numbers.

Pivot to Suppression and Lockdown 1: March 2020

The strategy of flattening the curve, reducing the strain on the NHS while slowly increasing critical care capacity, without totally suppressing the virus, was inevitably coming under pressure. As images from Northern Italy began to appear in early March the full scale of the impending horror began to dawn. The empty streets of Milan and waterways of Venice were appearing on British screens in all their beautiful, eerie desolation. In ugly contrast viewers saw the makeshift emergency wards lined with rows of patients, a desperate attempt to ease pressure on the overflowing hospitals.

The numbers from Italy, alongside Ferguson's updated modelling discussed in SAGE, suggested that the peak of the virus could be a staggering eight times larger than total NHS capacity. The more overwhelmed the NHS, the worse care would become, and the greater the number of total fatalities. NHS leaders discussed in private that they would be overwhelmed sooner than the scientists were predicting, but they were hesitant to put this on the record in calls with No. 10 and DHSC without the modelling definitively to back it up. If the UK went into an unnecessary lockdown as a result of them raising the alarm, they would be to blame.

The news from Italy and elsewhere caused a change of heart in Cummings, who together with Ferguson and others realized that social distancing measures and strict behavioural interventions were now absolutely necessary. Within SAGE, voices grew incredulous therefore at the 13 March meeting that more wasn't being done. Others in the meeting remained resistant to the idea of suppression. 'Why wouldn't enacting lockdowns like China, Singapore or South Korea work for us?' 'It absolutely won't work. No doubt at all,' replied a SAGE modeller endorsing a herd immunity strategy, 'because when you enact lockdown measures, you'll get a spike downwards, but the second you release them numbers will immediately come back up... One hundred per cent.' Behavioural Insights Team CEO David Halpern baulked at their lack of doubt, suggesting to him that some modellers had tipped into dogma rather than being led by evidence. He scribbled frustratedly in his notepad: 'WE ARE NOT READY!' Ben Warner was sitting next to him and saw his jottings. He leaned over, crossed out Halpern's 'NOT READY!' and wrote in its place one word: 'f**ked!'

Momentum was building that Johnson's mind had to be changed about the lockdown. But how? Cummings knew that with advice frozen around SAGE, and SAGE itself frozen and unable to put forward a single view, he would need to intervene directly with the Prime Minister with the support of others – or in the more critical view of an official who fell out with Cummings over his hardline attitude to Covid, 'Dom wanted to kettle the PM with people who had the same views as Dom.' Cummings was not unique in realizing the urgency, but he was uniquely placed as a still trusted voice with the ability to convince Johnson.

He worked with Warner and the No. 10 Private Office to build the case on the evening of Friday 13 March,[6] producing the famous whiteboard on which was scribbled the new strategy.[7] The government's 'Plan A' of mitigation would see cases surge to the point where the NHS was broken. But 'Plan A+', as Cummings dubbed it, demanded lockdown to prevent the NHS collapsing and mass deaths, starting aggressively from the following week, with restrictions loosening and tightening depending on the gap between hospitalizations and NHS capacity.

The following morning of 14 March Johnson was presented with the plan. He didn't like what Cummings and Warner were suggesting one bit. Imposing draconian restrictions on the nation went against every fibre of his being, every sense of freedom and individual choice. 'Boris was clear from the early phases that he would do more damage by government decisions than by the epidemic,' says a senior Cabinet Office source. 'He was motivated by a suspicion of the role of the state, of ceding power and trust to Blairite kind of people.' Was it for this that he had won a great landslide? To impose lockdown and great economic damage on the country?

At this point, fear kicked in inside the prime ministerial mind. Supposing the forecast proved correct, he would be blamed for the 4,000 deaths a day, and failing to lock down, unlike the rest of the continent, would leave him uniquely exposed. 'That was the moment Boris realized the strategy needed to flip, right then in his office,' says a source present. Cummings had rarely been more specific: 'Move now, move quickly, and move decisively.' Key in tipping the scales for Johnson were the timely interjections of Whitty and Vallance, whose opinions had flipped to believe that the numbers were now so dire that the UK could not wait for the 'optimal moment' but had to go hard and fast.

That weekend of 14–15 March was spent on pivoting towards a strategy of suppression and devising the necessary policy and communications, alongside recruiting a select few capable officials to run the new strategy within the No. 10 Private Office, sending the rest of the staff home. Hancock, upon hearing news of the awful numbers and SAGE disagreements, said to an official, 'Thank God, this is the best news I've had all week.' The official responded with a baffled look, until the Health Secretary explained: 'Me and the PM, we're tied to this cart of the scientific evidence. Now that's changed, we can actually do something.' Ferguson, not Hancock, had been significant in changing the system's view of the virus. Ferguson's numbers, published on 16 March and based on latest inputs, were grim: between 410,000 and 550,000 deaths if no interventions were made.[8] Although Ferguson sees the paper he compiled as relatively unimportant, it helped create an atmosphere in which the Prime Minister could go hard on lockdown, using the now-public numbers as his shield.

The response worked up between the Cabinet Office and No. 10 was to issue guidelines, namely strong advice, to encourage high levels of social distancing. 'Without drastic action, cases could double every five to six days… Now is the time for everyone to stop non-essential contact with others,' a notably measured Prime Minister told the nation on 16 March.[9] Addressing the country and striking the right note throughout the pandemic was one of his signature strengths.

The week that followed was unmatched in the history of the British state for sheer administrative reach. Schools were shut down, hospital beds vacated to make way for Covid patients, unparalleled compensatory schemes launched. 'The only thing that compares would be working during the world wars, it was utterly exhausting,' says a Private Office official.

But No. 10 and the Cabinet Office still lacked a clear idea about what to prioritize. Special advisers and officials at No. 10 were exhausted and baffled, their inboxes bulging with multiple potential disasters at crisis points and huge uncertainty as to which was most likely to blow up. 'We were setting up a wartime economy with no background to work from,' one recalls. Contingency plans were made from scratch, covering every area from food security to potential prison riots. The centre of government was not good enough at planning ahead, and mistakes were being made left, right and centre. Senior leaders struggled to leverage the UK's lagged spread of the virus to learn lessons from overseas, be it upcoming threats such as the care home crises in Italy and France or the effectiveness of potential responses such as South Korea's test and trace programme. Some officials attribute this to the pace of decisions: 'We were moving a hundred miles per hour, just trying to stay afloat. It was so difficult to apply learning when all you're doing is trying not to drown in the crisis.' Others point towards the lack of structure and the male-dominant culture combining to produce a machismo desire to own the issue of the day: 'Multiple senior Cabinet Office officials were chasing the same balls all day. We didn't have someone in the centre saying to us "we need to be doing forward planning, let's talk about this NOW".'

Not helping was the tension between various departments and No. 10, exacerbated by No. 10's principal actor, Cummings. In the firing line was NHS England, PHE and DHSC – not least its minister. 'Hancock arrived at meetings insisting that PPE, testing and care homes were being handled and he was on top of it all, when it was evident to all in the room that nothing was further from the truth,' says an official. 'Boris knew Matt was lying, but everybody was very conscious that there would be an inquiry, and that what they were saying would be recorded,' adds an aide. Hancock was desperate to appear competent and keep others (particularly Cummings) off his turf, even if that meant misleading the Prime Minister. Cummings despised Hancock even more than others, and wanted him fired. His ire fell equally on NHS England boss Simon Stevens. Highly knowledgeable (he'd overseen health in Blair's No. 10) and capable but thought to be very territorial, Stevens wanted as much operational autonomy from the chaotic No. 10 as possible, and Downing Street struggled to secure detailed data from him as a result. Despite the vocal frustrations of No. 10 staff, Johnson refused to confront either Hancock or Stevens, his chronic inability to initiate difficult conversations overriding all. Cummings wanted Stevens fired and replaced by, at one point, and there were many points, Dido Harding.

Mark Sedwill, with his background in the military and security rather than domestic departments, was not perhaps the ideal Cabinet Secretary for Covid. But he was strong on organization, noted the soup at the centre, and decided to act. A request to rework the structure had been approved. On 16 March, he called into his office senior officials Simon Ridley and Jess Glover. He slapped down in front of them his plan to bring control to the centre. There were to be five functions focusing on different areas of the pandemic response. Cabinet Office director general Mark Sweeney would lead the overall strategy and morning meetings, with policy issues sorted under health, economics, international affairs and public services, each led by a senior Cabinet Office official and the relevant Cabinet minister (Hancock, Sunak, Raab, Gove) chairing their respective sub-committees, all reporting to the Prime Minister. Sedwill's role was to coordinate and lead the end of day meetings.

A logical and coherent plan, or so it seemed? In practice, it dissolved near-instantaneously on contact with political reality. The five functions never had the firepower necessary to contend with No. 10's chaotic politics, above all a staffing chief in Cummings with a total disregard for structure, nor with a Prime Minister who lacked the focus and grasp needed to keep on top of the separate streams. Strong, assertive political leadership from the very top was required to take urgent decisions day-to-day; without it, this devolved decision-making structure with overlapping jurisdictions, overseen by often just junior ministers, was never going to work. 'Instead of making the system more effective as designed, the cast list and multiple overlapping meetings ballooned beyond reason,' records an official. In no time, Cummings became disillusioned with the system, and with Sedwill personally, and was furious at the lack of progress in solving questions of data analysis, which he prioritized above all else. The final straw was that almost everybody caught Covid. Within a week of the new system, Ridley and Glover were chairing meetings to cover for Covid-stricken colleagues, the rotating cast meaning responsibilities shifted and lines of communication rapidly became blurred. 'Giving authority to multiple chiefs had been intended to avoid a single point of failure if one had fallen ill: instead, it created even more complexity,' says an observer.

By the time in mid-April that staff had pinned down the organogram of each person's role, the situation had become so bad that all involved knew it wasn't working. Even Johnson, who rarely had a sense for structural issues in the machinery of governance, sensed something was awry. 'What on earth is happening? I never know who I'm supposed to be looking to, there are either five different people in the meeting all telling me what to do in a different voice, or it's just the one person, but who they are keeps changing week after week.'

Slow progress in testing and PPE procurement was one result of the confusion. Without a full-throated lead from the top, staff struggled to hold decision-makers in DHSC, PHE and the NHS to account, and were unable to challenge delays. One staff member recalls, 'By the time we in No. 10 realized PPE was a major issue we couldn't do anything about it, and could only watch the arm-wrestle over placing blame and abdicating responsibility between DHSC and the NHS.' Cabinet Office officials found that DHSC were woefully underprepared for the wider implications of a pandemic on society. 'When we came to them in the first week of March asking them to send us their people working on how we could do things like shielding the vulnerable from the virus, keep public transport safe and operational, ensure that provisions make it to those who are ill and have to isolate, they told us there wasn't really anybody solving those questions. They were focused on the NHS and didn't see it as a full system problem, leaving it up to us to plug the gaps in their preparedness planning where it hadn't accounted for a SARS-like virus.'

Failure to scale testing was similarly dismal. PHE communicated to Downing Street in March that they could run roughly 5,000 tests a day nationally, and hoped to reach 10,000 by the end of the month. The No. 10 health adviser knew this was light years away from the number needed to handle a full-scale pandemic, in part limited by a lack of testing machines. So, he drove cooperation with the private sector, including Thermo Fisher which had some 170 PCR machines scattered across the UK, centralizing testing efforts to three facilities in Milton Keynes, Manchester and Glasgow.

For Sedwill, progressively marginalized by Cummings, it was the beginning of the end. 'He wasn't influencing proceedings in No. 10 as he wanted and became irritated about it. He knew that Downing Street's decision-making wasn't working, but his solution hadn't solved anything,' says one Cabinet Office official. Feed into this Johnson and his team's visceral suspicion of the civil service and it became toxic. Johnson had been in two minds about retaining Sedwill, and now had to contend with Cummings badmouthing him at every opportunity. At the same time, Sedwill felt obliged to defend the Cabinet Office and the civil service from the politicians, including systems exposed as dysfunctional in the early months of the pandemic.

Into this mix had stepped Tom Shinner, a former Brexit mandarin, to try to aid coordination. Cummings admired him greatly, and with that authority behind him Shinner quickly became a lead force on Covid, asking structured questions at increasing levels of detail until he finally got his answer. Esteemed by some, others found his manner unproductive and unsympathetic, and the introduction of his parallel operation a source of confusion for officials who did not know which way to turn when reporting on progress.

One Whitehall area which at this time was not dysfunctional was No. 10's relationship with the Treasury, too often chronically bad in history. After Cummings engineered Sunak to be Javid's replacement in early February the new Chancellor enjoyed his patron's total support. 'For the financial packages, it was all Rishi directing,' says Eddie Lister. 'He told the Prime Minister at the morning meeting, "Look, if we're telling people to stay at home, we need to give large-scale financial support to businesses and workers." Rishi was clear, and the Prime Minister was supportive.'[10] Sunak had committed to £12 billion of additional spending at the 11 March Budget; a week later, he had committed a staggering £350 billion more. Furlough and business support schemes were worked up in a matter of days (announced on 20 March), a far cry from the usual projections, forecasts and impact assessments the Treasury runs through before a Budget. The figure of 80 per cent of wages paid for furloughed workers had not been tested at all, and was selected for no better reason than Sunak thought it 'about right' – and that it gave Britain the most generous scheme in Europe.

The £350 billion package of loans and grants for business was equally unprecedented. 'This is not a time for ideology and orthodoxy. This is a time to be bold. A time for courage,' proclaimed Sunak in a pre-recorded broadcast speech.[11] Instituting aid at an unparalleled pace meant confronting the trade-off between speed and accuracy. Safeguards were dropped to encourage banks to lend and enable legitimate businesses to access loans as fast as possible, with an estimated £4.5 billion lost to fraud and waste.[12] If government does not plan ahead for crises, massive waste of public money is just one of the results.

Johnson kept bumbling along: there is little evidence that he was learning and improving his performance. His natural tendencies of avoiding the delivery of bad news, cracking jokes and changing his mind were too deeply ingrained. But his survival instinct was kicking in, helping to instil some seriousness necessary for tough calls.

Few were tougher than the Wednesday 18 March decision that schools were to be closed by Friday evening. Increasingly parents were refusing to send in children, and with cases rising Johnson reluctantly accepted in the morning meeting there was little choice but to introduce restrictions. 'We need this ready to announce in detail by 5 p.m. today,' Johnson and Cummings told staff. The policy was worked up in a day between No. 10 and DfE, who were largely unprepared as they had been getting ready for a phased transition away from in-person learning, as preferred by the department, rather than the instant lockdown chosen by No. 10. Gavin Williamson, his PPS and a No. 10 official spent the day producing the slides for Cabinet, deciding vast swathes of policy on an issue by issue basis. A rotating cast of officials traipsed through the office, specialists in everything from free school meals, to exams, to which children should still be able to attend school. Free school meals would be issued through a mixture of packages and vouchers, and all exams cancelled in the knowledge that the asymmetric experiences of pupils would make remote assessment impossible. Keeping schools open for key workers' children was one of few measures which had been prepared within the department in case of emergency, but the list of jobs covered was so old it contained now-defunct professions alongside the critical workers.

On 22 March the government's policy of shielding – protecting of the elderly and immunosuppressed – began. The struggle to get there had been emblematic of the system's failure in the first wave of the pandemic. Despite the policy being a priority of the government throughout late February and March, it was still not ready days before it was supposed to launch. The government needed to get over a million clinically vulnerable people to shield with support structures around them such as delivering shopping. In a cross-government initiative the NHS was in charge of sending out the letters, the DWP running a call helpline, MHCLG liaising with local authorities, and all coordinated by the Cabinet Office.

Three days prior to launch, No. 10 was notified that it wasn't ready. Deputy Brexit negotiator Oliver Lewis was sent by Cummings to look at the scheme, along with a No. 10 Private Office official, only to see that the DWP helpline – which needed to handle over a million people with urgent questions on shielding – had a capacity of a few thousand calls per day. Worse, it was unable to feed any data back to the local authorities assisting shielders, rendering it functionally useless even if callers could get through. Nobody in the cross-departmental effort had taken ownership of the glaring issue, and it fell to No. 10 to drive for an automated solution at scale.

As government efforts intensified, Covid cases continued to grow. By 17 March officials began to look at locking down London, worried that it was running ahead of the rest of the nation. By the 19th it had been discussed with the Prime Minister: if a lockdown were to take place, it could not be exclusively in London due to the likelihood of perverse effects regarding compliance elsewhere, NHS officials believed. It needed to be nationwide. At COBRA on 20 March there was little choice for the Prime Minister but to opt for lockdown, announcing that non-essential businesses and venues would be advised to close. Any other course, officials believed, would create a greater level of risk that the NHS would be overwhelmed, with intensive care units (ICUs) overflowing and fatalities skyrocketing. Johnson would not allow himself to be the Prime Minister who let the NHS, the UK's 'national religion', collapse.

Over the weekend legislation was worked up to ensure that lockdown could be enforced in law ahead of a Monday announcement. On the morning of Monday 23 March the data looked particularly bleak. SPI-M, the modelling body which fed into SAGE, found a three-day doubling time for cases. Combined with the nine-day lag, the NHS in London was on a course to exceed critical care capacity – even with immediate intervention.[13]

He duly addressed the nation on the evening of 23 March, the libertarian Prime Minister announcing the single most restrictive act to public life in UK history.[14] 'From this evening I must give the British people a very simple instruction – you *must* stay at home.'[15] People would only be permitted to leave their homes for basic necessities, medical aid, travelling to and from work where absolutely necessary, and one form of exercise a day. Johnson watched the broadcast as it went out, sitting with aides in the outer office. The tone in the room was half-sadness, half-disbelief at what they were having to do. He attempted to inject some humour into the surreality of the measures. His arm shot up into the air, clenched fist, mocking his own televisual proclamation as if a communist dictator: 'The people's government. Closing the people's schools. Closing the people's shops, closing the people's pubs!'

The speech was broadcast live on BBC1, BBC News, ITV, Channel 4, Channel 5 and Sky News, one of the most watched television events in UK history, with over 27 million tuning in. It was the first ministerial broadcast to the nation since Blair committed British forces to the invasion of Iraq in 2003, 'exercising a right only used by political leaders at times of great national turmoil'.[16] Johnson's ability to speak on television to the nation nightly at first, flanked by Vallance and Whitty, was indeed perhaps his most important positive contribution in tackling the epidemic. Johnson may have been woefully inadequate at governing, but he could at least campaign. The daily broadcasts came naturally to a Prime Minister who loved nothing more than being the centre of attention, performing day after day even where there was little new to say. Being Prime Minister might not have given Johnson his Olympics moment. But talking to the nation from No. 10 gave him his Churchill moment.

Advisers struggled to rein in Johnson's joviality and misbehaviour, given his general sense of immunity from illness in any form, a belief inherited from father Stanley.[17] Their best attempts found elegant 'Boris-like' solutions, but often they had to resort to blunter instruments to get the point across. 'We got him to go with the recommended fist bump in place of a handshake, which fitted his brand as an enthusiastic guy. But on masks, he was very difficult to persuade. We sent him a slide pack including one which showed all the other major world leaders wearing a mask, then him without,' says Halpern.[18]

On 23 March election mastermind Isaac Levido was drafted back into a No. 10 concerned that the message wasn't getting through to sections of the public, joined by three comms faithfuls from the 2019 campaign. They found a Downing Street in utter disarray. 'It was absolutely mad in there, they needed help translating all these policy changes into messaging and getting across to people why they needed to stay at home. We couldn't tell people that it was going to be OK, but we could find a message to put out that was at least consistent and that in itself can serve to reassure, which is in part how we came up with the "stay home, protect the NHS, save lives" slogan,' says Levido.[19]

By the end of March political aides in all areas were stretched to breaking point, including their leader. 'Cummings in particular had lost it, the pressure had really started getting to him. He'd sit at his desk, shouting and swearing at his computer,' says one official. 'Dom got unhinged – or more unhinged than usual,' recalls another. 'You had to be on your guard the whole time, he would switch from his rational analytical mode to absolutely apoplectic without warning.' The more stressful the situation, the more forceful Cummings became. Johnson, uncomfortable with such conflict, tended to withdraw and avoid challenging his senior adviser. Cummings vanished from No. 10 with little warning, stricken with Covid and self-isolating on 30 March.

During this period Whitty rose to be a shining light in the UK's response, gathering unanimous praise from those within No. 10 – even from those critical of his initial response during mitigation. 'He had an almost superhuman ability to be everywhere at once,' eulogizes a No. 10 official. 'Everybody wanted him in every meeting, yet he always arrived having read all the papers, completely up to date on the latest data, in addition to the latest journal evidence and pre-prints.' He exuded calm and control, imbuing a stability absent elsewhere. Johnson placed total trust in Whitty to lead him through the first lockdown and the non-pharmaceutical interventions.

Other officials, however, were in no less distress than the aides, some spending nights in No. 10 holed up in various state rooms and studies on camp beds: 'It felt like we had to make everything work in the most terrible circumstances. It was the closest thing I've seen to a systemic collapse,' says one civil servant. Like Cummings, Sedwill had contracted Covid, leaving Reynolds, MacNamara and Deputy PPS Stuart Glassborow to lead the officials, and Cain to lead the political team. In addition to the eighteen-hour days and breakdown of hierarchy was the constant fear that, as one by one their colleagues caught the virus, they would be next. 'We had to remain at our desks, and never socially distanced because we couldn't, there simply wasn't the space. Separating screens on desks came in the summer for some of us, but not between February and April. With so little support from the rest of Whitehall, we just had to carry on, working flat out in the most desperate circumstances,' recalls an official. Staff were being burned out by the fear of the virus, the brutal hours, the constant decisions. There was no rotation of staff, nor welfare measures to alleviate the stress. The No. 10 Private Office duty rota board, in normal times detailing which staff member would be stepping up and covering the evenings or weekend, simply read: 'EVERYONE, ALL THE TIME.' 'It was written like a joke but there was an immense pressure to always be present, and the longer it went on the more we became fatigued, and the harder it became to evaluate our own judgement. It just didn't need to be that way,' says a Private Office team member. 'We didn't think of that,' says a senior official, when the idea was put to him that, during the Second World War, calm and order were the keywords for the operation of the centre. 'We didn't think of history: the centre doesn't really do history.'

Illness: April 2020

On 26 March, as a group of officials and aides waited to go into the Prime Minister's study to brief him, they heard him coughing and spluttering behind the door. 'He's got Covid, hasn't he?' they murmured to each other nervously before he called them in. But they went into the airless room nevertheless. One present recalls that 'Cleo [Watson] brought in some Lemsip for him, as if that was going to help. I thought vaguely this isn't what we should have been doing. We all knew he was ill.'

The previous day he was due to meet the Queen for their weekly audience, with Palace and No. 10 officials going back and forth about whether the meeting could take place in person. Johnson was very eager not to be restricted by the new laws or his apparent symptoms, to the dismay of Palace officials deeply concerned at the risk of exposing the elderly Queen to the virus. After some convincing, both from the Palace and Cummings,[20] Johnson acquiesced and agreed to hold the conversation remotely by phone. The content of a Prime Minister's audience with the sovereign is sacred, with no special advisers in attendance and no official record of their discussion. The sanctity of this one would be easier to keep than most: afterwards the Queen turned to an aide and commented that she couldn't hear a word of what he had said, he was coughing so much. Had the meeting gone ahead as planned, the Head of Government would likely have given the Head of State the virus, a scandal not even Johnson could have downplayed.

On 27 March Reynolds organized a Covid test for the clearly ailing Prime Minister. Many felt like they already knew the answer. But the shock still rippled around No. 10 as the news was received. The Prime Minister had contracted Covid.

The Private Office scrambled to set up a working space away from the rest of the building, putting him in Sunak's No. 11 office below the flat. The doors connecting 10, 11 and 12 Downing Street – typically open such that one can look through the three buildings upon entering through No. 10's front door – were all shut, the ancient basement corridor the only connector.

Johnson was entirely unsuited to remote working and isolation, his early illness frequently breaking into farce. His fumbling constantly disconnected his iPad from Zoom and he was clueless as to how he could rejoin the meeting, so a series of iPads connected to the calls were placed outside his room. Once he had broken the first, he could grab the second, then third, then fourth.

Johnson tried to stay optimistic but he found the enforced loneliness unbearable. With the newly engaged and heavily pregnant Carrie also sick with Covid (isolating at their Camberwell townhouse) they were apart and distraught, the effects of the virus on pregnant women still uncertain and playing on both their minds. Johnson's attempt to regain sanity was to repeatedly ask staff to come and see him in the Chancellor's office to help with tasks, desperate for any contact with the outside world and people to entertain, and careless of the risk he put them under. His fears of being alone floated back to the surface. His appearance had visibly deteriorated on camera in both his health and presentation; at one point he joined a call with his broken glasses mended with Sellotape.

On Friday 5 April, the day on which the Queen was giving her address to the nation, his health began to decline alarmingly. He held on until it became clear he needed medical attention, lasting the evening so that news of his admission did not overshadow Her Majesty's speech. Feverish, he was sent to Guy's and St Thomas' Hospital, while Reynolds informed staff of his status. 'It was shocking to hear for us,' says one official who knew well Johnson's belief in illness as a sign of weakness. 'We figured it must be serious, he'd never agree to be taken to hospital if it wasn't.'

Reynolds, MacNamara and Glassborow were scrambling to keep the system operational. Johnson had previously lined up Foreign Secretary Dominic Raab to cover for him in case of illness, on the typical Johnson basis that he took a look at the alternatives and didn't want anybody else to do it for fear of strengthening their hand. Officials shared concerns with each other about political infighting breaking out between Johnson's excitable ministers. The Queen's private secretary Edward Young was kept up to speed. The questions rolled on. 'Matt's responsibility over the health portfolio gives him far more authority over operational decisions than the Foreign Secretary. What if he tries a power grab? What if Raab makes radical changes? Do we give him the security briefings?' The UK's constitution does not outline a formal position of acting or caretaker Prime Minister, leaving a large degree of ambiguity when the premier is incapacitated. If ministers decided to be 'creative' in the absence of Johnson, there would be few tools to restrict them.

MacNamara had drawn up a table of functions the Prime Minister usually carries out, and went through item by item with Sedwill, Reynolds and Cain as to what would be covered in the Prime Minister's absence and how. Sedwill made the call to Cabinet, informing them of the situation, and sat down separately with each of the so-called quad of Raab, Hancock, Gove and Sunak to issue a half-address, half-warning. 'The Prime Minister has designated the Foreign Secretary in his capacity as the First Secretary of State, and he will take the role of acting Prime Minister until the PM is back to health and ready to return to his duties. This is a moment of severe importance in the history of this country. We all have a responsibility to act in the national interest here, so let's do so.'

Private Office staff at No. 10 were presented with a different kind of warning on Raab's arrival. 'In advance we were told about his alleged bullying and shouting,' recalls one official. Raab was known as a 'tough boss' in the more diplomatic language of the civil service, demanding his personnel work until the early hours of the morning, deliver his boxes to his home in Esher and brief him well ahead of time for meetings – a difficult task considering the ongoing developments and information churn inherent in a fast-moving pandemic response. MacNamara and Cain spent his first few days guiding the newcomer into the role, or as Sedwill put it to staff, 'keeping him steady on parade'.

Despite his style, most political staff and senior civil servants have only praise for Raab's handling of the situation, not least for the contrast with his boss. 'He ran very orderly meetings in contrast to Boris,' says a Downing Street staffer. 'Raab could not have behaved any better,' concurs an official working closely with him in No. 10. In what could have been yet another constitutional crisis for the Johnson government, not least because of Raab's agile handling of his new responsibility, all ministers behaved, never overstepped the mark or acted beyond their station. It was a rare example of Cabinet as a whole rising to the occasion during these three years.

In hospital Johnson worsened. Struggling to breathe, he was given oxygen then admitted to ICU on 6 April. Staff were told that, at a rough estimate, around half of those who went into ICU were subsequently put on ventilators; half of those on ventilators died. Three in four odds of survival. Hushed whispers and WhatsApps flew around as a Personal Protection Officer overheard the medics discussing putting Johnson on a ventilator, a measure the PM was desperate to avoid. Even if Johnson survived but required a ventilator he could be incapacitated for months, and possibly never recover to full health. A deeply distressed if composed Carrie Symonds was informed that the doctors might have to take that step. Sedwill had been isolating at home following his bout of the virus, but when staff knew Johnson was going into intensive care he was called back in ahead of schedule in the hope that his presence would project the message to ministers that they needn't worry. He spent the evening discussing with other officials their grave concerns that the country would be without a Prime Minister capable of giving direction, with an unclear procedure for the selection of a successor, and whether Raab himself could stand and still be acting PM. 'We considered locking Cabinet in a room and telling them they wouldn't be let out until they came up with an agreed choice for Acting Prime Minister. It was a very delicate moment for the constitution,' says a senior official talking to Sedwill that night.

Not since Churchill's acute stroke in the summer of 1953 had a Prime Minister come so close to succumbing to illness, complicated by the fact that Churchill's de facto deputy, Foreign Secretary Anthony Eden, was in Boston, Massachusetts, having a serious operation. A closer comparison still to Johnson is Lloyd George in September 1918. Both aged fifty-five, they fell victim to their respective pandemics mere months after the viruses had entered the country and were forced to delegate their responsibilities to a small group of ministers (though Raab, Gove, Sunak and Hancock were hardly of the same stature as Curzon, Bonar Law, Austen Chamberlain and Smuts).[21]

As with his prime ministerial progenitors Churchill and Lloyd George, Johnson had spent a lifetime travelling with Fortuna.[22] His luck was not to abandon him at the moment of greatest vulnerability. No sooner had he been admitted to ICU than his condition improved, and by 9 April he was moved out of intensive care. He was quickly glued back to his phone, keeping abreast of updates in No. 10 and attempting to remain upbeat. 'What do I hear about Andrew Gilligan trying to cancel HS2? Can't I even die in peace?' he half joked to one aide.

Johnson had spent a week at Guy's and St Thomas', just shy of Lloyd George's ten-day stint at a makeshift room within Manchester

Town Hall. Both were poor patients: irritable, restless, desperate to rush back to work and forced to convalesce in the countryside: Lloyd George at Danny House in West Sussex, accompanied by both wife and mistress, and Johnson at Chequers, with his heavily pregnant fiancée now recovered from Covid herself.

Near-death experiences tend to change ordinary mortals. But Johnson was no ordinary mortal, and opinions differ if and how far it changed him. Some close to him saw a genuine difference in attitude towards Covid and sickness in general, the seriousness of the matter a rare piercing of the 'Boris' persona that demanded authenticity and genuine reflection. Others saw Johnson reverting to his insouciant norm within weeks, as if his behaviour was too deeply ingrained to be changed by anything as frivolous as nearly dying.

Johnson was phased back in as he worked from Chequers, Raab gradually phased out, creating in effect a dual premiership for a few weeks. But Johnson was anxious to grab the reins back fully, despite Raab giving him no cause for concern, thus squandering an opportunity to make him the proper Deputy PM he so transparently needed. Upon his recovery from the brink Johnson lost the modicum of focus and fear that had come with March's developing crisis. With his return, short of breath and weary, came the habits officials struggled to cope with, and they soon found themselves pining for Raab's ability to do the job of Prime Minister. 'It's astonishing that we were grateful for Raab,' an official says. 'Being decisive and being willing to let people down are so basic but the Prime Minister we had just couldn't do them.' Johnson returned no more consistent than ever, in the words of another official: 'He wildly oscillated in what he thought. In one day he would have three meetings in which he would say three completely different things depending on who was present, and then deny that he had changed his position. It became difficult when he took a decision to know whether it would hold, and how much importance to give it, because so often he changed his mind even on Covid.' Yet another recalls how 'at one point, I had to show him the printout of what he had said in a meeting because he was denying completely what he'd decided upon earlier that day now that he was unhappy about the decision.'

He would chair meetings chaotically in contrast with the orderly Raab, drifting from one point to another, occasionally hyperfixating on the issue that interested him most; it could be the most important point on the agenda, it could be trivial. There was little distinction in his mind. Where he attempted to drive at problems he either wouldn't wait for a full answer where a lengthy explanation was justified, or moved the conversation on when the discussion became awkward. Officials present are almost uniformly damning of his ability in meetings, as one describes: 'It was astonishing how hard he found it to grasp the finer points of Covid policy. We found it difficult to tell whether he was being wilfully ignorant or genuinely didn't know at times, but what is certain is he couldn't process the volume of information and was obsessed with the interpersonal politics of it all.'

Roadmap and Reconstruction: May–June 2020

With Johnson, Sedwill and Cummings all back working in Downing Street (Cummings back on 14 April, Johnson on 26 April[23]), the search was on for a reopening from lockdown. The government had set out five tests for reopening which, echoing Brown's five economic tests on the Euro in 2003, were cautious to the point of being impossible to meet with the tools at the government's disposal. Particularly challenging was the fifth test: 'no risk of a second peak that would overwhelm the NHS'.[24] With a vaccine still a distant prospect, and the UK's Test and Trace system ineffective in clamping down on community transmission compared to successful programmes such as South Korea's, an increase in infections and eventual second peak breaching critical care capacity would be inevitable.

As with Brown's Euro tests, achievability was secondary to the politics, and Johnson's politics had him champing at the bit for reopening, particularly in schools – which proved a textbook example of how indecisive his leadership could be. No. 10, DfE and the Treasury were all eager to get pupils back in classrooms, with the Treasury and Education arguing over whether they should send back primary school pupils to alleviate childcare burdens on parents (for maximum economic impact) or pupils in the crucial transition years (i.e. those supposed to be taking exams, for maximum educational impact). Johnson, however, struggled to grasp the basic level of detail needed to triangulate. 'He wanted them open as soon as possible for as many as possible, but he was less interested in probing the possibilities. He liked declamatory statements and thought things would get done as a result,' says an official. Education Secretary Williamson entered meetings in April, armed with the official advice to send only half the children back, but folded when Johnson pushed back. 'Honestly, we can't have half the children going back half the time. If they don't go back full time now, they'll never go back,' the Prime Minister told him. 'And don't give me this nonsense about them coming in later – if they can come in later, they can bloody well come in now.' Officials were bemused by his position, which did not seem to be informed by any of the briefing or advice provided. The two-metre social distancing restrictions made it physically impossible for all children to return at once, and would clearly be a temporary measure, but the Prime Minister was in denial. 'I want them all back, just get them all back with social distancing.' 'Why didn't you forewarn us the Prime Minister would say that?' the Education official asked his No. 10 counterparts after the meeting. 'We didn't know he would.' Not for the first time, the DfE official was left with the sense that 'he [Johnson] never reads the papers for meetings like this, he just makes it up in the room'.

Johnson pushed ahead regardless, feeling pressured to announce easing up by the forensic and increasingly sceptical media scrutiny of the Covid press conferences. The *Daily Mail* and the *Telegraph*, liberal commentators and Conservative MPs were joining forces to demand 'freedom'. 'The advice was that returning all primary school children for a month before the summer holiday couldn't happen,' says Williamson. 'But he inserted it in his speech anyway. We knew it couldn't happen because it wasn't physically possible to do – the rules said a maximum of fifteen students in any one classroom due to social distancing, and we didn't have the teachers or facilities for it. Multiple times he would commit to these policy decisions that we knew we couldn't deliver.'[25] After another unfruitful meeting, Cummings concluded that No. 10 would have to take it on and sort it out. But confusion still reigned. Johnson said he was inclining towards the DfE's position, but he still changed and unchanged his mind. Eventually the Treasury got most of what they wanted: nursery, reception and year 1 children would return, with the DfE-favoured year 6 coming back too.

As with schools, the entire Covid strategy was more revealed than designed within No. 10. 'We had the vague goals of suppress the virus, minimize the economic damage, keep R [the Covid infection rate] as close to 1 [i.e. steady] as possible. But the whole strategy was never fully worked out and stated; it was more implicit in the decisions the PM took along the way,' says an official.

An attempt to turn Johnson's inconsistent goals into a viable agenda for unlocking was found in the first 'roadmap' in early May. Shinner, Sweeney and Jonathan Black (the Cabinet Office official overseeing the economic response to Covid) had led on setting out the government thinking for this, with the aim to 'return life to as close to normal as possible, for as many people as possible, as fast and fairly as possible in a way that avoids a new epidemic, minimizes lives lost and maximizes health, economic and social outcomes'.[26] Under the plan announced on 10 May by the Prime Minister, schools were to be slowly reopened, followed by non-essential shops, finally followed by pubs, restaurants and hairdressers on 4 July.

In the weeks after the publication No. 10 and the Cabinet Office made yet more machinery of government changes. During Johnson's absence in April an internal review had been ordered by MacNamara and Reynolds into why government wasn't working and how to fix it, interviewing everyone in the centre and concluding that the Sedwill system of five functions under ministers and matching officials was not working. A single permanent secretary with a focus on the longer-term was needed, and greater collaboration between the Cabinet Office and No. 10 with clearer roles and responsibilities so that officials drafted in could return to their previous work on Brexit and departmental policy.

Sedwill was overworked and overwhelmed, and still recovering from the illness. Cummings had long lost faith in his ability to do the job as he wanted it done, thinking him more suited to his contiguous role of national security adviser, and was eager for his replacement. Removing him would also have the added benefit of disempowering one of the few with sufficient standing to challenge him. The point of maximum awkwardness had come in early May, as the plan for reopening was being developed. 'Who's in charge of all this? Is it you?' Johnson asked his Cabinet Secretary. 'No, I think it's you, Prime Minister,' Sedwill replied.[27] Very clearly, the Prime Minister was not 'in charge of all this', and Sedwill's riposte solidified in his mind that Cummings was right in his assessment that the Cabinet Secretary was not gripping matters. Cummings wanted someone alongside him who would be both more effective and more pliable. He had already shown himself to be far more powerful than the Prime Minister in the conduct of Covid policy: he was fearless.

Cummings equally knew who he wanted to bring grip to the centre: Simon Case.[28] The former No. 10 principal private secretary, then private secretary to Prince William, possessed a rare institutional knowledge of No. 10 and the Cabinet Office and a canny ability to navigate court politics. The supreme courtier indeed, untainted by the general disdain for his fellow officials at large. Case duly came in and set out to staff his role in drawing together the Covid effort in 10 Downing Street and 70 Whitehall (Cabinet Office). One prong of his pitch was to change the culture at the centre, which staff in No. 10, and not just women, found unbearably macho. 'It was men fighting for space rather than taking responsibility, talking over each other with no medium- or long-term sense,' says one. Civil service leaders belittled their juniors to the point of tears on multiple occasions, unacceptable conduct for all the unique tensions of the epidemic.[29] Senior male officials left women in particular excluded from meetings and decisions, leading MacNamara to issue an email to the men leading the Covid response that summer setting out the basic behaviours expected of them. Johnson had sought to emulate Blair with his ten years, but it was not that New Labour leader he was actually emulating. A macho culture with a blithe indifference from the PM's Office had been a feature of Brown's No. 10.

Case's efforts involved marginalizing the multiplicity of figures who were offering advice to the Prime Minister from within the system, and centralizing authority in a newly established Covid Task Force (CTF) based in the Cabinet Office. 'I don't want five people to be going and telling the Prime Minister different things, I want one person giving him a clear view,' he told civil servants. He excelled at managing the politics and calming down the decision-making process, countering egos desperate to be in the room during the initial response and moving the decision-making and advice process away from the diverse cast of characters spread throughout No. 10 and the Cabinet Office, towards a single body with defined responsibilities.

The effect was felt overnight. Exceptional officials including Simon Ridley, James Bowler and Kate Josephs drove improvements, with practices such as 'red-teaming' (introducing a set of critical opposition with significantly different views when making crucial policy decisions) working to stress-test policy advice, correcting for the early mistakes blamed in part on groupthink. With Case's two hats, as No. 10 permanent secretary and leading the Cabinet Office CTF from 70 Whitehall, the connections between the two buildings were much enhanced. This was Case at his most effective.

The CTF helped address the short-termism of the early response with its overload and fragmentation leading to ministers and officials alike struggling to think beyond tomorrow. The erratic ministerial inputs to date were streamlined in June by two new

Cabinet committees: Covid Strategy (S) and Covid Operations (O). The former was charged with the broad direction of the government response, the latter with the granular day-to-day policy, preventing strategy from getting bogged down by implementation.

Some organizational tensions remained. 'Sedwill still attended meetings, but the Prime Minister now looked to Case on Covid. Case took the end-of-day meeting from Sedwill, and led on it within the building,' says an official. Establishing authority was not limited to the civil service staff – early on, Case had a bruising exchange with Mirza, who felt she was being excluded from inputting on Covid policy and providing advice to the Prime Minister. The permanent secretary, believing the issue to be too many cooks, stood his ground and the Policy Unit had no alternative but to take a back seat.

Cummings remained the domineering figure in No. 10 throughout the period, Johnson knowing that he needed his senior adviser to see him through these terrible times. One particular policy issue into which Cummings threw himself was testing. 'He was totally obsessive about it,' says an official. Cummings' long-running contempt for Hancock led to him wanting to take testing away from his portfolio, along with vaccinations and PPE. April was spent with Cummings establishing bodies bypassing the Health Secretary, led by allies who would report directly to the Prime Minister – despite their briefs being firmly within Hancock's remit. Dido Harding was duly appointed executive chair of NHS Test and Trace, Kate Bingham to the Vaccine Task Force and Lord Deighton on PPE procurement. Hancock was not present for the appointments of Harding and Deighton, and even excluded from their WhatsApp groups raising and addressing policy issues, with the governance structure cutting him out completely. 'It was an extraordinary expression of no confidence in him as Health

Secretary,' says one No. 10 official. Although Cummings had latched on as a champion of the Vaccine Task Force, it was the brainchild of Vallance and heavily supported by Sedwill, who saw the need to create a streamlined, agile team to drive procurement outside of the usual processes of the DHSC. 'I can say categorically that without Mark and Patrick taking those risks, we would not have had vaccines as early as we did,' extols a senior Covid official.

Cummings badgered Johnson incessantly about getting Hancock replaced, preferring alternatives such as Alok Sharma. Johnson would moan in response, calling Hancock 'totally f**king hopeless'.[30] But when Cummings asked officials to exclude Hancock from meetings, Hancock called the Prime Minister. 'Oh, of course you can come to that, Matt,' Johnson replied, getting Hancock back on the meeting list. 'It was like secondary school gossip about who can sit next to who, all in the middle of a pandemic,' says one of the officials coordinating the meetings.

The level of respect for the Health Secretary had so depleted that, after months of Cummings and allies referring to Hancock as 'that c**t', by summer even the Prime Minister started joining in. While doing some regional interviews Johnson let the phrase slip out – his blushes spared by it being a pre-recording rather than live broadcast. Cain forced the Prime Minister to call Hancock and apologize in case word got out, downplaying it as a one-off accidental joke.

So why didn't Johnson get rid of his Health Secretary if he too felt he was not up to the job? Simple. 'Boris thought it would be useful to keep on Hancock so he could blame him when the inquiry came out,' says a No. 10 aide. 'It was like a group of rats trapped in a pipe.'

Cummings' attempt to defenestrate any figure he either felt incompetent or able to challenge him was unrelenting. Execution was his stock response, devoid of empathy, or with regard to collateral damage. Having failed to replace NHS boss Simon Stevens with Harding earlier in the year, he was after Harding's blood months later following the failure of the Test and Trace programme. Stevens and Harding remained, but more often than not, Robespierre got his way.

The Svengali's strength indeed was indicated not only in No. 10 and Westminster, but to the nation, by Johnson's handling of his leaving London for County Durham in contravention of the national lockdown rules (discussed in the next chapter). Johnson stood by his man, but at what cost? Within the building the atmosphere became surreal, officials afraid to speak up about the issue. 'Lots of people wanted to influence Dom, but nobody wanted to become his enemy so there was this bizarre silence. After Barnard Castle, everybody hushed to a whisper as Dom took on the handling of the response himself.' Officials and aides were terrified of incurring Cummings' wrath, which could be terminal to their careers, so lockdown compliance issues highlighted by the scandal were not discussed in meetings for fear that word could get back to the man himself.

Reopening and the Road to Lockdown 2: July–August 2020

As reopening rolled on, Sunak delivered his 8 July package of £30 billion additional spending, including a number of non-Covid programmes such as the Kickstart Scheme, subsidizing wages for unemployed young workers. The policy which would receive the most cut-through, however, was 'Eat Out to Help Out'. 'Sunak was concerned about the damage to young people that lockdown had brought and wanted to reduce the numbers who would become NEETS [Not in Education, Employment or Training],' says a Treasury official. The Chancellor was equally wary of leaks, and cooked up the policy internally and secretly in the Treasury. The scheme, offering discounted meals to diners on Mondays, Tuesdays and Wednesdays in August, led to a surge in demand and helped ensure that young service workers would remain employed, at least for a time.

Sunak presented his plan to the Prime Minister as part of the ongoing summer reopening, alongside £30 billion in economic measures, and Johnson found it hard to say no. 'It is very difficult to decline a Treasury offer when they advocate a giveaway or tax cut,' says a No. 10 official. Johnson was even happy to let Sunak own it: when the suggestion was raised at a bilateral meeting that they could jointly present the scheme, he insisted, 'No, no. The Chancellor came up with it, therefore the Chancellor should go ahead and announce it.' Sunak had shot to stardom in his initial furlough measures; images of him serving food at restaurant chain Wagamama ahead of the launch were the mouth-watering gift to the young Chancellor taking his early steps into the political stratosphere.

Absent from the decision, though, was any health advice on the effects of subsidizing meals in largely indoor public spaces. Hancock first found out about it when the press release went out, as the policy process and decision was pushed solely through meetings between No. 10 and the Treasury. Insufficient consideration had been given to the trade-offs between the economic and health impacts of the policy. Given Covid's still high reproduction rate, the snowball of infections was bound to be affected by it before the winter. Later research suggested that the scheme, costing a total of £850 million, caused around 5,000 additional symptomatic infections in the period it was active – responsible for between 8 and 17 per cent of all newly detected infections in late summer.[31] Sunak had inadvertently subsidized the virus, with the Prime Minister the complicit bystander.

It was a worrying indication that organizational enhancements to the Cabinet Office and No. 10, for all their improvements, had not removed the first wave's lack of strategic thinking, nor interdepartmental conflict which was again to dominate the second wave. The tension between prioritizing health and prioritizing the economy that the Treasury imagined during the second wave was a mere artifice, with many officials now believing that the Treasury had missed an obvious lesson: that doing the best thing to fight the virus was the best thing for the economy for most of the pandemic. 'Eat Out to Help Out was a complete disaster. Not linked to health at all, the result of having two warring stations of power [the Treasury and DHSC] and no coordinator to keep them in check,' agrees another.

Instead of Health and the Treasury working with No. 10 and the Cabinet Office to integrate epidemiological and economic models to help understand the trade-offs of any policy decision better, they remained in their silos and left No. 10 officials frustrated. Sunak had built a shadow modelling team, working parallel to the Cabinet Office, causing frequent disagreement between them and the CTF on evidence. Many felt the relationship was more oppositional than collaborative. The Prime Minister was ineffective at banging heads together. When the Treasury did examine 'epi-macro modelling', which integrated health dimensions, it was too readily dismissed due to the sensitivity of the model's underlying assumptions. The saying 'All models are wrong, some are useful' was not heeded, and with its dismissal went the Treasury's ability to think accurately about the implications of its policy agenda.

As the country reopened for business on 4 July, the policy switched to a system of local lockdowns where high numbers merited it, as in Leicester. But with cases growing nationally the scientists became sceptical of their efficacy. 'It was a levelling-up approach to Covid,' says one. 'When we had a large number of cases in an area then we'd order a lockdown, and where you didn't, you'd let the cases increase until they became large enough in number.'

Ministerial involvement in decisions continued to be hit-and-miss, driven by the quad: Hancock and Gove were both hawkish favouring tougher action; Covid-sceptic Sunak believed it was imperative to avoid lockdown measures and protect the economy; Johnson was biddable as ever, but at decision time fell back on his libertarian instincts. Whereas the scientific advice was relatively unified, the political advice Johnson was receiving was decidedly not, making even more for zig-zag policy.

Defying the Science: September–November 2020

If the first wave had been led by the science, the second was far more led by the politics. SAGE was sidestepped, most notably in its 21 September advice to pursue a 'circuit-breaker' national lockdown to halt the spread, banning household mixing and closing all bars, cafés and restaurants. At first it seemed, with autumn drawing in and schools reopening, Johnson might listen to the scientists' demand for tougher measures during September. In meetings he would nod along, and hawkish aides thought he was finally beginning to understand the seriousness of the situation. 'Lock down, we must lock down,' he would utter. But his resolve lasted until he met with somebody of the opposite persuasion who said he could have his cake and eat it. Inside No. 10, a battle was raging over how far the measures should go. The approach adopted in September was meagre in comparison: advising people to work from home, given out by Johnson at the following day's press conference.

So why did Johnson sidestep advice?

Johnson and Carrie Symonds had found the restrictions of national lockdowns personally unbearable, cooped up in the flat, unable to get away from the bustle of No. 10. There was little privacy: when Carrie wanted to go outside she had to go through the office; if she wanted to take baby Wilfred to the garden, every step could be seen by multiple staff through the windows. One positive change aides noticed after he recovered from Covid was that Johnson was far more conscious of his weight, and took to his regular jogging more seriously. But for security reasons he could not go running as he would like, a matter the Queen took pity on. So she granted him special permission to run at Buckingham Palace, as well as allowing his family to use the gardens. Delighted as he was at such kindness, he still chafed at lockdown as a restriction on his freedom, and that of the country at large. To be the Prime Minister who constrained Britain in the immediate crisis was discomforting; to do it a second time less agreeable still.

The noises of his party were also growing louder in Johnson's ear. The scepticism of right-wing MPs about the health benefits of lockdown, and the economic costs, was turning to anger. 'The vote on the 10 p.m. curfew on 13 October was the turning point for many colleagues,' says 1922 Committee Chair Graham Brady, himself, ominously for Johnson, part of the rebellion.[32] 'It was so utterly senseless that it was relatively easy for them to vote against it,' he says. Forty-two Tory MPs voted that night against the measure to force bars, pubs and restaurants to close after 10 p.m., and they would form the core that later made up the anti-lockdown Covid Recovery Group.

No. 10 attempted at first to manage the rebels, a sensible strategy given its record for having a tin ear for its MPs, but to little avail. 'To satisfy their demands there was a lot of outreach. We were giving them impact analysis, we tried to do as much as we could and it still wasn't enough,' says a senior adviser. At that point, the policy pivoted. 'Because we couldn't satisfy them, we began to think it wasn't worth trying, that the PM just had to accept that level of rebellion.' The MPs believed Johnson had allowed himself to become intellectually captured by the scientists, despite his growing doubts about them. Criticisms of the man they had backed as their leader just a year before were increasing, not least about his support for an expanding state and higher taxes.

The right-wing press, for so long his natural allies, were nipping ever more ferociously at his heels. The *Telegraph* and *Spectator* had both shifted to strong anti-lockdown positions in the summer, despite the public remaining broadly pro-lockdown regardless of political affiliation. Many figures he followed carefully were also messaging him on WhatsApp, urging him to keep the country open. Should he trust his tribe more than SAGE? For an avid reader of the papers, but not his official papers, it was an uneven fight.

Even more influential than the columnists were the editors and proprietors. In April that year a cash subsidy had been arranged called 'All In, All Together'. It was in part the product of Johnson's relationship with the press barons, who spoke to him directly requesting aid, as later alleged by Cummings.[33] Fearing another lockdown, Johnson's phone blew up with their messages too. 'He was under huge pressure from newspaper editors at the time, terrified about the reduction in circulation if there was another lockdown,' recalls a senior No. 10 media adviser. 'He was very torn between doing what the public wanted and what his friends in the press wanted.'

Pressure was mounting on Johnson from Sunak as well. 'Boris himself was reluctant, but not opposed to a lockdown,' says Gove, who comments that the key figure 'pushing against Rishi' was himself not Johnson.[34] The Chancellor was at the peak of his popularity and power, and Johnson found it near impossible to tell him no. Like Gove, Hancock was frustrated with Sunak, and felt that discussions with him were pointless, demonstrating to him the intellectual hollowing out of the Treasury with economic thinkers replaced by 'mere accountants' whose models could not see that health costs were economic costs too.

Pushback was coming at the hapless Johnson from the scientific community as well, disconcerted that they were no longer in pole position. 'It was the most depressing time to be a scientific adviser,' says one, 'because we had stated back in March that lockdown is not something you can just do once, which is part of the reason it took SAGE a while to come round. There would be an initial lockdown and then release and need to do it again.' Whitty and Vallance were thus now pushing hard in No. 10 and COBRA for decision-makers to learn the lessons of the first wave, and not repeat them.

The stage was ready for one of the great set-piece debates over Covid strategy, a virtual meeting with Johnson and Sunak on Sunday 20 September. The stakes could hardly be higher. On the one side, a presentation by Oxford's Professor Sunetra Gupta, who was to co-author the 'Great Barrington Declaration' (an open letter in October) advocating 'focused protection', and a proponent of the widely contested view (later proven incorrect[35]) that Covid was far more widespread than most scientists thought due to an overestimation of mortality rates. Joining her was Anders Tegnell, the Swedish state epidemiologist who had delivered Sweden's light-touch approach during the first wave. With the argument that the British population were closer than SAGE thought to herd immunity, they argued to Sunak and Johnson that any further lockdown would be counterproductive. Let the virus spread through the community, while protecting those most vulnerable to serious illness, and the pandemic will become an endemic non-issue in three to six months.[36]

Presenting the oppositional SAGE view was Professor John Edmunds. For a group generally hesitant to convey certainty in their advice, his case was as conclusive as it got. 'As over 90% of the population remain susceptible, not acting now to reduce cases will result in a very large epidemic with catastrophic consequences in terms of direct COVID related deaths and the ability of the health service to meet needs,' read SAGE's official summary the following day.[37] But the other side told Johnson he could keep the economy open, pacify his Chancellor, appease the right-wing press – and at the low price of a few regrettable deaths.

The meeting over, Cummings railed against the lockdown sceptics, to little avail. Furious at the Prime Minister's ignorance of the policy realities, it set in motion their final fallout. 'We're going to kill thousands of people if this is the f**king decision,' Cummings and Cain told him. 'What about the economy? Rishi and Eddie [Lister] are telling me we have to keep businesses open,' Johnson responded. Cummings wasn't comfortable when Johnson argued back at him, his discomfort added to by being on the opposite side of the argument to his protégé Sunak.[38]

The science and politics had so diverged that even Johnson's once-trusted team could not bring him around. He began to display, observers thought, elements of paranoia. 'I am being pushed towards a decision to lock down by Dom, who is excluding ministers and surrounding me with lockdown-friendly experts,' he began to think according to one aide. 'Why should I listen to Chris and Patrick telling me to make hard choices? That's precisely what Dom wants. It's nonsense, it's a trap. I can have it all,' was how another described his thought processes.

The country would remain open, he decided that evening. The 21 September restrictions were next to non-existent: pubs, bars and restaurants closing at 10 p.m., limits on attendees at weddings, and recommendations to work from home if possible.

It took just three weeks for the fantasy to be revealed for what it was. By 8 October SAGE had found that the case numbers were exceeding the reasonable worst case scenario levels for which they had planned, advising that serious measures would need to be adopted to reverse the exponential rise.[39] Sunak nevertheless continued to resist the full recommended circuit-breaker lockdown, believing it too damaging to the economy, as did Johnson.

The 'figures are flashing at us like dashboard warnings in a passenger jet', the Prime Minister told the nation on 12 October, but the solution was not commensurate with the scale of the problem: a simplification and standardization of the local lockdown rules, introducing three tiers of restrictions depending upon the severity of the virus. Whitty was as unsupportive as an official can be within the confines of a press conference (without losing their job), admitting he was 'not confident, nor is anybody confident' that Tier 3 (the highest) would work in limiting the spread of the virus. The following day SAGE rushed out their advice which had previously been given on 21 September, three weeks before Johnson's 12 October non-intervention. It was a desperate bid to provoke the government into seeing sense and taking stronger action by making public what SAGE had been saying internally for weeks, their view chiming with the public's pro-lockdown mood, to no avail.

Johnson had inadvertently chosen the worst of all outcomes. 'It was completely indefensible. We had all the information to make the right choice then,' says a No. 10 Covid official. As with earlier local lockdowns the measures would suppress Covid numbers only where the case numbers were high, and therefore failed to prevent the spread of the virus in less affected areas until they were critical, straining the NHS and resulting in a huge number of deaths. It suppressed businesses in affected areas, which Johnson had sought to avoid on the advice of Sunak, and, worse than in a time-limited national lockdown, businesses would not be able to predict restrictions and adjust plans accordingly. In both economic and health terms, it was disastrous. The economic bounceback stalled, with low growth through September and October, and the health figures were deeply sobering: the Office for National Statistics estimated 568,000 people in England, over 1 per cent of the population, had Covid for the week of 17–23 October.[40]

The local lockdown plan proved politically difficult too. Sunak had resisted broad measures as suggested by the CTF on the basis that universal financial support packages would be too costly, and insisting that each area placed into Tier 3 negotiated with the Treasury independently rather than instituting uniform compensation. This meant scrapping with local mayors, the most prominent of whom was Manchester's Andy Burnham who attacked the government for offering two-thirds of wages in furlough, down from the earlier 80 per cent.[41] Avoidable regional battles sapped the Prime Minister's time during a crucial moment of the pandemic; he spent nearly a day negotiating terms with Burnham who was determined to get a better deal than Liverpool.

By the end of September, Johnson's data dashboard was looking particularly grim. On 1 October there were sixty-seven daily recorded Covid deaths. By 31 October the number stood at 326, a fivefold increase. It had been obvious to advisers and officials that the Prime Minister would regret his decision. 'Everybody in the building knew that he would U-turn in a couple of weeks because it's what he does, and that's exactly what happened. He just couldn't focus on Covid long enough to stay consistent,' says one.

The U-turn came, as it surely would, on 31 October, though even on the very day before as the decision was being made Johnson was still prevaricating. At a meeting of the Covid Strategy Cabinet committee Hancock and Gove were at their most influential. The two biggest advocates of a lockdown within Cabinet, with help from Whitty, finally swayed Johnson into submission. The clincher came from Gove: 'Prime Minister, if you don't do this then ambulances will be arriving at hospitals and getting turned away because they don't have the space. We will be sending in soldiers to guard hospitals to keep people out if we don't lock down now.' Johnson's response was frustration, followed by begrudging acceptance. 'It was the most fruity I've ever seen a Cabinet committee get,' notes a senior official. Leaving the meeting, Johnson's frustration allegedly spilled over into a callous amorality as he exclaimed to Cummings, 'No more f**king lockdowns. Let the bodies pile high in their thousands.'[42]

Bitter recriminations now showed that the love-in between Cummings and Johnson was well and truly over. To force the issue, and prevent Johnson from his typical U-turning, the government's 'decision' was then leaked to the press – that a national lockdown would be going ahead. Johnson had been bounced into acting. 'When I told you two weeks ago that we were pursuing a local and regional approach to tackling this virus, I believed then and I still believe passionately that it was the right thing to do... But as we've also seen from those charts, we've got to be humble in the face of nature,' Johnson told the nation.[43]

A leak inquiry was established the following day.[44] It did not find the culprit, but Johnson had no doubts as to who the 'chatty rat' (as No. 10 staff dubbed the leaker) was. ITV's Robert Peston and the BBC's Laura Kuenssberg both went hard on the story independently, their confidence indicating to the Prime Minister that it had come from a definitive source. Cummings was believed to have leaked to both in the past, and Johnson readily saw his motivation for doing so again: locking the government into its position and preventing any more of Johnson's infamous trolleying from undoing the decision. 'It took several weeks to properly ignite, but that leak set in train the ending of their relationship,' says an official.

The second national lockdown came into effect on 5 November, time-limited to end on 2 December. The legislation passed the previous evening with thirty-two Tory votes against the motion, and prompted the Covid Recovery Group's official formation, led by Steve Baker and Mark Harper, advocating for minimal restrictions and maximum freedoms despite the pandemic. The combined organizational ability of the ERG leader and the former Chief Whip was formidable, putting the government in an even more politically difficult position.

The Road to Lockdown 3: November 2020–January 2021

The best news of the entire pandemic hit No. 10 four days into the lockdown on Monday 9 November: there was a vaccine. Trials by the US pharma company Pfizer had shown its jab to be more than 90 per cent effective after two doses, and with the Vaccine

Task Force having pre-ordered 40 million jabs, the UK would have enough to vaccinate 20 million people, starting with the most clinically vulnerable before the end of the year.

No. 10 and the Prime Minister were jubilant, a way out of the pandemic finally in sight. Their spirits only grew that month as further vaccine news rolled in. On 23 November, Oxford University announced that its vaccine, produced jointly with British-Swedish pharma company AstraZeneca, was effective and offered a high level of protection. This was the big one – the UK had ordered a diverse range of vaccines, but the 100 million orders of Oxford-AstraZeneca made up the largest chunk of the portfolio.

Later that day Johnson set out the government's Covid Winter Plan: a return after 2 December to a three-tier regional approach, with Tier 2 and 3 restrictions strengthened until a five-day relaxation at Christmas, allowing three households to mix. ''Tis the season to be jolly but 'tis also the season to be jolly careful,' Johnson japed.[45] Though strengthened, the tiers were still some way short of the full lockdown the country had just experienced. Some of the restrictions were semi-logical at best, the blanket 10 p.m. curfew and alcohol only being served with 'substantial meals' the result of interminable meetings between the hawkish (CTF, Hancock, Gove and health advisers), a Chancellor desperate to keep the economy maximally open and an inveterate optimist of a Prime Minister. Johnson believed that the country could be back to normal by Christmas if he bade it so; reasoning in part motivated by fear of what others might say if he went too hard. He couldn't bear to face a rebellion from his backbenchers, pick another fight with his Chancellor, receive swathes of angry WhatsApps from his *Spectator* kin, or go down as the Prime Minister who robbed people of their Christmas. 'In his mind throughout was this idea of being "back to normal by

Christmas", which wasn't even broken by his 30 October decision to lock down,' says one official.

News of the vaccines should have given Johnson the confidence to take a strong decision – to restrict 'earlier than you think you want to, harder than you think you want to, and broader than you think you want to', as Vallance advised him. Instead, he continued to oscillate between emphatic declarations of action ('Let's go hard, we can get ahead of this') and passivity ('We can't lock down now, the people want to have their Christmas, I want us to have Christmas!'), which inevitably ended in the latter. It was easier for Johnson to do nothing than do something.

The quality of decision-making was in part the product of fatigue. Johnson found the pace of the crisis exhausting, and was disheartened that Covid was becoming the issue defining his premiership. The nine whole months, his short attention span and ravenous hunger for novel ideas had been submerged in a single policy challenge, dominating meeting after meeting after meeting after meeting after meeting. Exhaustion turned to frustration, frustration to boredom.

Gove in particular was exercised by the Prime Minister's depleted capabilities, complaining to officials that 'We always find ourselves a step behind because we're doing three-quarters of the job necessary.' At a lengthy Covid Operations meeting towards the start of December, Gove was emphatic on moving London to Tier 3: 'If we don't do it now we'll have to do it later, and when we do it later we'll regret not acting sooner.' The Prime Minister, at that moment veering towards libertarianism, pushed back and the capital remained in the lighter Tier 2 restrictions. A week later on 14 December it was announced London was moving to Tier 3. 'We didn't restrict London because of the Prime Minister pushing back in the meeting, then we were back around the table a week later doing it anyway,' vents an official.

When it came to the emergence of a new (Alpha or 'Kent') variant that winter the government once again reacted too late. No. 10 had seen the numbers rising in the South-East, with infections beginning even as Johnson announced in November the Christmas relaxation. 'We saw the numbers shooting up but we couldn't convince the Prime Minister that action needed to be taken,' recalls one CTF official. The Prime Minister had to be talked down in stages, first in moving London to Tier 3, then offering the public more stringent advice regarding their Christmas gatherings on 16 December.

It took until 18 December for the scientists to finally articulate to Johnson that stricter restrictions were necessary. In a data dashboard meeting Vallance revealed that early studies had shown a causal link between the Kent variant and infections, the mutated virus spreading 70 per cent faster. 'There's not really a choice to be made here, Prime Minister,' he told him.

Johnson could hold out against reality no longer and acquiesced, decisive on shutting down the affected regions. 'The Prime Minister was aware it gave him an excuse, an out of control variant that justified strong action. He seemed almost relieved after Patrick told him it was bad,' says one scientist. Christmas bubbles were restricted to a single day in Tiers 1, 2 and 3, and a new Tier 4 was introduced in London and the South-East with 'Stay at Home' restrictions where the Christmas bubble policy no longer applied.

No. 10, simultaneously attempting to finalize the UK's future relationship with the EU, was still only stumbling into the third lockdown. On 30 December yet more areas were put into Tier 4, the inevitability of a full national lockdown still resisted by the Prime Minister despite how painfully inevitable it seemed to advisers.

The emergence of vaccines and the Kent variant had changed the dynamics of the debate among Cabinet ministers; Sunak had fought tooth and nail to avoid the second lockdown, but stayed silent at the prospect of a third. The most important ministerial resistance (besides that of the Prime Minister himself) was now Williamson, who had driven down through the snow from his South Staffordshire constituency on 28 December to find himself in a meeting in Johnson's office with Whitty, Vallance and incoming Chief of Staff Dan Rosenfield. Johnson was not only eager to tell Williamson what he wanted to hear, but had vowed never to repeat the school closures. 'I'm not closing schools again, I'm not doing it,' he said vigorously to his officials, refusing to consider alternative compromises such as extending the Christmas school holidays. Primary schools in all but the worst hit areas were to reopen on 4 January, as Johnson and Williamson agreed. 'We'll end up U-turning on this,' officials said to each other after the meeting.

The morning of 4 January came, and Williamson received a call from the Prime Minister, delighted to see children returning in person. 'You're going to get them *all* back soon, aren't you, Gavin?' he said. Williamson was buoyed by the Prime Minister's support that day, until he received a call from Rosenfield at lunch and his heart sank. 'This won't be what you want to hear, but we've been round the houses with Chris and Patrick looking at the numbers, and we're going to have to close schools. We're going to have to close everything really.'[46] There was less than six hours between Johnson stressing the importance of reopening to Williamson, and his chief of staff apologetically sweeping up the pieces after the position was reversed.

The Prime Minister had been converted to a full lockdown by the data dashboard meeting of that morning (less convinced by Hancock's plea the previous night).[47] The sharp incline over the previous days in both total cases and those in critical care was sufficiently worrying to convince the self-proclaimed 'mayor from *Jaws*'[48] (after his desire to keep the economy open) to go against his instincts and close the beaches. Johnson could no longer avoid the inevitable. It had taken a month from the 2 December reopening but the Prime Minister had finally moved the country haphazardly back into lockdown. As he made the announcement on 4 January, the first jabs of the Oxford-AstraZeneca vaccine were being administered to patients in the UK. The country was finally on its way out of the biggest health crisis for a century.

The Record

The record of how the Prime Minister performed during the pandemic can be seen in simple statistics. Britain came 15th when compared to the twenty-eight EU states in terms of excess mortality, but performed the worst of the G7 economically.[49] So did the Prime Minister 'get the big things right' as he and his supporters later claimed?[50]

Johnson should not bear the brunt of the blame for the delay in locking down at the beginning of March 2020. Few (if any) deviations from scientific advice were made, the litany of errors being systemic: absence of long-term thinking, insufficient preparation, poor departmental coordination, and groupthink within the scientific and health bodies. Prime ministers rightly and inevitably shoulder responsibility for decisions taken by them, not taken by them, or taken in their name.

The poor quality of the UK's response later in March and April 2020 rests more heavily on Johnson's shoulders. His inability to provide calm, consistent and decisive leadership, to grip policy issues and to appoint and trust strong people placed too large a burden upon others in No. 10 and the Cabinet Office, who fought with each other to fill the vacuum he left. He was too weak to rein back Cummings, who for all his positive contributions, brought panic, fear and confusion into a system crying out for calm and order. But even an exceptional Prime Minister would have struggled with a system at the centre not well enough equipped to coordinate government internally or hold external bodies to account in a crisis. The deepest lessons here are for the centre of government, and Whitehall's wider preparation. Johnson did not get all the big calls right, but he did not get them all wrong either, his decision-making improving in 2021, as we outline later in the book.

The most damning criticism must be reserved for his handling of the second wave. No politician can predict the future, and it is a fair mitigation that the arrival of vaccines in late 2020 renders decisions not to lock down worse in hindsight. But Johnson made serious errors in his disregard of the official advice, heeding the political beliefs of influential right-wing columnists, backbenchers and his Chancellor ahead of the scientific community. The failure to lock down until November was a preventable, predictable and irresponsible mistake. The failure to extend the lockdown once highly effective vaccines had been found even more egregious. The majority of deaths in the UK occurred during the second wave, including the very peak. The data was available, the advice to No. 10 clear. It was a political error and weakness not to follow it. His essential frivolity could not grasp the issues when gravitas was required.

The British state had been pushed to the very brink for the first time since 1945. Institutional and cultural shortcomings were not unique to the United Kingdom, but were laid bare to catastrophic consequence. The hard truths of the pandemic must not be filed away and forgotten, but institutional memory retained and ready to be redeployed in the event of another crisis.

Speaking to people in the process of writing this book we fear the memory is already slipping and becoming distorted. We encountered many cases where individuals during the pandemic were acting with an eye to how history might judge them. Where self-interest trumped public interest. Equally, witnesses told us that the fear of blame and for their careers impeded them from being fully frank with their superiors, such was the regime of trepidation and finger-pointing within No. 10.

We encountered concerns too that official inquiries would not reveal the full truth, and that lessons would not be properly learned. Sensible investments in excess capacity for low-probability, high-impact events are being scaled back in a time of economic crisis. Evidence-light assumptions, such as the South Korean or Singaporean approaches to the virus being ineffective due to a lesser appetite in the UK for authoritarian government intervention, still circulate in policy-making circles. Covid's political leaders rewrite history to downplay their own errors of judgement, whether arising from errant policy or passive inaction.

It is crucial to temper these criticisms with praise for the gruelling effort of public servants throughout the pandemic. Countless civil servants, aides and politicians worked tirelessly in the face of an unprecedented policy challenge for which they had little preparation or guidance, coming up with instant solutions to problems inconceivable the previous week. The selfless sacrifices of the unnamed who toiled away in their offices for near hundred-hour week after hundred-hour week – to great strain on their own personal lives and mental health – should not be forgotten amid the many recriminations and official findings to come.

The importance of those findings, however, cannot be understated. It is unlikely that the gap between Covid-19 and the next major pandemic will be as long as the century that passed since the Spanish flu. When that time comes, and the nation is once again plunged into a deep and transformative crisis, it is imperative that we learn from history, that the successes and failures of Boris Johnson and the team he led in Whitehall are roundly understood and built upon.

Dominic Cummings departs No. 10 for one last time as his 16-month tenure as chief adviser comes to an end

6

CUMMINGS

Dominic Cummings made Johnson's premiership – and he destroyed Johnson's premiership. No aide to a Prime Minister in British history was quite like him. None were so influential when in post, nor so destructive to their former boss once they left office.

We cannot understand the Johnson premiership without understanding the motivations and actions of this extraordinary man. What was it about Johnson that allowed Cummings to gain such vast power? What does it say about Whitehall that it didn't moderate his power and conduct? And why was his critique of the system so often devastating? Hence this chapter is devoted to what he did, how he did it, and the impact it had on Johnson and the entire premiership.

Johnson was gifted and flawed. Cummings was more gifted, and more flawed. Johnson had a unique influence on the fate of more than one British premier. Theresa May would not have become Prime Minister without him, and Johnson would not have become Prime Minister without her. But neither would have become Prime Minister without Cummings, who had earlier played his part in the demise of David Cameron, for whom he had total contempt. As he had for May. As he developed for Johnson.

Cameron had sacked Michael Gove as Education Secretary in 2014 partly because of Cummings, who was Gove's special adviser at the time. Cummings' rebarbative influence had poisoned Gove's relationships with both the education profession and the premier. Without that dismissal Gove would not have been so willing to defy his once dear friend Cameron and back Vote Leave in the Brexit referendum. After working for Gove, Cummings masterminded the close victory for Vote Leave. Without Cummings working with Johnson and strategizing the campaign, it is likely Britain would still be in the EU.

Not since Thomas Cromwell under Henry VIII in the 1530s and William Cecil under Elizabeth I had the country witnessed an adviser to a principal with so much political power. Not since John Maynard Keynes and William Beveridge in the 1940s has there been an adviser with such radical potential and desire to recast the mould of government thinking. Our quest here is in part to understand how cogent his ideas were and why, unlike these antecedents, his revolution was incomplete.

The office of Prime Minister was established in April 1721. Prime Ministers since have all had influential advisers. Most held onto them. Disraeli had Montagu Corry throughout both his periods as Prime Minister. Margaret Thatcher had Bernard Ingham and Charles Powell by her side for most of her eleven and a half years at Downing Street. Tony Blair had Jonathan Powell as his chief of staff throughout his ten years, a position Ed Llewellyn held throughout all six years that Cameron was in Downing Street.[1] All these advisers, like others who held senior positions working for the Prime Minister, saw their primary task as serving their boss's wishes, knowing the Prime Minister's mind and shaping the world around them accordingly.

They were the servants, not the masters.

Cummings saw himself as the master, not the servant, especially after the general election in December 2019.

Three recent Conservative Prime Ministers imported into No. 10 their high-octane male advisers who, like Cummings, brightly illuminated the whole Downing Street sky only to burn out prematurely after months not years, their tasks incomplete, leaving feeling bitter and frustrated with their former bosses. They had humble roots, were iconoclasts, were true believers in their causes, and all were intellectually capable, if prone to projecting a mythology of their total authority and ability across Whitehall. Thatcher had Alfred Sherman, a polymath and communist who fought in the Spanish Civil War before becoming an ardent convert to the free market. David Cameron had Steve Hilton, whose family had come to Britain after the uprising in communist Hungary in 1956, and who lasted little over two years in No. 10 as Cameron's left-field strategic adviser, longer than any of the others. Theresa May had Nick Timothy, the son of a car worker in Birmingham, who had absorbed the communitarian ideals of the city's great nineteenth-century mayor Joseph Chamberlain and visualized an activist role for the state in empowering its citizens, regardless of background. Timothy, predominantly focused on policy in the shared chief of staff role with Fiona Hill, had the most influence, because May was far more biddable than Thatcher or Cameron, if less so than Johnson. None were conventional Conservatives, nor lovers of Tory MPs. Sherman would pad around No. 10 in an old-fashioned three-piece suit, Hilton without shoes and Timothy with his Rasputin-esque beard. All three were described as 'oddballs', mavericks even, more alike than they might find comfortable to admit.

All four super-powered advisers to the Conservative Prime Ministers – Sherman, Hilton, Timothy and Cummings – were deeply anti-EU. Sherman wanted to head up the forerunner of

UKIP, Hilton departed No. 10 partly in horror at Cameron's pro-EU stance, while Timothy almost single-handedly drove May in a far more Eurosceptic direction from the moment she became Prime Minister.

Yet influential though the first three could be, none of them, nor any other adviser before them, had successfully engineered the departure of the most powerful figure in government after the Prime Minister, the Chancellor of the Exchequer, followed by the most powerful official in the country, the Cabinet Secretary, nor tried to install their preferred candidate as head of the nation's Secret Intelligence Service and the Bank of England. None so unsettled the monarch, nor engineered the gravest political crisis in the late reign of Queen Elizabeth II. No other adviser boasted so grandiloquently of having toyed with plotting to have the Prime Minister replaced, nor unleashed a procession of secret material to their advantage.

Did the state, or even the murky 'deep state' about which Cummings wrote, hold talks and plan to circumvent the influence of this revolutionary in their midst? Did it concern the intelligence services, whose job it is to defend the democratic and orderly conduct of government, that this unelected aide was riding roughshod through the system? If not, why not?

Who *was* Dominic Cummings, and how did he come to acquire the extraordinary position that he did?

The Formative Years

Born on 25 November 1971, his first thirteen months were spent with Britain outside the European Union he came to detest. His parents were a reasonably affluent middle-class northern family, who had pulled themselves up by their bootstraps. The family were not socially smart, his father a sometime builder of oil rigs and manager of a canoe paddle factory, his mother a special needs teacher. Cummings attended a state primary school but moved to the private Durham School for his secondary education, from where he gained a place at Exeter College, Oxford, gaining a First in Ancient and Modern History in 1994. So far, so unexceptional.

Cummings, unlike Johnson, was desperate for intellectual nourishment at Oxford, wanting to be shaped by the powerful minds he encountered rather than just joshing around. Norman Stone, the controversial, iconoclastic and virtuoso historian, was one such. Stone was a man never guilty of moderation, in manner, language, thought, women or alcohol consumption, and Cummings was utterly captivated by him. In 1983, Stone had published his book *Europe Transformed, 1878–1919*, which expounded on the prowess of Germany's first Chancellor, Otto von Bismarck, who used his masterly political skills to exert influence via Kaiser Wilhelm I. Cummings would unfavourably measure the performance of contemporary leaders against Bismarck's statecraft. In his review of *Europe Transformed* in the *London Review of Books*, left-wing historian Eric Hobsbawm said that Stone 'does not believe the course of history is determined by a combination of accidents, such as the unpredictable appearance of a Bismarck or Lenin'.[2] No, for Stone, as for Cummings, human agency and great men were the agents of historical change, seizing where need be on events of great moment. Lenin, creator of the Soviet Union, was another Cummings hero.

Stone's views on the importance of knowledge in the school curriculum and his abhorrence of progressive education were other topics on which he and his impressionable mentee chimed, to bear fruit when Cummings teamed up with Gove. Stone so mesmerized the young Cummings that his suggestion that after Oxford he go to Moscow 'to witness the New World being created behind the old Iron Curtain'[3] was seized on with alacrity. Cummings' three years in post-communist anything-goes 1990s Moscow later raised eyebrows in the intelligence community. 'But nothing untoward was found. He had a deep fascination for Russia, which we never got to the bottom of, but nothing came up on security checks,' a source says. 'He was intense, very clever, socially a bit awkward,' said Liam Halligan, the economics journalist on whose Muscovite corridor sofa he slept. 'He didn't initially have a job but wanted to see what was going on… There were lots of investment projects coming and going.'[4] In later years, his evident deep interest in Russia led several to take interest, as on the question of Russian interference during the Scottish referendum: 'Dom was very, very interested in Russia. He would interrogate Russian material very deeply.'

In 1997, the year the Conservatives fell from power after eighteen years, he returned to the UK. Friends describe him as 'intellectually restless, loving the good things in life, depending upon others for somewhere to live, and intent on pursuing "rich pretty totty": it was crucial that they were well-born and wealthy, and he was very open about it,' says one.

Two years later, he became campaign director for Business for Sterling, a cross-party group set up in 1998 to lobby against Britain joining the euro, a favoured project of Prime Minister Tony Blair. Norman Stone, a pronounced Eurosceptic, had helped broker the appointment. In post, Cummings honed his skills as a political operator, helping to manoeuvre out Business for Sterling's director Nick Herbert, so he could run it with his friend Alex Hickman. 'Dom in fact had very few friends: his relationships were mostly intellectual, not emotional,' a former colleague says. The group successfully campaigned for the Conservatives to include a 'save the pound' pledge in their manifesto for the 2001 general election, but played little part in the actual abandonment of the euro policy by the government, when Blair was outgunned and outclassed by Chancellor Gordon Brown and his wily lieutenant Ed Balls.[5]

Mission completed, Cummings enjoyed a major hike in status when promoted to director of strategy for Conservative leader Iain Duncan Smith (IDS), with a mission to reinvent the Conservative Party, then being mercilessly pulverized by Blair's New Labour. It was a bumpy ride: 'the 30-year-old got up the noses of Tory traditionalists – and not just for his determinedly casual dress-sense and allegedly astronomical salary', as journalist Andrew Gimson described in a 2014 profile.[6] A more improbable coupling than that between revolutionary Cummings and the traditionalist IDS could scarcely be imagined in politics. The wonder is that their crazy waltz lasted as long as it did before the music abruptly stopped.

While with IDS, he developed a loathing for Conservative MPs, including IDS himself, considering them complacent, landed or entitled. Eurosceptics such as Bill Cash and Bernard Jenkin too ranked high in his pet hates. 'Dom was searching, not like IDS to reform, but for a shock to destroy the old Conservative Party and replace it by a technocratic modern force, attracting intellectuals to tackle and solve Britain's national problems,' says a friend. In 2003, he moved to head up a new free-market and Eurosceptic think tank, the New Frontiers Foundation, which grew out of Business for Sterling. The money came in part from Tory grandee and former Leader of the House of Lords Lord Salisbury, whom Cummings revered, and who became the chair. On the Advisory Council were Norman Stone, who had moved from Oxford to Bilkent University in Ankara, and spread-betting magnate Stuart Wheeler, a major donor to the Tory Party and later to the Brexit campaign. Friends noticed how Cummings was becoming steadily more ideological and anti-EU: 'He was drinking less, becoming more serious, tribal and, indeed, more vindictive towards those he didn't rate,' says one.

Cummings' later preoccupations were foreshadowed at the New Frontiers Foundation including reform of the civil service, the creation of a body to fund high-risk scientific projects, the ending of the BBC's monopoly as public service broadcaster, and a fascination with the neoconservative movement in the US, whose ideas propelled President George W. Bush into war against Iraq in 2003. Indicative of his dislike of extending the tentacles of government, Cummings became concurrently a key figure in the successful campaign against Labour's proposed regional assembly in the North-East, called 'North East Says No', in which he honed tactics later to be used in the Brexit referendum, including suggesting that more money would flow to the NHS if the assembly was not created.

While Johnson was gallivanting through life, unsuccessfully dodging scandals, getting sacked from the shadow Cabinet and resigning from the *Spectator*, Cummings was systematically building his own career and agonizing about the future of the world. With victory against the regional assembly in the bag and the New Frontiers Foundation dissolved shortly after, he constructed a retreat at his family's farm in County Durham where he secreted himself away for two years reading and thinking deeply about history, science and the future.[7] The Canadian-American political science writer Philip E. Tetlock was one of the figures to intrigue him. In 2005, he published *Expert Political Judgment: How Good Is It? How Can We Know?*, which argued that experts could be no better at making predictions than anyone else, yet often evaded the consequences of their errors – not a long journey to Gove famously saying that Britons had 'had enough of experts'. Investor Warren Buffett's collaborator Charlie Munger was another to intrigue Cummings with his 'Lollapalooza effect' explaining how normally rational people can behave highly irrationally at times due to unconscious biases. Munger was a rare contemporary whom Cummings saw as an intellectual equivalent. His history reading focused on leaders who had made dramatic changes: Jean Monnet, the 'father of Europe', was one who fascinated him for springing the idea of European integration on people and making it happen – even if he scorned the institution that was created.

First Taste of Whitehall: The Gove Years 2007–14

Cummings' relationship with Michael Gove began on his re-entry to normal life, his retreat over. They had met on the campaign against the euro, and after Gove was appointed shadow Schools Secretary by Cameron in July 2007, he was eager to bring the firebrand on board. Cummings respected Gove as a serious intellect, intent, unlike IDS, on crashing through institutional resistance and driving radical reform. Gove was enchanted by the young Cummings, amused not troubled by his quirks: observers were surprised at how the impeccably polite and outwardly formal Gove embraced 'someone that mad and off the wall, who can have ferocious temper tantrums and looks like he's been sleeping in a hedge'.[8] Their relationship was to be the making of Cummings, his longest in politics, Gove being the only politician with whom he worked who did not induce his lacerating contempt. Tellingly, he invited Gove to give a speech at his wedding: although ideological fellow travellers, they were not close personally. During the Gove years, friends noticed Cummings becoming more introverted and serious-minded but still more intolerant and vituperative too. 'Dom ascribes inviolable qualities to those he currently admires, but it never lasts. When he's for you, he is 100 per cent for you, expecting 100 per cent loyalty; and when he's against you, there is no stopping his animosity,' says an insider.

Cummings was to remain with Gove for seven years. 'He never played Gove like he later did Johnson,' says Sam Freedman, who became senior policy adviser when Gove became Education Secretary following the general election in May 2010.[9] 'He could speak forcefully but always respectfully in the presence of Gove,' says the department's permanent secretary, David Bell.[10] Gove had wanted to appoint Cummings as his special adviser, but Cameron's director of communications, Andy Coulson, had different ideas. 'He knew that Dom would soon start briefing against Cameron. So he flatly refused to let Michael appoint him, who was utterly shellshocked to lose his right-hand man,' says an aide. On hearing the news, Cummings phoned Freedman and told him, 'Get to the department at once: Michael has no one with him.' The brutality of Coulson's act burned deeply into Cummings' psyche, planting ideas in his head of the potency of denying ministers their special advisers. For the following eight months, he brooded dangerously, coming into the department and sitting menacingly in the corner of rooms. 'He was incredibly frustrated that he couldn't formally attend meetings, and was denied email access; being half in, half out maddened him,' an aide says.

Coulson resigned in January 2011 following continued allegations into phone hacking while he had been editor of the *News of the World*. Cummings had not leaked to precipitate his departure, though he was almightily pleased by it, not least because it cleared the path for Gove to bring him into the department as de facto chief of staff. Once there, leaking to the press, while hotly denying he was doing so, became one of the hallmarks of his statecraft. Treating staff in a hectoring fashion was another. 'You can't treat junior officials in that way,' he was told in a dressing-down from a mandarin. He backed down humbly at once: 'the classic reaction of a bully', his reprimander noted. Another trait was an acute hatred for people and plans he believed to be inadequate. 'He utterly loathed and despised Tim Loughton [junior minister at the department],' a colleague recalls. 'A stupid total irrelevance', was his withering verdict on Gove's plan in 2011 on the four hundredth anniversary of the King James Bible to send one to every school by 2012. When an aide suggested that Gove tried working with the more amenable NASUWT teachers' union to isolate the more militant National Union of Teachers, Cummings shouted at him, 'Don't you understand – they're *all* our f**king enemies?' Many who found themselves at the wrong end of Cummings' ire felt traumatized by his aggression.

Gove should not escape criticism for failing to rein in his turbulent priest. 'Michael seemed to notice but not notice,' one witness recalls. Some point to a dark side in Gove, behind the carefully polished veneer, not troubled by dark arts. If Cummings could act as he did under a competent boss like Gove without restraint, 'just imagine', he must have thought, 'how I could transact business under a shopping trolley.'

DfE suited Cummings ideally: Gove and he shared a vision – and they had found an enemy, the 'blob', an amorphous mixture of teachers, officials and academics who they thought were blocking reform. Making enemies never deterred Cummings: it energized him. His whole way of working was predicated upon enemies. 'Conflict made him more comfortable, and he knew how to exploit the anxiety it generated. Dom came to believe the position of Britain was so grave, democracy wasn't working, and it needed a shove. He was utterly singular in his drive to get the things he believed in done,' says an ally. His disregard for democracy under the banner of progress and reform was a matter of dismay for the civil servants who worked closely with him. 'He is virulently and wholeheartedly anti-democracy. That is the truly frightening thing about him,' believes a senior official.

A belief in mass education thus wasn't part of the Cummings doctrine, though he did believe in skills, and drove their provision, as he did later in No. 10, for non-academic students. But he didn't share Gove's passion that every child could gain by an academic education. 'He was mostly interested in the top one per cent, the geniuses. That's why he wanted a difficult curriculum with exams that stretched the really bright ones, and you needn't worry about the rest. Super bright students he thought would later take the decisions that society would need in the future,' says an insider. Maths became a particular passion, and he pressed hard for the subject to be given priority. Specialist 'maths schools' were one of his greatest legacies: 'He created them,' says Alison Wolf, the economist and academic who worked closely with Cummings in establishing King's College London's Mathematics School.[11] Inspired by the Russian institutions of the same name established by renowned Soviet mathematician Andrey Kolmogorov, the first two at KCL and Exeter opened in 2014. The idea took hold within the Conservative Party: in January 2017, Theresa May said she wanted every British city to have a maths school.

Cummings was impatient to make change, but early on he decided the civil service was an impediment, not an ally. 'It cannot manage public services… It concentrates power in a small number of people who are increasingly crap,' he said.[12] Within a year of his joining, Permanent Secretary David Bell moved on, as did a number of other senior officials, including leading luminary Jon Coles. 'There was a lot of shouting from Dominic Cummings at the time. Most people in the department were scared of him,' recalls one. Yet despite all the Cummings-esque confusion and angst, he was successful in helping Gove push through a series of very significant reforms including toughening up the curriculum and exams, the free schools programme and major extension of academies.

The 'blob' was stirred to rebel in the form of a series of no-confidence motions in Gove by teachers' and head teachers' unions in autumn 2013. Cameron was irritated with Gove's faltering relationship with the 'blob', but it was Gove's proclamation that the concentration of Old Etonians in Cameron's inner circle was 'ridiculous'[13] which helped seal Gove's fate.[14] The Prime Minister decided to move Gove in the July 2014 reshuffle, despite him being his most effective departmental minister. Towards the end, Cummings had become the power behind the throne in Education, more dominant and domineering year by year. A fatal lesson that went unlearned by him was that making enemies leads to unfinished revolutions. Widespread support among state school heads for an Education Secretary sincerely committed to improving academic standards, above all for the least advantaged, was squandered. No Education Secretary since Gove – there were nine in the following ten years – has left more than a marginal mark. Goodwill, including across the 'blob', was needlessly squandered. Reflection and self-knowledge never ranked high in the Cummings Canon.

Cummings distilled his experiences in a 237-page manifesto, 'An Odyssean Education', in October 2013, his most thoughtful and constructive piece of work to date.[15] It contains, embryonically or in more developed form, more about his key themes, the case for those in government to understand statistics, science and mathematics, the dangers of misplaced trust in experts, such as PPE graduates with their 'superficial bluffing', and the benefits of proper training of departmental ministers in management prowess, procurement and project management. Outside government, he advocated interdisciplinary courses at university to expand minds, education to focus more on big questions, and the need for Britain to have its own version of the US's Advanced Research Projects Agency (ARPA; later renamed the Defense Advanced Research Projects Agency) to stimulate imaginative investment. The contrast with Johnson's dilettante peregrinations at the same time could not be starker. It was as if they were living in parallel universes.

Had Cummings focused on introducing the changes he identified, he might have become the most remarkable reformer in the hundred years since Richard Haldane, the intellectual, philosopher and politician fascinated, like Cummings, by German thought, by science, technology, intelligence and defence. Haldane helped found the London School of Economics and Imperial College, and pioneered a host of modernizations to government. Neither New Labour after 1997 nor the Conservatives/Lib Dems after 2010 had thrown up a mind of such depth and capability to reimagine the state and policy for the twenty-first century. It was sorely needed.

Haldane too was a creative force. He worked with the grain of government and with politicians and officials and channelled positivity to achieve extraordinary things. Cummings, on the other hand, channelled his intense energy in the form of negative emotions, allowing anger and frustration to militate against building the alliances which are essential to embed change in any system of democratic government. This negativity framed policy through problems, not accomplishments; blockages, not opportunities; what he hated, not what would be an improvement.

Cummings also chose a cause, Brexit, as a speedy fix for all that he saw wrong with the civil service, with the economy and industry, with productivity and science. But was he placing too heavy a burden on Brexit to solve these? Unlike the Boer War and the First World War, which Haldane turned to his advantage, Brexit was an elective event. It was not foolish to imagine that the shift in Britain's domestic and foreign politics could be a catalyst for change, just as his hero Bismarck used the unification of Germany in 1871. But, save for a few pet projects, Cummings' ideas never progressed to a level of complexity beyond railing against EU constraints he was desperate to be freed from. One official recalls their realization that the substance of Cummings as a thinker did not match the branding: 'I was massively disappointed to discover how thin his vision of Brexit was. I thought that finally I was meeting someone who had a prospectus for what we were going to be as a nation…'

Like Bismarck, he needed a champion, recognizing that he himself, unlike Haldane, would never be a minister. After Education, the search was on to find such a figure or figures whom he could bend and influence as much as he had done Gove. Of the four big beasts of the decade, he had burned his bridges with Cameron and Osborne; he decided Gove didn't have it in him to be the top man. That left just one figure. One who was everything Cummings wasn't.

Brexit: 2014–19

Never possessing Johnson's inchoate beliefs on the EU, Cummings' abhorrence of it still took time to crystallize. It was evolving at Business for Sterling, and by the time he started at New Frontiers, his language had hardened. Deep suspicion of encroachment on British legal and political sovereignty form part of it, discussions with his High Court Judge uncle John Laws a formative influence; where Laws differed from his nephew was in his view that it would be 'a mistake to assert… that our sovereignty was diminished by membership of the European Union' and that the 2016 referendum was 'constitutionally troubling'.[16] The EU's labyrinthine structures infuriated him, rendering it in his words 'extraordinarily opaque, extraordinarily slow, extraordinarily bureaucratic', totally ill-suited to the fast world of 'gene drives, lethal autonomous robotics, you name it'.[17] Leaving the EU he believed would provide the vital jolt needed to destroy the 'blob' and archaic practices, finish off the Conservative Party in its current guise, and usher in a brave new world of reform and innovation in which he himself would be the commanding influence and genius. 'He saw the referendum in 2016 as the only chance Britain would have to get out of the EU,' says Freedman, 'but he always saw it as a risk, because it could be overseen by idiots.'[18]

Cummings' contempt had grown for the Tory Party's Eurosceptic hardcore, who in his view had been pushing the same arguments for twenty-five years and getting nowhere. He despised the European Research Group which had been formed in 1993 and its leaders, notably Steve Baker, and had total disdain for Nigel Farage and UKIP. In part for personal reasons because he sought to be the boss himself, he wanted them nowhere near Vote Leave, whose strategy he masterminded. Johnson wasn't a fan either, saying he didn't want UKIP's 'stench of stale fags and booze' anywhere near their own campaign, as one Vote Leave figure recalls.

Gove and Johnson were happy to delegate Vote Leave campaign responsibility to Cummings as the strategic genius. 'Our approach,' as Cummings tellingly put it, 'was to match exactly the priorities of target voters who desperately wanted an Australian style [i.e. high skills only] immigration and more cash to the NHS… [and to] connect them to Vote Leave and "take back control".'[19] Cummings rated Johnson for his ability to speak to different demographic groups, especially in the final four weeks of the campaign, and Gove, whom he never saw as popular enough to win it alone, for his organizational grasp. Here was Cummings' dream team: Johnson the figurehead, Gove the organization man – and he himself, naturally, as the omnipresent brain.

Would the Brexit vote have gone the other way on 23 June 2016 without Cummings driving Vote Leave? With the result so close, 51.9 per cent to 48.1 per cent, the answer is quite possibly yes, especially if Farage's Leave.eu had been designated as the official campaign by the Electoral Commission rather than Vote Leave.

Cummings knew that creating a new world after the victory would be much harder than destroying the old one. But he had faith enough in Johnson in 2016, with proper support, to succeed as PM, so was angry with his old mentor Gove for stabbing Johnson in the back in the leadership election. Cummings had taken a break from the joint Johnson–Gove campaign following the referendum result, telling fellow staff that he'd be back 'once they were in No. 10'. Within days of his absence the whole operation had tellingly broken down. 'Dom leaving was the beginning of the camps [around Johnson and Gove] forming, and it didn't need to happen. A lot of people were projecting their own careers onto the principals,' says an aide. 'He was such a force of nature, he brought Boris and Michael together and held them together. The second he was out of the picture it all fell apart.' Cummings had had enough of high politics, so disappeared from the scene altogether. He had other priorities. *Spectator* journalist Mary Wakefield, whom he had married in 2011, gave birth to their first child in 2016, and according to a friend, 'she pretty much forbade him' from getting involved in politics at that time. He was regularly seen with their baby sitting outside a local café 'with a scarf over his head, bent double over a book. *Anna Karenina*, maths and Bismarck are his three obsessions.'[20]

Baby, blogs and brooding kept him busy, but increasingly Boris, Brexit and the 'blob' were insinuating themselves into his mind. He'd never had an easy relationship with Johnson, whom he hadn't seen in person since the referendum result, but from 2018 he began to offer comments on articles Johnson sent him prior to publication. 'Boris was *very* secretive about it,' says James Wharton, the MP who was Johnson's leadership campaign manager, 'but one Sunday evening [during the campaign] he sent me over a column to check on a Google doc and I saw it was hosted by Cummings.'[21] After two and a half years in hibernation, Cummings was ready to re-emerge. With May crumbling and the leadership competition revving up, he was not just positioning himself towards Johnson but 'had been working behind the scenes and trying to ride every horse until the front-runner emerged', according to one ally. Cummings was playing a long game, in regular contact with rival candidates Michael Gove and Dominic Raab, eager too to keep his relationship with the great loose cannon under covers. Johnson was just as secretive as Cummings regarding their behind-the-scenes alliance, for fears of upsetting both Whitehall and backbenchers. According to one working in the campaign, a *Daily Mail* journalist got hold of the story that Cummings was giving advice to Johnson, and was prevailed upon by a member of Johnson's team not to print, reluctantly pulling the story.

None of the ex-City Hall team, least of all Eddie Lister who was to be Johnson's chief of staff, wanted to see the ultra-tribal Cummings coming into No. 10. But days before Johnson became Prime Minister, the fateful meeting had taken place with the civil servants he would be encountering there. They asked Johnson's aides a series of questions on their plans, and it quickly became apparent that there was not sufficient thinking going on. 'It made Johnson petrified that the incoming political team was nowhere ready or in tune with the premiership's plans, above all on Brexit. Hence the eleventh hour decision to go for the nuclear option,' says one present. Having Cummings by Johnson's side with his almost Messiah-like status among the Vote Leave ultras, who would ram a deal through Whitehall, had obvious advantages. 'Without Dom, Boris would get eaten alive', was the view of a senior adviser, one shared by others who thought that, in meetings with him, Whitehall officials would run rings around the congenial Johnson. He talked it over with Symonds, who was strongly encouraging; 'She knew he'd find it very hard without Cummings,' said one intimate. Lee Cain and Dougie Smith, Munira Mirza's oddball husband who was to enter No. 10 as well, urged him on.

For Cummings, the moment of truth had arrived. The reservations he had felt about Johnson becoming Prime Minister in 2016, hence the need to plant Gove by his side as Chancellor doing the work and taking the decisions, remained. As Cummings later reflected,

Johnson was still 'unfit to be PM'.[22] With Gove (and Raab) now eliminated from the leadership race, he knew that Johnson would win, and that he would never now give Gove the top position in his Cabinet that had been part of the plan in 2016. Hence the dilemma, one of the biggest decisions of Cummings' life. If he chose, he could walk clean away, but with the risk of a second referendum or Jeremy Corbyn winning a general election. Or he could step forward to blast through the three-year constitutional crisis under May and engineer the breakthrough that the hapless Conservatives had been unable to achieve to date after he'd handed them Brexit on a plate. Could he indeed become the key figure himself, playing the role he had carved out for Gove of overseeing Brexit, and become de facto Chancellor of the Exchequer and policy chief? The idea had its attractions. Once Brexit was done, ARPA and other favoured schemes previously impossible due to EU state aid laws could be realized.

Could the Brexit impasse together with the sheer ineptitude Johnson would surely display as PM indeed be the very 'Bismarckian moment' for which he had long yearned?

'I need you with me,' Johnson said breathlessly when he phoned Cummings on holiday in Greece. His usual charm and patter were in overdrive, so he was disarmed that Cummings came across as quite detached and noncommittal, according to those he recounted the call to. So on his return, Johnson went to persuade Cummings at his house in Islington on Sunday 21 July, three days before D-Day. Johnson knew which buttons to press. 'The whole thing is a total mess. I don't know what I'm doing. Someone needs to galvanize Brexit. So much is at risk, the survival of the Conservatives, a second referendum, letting in Corbyn…'

'Let me think about it', was the most Cummings would say.

'Look, you understand Parliament, you understand No. 10 and the Cabinet Office, and the way the civil service works,' Johnson pleaded with him. 'Why don't you come in and we can do it together as in the referendum?'

'Let me talk to Mary and I'll come back to you.'

'OK, OK, of course.'

Cummings was minded to join, but feared that unless he fought hard on his working terms and bringing in his own crack team, he could be swallowed up by the labyrinthine Whitehall machine and end up on 'mundane tasks like preparation for Prime Minister's Questions' as an ally recalls. So he told him, 'I want a written agreement making it clear what I'll be doing.'

'I agree, I agree verbally to it all, is that good enough?'

'No, it isn't. I want it written down.' The meeting ended there, and Cummings submitted his list of requests to Johnson in what became known as the 'terror memorandum'.

Johnson was unhappy about the level of specificity, including a huge increase in spending on science and having special advisers reporting to Cummings, not to him. Knowing his man, though, Cummings was emphatic: his answer was 'no' until Johnson agreed that he would abide by it all. 'Dom is a tough negotiator,' says Conservative Party Chairman Ben Elliot. 'In theory there are lots of people who would want the top position at No. 10. But the post is so difficult, under such intense scrutiny, and it's not well paid: Dom knew his strength.'[23]

'It was a hell of a risk that Boris was taking, and potentially very dangerous to him,' says a close adviser, 'because Dom is not like the usual aide who wants a peerage and a well-paid job in the City after quitting No. 10. He wouldn't go quietly when it was all over.' Johnson knew it was a Faustian pact, but considered he had no option: 'The danger with Dom is he's like an organism that lays eggs inside you, and before you know it they blossom,' he once confided in a senior aide.

The decision to bring in Cummings was the most fateful of Johnson's premiership. Without him, Johnson would have been unable to navigate the Whitehall system. He would still have had David Frost and Oliver Lewis to drive through the Brexit negotiations, and the deal reached with the EU might have been quite similar. Whether he could have taken the brave steps necessary to push it through Parliament and win a general election on the deal is far more doubtful. History after the general election would have been very different too, and exactly how the Johnson premiership would have turned out without Cummings at the helm will never be known. But Cummings unintentionally contributed to the downfall of Gove, whom he admired, in 2014. What might he do intentionally to a man he thought a charlatan if Johnson spurned him?

A brisk ten-minute walk from Cummings' home in Islington is the site of the now-closed Granita restaurant in Upper Street. Here, over twenty-five years before, a similar political pact had been agreed between Tony Blair and Gordon Brown about how the spoils of prime ministerial power would be divided once the citadel was theirs. Different interpretations of that agreement later emerged, then as now, both culminating in the premature ending of a premiership.

Johnson was effectively bringing a sledgehammer into No. 10, and was almost gleeful at the prospect, feeling a childlike sense of mischief. 'Dom has some very big ideas on the civil service,' he told Mark Sedwill and Helen MacNamara after breaking the news to them that Cummings would be joining him in No. 10. 'Great, what are they?' responded Sedwill quick as a flash, anxious to dispel any notion that Britain's top civil servants were resistant to top down reform. Johnson's glee dissipated, the future Prime Minister not quite sure what exactly his senior adviser's big ideas actually were.

Johnson's parting words to the mandarins troubled Sedwill: 'It'll probably end in tears, but I need him now.' So the Cabinet Secretary took the precaution of having an intermediary call with David Bell for advice; based on his time as permanent secretary at Education, how would Bell suggest he handle this wildcard suddenly parachuted into the very apex of the British state? The message came back that Cummings, for all his brilliance, had lacked basic understanding of how government or politics work, and that his reputation as a high priest of hyper-rationality based on his command of data overlooked the simple truth that he was 'emotionally incontinent'. 'It will end in tears,' Bell concluded. 'I just can't tell you when or how.'[24] Not what Sedwill wanted to hear, but he was determined to make it work, somehow.

Necessary Evil: July–December 2019

Cummings needed Johnson to be the front man getting Brexit through Parliament and winning a general election so he could then set to work on his passions for government.

Johnson, very evidently to all, was not the dominant figure from the moment he walked into No. 10 on 24 July. Lurking in the corner as Sedwill greeted the Prime Minister, heavy with unspoken import, was Cummings.

His demonic energy, clarity of vision and willingness to take calculated risks resulted as we saw in Johnson's Brexit deal. 'Dom's biggest contribution was to keep the PM true and committed to the strategy,' says a senior adviser. For many in the building, Cummings was largely responsible for making it the most exciting and satisfying six months of their careers.

Cummings needed now to compensate fast for the weaknesses he saw in Johnson: ignorance of Whitehall and Westminster; lack of interest in and grasp of policy; and an inability independently to apply himself and work hard where there was no immediate threat. For Cummings, they all pointed to one end: him becoming chief strategist by seizing control of the levers of power inside No. 10, levers he only knew second-hand from his time with Gove at Education. It meant him supplanting Eddie Lister, whom he and the ex-City Hall team wanted to play the chief of staff role that James Baker had to Johnson's hero, President Reagan. Senior officials who had done the transition planning with the steady, avuncular Lister had quickly taken to him. Lister was more than discombobulated when he heard Cummings was coming in, and demanded he have equal status. The exact job titles were never precisely defined, Cummings rejecting the chief of staff title both to avoid the greater scrutiny that came with the role and to signal that he was not there for the grand job titles, but to work. A *modus operandi* nevertheless was established: 'Dom agreed to a split where I did Parliament, foreign policy and security and he did domestic policy. We sat facing each other at the table just outside the Prime Minister's study,' Lister says.[25] The split was largely academic. If Cummings became interested in an issue, he would pursue it; if the Prime Minister wished to balance his senior adviser's views on a given issue, he would turn to Lister for advice.

The officials in the Private Office headed by Martin Reynolds and his deputy Stuart Glassborow oversaw the machine, but their advice was not typically sought or valued by Cummings except on matters financial where Cummings, no economist, knew he would be outgunned by the Treasury. Liam Booth-Smith was one of few in Johnson's political team with experience of Whitehall. After heading up the Localis think tank he became a special adviser at the Ministry of Housing, Communities and Local Government where Sunak was a junior minister, a relationship that blossomed into Booth-Smith becoming his chief of staff when Sunak became PM. Apart from Nikki da Costa, James Slack and Sheridan Westlake, the new No. 10 didn't have any insiders from the May years or before, so they had no idea of the legislative agenda or upcoming Whitehall challenges in the immediate short term, such as uprating benefits. Booth-Smith brought these to the team, his capacious and quick intellect appealing to Cummings who later charged him with heading a joint No. 10/Treasury unit. Policy Unit head Mirza was the closest Johnson had to a key figure on domestic policy. Her seriousness about getting things done, if not always her policy priorities (including levelling up), appealed to Cummings, as well as his familiarity with her husband Dougie Smith, who had been a helpful sounding board at Education. The other key members of 'Team Cummings' were Lee Cain on communications, Cleo Watson on operations, and David Frost and Oliver Lewis on the nitty-gritty of Brexit.

Cummings decided for the time being to work with Sedwill. While he did not conceal his disregard for Sedwill's celebrated predecessor Jeremy Heywood ('The elevation of Heywood in the pantheon of SW1 is the elevation of the *courtier-fixer* at the expense of the thinker and the manager,' he wrote in June 2019[26]), nor for May's chief Brexit negotiator Olly Robbins, nor his dislike of the Treasury for not being on board with planning for Brexit, he went out of his way to reassure Sedwill and his fellow senior officials that he did not blame them for the failure after three years to achieve Brexit, but rather the politicians.

The Downing Street/Cabinet Office/Treasury nexus was what Cummings cared about. He had little time for Cabinet ministers and played no part in Johnson's initial ministerial appointments, nor had he any time for Parliament. Gove was the only minister in Johnson's first Cabinet whom he really respected. Though Gove's role was to be much smaller than the wide-ranging Deputy Prime Minister role envisaged in 2016, he was still given a broad brief in 2019: overseeing public service reform, Britain's trading relationships post-Brexit and the future of the judiciary after leaving the EU, which was a particular passion. Cummings regarded him as the Deputy Prime Minister de facto if not de jure, and put great trust in his daily chairing of the key Cabinet committees on Brexit. The First Secretary of State, the austere Raab, he laid rather less store by despite having considered him as a potential alternative to Johnson during the leadership campaign. Politicians were not allies or friends for Cummings, but tools to achieve his ends.

Divisions between Cummings and Johnson bubbled up to the surface less than two months in, when Johnson felt Cummings was pushing him harder on Brexit than he was comfortable with. The dismissal of Sonia Khan, a media adviser to Chancellor Sajid Javid, made front page news at the end of August when she was marched out of Downing Street by an armed policeman. She believes it was a deliberate attempt to humiliate her, and to intimidate others not to leak, the accusation against her being that she had leaked details of a no deal to the media.[27] Her treatment infuriated Javid. 'I caught her red-handed leaking information and I fired her,' Cummings insouciantly texted Javid. 'Totally unacceptable. The way to have dealt with it was to discuss it first with me,' the Chancellor messaged back. The next morning, Javid demanded an audience with Johnson (at which Cummings was present) before the 8.30 a.m. meeting in his study. Javid asserted that Cummings had acted deliberately to humiliate her, with a journalist present to record it, and a police officer on standby to manhandle her out of the building. 'It shows you are completely unfit to be in government,' Javid told him.[28] Cummings listened calmly and responded that he knew she had been leaking and that it was Javid's fault for not knowing what was going on, because he wasn't on top of his job. The two men glared at each other. Johnson, not knowing where to look, but certainly not at either of them, said, 'I can't reinstate her now that she's gone. It's a fait accompli.' Javid left the meeting in no doubt that had Johnson reinstated her, Cummings would have resigned – or at least threatened to – and Johnson was too needy to allow that to happen.

A few days later, on 5 September, a thoroughly disconcerted Johnson turned up more than an hour late to speak at a police training college in West Yorkshire, declaring he would 'rather be dead in a ditch' than agree to extend Brexit, while ducking questions on whether he would resign if it was forced on him. His internal confusion was reflected in him appearing 'dazed, lost and uncertain', his speech full of 'inexplicable pauses'.[29] 'Whenever Boris was panicking, Dom and Lee would tell him "there is no other way through. You'll be the shortest-serving Prime Minister in history unless you do this",' said an aide. A *coup de grâce*, if a mean one, was to remind him that Cameron and Osborne would like nothing more than to see him fail. 'The prospect of those two laughing at him would drive him insane. He'd move from "Oh my God we've got to ease up" to "I'll show those f**kers",' an insider says.

Shouting and expletives quickly reached new levels of acceptance. The F word had been common currency, insiders attest, since

Blair and his spin doctor Alastair Campbell's arrival in 1997; language and shouting deteriorated further under Brown, but improved under Cameron and May. 'What the f**k do you think I'm here for?' Cummings told a Conservative MP at a Downing Street garden party in September who had the temerity to question the threats to deselect any MPs who voted against the government. Cummings 'only does "angry" and "F**cking angry",' said a minister.[30] Johnson's language could be as bad. Critics in the party could be dismissed as 'c**ts' or even 'utter c**ts'. So too was the editor of the *Sunday Times*: 'Emma Tucker is a c**t,' he said when he didn't like a story her paper had run; when the epithet got back to her, he summoned her to apologize in person. 'He would use the C word a lot around Dom and Lee,' says an aide. 'It's what he thought working-class people did. Lee is definitely working-class, and even though Dom wasn't, he came from the North-East, which was working-class enough for Boris.' It all contributed to a male macho culture in No. 10 which some, and not just women, found hostile. Those accustomed to a certain formality in Downing Street found the self-conscious informality and male banter disconcerting.

Until the general election, a lid was kept on Johnson–Cummings divisions. 'I never saw any tension between the Prime Minister and Dominic Cummings in these first six months,' says David Frost.[31] Behind the scenes, though, Cummings was growing increasingly impatient with Johnson, regarding him as a time-specific useful idiot. Others closer to the day-to-day saw the tension grow in the early morning meetings, Cummings pacing the room as aides looked to him rather than the Prime Minister for direction and instruction. Why did Johnson tolerate his highhandedness? Easy: Cummings and Cain continuing to play mercilessly on his fear he would be the shortest-serving Prime Minister of all time, a mark only crossed on 20 November when (unlike his successor Liz Truss) he outlasted the 119 days of George Canning, who had died of illness in 1807. 'For that reason, Johnson was willing to accept directions from Dom because it was clear fate depended upon it,' says an aide.

Divisions over the Landslide, the Agenda and Brexit: January–February 2020

Willing, that is, until he won the general election on 12 December 2019. Johnson regarded it as his personal victory: 'He thought the landslide was a total endorsement of his brilliance personally, not the Conservative Party's victory. He would regularly refer to "my majority" and say "they would be nowhere without me",' an official recalls. Johnson drew on his proven strength as an election winner to validate himself – 2008, 2012, 2016, and now 2019. The last really irritated Cummings, who had set the strategy and seen the research that showed Johnson's personal popularity had been only a minor factor in the result. He worried that, emboldened by the success, the PM might even choose to ignore their secret understanding of July 2019. If anything, Cummings regarded it as *his* victory, confiding to friends, only half in jest, 'I will make the victory speech. The People's Government. I won the fourteen million votes. I'll get rid of the Chancellor.'

The victorious Johnson, no longer politically vulnerable, came to resent his rudeness and domineering manner. Johnson wasn't anywhere close yet, however, to replacing him. 'He gave no other thought to a different way of running No. 10 after the landslide than relying still on Dom almost exclusively. Dom would treat him, if not like Jeeves and Wooster, then perhaps like the Lord Protector with a young and inexperienced king,' says Gove.[32] Cummings was taking nothing for granted. Lord Protectors he knew could easily be ousted, hence his fearful comment 'He won't need us now' to an ally on election night. 'I didn't feel Dom was overjoyed with the victory like the rest of us: part of him seemed annoyed,' says a senior party official.

To Cummings, the clock was ticking. 'My understanding is it was always their agreement Dom would step away as soon as possible to, at the most, think about long-term reform projects,' says Cleo Watson, a close ally of Cummings when in No. 10.[33] Staying on under Johnson's successor maybe? But for the time being he still thought he could manipulate Johnson as readily as he had done before the election – though he was wont to wonder whether he could engineer a successor quite as malleable and as indulgent of his own agenda. But he'd been kingmaker once. Why not a second time?

For now, though, Johnson was the Prime Minister, and Cummings would have to work around him. He wanted No. 10 to be the NASA-style powerhouse again it had been in the first six months, driving change and centralizing policy into his hands. Instead, he found himself in a bowl of syrupy porridge. Johnson and the party managers decided the reshuffle should wait until after Christmas – it would be cruel to cause people upset just before it, thought Johnson. His hesitation to deliver bad news, even at the height of his power, was compounded by fatigue within the building, as an official recalls: 'Everyone was utterly exhausted after the leadership election, Brexit then the general election rolling on one after the other.' 'After general elections,' another says, 'there is normally a huge burst of activity, it is all systems go, roaring ahead. This time, lassitude pervaded the building. It was very noticeable. Nothing was coming from the Prime Minister, who was quite downbeat once the immediate euphoria wore off.'

Johnson felt in desperate need of a holiday, and just after Christmas at Chequers he and Symonds set off for ten days over the New Year to Mustique, paid for by Tory donor David Ross.[34] Johnson, never far from his mobile phone, was receiving a deluge of conflicting advice on the Caribbean island. 'You've done Brexit, you've won the general election. You should now heal the party and command the centre ground,' former comms adviser Will Walden messaged him. 'He could've remodelled his entire premiership like he did as Mayor, bringing in divergent voices and getting rid of the ultras.'[35] Guto Harri was another ex-City Haller texting him to say: 'You've got to get rid of Cummings.'[36] But he didn't do it. 'The PM came back not in a great mood,' says an aide. Questions being asked about the holiday, and how exactly it was paid for, irked him.

Irked doesn't begin to describe the exasperation Cummings felt at the 'wait, wait, wait' philosophy. He was deeply suspicious of the stench of post-landslide hubris he detected emanating out of Johnson's study. 'There was no take-off after the general election because from mid-December to the end of January, it was all self-congratulation,' recalls Gavin Williamson. 'There was no "first 100 days" document as in July 2019, even after it became clear the general election would be won comfortably.'[37] To Cummings, it was incomprehensible. 'This was the very moment to spend physical capital and do unpopular things now,' says a senior Cabinet Office official. But all Cummings got back was 'torpor, torpor, torpor'. While for Cummings the work was only just starting, for Johnson, he suspected it was all but over. This was not of course entirely to Cummings' displeasure: while he would have ideally liked a Prime Minister committed to his ideas and eager to achieve them, the next best thing was a detached Prime Minister who would let him rule the roost. One official recalls Cummings being eager to keep Johnson out of No. 10 at the start of 2020, repeatedly suggesting that he could work from Chequers instead.

'Get Brexit done, then ARPA', was Cummings' WhatsApp profile status. He barely contributed to policy discussions at the long-awaited January away day at Chequers – Mirza's show primarily – talking about the 'Johnson project' over the following ten years. Her aims, focusing on levelling up social care and skills, weren't his first priorities, nor was the forensic work on which her Policy Unit team was engaged, itemizing and costing some 500 manifesto commitments.

Cummings had his vision, and it wasn't the same as Johnson's. Nor was it Mirza's. Nor was it Frost's. And it certainly wasn't the same as the Chancellor's. 'It seemed to us at the time that they all had a coherent view and a unity brought about by Brexit,' says an official. 'But from this vantage point, it might have been a chimera.' 'Science and technology funding, defence procurement, civil service reform, data, supply side reform, deregulate planning and ARPA, that is what Dom now cared about,' says Gove. 'The PM had an impressionistic view of what Dom was talking about, a romantic notion about Cornwall becoming the UK's Cape Canaveral, revolving satellites and all that stuff.'[38] This was Cummings' vision for post-Brexit Britain, but Johnson didn't read up or engage with it. His wasn't even a British but an English vision: Cummings cared no more for Scotland or Wales than we've seen he did for Northern Ireland.

Strategic narrowing to ensure mission success wasn't part of his *modus operandi*: his field of interest remained vast, despite help being so limited and his own time horizon in government so short.

Science and intelligence continued to be his deepest passions, and he was rigorously seeking evidence to probe lazy assumptions. Aspects of defence intrigued him: his intellectual input and support were essential to the Integrated Review of security, defence, development and foreign policy published in March 2021.[39] John Bew, who led the process, marvelled at his zest. Defence modernization, research and development (R&D) spending, artificial intelligence (AI), unmanned weapons and Project Solarium thinking (Eisenhower's US strategic planning programme in the Cold War) were utterly intriguing to him. So too was intelligence, and he pushed for more spending for the agencies. 'He wanted MI6 to be much more risk-taking and insert itself in new directions, with some quite wild thinking,' an official reflects. The system pushed back in mid-2020 when he tried to insert his own candidate, supportive of his agenda, as head of MI6 to replace retiring Alex Younger, who'd been close to Johnson personally. The intelligence community equally, seeing Cummings as an ally, was not above playing him: 'Everybody was very nervous about giving him anything secret at all because nobody trusted him. Because he was so in love with the intelligence world he was easy meat, and we were able to use him to fight for extra money and better terms,' one says. Another concurs: 'Because he was untrustworthy it was therefore very difficult to let him know about very sensitive personal and security material. The fear always was that Dom would use it as collateral. Ken McCallum [director general of MI5] was very good at making Dom feel in the know without actually making him in the know.'

Johnson hadn't a clue what Cummings was up to most of the time. 'Let's not kid ourselves. Dom briefed endlessly and had a huge ego, always thought he should be the PM and was telling everyone Boris was just his vessel,' says one Johnson loyalist, 'but that is just insulting, and has no recognition of the qualities Boris had nor why the British public so liked him.' 'After the election Boris no longer wanted to be treated as a tempestuous thoroughbred, with a strong whip and bridle to keep him in order. Dom could be insulting and rude; some days the Prime Minister could laugh it off, but other days he didn't,' says Gove.[40] Carrie Symonds was growing resentful too of the man she had once lobbied to come in, and was antagonized by his barely concealed contempt for her partner. Cummings' allies believed in turn she was constantly whispering in Johnson's ear that he 'didn't need Dom now'.

Tension grew when it became obvious to everyone in the building that Team Cummings had no respect for Johnson's 'legacy' projects. They found his desperate search for personal projects risible and contemptible. 'Lacking an agenda of his own, he alighted on Net Zero despite knowing nothing about it, the Scotland–Northern Ireland bridge, nonsense, COP26 as his "green Olympics", the "Festival of Brexit", the Commonwealth Games,' says one Cummings supporter. Another believes 'he was always desperate to relive the glory days of the Olympic Games, with him taking the applause'. Cummings had no time for any of this nonsense. He saw Johnson's infrastructure projects as 'massive white elephants' and he bitterly resented Johnson getting his way on HS2, another marker in their deteriorating relationship.

The Brexit-night party in No. 10 on 31 January 2020 – the date that Brexit officially came into effect – saw the jealousy burst through to the surface. Earlier that day, Johnson had taken the Cabinet to Sunderland, viewed as 'Brexit central' because it had been the first to declare its result in the referendum, to mark Britain's last full day in the European Union. Cummings took a dim view of this vanity parade and the focus on Johnson himself, and was not placated when, at the party in No. 10 that evening, Johnson credited him with devising the two resounding slogans, 'Take Back Control' and 'Get Brexit Done'. The raucous excitement in No. 10 contrasted with the sober evening in October 1971 when Parliament voted to enter the EU, and Prime Minister Ted Heath sat at his clavichord and played Bach. Johnson's chosen musical instrument was a gong, and as he ushered in the countdown to 11 p.m. (midnight EU time) he hammered it with wild abandon to mimic Big Ben, silenced for repair work. 'A fantastic moment in the life of our country,' he proclaimed prosaically. Something told him he was not the figure who the party attenders yearned to hear. But when the man they did want came to the microphone, he was unable to speak. 'Dom was so overcome with emotion. So much of his life had been invested in this project,' recalls Frost.[41] Taking a full minute to compose himself, head in his hands as supportive shouts echoed around the room, Cummings could muster just one sentence about the culmination of his life's work. 'Lots of people in this room know what happened, thank you.'

Cummings, Frost, Gove and Mirza, and even Johnson by the end, were united in their belief that Brexit was the right thing to do. But what was Brexit *for*? Frost had ideas about creating a bustling free-market Thatcherite economy, a Singapore-on-Thames. To Mirza, it was more about higher tax opportunities to support the Red Wall with high spending, and new possibilities in justice. To Cummings, an opportunity to push the UK's comparative advantage in technology and innovation, and to reinvent the state. For Gove, it was about maximizing opportunities outside the EU for British sovereignty without stripping away safeguards and regulations. Johnson, coming to the cause late in the day, seized on Brexit as the portmanteau chance to rebuild the British state and economy, and rethink its position in the world. 'What became increasingly clear to us throughout 2020/21,' an official says with devastating accuracy, 'was a total lack of agreement about what they wanted to see post-Brexit.'

Cummings couldn't wait for Johnson to decide. He wanted to focus on what needed to be done now. First, a reshuffle to place the Cabinet ministers he wanted into the key posts. Delayed initially because of Christmas, it was postponed again for the machinery of government changes he'd been working on with Sedwill. 'Let's rub all the names off the whiteboard and put in people purely on the basis of ability,' Johnson was told by Cummings and Cain. Gove was earmarked as Home Secretary, Sunak as Chancellor, and Patel and Truss were to be demoted. 'While we needed a Brexit Cabinet in July 2019, this was now the moment to appoint the very best to the key positions,' they said. Johnson harrumphed. Of course he knew his Cabinet was mediocre, and far too right-wing for his taste, but he hated reshuffles – the anxiety, the animosity, the agony of choice. No manager himself, he hadn't a clue who would be good performers in different departments. Dodging a root-and-branch reshuffle after the election to power Brexit and government policy forward was a massive lost opportunity. But Cummings was never seriously a fan – it would have created too many rivals – officials recalling Cummings' keen support of the delay. Neither did Johnson ever have it in him as Prime Minister to understand what Cabinet ministers did, and why he needed to pick and back the very best to make it a successful government.

War on the Chancellor: February 2020

Cummings set his sights instead on the more limited objective of finally getting rid of Javid, and building a smaller and more pliable reshuffle around that. For a mere aide to the Prime Minister to unseat a Chancellor of the Exchequer, especially so soon into post, is a very big deal. Not accomplishing his dream team in 2016 with Gove at the Treasury had gnawed away at him. The historic tensions between No. 10 and the Treasury had to end, he decided in his mind. He'd played no part in Javid's appointment in July 2019 and never accepted his legitimacy. His written understanding with Johnson stated very clearly, much like Brown and Blair in 1994, that he would be overseeing domestic policy. Sonia Khan's dismissal in August revealed how poisonous the relationship with Javid was from the off.

Javid, as George Osborne says, 'made a real effort to become a partner to Boris, to have a similarly close relationship to the one I enjoyed with David Cameron'.[42] Javid himself agrees. 'He absolutely hated the relationship between me and Boris, because he felt it undermined his own authority, so very early on concluded that he couldn't countenance continuing with an independent-minded Chancellor.'[43] In early December, Boris and Carrie were filmed dancing at Javid's exclusive fiftieth birthday party. It riled Cummings as did the fact that both men lived next door to each other in Downing Street, and talked directly at weekends without him being there. Javid's warm friendship with Symonds helped secure him the job; having the continued support of the Prime Minister's partner, to Cummings' chagrin, similarly strengthened his position.

Rows between Cummings and Javid followed in quick succession. In the week before Christmas, the Chancellor presented Johnson with a nineteen-page memorandum titled 'Delivering on Levelling Up', which looked at the investment required to turn his signature policy into reality. Cummings was aghast at this activism from the Chancellor, which he considered impinged on his turf. Tempers also flared over the appointment of Andrew Bailey as Mark Carney's successor as Governor of the Bank of England. Javid had interviewed candidates before the general election and had decided who he liked, which, as convention required, had to be agreed by the Prime Minister himself, who could veto the Chancellor's choice. Cummings, though, had his own candidate, the Bank's chief economist, Andy Haldane, whom he thought far more intellectually capable and able to inject the Bank with some fresh thinking. Haldane had not applied for the role, but this did not stop Cummings from pushing his man. Javid had no time for this and requested a meeting with Johnson to finalize the selection alone, bar officials minuting it. When Cummings insisted on being present, Javid protested on the grounds that the meeting was to discuss market sensitive information, and he didn't trust him not to leak. Cummings lost out, and the bilateral went ahead, Johnson readily signing off Javid's first choice: 'Absolutely fine, you are the Chancellor.' Cummings was incandescent and shouted down the line to Javid's chief of staff, Matt Pearson, 'I'll get my own back.' Andrew Bailey's appointment as the new Governor was duly announced on 20 December 2019, but Javid was a marked man, and so were his staff.

Relations between No. 10 and No. 11 had become toxic – but, unlike twenty years before with Blair and Brown, it was not the principals who were warring. Rather, the rivalry was between the Chancellor and the chief aide. Cummings decided to turn up the heat, his ire directed against Javid's special advisers, who he thought were plotting against both Johnson and him, and who he proclaimed were incompetent at handling economic policy. 'Saj was really struggling to take command of the brief. Most of his political team appeared more interested in how they could get the Chancellor on the front page than working out any sort of economic strategy,' says a Cummings supporter.

He became dismissive too about Javid's Treasury officials, whom he didn't trust over Brexit, and for their parsimony. Javid in contrast thought highly of his Treasury team. He had worked closely with its senior official Tom Scholar on the emergency no deal Budget at the end of 2019, which in the end was shelved when overtaken by the general election, and on planning for the Budget due on 11 March. He encountered none of the Treasury's alleged hostility to Brexit, nor evidence of resistance to the will of the government. Word came that Scholar was on Cummings' hit list, and he had sounded out Treasury Chief Economic Adviser Clare Lombardelli as the replacement. 'Over my dead body', was Javid's livid response at the intrusion on his turf. Javid was also tensing himself to repel Cummings' nascent aspirations to split the Treasury, though no precise plans had yet been put forward. 'It wasn't something I would have supported,' Javid says.[44]

By January, he had come to regard Cummings as a danger to the government, and to Johnson personally, and made no secret that he wanted him dismissed immediately after Britain left the EU on 31 January. He had form on unseating the PM's special advisers, demanding that May sack her two key aides, Nick Timothy and Fiona Hill, immediately after the general election in 2017. 'The tension between No. 10 and No. 11 became even more noxious when it became clear Sajid was trying to get rid of Dom. He wanted a Chancellor to make the Treasury more imaginative, a less fiscally conservative Chancellor and one more in tune with the government's [i.e. his] programme,' says an official. Symonds intervened and flatly refused to let Javid be sacked. Tension intensified when discussions opened in earnest on the Budget planned for March. Cummings demanded Javid find money to spend, while he insisted on sticking to the fiscal rules. 'No. 10 believed Javid's team was positioning him in the press as an alternative leader to Johnson,' says Chief Whip Mark Spencer.[45] The HS2 debate was the final straw. Javid insists his stance was consistently positive, but it appeared otherwise to Team Cummings. 'Saj tried to get ahead of the PM by second-guessing him, then changing his position. With the Budget fast approaching, we had to act,' says a Cummings ally.

How to devise a plan to chop out the Chancellor with a Prime Minister flatly refusing to let it happen? Cutting him off at the legs was the answer by telling him that all his special advisers would have to resign, to be replaced by a 'Joint Economic Unit'. 'It was clear that no Chancellor could go back to Treasury and announce he's lost all his special advisers: it would be too big a loss of face,' says an official. Many around the Prime Minister saw what was about to unfold, but not the man himself. 'No one would give up such a big job for something so small,' he told aides.

The Chancellor was summoned to a meeting in the Cabinet Room on 13 February, Cummings absenting himself as his presence would have been too incendiary. The meeting opened cordially enough: 'Saj, you're doing a great job, I love what you're doing, I want you to go on.' Javid didn't know what was coming next, but had a sense that Johnson had a faux joviality and was reading his lines from a script. 'I want No. 10 and No. 11 to work together, with joint special advisers in a team. What I'd like you to do is for you and Dom to pick the special advisers together.' Javid had not expected Johnson to deliver what was sounding suspiciously like an ultimatum. He was shocked. Johnson proceeded to read out a list which included Booth-Smith, suggesting strongly to him that the selection had already been made, and that Cummings was going to be insisting on his own people.

'What will happen to my six special advisers?' Javid asked.

'They'll all have to go I'm afraid, Saj.'

'But they've all been working loyally for the party. They're all good people.'

'Ah.'

'I'm not at all happy.'

Johnson persisted. 'I want you to do this. Please agree to it. Dom will work with you, I know he will.'

Javid was reeling, trying to take it all in.

'Saj, look, your advisers, they're just people.' Johnson's words shocked Javid to the core. 'Just people'? He couldn't believe what he was hearing. Now he was indignant.

'No, they're not, they are *our* people.'

There followed what embarrassed observers, eyes firmly fixed on the carpet, described as 'a mighty row'.

'If this is what you want, I will resign,' Javid told Johnson.

'Come on, Saj, I need to do this with you,' Johnson pleaded. When he saw the Chancellor wouldn't budge, Johnson asked, 'Can I have time out?' Javid went into the side room. First Lister came in and spoke to him, then Helen MacNamara, who had worked for him as an official. 'Dom has the PM by the balls. Just agree to it and he will soon be gone', was the gist of what he heard. For half an hour, they tried hard to persuade him that a middle way could be found and the options weren't simply accept or resign – to no avail.

No. 10 was in meltdown. When Johnson appeared to have second thoughts on dismissing Javid's advisers, it was Cain who stepped in and threatened to resign. 'God, not you, Commissar, I can't do it without you,' Johnson said, now in an almighty fix. Risk losing Cain and possibly Cummings, or lose his Chancellor? He opted to make one last attempt on Javid, who was asked to join him in the Prime Minister's study.

Javid shot straight at him. 'You don't see what's happening, do you? Cummings is running rings around you. He's running your government.'

'That's absurd. I am in charge. It's just not true. You can't say that,' countered Johnson.

'He [Cummings] will not be content until he burns the house down.'

'Please say, Saj, that you'll accept it.'

'But you've already made up your mind. I'm not accepting it.'

It was clear to Javid that there was not going to be a resolution and equally obvious that Johnson dare not fire his Chancellor: 'He didn't have it in him to do it,' he recalls. So he took the matter into his own hands and walked out to tell waiting cameras that he had been asked to replace all his political advisers, saying, 'I do not believe any self-respecting minister would accept the conditions.' His resignation letter fired a number of parting shots directly at Cummings.

No Prime Minister since 1945 had lost a Chancellor to a dispute so quickly. The profound turbulence that it would have unleashed was mitigated only because of the pandemic that began just days later. The evening of his resignation, Johnson called him, saying, 'Look, Saj, I can't believe that it happened.' He apologized and told him that he would like to see him return to government: 'We will have you back, Saj.'

Did Cummings lull Johnson into believing that Javid would not quit? Many present in the building believe Johnson was shocked and surprised by his resigning, with one official reflecting that the Prime Minister had crucially misread the situation: 'The PM did not always understand human feelings, so didn't anticipate that Saj's pride would never let him walk away from the humiliation.' Cummings later claimed that he deliberately 'tricked' Johnson into sacking Javid.[46] Cummings makes many claims; sometimes they are true. On this occasion, though, it suited Johnson to feign ignorance. He rid himself of a Chancellor whose wholehearted support for his agenda he increasingly doubted, he avoided a difficult confrontation with his senior adviser, and he directed the blame for a decision his partner would otherwise have railed against away from himself and towards Cummings. 'The PM absolutely knew that Dom forcing Javid's staff out would make him walk,' says one Cummings ally, 'but he wanted to make Dom the lightning rod so he could say to Carrie: "I didn't sack him, he resigned all because of Dom!"'

Any attempt to completely absolve himself from his partner's ire was not a total success, however; he received what one official describes as 'a clattering from Carrie later that evening'. To appease her Johnson offered a junior ministerial post in the Department for Digital, Culture, Media and Sport to her former boss, John Whittingdale, reshuffling Johnson ally Nigel Adams to the Foreign Office, a worry to moderates because he was better known for his acute tribalism than for his intellect or polish. The brazen horse-trading was shocking, even for seasoned officials, the first of many such moments.

Who then to succeed Javid? Enter Rishi Sunak, who'd impressed Cummings as Chief Secretary to the Treasury in the 2019 Autumn

Statement ('Dom thought him smart, competent, didn't leak, no fuss,' says a political aide). The choice belonged 100 per cent to Cummings: 'He thought he would own him, and he would underwrite his plans on R&D spending and to back ARPA.' Most immediately, it brought one step closer his dream of No. 10 and the Treasury working as a single unit, and rewriting the fissiparous history between both. Cummings' belief was that he could control the Treasury not by owning the machine (the Treasury was too large a beast for the small No. 10 to tame) but by installing his own people at its head and enabling closer personal collaboration, integrating the Treasury's financial considerations into No. 10 decisions and No. 10's political considerations into the Treasury. The key figure was Liam Booth-Smith, who went straight across from No. 10 to work for Sunak; aligned with Cummings, the change improved relations overnight, bearing fruit in the harmonious March 2020 Budget. It was reminiscent of the relationship between Osborne, Cameron and Osborne's senior aide Rupert Harrison, with Harrison and Booth-Smith both regularly attending the respective No. 10 morning meetings and feeding into decisions from the Treasury and Chancellor's perspective.[47]

For a while, coordination between No. 10 and No. 11, if not the utility of the joint unit, worked as Cummings envisaged. 'We were surprised when we heard about a joint unit,' says a senior Treasury official, 'but in no time, we had comfortably absorbed it'. What Cummings didn't envisage, but a better student of history would have known, was that once in the saddle the Chancellor soon wanted to be his own man and had absolutely no intention of being Cummings' (or the PM's) man. It took very little time for Johnson to work out that the switch of Chancellor was not to his benefit. With Booth-Smith now working for Sunak, as was Douglas McNeill, he had no political economics aides left in No. 10. He didn't understand economics and was worried that Sunak was running circles around him – as indeed he soon was. Economics was not a particular strength of Mirza any more than of Cummings. And Johnson had furthered his economic isolation by wilfully choosing a principal private secretary in Reynolds who was not ex-Treasury and could not compensate for Sedwill's lack of experience of domestic affairs. For economic and fiscal advice, he had to lean heavily on his deputy PPS, Stuart Glassborow, but a single official – and one Cummings was eager to get rid of – could not act as a complete counterweight for No. 10 against the Treasury machine. 'I want Liam back,' he soon started saying. But Booth-Smith, who found Sunak a far more competent and impressive boss than Johnson, was going nowhere, so the Prime Minister cast a fly over figures such as long-serving MP John Redwood and pro-Brexit economist Gerard Lyons, to no avail. Johnson hated the praise that Sunak was getting, which started with the Budget, the *Daily Mail* describing him as 'PM in waiting'.[48] Under Sunak, the Treasury became stronger and more independent than it had ever been under Javid.

Javid's departure aside, the 13 February reshuffle paled into insignificance compared to the hype that up to a third of the Cabinet would be dismissed, Whitehall departments abolished and civil servants replaced by special advisers. Other sackings included Julian Smith as Northern Ireland Secretary for the more biddable Brandon Lewis, and Geoffrey Cox as Attorney General replaced by the more aligned Suella Braverman.

War on Special Advisers and Media: January–March 2020

Shaking up special advisers so they became a cadre of centralized revolutionaries committed to Cummings and the project came next. Whitehall had singularly failed to attract divergent thinkers of the kind he needed, and he would correct it. In January he famously advertised for 'weirdos and misfits with odd skills' to apply for jobs in No. 10 as special advisers or officials with 'deep expertise in specific fields' such as data science and economics. 'Public School bluffers' were told not to bother in an attempt to overhaul the government's usual tendency to hire PPE generalists. The regime would be tough: it will 'frankly be hard having a boy/girlfriend at all'.[49] James Phillips was one such recruit who remained with great success in post till 2022 to see ARPA established in the form of the Advanced Research and Invention Agency (ARIA). Andrew Sabisky was not so successful: within just a few days of joining he had picked a spectacular row with Defence Secretary Ben Wallace, and after online comments about eugenics and race came to light was promptly forced to resign.[50] Cummings suspected Wallace of leaking and briefing as No. 10 took increasing control of their turf in producing the Integrated Review.

Cummings' stance entailed weeding out 'duffs'. Three days after the dismissal of Javid, two No. 10 Policy Unit staff, Christopher Brannigan and Elliot Roy, were sacked. The evening before, a special adviser at Defence had stood up to Cummings at his weekly meeting in No. 10 demanding he show them more respect – the week before he had humiliated young aides to Theresa Villiers and Andrea Leadsom. Cummings exacted his revenge by helping ensure that both Cabinet ministers, and with them their special advisers, were sacked in the reshuffle on 13 February. While Cummings' intellectual spark and ideas had many admirers, his *modus operandi* did not. 'His Friday meetings, famous for being held late to keep people at work, were extraordinary: totally egocentric, just Dom on transmit or ranting, no opportunities for questions, no uplifting message, no empathy: just total self-absorption', was the view of one regular. 'He had no empathy. He wanted to shape and centralize special advisers, and many were inspired, or cowed, but he would be so rude and offensive,' says another.

Changing the media approach so it focused less on the day to day and more on long-term plans was another core Cummings and Cain aspiration. 'Dom hated the way that Prime Ministers constantly responded to the twenty-four-hour news cycle. He wanted the morning meetings to lead with strategy and finish with media issues,' says a senior adviser. 'We're going to f**k the rules governing the lobby and politics and rewrite them', was their stated intention. 'Alastair Campbell could've walked in here and noticed no change in twenty years. The focus was still on print and lobby briefings. It was a time-warp,' says one of Cummings' team. Terminating the convention whereby the Prime Minister visited distressed areas would put down a marker, they thought. So when the Welsh Borders and the Pennines suffered floods in February 2020, Johnson remained resolutely in London. 'Don't you think I ought to go?' he asked plaintively. 'No. It's Westminster bulls**t. They can f**k off', came the blunt response according to one present during the discussions. Fresh in their minds was a visit he had made to flood-hit Derbyshire in November 2019 when he'd been mocked for mopping up water in a flooded shop in Matlock. Pressure mounted with Corbyn, in a late flourish in his last weeks as Labour leader, attacking the ('part-time') Prime Minister for desertion of duty, until he eventually had to relent.

'Divide and rule' was another tactic for dealing with the lobby, influenced by the tactics of Campbell, based on the idea that No. 10 possessed the gold for which all political journalists yearned, but they could only receive pieces of it if they behaved. Cummings loved playing the media and had his favourite journalists, Robert Peston of ITV News, Tim Shipman of the *Sunday Times* (till they had a bust-up), Simon Walters of the *Daily Mail* and above all Laura Kuenssberg of the BBC (he would instruct colleagues to focus primarily on BBC headlines, saying three-quarters of the media consumed on any given day is via the BBC). Likewise, Cain felt a frisson in creating divisions within the lobby, excluding journalists from unfriendly publications from government briefings.[51] 'They wanted to have a proper system of open lobbying that would put the fourth estate in their place,' says one ally.

Divide and rule proved no more tenable than for Campbell two decades before. So Cain came up with a plan of a new 'Prime Minister's spokesperson', akin to the press secretary at the White House, who would give public briefings. The on-camera briefings during the 2019 election planted the idea, which were reinforced by the daily Covid conferences. The television briefings during the pandemic reaching peak viewership of millions cemented the idea of directly appealing to the nation, bypassing journalists and conveying the government's message directly to voters. They knew Johnson would be shown up, and his time sapped by preparation, if he himself stood at the lectern; but the later row over the choice of external spokesperson was to precipitate both Cummings' and Cain's departures.

The model of government in the US, a country Cummings admired, was also an influence behind his wish to terminate the 285-year-old (if punctuated) practice since Robert Walpole took up residence in 1735 of the incumbent working at No. 10: 'Dom thought the ramshackle building a rabbit warren and very bad for delivery, just hopeless as a government headquarters,' says an ally. His aim was to create a modern 'department for the PM' by shifting Johnson into the Cabinet Secretary's much larger room, and for all key personnel including the Policy Unit to move into capacious state-of-the-art rooms close by, as in the West Wing of the White House. It was a reasonable solution to the chronic problem of No. 10, but apart from the Policy and some other units temporarily moving in the summer, the plan faltered. It was in part a victim of Covid, but would likely have failed regardless. The resistance of those – including the Prime Minister – to departing from the institutional inertia and iconography of 10 Downing Street was significant, particularly among those who worried they might lose their proximity to power. Many believe that the plans were more valued by Cummings for their ability to strike fear into those in the building than any potential for improving government. 'If he had actually wanted a PM's department it would have happened, but he didn't really want to follow through. Dom liked discombobulating people, and it sent absolutely everyone into panic about where they would sit,' says one official. Why was this man allowed to pursue such unevidenced schemes and a style of personnel management known to be conducive of poor performance on a mere whim? Johnson above all must take the blame for licensing his idiosyncratic sidekick.

The most radical reform to the civil service in the public sector since the Fulton Report of 1968 was the ultimate aim of Cummings' agenda, a worthy aim and long overdue. 'His DfE experience had really scarred him with the inefficiency of Whitehall bureaucracy, computers not working, the system moving so slowly, promotion of safe mediocrities: he wanted to break things to free up processes,' says a senior No. 10 adviser. With his great machinery of government changes on ice, Cummings turned his revolutionary zeal to executions, in the belief that stronger and abler individuals would step into their shoes. 'People, ideas, machines – in that order', was Cummings' mantra, a quote borrowed from his hero, the Pentagon's Colonel John Boyd at the height of his influence in the Cold War.[52] Ten permanent secretaries were dismissed or moved on, a rate of politically engineered change never seen before with Britain's tradition of a politically impartial civil service.

War on the Cabinet Secretary (December 2019–July 2020)

Cummings' most-prized scalp was the biggest chief in the tribe, Cabinet Secretary Mark Sedwill. The relative harmony of the first six months between Cummings and Sedwill (prorogation being an exception) began to break down soon after the general election. In this new world, Sedwill was no longer doing the job that Cummings thought the Cabinet Secretary should be doing. 'I know you want to manage the Prime Minister to do the job *you* want,' Cummings revealingly told him, 'but I want to manage him to *make the change we need*.'

Though the prorogation saga had already strained their relationship, any hopes of a reset following the election were soon dashed by a bust-up over the pre-Christmas appointment of Melanie Dawes (previously permanent secretary at the Ministry for Housing, Communities and Local Government) as chief executive of Ofcom, the broadcasting regulator. Dawes was highly rated within the civil service, and Sedwill thought it a good appointment providing continuity with the previous head, Sharon White, another ex-civil service talent. It was a view with which the Prime Minister concurred. Cummings, however, didn't rate her, seeing her as too much of an establishment figure, and opposed the appointment in a blazing row with the Cabinet Secretary.

Irreparable damage was done in two other rows between them over how to respond to the 31 December 2019 attack on the US embassy in Baghdad and the 11 March 2020 attacks on Coalition Forces at Iraq's Camp Taji. Cummings was much more isolationist in how he thought Britain should respond, Sedwill much more eager to align with the US if retaliation was pursued; both thought it was their area of authority. Defence and security were Sedwill's areas of expertise, and he believed that it was his job to reach agreement on such a question directly with the Prime Minister, not with his adviser. In the first meeting they clashed over authority: 'Both Mark and Dom thought they were in charge of the [31 December] meeting, simultaneously trying to lead it,' says an official present. Sedwill wanted the Prime Minister to take any decision in a structured, controlled way, listening carefully to a wide range of advice. Cummings thought it a self-indulgent distraction and wished to go away and take an ad hoc decision rather than wasting time on frivolous foreign affairs decisions.

During the second row they clashed over policy. Other officials involved in the decision believed Cummings was coming at the issue 'from no basis of knowledge. He kept saying "we need more evidence" as a tactic to put the bar for any intervention so high that no decision could be made,' one recalls. President Trump eventually decided not to proceed with military action in March, to the further chagrin of Johnson's chief adviser. It highlighted Cummings' dislike of Sedwill combining his job of Cabinet Secretary with national security adviser. 'The disagreement was over substance *and* process. There could be no rolling back from it,' says another senior official.

It was Covid, though, that broke them apart. Sedwill became concerned that Cummings wanted to present a single view of how to proceed to Johnson as a *fait accompli*, and insisted he listen to diverse opinions. From as early as April, Sedwill thought he was a 'marked man'. Cummings couldn't brook others having influence on Johnson. The most serious clash came over Sedwill's streamlining the Covid response under the four different strands of health, economics, international and public services. 'Total f**king nonsense', was Cummings' view. He thought the Cabinet Office was out of control, there were too many overlapping meetings and a total lack of clarity. Gove and he wanted it replaced with the Covid Task Force. Bitter rows ensued, including who should oversee it. Cummings became so frustrated he used it as a lightning rod for when Johnson returned from hospital to get rid of Sedwill. 'You have got to get rid of him,' Cummings told Johnson, according to one minister who later heard accounts of the conversation from both Cummings and Johnson.

'Who are you to tell me that? He's a good guy.'

'You have still got to sack him, we need someone better.'

'I'm not going to do it.'

Cummings saw he couldn't knock Sedwill out yet, but continued to chip away at his authority, including the May 2020 addition of Simon Case to lead the response on Covid as permanent secretary at No. 10. Cummings kept the pressure on him until Sedwill finally had enough. Britain was on the path to recovery, and it was announced in June that he would depart in September. Sedwill had jumped before he was pushed. 'Everyone knew that it was a dismissal. It had a very sobering effect,' says one official.

If Sedwill wasn't safe from the wrath of Johnson's chief adviser, who was?[53]

Cummings urged Simon Case to take the role. Case's doctorate had been supervised by legendary contemporary historian Peter Hennessy, who once described him to an official as 'the most intellectually able student I've ever recognized'. Cummings saw in him an intelligence capable of handling the Prime Minister, but one without the seniority which would impinge upon his own authority. Cummings thought that, like Sunak, Case would be more amenable to his agenda. As with Sunak, Cummings was to be disappointed – Case proved adept at navigating the divide between Prime Minister and his senior adviser. And as with Javid, Johnson was to have regrets. 'I should never have let Mark go,' Johnson was heard to say on several occasions. Cummings was now responsible for Johnson losing his two most powerful figures: the Chancellor and the Cabinet Secretary.

Cummings' strategies harked back to his DfE days. He wasn't interested in democracy: he was interested in change. Party politics bored him, and he thought Conservative MPs stupid or boring, or both. Keeping Johnson away from MPs, not least because of Cummings' fear that he would say stupid things, was an article of faith. The fact the Prime Minister owed his position solely to the support of MPs no longer troubled him now they had such a large majority. Graham Brady, chair of the 1922 Committee, was a particular irritation. Cummings so mistrusted Johnson with him that he forbade Johnson seeing Brady alone. Inevitably, perhaps, the injunction leaked. 'It was a very odd insight into the mentality of No. 10 and resulted in a grovelling phone call apology,' says Brady. 'Cummings had contempt for our MPs, and thought that we should be grateful for being in government, for the general election result, and that our job was now merely to behave.'[54] Cummings had no time for Parliament, almost never visited it, and thought Cabinet a waste of time too. 'Symbolically he refused to attend Cabinet as a symbol of his disdain for the institution. He governed round rather than through Cabinet,' says an official.

Civil War: April–May 2020

By the time Johnson returned to work after hospitalization from Covid, if not before, Cummings was adopting the voice of the Prime Minister brazenly. Civil servants began to talk openly about what they termed 'Potemkin Government', with the system no longer knowing who was running the country. 'It would have been perfectly acceptable had Cummings gone into the PM's study, talked to him, and come out and said "the PM wants". But he began giving instructions in the name of the PM with no cover for the PM,' says an official. 'Don't tell the PM', was a regular Cummings utterance to staff, or 'Oh, don't bother him with this'. Limiting the flow of unnecessary information to the Prime Minister is a core task of the Prime Minister's most senior adviser, but Johnson's reluctance to seek out additional papers meant there was no counterbalance to Cummings' view of what mattered, which did not necessarily chime with the Prime Minister's. 'The concept of the Prime Minister's box became completely opaque,' says another official. 'Dom would take things out and block papers getting to him, either overtly or covertly.'

It was a struggle not just for officials, but ministers too. One Cabinet minister recalls, 'He would increasingly take Johnson's name in vain, talking with a level of precision that Whitehall knew was not authentic because that was not how the PM's mind worked. Cummings would say that Boris wanted a certain bill to include X, Y and Z when everyone knew that the Prime Minister hadn't a clue about this level of detail.' Even the most domineering predecessors in the role, including Nick Timothy and Fiona Hill, had been careful not to overstep and invoke the Prime Minister where a proposal could be against their wishes. Ministerial private offices across Whitehall would receive messages from No. 10 which they knew, implicitly or explicitly, came from Cummings. Some Cabinet ministers hitched their wagons to the Cummings star, knowing that, 'with a semi-detached Prime Minister, his impetus was essential to drive things through Whitehall and Parliament'. One such was Housing Secretary Robert Jenrick, who worked with him to liberalize planning reform, an impetus that slowed down after he left.

Within No. 10 during much of 2020, some third of the political staff would report to Cummings, a third (above all communications) to Cain, and a final third, including Mirza, direct to Johnson through his Private Office. But as a senior adviser says, 'This last group realized that the PM would say anything to them and there would be no follow through, nothing happened.' An official comments, 'It was desperately worrying, because he would say three different things on the same day to three different sets of people, and then deny that he had changed his mind or that the positions were mutually contradictory.' Another says, 'The PM's wishes were no longer holding, because everyone knew he would change his mind.' Those close to Johnson noticed him becoming increasingly troubled by being bypassed. '"I am meant to be in control. I am the *Führer*. I'm the king who takes the decisions," he would say in frustration. It was totally dysfunctional,' says a special adviser. Martin Reynolds, heading his Private Office, found it impossible to impose order over Johnson's unruly 'divide and rule' court politics.

For the most creatively dysfunctional relationship in modern politics as that between Johnson and Cummings finally to break up, with the bond of mutual need still so powerfully strong, required a conflict so public and so explosive that there could be no way back.

Would their relationship have gone wrong so quickly without Covid? It was an event of such immense importance on which they had such fundamentally differing views about the gravity, the process and the solution. It exposed Johnson's weaknesses in a brutal fashion. 'Covid broke the relationship. Dom always thought Boris very limited, but Covid made him conclude that he was an idiot,' says a Cummings ally. The intense focus by Cummings on pushing for early lockdown, on rapid testing and on vaccines meant, to his frustration, he no longer had time to drive his other pet projects, ARIA being the exception. Johnson equally, to Cummings' intense irritation, pulled back on his support for his projects.

But he didn't pull back from supporting Cummings over the Barnard Castle escapade in May. Cummings' wife Mary Wakefield had contracted Covid on 27 March, the same day as the Prime Minister, and Cummings knew he was likely to be infected shortly after. Concerned for the wellbeing of their four-year-old son if both were incapacitated, Cummings drove them to his parents' home in Durham and stayed at a separate house on the grounds. As both recovered from the disease, on 12 April Cummings found his 'eyesight seemed to have been affected by the disease' and drove his wife and child to Barnard Castle to test whether he could safely make the 260-mile return journey to London the following day.[55] The truth of this explanation is hotly contested. Some believe that Cummings had cracked up under the pressure, had a mini-breakdown and had fled London for the solace of his parental home.

As the story of his trip broke in the *Daily Mirror* and the *Guardian*, Cummings became the subject of national ire. Johnson flip-flopped hopelessly: standing by Cummings, changing his mind, then bitterly regretting the damage it had done to his own reputation in the party and the country. 'What's going on? Sort it out,' Johnson was overheard telling Cain. 'I want you to get him to put out an apology at once.' 'He's your chief of staff: *you* tell him.' As Cummings became the leading story in the country, Johnson was inundated with advice from former advisers, backbenchers and Cabinet ministers to drop him. 'You are trashing your public health strategy if you continue to support him. Either he should apologize or he should resign,' Walden told him.

'This is a total *Guardian*/*Mirror* conspiracy. Total tosh, matey. The story is total balls. It will blow over.'

'No, it won't.'

'You don't know the story. If you did you would see it's just a f**king conspiracy,' the Prime Minister snapped back before hanging up.

Walden messaged back: 'Wow, please tell me you didn't just hang up.'

When Johnson called him back, he insisted Walden was wrong. Walden told him, 'That doesn't sound like a leader of the free world talking.'[56]

Crosby received a call from Johnson, asking for his views. 'He's got to go, mate,' Crosby insisted (as relayed to the authors by a third party). Johnson's rock was absolutely clear. 'This is your chance.' By the time they finished talking, he'd convinced Crosby that he was going to get rid of him, once the media storm had died down.

'He's got to go,' advised Ben Elliot also, who in February had warned Johnson 'he's running a Stalinist cell'.[57]

In a similar vein, Javid texted: 'Everything I told you about Dominic Cummings is coming to pass. He's got to go now.'

'You're right, you're right, Saj,' he messaged back, making Javid think that at last he got it and would let Cummings go.[58]

But Johnson remained in two minds. With his judgement still affected by his battle with Covid, as friends assert, he stuck relentlessly to his belief in 'standing by your man'. Unlike previous Prime Ministers who would cave in, Johnson believed he himself was 'a man of principle' who wouldn't let the media force a resignation for the mere act of breaking the rules. Judgement impaired or not, Johnson's tendency was to let others get off the hook for bad behaviour. He'd got away with far worse things: who was he to drag someone down? Cummings agreed. He was defiant to friends: 'After all the s**t I've had to face, I'm not going to let this end my time.' He would not resign of his own accord. Dougie Smith was one of the strongest voices telling the Prime Minister 'under no circumstances' to let him go. 'Dom was Dougie's security: he was petrified about his own position if he was to quit,' says one aide. 'The backbenches were mostly opposed and very angry,' Chief Whip Mark Spencer recalls, 'especially those with seats near Durham.'[59] Cabinet ministers were more divided: Gove (above all), Sunak, Raab and even Hancock were supportive of him staying, while others were horrified at the damage and the mixed messaging keeping him would create.

Early on Sunday morning, 24 May, Johnson held a conference call with Cummings, Lister and Cain in which Cummings gave his version of the events. Johnson listened carefully. 'It's totally fine. I don't think you've done anything wrong,' he told him. 'Dom was only too happy for Boris to take the hand grenade and fall over the episode. He sold him the story, and he bought it,' says an aide. 'Just so you are clear,' Cain was heard to say, 'if you decide to stand by Dom it will be the most difficult headwind in your career. The very very worst thing you can do is to back him and then change your mind in two or three days.'

'Don't worry, I am with him shoulder to shoulder. We can't lose Dom. He's integral to us.' Johnson went into the press conference on Sunday afternoon thinking he could win people over. The pounding he took caused him to rethink, telling his team after it, 'We can't hold the line. We've got ourselves in a ridiculous position.'

On Monday, Johnson had a fresh escape plan. 'Why doesn't Dom hold his own press conference, and let people decide?' Lister and Cain were sceptical, but Cummings himself was up for it. He promptly took control of No. 10, making all the arrangements. Cummings' highly public humiliation, televised to 4.5 million viewers, was unenviable to most people.[60] Johnson, however, was not most people. He hated that Cummings had made himself the star of the show – no matter how poor the reviews. As one aide recalls, 'You could see the jealousy in the Prime Minister's eyes, unhappy that Dom was so decisively taking centre stage and calling the shots.' 'I don't regret what I did,' Cummings asserted in the No. 10 Rose Garden that afternoon.

Anger on both sides was inflamed further by the event, with many commenting on the constitutional oddity of the PM's adviser holding a press conference, not least in an unconventional spot previously reserved for occasions such as the Cameron/Clegg launch of the Coalition government in 2010. Johnson was now panicking, calling new names on his speed dial list of trusted advisers in crises, including Gavin Williamson: 'Should I sack him?'

'If you were going to, you should've done it on day one. It needed to be swift and brutal. It's far too late, Prime Minister,' he replied.

Conservative MPs were complaining that they had never experienced such voluminous and furious messages from constituents. The gist was: 'While we were making huge sacrifices, the PM's very own senior adviser was breaking the rules.' Mark Spencer realized that No. 10 underestimated the fury: 'Frankly, we had the confidence of an eighty-seat majority, and we were certain we could tough it through.'[61] For MPs, it was payback time. 'These guys have no idea what they're talking about. They're all morons,' Cummings would regularly say of Tory MPs and they knew it. 'Many on the Conservative side turned on Boris because they were frankly fed up with Dom, and with Boris for supporting him,' says a party official.

Johnson standing by his man when under media attack was a dress rehearsal for the later scandals of his premiership. Lacking moral compass, his judgements were made on faux loyalty and political expediency. Cummings himself survived until November, but at a cost. 'A lot of MPs became very angry indeed with the Prime Minister. With hindsight, his unwillingness to listen on Barnard Castle set the tone for the crisis that finally brought him down – Owen Paterson and Chris Pincher,' says 1922 Committee Chair Graham Brady.[62]

Johnson's failure to dismiss Cummings over Barnard Castle, to cling onto his belief that nobody should resign merely because they've broken some rules and the press want them to walk, was the first great misstep of his premiership, as he later realized. Not dismissing him further entitled Cummings, and vividly showed Whitehall and Westminster who was calling the shots in No. 10. Post-Barnard Castle, Cummings decided to step away from Covid to become more involved again in No. 10, 'treating it as his personal fiefdom', says an aide.

Johnson tried to lean more on Lister, which Cummings hated. No. 10 was about to descend into its most anarchic period in the modern era.

The End of the Affair (June–November 2020)

Cummings had dispatched the Chancellor and the Cabinet Secretary, and for the time being their successors were pliable to him. Only one figure was capable of ejecting him. On Saturday 11 July, Johnson and Symonds hosted Javid for lunch at Chequers. The hosts felt remorseful about his departure. 'I want you back in the government,' Johnson said. 'Not if Cummings is still there,' Javid countered. 'Why not come in and you can work together?' Johnson said. The conversation was going nowhere, and they moved on to more congenial subjects.

Symonds was beginning to focus back on politics. As she adjusted to her new reality in the very different and restricting world of the Downing Street flat, and to the birth of her first child Wilfred in late April, she became clear that Cummings was no longer an asset. The departures of Javid and Sedwill had unsettled her confidence in him, no longer perceiving him to be a strategic necessity as he had been in the summer of 2019. Her relationship with Cummings deteriorated further after Johnson's illness. 'It was toxic during that period. Anyone who was a friend of Dom was under constant scrutiny. Carrie and her allies were on the warpath,' says an ally of Cummings. She had grown to resent his unabashed contempt for her partner and the way he pushed him around. Johnson in turn regularly vented his frustrations with his chief to her. Cummings too had grown frustrated with the woman whom he and allies now referred to as 'Princess Nut Nut'.[63]

By the late summer of 2020, No. 10 was in meltdown. One adviser notes that 'No. 10 was completely unrecognizable compared to 2019. Everybody was knackered, weary, meetings lacking any structure. People were focused internally on the disarray within No. 10, and the briefing wars between the teams didn't help.' Cummings' efforts on Covid had neutered his ability to control No. 10, culminating in the 2020 exams failure discussed in the next chapter. 'It made clear there was nobody in No. 10 who had a grip across government. The Prime Minister basically had no chief of staff, Dom was too busy elsewhere,' says an aide. Rather than working in the outer office, he was tucked away pursuing his own agenda.

Cummings and Symonds, both able and demanding activists, were more alike than they might care to admit. Both in their different ways helped propel Johnson into No. 10, but, once there, had their own agendas and very pronounced views on people. Cummings believed that Johnson was most useful as a vessel, while Symonds' firm views often didn't chime with Johnson's own. Both inspired great loyalty in their teams of ultra-loyal supporters, but they also struck fear in those around them: 'Some found her difficult, precious, terrible temper, scary,' says an aide. Neither Symonds nor Johnson steadied each other with constancy as Denis Thatcher, Sarah Brown and Philip May did with their partners. Rather, 'Boris and Carrie added to each other's paranoia', was a view repeated by several. She was capable of great kindnesses, but like Cummings, she could be scornful in public towards him (or 'dismissive and mean' as one aide puts it).

But their greatest similarity was Johnson's tendency to use them as an excuse. 'I'd love to do that but I can't [pointing upwards] because of her,' he would often say in meetings. 'It suited him to make people think she was to blame for things not happening,' says an official. An aide believes, 'He played us all off against each other. He would tell us that she was impossible to deal with and he couldn't control her and she would do whatever she wanted. Then he'd go upstairs and tell her that we were impossible and he couldn't control us. He liked to pour petrol on both sides and see what happened to the fire.' Formerly trusted figures were caught in the crosshairs for their association with either camp. 'I went from someone who seemed rated to suddenly being heavily briefed against and having all sorts of unfounded accusations thrown at me,' says Oliver Lewis.[64]

The position of spouse to the Prime Minister is not an easy one to navigate, doubly so for Symonds who had a history and interest in party politics exceeding most of her predecessors. No. 10 officials wanted to help her find a place: 'We looked at establishing the position of first lady on a much securer footing for her,' says one official, an impetus smothered in the row over decorating expenses in the No. 10 flat in early 2020 dubbed 'Wallpapergate', then swallowed up by Covid. 'I have no doubt that she really loves him and that she bolsters him, and that she's been much maligned for being young and political, and for the affair breaking up a family when it's the woman who is always blamed,' says a member of Johnson's family. To one of Johnson's most trusted advisers, however, as to others caught in the middle, she was not a net help to his premiership. 'He would have been a much better PM without her. History will say that she was a distraction, encouraging him to spend time with her friends half his age rather than with serious people, figures who were intellectually his equal. I can't blame her for first one child, then two, nappies, sleepless broken nights, but the other distractions I do. The dog, the parties, the flat...' Others speak of their concern at how he would go upstairs to the flat, and it would be full of Carrie's friends giving him countervailing opinions. Lister concludes ultimately that Johnson must take the blame: 'He thrives on chaos: they were all his decisions.'[65]

Any blame indeed falls foursquare on Johnson, not Symonds. He had broken his relationship with a woman who had the measure of him for someone nearly half his age. For three years in Downing Street, Boris was being Boris, and Carrie, Carrie. But he was the one who held the elected office, the highest position in the country. 'I suspect history will be harder on her than she deserves, with the idea she was a power behind the throne manipulating him,' says an official, 'but I didn't see it like that. His tendency is to manipulate women, not vice versa.' Indeed, Carrie Symonds with her many accomplishments could have been a major asset had Johnson managed the relationship differently.

The search for a No. 10 spokesperson to give the daily press conference was the catalyst for his final bust-up with Cummings. Johnson agreed that Cain should oversee the process to decide the appointment. Fearing Symonds intervening, Cain was emphatic that the choice should be his and Cummings' as outlined by the so-called terror memorandum. After interviews, a front runner was identified. The quest was not easy. Cain favoured Sky's Sophy Ridge, but she turned it down, as did others. But behind his back, Johnson had invited Allegra Stratton, highly rated by Symonds, to dinner at Chequers, who had been helping Chancellor Sunak become the nation's most popular politician. Johnson sensed a double gain – acquire someone with magic dust, and deny his rival his media champion. The fact that it riled Sunak, for whom she worked, didn't lose him sleep. He had found his woman.

But Cain had alighted on another candidate, the BBC's Ellie Price. Johnson and Symonds stuck with Stratton. Cain, the inventor of the idea of a regular No. 10 press conference, and who Johnson had promised authority over the process, said he would resign. 'You can't do that, Commissar. I need you. You have my word I haven't offered Allegra the job,' Johnson told Cain, shaking his hand and looking him in the eye, 'to show him it was not his usual nonsense'. The house of cards at this point suddenly began to crumble: Johnson insisted on Stratton for the job. Cain was promised the chief of staff post (with Cummings' enthusiastic nod) as a *quid pro quo*, but Stratton said she couldn't work with him; nor he with her. Johnson in all his weakness and indecision found himself boxed in one ear by Carrie and in the other by Cain and his supporters. Court politics, in the power vacuum in No. 10, was at its height, with threats, rows, leaks and talks of resignation on all sides. Stratton, highly accomplished but ill-equipped for this post, duly started as Downing Street press secretary. On Friday 13 November, Johnson held a warm meeting in his office with Cummings and Cain, with laughter peeling out through the closed doors. Both bowed to the inevitable and agreed to depart that day. There was talk about a future role for Cummings in science, and Cain in comms, 'getting the gang back together to smash the next election victory out of the park'. It was an amicable departure with reminiscing about victories on Vote Leave, Brexit and the 2019 general election, and Johnson signing a pair of 'Get Brexit Done' boxing gloves for Cain.[66]

All sweetness and light.

The Reckoning

Cummings left by the front door of Downing Street carrying a box, widely thought to contain secret papers that he could use if needed to counter-attack against Johnson and Symonds. The box was empty, but the implied threat was not. Deputy Chief of Staff and ally Cleo Watson had left unobtrusively by the Cabinet Office's Whitehall entrance with Cummings' 'personal belongings', including documents. Johnson feared what fury he and Cain could unleash, but the hook among his team was that, after months of turbulence, the departure would be amicable and everyone could move on. That is exactly what Cummings maintains that he and Cain would have done.[67] The fact that they most emphatically did not is blamed by them on Symonds for a series of briefings the evening after their departure which 'left them no other course of action'. 'Not content with killing them off, Carrie and Henry Newman wanted to burn their bodies', says a member of Team Cummings. From there the briefings escalated with devastating effect.

How did Cummings achieve so much more influence than other Prime Ministers' advisers, including Sherman, Hilton and Timothy? The weakness of the Prime Minister explains much, his lack of ideas and decisiveness, and surrounding himself with amenable staff. Johnson disliked confronting him and slapping him down. The principal reason Johnson didn't 'stand up to him' was the same reason why Gove didn't at Education. They needed him – and they were afraid of him.

A more difficult question is why did the system tolerate someone as destructive as Cummings? The UK's unwritten constitution allows a Prime Minister to invest almost the complete authority of the office in their chief adviser. Most of Johnson's Cabinet ministers, grateful for his Brexit leadership, did not object to Cummings. When they did, like Javid, they were swept aside. Fear explains why some, above all Johnson himself, didn't stand up to him – fear of losing him, and fear of the damage he could do. The Cabinet Secretary was the one figure within the civil service who could have stood up to what was going on; but when he did, Sedwill too was swept aside by Cummings, and a more pliable successor Case put in his place. Officials, ministers and special advisers alike admired much of what he wanted to do, not only on Brexit, but also his wider and searching analysis of what had gone wrong with the British state, and how to remedy it from its hollowed-out condition.

The hollowing out of the centre explored in the penultimate chapter provides a deeper way of understanding how Cummings penetrated so far and for as long as he did. Ultimately, the centre had become too weak to resist him. It was far too dependent on an omnicompetent Cabinet Secretary. Had Heywood not died of cancer in 2018 he would have been Cabinet Secretary for almost all of Johnson's premiership – he would have been sixty in December 2021. Though it is unlikely he would have been able completely to tame Cummings' treatment of staff (he had not previously managed to do so for Timothy and Hill), he would have channelled Cummings' robust ideas and worked to realize them with the engagement of the Prime Minister. Instead, his absence and the lesser authority of his replacement in Sedwill meant that for some civil servants Cummings became a career opportunity. The nature of his complete and often capricious confidence in a select few favoured individuals, placing these above any system or process, deepened the perverse incentives of Whitehall he claimed to be stripping away. Several civil servants, mostly male, gained promotion as a result of allying themselves with the chief adviser, rather than serving the Prime Minister and the nation as a whole.

How far did he succeed in changing the country in a Bismarckian way? A greater focus on science, data and R&D was achieved in part, and ARIA established after he left. Skills and technical colleges were a work in progress. The revolution was unfinished, though: the civil service, public services and planning, where he had some of his best insights, were largely unreformed; No. 10 did not become the powerhouse he sought nor were institutional links with the Treasury built; defence procurement still awaits reform, though some defence and strategic modernizations were realized in the Integrated Review; development spending was reduced and the Department for International Development merged with the Foreign and Commonwealth Office; Brexit was achieved but a Brexit dividend still awaits being realized. His major post-election impact was on Covid, with the first lockdown, testing and vaccines his most significant legacy, for all the damage his chaotic leadership brought in its wake.

The tension between his analysis and his abilities as an actor explains part of the disappointing performance. He held aloft his favourite rationalist thinkers as truth-seekers, beacons of knowledge which could help secure a better future for humanity, then treated the truth as an irrelevancy at best not least in his campaigning.[68] He wanted robust institutions across Whitehall no longer dependent on flawed humanities-educated bluffers, but in post relentlessly centralized power to himself. He dismissed the personal courtier office politics of Whitehall, then unrelentingly pursued personal vendettas against those who crossed and challenged him. He was able to see that Johnson would fall victim to his tendencies of complacency and indecision following the election, but failed to build the structures and alliances around him to keep the premiership on the rails. He saw the opportunities Covid presented for a revitalization of the British state led by effective and specialized technocrats, but instead of replacing the systems of appointment and incentives, his war on the senior civil servants merely succeeded in replacing one generation of bureaucrats with the next.

Then unrealistic ambitions (both breaking up the Treasury and reforming the Cabinet Office) needed more detailed preparation, and insufficient time explains why so little happened, beyond blood spilt. Bismarck and Richard Haldane were at work for twenty years reshaping the state, Thomas Cromwell ten, but Cummings for barely more than fifteen months. Despite his prodigious blog posts, he did not write or codify his plan for reform in the necessary detail and he hesitated to provide it to those within the system who were willing and able to help. 'He just didn't get into the nitty gritty and direct people on it, he wasn't prepared to do the planning and graft. I think he was afraid of actually owning it, nailing his colours to the mast,' says one official supportive of his ideas. Another would-be admirer says, 'In the last analysis, Dom understood neither government nor people.'

Cummings ultimately failed to match the achievements of the great reformers in history he admired because he didn't understand the history. He failed, unlike them, to carry people with him. His conduct ensured that as enemies multiplied exponentially, allies dwindled. Unnecessary skirmishes with the BBC, the press lobby and Conservative MPs alienated those within the system who could have otherwise carried his ideas when he was a spent force. His total disregard for the democratic processes of British politics as a tedious parlour game meant that when the fruits of his work on Brexit and securing a general election majority ceased to be relevant, there were but a handful of individuals who would fight his corner.

The Cummings era was over. The Carrie Johnson era was about to begin, aided by Munira and Stratton, and by her friends who were about to be promoted to commanding heights within No. 10. The promise was of a less rebarbative and more inclusive style of politics such as Johnson had championed at City Hall. A newly confident Johnson, pleased he had at last seen off the intrusive Cummings, finally had the chance to be the leader he always wanted to be.

But Cummings would destroy all these hopes and set in train a series of events that would end the premiership.

A renewed Johnson outlines his Build Back Better agenda at the 2021 Party Conference

7

DOMESTIC

The 2019 general election had seen Johnson secure an eighty-seat majority, vanquish Corbyn and set out his wide-ranging ambition to transform Britain. His was an opportunity for which all premiers yearn: Harold Macmillan (in 1959) and Thatcher (in 1983 and 1987) were the only other Conservative leaders since 1945 to secure landslide majorities for their electoral programmes.

Johnson thus had a breathtaking vista. While his re-emergence as the pre-eminent candidate for the Conservative Party leadership in July 2019 left him without time to prepare detailed plans, such as was available to Thatcher (four years as opposition leader), Blair (three years) and Cameron (five years), the premiership had been within his sights for years and the object of his desires for longer still. Finally within his grasp, what was he to do with his time in No. 10? We looked at Johnson's ideas ('Dreams') in Chapter 4, and turn now to examining how far his amorphous 'impulses' were translated into domestic and, in the next chapter, foreign policy. We look too at the critical question of how far his idiosyncratic agenda was what Conservative MPs wanted: they had voted him in as leader to do a job, but would they continue to support him once he started trotting out his often quirky and unconservative plans?

With three years lost under May to Brexit with its bitter divisions in Cabinet and Parliament, the country was long overdue a period of policy activism. Breaking the Brexit deadlock and winning the general election sucked much energy out of the first six months of Johnson's government, save for the slew of announcements signalling big spending. January and February 2020 passed in elective tranquillity before Covid struck. From March 2020 until early 2021 there was precious little bandwidth for the government to achieve anything other than crisis mitigation. No single issue since 1945 had been so all-encompassing or placed such a burden upon the state. But the reopening of society in 2021 didn't give the green light for Johnson to return to domestic policy as usual. The virus had shifted national policy dynamics, creating new challenges in health, education and the economy. While the needs had multiplied, the means were divided. The Treasury and Chancellor were clear: the costs of the pandemic would not go away, and the books needed to be balanced on day-to-day spending accordingly.

The political world gave Johnson less room too. While Johnson's political capital earned in the general election had dwindled, Sunak had grown in strength and he, not Johnson, was now the most popular politician in the country. Backbenchers had grown in confidence and restlessness, their divisions and contradictions with both the Prime Minister and each other seeping through the corridors of the reopened Westminster. Lockdowns had cost him significant support in the party and the press.

Yet Johnson was not without his domestic achievements in the curtailed time he had, despite these handicaps. The question was, could more have been achieved if he had led better? We look at his response to Covid, why he fared better in 2021 than in the first year of the pandemic, and at the lasting impacts of Johnson on both policy and public debate.

The Road to Freedom (January–July 2021)

The Covid crisis left little space for thinking or activity, officials and politicians alike working ungodly hours with relatively few periods of rest between the inflection points of the pandemic. The start of the vaccination programme in December 2020 had marked the turning point, providing a clear path out by the protection of the population against serious illness when contracting the virus. Johnson could at last return to the rhetoric of sunlit uplands where he felt most comfortable, banging the drum for the vaccine in government and the country at large.

Principal among the UK's successes during the pandemic was the Oxford-AstraZeneca vaccine. Oxford had been considering partnering with US biopharmaceutical giant Merck in April, which raised alarm bells in Downing Street. President Trump was so unpredictable, and advisers thought it likely he would intervene to ensure US-produced vaccines would go to the US population first. After No. 10 had pushed for AstraZeneca as a partner, Chief Scientific Adviser Patrick Vallance intervened to secure vaccine rights and onshore manufacturing in the contract. If they were indeed successful in developing a vaccine, there was no question as to whether the UK would be assured access.

One vaccine was not enough, and Vallance pushed hard the idea of a 'vaccine task force' outside the usual rules of the procurement process, cutting through any bureaucracy or red tape. From a list of potential leaders given to Johnson after he returned from illness, the Prime Minister picked out Kate Bingham – a name he was vaguely acquainted with through familial relations, her mother's first cousin being married to Johnson's sister Rachel. Having been offered the job by Johnson (via phone calls from Hancock) she agreed on two firm conditions: a ring-fenced budget with 'no regrets' funding which would see the government buy vaccines in advance before it was known whether or not their trials were successful, and single lines of reporting, with support from the Prime Minister when needed, so that she could push back against departmental blocks. Johnson agreed to her terms, emphasizing that the priority was not minimizing the cost of delivery but maximizing the speed.

As development of the vaccine progressed Johnson was only lightly involved in the process, but remained a rhetorical driver for vaccination within No. 10. His media team were careful to tread the fine line between arousing expectations and creating disappointment, knowing that Johnson was prone to overpromising, and kept him strict. The finer points of the vaccine process often escaped him, with Bingham told firmly by his office 'you can't give him more than three slides of information'. He was enthusiastic nevertheless, including embracing the risk that came with rapid development. 'He got everybody comfortable with the idea of unlimited indemnities, where officials were swooning at the risk, but I felt it was necessary for urgent delivery,' says Bingham.[1]

Those around Johnson were not uniformly supportive. Into autumn Bingham found that No. 10's support was waning, and she was barred from doing media rounds to encourage people to join Covid vaccine trials and enrol via the Covid vaccine NHS registry. As the first details of a vaccine developed jointly by the US pharma company Pfizer and German firm BioNTech came out in early November, briefings were under way, including the leaking of Bingham spending £670,000 on PR support for the Vaccine Task Force. Bingham felt No. 10 had been briefing against her in their annoyance that she was stealing media exposure from ministers and asked Johnson to call her, issuing an ultimatum down the line: 'If you don't like what I'm doing, I'm happy to step back. You can come out and be energetic in support, or I won't be staying.' Johnson immediately put a halt to any No. 10 media activity, and the following morning Hancock was on BBC Radio 4's *Today* programme offering unequivocal support.[2]

The announcement on 30 December 2020 that AstraZeneca's vaccine had been approved for emergency supply, with the first doses available in early January, transformed Johnson's thinking. He understood immediately that this was the way out of this terrible trauma the country had been through. He was desperate now to exploit the advantage of the UK getting a vaccine early, and pushed and pushed for the most ambitious vaccination targets in meetings,' says a No. 10 aide. The vaccine gave him some immunity against the earlier criticisms of backbenchers by providing an endpoint to the virus where herd immunity could be achieved through vaccine-induced antibodies.

The vaccine rollout has since been claimed as a major personal success of Johnson's. 'Let us never forget, and make sure our country never forgets... he was the man who delivered the fastest vaccine rollout in the world,' Gove told the Conservative leadership hustings in August 2022.[3] His willingness to follow the advice of officials, appoint effective people and embrace risks certainly deserves credit. But the principal architect of the rollout was not a man at all; Dr Emily Lawson, as suggested by NHS chief Simon Stevens, receives universal praise from civil servants in her oversight of the first and second jabs, then later the booster programme in late 2021. With Vallance and Bingham pushing the procurement and Lawson the delivery, the Prime Minister's primary credit is for being at best a vocal champion, if periodically an unobstructive presence.

The vaccine rollout proceeded through second jabs, with five million receiving them by the end of March 2021. With cases declining, the UK looked as if it was through the worst of Covid. Johnson led from the front announcing the second roadmap for reopening in March. The country would be open to the maximum degree compatible with placing limited stress on the NHS. Johnson had at last landed at a consistent, measured position, not cowed by ministers and backbenchers urging him to throw caution to the wind. 'There will be others who will believe that we could go faster on the basis of that vaccination programme, and I understand their feelings and I sympathize very much with the exhaustion and the stress that people are experiencing… but to them I say that today the end really is in sight and a wretched year will give way to a spring and a summer that will be very different and incomparably better than the picture we see around us today,' he told the Commons.[4]

In leading the second roadmap, Johnson and officials Bowler and Case had absorbed the lessons of the first, committing to be led by 'data not dates' and allowing for a variable pace in the four-step unlocking: first reopening schools and limited outdoor gatherings, then non-essential retail, then limited indoor gatherings, and finally a total unlocking with all legal limits removed. Changes in outlook and potential Covid mutations were anticipated in the more gradual process, allowing the government to assess at each checkpoint the best way forward. Sunak and the Treasury, who had proved central in pushing for maximum economic freedom earlier, began to take a back seat. 'We were all exhausted, everyone was burnt out,' says a Treasury official.

Another helpful stabilizer was the absence of Cummings. 'Dom had his strengths but the February roadmap was much better without him, there was a lot of trust between us and No. 10,' says one Covid Task Force official. 'The machine was better not because of the inputs, but because Dom's gravitational pull was no longer warping our coordination.' Henry Cook, who had taken the lead on Covid policy within No. 10, was a far more stable influence and officials were relieved to have a steadier hand advising Johnson. Cummings' absence changed the system's response to the data, but also made the Prime Minister more measured in how far he would push conventional opinion on the virus. 'He became much less libertarian. He realized that he didn't have that equal and opposite force pushing back,' says a No. 10 official. The success of the rollout saw a 'vaccine bounce' in the Prime Minister's popularity, with the Conservative Party handily outperforming Labour in the 2021 local elections in May, swinging Hartlepool from Labour to Conservative in a by-election, and finishing the month leading Labour in the polls 46 per cent to 28 per cent.[5]

The surge in cases due to the emergence of the Delta variant that month would challenge the strategy, with one of the four tests to progress being that the risk assessment was not changed by new 'Variants of Concern'. Returning to Downing Street from the Carbis Bay G7 summit on the evening of Sunday 13 June, Johnson was greeted by doom-and-gloom projections from the government's 'Scientific Pandemic Influenza Group on Modelling'. The Prime Minister was pressured to finish unlocking at the earliest 21 June deadline set out by the roadmap, not least from the rowdy backbench Covid Recovery Group led by Steve Baker, who texted the group a quote from *The Great Escape*: 'It is the sworn duty of all officers to try to escape. If they cannot escape, then it is their sworn duty to cause the enemy to use an inordinate number of troops to guard them, and their sworn duty to harass the enemy to the best of their ability.'[6] In contrast with WhatsApp histrionics was the measured performance of Chief Medical Officer Chris Whitty putting the case for delay to Johnson. 'He was at the top of his game, and gave the Prime Minister a hugely significant speech explaining the dividends waiting another month would bring,' says a special adviser. Whitty did not refer to models or forecasts, knowing Johnson had not relinquished his scepticism on their soothsaying powers, but grounded it in the concrete. 'If we open up now, Prime Minister, there will be huge pressure on the NHS. All we need is a slight increase and the pressure on beds will overwhelm the system. But if we hold on for another month, let the vaccine rollout continue to weaken the link between cases and hospitalizations, it will all come right.' Johnson heeded Whitty's advice, delaying the unlocking a month to 19 July, to the fury of Baker and company.

A more sympathetic interpretation of Johnson's development as Prime Minister can be found here: that he learned – albeit slowly – by doing. The 19 July date (or 'Freedom Day') was criticized by several scientific advisers as being too rapid in the face of rising cases and the possibility of new variants, and labelled 'reckless' by Keir Starmer. The Prime Minister's position marked an increased stability, however, even if some thought the pace of reopening on the riskier side. It was a welcome relief for those who had been through his trolleying prior to the second and third lockdowns. 'It was much easier to operate as a scientist in that environment,' says one SAGE member.

As it emerged, Johnson had not made an error in his risk assessment to proceed with reopening on 19 July. Although the UK's cases were the highest in the world, the numbers largely flatlined with R (the Covid infection rate) at around 1. The daily average of new cases remained under 50,000 until the Omicron wave later that year, and hospital admissions did not exceed 1,000 in a day. The biggest hiccup was that of the 'pingdemic', during which the NHS Covid app told increasing numbers of people (peaking at 600,000 the week of 15–21 July) they had been in contact with somebody who had tested positive for the virus and should self-isolate. Backbenchers were naturally indignant, with the self-isolation of those who had not caught the virus causing large-scale disruption to businesses. But as the pandemic began to fizzle, so too did the pings, before a step-change on 16 August as those who had received both doses of the vaccination were able to avoid quarantine even if they had come into contact with the virus.

With Covid no longer the sole first-order issue, as the nation reopened No. 10 had begun to look outwards across Whitehall too, seeking to get the premiership back on track. The government's post-Covid relaunch in 2021 came in two phases. The first was ostensibly led by the Treasury, labelled 'Build Back Better: our plan for growth'. Wrapped in the flag of recovering from Covid and improving the UK's long-maligned productivity growth, it was more an exercise in appeasement than a genuinely significant long-term growth agenda. 'Rishi didn't see it as particularly significant, he did it because the PM wanted it,' says an official. It provided an excuse, though, for Sunak – alongside Kwasi Kwarteng at BEIS – to scrap Theresa May's Industrial Strategy document and sectoral deals, in order to put their own framing on government plans. Johnson came to find the framing grossly inadequate, and became progressively frustrated by Sunak's tin ear to stimulating growth through fiscal policy.

The second was a machinery of government change within No. 10 – a new delivery unit.[7] Case had put forward replicating the successful Delivery Unit model established by Michael Barber under the 1997 New Labour government, and in January 2021

Barber was drafted in to help Johnson's deputy principal private secretary Stuart Glassborow focus the Prime Minister's priorities. 'People tell me you don't like outlining your priorities,' Barber told Johnson.[8] 'So let me ask you a different question. When it is time for you to leave No. 10, what do you wish that you had done?' Johnson listed four things, down from his typical list of three dozen: levelling up, jobs and skills, public sector delivery, Net Zero.[9] By July 2021, the Delivery Unit was set up, with Emily Lawson recruited from the vaccine delivery programme to oversee it. The policy premiership was at last to begin in earnest.

Levelling Up, Infrastructure and Skills

In as far as his team was capable of defining what he wanted to do as Prime Minister, and they tried hard on several locations to get him to elucidate why he had so badly wanted the job, it came down to what we have described as his 'three impulses'. We now consider the first two, levelling up and infrastructure, emblematic of his desire to rebuild the country and be a Prime Minister in the mould of US Presidents Roosevelt or Reagan. The third impulse, 'patriotism', we examine in the next chapter.

'Levelling up' encapsulates Johnson in a nutshell – boosterish, inchoate and self-serving. No longer able to rally the forces to get Brexit done and destroy Corbyn, he was also no longer able to justify himself as the defiant challenger – his natural habitat. Rather, he needed to show himself to be a successful *governor*, a transition he achieved in the London mayoralty. Levelling up Britain ticked every box. It even promised to retain Red Wall seats in the North, a far cry from the party's natural heartland. Levelling up was win, win, win.

Then reality began to dawn in the course of 2021: levelling up was politically difficult, cross-cutting and very expensive. Johnson had never sought to articulate or substantiate it in any great detail, happy to leave it as a fluffy aspiration – only periodically visited where a speech called for the recurrent motif. Johnson taking little responsibility for its progress would have worked if he'd charged other ministers to do so. But being so broad, the policy lacked a natural home and ministerial sponsor to own it. Very little flesh, therefore, was on the bones of levelling up by early 2021 despite Johnson's repeated and undoubtedly sincere insistence that 'talent and genius is distributed equally, but opportunity is not'.[10]

The Treasury, the Whitehall department that was most sceptical about the policy, had been left to drive change, its partial move to Darlington in the North-East following on the slow rollout of the 2019 Towns Fund and 2020 Levelling Up Fund. 'These funds weren't actually intended to achieve the levelling up agenda,' says an official. 'They were merely short-term financial support to pave the way for longer-term transformative programmes.' With Covid mostly under control, Johnson appointed Neil O'Brien to a junior ministerial post for Levelling Up within the Ministry of Housing, Communities and Local Government (MHCLG). A rising star in the wonkish mould and a protégé of Osborne, O'Brien was on paper a natural fit, having written the first serious piece on how levelling-up progress might be measured for centre-right think tank Onward in September 2020.[11] Heading a unit of fewer than a dozen officials, he rolled up his sleeves and began articulating the long-awaited details of levelling up.

Few of them made it into Johnson's speech delivered in Coventry on 15 July 2021, billed as the seminal relaunch of the levelling-up policy. Couched in the 'recovery from the pandemic' vein, the speech was effective in its analysis of regional inequalities – drawing extensively on data on regional disparities and citing Germany's successful levelling up after reunification in 1990. Johnson articulated some of the thorny trade-offs, such as levelling up not being zero-sum, or 'robbing Peter [London] to pay Paul [deprived regions]'.[12] But otherwise the speech left the levelling-up rocket, if that is what it sought to be, firmly on the launch pad. It lacked detailed solutions and substance, largely rehashing 2019 pre-election promises as a panacea. It did little to reassure growing numbers of sceptics that Johnson was serious about his flagship policy. Why was it such a failure? 'In fairness to the new team, the speech was thrown together by the principal the evening before. It didn't draw extensively from the research they had constructed,' says one official. 'There was just so much drift, the team running the process weren't given political oomph and authority,' argues another. It's difficult to conceive of any other modern Prime Minister launching their flagship policy with such a ramshackle speech.

In a second attempt in September to launch the rocket, this time with oomph, Gove suggested bringing in Bank of England chief economist Andy Haldane to head the Levelling Up Task Force. Haldane was a celebrated thinker with a rare ability to communicate complex economic concepts. Gove needed a point man to develop and explain their analysis in prose and relay it back to the Prime Minister in poetry, stimulating his intellect without losing his short attention span. Concurrent with Haldane's arrival came a refocusing of the machinery of government with a 'new' Department for Levelling Up, Housing and Communities to replace the MHCLG. Gove himself, near-universally considered to be Johnson's most capable minister, was to lead the agenda. He was replacing the sacked Robert Jenrick, who had been reshuffled out as the result of mounting backbench discontent over his proposed planning reforms, a lack of progress on cladding and growing public unpopularity following a series of stories of him overruling civil servants to push through the £1 billion property development of Conservative donor Richard Desmond. Johnson had not grown to trust Gove, but he was again forced to delegate to him as he had on Brexit and Covid. The man he least trusted in Cabinet was being charged with the make-or-break oversight of his most important domestic policy.

Sunak, critically, was less certain of Haldane's appointment, and indeed of the entire impulse. The Industrial Strategy Council he killed off in March had been chaired by Haldane and provided potential challenge to the Treasury's authority. The Chancellor was doubly sceptical of the appointment following the June 2021 Covid recovery education spending botch (discussed later in the chapter) and needed several attempts to be convinced by No. 10 that Haldane would not be suddenly asking for more money. Johnson seemed to have learned a lesson and didn't overpromise to the incoming adviser: 'No. 10 were very candid that we needed to produce a concrete plan without a huge pound sign,' says Haldane.[13]

The Treasury was Johnson's *bête noir* because he thought it irredeemably short term, whereas great leaders introduced changes which yielded economic benefits in the long term. Technicalities such as finance never unduly troubled him, and he was excited by the prospect that, two years after the general election, levelling up might be taking off at last. 'Let's have an away day to galvanize the Cabinet on it.' The Prime Minister had spoken, and it took place in November (though it was neither away nor a day, moved from Chequers to No. 10 due to the pandemic and shortened to a half-day session). The jamboree was jointly led by Gove and Sunak, with inputs from Johnson and Haldane. The Chancellor had been talked into chairing as a way of No. 10 binding him into the policy, against his Treasury instincts. 'The Chancellor's desire to raise his profile overcame his ambivalence about levelling up,' says one present. To corral his colleagues behind the mission, Johnson insisted they all had to outline the progress their department was making on levelling up. 'Let there be maps,' he said. So each Cabinet minister was told to make reference to a map. '[Lord] Bamford has a map of where every single JCB digger is in the world,' he repeatedly told staff. 'I want that – a data dashboard like we have on the virus where I can track the fortunes, the successes of levelling up in every area.' Amid the gathering clouds of Partygate, it proved a rare moment of jollity and harmony within Cabinet. 'One of the Prime Minister's favourite moments of his premiership,' says an official.

Any meeting of minds was, of course, temporary and concealed a myriad of disagreements among his colleagues about what levelling up actually meant, and the sacrifices that would be needed to achieve it. Tensions occasionally bubbled up into the open. In response to Gove asking ministers what the success of levelling up meant to them, Simon Clarke (newly Chief Secretary to the Treasury) responded, 'Every part of the UK having fully devolved powers.' Rees-Mogg (Leader of the Commons) spoke next: 'I believe the opposite of what Simon just said.'

A White Paper tying together policy and providing legislative direction had been advocated by Glassborow and Policy Unit staff earlier in 2021, to be paired with the Autumn Statement and Spending Review in late October. But substance was not yet ready following the fresh appointments of Gove and Haldane, while an increasingly hostile Sunak made clear anyway that he would not be giving up any ground on spending. Johnson had extracted quite enough from No. 11 for him, with new funds going towards Covid recovery in the NHS, schools, Johnson's new social care policy (albeit offset by tax increases), tackling crime and the Net Zero ten-point plan; the Prime Minister would not receive yet more for a pet project the Treasury did not believe in. 'Their lens for supporting regions through skills and cities was a far narrower view than the PM's,' says an official.

Sunak's disagreement with Johnson on levelling up spending was becoming personal. Johnson's allies noted ruefully how Sunak had embraced the Levelling Up Fund, similar to taking ownership of the furlough and Eat Out to Help Out schemes during the pandemic, and suspected he was positioning himself for any future leadership contest. 'Sunak effectively commandeered the fund as leverage for him with Conservative backbenchers,' says a No. 10 aide. He was far from the first Chancellor to use the Treasury to flex political muscle and build a leadership challenge. But No. 10 saw it as brazen ambition: levelling up was supported where Sunak had ownership, and discarded where the Prime Minister possessed control.

Gove and Haldane found themselves in the unenviable position of producing a transformational White Paper on a shoestring budget. Gove led the politics and Haldane the policy. The negotiations over how far the White Paper could go were decided in a quad, with Sunak up against Gove and Haldane, and Johnson taking the role of peacekeeper, conscious of his political weakness against his Chancellor. Spoils were unevenly split: Gove and Haldane received a Levelling Up Advisory Council, though not the statutory one they sought with power to push the government further in meeting targets. The targets themselves (to be achieved by 2030) were watered down from the original numbers; Sunak was wary of being locked into broad missions with large spending implications, and a halfway house was found on skills, R&D and education targets. Where the paper was most ambitious was in its plans for devolution: eleven new or deeper devolution deals by 2030, with a simplified long-term funding settlement. 'We got about half of what we asked for,' says Haldane.[14]

The paper, published in February 2022, at last gave some structure and definition to Johnson's amorphous 'levelling up' it had been crying out for. Haldane, while mocked for his comparisons, cleverly grounded the proposals in Johnson's sense of grand history, reaching as far back as Jericho, one of the world's earliest continuous settlements, founded around 8000 BCE, in explaining the history of economic geography and how the UK could today replicate the successes of the Renaissance and the Industrial Revolution to boost productivity and spread opportunities.

More recent economic history, however, was proving troublesome for the Prime Minister's legacy project. Large swathes of the parliamentary Conservative Party and membership were still persuaded by the long shadow of Thatcherism, and were allergic to both devolution and increased government spending. While Johnson was able to make the case to the public that regional spending was necessary, he was unsuccessful in communicating that changes were not zero-sum, and could instead expand growth for all through a new term planted in the Johnson lexicon, 'Pareto efficiency' – cakeism reborn as he saw it. Even his economically right-wing aides in No. 10 baulked at it. 'Boris would never convince the party that you had to rob Peter to pay Paul. The White Paper was all New Labour rubbish: you could never get the Red Wall paid for by the Blue Wall,' says one political adviser.

Ultimately, levelling up ran out of road because of the collapse of Johnson's political authority from early 2022. With terrible irony, the day following the launch of the White Paper saw the unprecedented resignations of his four most senior staff in No. 10. Johnson, battling unforced errors on Partygate and the uproar over his clumsy blaming of Starmer for not prosecuting serial sex offender Jimmy Savile when he was Director of Public Prosecutions, did not even attend the White Paper's presentation to Parliament later that day. The Levelling Up and Regeneration Bill could not be passed before his resignation in July. Levelling up, ultimately, was killed off by his inability to hold his team together.

Johnson had shown courage and some statesmanship in pushing ahead with an idea that cut through to a public who felt that the North did not receive its fair share.[15] 'One metric of success is whether your ideas are adopted by your opponents, and Labour certainly will borrow from Levelling Up,' says an official. But a present to the opposition while disillusioning Red Wall voters was not the grand legacy that Johnson sought.

The infrastructure projects Johnson had trumpeted in the heady days of 2019 and early 2020 fared even worse. Johnson's victory over HS2 in February 2020 was Pyrrhic. 'This is not an either/or proposition,' he told the Commons when announcing the news. 'Both [HS2 and Northern Powerhouse Rail] are needed, and both will be built – as quickly and cost-effectively as possible… Those who deny this… are effectively condemning the North to get nothing for 20 years.'[16] But the Integrated Rail Plan in November 2021 dropped HS2's eastern leg from Birmingham to Leeds and Northern Powerhouse Rail from Liverpool to Leeds. The projects were already controversial, but the financial and travel implications of Covid rendered both indefensible for No. 10 and the Department for Transport to pursue. A year and a half later, three-quarters of the plans had been cancelled. Condemned indeed.

Neither did Johnson's fabled crossing to Northern Ireland proceed. 'The Prime Minister thought it would greatly strengthen the Union and particularly the relationship with Northern Ireland,' says an aide. 'But Grant Shapps [Transport Minister], Network Rail Chair Peter Hendy and No. 10 advisers made it totally clear that it was a non-starter and would have led to a catastrophic clash with the Scottish government.' At least some of HS2 will survive, unlike his hopes for the link to Northern Ireland. Hendy's technical feasibility review of November 2021, commissioned at the Prime Minister's insistence, found the costs of any bridge or tunnel to be so vast and fraught with potential difficulties (if just about possible with current technology) that the project was an impossibility.

Johnson's rare prime ministerial interest in transport bore fruit in several closed 'Beeching' lines reopened through the £500 million Restoring Your Railway fund. £5.7 billion was provided for cities to invest in their transport networks, and Johnson's two mayoral transport loves (buses and cycling) were embraced with £3 billion for new bus lanes and £2 billion for cycle highways. Shapps proved one of Johnson's very few Cabinet ministers capable of driving and communicating policy, formulating with Rail Review Chair Keith Williams the Williams–Shapps Plan for Rail. The proposal, rolling back franchising and cohering the rail network under a single body in the wake of the pandemic, though, proved yet another victim of Johnson's messy descent: reforms could not be enacted before he himself ran out of track, and were put in limbo by his departure.

The Union might have been expected to be an incidental beneficiary of levelling up's regional ambitions, Johnson's self-appointment as Minister for the Union at the outset as an indication of such a priority. 'We had gone round in circles about how to oversee the Union – a Minister of State, a Secretary of State, a minister in the Cabinet Office? "I'll do it myself," he suddenly said,' recalls an aide. Wanting to take control himself, but then not knowing what he wanted, was a typical Johnson response. He was very aware that Scotland and Northern Ireland had voted Remain in 2016. Aware too that Covid further heightened tensions, when England was first to come out of lockdown. He knew too he was unpopular in Scotland, with only a quarter of Scots regularly saying they had confidence in him. He knew the Northern Ireland protocol was a fudge. He would lead from the front, but he ended up spending less time and energy on the Union than any Prime Minister in fifty years.

His early thinking was of a 'muscular Unionism', bolstered by his belief that Westminster was not getting the credit it deserved and devolved administrations were stealing the limelight, particularly in Scotland. The philosophy was shared with his first two Union advisers, ex-MP Luke Graham (in post until February 2021) and Oliver Lewis (leaving after just two weeks following hostile briefing), who both headed up an underpowered Union Unit in No. 10. The appointment in July 2021 of Conservative peer Mark McInnes, however, was a major change of direction and fit with the levelling-up agenda. In concert with Gove he sought to convert Johnson to a new philosophy of consensus building with the devolved administration. Johnson took some convincing – his working relationship with SNP leader Nicola Sturgeon was poor – but eventually he was won over by their idea of 'killing them with kindness'. Overreaching the SNP administration with spending in Scotland, working directly with local authorities and taking up a tone of emollient consideration was the core of an effective strategy. Despite Johnson's abysmal personal ratings in Scotland, support for the Union remained a steady majority. He even admitted to Gove that his more muscular approach had 'been a mistake'.[17] He bequeathed a Scotland, little thanks to his own efforts, more securely in the Union, but Northern Ireland in a mess. The first holder of the title 'Minister for the Union' cannot be deemed a success.

By the end of his premiership, the only real progress made on levelling up was in skills. The academic Alison Wolf had been appointed to the Policy Unit to drive reforms in January 2020. She had worked with Cummings on the 2011 Wolf report on technical education and on maths schools at DfE, as well as with Johnson when Shadow Minister for Further Education, and was respected by both. She knew the subject better than anyone, and had an 'oven-ready' vision prepared for the Augar Review of post-eighteen education in the dying embers of the May government. Wolf pressed for a lifelong skills guarantee at the heart of the initiative, a funding of technical courses equivalent to A levels for all through a loan scheme which, after compromises with the Treasury, was to commence in 2025. Johnson announced the policy in a keynote speech in Exeter on 29 September 2020, promising £1.5 billion additional funding for colleges, an expansion of apprenticeships and the loan scheme. He hailed it as an end to 'the pointless, nonsensical gulf... between the so-called academic and the so-called practical varieties for education'.[18] 'The Prime Minister's speech will provide the momentum to move the system,' Cummings told the team – and he was right.

So why was the skills agenda delivered in practice, while the bulk of Johnson's levelling-up reforms remained on the table? For one, there was a rare alignment of powerful forces within No. 10, a troika where 'Alison was the architect, Dom the sponsor and the PM the champion – even if he wasn't into the detail', says one official. 'Dom was completely behind it and that made all the difference,' believes Wolf.[19] It was the perfect set-up, granting a glimpse of what a successful Johnson premiership could have looked like. Less replicable, however, was the Treasury's acquiescence. Though still a challenge ('Sunak was hard work,' Wolf recalls[20]), it was convinced enough by the case for skills as a post-Covid growth measure with a sufficiently low price tag as to be acceptable, unlike the sky-high labels on levelling up and Johnson's infrastructure dreams.

Social Care and Health

Johnson had form on levelling up and infrastructure from his time as Mayor. 'Wow, where the hell did that come from?' was the reaction from his staff when he suddenly announced on the doorstep of No. 10 in July 2019 that he would be focusing on social care and had a 'plan'. 'I used that trick when I was Mayor,' he told staff with a self-satisfied grin afterwards. 'I would announce a plan out of the blue, and wait for the system to catch up.'

He could scarcely have picked a trickier rabbit to pull out of his hat. 'It was near impossible to see how to do social care reform without paying for it,' says a No. 10 official. 'There was huge resistance within the machine to getting anything done on it.' There was little electoral benefit to be gained, enormous risk and the Treasury was opposed to anything for which it would have to fork out. Yet 'he pushed it through personally, despite almost everybody in No. 10 on the political side being against it. "I want to do what no other PM has been able to achieve and fix," the PM told us,' says Dan Rosenfield, Johnson's chief of staff.[21]

Ironically, it was the funding of social care, when Johnson was at his most altruistic, that set the wheels in motion that led to his downfall.

The model chosen was that of economist Andrew Dilnot, author of the Cameron government's 2011 report on Funding of Care and Support. No. 10 health lead Will Warr put it forward as the most practical, cheapest and detailed of the schemes on the table (voluntary insurance, the alternative pushed by Hancock at the time, was quickly dismissed). Dilnot was brought in to consult during January 2020 and, in his words, 'left feeling uncertain whether there would be the political clout to make it happen, or if it'd be like all my other meetings since 2011 which went nowhere'.[22] Johnson was captivated by Dilnot explaining to him that social care affects 80 per cent of people before they die, but nobody knows who will need it or when. The market cannot thus pool the risk, so the public sector needs to step in and ensure that the costs of social care are fairly distributed so that individual families avoid catastrophe. Dilnot was a subtle reader of Prime Ministers and concluded his pitch with an excerpt from Martin Gilbert's Churchill biography, quoting the great man on social insurance: 'a real opportunity for what I once called "bringing the magic of averages to the rescue of the millions"'.[23] Johnson was engaged for the full ninety-minute meeting (an unusual occurrence) and went away prepared to do battle with the Treasury.

The policy progress, paused during the outbreak of the pandemic, resumed in September 2020. Failures in care homes during Covid had only highlighted the need for a joined-up and better-funded social care system. Not that it softened the Treasury to the cause. On 20 September an intrepid Dilnot presented the case in the Cabinet Room to Sunak and Johnson. 'The Treasury will tell you this is not the right time to do it, that Covid and the debt-to-GDP ratio says we can't. But this is far too short term,' he said, avoiding Sunak's eye. Onto the screen was then projected national debt as a percentage of GDP from 1974 to 2020. Then, his own rabbit out of the hat, he zoomed out, showing national debt as a percentage of GDP since 1691, revealing the UK to have unexceptional levels in comparison to previous crises. Johnson was convinced, but the presentation 'infuriated the Chancellor', says a No. 10 adviser. Dilnot, a past director of the Institute for Fiscal Studies, knew his pounds, shillings and pence. But Sunak and the Treasury were incensed that Dilnot was attempting to step on their turf and own the argument on economics, in addition to health.

While Hancock favoured exploring private insurance, he and the Department of Health and Social Care were happy to fall in behind the Prime Minister on what he was describing as 'my number one priority'. The introduction of a cap on the lifetime costs of social care at £86,000 was the core of No. 10's desired changes, the government also covering costs for those with assets of less than £20,000 (up from £14,000) and means-tested support for those with assets of between £20,000 and £100,000. The additional spending implied ensured that Treasury resistance to the proposals continued, undeterred by Dilnot and No. 10's arguments. 'We really didn't want to do it, and spent nine months protesting. In our view it was a bad policy with no delivery capabilities, Boris just wanted to do it for his legacy,' says a political aide to Sunak, signalling how much damage the issue was doing to their relationship. The issue came to a crunch in April and May 2021 in a series of bilaterals in which Johnson insisted on the policy and Sunak stonewalled, as one aide present recalls. 'Neither Dave nor Theresa cracked this. This is our opportunity,' said Johnson. 'If you insist on it going ahead, the roughly £5–£8 billion bill will have to be funded by new taxation,' Sunak replied, knowing full well that the 2019 manifesto ruled out tax rises. He was deeply unhappy:

'You will need to fund this long-term if we're expanding the role of the state,' he told Johnson.

Relations between the First and the Second Lords of the Treasury, once, if briefly, so amicable, were strained to breaking point. Sunak insisted that social care needed to be taxed as a long-term structural change, but also that it should be bundled with the short-term health goals of pandemic recovery in the NHS and vaccine payments. 'It was completely unnecessary,' No. 10 officials believe. 'It didn't make sense. He combined long-term transformation with short-term measures to tackle the impact of the pandemic, and you ended up with a hypothecated tax trying to pay for everything,' says one. Another saw a more sinister hand at work – 'an attempt for Sunak and the Treasury to flex their muscles' against the Prime Minister: 'As soon as they gauged Boris was serious they insisted that there needed to be a tax, knowing it would break the manifesto commitment. It was a deeply political move.'

To the surprise of some officials and aides considering the jeopardy, Johnson agreed to Sunak's proposed tax increase: 1.25 per cent on National Insurance Contributions (NICs), raising £12 billion a year.[24] His acquiescence to the Chancellor's demand was a signal of his political naïveté and how seriously he wanted the policy: 'He was incredibly focused and into the detail on social care. He asked the awkward questions and was very dedicated to it,' says No. 10 media strategist Meg Powell-Chandler.[25] 'We felt that it was an example of the Prime Minister taking on the big problems and showing conclusively that he was in charge,' agrees an official. 'Alongside HS2, social care was one of two moments during his premiership where Johnson had taken on the naysayers and won.'

His competitive streak, to succeed where Cameron and May failed, was just one motive. One for the scorecards the next time the living Prime Ministers met! But it was equally his closely guarded sensitivity which drove him: his mother Charlotte's experience with social care was a constant reminder of his mission, and that he could not sway to the path of least resistance lest he disappoint her memory. Just one week after the Prime Minister laid out his health and social care plan to the House of Commons on 7 September 2021, his much-loved mother died at the age of seventy-nine.

The September announcement went down terribly among Tory MPs resistant to tax rises, murmurs which grew as Johnson's position became weaker and weaker ahead of the levy's introduction in April 2022. 'I think this did huge damage psychologically, even bigger than Partygate,' says a senior aide. Sunak would not let him back out of his position and borrow to fund it, so Johnson had to stick with the policy or lose it all. One Treasury official believes it was a classic case of buyer's remorse: 'The Prime Minister felt that he'd been backed into a corner on it when he saw how unpopular it was within the party, and became very angry with Sunak indeed, blaming him for it all.' Seller's was Johnson's usual brand of remorse: he'd just added a new variant.

So much damage caused for so little gain to either figure. The Truss and Sunak premierships undid first the levy then, in the 2022 Autumn Statement, delayed the Dilnot reforms for two years, effectively ducking the issue until after the next election.[26] Unlike on levelling up, Johnson never won the rhetorical battle and convinced the public of his ideas. 'We squared off the right-wing papers in the general election, but if you don't have a mandate or level of public support, then social care changes are easy to unwind,' says a campaign strategist.

Johnson's legacy of social care may have disappeared as his premiership fades into the rear-view mirror; the legacy of health, as much as he may want it to, will not. The pandemic posed evident structural challenges for the NHS and healthcare provisions which went largely unresolved through the second half of Johnson's premiership. Covid infections had hugely diminished NHS capacity for elective treatments, thus the backlog ballooned: in February 2020 there were 4.4 million people on NHS England waiting lists; by May 2021 this had increased steadily to 5.3 million, and by the time Johnson left office in September 2022 it stood at 7.1 million – over 15 per cent of the UK population.[27] Prior to the pandemic A&E waits of twelve-plus hours were rare, peaking at just under 3,000 in January 2020. In September 2022, that figure amounted to 32,700 people who had waited over half a day to be admitted.

The twin pressures of austerity and Covid had driven the NHS further and further into crisis, while the NIC hypothecated tax aimed at the NHS was wholly insufficient to resolve the long tail of the worst pandemic in a century. Covid and long-term underfunding do not absolve Johnson for blame for the NHS problems under him. Key to the crisis were staffing issues which the 2019 manifesto had vowed to eliminate – the promised 6,000 GPs had not materialized, and although there had been some progress towards the target of 50,000 additional nurses, there remained a shortage of 50,000 nurses as well as 12,000 hospital doctors by the time of Johnson's departure.[28] The government refused to commit itself to regularly publishing workforce shortages and plans to address them.[29]

Many Prime Ministers struggle with overseeing the NHS, but Johnson was one of the less effective. His near-death experience at Guy's and St Thomas' Hospital in April 2020 gave him an altogether new and deep respect for the NHS. But he was never interested enough to assimilate the detail or to perceive systemic challenges to it, refusing to act as the threat of a collapsing NHS was not yet clear and imminent by the time he left. He was happy to visit hospitals, especially in elections, but was bored by spreadsheets and trade-offs. He never understood numbers, or the need to plan long-term in spending reviews, despite what his officials were telling him. A more orderly No. 10 would have served him better. But he preferred chaos and factions to order and prioritizing issues like health that really mattered to the country. Instead of providing gravitas, too many elements within the building were far more excited by the ephemeral, as we now see.

Culture

Three months after Covid arrived from the East, a tornado arrived from across the Atlantic. The May 2020 killing by the police of the African-American George Floyd in the United States triggered a cascade of anti-racist protests across the world, and pushed debates about culture and identity to the very top of the agenda in the UK.

Johnson's personal views on cultural issues were as inconsistent and fluid as any of his positions. He was proud of appointing the most ethnically diverse Cabinet in history: more members indeed than in every previous Cabinet combined, with all his three Chancellors (Javid, Sunak and Zahawi) from minority backgrounds. The left might respond that two-thirds attended private schools, but Johnson could retort with reason that his Conservative Party was far more progressive than the male and predominantly white Labour frontbench.

He had a real opportunity, as an intellectual, editor and writer, to give British culture a decisive lift, not least after Brexit. After initially regarding it as a 'grand project' akin to the Olympics, 'the next big thing' according to Nicky Morgan, he gave a wide berth to the 'Festival of Brexit'. First announced in 2018, it became 'UNBOXED: Creativity in the UK'; watered down by Covid and divisions within DCMS, it opened to muted applause in 2022. 'He was particularly fascinated by museums, not just Greek and Roman, but modern history as well, and always had at least one serious book on the go,' says a close aide. But as Prime Minister, he rarely if ever went to galleries, attended ballet, opera, concerts or theatre, and sacrificed the opportunity to be a Prime Minister of the arts. When the arts came to him, in the form of the Royal Shakespeare Company performing in Downing Street, he did not attend.[30] The Culture Recovery Fund was set up in July 2020 with £2 billion of capital and powerful backing from DCMS and Mirza in No. 10 to help arts bodies in England survive through Covid. The Fund proved a huge success, helping 5,000 cultural bodies across the country, and enabling the sector to survive intact through Covid. It proved the most important culture event of his premiership. 'Johnson surprisingly did not associate himself with the Fund,' says Damon Buffini, invited to be chair at the suggestion of DCMS, 'possibly because the idea came from the Treasury.'[31]

Johnson instead let culture be defined as mere 'culture wars' in a way that a more capable leader would not have let happen. On some days he cheered on whatever *Daily Mail* or *Telegraph* article fulminating about the latest 'woke' excess he had read over breakfast, on others he expressed outrage to aides on their narrow perspective. 'It depended on the day of the week,' says Oliver Dowden, his Culture Secretary and one of the most vehement on the need to push back against what he perceived as 'an attempt to delegitimize the Western enlightenment' from the left.[32] Above all, Johnson sought to avoid conflict and being disliked. As most cultural war issues had vocal backers on opposing sides, this led most often to his detachment. 'He was never particularly interested in the culture wars as he saw himself as an instinctively liberal unifier,' says one No. 10 official. 'The risqué comments on race earlier in his career put him on a sticky wicket, and he didn't want to invite accusations of racism,' says an aide. 'But on trans issues he didn't want to take a strong stand because frankly he didn't like to be unliked.' 'We want to Dodge, Duck, Dip, Dive and Dodge the issue,' Johnson told his aides whenever transgender questions came up, as they did increasingly, aping a line from one of his favourite films, the 2004 sports comedy *Dodgeball*.

Where the principal lacks strong views, the direction at No. 10 is often influenced by the team around the Prime Minister. The two most 'fiercely anti-woke zealots', as they were called, were married to each other, Munira Mirza and Dougie Smith. They regularly railed against individuals and institutions perceived to be pushing a 'woke' agenda. The list of those to be purged was long: the BBC, the civil service (especially the Treasury), the National Trust, universities and the NHS among those whose socially conscious tendencies needed to be stamped out. Supported by several ministers, notably Dowden, Truss and Kemi Badenoch, they were convinced of a need for the party and No. 10 to be ever more vocal on the emergent cultural fissures – not least on footballers' activism and new revisionist views of history and empire.

The difficulties over the first came in the government's response to England football star Marcus Rashford's campaign to extend free school meals over the summer holidays in 2020. The campaign was massively popular, forcing No. 10 into a U-turn in the form of a £120 million Covid summer food fund, then again in November 2020 over Christmas holiday provisions.[33] 'They were very rude about Rashford in meetings. He was winning the public battle and the senior political team didn't like it. They didn't think someone like him could win, that he was just a footballer, but he kept winning because he was right,' says an official.

Smith became exasperated when football players from the start of the 2020–21 season began 'taking the knee' in support of the Black Lives Matter movement. So he took things into his own hands, telling a special adviser at DCMS to put out an official statement banning the action. The aide contacted No. 10 and was told 'under no circumstances' to proceed, as the Prime Minister had given no such authority. A meeting was hurriedly convened in the Cabinet Room to resolve the issue. Cummings slouched in and muttered, 'No way.' The plan was dead, Smith going 'ballistic' at being blocked.

In June 2020, Raab had stoked controversy when he had said he saw the kneeling gesture as 'a symbol of subjugation and subordination rather than of liberation and emancipation'.[34] Johnson remained under pressure to make a stand against it. 'But the players are intelligent people and they'd have just done it anyway, then the PM would have looked weak,' says an official. Johnson didn't care for intervention either way – 'Stop giving it oxygen,' he would say to aides, so the decision to overrule Smith was made without his knowledge, witnesses attest.

The *Kulturkampf* intensified after Cummings' and Cain's departure. Dan Rosenfield, who took over as chief of staff in 2021, 'didn't give a toss about it', according to one official. Mirza and Smith maintained the pressure for Johnson to make stands while fresh impetus on the progressive side came from adviser Henry Newman and a renewed impetus from Symonds, while Home Secretary Patel was particularly vocal in moving the government's position against support for taking the knee. Johnson's own view was equivocal:

supporting the players' right to protest but refusing to condemn boos directed at them. As the Covid-delayed opening of the Euro 2020 football tournament in June 2021 came ever closer, the topic shot back up the agenda. 'When it looked like England might win the Euros, Johnson's mind suddenly switched and he became in favour of taking the knee and making a public stand,' says an insider. 'He became particularly gung ho when there was a prospect that he might host the celebratory party in No. 10 – possibly the first major football win since England won the World Cup in 1966. But even before England was defeated in the final, the players refused,' says an insider. Most damning was the comment of England player Tyrone Mings, following Patel's criticism of racial abuse towards the team after the penalty shootout loss. 'You don't get to stoke the fire at the beginning of the tournament by labelling our anti-racism message as "Gesture Politics" and then pretend to be disgusted when the very thing we're campaigning against, happens.'[35]

There was one football debate on which Johnson did opine very strongly from the start, though, precisely because he was told 'all the good guys are on the same side'. This was the announcement of the breakaway European Super League in April 2021, which would see the 'big six' clubs (Arsenal, Chelsea, Liverpool, Manchester City, Manchester United and Tottenham Hotspur) join nine of the top clubs from Europe in a competition where they would not be required to qualify on sporting merit. The proposals would widen the financial gap between the 'big six' and the rest of the Premier League, damaging English football. Johnson knew little of the beautiful game (he was a rugby man) so when No. 10 communications director Jack Doyle phoned him on Sunday 18 April he asked, 'What's all this stuff about?' 'It will be bad for football and hated by the fans,' Doyle told him. Johnson picked it up very quickly: 'This is a cartel. It's not fair,' he said. He sprung into action with singular vigour, convening a meeting for the top football brass in No. 10 and talking about using all the powers that Brexit gave him to ensure the plan would be destroyed. He'd use 'a legislative bomb', he said, to scupper the breakaway competition if football authorities were unable to stymie the move on their own.[36] Johnson was in his element, harmonizing with the backlash of fans and players, proclaiming at the Covid press conference in Downing Street that evening that football was 'one of the great glories of this country's cultural heritage'. Within a few days, aided if not unduly by his interventions, the plan was dead in the water.

History was at least an aspect of the culture wars on which Johnson was more confident, though still hesitant to elevate it to a first-order priority of the government. 'He was vehemently opposed to statues being pulled down, paintings removed, history edited,' says one close source. Johnson's clearest intervention came on 15 June 2020, in a *Telegraph* op-ed stating that he would 'resist with every breath in my body any attempt to remove [Winston Churchill's] statue from Parliament Square' after the statue became the centre of attention when right-wing extremists flocked to protect it after an activist sprayed 'was a racist' below Churchill's name.[37] Johnson's outspoken defence of an historical idol contrasted with his hesitancy to strike too bold a stance over the tearing down of statues associated with racism, such as that of slave-trader Edward Colston in Bristol. His brain was split between the metropolitan liberal mayor brain and a very different mode of thinking which hates the puritanism of 'woke'. 'But Churchill clarified the issue and gave him such a strong gut reaction,' says Doyle.[38] From then on the position on historic statues was clear, and a series of planning reforms were introduced to make them more difficult to take down.

Johnson's *Telegraph* article simultaneously called for 'a cross governmental commission to look at all aspects of inequality', laying the foundations for the launch of the Commission on Race and Ethnic Disparities, led by education expert Tony Sewell. Mirza had been pushing for his selection as a fellow critic of the concept of structural racism, and she recruited Commission members. The report concluded that the 'claim the country is still institutionally racist is not borne out by the evidence'. Publication in March 2021 provoked considerable angst across the political spectrum. Johnson himself took little interest in the report, and was content to let others get on with the task without publicizing it himself – an attitude Sewell later stated was due to Johnson's 'bad track record', including an admission from Johnson that 'the race thing's difficult for me'.[39] One facet of that was in discussing the impact of lone parent families, with 63 per cent of Black Caribbean children growing up in a lone parent family as the report found. 'That's dynamite, I don't want to go anywhere near it,' Johnson told aides. 'Having had his own share of children born out of wedlock, he didn't feel that he could take the moral high ground on the issue,' an adviser says. Best stay out of it altogether than upset more people and risk difficult questions, Johnson thought, letting Badenoch lead the response as Minister for Women and Equalities. The commission did little to build on the effective work of the Race Disparity Audit carried out under Theresa May, with few original suggestions.

Johnson was hailed as the leader who would take on the 'woke'-Remain establishment, planting solid, Brexiteer Conservatives in the commanding heights of national life. Some appointments he did shape, like occasional advisor and Tory donor Richard Sharp to chair the BBC in February 2021, and his campaign manager James Wharton, a Gavin Williamson suggestion, to chair the Office for Students two months later. He had previously tried to appoint former *Telegraph* and *Spectator* editor Charles Moore as chair of the BBC, but his biggest miss was failing to appoint former *Daily Mail* editor Paul Dacre to chair Ofcom. The independent appointment panel concluded that Dacre was 'not appointable' because of the 'robust' views he expressed in interviews, and broadcasting aficionado Michael Grade got the nod instead. Overall, Johnson's record of transforming the landscape by brave, new appointments was considered lacklustre at best, while his reluctance to take a stronger lead opposing 'woke' disappointed not just Mirza and Smith within No. 10, but many on the right of the Conservative Party, in the press and voters in traditional working-class heartlands.

The last group in particular felt betrayed that Johnson did not stand up more strongly as an opponent of immigration, a key factor in their voting for Brexit in 2016, and for Johnson in 2019.

Immigration

David Cameron said he didn't want his premiership to be overshadowed by Britain's membership of the EU, but it was. Boris Johnson didn't want his overshadowed by immigration, but it was. The 2021 census revealed that the ethnic minority population in England and Wales had increased by eight million over twenty years, with immigration playing a key role.

Johnson was as blasé about it, though, as Cameron tried to be about the EU. But following the Owen Paterson lobbying scandal and Partygate affair in November and December 2021, discussed later in the book, Johnson's survival instincts kicked in. The immediate threat was his MPs, but how to calm them? No more Brexit to deliver, no country to free from the shackles of lockdown, tax cuts blocked by his Chancellor. What, he wondered, was he to feed to the ravenous lions threatening to devour his premiership? The pantry was almost bare but for one remaining slab of red meat: immigration.

Immigration might have been the issue that more than anything was responsible for voters choosing to leave the EU, ranked by Leave voters as the most important reason for their choice ahead of the EU's role in law-making, contribution to the EU budget, and teaching British politicians a lesson.[40] But it was still an issue over which Johnson felt, in Rhett Butler's words from the film *Gone With the Wind*, 'Frankly… I don't give a damn.' The trouble was, that was exactly the attitude that Red Wallers suspected from a man whose privileged life had never been negatively impacted by immigration. It was one of the key issues of concern of the Common Sense Group, an informal band of some sixty Conservative MPs formed in the summer of 2020 by Edward Leigh and John Hayes. It was concerned by Johnson's decision in September 2019 to reverse May's policy and allow international students to remain in the UK for two years after graduating to look for a job. Johnson may have committed during the election campaign and in the manifesto to ensure that 'numbers will come down'[41] but he had no intention of seeing through that promise, and it riled many of his MPs and voters in the country.

Over the course of Johnson's premiership the balance of immigration tipped. The UK's departure from the EU had slowed flows from Eastern Europe, with a far higher number and proportion of immigrants coming from non-EU countries following the introduction of a more liberal points-based system from 1 January 2021 which decreased the skills and salary thresholds and suspended the cap on work visas. Johnson was content with this, and saw it as imperative that Britain extend an arm to those in Hong Kong and Ukraine threatened by oppressive regimes – the crises, as well as the economic necessity, meant total immigration had reached 504,000 in the year to June 2022 (up from 397,000 the year before).[42] The popularity of the Hong Kong and Ukraine schemes, as well as the decline of immigration as a political issue after Brexit, meant Johnson faced few protests for immigration numbers which would have been seen as politically disastrous for Cameron and May.

Where the Prime Minister tended to be firm was over uncontrolled immigration. The number of small boats bringing migrants across the Channel from France had been growing steadily since 2018. 'Initially, Johnson was persuaded the problem was unsolvable,' says an aide. 'But as the political pressure mounted, like with Afghanistan, he decided he would try to run it himself, which is not his forte.' His conversations with Patel went nowhere: he was frustrated that she couldn't deliver more viable options for him, and by the sheer level of systemic failure within the Home Office. His conversations with Macron went nowhere too, the French President telling him, an aide recalls, 'It isn't primarily a French problem, but a Belgian, Dutch, Spanish issue because they make landfall there and by the time they reach France, they are committed.' The Small Boats Task Force was a response in late 2021.[43] But the Border Force couldn't deter the armada and still the boats came. 'The Prime Minister saw it as an electoral issue certainly, but also a very good wedge issue to give him some positive headlines,' says an official.

Johnson came back from his Christmas holiday in January 2022 absolutely determined to be resolute. But then… he hesitated, to the consternation of all. His urge not to provoke dissent and his flickering deference for the status quo led him headlong into conflict with growing numbers of his MPs, whose irritation was funnelled by Patel. 'Some days he would say "we have to send them back, be tough", the next he would ignore his MPs completely,' recalls an official. For a while, to widespread confusion, he tried to run the policy himself from No. 10. But he wavered back and forth, before ultimately coming down against harsh measures such as dumping migrants back on French beaches or leaving the European Court of Human Rights (ECHR), as his right-wing MPs and advisers in No. 10 were advocating. 'Munira absolutely hated the ECHR and was *so* fired up about it,' says an aide. 'Push them back. Leave the ECHR,' hardliners persistently told him after she left in February 2022. But 'he knew in his heart of hearts it would be morally reprehensible to risk life and court illegality', says an insider.

Where he did not hesitate was on the controversial programme of deporting asylum seekers arriving by boat to Rwanda. 'Rwanda was a classic [attempt at a wedge issue],' continues a mandarin. 'No. 10 was absolutely gung ho about getting the deal over the line, money no object, with huge publicity and priority.' The merit of the plan was that it would act as a deterrent to would-be migrants, making them think again: 'a message to migrants that even if you got here it wouldn't be a land of milk and honey'. The scheme polled divisively, but was widely supported by Conservative voters – the precise tonic Johnson desired to remedy his ailing premiership.[44] Concerns from officials that the scheme was dangerous and unworkable, based upon significant human rights concerns with the Rwandan government and unproven efficacy as a deterrent, were ignored. Johnson was not about to let such doubts get in the way of rescuing his premiership from the brink, and drove the policy against resistance from the Foreign Office and the Home Office. His MPs were rallying to him, but then, he wobbled. On Tuesday 14 June 2022, the first asylum-seeker plane was waiting on the tarmac to fly the deportees off to

Rwanda when the ECHR intervened to stop the flight. 'Overrule the ECHR. This is your Churchill moment,' said a senior member of the Common Sense Group to Johnson in the Smoking Room of the House of Commons. 'A defiant stand against the ECHR is exactly what you need to win back your MPs.' 'I can't. We must show strategic patience,' he replied. The MP believes it cost him hugely.

Environment and Energy

'I used to think that all this green stuff was a load of nonsense,' Johnson regularly said. 'But I've seen the science.' As with social care, Johnson led from the front on the environment, a rare example where he was happy to upset people, principally on the right, and without being able to cite strong manifesto support. It gives us another glimpse of the leader that Johnson might have been.

Theresa May's late-premiership intervention on climate, committing to Net Zero by 2050 and the COP26 presidency, was one of her most influential. Her advocacy might have been used by Johnson as a reason for turning his back, but he found himself on a journey in the same direction. 'He always reacted against preachers, and the environment lobby with their strong views on Net Zero were up there,' says one official. But once in Downing Street he found aides and officials persuasive,[45] above all in appealing to his adventurous love of novel technologies and his columnist's weakness for a good tagline – as in his marketing the UK as 'the Saudi Arabia of wind'.[46] Johnson dispensed with hot air on this subject, wanting to bore down into the detail, his intellect fully engaged with the potential of carbon capture technology transformation, and the dire implications of failure.

Johnson's curiosity was bolstered by aides, officials and his wife Carrie – herself a lifelong environmentalist and lover of wildlife like his father Stanley. He was warned of severe opposition in the party, which contained a significant number of climate change deniers (Downing Street accordingly ditched proposals to undo Cameron's restrictions on onshore wind as a measure to appease them, opting to expand offshore wind instead). No. 10 too had its naysayers, in particular Cummings who bounced between uninterested and unsupportive of the plans. Ben Warner's testing of the proposals, worked up by Dhadda with official Emily Beynon, helped to reassure him.

Early progress came in a meeting on 10 January 2020 that Johnson held preparing for COP26 with chief scientist Vallance. Six months were then lost to Covid, as with other policy areas. But in June, a meeting with recently departed Governor of the Bank of England Mark Carney and business-climate supremo Adair Turner re-energized Johnson on green recovery and he started speaking about a 'ten point plan' for a 'green Industrial Revolution'. This was worked up by the Net Zero and energy lead in No. 10, Anouka Dhadda, with the help of Warner, in the summer of 2020 prior to publication in November.[47] 'We are going to change the country for the better,' he wrote in his note to thank the Policy Unit.

Differences in his increasingly fractious relationship with his Chancellor impeded progress. 'It shone a penetrating light on their different world views,' says a partisan aide. 'To the Prime Minister, he felt that the modern Conservative government should work with the private sector and set the signalling for how we could together shape decarbonization over the next decade. But to the Chancellor, the job of government was merely to set the framework and let the market get on with it.' But even Sunak had to concede ground when he realized how intent Johnson was. 'The PM was very effective in communicating to those in the party concerned about decarbonizing energy,' recalls an official. 'He always used the same script. "I used to be a sceptic, but I've seen the science. Let's go ahead and invest in the technology of the future. We can decarbonize and turn Britain into a green superpower."'

Johnson would forever gyrate between being a PM with an almost Brownite obsession with detail to a figure of frivolity, demanding throughout early 2021 that a mascot be found for the COP26 opening ceremony akin to the 'Olympic spirit'. 'After much perseverance from us, his mission got taken seriously by the system,' says an aide. Johnson's constant refrain 'I don't know what success in Glasgow looks like' was finally answered on 22 July at a meeting in No. 10 when Allegra Stratton came up with the catchphrase 'coal, cash, cars and trees', which he trailed at his speech at the UN in September. The event in Glasgow in November was the culmination of Johnson's efforts on the environment; as we see in the next chapter, COP26 also shows how much more he might have achieved with a more single-minded focus, undistracted by political turbulence.

The switch from Cummings to Rosenfield, who needed to be persuaded afresh on the necessity of the Net Zero programme, was another judder on progress, further evidence of the harm done to policy development by Johnson's inability to appoint a stable team at No. 10. Progress was handicapped too by the long-term impact of austerity and the Cameronite agenda – or cutting the 'green crap' as Cameron put it, referring to eco taxes on energy bills[48] – which saw the number of home energy efficiency installations collapse from over 2 million in 2012 to under 100,000 in 2021.[49] Although the Heat and Buildings Strategy published in October 2021 aimed to undo some of the damage, substantial improvements had not been made by the time energy prices began to rise, and the opportunity to dramatically improve the UK's energy efficiency was passed up.

Energy questions dominated Johnson's final months in No. 10. As 2022 began, energy prices were forecast to skyrocket as the world economy opened up following Covid, with global supply chains stretched by the surge in demand. In February, Sunak introduced a package of £9 billion to help households keep the lights on, but after Russia invaded Ukraine three weeks later it became clear that the knock-on effects would drive prices to unacceptable levels. In May, Sunak announced a further £15 billion package, part funded by a 'timely, temporary and targeted' £5 billion windfall tax on energy firms. The levy was stiffly contested by the new political team at No. 10, including Steve Barclay and David Canzini, as 'unconservative'.[50] Cabinet free marketeers including Truss were no keener, insisting it would deter investment, a position unexpectedly challenged by BP chief executive Bernard Looney.[51] If the social care levy had unintentionally damaged Sunak's reputation within the Conservative Party as a low-tax Chancellor, the energy levy, for those of the Truss persuasion, was the nail in the coffin.

No. 10, in one of the last domestic interventions of the Johnson premiership, led on the invasion's impact on energy prices with its energy security strategy, written by Dhadda and Glassborow and launched at Hinckley Point nuclear power station in April 2022.[52] It was intended to set a long-term strategy to decrease the UK's dependence on foreign, non-renewable energy sources, centred around the aspects of energy policy Johnson most enjoyed – technology and nuclear developments. It included a delivery body to drive eight new large nuclear reactors to final investment decisions by 2030, one a year, and investment in carbon capture. 'If we had built nuclear power ten years ago, we wouldn't be in this position now,' he said to his officials. The outbreak of the war highlighted afresh the need for independence from Russian natural gas and oil for Europe. But Johnson's long-term vision now ran headlong into domestic political turbulence. Johnson's fast-growing jeopardy militated against further short-term spending from the Treasury in support of his ambitions. Backbench pressure meant the continued exclusion of onshore wind to shore up support from the NIMBY wing of the party and a commission to explore the viability of fracking (popular among the party's right) despite the 2019 manifesto's moratorium and the Prime Minister's personal dislike of the practice. 'The politics were spiralling out of control,' says one official working on the strategy. However grand his vision, Johnson's premiership was deteriorating faster than legislation could be passed, all his remaining political capital spent on just surviving. As with Levelling Up, the Energy Security Bill was left in limbo as he departed from 10 Downing Street, more potential unrealized.

Education and Housing

When Johnson announced to his new Education Secretary, Gavin Williamson, at the start of the premiership 'I want every student to be ranked from one to two hundred in each year group. It's what happened at Eton,' he was disconcerted to be told by an official. 'But Prime Minister, I've been told that Eton stopped that practice many years ago.' Johnson harrumphed and changed the subject. He would have to come up with other ideas to address the policy vacuum beyond the wafer-thin promises in the manifesto.

The story highlights Johnson's strange lacuna on schools, as indeed on universities. The genuine if uneven interest he displayed in other areas of domestic policy was largely, bar the odd spasm, absent. As education played such a crucial part in solving levelling up, and had become in the previous twenty-five years such a core field of interest for the Prime Minister, the omission is puzzling.

The pandemic had been deeply damaging to education, widening inequalities and hampering student progress at all levels. A perfect storm blew in early with the exam fiasco of summer 2020. As the pandemic's interruption of the academic year made examinations impossible, an alternative method of grading had to be found. DfE had agreed that moderated teacher-assessed grades were the fairest method, using the best-available evidence of ability while minimizing the levels of grade inflation which would make it difficult to use results as an accurate gauge of ability. Usually reserved for students with extenuating circumstances, now it was being rolled out to the whole country.

But the grading caused uproar in Scotland, which had independently decided to moderate grades and, in any case, publishes its results ahead of the rest of the country, with many students failing to achieve their required results for university after their teacher-assessed grades were moderated downwards. The psychological toll on students missing their grades was particularly damaging, given no exams had been sat. A handful of officials and aides had been warning of the risk that DfE was not gripping the problem earlier that summer, but it was only then that the wider No. 10 system began to appreciate the scale of the problem about to hit England days later. It was feared that there would be unprecedented numbers of high grades awarded by teachers which would require heavy moderation down. DfE and Ofqual, the exams regulator, had not set up a sufficiently robust appeals process to cope with complaints despite having months to prepare, leaving few outs for the government. Making matters worse, the impending crisis had not been flagged up the chain of command in No. 10 until the results were nigh, meaning the Prime Minister had little clue how bad it would be until, at the eleventh hour, he had moderation explained to him. He was not amused at the lack of warning about the 'mutant algorithm', as he dubbed it, which produced the problematic grades. There were no palatable choices. If the Prime Minister stuck with moderation, thousands of pupils would be furious at their downgrading. If he twisted and opted for unmoderated teacher-assessed grades, there would emerge rampant grade inflation favouring students from more privileged backgrounds, widening the attainment gap.

The crisis highlighted the vacuum in the No. 10 he had created. Senior officials and aides sprinted away from the problem at breakneck pace rather than taking responsibility. 'Case, Cummings, Cain, they were all gunning for someone to blame,' says an official. When the crisis eased, officials were warned off trying to draw lessons for the future by a benign No. 10 figure for fear junior colleagues would end up taking the rap. 'Don't get involved – everyone is trying to shoot each other', was the advice. In the end it was DfE permanent secretary Jonathan Slater who caught the bullet; disliked by Cummings, and the department falling transparently short in their handling of grades, he made an easy scapegoat.

The fiasco was a sobering experience for Johnson, and he vowed to do better. The next year's handling, with teacher-assessed grades leading from the start, received criticism for disproportionate inflation among private schools in particular, but the measures (including plans to gradually deflate grades over 2021/22) were broadly successful in protecting admissions to university. Grades aside, there remained two questions: how do we get students back to the desired level of learning, and how can we mitigate the widening of the attainment gap between wealthy and poorer students which had worsened during the pandemic? In late 2020 Johnson became convinced that an 'education recovery plan' was what was required to redress the learning lost. 'He didn't have great confidence in the Education Secretary to sort it out, so he proposed the idea of getting in an external expert,' says an aide. At the recommendation of his Policy Unit, Johnson duly appointed respected educationalist Kevan Collins to be his 'education recovery tsar' to lead an ambitious programme. For a few weeks, Johnson became immersed in schools, quickly alighting on the 'three Ts' – tutoring, time and teaching – as ways forward. 'Tutoring programmes for disadvantaged students, which worked in Bradford, became his particular passion,' recalls schools adviser Rory Gribbell.[53] He drilled down to a level of detail not normally seen, wanting to know that teaching materials for the new teachers being trained would pass the 'Prof Mirza' test, the gold standard he ascribed to his long-standing education specialist.

Johnson whipped himself up into a fervour, ignoring amber lights flashing from the Treasury, driving Collins to be as ambitious as possible. Johnson was not blind to the sheer costs: 'Bloody hell, how many children are there?' he baulked whenever the price of measures for all students was mentioned, but he had not reconciled this reaction with the reception he would likely get from his Chancellor if he were to seriously pursue the policy. Little was done to temper the expectations of the new tsar, and no one explained to him Johnson's known tendency, oddly unnoticed by Collins, to build castles in the sky. 'It's not big enough, it's not big enough,' the Prime Minister would say in meetings, wanting the package to be ratcheted up as far as it could go. In the words of one No. 10 official, 'Kevan mistook the Prime Minister's enthusiasm as backing his ambitions to the hilt.'

Collins soon found himself the unwitting victim stranded in a no man's land in a firefight between No. 10 and No. 11. Having agreed with Johnson a £15 billion package – which No. 10 promptly briefed to the media – Collins' proposals fell apart upon first contact with the Treasury. 'The evidence was absolutely rubbish, there was no groundwork done with the sector, it was just a big list of mad demands,' argues a Treasury aide. Sunak's officials were particularly unconvinced by Collins' proposals for lengthening the school day, and the Chancellor was characteristically unwilling to dip into funds for yet another of Johnson's schemes. With the Prime Minister unwilling to have a row with his Chancellor, and the Education Secretary possessing little personal investment in the plans, Sunak easily talked them down over pizza in Johnson's flat one Sunday evening to a figure of £1.4 billion of additional funding, just a tenth of the original proposals.[54] Collins' resignation inevitably followed, and he publicly criticized the 'feeble' proposals of the government in compensating for educational loss and bridging the growing attainment gap.[55] Coming on top of the exams fiasco, it shot the government's credibility for having anything valuable to say on schools.

Universities were another area where Johnson, as one of the most academically interested of recent Prime Ministers and the first author in the post since Brown, might have been expected to make a positive impact. He had moreover, when shadow Higher Education Minister, written his one and only think tank pamphlet, *Aspire Ever Higher: University Policy for the 21st Century* (2006). He railed against Britain's universities being weakened by ever tighter control from government and its bureaucracies, with their freedoms under threat from 'the political and ideological preferences of governments'. His three-point plan was for 'proper funding', 'less interference' and 'greater freedoms' to allow these 'hierarchies of excellence' to flourish. His brother Jo's early action as Universities Minister in liberalizing visas for overseas students was in tune with the pamphlet's spirit, and delighted the sector as much as it had antagonized the right.

He might have built on this start to enlist universities in his drive for levelling up and helping the economy thrive better post-Brexit, given how integral the sector is to the success of the British economy. A meeting with university vice chancellors arranged in July 2019 with Williamson showed the Education Secretary they were not a bunch of wild 'wokers' but serious professionals willing to work as partners with the government.[56] But little followed to build on this spirit beyond greater flexibility on visas and the Turing Scheme for student exchanges to replace the EU's Erasmus Programme after Brexit, driven by Johnson against Treasury parsimony.

Instead of partnership, imagination and shared ambitions, policy was dictated by the elements with No. 10 who chose to tar all universities with the actions of a radical and 'woke' minority. Cummings, a rare imaginative force in the debate, wanted to abolish the laborious Office for Students to free up universities, but was deflected by Williamson. Where Cummings had more success in his attempts to free the sector from bureaucracy was in pushing for its place at the heart of the UK's research and development space, boosting UK Research and Innovation funding as a benefit of the uplifted science budget (£22 billion, up from £14 billion) and simplifying funding criteria. Without Cummings, suspicion and mutual incomprehension began to grow. The government went on the rampage to defend free speech without boosting it. Sunak too had an oddly restrictive vision, dictated less by culture than by finance: 'Rishi had a driving ambition to reduce the cost of universities to the taxpayer and an absolute determination to reduce the student loan book which was not paid back,' says Alison Wolf.[57] His policy bore fruit in changes to student loans in spring 2022 as a long-overdue response to the Augar Review under May's premiership.

Education cried out for an imaginative approach post-Brexit after some lacklustre years with three changes of Education Secretary since Gove's defining regime ended in 2014. New AI and digital technologies were transforming schools and universities globally, fresh approaches to mental health were waiting to be developed and educational institutions at every level cried out for more independence from the dead hand of state regulation. Geographic inequality in education was begging for a 'levelling up' solution. Instead, Johnson had five Education Secretaries, but no defined education policy.

Yet more opportunity was foregone in housing policy despite Johnson's obvious relish for the subject as Mayor. 'Build, Build, Build', was his announcement in June 2020,[58] allied with Cummings in believing that Britain's archaic planning system needed a complete overhaul. Building more houses was a moral cause, home ownership a 'most fundamental' value as the 2019 manifesto stated. It was political too; ownership strongly correlated with voting trends, with renters far less likely to vote for the Conservative Party. Building more houses was thus necessary medicine to enhance the future health of the party, but Conservative MPs couldn't stomach the taste.

Cummings was thus the primary driver of policy, with Johnson willing to join him in revolutionary rhetoric, as ever until things got tough. 'He always chose the radical policy choice, but never thought it through, and was never willing to be unpopular – especially with Tory MPs,' says a senior Conservative. 'But you would leave a meeting where he backed certain reforms only to discover the next week that he'd withdrawn support.' After Cummings departed in November 2020 the engine lost steam, the Prime Minister more easily swayed by vociferous NIMBY backbenchers. At the No. 10 strategy day in April 2021, Johnson toyed with the idea of giving housing an extra impetus again, but, despite himself, pulled back. The seminal Chesham and Amersham by-election in June proved the turning point. The loss of a Blue Wall seat to the Lib Dems campaigning against the government's plans for housing was an omen that the party would struggle to please both sides of their coalition at the next election. Planning measures, part of the Levelling Up and Regeneration Bill, did not make it through Parliament during Johnson's tenure, with the threat of over eighty MPs rebelling against it. Johnson's domestic policy required money.

The Second Chancellor

After the 'spend, spend, spend' promises of the first six months, reality dawned. February 2020 brought Covid, and a new Chancellor. Javid had been willing to go along with the pre-election bonanza, but the March 2020 Budget which he wrote and Sunak delivered was overshadowed by largesse dictated by a new impetus, the pandemic. Within weeks, Sunak showed that he was going to be a more formidable and independent force than Cummings had reckoned, not least smartly putting paid to the plans for a 'joint economic unit' between No. 10 and the Treasury. Liam Booth-Smith and Douglas McNeill went across from Downing Street to join Sunak and the Treasury, and in no time went native. 'The joint unit was never a serious idea. It had no advocates with the power to make it happen,' says a Treasury official, and Cummings, immersed in Covid, had no spare capacity to fight.

Relations between PM and Chancellor were mostly good for 2020. Sunak had not expected to find himself suddenly leading the Treasury, and was very conscious of his inexperience and junior status: he had entered Parliament less than five years before and had only been made a minister in 2018. 'Sunak started off saying "Johnson is the person running the government as the First Lord of the Treasury",' says a senior Treasury official. 'But then over time, he realized you can't survive like this, and that he was getting no direction from the Prime Minister, or at least no consistent direction. He had to step up.'

Sunak had shown confidence and resolution in coming up with the furlough and Eat Out to Help Out schemes, and Johnson had let him take the credit. November's Spending Review caused yet more conflict within No. 10, between Johnson and Cummings' different priorities, rather than a battle against the Treasury – though Sunak insisted on it being a multi-year settlement to lock in the future. Both sides realized that with the return of the pandemic it would be prudent to make it a more short-term, one-year exercise.

The March 2021 Budget, which saw capital allowance reforms coupled with a corporation tax rise and thresholds freeze, was reasonably harmonious. The ideas were mostly driven by Sunak and Booth-Smith in their regular weekly meetings, where Johnson was supported by his civil servants: Glassborow and occasionally Case. A growth strategy formed part of their conversation with elements making it into the Budget, but then became lost in the detail with Johnson keen, Sunak less so, but neither principal exerting themselves to push it. It was only afterwards when the relationship began to break down that Johnson started to drive ahead on his favoured policies. Their fallouts over Net Zero, social care and education were not helped by Sunak taking an almost instantaneous dislike to Johnson's new chief of staff, Dan Rosenfield, who knew the Treasury well and who he felt talked down to him. Johnson and Rosenfield toyed that summer with finding a more pliable Chancellor, but concluded it would be too risky to do so in the September 2021 reshuffle, so settled for challenging his growing powerbase by moving his leadership rival Truss into the Foreign Office.

Tension broke seriously out into the open over the 2021 Spending Review in October. 'The PM was desperate for a legacy, but with all the broken promises over the year, Rishi was not minded to yield,' as a Sunak aide recounts, indicative of the bad blood. Sunak and his team had become disillusioned, regarding Johnson as not serious about holding ministers to their spending commitments. 'We no longer thought Johnson would back us against the departments: No. 10 had become an agent for the Ministry of Defence, DHSC, and even for Business,' says another Treasury source. A confrontation was only a matter of time. 'I am done,' announced Sunak to No. 10 two weeks before the statement. 'I'm not signing off any more spending.' With ten spending decisions still to be taken, it made for the most turbulent time to date between No. 10 and the Treasury.

Two days before the Spending Review, a crisis meeting was held in No. 10 for the PM and the Chancellor, with their teams to break the deadlock. 'Here are my demands,' Johnson said at the beginning of the meeting. 'Everyone out,' snapped Sunak. Silence. 'Give them the room,' someone said, as the teams filed nervously out. Both men, left alone, were uncomfortable: neither liked conflict. As was later recounted to aides on both sides, Sunak explained that he believed that Johnson had been led up the garden path and set up to fail, blaming Rosenfield squarely for the strategy of asking for a further £20 billion spending at the last minute, hoping for at least a third. Sunak held all the key cards: he knew Johnson couldn't afford to dismiss another Chancellor when he was so politically weak, and Johnson was left with no further money. He realized he could not continue to push his Chancellor.

From this point to the end, Sunak and his political team had given up on Johnson, and began thinking how he might impose his agenda. Sunak was the most forceful figure in the tense Cabinet meeting on 20 December, deciding against lockdown. His distaste for Johnson increased further over Partygate. He was angry at being fined himself, but most of his fury was directed at Johnson for his handling of the entire affair.

Rows over energy policy and funding for Ukraine dominated the spring, difficulties caused by the rising levels of inflation plunging the relationship to new depths. Sunak's caution ran up against Johnson's desire to build an enthusiastic response to the worsening economic situation. 'We felt suffocated by Rishi, who didn't seem to see the need for growth. His only interest was cushioning the blow for households in the short term by subsidizing bills,' says a No. 10 adviser. To make matters worse, in April 2022 Sunak came close to resigning over attacks on the tax affairs of his wife Akshata Murty, with her non-domicile status. In the toxic atmosphere, the belief was widespread that it had been leaked in retaliation from those close to Johnson. Sunak's resignation was only a matter of time.

For all Johnson's frustrations that he could never obtain the money he wanted for his grand visions, it was his Heseltinian philosophy of a higher tax, higher spend state that triumphed rather than Sunak's Thatcherite approach. Johnson's three years as Prime Minister mark a clean break from the austerity and parsimony of

Osborne and Philip Hammond. Spending on health, education and crime were all significantly up. Not quite F. D. Roosevelt perhaps. But Johnson outspent Cameron and May while taxing and investing not insignificantly, which he regarded as success of a kind.

Omicron (November–December 2021)

Following 'Freedom Day' on 19 July 2021, Covid declined from its status as a first-tier issue, with vaccination and testing both wide-scale throughout the country, and Whitehall bandwidth had been freed up to focus on the policy matters neglected during the pandemic. There was to be one more twist in the tale, however. In late 2021, a new variant had arrived in the form of Omicron. Early data from South Africa, where the variant originated, suggested it was highly transmissible and outcompeting other strains, with SAGE forecasting up to 6,000 deaths a day at the peak if no intervention was carried out. Initial murmurings in early December were that the mutation might affect children as badly as adults, a nightmare scenario with deeply worrying implications for education and healthcare.

Johnson had been adamant that 'Freedom Day' meant freedom; that belief was to be tested. Whitty and Vallance informed him that to avoid the NHS being overwhelmed and the risk of another lockdown, some measures needed to be taken to bolster immunity and minimize the spread in a non-intrusive manner. This solution was labelled 'Plan B', worked up earlier that autumn, and laid out by Johnson on 8 December. Plan B contained a package of measures to limit transmission without the imposition of severe restrictions, including working from home, the mandatory wearing of face masks indoors where practical, and 'vaccine passports' (proof of vaccinated status or a negative lateral flow test) being made obligatory for nightclubs and large venues. The restrictions, though moderately effective at slowing the spread of the virus, were deeply unpopular among Conservative backbenchers. Ninety-nine Conservative MPs voted against the measures on 14 December – Johnson's blushes were saved only by Starmer whipping Labour MPs in favour of the changes.[59] It was the nadir of Johnson's relationship with the Conservative Party over Covid, and the largest parliamentary rebellion he would experience in his time as Prime Minister. 'No. 10 simply hadn't caught up with the fact that MPs wouldn't tolerate it any longer,' says one rebel.

Partnered with the restrictions was a major drive on booster jabs, propelled by Johnson's conviction that vaccinations were the way out of the pandemic. 'He recaptured the sense of a national mission,' says an official. The Prime Minister, concerned about the rate of the rollout ahead of an inevitable winter wave even before the emergence of Omicron, had asked that Emily Lawson return to the vaccine programme in October and oversee the provision of a third jab to the population in order to boost immune responses. The emergence of Omicron kicked the upscaling into overdrive, with Johnson addressing the nation on 12 December to say, 'We must urgently reinforce our wall of vaccine protection to keep our friends and loved ones safe… And I know there will be some people watching who will be asking whether Omicron is less severe than previous variants, and whether we really need to go out and get that booster. And the answer is yes we do.'[60] Early research showed booster shots were up to 75 per cent effective against symptomatic infection from Omicron, numbers which would dramatically cut the level of infection if widespread uptake of third doses could be achieved.[61] 'We must race the variant,' Johnson told officials, urging them to spread immunity through vaccination faster than the variant could make its way through the population. The campaign to 'Get Boosted Now' proved a success and saw the UK's daily jabs reach their highest ever level, peaking at a seven-day rolling average of 970,350 daily administered jabs on 21 December.

Despite the successful vaccine rollout, cases continued to rise throughout December, and scientists became increasingly nervous that the rise in infections could result in a collapse of healthcare services in early January 2022. Deputy Chief Medical Officer Jenny Harries labelled it on 15 December 'probably the most significant threat we've had since the start of the pandemic'.[62] While many were urging Johnson that a lockdown could not be avoided, including the Covid Task Force, Whitty and Vallance were not among them. 'Chris and Patrick didn't come down either side, they were balanced and very straight, holding their nerve and giving the PM space to hold a judgement,' says an official. Though still early and unable to ascertain the severity of the variant (although concerns about it affecting children were by this stage relieved), preliminary data indicated that hospitalizations in South Africa from the variant were below the expected range.

Johnson again had a choice: caution or confidence. The evidence was more finely balanced than in 2020, and the Prime Minister himself in a far weaker position following the double hits of Paterson and Partygate. The first had damaged his reputation with his backbenchers, the second with the public. Johnson unilaterally declaring a lockdown amid reports of No. 10 staff engaging in brazen rule-breaking during the first two was therefore a non-starter. Johnson's own instincts were that lockdown should be avoided, officials recalling that he found Sunak's argument to be very persuasive: 'If we lock down now, with all the vaccines, when won't we lock down in the face of a wave? We'll be sunk to this virus forever.' Those instincts were finely tempered by now, though, and Johnson was cautious of having another disaster on his hands. 'The Prime Minister didn't *want* to lock down, but he was genuinely unsure whether or not he *had* to,' as a Covid official puts it.

This dilemma produced the only formal Cabinet debate of significance during Johnson's entire premiership. Whichever way his ministers went, if later found wrong, the Prime Minister would not shoulder sole responsibility for the decision; if proven correct, he would be able to champion the decision as exemplary political leadership. In the 20 December meeting the Covid Task Force opened with a short presentation on the numbers and the threat, before the Prime Minister urged his Cabinet, 'Each of you, speak freely.' Those round the table gave their view one by one, it soon becoming clear that the majority were against another lockdown. Hancock had resigned in June following the revelation he had breached social distancing guidelines by having an affair with his special adviser Gina Coladangelo. His successor Javid did not hold his strong views, leaving only Gove holding the fort for the lockdown hawks. He found himself heavily outnumbered: on the other side of the debate Sunak, Truss and Shapps had coordinated their position, drawing upon external JPMorgan modelling projecting that deaths would be far lower than the SAGE figures based upon South African Omicron data.

Even after the position was decided, officials saw Johnson working effectively: chairing daily meetings, tracking the data carefully and keeping on top of any developments. Just two days later Johnson and his Cabinet would be partially vindicated in their approach, when the UK Health Security Agency published its finding that Omicron would cause a milder disease than the Delta variant it was outcompeting with its rapid spread. SAGE's projected minimum peak of 3,000 hospitalizations a day without further intervention did not transpire, with numbers peaking at 2,000 in early January (just over half of the second wave peak of 3,800). The link between cases and deaths was hugely diminished thanks to the vaccine efforts, peaking at 250 deaths a day in the Omicron wave – a massive reduction compared to the second wave's peak of 1,200. Gove later issued a *mea culpa* to the Cabinet on his position: 'One of Boris's strengths was his willingness to be convinced, to admit when he's changed his mind. I felt it was the right thing to reciprocate over Omicron,' he says.[63] Although he had got this one wrong, Gove's overall record provided a stark contrast to a Prime Minister who had often erred. 'Michael was right on everything Covid, apart from Omicron,' says a No. 10 official.

For all the multitude of flaws found in the government's 2020 Covid response, Johnson deserves credit for his handling of the pandemic response in 2021. The vaccine rollout, roadmap, booster programme, June pause on reopening and holding his nerve over Omicron all demanded difficult decisions, the bulk of which the Prime Minister made correctly.

How can we explain Johnson's differential performance? Not all Prime Ministers improve greatly over their tenure. To his credit Johnson showed he was capable of 'learning through doing' given a sufficient number of opportunities: he had become better at executing the basic competencies of crisis handling in 2021 than in 2020. His data literacy had improved, if only marginally, and he had become more effective at considering the credible arguments on any given Covid issue rather than grasping onto those he wanted to hear. But there is also the fortune that the latter period aligned with Johnson's own instincts, to take risks and push boundaries as to how far and fast the UK could return to normalcy. Johnson's relentless triangulation of public opinion, party opinion, Cabinet opinion and expert opinion was eventually successful, through a mix of conscious effort and luck.

Underweighting the opinions of cautious officials and a scared public due to the pressures of Sunak and backbenchers in the first half of the pandemic was a critical mistake. 'He was far too ready to be driven by the noise in 2020,' says a Covid official. Although his weighting had improved by 2021, it was fortuitous for his position that the danger of Omicron had been overplayed by experts. 'You could argue that the real difference is when it came to the third wave, the politicians decided to ignore the advice and got away with it. They did the same thing in the second wave; the difference is they didn't get away with it then,' says a senior NHS official.

Britain in 2022: Dreams and Reality

Cabinet Secretary Simon Case, delivering a lecture in October 2021, spoke of what kept him awake at night: his doctoral adviser Peter Hennessy's greatest fear for government, the 'Curse of the Missed Opportunity'. That, as after the Second World War, Britain would not use great disruptions, in this case the pandemic, to fix the state's emergent weaknesses. These he defined as poor coordination between national and local government, low-quality data use, and lack of specialism and technical ability.[64] 'We need to fix these weaknesses – and I know we can – to help spearhead a recovery from Covid and truly deliver levelling up,' Case told the audience. Johnson departed from office less than a year after Case's speech, during which time those opportunities had slipped gradually like sand through Johnson's fingers.

Covid provides a partial explanation as to why more domestic policy achievements were not notched up. The 2019 manifesto was thin and detail-light, not written to govern but to win. Johnsonism, in all its vague definition, and lacking a settled locus in any Conservative tradition, therefore lasted only as long as the party's belief in the man and his policies. Nobody had been lashed to the mast of detailed commitments and plans, not even Johnson himself, thus the ship of state set sail perilously, devoid of a clear map or destination.

The inevitable loss of political capital and the entirely unpredictable Covid pandemic could have been countered by a stronger leader able to both articulate why the Conservatives would need to act if they were to set themselves upon a path to win in 2024, and execute the policies with intent and authority. But Johnson's indecision, biddability and eagerness to agree with the last person he spoke to plunged programmes into a state of constant flux. 'It was so difficult to work with him because it is genuinely hard to tell what he believes. He's so good at convincing others, you never know if he's quite convinced himself,' says a senior domestic policy mandarin. He swayed like a willow in the wind, bending to the preferences of all he wished to please then meekly backing down when confronted on the feasibility, detail and trade-offs. Often unserious, unable to focus for long and lacking any kind of grip on the machine, his mentality was ill-equipped for the task of governing for an extended period.

It is tempting to explain away his lack of domestic success by his not being afforded a lengthy period of preparation for his spell in No. 10. But as we have seen, he didn't use his journey on the way up to No. 10, despite a lifetime of dreams of its front door opening to him, to prepare for the rigours of the job or to develop his personal credo. Very likely, a prolonged period as Leader of the Opposition, as Thatcher, Blair and Cameron enjoyed, would have shown up his glaring faults earlier for all to see. At his core, Johnson is driven by the thrill of the deadline, that flirtation with failure which quickens the heart and focuses the mind. Having longer to prepare would not have been seized by a man whose nature was to treat time as a challenge, not an opportunity.

Johnson's ambitions will not leave a totally empty legacy. He was hardly the first to declare an end to austerity, but it was his premiership which marked a definitive break with the central project of the Cameron government in both policy and rhetoric. The UK's tax burden rose to the highest level since the Second World War, with a marked increase in expenditure through conscious choices to embrace a more activist state. Johnson disavows this legacy in his post-premiership call for a 'low tax Global Britain', but his imprint is undeniable.[65] The benefits of investment decisions in nuclear energy, infrastructure and R&D will not provide an immediate return, but they will be reaped in years to come in a stark and favourable comparison to the dearth of capital projects in the Conservative governments immediately before him. His push of skills will leave a legacy throughout the country too for decades to come.

But there still feels the sting of wasted opportunity. Here was a genuinely innovative and heterodox set of aims, with some lofty ambitions – reducing regional inequalities, resolving the unrelenting issue of social care, ending the housing crisis – which at his best the Prime Minister could invoke to span left and right, a 'squatting toad' over British politics as characterized by Brexit's great chronicler Tim Shipman.[66]

Before him lay the grand opportunity to reshape the country, to use his majority and the critical juncture of the pandemic to build a new national settlement, just as the great Prime Ministers before him had used their own crises. How much more could have been achieved if not for the indecision, the people-pleasing, the procrastination and the mistrust at the very top? The failure to do more to prepare for Covid cannot be laid at his door; the failure to do more to prepare for the cost of living, energy and NHS crises can. All Prime Ministers look back on their premiership with regret that they did not do more to seize their moment and secure their domestic legacy when the fruit was fresh. Johnson has reason to be regretful more than most.

If Johnson was to have a legacy, it would have to be on Britain's position in the world.

Johnson walks the streets of Kyiv on a surprise visit to see Volodymir Zelenskyy on 9 April 2022

8

GLOBAL

'I want the UK to feel different. I want in fifty years' time people to say Brexit has transformed the life experience of Britons,' Johnson told his team on his first day as Prime Minister. Glad confident morning, when everything seemed possible. 'He continued to believe in Brexit. I don't remember him ever having doubts about whether it was the right thing,' says a diplomat. 'He saw Brexit as the chance to reinvent the country. He saw it as a unique fillip to Britain in the world.'

Johnson's Brexit co-leader Michael Gove, the only other one of the four big beasts of the 2010s still standing, confirms how serious he was. 'He believed that post-Brexit Britain presented a unique opportunity, once we were at last untangled from the EU, for free trade, to exploit its defence and security assets, the English language, soft power and place in the world. He saw this as the time of pivot for Britain.'[1]

Prime Ministers only rarely enjoy a pivot moment, the chance fundamentally to reset the country on a new global course. Lloyd George after 1918 and Clement Attlee after 1945 both did. Harold Macmillan after Suez in 1956 and Blair after 9/11 both tried. Johnson, his sense of history to the fore, rose to the challenge rhetorically. Just three days after Britain formally left the EU at 23:00, 31 January 2020, with his blood strongly up, Johnson declared in a landmark speech in London's Greenwich, 'We are embarked now on a great voyage, a project that no one thought in the international community that this country would have the guts to undertake'. Britain would prevail, he continued, 'if we are brave and if we truly commit to the logic of our mission – open, outward-looking, generous, welcoming, engaged with the world championing global free trade now and global free trade needs a global champion'.[2]

To find a historic comparison for the opportunity facing Britain, Johnson went back further than 1918. His inspiration was the 'Glorious Revolution' of 1688, depicted in the painting above his audience's heads in the Painted Hall at Sir Christopher Wren's Royal Naval College. This opportunity, he said, was like that, a moment of 'supreme national self-confidence', with Britain 'on the slipway' to nothing less than global economic dominance. Johnson's extravagant vision would need to commit people and resources to achieve it. It would require him to impart a purpose, substance and drive which, as we have just seen, were so lacking in his domestic agenda. Above all, strategic clarity would be needed if the opportunity was not to be lost, not least during Covid, about which he made so light to his audience at Greenwich. Britain, he said, was 'ready to take off its Clark Kent spectacles, leap into the phone booth and emerge with its cloak flowing as the supercharged champion' of economic freedom in any standoff with public health restriction. We should be on the alert, he said, for the 'risk that new diseases such as coronavirus will trigger a panic and a desire for market segregation that go beyond what is medically rational, to the point of doing real and unnecessary economic damage'.

It was the most optimistic, and the most hubristic, speech Johnson was to deliver as Prime Minister. Indeed, it's hard to find many speeches by a Prime Minister on such a serious topic that are more hubristic.

Johnson's foreign policy team

The PM might not have had a plan, but he had a plan on how to arrive at a plan. 'Put down in 3,000 words what you think my foreign policy should be,' Johnson told his startled officials in No. 10 soon after becoming Prime Minister. The diplomats looked at each other in dismay. 'The thing about Boris was he didn't know what he wanted,' says one. This is puzzling given foreign policy was his solitary area of ministerial expertise. Before 1964, it was not uncommon for Prime Ministers to have served as Foreign Secretary, the second most important position in government till replaced by the Chancellor of the Exchequer in the 1960s. But since then, only three others have done so, Jim Callaghan and, very briefly, John Major (now also Liz Truss). Johnson's two years should have given him a vantage point on a field denied most contemporary incomers. But as we have seen, he was an aimless Foreign Secretary, 'nothing more than a translator' for the Prime Minister as he told officials.

Johnson appointed Dominic Raab as Foreign Secretary, but apart from cutting him a bit of slack in areas like Hong Kong, he gave him no more meat than Theresa May had given him despite Raab's continual attempts to be involved and control policy. The Prime Minister thought Raab altogether too cautious, and the Foreign and Commonwealth Office, partly as a result barely featured in his thinking. Occasional backer and Defence Secretary Ben Wallace was marginally more influential, and their relationship improved critically on Ukraine; until then Johnson found him rather 'needy' (exactly the word May had used to describe him as Foreign Secretary) and unpredictable, always trying to set up meetings with him no matter the importance of the subject. He would largely ignore them both. Rather, he would plot his revolution in Britain's foreign policy position from within No. 10. David Frost, his Europe adviser from July 2019, was given even more independent authority than his predecessor Olly Robbins had under May. 'Boris was quite content to delegate a lot to me. We had a couple of meetings where I talked things through, but it was clear that the PM and I agreed, and there wasn't room for other views,' says Frost.[3] Not having room for the views of others suited Johnson just fine.

Planned changes for the foreign policy apparatus in Whitehall went ahead, with Johnson merging the Department for International Development (DfID) into the Foreign and Commonwealth Office. Though adopted by Cummings, the idea had long been a Johnson passion, and according to Foreign Office officials came to him after a visit to an African nation as Foreign Secretary. As the trip came to a close he told the local protocol officer that he'd had a good time, but expressed disappointment that he'd not been able to meet the President or Prime Minister, to which came the reply, 'Really? They saw the DfID Director who was here last week.' Johnson thought anything less than a full merger would leave DfID's healthy budget and leading policy in Africa diminished and forgotten, rather than joined-up thinking connected to the goals of the FCO. With support from Sedwill, Cummings, McDonald, Bew, Reynolds and Raab, in June 2020 two became one under the banner of the Foreign, Commonwealth and Development Office (FCDO). All felt foreign policy would be better served having both under one roof, but the difficulty of the merger soon became apparent: both Foreign Office and DfID officials describe it as highly dysfunctional in process and outcome, with diplomats criticizing Johnson's approach to it as 'distracted'.

Shortly following the merger came a second major change, this time pursued by the Chancellor. In the 2020 Autumn Spending Review Sunak announced the cutting of the aid budget from 0.7 per cent of gross national income to 0.5 per cent, a major cost-saving measure in the face of the pandemic which broke promises set out by both the manifesto and Johnson himself. Though Johnson was not enthusiastic about the change, Sunak found allies in Raab, Cummings and Conservative backbenchers who had long felt the aid target far too high. Also in favour was McDonald, to the chagrin of ex-DfID civil servants who had merged in. 'They wanted to ensure that there was no ongoing competition to be a voice of the department separate from the FCO, they wanted development to be totally subservient,' says one. To Foreign Office officials the change was simply joined-up government.

On national security and defence, Johnson set great store by the seasoned Mark Sedwill, a state of affairs that Cummings found intolerable. After Sedwill's departure Johnson dropped the ball. At the behest of Cummings, he asked Frost to become national security adviser (NSA), a role for which his long-time Europe sherpa experience did not in any sense equip him. Cummings saw foreign affairs generally as a frivolous distraction for the Prime Minister ('foreign masturbation', he dubbed it) and was no fan of the National Security Council (NSC): 'Why the f**k are you bothering to go to it?' he once shouted after Johnson who was scurrying off late to one of its meetings. His solution was to take power away from the securocrats and appoint someone in Frost who Johnson trusted completely, making the body take a more political lead. Following backlash around the announced appointment, including an intervention in the Commons when Theresa May at her most scathing asserted that Frost had 'no proven expertise',[4] the appointment stalled. The off-ramp of an alternative role (leading an international affairs unit in No. 10) was arranged, until Frost, realizing he was ill-equipped for the NSA job, decided to re-focus on the Northern Ireland Protocol and Brexit full time. David Quarrey stepped in as acting NSA, eminently qualified and adept at handling interdepartmental disputes, but not rated as sufficiently exciting by Johnson. The post, at the head of the NSC, matters: set up in 2010, it oversees Britain's security, foreign and defence policy, and its response to crises. After six months, Stephen Lovegrove took over in March 2021. But Johnson never took to him, despite Lovegrove's five years as permanent secretary at Defence; the Brexiteers around the Prime Minister found him patrician in his demeanour. Indeed, the entire NSC process 'Johnson found tedious, just moving pieces around the board', says an official. 'They would want to boil meetings down to three questions which he found impossibly anodyne. He thought it Byzantine and clunky, like the EU.' Instead, he wanted big picture and blue sky thinking. He would regularly miss its meetings and cancel at the last minute. On Ukraine in his final months, he found the NSC with its safety-first approach bothersome, and its heads could not trust Johnson to back them on any issue where ministers such as Raab and Truss differed in view. By the end of his premiership, lacking prime ministerial engagement, the NSC was flagging. Johnson always much preferred talking not to leaders with general knowledge but to those, however junior, who had a deep command of the subject.

Day to day, Johnson relied on his foreign affairs private secretary, Will Gelling, who, after serving just a single day as one of May's final appointees, was retained. The role has been at the heart of the emergence of the Prime Minister as the key decider on foreign policy,[5] with the long-serving Charles Powell under Thatcher the pivotal figure in the eclipse of the FCO, and Gelling as influential as many, given the wayward nature of his premier.[6] Johnson felt he had covered off foreign affairs by bringing Martin Reynolds, his principal private secretary at the FCO, to the same position at No. 10. But as Johnson quickly came to trust Gelling on foreign affairs, Reynolds shifted to be more of a fortifying figure on Brexit. He fully shared Johnson's vision of it, and believed that 'the more upbeat Johnson was on Brexit, the better, and don't get too hung up on processes', says an aide. If there was one kind of figure Johnson disliked, it was those he called 'stuffed shirts', diplomats and those in the armed services who came across as overly formal and gave him dull, predictable answers. An initial meeting with twenty officers went badly, but Tony Radakin, then First Sea Lord, was a straight-talker to catch his eye. No surprise that he gave him the nod for the top job, Chief of Defence Staff, in November 2021.

For intellectual heft and coherence, and to create his foreign policy vision (which saw light as the Integrated Review of March 2021), he turned to John Bew, one of his best appointments, and an excursion at No. 10 into the big tent thinking he practised as Mayor. 'Johnson felt the FCO was a pretty miserable place, everyone critical of Brexit, so he wanted a fresh figure to come in to bring a critical perspective,' says an aide. As a professor in History and Foreign Policy at King's College London and author of *Citizen Clem*, an acclaimed life of Labour's most successful PM, Attlee, Bew fitted the bill. His political identity was neither tied to the Conservative Party nor Brexit, and provided a heterodox way of thinking Johnson liked.

Until Ukraine landed on Johnson like manna from heaven, his focus was on obtaining the best possible Brexit, with bountiful free-trade deals and maximizing inward investment. He fondly believed free-trade deals would fall into Britain's lap once released from the shackles of the EU. He retained Liz Truss as his International Trade Secretary for two years until, in September 2021, he made her Foreign Secretary, despite thinking her flaky. He had great faith in his own powers of persuasion with foreign leaders and had been inspired by his trip in July 2017 when Foreign Secretary to Australia, New Zealand and Japan. These countries, he believed, were vital for the future of Britain, and as a result he wrestled control from Truss over Britain's first post-Brexit trade deal with Australia, only to cave in and settle on terms in December 2021 no better than she would have achieved. Even his Environment Secretary George Eustice savaged it after Johnson had left office because it 'gave away far too much for far too little in return'.[7]

The dissatisfaction was mutual; Truss was frustrated by Johnson's inability to set a strategy and his constant desire to set out impossible positions and unnegotiable mandates, rather than adopting Truss's preferred 'salami tactics' which would take as much as she could initially get then slice away more and more as the deal progressed. The lack of vision on what a post-EU trade policy looked like was not helpful, with officials particularly critical of Frost, as one makes clear: 'He could boil down complexity to simplicity for the Prime Minister and get a decision out of him, but he doesn't understand modern trade policy. Goods he got, as a former whisky salesman, but not services like data, digital and investment.'[8]

Johnson saw inward investment into the UK as a barometer of Brexit's success, not least with the media and the political world. He longed to show that money was flooding into Britain as never before to prove Brexit was working, despite Britain being in a weak position to capitalize on capital flows. But he was hopeless at understanding how to convert his woolly dreams into substance. Only late in the day did he realize post-Brexit Britain needed to be a more attractive place to invest: 'Prime Minister, we need somebody to work on freedoms and getting rid of regulations, because David Frost isn't doing the job, and nobody else is,' his aides would remind him. But nobody did, until Jacob Rees-Mogg was appointed Minister for Brexit Opportunities in February 2022. And by then, it was far too late – the Trade and Cooperation Agreement had been decided and Johnson's premiership was on the wane.

Johnson's other core objective was to snuggle up as closely as possible to the United States, 'to show that Britain had no better friend in the world', says an aide.

No special relationship

Johnson had loved America since his childhood years there, but had been disappointed not to have made more of an impression on the country as Foreign Secretary when Obama was still President. 'He couldn't really warm to John Kerry [Obama's Secretary of State], who he found too controlled, too humourless and too work-focused,' says Simon McDonald.[9] Kerry found Johnson incomprehensible, 'baffling, very very English public school, trying to be funny, starting down one track then changing to another', says an insider. Johnson's staff winced with embarrassment. Had he asked how to create a better impression, they might have told him: 'Think through before what you want to say. Stop trying to make jokes and be more serious.' But Johnson didn't ask, it was not his way to enquire, and carried on making the same mistakes.

Donald Trump's victory against Hillary Clinton in the November 2016 US presidential election had created an opportunity for a fresh start, but also a quandary. 'The only reason I wouldn't go to some parts of New York is the real risk of meeting Donald Trump,' Johnson had said in December 2015 after Trump called for Muslims to be banned from the United States to ensure the country did not end up with 'radicalized' no-go areas 'like London'. Trump, he concluded, was 'unfit' to hold the office of President of the United States.[10]

But following Trump's election, Johnson deftly changed his tune and praised him as a dealmaker, calling for an end to the 'whinge-o-rama' over his victory.[11] The new boys in DC couldn't get enough of him. 'The guy we would really like to meet is Johnson,' they told the British embassy. 'Why?' staff enquired. 'Because we are big fans of Brexit, and he's the man who made Brexit happen,' they were told. Trump's interest in him rather than Prime Minister May was delicate for diplomats in Washington, eager to nurture links with the new team without affronting their boss in Downing Street. So they messaged London to say they realized the Prime Minister would be very tied up at short notice, but wondered if she could possibly send the Foreign Secretary to meet the new team in Washington instead. 'Absolutely not', was the furious response from No. 10. 'The Prime Minister will be the first to meet the President, not Johnson.' Trump's team were persistent, however: 'We want to meet Johnson.' The embassy went back to London stressing Johnson wouldn't be meeting Trump himself, just his team. But that still did not satisfy May's team, desperate not to be upstaged by their nemesis. Eventually No. 10 relented, and Johnson duly came to New York for a meeting in Trump Tower with chief strategist Steve Bannon, Trump's son-in-law Jared Kushner and senior adviser and speechwriter Steve Miller. Iran was the main topic, on which they disagreed, with Johnson and Mark Lyall Grant (UK permanent representative to the United Nations) deploring Trump's antipathy to the Iran nuclear deal negotiated by Obama. But it didn't seem to sour one bit Team Trump's enthusiasm for their new British best friend. One condition No. 10 set for allowing Johnson to go was the understanding that Trump would be safely tucked away in his Palm Beach resort of Mar-a-Lago. But Kim Darroch, the British ambassador, could not be 'stone cold certain' that Trump was not in New York and spent the meeting in a cold sweat that he might suddenly burst through the doors, creating a major diplomatic embarrassment.[12]

Johnson was cock-a-hoop after the visit, praising Trump's 'exciting agenda for change'.[13] 'He sensed there was something in the way the new President did business that he liked, how he connected with voters, never apologized and dominated the twenty-four-hour news cycle which gave him ideas about becoming a national leader,' says an official. He hit it off particularly with Bannon, Trump's maverick strategist, who intrigued him: they exchanged mobile numbers and in the following months, behind No. 10's back, regular texts flowed between them. Johnson was reminded by his officials that Bannon had extensive contacts with the far right in Europe including with France's Marine Le Pen and Dutchman Geert Wilders, but 'it didn't seem to concern him', according to one. Johnson acknowledged there was something distasteful and unsavoury about 'the Trumpies'. But something beguiling and fascinating as well.

Trump too was intrigued by Johnson. 'It was obvious to us that Trump liked him, loved the Churchill patter, and saw him as a mini-me, all a bit awkward for Boris,' says one of his London team, especially when Trump started integrating some of Johnson's words into his speeches. Their superficial similarities were much commented upon: 'both have flamboyant blonde hairstyles, rail against political correctness, are slippery with the truth, sound populist themes, and are willing to buck the establishment for political gain', as news outlet Politico put it.[14] Devoid of ultimate responsibility, Johnson was able to share enthusiasm for areas of the Trump agenda, including Israel and Brexit, but was not a close policy bedfellow.

Apart from Bannon, Johnson kept in touch with Miller and Kushner, showing great acumen at the interpersonal relations. But his relationship with Trump himself dwindled after he resigned as Foreign Secretary. Trump, meanwhile, had been appallingly rude to May, was glad to see her quit and continued to be rude with offensive impressions of her down the telephone to Johnson, as an official recalls. Both principals laughed, though No. 10 staff were sure Johnson was merely playing along.

Trump's distaste for May had surfaced again in her final month at No. 10. Ambassador Darroch's classified cables were leaked in early July 2019 to the Brexit Party, which described Trump's administration as 'inept and insecure'. Darroch protested that the message was private and he was merely saying what was widely known. Farage, who was eager for the ambassadorship himself, declared Darroch was 'totally unsuitable' for the office, while Trump tweeted that Darroch was 'not liked or well thought of within the US' and that 'we will no longer deal with him'. May, to her credit, expressed support for the ambassador, but Johnson pointedly did not. 'He rated Darroch, but refused to condemn Trump, because he expected to win the ongoing leadership contest. He thought, "I'm going to win so I don't want to close down my options",' says an aide. On 10 July, Darroch resigned, uniquely forced out by an American president. He believes Trump's vehement reaction 'was a function of his giant ego under which lies a massive hole of insecurity. He had absolutely no ability to take criticism.'[15]

Exactly two weeks later, Johnson became Prime Minister. Trump could barely conceal his elation at a potential alliance of the two leaders who, in his own mind, embodied the rise of right-wing populism in the West. While reality was dawning on Johnson, Trump still had hopelessly idealistic expectations of the Prime Minister. They met face-to-face three times in 2019 in the margins of large meetings: for the G7 summit at Biarritz in August, in New York for the UN General Assembly in September, and at the NATO summit during the general election campaign. Trump was only too glad to escape the summit at which he had given a chaotic performance including gratuitous aggression towards France's President Macron and lobbying for Russia's return to the G7/8. He breezed through the black door of No. 10 for their first proper conversation on 3 December, Trump still finding it hard to contain his delight at having an imagined fellow traveller at the head of such a major ally. White House intelligence had predicted a strong Johnson victory, a good omen, Trump thought, for his own re-election the following year, as the referendum result had been for his first victory in 2016. He heaped blandishments on his host, telling him in front of his officials, 'We've got the world by the balls Boris: what can we do?' The President treated him like a fellow campaigner and intimate friend. He knew Johnson was eager to reshape Britain's position in the world. How could he help?

Johnson no longer had illusions about Trump's help ('he'll do us no favours', he said), and didn't want to hitch his wagon to a star that looked to be on the wane. Trump's pro-Putin outburst at Biarritz had shocked him greatly. He had realized too just how much of a liability Trump was to his brand domestically, and was cautious about encouraging any further comparisons between the two as populist demagogues. Johnson had learned how to play him, his vanity and thin skin. 'People really love you in the UK, Donald, ignore the media, they've got it all wrong,' he would say. Trump purred. 'You are the most popular leader in the UK, the biggest thing,' Johnson shamelessly told him. Before the NATO trip, Johnson's election managers had been spooked by the fear that the President would extol the virtues of privatizing the NHS. The situation called for peak Johnson diplomacy: 'Some people in my party and other parties might make mischief if you were to talk about doing that, Donald,' Johnson said to him on a call before their meeting in December 2019. 'Let's talk about it all you like in private when you're here, but can we keep it to ourselves?' 'I understand,' Trump said meekly. Throwing the election at the last minute with an inflammatory remark on the NHS was one of many dreads Johnson had about what the President might dredge up to show his self-identification with, as he described him, 'Britain's Trump'.

Trump continued to be useful to Johnson throughout 2020 as the only leader in the free world supportive of Brexit. But Johnson's admiration for his bombastic style had long since waned, and his underlying contempt for his opinions came to dominate. 'He never thought Trump very bright and regarded him frankly as a bit thick. He thought his views on most subjects were bonkers and wasn't remotely interested in what he had to say on any policy subject,' says an aide. Johnson was not unduly sentimental towards the concept of the special relationship, and thought Trump's behaviour damaging to both America and the world, disliking the President's tendency towards withdrawal, isolationism and protectionism.

Whenever they spoke by phone or in person, Trump was the dominant figure and talked far more. He saw himself as the old hand, eager to dispense his wisdom on his protégé. Top of the Trump gift list was how Johnson could use some of his own mastery at dealmaking to knock the pathetic EU into shape. But before long, he was criticizing Johnson's decisions: 'How on earth did you manage not to get a better deal from that drunk Juncker and the pack of socialists, Boris?' he demanded to know. The intricacies of the Northern Ireland Protocol evaded him, as they did Johnson, but he was forthright about it nevertheless: 'You should've ripped up the contract and played hardball with the Europeans.' Differences progressively clouded their relationship throughout 2020. Trump told Johnson he was 'totally wrong' to prioritize the environment and to support the Iran nuclear deal. The relationship soured further after a furious call over the UK's decision to allow Chinese company Huawei to help build its 5G network. Trump was apoplectic and swore down the phone at Johnson before 'abruptly ending the call', an aide recalls. Covid meant Johnson postponed plans for a trip to Washington scheduled for early 2020. After the subsequent US decision to sanction the companies making it possible for the UK to import Huawei into the network, Johnson was left fuming at Trump's temerity to interfere directly with the UK's supply chain, as well as the lack of room for manoeuvre bequeathed to him by May.

The two leaders rubbed along for the remainder of the year, but gone was Trump's notion that he and Johnson could remake the world, while Johnson, with the increasing likelihood that his first full year in office would be the President's last, was not sorry that Covid had effectively shredded their personal contact. The Prime Minister's struggle with the virus had provoked an uncharacteristic gesture of goodwill from the President, with Trump 'calling the hospital daily and offering to send his personal physician' according to one diplomat, but their contact was otherwise slim. Johnson's own court was divided on the looming presidential election result: Lister took out a bet against Cummings that Trump would win.

Johnson, like Cummings and the pollsters, believed in a Biden victory, though was temporarily thrown by the early Florida result where the Democrats fared less well than they had done in 2016.

Momentum had not been aided by the hiatus in the British ambassadorship after the Darroch furore. Farage, publicly favoured by Trump, and who beat Johnson to seeing him, hoped he was still in the picture, 'but the idea never crossed Johnson's mind or desk. Not once,' says an official. Sedwill was actively considered as a suitable big-hitter well known in Washington, but the appointment eventually went to Karen Pierce, formerly Johnson's political director at the FCO, whom he trusted to give independent advice. The political right were not pleased, complaining that Johnson was 'selling out to the blob' in the words of free-market economist Gerard Lyons by not using the precedent of a political appointee to Washington and choosing a true Brexiteer.[16]

A quick post-Brexit US trade deal had been central to Johnson's ambitions, prior to his striking a trade deal with the EU. Obama had been explicit in 2016 that Britain would go to the 'back of the queue'[17] for a US trade deal, so Johnson was exuberant when in 2019 Trump's national security adviser John Bolton echoed Johnson's words as Foreign Secretary that the UK would be 'first in line' for a free-trade deal.[18] Trump was no advocate of international free trade, but saw it as a logical follow-on from Brexit, and a gift to US agriculture. Trump continued to dangle the prize, and when he received news of the Conservative general election victory in December 2019, he tweeted, 'Congratulations to Boris Johnson on his great WIN! Britain and the United States will now be free to strike a massive new Trade Deal after BREXIT … Celebrate Boris!'[19] Beneath the airy rhetoric lay a concrete block: US standards on food production and animal welfare were far below British ones:

what was regarded as perfectly normal by consumers on one side of the Atlantic was anathema on the other. With a trade deal not going to happen ahead of one with the EU, he thought it better to put it on hold than rush into a bad one. As a substitute Sedwill and Larry Kudlow, director of the National Economic Council in the White House, developed the 'Special Relationship Economic Working Group', which saved face but proved neither special nor a relationship, meeting on fewer than a handful of occasions – 'It was a fig leaf for not doing a trade deal,' says one official.

Johnson was mightily relieved that Trump had lost the presidential election in November 2020. His No. 10 office promptly suggested that he should call Joe Biden first, then call Trump, 'to prepare the ground in case he made a comeback in the future'. But Johnson's nous made him very reluctant to do that. He discussed with his aides relaying a message to Trump instead through Kushner, but even that made him queasy. He was then very quick to condemn the riot by Trump supporters on Capitol Hill on 6 January 2021, all of which incensed Trump. To him, Johnson became just another traitor who had let him and the cause down.

The new President presented formidable challenges of his own. Biden was extremely proud of his Irish heritage, so was deeply concerned by the Johnson government wanting unilaterally to rip up the Northern Ireland Protocol. His new team thought that Johnson had been far too close to Trump, more so than any other leader in Europe, and they criticized Johnson for his gall in making out he was their friend. Worse, as White House veteran Ben Rhodes relayed to a British diplomat, Team Biden really disliked what Johnson had said about Obama, whose Vice President Biden had been, deeming it borderline racist when Johnson alleged Obama was unable to get over his colonial past.[20] Significant also in relegating the UK down their international league table, they thought Brexit a disaster and utterly stupid for Britain, as well as damaging to Europe.

Johnson was all too aware of this long list, so invested time in working out how on their first phone call to hook the new President, whom aides said he regarded as 'an old-fashioned, smalltown American politician'. His team, thrilled to have dug up Biden ancestral history beyond Ireland with family roots in Sussex, ensured Johnson was armed with high-quality titbits about Biden's family tree to pull out of his hat. Much hinged on the rapport established on the first call. If the new President came in hard on the Protocol on their first exchange, it could herald four very difficult years for the special relationship, which was all the more important given Johnson's failure to make an ally of any leader of a heavyweight country in his first eighteen months. Johnson, 'turning on a sixpence' as aides recall, told Biden, 'It's so good to have somebody back in the White House who understands the meaning of duty,' a soft dissing of Trump. The Protocol barely came up as an issue on the call, and they spoke about the G7 in Cornwall: 'Joe, you'll be very welcome to come.' Biden came across as 'pretty stiff', mouthing warm enough words, but Johnson's team listening in 'felt he was reading from his script'. All in all, not bad though, Johnson's team reckoned: a score draw.

Within weeks, it became obvious to No. 10 how different the new White House was. Trump had handed Johnson his personal mobile number, and whenever their offices wanted to speak, they connected almost immediately. But with Biden, his staff gave out no direct contacts, so No. 10 had to call the White House switchboard: 'Days went by with no response, and we didn't know if his team just didn't want to talk, or if he hadn't yet mastered the system.' Johnson's team noticed how Biden could be repetitive and anecdotal, and appeared to follow his briefing script assiduously – a reversal of the position seventy years before when a White House briefing for President Truman said Prime Minister Churchill 'was apt to be repetitive, and to fall asleep'.[21] Whitehall as a whole, though, found it far easier to deal with the new administration, with much of the relationship-building done on the spot by Karen Pierce in Washington, supported by John Bew and G7 Sherpa Jonathan Black.

The withdrawal from Afghanistan in the summer of 2021 marked a low point in the Johnson–Biden relationship. Trump had been responsible for the plan signed in Doha in February 2020 with the Taliban (which excluded the Afghan government) for the withdrawal of all NATO forces. Dubbed a 'surrender agreement' by Trump's former NSA Herbert McMaster, it promised that foreign forces would leave within fifteen months, without any promises from the Taliban to stop its campaign of violence, and with no verification or enforcement measures.

In April 2021, Biden, with effectively no consultation with the British, decided that all US troops would be out by 11 September. Given that the British had borne the brunt for twenty years alongside the US in Afghanistan, a commitment that stemmed from the intimate relationship between President Bush and Prime Minister Blair and with a loss of 454 military personnel and civilians, Washington's unilateral decisions spoke of how cool the relationship had become. 'David Quarrey spent a lot of time with Karen [Pierce] and the FCDO trying to extract what the US were thinking in 2021, and we didn't succeed,' says an official. Equally, the whole twenty-year failure to find a coherent and consistent strategy in Afghanistan after 2001 can be viewed as a fruit of policy differences between Washington and London. 'That legacy of failure to find a strategy on Afghanistan was the basis of Johnson's scepticism about the securocrat community,' adds another official. The British government, apt after the Doha agreement to think it could wash its hands of the problem, suddenly found itself caught on the wrong foot, with key figures including Foreign Secretary Raab on holiday. Even the most cautious voices in the NSC had not anticipated the speed of the collapse, which culminated in the Taliban taking over Kabul on 15 September amid scenes reminiscent of the American scramble out of Saigon in 1975 at the conclusion of the Vietnam War.

Johnson had a feeling for the country, informed in part by his brother Leo marrying an Afghan woman. Grandstanding from Defence Secretary Wallace, who said Britain could remain in Afghanistan alone, irked the Prime Minister but he tested the idea with officials nevertheless, including whether the Turkish forces could hold the airport as an international zone. The reality that Britain had long drawn down the military campaign in Afghanistan was too strong, however. 'He was very clear that there was no option for the UK to remain behind with the US gone. It was "in together, out together",' says an FCDO official. Johnson, after chairing an unsatisfactory meeting of the NSC on 13 August, decided he had had enough, and centralized control within No.10. 'At first, Johnson had tried to chair almost everything himself, going down rabbit holes, impossible to get good information about what was happening on the ground. People were texting him about individuals in Afghanistan. It was unsustainable,' says an official. But order grew after he banged Wallace's and Raab's heads together, and set up a control centre in the Cabinet Room. 'You couldn't make up how disjointed it all was,' says an adviser. 'One lesson we learned is that No. 10 and only No. 10 can pull everything together.' Thus when the Ukraine crisis broke nine months later 'we made absolutely certain that No. 10 led everything. We had to grip it.'

The House of Commons Foreign Affairs Committee's review into the failure of the withdrawal was scathing towards the Foreign Office, and no more complimentary to No. 10 with the scandalous suggestion that the Prime Minister had intervened to enable pet charity Nowzad to secure a plane in order to airlift over 160 stray cats and dogs from Kabul while many eligible Afghans were left behind. Even officials are unclear exactly how the order happened: 'In every meeting I saw where it was raised with him the Prime Minister said, "We're not putting pets ahead of people." It was totally clear he wasn't supportive, so if he did change his mind it was in a remarkably underhand way.'

While there was never any warmth between the two principals, events were pushing Johnson and Biden closer together on policy. Their teams worked productively on preparation for the G7 in June and COP26 in November 2021, though Washington says the apparent warmth of the iconic photos of both leaders with their wives on the Cornish beach at the former was prompted less by personal affinity than the needs of the American audience. The G7 summit was a success for the development of their relationship, with Second World War archival documents brought down from London for Biden, who responded warmly over their shared interest in history. Alignment over China in the AUKUS defence and security partnership between Australia, the UK and the US agreed in September saw them join to counter Chinese ambition in the Pacific. 'Johnson was very proud of the deal. He wanted it to project a perception of UK closeness to the US globally which would impart an aura of foreign policy glamour,' says an official. The fact it was one in the eye for Macron was the icing on the cake.

Whereas Johnson had fought Trump over Iran, the environment and NATO, he was in alignment on each with Biden. But genuine respect for Johnson from the White House came only in his final months over Ukraine.

Johnson invested great personal energy in trying to have a meaningful relationship with the United States, and in achieving a trade deal as a cornerstone of his foreign policy. But he had to admit in 2021 that a trade deal would not transpire. Overall, indeed, he failed to achieve his ambitions with the White House. Trump would have been difficult for even the most agile British Prime Minister to handle. Johnson then ran headlong into Biden, who disliked what he saw of his insincerity and values on many subjects. Not since Harold Wilson (1964–70) did the Prime Minister fail to bond with two presidents in a row (Lyndon Johnson and Richard Nixon). The question is, with Johnson determined to achieve Global Britain post-Brexit, did it matter?

EU Trade Deal and Northern Ireland Protocol

Britain formally left the EU on 31 January 2020, but until 31 December 2021 a transition period applied in which the UK was still considered for most trade matters to be part of the EU. Here was the opportunity for Johnson to confound the sceptics and show that he could strike a good working relationship with his EU counterparts, and secure a great trade deal for Britain to maximize economic opportunities outside of the EU.

Negotiations were to begin at once to reach an agreement by the end of the year on trade and all other relations between the EU and the UK. 'Task Force Europe' was charged with the mission, headed by David Frost, with Oliver Lewis his key political aide, and Jonno Evans the lead official within No. 10. Johnson, bar a few interventions, was detached from the process and was happy to let Frost 'prioritize freedom: hence any deal to give the UK the maximum number of freedoms and the fewest number of constraints in the future'.[22] How would he achieve that? 'Leaving the Single Market and Customs Union, and ending the European Court of Justice's jurisdiction were givens: so some minor stuff was up for grabs in the negotiations, but it was all tactics really,' says Frost.[23] Johnson told him in their periodic sessions that he wanted to ensure that the future relationship wouldn't be trapped by 'the tractor beam' from Brussels, i.e. that the UK would be truly free, and not imitating the EU way of doing business burdened by petty rules.

A rare Johnson intervention was over the length for the negotiating period, with the twenty-one months in May's original Withdrawal Agreement already cut back to eleven under Johnson's agreement, and further constrained by Covid when the conversations with Brussels switched online. The initial conversations had gone badly and were described as little more than 'a shouting match' between both sides.[24] 'Officials thought we needed another year to do it all properly,' says one source, 'but we were wrong. The Commission always needs a deadline and won't focus until it is imminent.' The critical decision was taken when Johnson was recuperating from Covid in April. 'He told me from his sick bed as he was recovering, "We're not delaying, we are going to leave at the end of the year. We have to do it by then. Final,"' recalls Frost.[25] The direction of travel had been set by Gove in a 12 June meeting with European Commission Vice-President Maroš Šefčovič where he declared that the UK did not wish to extend the negotiating period, and reiterated on a video conference with European Commission President Ursula von der Leyen on 15 June, during which Johnson confirmed no extension of the transition period. 'We agreed beforehand three or four conditions for reaching a deal, which the Prime Minister read out in the meeting: that effectively shaped everything that happened afterwards,' says Frost.[26]

The Prime Minister's interventions were otherwise uncommon. Cummings recalls that 'we had to keep the PM out of the negotiations as much as possible. He didn't understand them. He wouldn't read the papers. He was constantly shifting positions, sometimes using maximum aggression, then suddenly collapsing.'[27] Cummings claims it wasn't until 25 September, with three months left before negotiations ran out of road, that Johnson understood the implications of leaving the Customs Union. 'I will never forget the look on his face when, after listening to Frost… he said, "No no no Frosty, f**k this, what happens *with* a deal?" And Frost looked up from his paper and said, "PM, this is what happens *with* a deal, *that's what leaving the Customs Union means*." The PM's face was priceless. He sat back in his chair and looked around the room with appalled disbelief and shook his head.'[28] 'You should never take Johnson at face value,' says an aide in response. 'Feigning ignorance was his way of drawing people out. The problem, though, is that sometimes he actually *was* ignorant. The challenge was, you could never tell when it was an act.'

'The clock is ticking', a 2017 catchphrase of Michel Barnier, the EU's chief Brexit negotiator, became a leitmotif as 2020 ground on. Northern Ireland was the biggest single nut that needed to be cracked. The 'Irish Trilemma', as discussed in Chapter 2, continued to be a thorn despite Johnson's repeated insistence that there would simultaneously be no barriers to trade, divergence from the EU or border in the Irish Sea under the agreed Northern Ireland Protocol. In reality, the Protocol was always a costly compromise between sovereignty and trade – and Johnson knew it, even if he was hesitant to admit that freedom was not free. The day before Frost reached an agreement, Attorney General Cox had warned the Prime Minister that, despite a supposed 'carve out' for tariffs on some goods passing between Great Britain and Northern Ireland and a majority consent vote in the Assembly every four years, the deal would amount to a permanent arrangement in which Northern Ireland feels to be in a different market – with implications for Unionism and the stability of the Good Friday Agreement. Frost was called, and agreed with Cox's assessment that Northern Ireland would effectively be a third country, but that it was too late to make any changes. Johnson and Frost may have been ignorant to the exact implications of their deal, but they undoubtedly understood that they were weakening Northern Ireland's place in the UK's internal market. It would also have been plain to Johnson and Cummings in considering subsequently whether to violate or circumvent the treaty that Cox would not have gone along with it, and he was in turn pre-emptively briefed against by No. 10 as 'not a team player'.

Northern Ireland Secretary Julian Smith was also uncomfortable with the agreement. 'My sense was that Northern Ireland policy was being driven by Brexit, which has been driven by Cummings and Frost, though Johnson was ultimately responsible. There was no humility, no recognition how fragile the Northern Ireland ecosystem was, but arrogance and confusion,' he says.[29] The consequence of their concerns followed inexorably: both were replaced by more pliable figures in the February 2020 reshuffle – Cox by Suella Braverman, and Smith by Brandon Lewis. An Attorney General who would help them get around the Protocol, and a Northern Ireland Minister who would not fight them hard over its status. 'The price of survival in Johnson's Cabinet appeared to be subservience.

That was short-sighted. In advising on the law, an Attorney General cannot be an acolyte', is Cox's verdict.[30] Smith concurs: 'Johnson couldn't cope with any pushback. Any self-respecting Northern Ireland Secretary would have taken the same view. What he needed was confident independent people in Cabinet, not a bunch of nodding donkeys.'[31]

The donkeys had nodded through a bad agreement which was never going to satisfy all parties. The buck stopped with Johnson, but the responsibility was shared with those who reassured him there would be no problem. One of these was Gove, who believed that the Protocol could easily be tinkered with later. 'He sought assurances from Gove, which he received, but the EU doesn't sign things casually,' says an official. Frost's culpability is more in question: either he didn't understand the Protocol himself, and no one pointed it out in the very tight circle that he ran. Or he did, and he deliberately misled Johnson about how easy it would be to reconcile in the future. Or they both were equally and knowingly guilty of the fudge. Officials who were in the room are of no doubt that the last of these is the case. 'David Frost understood trade, but never grasped the complexities of Northern Ireland,' says one. Another says, 'The PM had no interest in what was agreed on the Protocol, wilfully or not wilfully. He was told repeatedly how the Protocol would work, and what it meant. "I just want it done", was his response.' The quality of the deal itself was secondary to the fact of achieving Brexit from the set of negotiating constraints in which May had left him.

A solution, the UK Internal Markets Bill (UKIM), was dreamed up by Oliver Lewis and workshopped by the Union and policy teams in the summer, intended to blast through the Protocol concerns by asserting British sovereignty over the whole of the UK. 'Like prorogation, it was intended to show we meant business, and there were only certain arrangements that we would agree to,' says Frost.[32] The device was intended to prevent internal trade barriers among the four countries of the UK, and to restrict certain legislative powers of the devolved administrations. 'It stopped the trend since Blair's late 1990s reforms of devolving power, reassessing parliamentary authority with a bigger role for Westminster going forwards. I was very proud of it,' says Oliver Lewis. He worked closely on it with Gove, presenting it to Johnson as only the Scottish National Party objecting to it. 'Johnson didn't understand the minutiae. But he got the logic of UKIM and the rewriting of the British constitution,' Lewis continues.[33] Johnson might not have fully understood it, but was right behind UKIM; 'He was always the toughest person on it,' says Frost.

On 9 September, the government published the UKIM Bill, including a clause enabling ministers to unilaterally disregard measures within the Northern Ireland Protocol and overrule EU customs law. Only nine months before, Johnson had agreed to the Withdrawal Agreement with the EU; now he was enabling his ministers to breach it. Not only was he granting ministers the power to breach the agreement, granting them that ability was a breach of the agreement in itself: Article 4 stipulated that only primary legislation may be used in domestic implementation, therefore enabling ministers to enact policy by means of secondary legislation violated the Withdrawal Agreement's terms. Brandon Lewis admitted to a startled House of Commons that it meant international law being broken 'in a limited and specific way'.[34] Jonathan Jones promptly resigned as head of the government Legal Department. Labour, the Liberal Democrats, the SNP and Plaid Cymru all opposed the bill. So too did all five living former

Prime Ministers from Major to May, the last asking, 'How can the government reassure future international partners that the UK can be trusted to abide by the legal obligations of the agreements it signs?'[35] Major drilled the point home: 'For generations, Britain's word – solemnly given – has been accepted by friend and foe. Our signature on any treaty or agreement has been sacrosanct. If we lose our reputation for honouring the promises we make, we will have lost something beyond price that may never be regained.'[36] No. 10 could dismiss them all as a bundle of Remoaners, but could not so easily distance itself from the criticism of lifelong Eurosceptic Michael Howard, who asked in the Lords, 'How can we reproach Russia or China or Iran when their conduct falls below internationally accepted standards when we are showing such scant regard for our treaty obligations?'[37]

There shortly followed a list of the UK's demands: in exchange for dropping the offending clauses, the EU would shift its position on the application of the Northern Ireland Protocol towards import VAT, paperwork requirements and the application of state aid provisions.[38] As so often with Johnson, he was gung ho about a course of action only to backtrack once the deed had been done. He found the furious reaction to UKIM surprising and disconcerting: 'I didn't expect people to be this angry,' he complained to his staff. International condemnation at the blithe abandoning of international law was heaped upon the top-level domestic criticism. It was not how Johnson intended events to turn out when trade talks had begun at the start of the year. He fondly imagined that getting Brexit over the line for 31 January 2020 was the real thing and, as Frost reassured him, sorting out a trade deal subsequently was relatively simple and need barely trouble him.

In fact, the trade talks were stalling inside the EU's Borschette Building, described by an official as 'like negotiating in a 1970s car park'; the basement at the Department for Business, Energy and Industrial Strategy for the London talks was even worse: 'there was no light, very disorientating'.[39] Little progress had been made in particular on fisheries and the so-called level playing field binding the UK to EU regulation and state aid rules that would need to be resolved before any trade agreement could be finalized. Discussions continued in a desultory fashion over the summer and into the autumn. 'We can leave without a f**king trade deal', was Cummings' regular response when he thought the EU was being particularly difficult, an eventuality that Johnson himself was anxious to avoid.

By October, with just weeks to go, he was becoming seriously irritated with the EU leaders of its principal countries. Bad blood ran deep. Johnson couldn't forget being badly stung by his treatment at the Munich Security Conference in February 2017 where he asked why the EU was necessary when there was NATO, and said Britain would be 'liberated' by Brexit. 'The reaction, with booing and shouting-down by people on the floor, was formative. "I'm never coming back here," he said,' as an aide recounts. He did not develop a good working relationship with Macron or Merkel, or with any other national leader except Ireland's Varadkar. 'He was always perfectly polite, courteous, and gave the impression that he liked them. But actually, his opinion of almost all EU leaders was disdain,' another says, while Frost adds, 'They all predicted disaster for Britain after Brexit, and he had proved them wrong. We had spent four years disentangling ourselves from these people, and we weren't going to let them lecture us any longer.'[40]

Johnson spoke to von der Leyen on 3 October and agreed to intensify talks. But with just three days a week set aside for negotiations, and a meeting of EU leaders on 15 October appearing to be dragging its feet, London let it be known they would walk away from talks altogether, known as 'the madman strategy'.[41] Preparation for no deal, including medicines and other vital supplies, accelerated on both sides of the Irish Sea.

By the end, 437 British officials from twenty-five government departments and agencies took part in some 1,000 negotiating sessions. Suspicion on both sides continued right to the end. On Wednesday 9 December, Johnson travelled to Brussels to meet von der Leyen for a make-or-break dinner, with Frost and Barnier present, ahead of the two-day summit for the twenty-seven EU heads of state and government. The previous day Gove, eager to avoid no deal and uncertainty in Northern Ireland, had agreed with EU Commission Vice-President Šefčovič to drop the controversial UKIM clauses which violated international law after the two came to an agreement over implementation of the Northern Ireland Protocol. Johnson, however, announced that he could not accept the broader terms that would tie Britain to EU rules. The atmosphere was acidic as they debated whether the deadlock could be broken in time: 'the most awkward experience I've ever heard in a diplomatic event', says an official. 'Discussions were at breaking point. The commission sat in silence – they had clearly decided beforehand that stonewalling the Prime Minister was their strategy. They gave nothing away. We had prepared for something like this but it was very odd.' 'Completely appalling. If that was the negotiating strategy, it backfired badly. The PM was thoroughly pissed off,' says another. The UK and the EU had proved themselves equally capable of frustrating each other with petty tactics, neither convinced the other was truly mad enough to walk away.

Johnson returned to London where he was regularly on the phone to Frost, who remained in Brussels. The 'level playing field' dispute was about the EU's concern that the UK should not undercut it on environmental and social protection, nor on state aid, to gain a competitive advantage. The EU continued to demand heavy penalties if Britain was to diverge, with Frost saying British sovereignty didn't allow it to do so. 'The Prime Minister was following it anxiously but was not into the detail of it all. We tried explaining several times the difference between "ex-ante" and "ex-post" states and systems, and on one level he got it. But what he wanted above all was a resolution,' says an official. With the Christmas break approaching, and mutual trust still very low, it was touch and go. At the last minute a way through was found by Oliver Lewis's proposed 'rebalancing mechanism', with agreement to limit divergence and a provision for retaliatory sanctions if either side was to undercut the other. Johnson promptly dubbed the entitlement to diverge 'the freedom clause'.

If this first issue in contention was a score draw, agreement on fish was an EU win, with Britain conceding a more generous settlement than needed. Johnson was much more involved, believing that for the UK's fifty years in the EU, the government had sold out the British fishing industry. With Brexit, he wanted the industry proudly revived, arousing expectations that could not possibly be met. Knowing how much the French cared about the subject, he saw a fish settlement as a chance to get even with a victory over them. He was further stirred by his anger at what he considered French perfidy, evidenced, for example, by France not allowing British researchers to participate after Brexit in the Horizon Europe scientific research scheme. 'The Prime Minister alighted on fish as the battleground to win a victory,' says an official. But neither he nor Frost were a match for the formidable Stéphanie Riso, negotiating for the EU, who completely outplayed them. The settlement, based on reduced quotas and a five-year transition period on access to UK waters, stoked intense fury: 'bottling it', 'sold out', 'betrayed' and 'the PM caved in to the EU to save the deal' were among the reactions over the Christmas holiday from the British fishing industry.

'Like Alexander the Great, Boris has cut the Gordian Knot,' lifelong Eurosceptic Bill Cash declared in the Commons on 30 December,[42] claiming that Johnson in achieving the EU–UK Trade and Cooperation Agreement (TCA) was walking in the footsteps of Churchill and Thatcher. Jubilation at the deal among the Brexiteers ran high, though some ultras would still have preferred no deal. 'Sovereignty with free trade with the EU' has been achieved, declared Johnson to the BBC. He cited critics who had said 'you couldn't have free trade with the EU unless you conformed with the EU's laws [but] that has turned out not to be true… I want you to see that this is a cakeist treaty.'[43]

In fact, the TCA was a bad deal for Britain, dishonestly sold by Johnson, who refused to acknowledge its full limitations as the inevitable outcome of placing such a high value on legislative autonomy. It lumbered British industry with red tape and trade bureaucracy that May tried to remove with her own deal. It was silent on how the highly prized sovereignty and regulatory freedom would benefit the British economy. 'They haven't got the first clue,' said a banking executive at the time.[44] As if to underline the point, Johnson asked 250 business leaders on a Zoom call on 6 January 2021 to come up with ways in which Britain could benefit from its newfound freedoms. Barriers to trade between the UK and the EU were erected, as they were, fatally, between the mainland and Northern Ireland. Some cake.

The implications of Johnson's Withdrawal Agreement and the TCA dogged the final eighteen months of his premiership, and remained unresolved at its conclusion. Vaccine wars broke out in early 2021, with the EU threatening to invoke Article 16 of the Northern Ireland Protocol, designed to be a last resort, to impose border restrictions on vaccine movements in Ireland, resulting in a humiliating U-turn by the EU. The pandemic still raging and deaths near their peak, the move was utterly incendiary. 'It was probably the most dramatic day I can remember in No. 10,' says an official. On 5 February, Johnson had a furious phone call with Macron, the low point of their fraught three-year relationship. 'I've never listened into such a bitter call,' says one seasoned official. Johnson was seething that Macron had queried the efficacy of the Oxford-AstraZeneca vaccine and its safety with people aged over sixty-five,[45] which had a huge negative effect on confidence especially in the developing world which needed it badly. 'How dare you call into question the efficacy of the vaccine that has been approved by my regulator and by your regulator: you're doing it for purely political reasons,' Johnson said. The row escalated even further due to the EU's prevention of vaccines, produced in the UK then exported for bottling in the Netherlands, from being imported back. 'I will hold you personally responsible for the deaths of the British people from this decision,' Johnson told Macron, a sentiment he then echoed to Dutch Prime Minister Mark Rutte.

For a long time afterwards Johnson would refer back to that call when talking with both officials and the French President himself, but Macron's disdain for his British counterpart was long evident by then. 'The truth is that Macron could never forgive Johnson personally for Brexit and didn't think he was a worthy character,' says an official. 'Boris, you're just not being serious,' he would repeatedly tell him on calls. The talented ambassador to France and former No. 10 Chief of Staff Ed Llewellyn was not able to salvage the relationship, nor was his successor Menna Rawlings. The final nail in the coffin was over small boats: having offered a reset and technical route forward in November 2021 on the condition that the British government would not make any proposals public until France was ready, Macron was shocked to find that Johnson had publicly tweeted his response the following day.[46] 'We do not communicate from one leader to another on these issues by tweets and letters that we make public. We are not whistleblowers. Come on,' commented Macron at a press conference later that week.[47] The incident underlined the lack of seriousness with which Johnson could be treated, Macron believed.

Frost sensed that the EU's attempt to invoke Article 16 over vaccines had opened up opportunities for yet more hardline strategy. 'If the EU had not tried to use it first, it would have been much more difficult for us to get it on the agenda. That they broke the taboo, even if they retreated rapidly, made it impossible to contain.'[48] In July, the UK attempted to address outstanding issues in Northern Ireland with its 'command paper', seeking to eliminate as many checks in the Irish Sea as possible, and Frost threatening to invoke Article 16 if the EU refused to reopen negotiations and accept the UK's position.

Once more the UK set out a hardline negotiating stance in an attempt to cow the EU, as it had done in autumn 2019 (threatening no deal) and 2020 (threatening to break the deal). And once more, the UK government backed down as crunch time approached.

As the UK retreated on issues surrounding the European Court of Justice jurisdiction in December, an increasingly disillusioned Frost resigned over tax changes and Covid restrictions. 'We always had him on resignation watch, he'd been in the departure lounge for some time,' says Andrew Griffith, Johnson's business adviser.[49] Power-sharing collapsed in Northern Ireland in February 2022 with the province riven by divisions over the Protocol. One of Johnson's final acts as premier was to push the Northern Ireland Bill with Foreign Secretary Liz Truss in June 2022, aiming forlornly to resolve concerns with the Protocol he created.

After Johnson's departure, even Brexit's media cheerleaders such as the *Spectator* acknowledged that their hopes had not been met.[50] The fault was not the deed itself, but the implementation by Johnson, his lack of drive and sense of purpose. To Johnson's co-leader Gove, Covid was partly responsible: 'It sapped the bandwidth, departments weren't thinking about it, ministers like Sharma and Kwarteng couldn't apply themselves to it, and the Chancellor was distracted by all that the Treasury had to do.' He remains optimistic, nevertheless, that 'divergence will occur over time: benefits will reveal themselves. Only in the 1820s was it clear that the US leaving the British Empire was demonstrably for the better.'[51] One senior aide acknowledges that 'Brexit could indeed have been a revolutionary moment like the Glorious Revolution (which wasn't in fact so glorious), one of the great resets in British politics. But it hasn't worked out like that.'

Maybe Gove is right, and Britain will have to wait fifty years, as did the United States, to see the benefits. But as of 2023, we can say that Brexit has not achieved the benefits that Johnson proclaimed, and the deal he achieved looks less successful than that negotiated by Theresa May.

A Better 2021: Integrated Review, Carbis Bay and COP26

Johnson was frustrated with the never-ending Brexit rows, and was anxious to make progress on his aim to make Britain a global force again. John Bew, following a half-year Covid delay, laid his egg in March 2021; 'The Integrated Review of Security, Defence, Development and Foreign Policy', which set out the government's vision for Global Britain after Brexit, was the best piece of thinking to emerge on Johnson's three-year watch.

Bew described his brief as 'to think about Britain's place in the world and how to deploy our influence'. Johnson's confidence in Bew was apparently enhanced when he read an article in the *Telegraph* in August in which one of his favourite writers, Andrew Roberts, praised the historian.[52] Every month or so thereafter Bew would put 'direction of travel notes' through to Johnson in his box – essential to his success was the PM's authority behind him. 'Johnson always wanted to pop and pick away at lazy intellectual thought in briefs, so was definitely in tune with the instincts and spirit of Bew's work,' an adviser says.

Two important influences were Sedwill, who pressed the special forces and defence modernization causes, believing the Ministry of Defence was bloated and overdue reform, and Cummings. Bew spoke to Cummings at the NATO summit during the general election campaign and was interested in his ideas as to how serious change could be brought about. They sat down with a piece of paper and discussed Labour's intentions of a similar review. 'We should definitely undertake a wide-ranging review,' Cummings said. He had a deep interest in modernizing defence, including AI, drones and the need for serious investment in new technologies, and he became 'a huge influence' on Bew. As a result, a broad review was announced in the Queen's Speech at the state opening of Parliament on 14 October 2019.

Bew was at one with Cummings on stale thinking across Whitehall, the plodding British state several years behind the US community on the rise of China. Bew believed that the UK needed to move away from the homeland security focus which had dominated thinking since 2001, and prepare itself for the end of US hegemony and a return to a period of multi-state competition driven by technology. Brexit, for which he had not voted, provided the very opportunity for a fresh start that Cummings argued for on the domestic front; crucially the review was not tethered to the UK's decision to leave the EU, and able to build consensus across Whitehall in its measures.

Failure to foresee the rise of China with the risk of the Huawei relationship was a particular angst. The UK's intelligence, security and cyber agency GCHQ believed it had found a way to keep the Chinese firm out of the core of the network and let it be used for non-sensitive 5G devices such as bus stop signs, thereby keeping some of the savings without risking the UK's security. To Cummings, Huawei was totally subservient to the Chinese state, and the risks were unimaginable. Johnson had castigated May for her folly in agreeing to work with the firm initially, but found that there was little alternative given the sunk costs and acquiesced until the introduction of US sanctions, at which point a *volte-face* on the policy became possible. The experience made Johnson much more sceptical of official advice and wont to be much more robust on defence and security matters.

Bew was a happy choice to spearhead the quest. Indicatively, he turned for inspiration to history, for which Whitehall has traditionally had little interest. The Second World War work of

Arnold Toynbee and his team at Oxford analysing why order had broken down in the 1930s and how best to rebuild it after the war was one influence. Another was the sweeping review that Blair's Defence Secretary George Robertson produced in 1998. Also refreshing was his eagerness to take influence from beyond the UK, turning to the US, Europe, Israel and Singapore. 'We found that the further we got from London, the more genuine interest and engagement there was in the future,' an aide working on the Integrated Review recalls.

The six-month delay in publication over the winter saw the Treasury frustrated with No. 10's demands for greater defence spending, but Liam Booth-Smith had acknowledged that alongside R&D it was a priority of the Prime Minister (or, at the very least, a priority of the Prime Minister's senior adviser) and worked hand-in-glove with Cummings to carve out funding until Cummings' departure in November 2020. The stage was the Autumn Spending Review, and the result the biggest increase in defence spending since the end of the Cold War. Johnson personally launched the Integrated Review in the Commons on 16 March 2021, and his own imprimatur was further highlighted by the Foreword setting out his vision, that the UK is at its best when it leads, while recognizing that it needs to do so working with other powers.

Opinions were divided on what was billed as 'the official opening of Global Britain'.[53] To many foreign policy experts, including FCDO mandarins, its sidelining of the EU in a vain pivot to the Indo-Pacific could not possibly deliver as well for Britain. 'China are not interested and India is very tricky, while New Zealand and Australia don't want to go back to the relationship they once had with Britain,' says former No. 10 foreign policy adviser John Holmes.[54] But others such as Gove see it differently: 'Global politics is moving away from the EU, and in the report John Bew anticipated this, as originator and a deliverer.'[55] Cummings agrees on its visionary aspiration: it 'set a different course for defence... From nuclear policy to the intersection between intelligence and special forces.'[56] The Review did indeed offer a bold vision: 'we will lead where we are best placed to do so', it said, while recognizing that cooperation in alliances new and old will be essential for optimizing Britain's interests in security, climate change and cyber warfare as in other areas of concern. In another victory for No. 10 over the Chancellor, the review committed to restoring the 0.7 per cent foreign aid commitment 'when the fiscal situation allows', which the Autumn Spending Review just six months before had said would be cut to 0.5 per cent. 'It looks ludicrous in hindsight,' says an official, 'but the Prime Minister faced down the Chancellor in his office in No. 10, a rare example where he got what he wanted because he was determined and properly primed.'

Johnson's remaining fifteen months in office provided opportunities for him to put into action all four of the Integrated Review's broad international priorities: bringing together a wider community of countries through his use of the G7 presidency and hosting that year; being a leading defender of the liberal democratic community with his leadership in the Ukraine War; promoting global resilience to the challenges of climate change at COP26 in Glasgow; and finally, supporting the welfare of British citizens through its international economic policy, albeit with limited success, through trade deals.

The timing of Britain hosting the G7 in June 2021 could not have been more fortunate, with the institution in dire need of resuscitation. The forum, consisting of the seven leading like-minded countries, plus the EU, but excluding China and now

Russia following the invasion of Crimea in 2014, had first met in 1973. But it had never experienced an American President like Trump who had no time for it and proved a menace. 'He hated international gatherings because it was not all about him, and he loathed sharing a stage with other leaders. He also worried, accurately, that the other leaders were talking about him behind his back,' says an official. He had all but sabotaged the summit when, in 2018, Canada was the host in Québec, by walking out from the final communiqué. The French at Biarritz in 2019 then fudged or finessed it by avoiding direct confrontation with the US President by not having a communiqué at all. In 2020, Trump himself was due to host, controversially at Camp David in June, but Covid intervened. Instead, two conference calls, described as 'terrible' by officials, took place. Had Trump been re-elected, the future of the fifty-year-old gathering might have been called into question, especially with European members ambivalent about its continuing relevance. None in the G7, though, wept any tears when Trump was defeated.

In the summer of 2020, Johnson's G7 Sherpa Jonathan Black went to talk to his boss about his aspirations. 'I want you to project the image of both Britain as a soft and a hard power,' Johnson said, telling the team that he wanted his top three G7 themes to be health (because of the pandemic), climate (with Glasgow imminent) and the economy (how to rebuild after Covid).

Ascertaining the attitude of the new US administration to international relations after four years of Trump was now the priority. So at the start of 2021, Black, with his opposite number on COP26 Peter Hill, flew to Washington. With so much hinging on the result of the November 2020 presidential election, they had prepared separate Trump and Biden versions of their plans for the

G7 and COP26. They now needed to find out what the new White House wanted from both events, knowing it would be crucial to success. They rapidly realized that the new strategic ambition was 'we want the world to know that the US is back in multilateralism and back in business after Trump'. They reported back that this was the chance for a major reset in the special relationship post-Brexit. One early impact was that the G7 plan developed a more China-critical edge. Much of the success of the G7 and COP26 was down to listening to the White House and securing its backing.

To stiffen resolve and to prepare the ground for the plenary in June, a one-off G7 video conference for the leaders was arranged in February 2021, 'designed to show everyone that the G7 was up and running again', says an official. Establishing Johnson as a credible figure with other leaders was not a given. He had difficult relations with several, including Biden, Merkel and Macron, as well as with the EU who were regular attenders, represented by von der Leyen. His relations with Italy's Mario Draghi and Japan's Yoshihide Suga were cordial but distant, and only with Canada's Justin Trudeau did he enjoy a good if punchy connection. He would have work to do if he was to optimize the summit in June.

Where to host the G7 was the next question. With Blair holding the 2005 G7 at Gleneagles in Scotland, and Cameron the 2013 G7 at Loch Erne in Northern Ireland, it was England's turn. Whitehall pressed for the North-East or South-West, with a scenic hotel projecting Britain's soft power in Yorkshire or Devon. But Johnson decided on Cornwall where he had spent happy family holidays, specifically a small coastal resort with a wide beach twenty miles from Land's End called Carbis Bay. He was told that the location was considered remote, very reliant on the weather, unusually 'intimate', was too small to accommodate all guests and that it would present all manner of practical difficulties. But Johnson was determined. Hosting the first major event after Covid presented further practical tests, including the nightmare risk of the leaders catching the virus. During a last-minute security sweep, one of the team tested positive, which meant the whole unit had to be isolated, and a new sweep done to confirm the venue was safe while Biden was already in the air on his way.

Johnson's mind had been on other matters, and he arrived in Cornwall, to the frustration of his team, having given little serious thought to what he hoped to get out of it beyond wanting it to be a very good show and to display to the world how Britain was opening up. One of his three priorities of the previous summer had now flipped from economy to trade. As often happens at such events, the big idea only came together at the last moment – namely the G7 pledging a further one billion vaccine doses to be shared with the rest of the world. The final days saw an internal spreadsheet being constantly updated on which member countries made their pledges. AstraZeneca and Pfizer responded that they had vaccines aplenty, and Johnson and Sunak agreed in a late meeting at No. 10 to find the funds. Regrettably, the UK then failed to follow through to ensure G7 countries deployed Covid vaccines in the most vulnerable countries anywhere near equivalent to the need.

Johnson's chairing of the G7 was idiosyncratic. 'He switched on late and hadn't read his briefing papers properly to prepare. But he chaired sessions with style, charm and humour even if he was winging it without particular structure. The session he chaired at the end on democratic values showed what he could achieve,' says an aide. The long separation meant all the leaders arrived in Cornwall genuinely wanting to see each other and to make it a success. Even Macron, who had been sat upon by the White

House, behaved. As a result, Carbis Bay helped re-establish the G7 on a firm footing. Showing the emerging and the vulnerable nations that the G7 was serious about Net Zero and taking hits themselves was a particular objective. A twenty-page communiqué was produced to show the rest of the world that the G7 was back. It talked about 'future frontiers', which was about getting ahead of the curve on a whole range of issues that affected all the nations. The communiqué was significant, shaped by the US, for calling out China for the first time in the G7's history: 'to respect human rights and fundamental freedoms, especially in relation to Xinjiang and those rights, freedoms and high degree of autonomy for Hong Kong'. During its presidency of the G7, Britain put together a wider community of countries, including allies in the Indo-Pacific, in a 'G7 Plus' to underline common cause against China, and deployed a Royal Navy carrier strike group of ships and aircraft to the region, an initiative in tune with the Integrated Review's tilt eastwards.

The icing on Johnson's cake was Buckingham Palace saying the Queen wanted to come to Cornwall rather than host the leaders at Windsor as originally planned. All delegations responded enthusiastically, with the US saying, 'Tell us the plan and we will help.' The nearby eco visitor attraction, the Eden Project, was selected as an ideal location for her to host as it was very secure, provided an arresting backdrop, and it chimed with the whole green theme of the G7. The aura of the monarchy, and the special quality of Queen Elizabeth herself, helped re-establish the G7 as a worthwhile forum, and Britain as a credible presence again on the world stage.

Attention now turned to COP26 in Glasgow, just five months away. COP (Conference of the Parties) had been held annually under the auspices of the UN since the 1990s. The Glasgow COP, delayed by Covid for a year, was particularly significant. At COP21 in Paris in 2015, every country had agreed to limit global warming to well below 2 degrees and to aim for 1.5 degrees. Under its Paris Agreement, they agreed that every five years they would come back together with an updated plan on reductions. Glasgow was the forum where they would be presenting their plans.

For a Prime Minister who had previously thought green policies a load of nonsense, hosting COP26 provided a transformative opportunity to make a difference. But as at the G7, the team were frustrated with Johnson and found it difficult to engage him till the event was imminent. Had he done so earlier, and in a more focused way, far more could have been achieved.

The selection of the COP president was one aspect he mishandled, before alighting on Business Secretary Alok Sharma, without a full appreciation of the skills required for the post. Johnson wavered over Sharma's appointment even after the UK's presidency had begun, but by then it was too late and too embarrassing to change his mind given Sharma had left BEIS to take the role. Fortunately, he proved adept at the job. Johnson's team worried that it would look bad if it leaked how many people he had asked to fill the role, including his casting a fly over several of his predecessors including Cameron, who turned it down. In the autumn of 2019, Theresa May's photograph was placed, as is the custom, with those of other former Prime Ministers on the wall at the top of the main No. 10 staircase. Johnson's team suggested that it would be a nice gesture to invite her back in for tea to see it in situ, and she duly accepted with Philip. 'What am I to say to her?' he asked before they arrived, panicking about meeting one of his least favourite people, who was entirely immune to his charms and disengaged from his conversational style. 'Whatever you do, don't offer her a job that you will regret,' they said sternly, knowing his penchant for doing exactly that. When he met up with his team afterwards, he confessed he'd offered her the presidency. But he had no intention of giving it to her, as he wanted COP26 to be his legacy not hers, so, in a grave discourtesy to her, it was fudged.

May herself had a good record on the environment and had been eagerly looking forward to hosting the event, deciding on Glasgow as the venue before the end of her time as Prime Minister. But when Johnson succeeded her, his team protested that it was the wrong location, hard to police, and would prove a headache getting him up and down to it. 'You couldn't fly because of the optics, and the train takes five and a half hours. Nightmare,' says Anouka Dhadda, his environment specialist in the No. 10 Policy Unit.[57] But Johnson was emphatic. 'This is about the Union, and about levelling up,' he said.

His team yearned for that same degree of decisiveness elsewhere. But for months, flippancy and humour were his stock responses. At Biarritz in July 2019, during his first international conference as Prime Minister, he started talking about the importance of planting trees. 'Let's make it a Vote Leaf campaign,' he joked. But at a pivotal meeting in his office in January 2020, with chief scientist Patrick Vallance in support, Dhadda talked him through a slide pack she had prepared on COP, and what their objectives might be. He was intellectually very curious and asked a range of searching questions: 'Has the climate really changed?' and 'How reliable is the science on this?' He wanted to be convinced the evidence stood up, but was aware of the sceptics on his right-wing. Cummings started from an even more sceptical position on the effectiveness of climate policy and the potency of environmental issues as a vote-winner, but once he and his data specialist Ben Warner came around to the set of proposals centred on technological advancements they helped get Johnson over the line, even if Cummings never fully bought into it. 'To get anything done in 2020 in No. 10, one needed Dom on side,' says an aide. Once convinced, Johnson was a huge supporter of the plans. 'He'd spend a disproportionate amount of time on it, ultimately he was the big driver of all the green stuff,' says an official. Then Covid struck, and for vital months focus on COP in No. 10 was lost.

Johnson, apt to fall back on his crowning glory as Mayor, started talking about COP as his 'Green Olympics'. 'For a painfully long time, he didn't understand what COP actually was. It was just about his own experience and how he could feel statesmanlike and popular, getting pats on the back from world leaders and toadying up to celebrities. Glitz and glamour,' says Cleo Watson. 'COPs are a very dry, painful and complicated negotiating process, set against the backdrop of climate activists and drowning small island states protesting out of a genuine fear that this summit won't move the dial, to secure a non-legally binding agreement. He simply couldn't see why treating COP as the "Green Olympics" was actively damaging to the atmospherics of the negotiations.'[58] At a meeting in February 2021, tempers frayed when he refused to take the substance seriously, saying, rather, 'we need a logo, we need a jingle, we need a mascot'.

Sharma, who began his duties that January, and Peter Hill, COP's CEO, were more frustrated than any at the lack of clarity and decisions, and for a long time saw Johnson as a liability in trying to achieve international credibility. Mighty international forces were at play, with China trying to wrongfoot Washington, and as Sharma and Hill lobbied leaders around the world on topics including coal and subsidies, Johnson was at best a distraction. 'Sharma deserves a significant amount of credit for building up a lot of goodwill ahead of the conference,' says an official. But when at the eleventh hour he did lock in, he made a significant impact. The official opening in Glasgow on Monday 1 November was preceded by a flat G20 in Rome, minus China's Xi and Putin, the Italians proving an unfocused chair. Johnson sprung into life on Saturday morning standing in front of the ancient Colosseum, likening the impact of unrestricted climate change to the fall of the Roman Empire. The world could be heading for a new 'dark age' if it failed to tackle global warming, he said. 'Civilization could go backwards and history could go into reverse,' he said, if emissions were not tackled. Frantic last-minute work by Black and Hill overnight on Saturday resulted in a G20 communiqué which achieved agreement on Net Zero as a target and also on financial subsidies.

An energized Johnson boarded the plane on Sunday night bound for Glasgow: 'Even the climate ultras were not going to suggest he should've spent four weeks coming by boat,' says an aide. Standing in the aisle, he regaled his team with stories from classical mythology before disappearing into his cubicle to work on his speech. He had absorbed the message from his team to focus on the big picture – 'coal, cars, cash and trees', the strapline coined by Allegra Stratton, appointed Johnson's COP26 spokesperson earlier in the year. Johnson's speech, delivered on the first day, saw him at his best. 'It's one minute to midnight on that doomsday clock and we need to act now. If we don't get serious about climate change today, it will be too late for our children to do so tomorrow,' he opened. '… if we fail, [children not yet born] will not forgive us. They will know that Glasgow was the historic turning point when history failed to turn. They will judge us with bitterness and with a resentment that eclipses any of the climate activists of today, and they will be right,' was his peroration.[59] It provided exactly the momentum and global attention that was needed.

Once his mind was committed, Johnson made a significant impact, bolstered by his willingness to make calls and lobby countries such as Indonesia and South Africa, and to listen to the concerns of Congo and other vulnerable nations. Much was made at the conference's conclusion on 14 November about India and China watering down the final agreement, from 'phasing out' coal to merely 'phasing down' its use, resulting in an exhausted Sharma, who had worked tirelessly to gain the support of almost all the 190 nations, shedding tears in his concluding speech. But Glasgow succeeded in achieving much, including building on the Paris Agreement and finalizing the rulebook. As Johnson told the Commons, they were 'keeping 1.5 alive' – the aim of limiting global temperatures to 1.5 degrees C.[60] So Glasgow was not an opportunity altogether lost, but one where so much more might have been achieved, not least on financing, had Johnson engaged earlier and taken it more seriously.

War in Ukraine

Johnson became immediately embroiled after COP26 in the Owen Paterson affair (see Chapter 10), with a low engagement in foreign policy until February 2022, when Russia invaded Ukraine. It resulted in the most impressive example of his leadership on foreign or domestic fronts, and a partial reframing of his entire premiership. Our questions are: what exactly were his contributions, why did he become so much more committed in Ukraine than elsewhere in foreign policy, and what was the impact of his net contribution?

His speech on 19 February 2022 at the Munich Security Conference on the eve of war stands out for the early gauntlet he threw down to his international counterparts. He spoke about how every time Western ministers visit Kyiv, assurances are given that 'we stand four-square behind [Ukrainian] sovereignty and independence'. It built up to his powerful conclusion: 'How hollow, how meaningless, how insulting those words would seem if – at the very moment when their sovereignty and independence is imperilled – we simply look away.'[61] The same pugilistic spirit informed his 'Six steps the West must take to help Ukraine right now' article in the *New York Times* on 6 March.[62] 'The lesson from Russia's invasion of Georgia in 2008 and seizure of Crimea in 2014 is that accepting the results of Russian aggression merely encourages more aggression,' he wrote. It was a far cry from his early time as Foreign Secretary in which he attempted a reset with Putin and Russian Foreign Affairs Minister Sergei Lavrov, culminating in a late-2017 visit to Moscow. The attempt to thaw relations was later described by Johnson himself as 'a fool's errand',[63] but the Salisbury poisonings had made him adamant not to be fooled again.

Providing weapons to Ukraine was one of Johnson's most significant interventions. In mid-January, well before the invasion, the UK was the first to talk loudly about the need to give material help and then was the first to supply the Belfast manufactured NLAW shoulder-fired anti-tank missiles. Even if they did not deter the invasion, they helped Ukraine combat the advancing Russian convoys. Johnson had to punch through Whitehall taboos against supplying the weapons – the initial advice was that Russia would win so quickly there was little point in providing Ukraine with any military aid. The initiative was largely the impetus of Defence

Secretary Wallace, who was ahead of everyone on advice that the UK needed rapidly to supply Ukraine and move to ensure that the situation could neither become nor be seen as a Russian victory. Wallace worried that 'if you left it to the Whitehall blob, nothing would've happened'. So he sent a secret letter to Johnson in the early summer of 2021 to warn him of the likelihood that Putin would choose to invade, and that the UK needed to step up in response with practical support. 'If I'd sent it by open channels, the system would have stopped it getting to the Prime Minister,' he says.[64]

Johnson was influential too in pushing for sanctions, even getting into a competition with the EU on who was the more vocal on their need. It is time to 'squeeze Russia from the global economy, piece by piece,' he said in Parliament on 24 February as he announced a wide-ranging sanctions package against Moscow, including freezing the assets of all major Russian banks and banning hi-tech exports.[65]

Boosted by his new Carbis Bay profile and confidence, he pushed the G7 to move beyond the cautious approach of the Minsk Agreements/Normandy Format response to the Russian invasion of the Donbass/Crimea in 2014. On the very day of the invasion, he urged his fellow G7 leaders to eject Russia from the international SWIFT payment system such that Russian banks would be crippled and severed from the global markets. It was a move resisted by Germany's new Chancellor, Olaf Scholz. To circumvent caution from some of his G7 colleagues, he drew on his underutilized coalition-building skills, allying with the Canadians and the Japanese and highlighting the global consequences of letting Russia succeed, not least the encouragement it would give China over Taiwan. Despite his tack frustrating many of his fellow leaders, Johnson helped make the G7 a more action-oriented foreign policy vehicle. Johnson's impact on the Biden administration is harder to ascertain. The White House was initially fearful of the consequences of escalating the conflict, as it said, vertically by making it more intense, and horizontally by broadening it out to other countries and taking war into Russia itself. Johnson certainly played a role in shifting Biden, if more through his direct actions than one-to-one persuasion.

Finally, Johnson's impact was felt through his four visits to Kyiv, on 1 February before the war, 9 April, 24 June and 24 August. While the last two visits were more for domestic consumption in a fractious Westminster, the first two visits were highly significant. The Cabinet Office, and Cabinet Secretary Case in particular, gave him strong advice not to go on 9 April, with Russia menacingly close to the capital. British intelligence didn't have much of a grasp of the risks that he would be under, with a credible possibility of him being killed. Not since 1812, with the assassination of Spencer Perceval, had a British Prime Minister been killed in office, and with all the domestic instability, and the Queen in frail health, the system was close to panic. The Cabinet Office and intelligence services drew up a risk statement, getting the Prime Minister to sign and accept that the decision to visit went beyond the level of risk they found tolerable; to Johnson this was yet another example of a system that was too cautious, and was only too happy to do as he was told: 'Prime Minister, you sign here.' He was warned too of the grave embarrassment that a bungled visit would cause him personally, and to Britain's standing abroad. Still Johnson persisted. If anything, the physical risk emboldened him, as it had done when he had walked the streets of Lahore when Foreign Secretary amid adoring crowds in November 2016. Jaimie Norman, the military attaché at No. 10, hatched a plan to punch through the delays, whereby Johnson flew to Poland and then travelled to Kyiv by train, with just Norman and his security detail in tow. Johnson was speaking regularly to President Volodymyr Zelenskyy by telephone, but even the secure line was not free of the risk of Russian eavesdropping, so the face-to-face talks allowed for more confidential exchanges, and the bond to deepen. Von der Leyen had visited Kyiv just the day before, to Johnson's annoyance, but he was the first national leader to visit the country, a powerful statement still.

Why then did Johnson have much more engagement in Ukraine than in any other area? Several factors were working strongly in the same direction. From the outset, the historian within him was utterly gripped. Not unlike his hero Churchill, he saw Britain leading the world against forces of darkness epitomized by Vladimir Putin. He took a long-term view that the risks of standing up strongly, which the world had failed to do over the Donbass, or indeed against Xi's provocations, were less than the risk of appeasement. Unlike Eden, who had equally seen his nemesis Abdul Nasser of Egypt as a Hitler-like figure in 1956 over Suez, Johnson was running with the grain of history. After he was woken at 4.10 on the morning of 24 February to be told Putin's troops had crossed the border into Ukraine, as military intelligence on both sides of the Atlantic had been predicting, he spoke to a very demanding Zelenskyy. At five o'clock that afternoon, he told a silent House of Commons, which for weeks had been baying for Johnson's blood, that Putin was 'hurling the might of his military machine against a free and peaceful neighbour, in breach of his own explicit pledge and every principle of civilized behaviour between states'.[66] Even his greatest critics sensed that they had a real leader speaking.

With Zelenskyy, Johnson formed his closest relationship with any foreign leader, which further spurred him on. Officials speak of the importance of Zelenskyy's visit to London in October 2020, a visit that forged their bond, and one which so nearly didn't happen. For months, it was on-off, not enough time in Johnson's diary and it was often cancelled. But when it happened, they immediately hit it off. Johnson arranged for him to meet the Duke and Duchess of Cambridge, which he enjoyed, and a visit to Portsmouth to visit an aircraft carrier and talk to the military engaged in training Ukrainian troops (on which Britain and Canada were in the lead). An agreement was signed promising £1.25 billion to help rebuild the Ukrainian Navy against Russian threats. The personal chemistry between the two leaders was evident for all to see: both natural comics, lovers of crowds and adulation, neither machine politicians but masters at putting themselves across in the media, and both with a historic sense of their mission. It was the only light in Johnson's tortured final months as Prime Minister. 'Zelenskyy thought Johnson was protecting his back, the one person he most trusted among international leaders,' says a senior Foreign Office official. 'That very human relationship with Zelenskyy was significant in bolstering the Prime Minister's morale at a very lonely and difficult time for him,' agrees another.

Johnson arranged for Zelenskyy to address Parliament on 8 March and Zelenskyy invited him to speak to the Ukrainian parliament on 3 May. In his final weeks as premier, Johnson presented Zelenskyy with the Sir Winston Churchill Leadership Award, bringing together two of his heroes: 'In that moment of supreme crisis, you faced a test of leadership that was, in its way, as severe as Churchill's challenge in 1940… you chose to stay in Kyiv, among the Ukrainian people, just as Churchill stayed in London in 1940… I imagine his spirit walking with you,' he said.[67] Further proof of their deep relationship is that they remained in regular touch long after Johnson quit No. 10; indeed, Johnson visited Zelenskyy in Kyiv in January 2023.

Johnson had a deep empathy for the Ukrainian people at large, one reason why he wanted British Ambassador Melinda Simmons to go back to Kyiv from the western city of Lviv in late April as a show of solidarity. He was emotionally engaged in a way that he never had been over Brexit, or over broad swathes of policy. Every evening at 10.10 p.m., he would call his close officials to say, as one recalls, 'What the f**k are we doing about Mariupol?', 'What the f**k are we doing about X, Y, Z?' They worked out that he'd been watching the 10 o'clock news up in the flat with a baby on his lap and was 'very emotional about it all'.

Johnson had real personal animus against Putin. When he first became Foreign Secretary, he made overtures to the Russian leader in an attempt to reset the relationship. He felt that Putin then snubbed him, and behaved appallingly in the Salisbury poisonings in March 2018. He then invested himself in organizing the response across the EU on the mass expulsion of Russian military intelligence officers, the way he conducted those discussions helping shape the judgements he would make over Ukraine on the gains from standing up firmly to Putin. 'He realized then that you can stand up to Russia and it works,' says an official. When Putin called him on 2 February, insisting the hostile Russian activity near the Ukrainian border was simply military exercises, Johnson remained stiff. The Russian premier used his typical tactics for Trump, lauding Johnson as wise for his decision to leave the EU, but Johnson was not so easily taken in by flattery. According to Johnson, 'He was being very, very familiar. I said to him, "Look, if you do this, it will be an utter catastrophe. It will mean a massive package of Western sanctions. It will mean we continue to intensify our support to Ukraine. And it will mean more NATO, not less NATO, on your borders." And he said, "Boris, you say that Ukraine is not going to join NATO any time soon," he said in English, "any time soon. What is any time soon?" And I said, "Well, it's not going to join NATO for the foreseeable future. You know that perfectly well."' Then Johnson made an extraordinary assertion: 'He, sort of, threatened me at one point and said, you know, "Boris, I don't want to hurt you, but with a missile, it would only take a minute."'[68] The system did not, however, regard it as a credible threat.

It was the first time they had spoken since VE Day 2020, and the last time. After the war broke out Johnson decided that he would not speak to Putin personally, a call which the Kremlin would have been pleased to accept. His quarrel he always stressed was with Putin and the Russian government, not with the country at large. When he wanted to give a message to the Russian people to say precisely this, voices in Whitehall and at the British Embassy in Moscow resisted. But he persisted, using social media to read out the short message in Cyrillic script, many of the letters of which he knew from Greek.

Outplaying the EU on Ukraine was another powerful incentive, especially as the main foot-draggers were France, anxious not to humiliate Putin, and Germany, which had allowed itself to become too dependent on Russian gas. 'The Prime Minister believed that if you don't use force, Putin thinks that the West doesn't care,' says an aide. He saw Putin's amassing troops on the border of Ukraine in April 2021 and not going ahead as a test, with an insufficiently robust response from the EU. The fact that critics of the EU in the British press applauded his calling them out made him even more determined to forge ahead. Johnson then showed agility in working with EU countries with whom Britain had a better relationship – the Baltics, the Nordics and the Dutch. He strengthened Britain's military presence and support for the northern European countries that form part of the Joint Expeditionary Force, fulfilling an ambition of the Integrated Review for Britain to be a leading European force within NATO, in defence of the liberal democratic community. In so doing, he helped delineate a future role for Britain as a European power outside the EU.

His disregard for many of the niceties of diplomacy aided him in striking a bold, influential stance and being truly catalytic in leading effective interventions. His November 2021 Guildhall speech urged the EU to drop the Nord Stream 2 gas pipeline with Russia. 'Don't include that, it'll just piss off the Germans', was the advice from his foreign affairs officials, but he kept it in the speech. It did indeed annoy them – but three months later the German authorities put a halt to the project. At G7 meetings he could be just as strong, and though he had had to struggle to shift Biden into a more ambitious position, 'he did manage to move the centre of gravity of the G7 position', says an official. His crowning performance was at the NATO and G7 leaders' summit on 24 March 2022. 'Everybody went through their positions and took stock, all pleased about the unity, until Boris came in right at the end frustrated by what he'd just heard. He was determined that everybody could be more ambitious in helping the Ukrainian people together,' says an observer.

The absence of serious dissent at home, with Labour's Keir Starmer falling in strongly behind the government's response, was another factor explaining his impact on Ukraine. While leadership contender Sunak was subdued on the subject, concerned that action could have negative economic implications domestically, Truss was out at the front with Wallace. With both yapping at his heels, it would have been tempting for him to have taken an even stronger stance. Initially, he thought they were over the top. But then he thought the NSC, which had put in the work preparing the British response, too cautious, which resulted in him making No. 10 his command base. On Ukraine, if not generally elsewhere, he put his trust in his officials, who helped him establish a strong middle way.

Johnson was finally motivated by domestic Tory turbulence, and the opportunity the war gave him to restore credibility and prolong his tenure. On at least a dozen occasions, calls with or visits to Zelenskyy were announced by No. 10 concurrently with embarrassing domestic news, including Partygate, scandals and unrest from his MPs. All Prime Ministers are motivated by ego, Johnson more than most, but on Ukraine, he was driven by far more than ego. Unlike Brexit, he believed in standing up for Ukraine with every fibre of his body.

What difference to the war will history say Johnson made? Above all, it will focus on Zelenskyy himself and the exceptional unity of the Ukrainian response. Compared to that, Britain was a small player. The belief among the right that Johnson led an indecisive EU, after the initial period, does not stand up. The rapidity of the switch within it, not least by Germany, was remarkable, with von der Leyen strengthening its resolve and bringing in countries like Poland. By the time Johnson had ceased to be Prime Minister, Zelenskyy saw her as the principal European figure supporting him, and Biden, the key figure overall.

Johnson might have encouraged Biden, who was impressed that Britain was the second largest national provider of weapons, but Britain's support pales into insignificance compared to the US and indeed the EU. As Johnson regularly remarked, and as his predecessors Lloyd George and Churchill equally felt, the US might be slow to respond, but when it does, the extent of its support changes history.

None of which is to take away from Johnson personally for his very clear position and lead. His staunch line that 'you can't be scared of victory' had been important early on in getting the West to take a strong line. He took enormous risks, not least downplaying the threat of nuclear war, and if he had been proved wrong, he would have been roundly castigated and worse. But his judgements were overwhelmingly correct, a reminder of what he might have achieved more widely.

Global Britain Achieved?

Foreign policy revealed Johnson's strengths and potential as Prime Minister far more than domestic policy. True, he fell far short of his 'Clark Kent' ambitions for an unleashed Global Britain. True also that while he made Brexit happen, he never made sense of Brexit. But given the constraints that Brexit, Covid and the weak UK economy imposed, to say nothing of two tricky Presidents in the White House, the G7 and COP26 can be considered qualified successes, still more so the response to the Ukraine War. 'At the G7 and COP, we made a little of Boris go a long way. In 2022 with the Ukraine War, we got an awful lot of him and it allowed us to go much further,' says an aide. Frustration remains the dominant word, as his Eton housemaster observed at the start of the book. How much more he could have achieved in foreign policy, as in domestic policy, if he had displayed more gravitas, applied himself more consistently and worked harder at meetings with leaders.

Erratic to the end, he made a thoroughly gauche and provocative comment in mid-March 2022, that Brexit showed British people 'loved freedom in the same way as Ukrainians fighting Russia's invasion', a comment as poorly received by EU leaders as by people across the Brexit divide in Britain. His quality could be seen, though, in his popularity within NATO circles as a result of his commitment to Ukraine. Near the end, he held one of the best meetings of his premiership with non-members Finland and Sweden, both delighted by the security guarantees. A conversation at No. 10 with Germany's Chancellor Olaf Scholz in April, a man utterly unlike him in every conceivable way, saw him at his best. It showed what he would have achieved with EU leaders had he been prepared to make the weather and be more constructive. 'I understand Olaf now. I like him,' he told staff afterwards. Two weeks later, he visited India, spun a charkha at Mahatma Gandhi's Sabarmati Ashram, hopped onto a bulldozer at a JCB factory in Halol and was mobbed by adoring crowds wherever he went. He handled Prime Minister Narendra Modi with a skill he rarely displayed with other foreign leaders, with whom he was too apt to spar. Not since Thatcher and Blair had Britain had a Prime Minister who was such a large presence abroad, with a degree of interest normally given only to visits by senior royals.

Diminishing the Commonwealth was one argument given for not entering the EU in 1972–73; re-engaging with it was also popular among some, the potential for alliances such as CANZUK (involving Canada, Australia, New Zealand and the UK) touted by Brexit enthusiasts such as Daniel Hannan, adviser to the Board of Trade. 'Complete bollocks', was how one retired diplomat dismissed the prospect. But Johnson got on well with the Australians and Canadians, and invited South Africa's President Cyril Ramaphosa to the G7 in Cornwall. There were foundations there on which he could have built, so it was perverse that he engaged so little with it: he only fleetingly visited Africa once for its biennial heads of government meeting in Kigali, but never the other fifty-three countries, despite much encouragement to do so. In part the lack of engagement was due to a frustration with the Commonwealth Secretariat: 'He was exasperated by the inefficiency of it all, but couldn't do anything about it,' says one FCDO official. National leaders always encounter hurdles: the best transcend them, not complain about them.

Prime Ministers with grand foreign policy visions, such as Macmillan, Thatcher and Blair, find that, as soon as they quit No. 10, no one abroad really wants to know. They have just the one shot at goal. Johnson had the historic opportunity after Brexit, as he laid out in his Greenwich speech, to reforge Britain's place in the world in the twenty-first century, a goal none of his predecessors since the millennium had achieved. He had the gifts too, which many Prime Ministers do not, to be a global leader. He even had the team, somehow conspiring to work with officials productively unlike in much of domestic policy. The fact he fell short was his fault alone.

Johnson struts out of No. 10, accompanied by his new team: Simon Case (left), Dan Rosenfield (right) and Stuart Glassborow (background)

9

GROWN-UPS

Every Prime Minister is different. But every Prime Minister is the same.

All fifty-seven arrived in office with very different ambitions and understandings of the job.

But all Prime Ministers since the creation of the modern office by David Lloyd George in 1916 have had fundamentally the same nature of job to do.

They all wanted to be successful. To achieve that, they needed a talented, experienced and loyal team around them. If loyalty was prioritized over talent and experience, Prime Ministers stalled. If loyalty was absent, their premierships imploded. The most effective Prime Ministers since 1900, Lloyd George himself, Winston Churchill, Clement Attlee and Margaret Thatcher, had teams who balanced all three attributes.

Nothing in their previous lives ever prepares the incoming Prime Minister for what is now expected of them. They might have held all the great offices of state with distinction, or been proven leaders of their party in opposition. But once through the black door on their first day, they move into a liminal world unlike anything they have ever known. They cannot achieve all they want. To be Prime Minister is to choose. Time is no longer their own, with decisions required on every subject, many unfamiliar to them, and too many people to meet, all of whom want things from them. Impotence rather than power is what many Prime Ministers find, victims to events that crash in upon them over which they have little or no control.

The Prime Minister thus has to be extremely clear and to rely utterly on staff to operationalize their policy objectives, manage their day-to-day business, handle No. 10's communications, build bridges to their party and advise them on how to play the role of an important international leader.

PMs have little or no space to think. They have to trust the powers behind the role. In the most effective premierships, No. 10 *becomes* the Prime Minister. It becomes one mind. Trust is the cement that binds the different entities within it together. Without it, premierships unravel.

The first months define whether and how the premiership will work. The initial decisions, appointments and behaviour have defined every premiership since Lloyd George.

Even if a Prime Minister is omnicompetent, with skills across the range required for the job, an Attlee or a Thatcher, they still have but twenty-four hours in a day. They need teams with that mix of talent, experience and loyalty to help them fulfil their role. Still more so if there is a Prime Minister, like Anthony Eden, Gordon Brown or Boris Johnson, deficient in several core attributes. No. 10, even though nowhere laid out, has clearly defined tasks: it only works if the Prime Minister appoints the right people to the key posts and backs them to do their jobs.

Johnson thus needed, as we wrote before he entered No. 10, a DPM to take over much of the routine work. Even hyperactive Thatcher had Willie Whitelaw as DPM, and was weaker without him after 1988. Johnson additionally needed a formidable Cabinet

Secretary and principal private secretary to ensure the Whitehall machine ran smoothly, a chief of staff to run No. 10, and directors of policy, communications and party relations to oversee each function effectively. Without these, his premiership would never reach the heights he so desired once the initial Brexit crisis had been resolved.[1]

Because he had never worked in a domestic department, knew very little about central government and had avoided engaging with fellow MPs in Parliament, his team needed to be particularly rich in knowledge of Whitehall and Westminster. Johnson was known to be a chaotic administrator. But once in No. 10, would he learn about governing processes and structures rather than individuals and the problems they could solve for him?

If his premiership was to work optimally, he would thus have to use the tried and tested systems of Cabinet government and the civil service. Improve them certainly, but not bypass or trash them. He would need to appoint the best to recognized positions, keep them in place, and build institutional memory and trust. What he needed to avoid was competing power centres, and bringing in mavericks whose job descriptions were unclear, who unsettled order and clouded trust and propriety. Lloyd George imported such characters with Maundy Gregory, and Harold Wilson with figures such as Paymaster General George Wigg and his personal and political secretary Marcia Williams after 1964. Prime Ministers need to be, and be seen to be, beyond reproach, and to surround themselves with figures of principle and repute, or the premiership rots from the inside out.

Grown-ups with experience are required in every premiership, none more so than in Johnson's. But as this chapter shows, he either didn't appoint them, didn't use or back them, or he spurned them.

Ultimately, the whole tone of a premiership is determined by the conduct of the incumbent. If they do not rise to the challenge with decorum and principle, then men and women beneath them, however good and however talented, will be dragged down into the mud.

The entire trajectory of Johnson's premiership was foreshadowed by 1 August 2019, the end of his first week.

In his beginning was his end.

Primi ordines: July–December 2019

With a top team, experienced, capable and loyal, who stayed put, Johnson would have achieved much more as Prime Minister.

Thatcher had essentially one leadership team in place in No. 10 for her eleven and a half years, as did Blair for his ten years and Cameron for his six years. Johnson had three teams in three years. Three leadership teams, or to use the Latin term *ordines*, was extravagant.

Like Henry VIII, he liked to play his cards close to his chest, with shifting alliances, and people vying for his attention. Like Henry VIII, he had a succession of courts. For Henry, Catherine of Aragon's court was succeeded after the breach with Rome by the fractious Anne Boleyn court, and then by the Seymour court, who fell out with the Howards/Norfolks in a crescendo of squabbling until Henry's death in 1547. 'F**king hell, this is Boris's court,' a shocked Cabinet minister suddenly exclaimed when watching the RSC's stage adaptation of *The Mirror and the Light*, the final part of Hilary Mantel's *Wolf Hall* trilogy about Henry's court.[2]

The first period of Johnson's premiership was the most successful, because he had effective people in post, he trusted them and they were wholly aligned on two overwhelming objectives: getting Brexit done and winning the general election. Fear of abject failure and the shortest premiership in history was very real. And very bonding.

But once the common purposes were achieved, the underlying flaws and differing ambitions in his team began to unpick his premiership thread by thread.

Cabinet Secretary Mark Sedwill explained to Johnson shortly before he took over that, more than any other post in government, the PM can shape the job to their own personality. The model he thought would work best for him was that of laid-back US President Ronald Reagan, with maximum delegation. James Baker, Reagan's redoubtable chief of staff (1981–85), was a figure in Sedwill's mind, as he was in Eddie Lister's. 'The PM does just three things: define the big picture, communicate it and appoint the people to deliver on it,' Sedwill explained to Johnson. 'Reagan appointed people from different camps, didn't interfere, and trusted them.' Reagan was Johnson's hero: it should have been a slam dunk. But he looked at Sedwill blankly, his mind elsewhere.

He then proceeded to do exactly the opposite. True, he didn't interfere with his team in his first six months and largely did what they asked. Just as long as the threat of a general election defeat hung over him, he trusted them. With Johnson, trust was always transactional and temporary. 'What Johnson did believe in was *mistrust*. He wanted to run No. 10 with responsibilities fuzzed, everyone distrusting each other, currying favour and owing their loyalty to him,' says an aide.

Johnson's innate incomprehension of bureaucracy and his unwillingness to listen meant that those trying to help guide him, Sedwill, Lister and MacNamara, were unable to construct a No. 10 to allow him to optimize his strengths and run an effective ship. It was as if he didn't want to acknowledge that much of what he had been able to accomplish in the vastly simpler world of City Hall had only been made possible by his team, led by Milton and Lister.

Above all, Johnson needed a superb chief of staff at No. 10, a post which has become the most important aide to the Prime Minister. The position was only created under Tony Blair in 1997 (Thatcher appointed David Wolfson to a more junior post with the same title in 1979, and it fell into disuse when he left). When Blair appointed Jonathan Powell, who had been a diplomat in Washington, they were influenced by the chief of staff position in the White House, which dates back to President Harry Truman in 1946. Prime Ministers, like Presidents, have used their chiefs of staff in very different ways. Powell was granted 'unprecedented powers' to give orders to officials, was senior to the PPS within No. 10, and became a more dominant figure advising the PM than even the Cabinet Secretary. The position became established after a brief period of pandemonium under Brown: Ed Llewellyn (2010–16) focused on foreign policy under Cameron, while Nick Timothy (2016–17) and Gavin Barwell (2017–19) under May emphasized domestic/EU policy and parliamentary management respectively.

Johnson hadn't a clue what the chief of staff did, displayed no interest in finding out, and promptly appointed two. The Cummings appointment as senior adviser and chief of staff in all but name came, as we have seen, late in the day. 'I don't trust the civil service. They want to destroy me,' Johnson told a startled Lister a few days before they moved into No. 10. He believed he needed a Rottweiler to save him from officials and to get Brexit done, and that man was Cummings. But he had told Lister, 'I want you to be chief of staff,' then didn't consult him on the appointment of his new Rottweiler. 'Eddie was more than put out that Dom effectively became chief of staff, especially when he said all the critical staff were to report to Dom,' says an official. They worked out a *modus operandi* in the first six months, but after the election, it became a standoff between the two, Johnson refusing to adjudicate and rather enjoying the scuffles. There were two main mavericks in Johnson's No. 10. Both helped bring him down. Cummings was the first.

Sedwill, after much leak-informed speculation, was retained as Cabinet Secretary. 'I will remain until after the general election and Brexit is done,' Sedwill told Johnson firmly. The post had been created in 1916 by Lloyd George to head up the new Cabinet Office and oversee Cabinet government, since which the continuation of the incumbent during the transition of a Prime Minister was never in question, given that the essence of the job was to give the PM impartial advice. Successful premierships since 1916 have been built on a strong relationship with the Cabinet Secretary: Churchill with Edward Bridges, Attlee with Norman Brook and Thatcher with Robert Armstrong and Robin Butler. A Cabinet Secretary draws their strength from the unalloyed approval of the Prime Minister, and affirmation of the permanent secretaries scattered across Whitehall, but Sedwill had neither in full after May fell. Initially appointed as an interim in May 2018 to fill in for the ailing Jeremy Heywood, his appointment had been formalized in October 2018 shortly before Heywood died aged fifty-six.

Despite Sedwill being the standout successor, as a proven leader and successful permanent secretary at the Home Office, some permanent secretaries questioned the legitimacy of the process as well as his suitability, given that he had not come from the Treasury or had wide experience of policy delivery. A more valid concern was over Sedwill doing three jobs: in addition to Cabinet Secretary and head of the home civil service, he continued as national security adviser, the job he particularly liked and was equipped to do. Senior mandarins past and present advised him it was too much to continue with everything once his job was made full time, but Sedwill told Johnson he would not continue unless he remained NSA.

In the first six months, he worked well enough with the new team, though his goodwill was often tested such as when Johnson sidelined him over prorogation and damaged relations with the Palace. But he was a marked man, not least for standing up to Johnson and Cummings.

Heywood's ghost hung over the entire Johnson premiership. His absence was compounded by the death, also from cancer, of Chris Martin, aged forty-two, Cameron's PPS. 'You can't underestimate their brilliance. I've lost count of the number of times we asked ourselves in the last few years what would've happened if they had still been here. Their loss was immeasurable,' says a senior official. Johnson's most impactful early decision on the civil service was summarily to cast aside PPS Peter Hill, universally praised as tireless and impartial. His sin? Working for Theresa May, and before that for a period for Peter Mandelson when EU trade commissioner in Brussels. 'Peter Hill had had some run-ins with Boris when Foreign Secretary,' says an official. The assumption was made that he was a Remainer who would resist Brexit including no deal, rather than loyally execute what his political masters wanted. At the pre-meeting before the transition, Hill had asked Johnson's team several robust questions which made it obvious they didn't know what they were doing.

Johnson did not tell Hill himself, never keen on breaking bad news, but left him to find out inadvertently via his replacement Martin Reynolds, who let slip that he would be replacing Hill before Johnson's team had informed the PPS. Coming on the back of Johnson's refusal to support Kim Darroch during the US ambassador's leaked cables debacle, it was a further signal that here was a Prime Minister who would not stand up for an independent civil service. Hill's meeting to tell staff in the Pillared Room at No. 10 about his departure was a sombre affair: 'Some people were in tears, no one could understand it or what it foretold,' says one. 'Within three weeks, when Boris saw him in action, and realized he was impartial and clued-up, he said "I want him back." But it was too late,' says an aide. 'A terrible mistake to lose Peter. It took some time to realize quite how stupid it was. None of us knew Whitehall like him,' agrees another. Typically after exits, Johnson had seller's remorse, insisting to Alok Sharma in 2021 that Hill was 'brilliant' and must be kept as the senior official on COP26.

For a replacement Johnson brought in Martin Reynolds, his first PPS when Foreign Secretary with whom he had worked closely and who had to be promptly recalled from his post as ambassador to Libya. Only after he heard Johnson had phoned Reynolds did Sedwill remind him that there would have to be an appointment process. Reynolds is a highly intelligent, able and empathetic figure. But he wasn't the right fit for that post, as anyone who knew No. 10 would have told him, had he asked. Johnson called him 'my golden retriever', and appointed him without giving him any instructions, precisely because he wouldn't be challenging. '"He looked after me at the FCO",' a senior Cabinet minister recalls Johnson saying by way of justification. 'Keeping the civil service and fuss away from me', was the primary goal of the appointment. Keeping him away from embarrassing matters was another reason why he wanted Reynolds, who had performed the same role for him at the FCO. Indeed, 'Martin spent up to half of his time getting

Johnson out of administrative and personal scrapes,' says an aide (the proportion of time the PPS normally spends on matters of personnel and proprietary issues for the PM is about 10 per cent). On issues such as appointments and honours, where Johnson was at his worst in wanting to give gongs and posts to everyone, Reynolds had to frantically run around solving the problems his incontinence created, officials recall. Reynolds agreed that Johnson would be up against formidable opposition from Parliament and Whitehall. Like Johnson's new team, Reynolds thought the civil service was dripping with condescension towards the incoming Prime Minister, fortifying rather than challenging his prejudices and optimism. We should not blame Reynolds himself: Johnson picked him, and knew exactly what he was getting.

The job of PPS at No. 10 is to link the PM to Cabinet ministers' private offices across Whitehall, to organize their day and flow of meetings, and to oversee what happens in the building. 'You have to be a tough bastard, a bit of a control freak, to hold people fiercely to account and keep pressure on to ensure that everything is happening properly,' says a former PPS. They need deep knowledge of finance and domestic policy. With Johnson's giant personality and ego, he required a PPS who was out of the ordinary to keep him under control. No. 10 bravely sought to defend the switch: 'These kinds of job often change hands with a new Prime Minister.' They didn't in the past. Brown brought in the admirably equipped Tom Scholar from the Treasury as his PPS in June 2007, but when it didn't work out, he replaced him with Heywood. Johnson might have emulated the precedent of his biography subject, Churchill. When he returned to No. 10 in October 1951 disgruntled to find the perfectly capable David Pitblado in situ, Churchill retained him to oversee domestic policy, but brought back his much-loved wartime private secretary Jock Colville to work in tandem to oversee foreign policy.

Reynolds wasn't biddable enough for Cummings, who tried to get rid of him, but Johnson would not let him go then or later. Cummings tried late on to get rid of the deputy PPS Stuart Glassborow, who oversaw relations with the Chancellor and came from the Treasury. With Reynolds so involved minding the PM, Glassborow took over several of the wider functions of the PPS liaising across Whitehall and oversaw the Private Office response to Covid.

As director of strategy in July 2019, Johnson's first choice was Isaac Levido, one of only three people who would stand up to him (the others being Crosby and Cummings). But when Levido heard about the Cummings appointment, he agreed to run the election campaign instead. Cummings then became de facto director of strategy/chief of staff/Deputy Prime Minister. So well did Levido run the election campaign that Johnson then tried to get him into No. 10 *after* the election – he was never fussed about the technicalities of job titles and descriptions – but Levido would have none of it.

Lee Cain became director of communications. The post, initially formed in 1945 by Attlee, and under its present title and role by Blair for Alastair Campbell in 2000, oversaw every aspect of government communications within No. 10 and beyond, a formidable job. Cain's trajectory of Ormskirk Grammar School/Staffordshire University/the *Mirror* was miles away from Johnson's Eton/Oxford/*Spectator*. Where Johnson had rugby and classical references, Cain had football and the legacy of dressing up as a chicken to taunt David Cameron.[3] Instinctively drawn to prestige and heritage, it was a rare example of Johnson forming a close bond with someone from a wildly different background (Ben Gascoigne was another), his own slice of levelling up at the heart of his inner sanctum. Johnson took to Cain almost at once when they met on Vote Leave, and he brought him into the FCO as a special adviser, their relationship deepening when he stayed on with him after Johnson resigned as Foreign Secretary. Cain was a rough operator, in the mode of a Campbell (2000–03) or Andy Coulson (2010–11), rather than an easygoing and equable comms lead in the vein of Simon Lewis (2009–10). Cain ran a tight and effective ship for Johnson, stiffening his resolve when he was losing his head over Brexit and the election and broadening the Prime Minister's horizon beyond the initial headline. The key figure working alongside him was James Slack, the PM's official spokesman, a very rare senior retention from the May regime. His relationship with Vote Leave when he'd been political editor at the *Daily Mail* spared him suffering the fate of Hill.

Munira Mirza, fiercely intelligent and widely liked, was appointed head of the No. 10 Policy Unit, having worked closely with Johnson at City Hall. Created by Harold Wilson in 1974, the unit oversees the manifesto commitments, helps drive the PM's policy agenda and legislation, and works on the party conference and other major announcements. The first six months were the most successful period for the unit, working on the manifesto and preparing policy for what happened after. It presaged well for the future.

The final key position was political secretary, possibly the least understood by Johnson, building relations with the party in Parliament and country. Wilson created the post in 1964 for Marcia Williams. A party rather than a government appointment, Danny Kruger divided his time between liaising with CCHQ and managing backbenchers in Parliament. After three years of infighting under May, and with morale battered by the dire 2017 election result which made the Tories a minority, he had a tough challenge to get MPs behind whatever Brexit deal Johnson's team could procure. Kruger's acumen was sorely missed after he won the seat of Devizes at the 2019 election, being replaced as political secretary by Gascoigne, who had little knowledge of MPs.

The general election victory on 12 December 2019 should have ushered in a glorious period for Johnson and his team. It did anything but.

Primi ordines: December 2019–November 2020

The greatest triumphs of Johnson's life, the witching hour of 13 December 2019 when he knew he would win the election by a landslide, and 11 p.m. on 31 January 2020, the moment Britain left the EU, were when it all began to go wrong for him and his team.

It was like a group of bank robbers who have spent months planning the perfect heist. They pull it off brilliantly. But no sooner have they done so than they start turning on each other over whose genius has been responsible for the success, and what to do with the spoils.

The *primi ordines* remained the same after the election, but by November 2020 his top three aides had all departed and his premiership was on the slide, even if not apparent at the time. The unity of the first six months when interests were aligned was over. With general election victory won and Brexit done, what held them together? It was neither respect for Johnson himself, which was always conditional for some, nor alignment behind his vision, which remained inchoate, nor deep shared roots, shared by many PM teams, which didn't exist.

Ah, but Johnson was in no great rush. This was a time to savour, celebrate and enjoy. Why the hurry? Hadn't they achieved the impossible? His ministers were chafing but he no more understood the role of Cabinet than he did anything else. He accepted they were weak, and that the Brexit wars and exhaustion had deprived him of much of his best talent. The two ministers he rated most in this phase, Gove and Sunak, were problematic, because he trusted them less than most. He didn't want to be bothered unduly by their issues – he would have been content to have kept them in post for what he imagined would be five years of power until the next election. Someone, though, had different ideas. The *agent provocateur* was Cummings.

While content in the first six months to work with Johnson, staff in No. 10, Whitehall and Conservative MPs, Cummings' patience snapped after the general election. Like Brown under Blair, he became angry that Johnson was not honouring their prior understanding to let him run domestic policy. Frustrated by Lister whom he thought ponderous and lacking grip, he impeded him as chief of staff with the result that no one was overseeing No. 10 properly, which became a serious problem during the pandemic. His reach extended across Mirza's brief at the Policy Unit, which clouded clarity on strategic direction too.

To activist and energetic staff, Cummings was the answer to a prayer, providing decisiveness and clarity where Johnson offered custard and frivolity. Some women, not all, who felt marginalized by the dominant male culture around Johnson, rated him too. He was evidence driven, immensely industrious and got things done.

Cummings was exploding with energy to seize the opportunity to transform the British state. Brexit had showed him that extreme measures worked. No matter that his goals didn't chime with

Johnson's. To achieve his revolution in this new phase meant knocking out top officials, including king of the jungle, Sedwill. Only the twelfth holder of the Cabinet Secretary post since it was established, no predecessor in 104 years had ever been dismissed or left before the age of sixty. To sacrifice him thus was a very major statement. It was clear to Sedwill that Cummings wanted him gone. By April it was unrecoverable. Sedwill spoke to friends about whether he should stay put to see out the Cummings tsunami. He sensed that Cummings would explode eventually, but did not expect it to happen so quickly. But the attacks and leaking against him proved too much, and in May he told Johnson, who had begun to suggest it might be best if Sedwill were to move on, that he would step down once Covid (subsequent waves not envisaged) was resolved. Johnson, his judgement clouded perhaps by post-Covid recovery and not wanting to take on Cummings, made his decision, then regretted it.

Johnson could never quite work out what he thought of Sedwill, telling him at one point, 'We are in some ways equal!' 'At times they were very close, obviously the PM had the last word, but Mark could say tough things to him,' says an official. But it was never a settled relationship. At their final meeting, Johnson, ever enigmatic, presented him with framed portraits of Thomas Cromwell, Henry VIII's equivalent Cabinet Secretary, and Francis Walsingham, Elizabeth I's head of security and intelligence. The gifts were heavy with symbolism.

Never quite knowing what the Cabinet Secretary job entailed or what he wanted from it, Johnson was at sea when contemplating what he sought from his successor. 'Boris had no concept of how the centre should operate. He knew good people when he saw them, but he didn't know why they were good,' says a senior Cabinet minister.

'I want my Jeremy,' Johnson then blurted out, without a clue what Heywood did 'beyond Dave and George rating him'. Cummings, the executioner of Sedwill, didn't want to look to the past. Rather, he was thinking ahead, like his former boss Gove, who set out his manifesto for reforming the civil service at the end of June in a lecture entitled 'The Privilege of Public Service'. US President Franklin D. Roosevelt was enlisted to the cause, who had said the centre of government had to be reformed to improve delivery and policy for 'the forgotten man'.[4] 'To Dom, Mark Sedwill was a symbol of the old ways of doing things, and we needed significant change at the top of the civil service, and to him that meant changing the top civil servants. He is an idealist. He had a vision of the qualities of a permanent secretary where they were all expected to be outstanding [without really knowing what outstanding looked like],' says a senior Cabinet minister.

Cummings didn't find an outstanding Cabinet Secretary. Such a candidate probably never existed. Even if they had, Cummings would never have approved them for fear of being unseated or his hegemony undermined. The search for a successor had been much harder than Cummings or Johnson expected. What happened next is without precedent in the history of the civil service: the best didn't want the top job. The obvious choices were ruled out: Tom Scholar, permanent secretary at the Treasury, wasn't interested. Chris Wormald, the most tipped choice, was never going to be appointed because of his department's performance during the pandemic. The big beasts, including Stephen Lovegrove at Defence (who, like Wormald, was running his second department), agreed that none of them would apply given their unhappiness at events ('mad and wrong', says one). The machine was kicking back. Permanent secretaries at large were disgruntled that they were not consulted for their views on the succession. 'Top candidates didn't want to do it with Cummings pulling the strings. They knew that, if successful, they and their families would soon become targets and be briefed against,' says a permanent secretary. They looked at the defenestration of Sedwill, and several of their colleagues, and said no. 'Did Cummings and Johnson really want someone to come in and stand up for the civil service? Obviously not,' says one. Worse still, the second set of likely choices said no on the same grounds: Case had lobbied hard for DCMS Permanent Secretary Sarah Healey to apply, as had Scholar and Alex Chisolm for Deputy Cabinet Secretary Helen MacNamara. Both prospective candidates were all too aware of the impossibility of the job under Johnson, and refused to apply.

Nevertheless, Sedwill and Simon Case, in his capacity as Covid permanent secretary, worked hard to build a list of those still willing, and four candidates made the shortlist drawn up by First Civil Service Commissioner Ian Watmore: Wormald made the list, for all the doubts about him, as did Antonia Romeo (Justice), Peter Schofield (Work and Pensions) and Charles Roxburgh (second in command at the Treasury). The 'process' consisted of a thirty-minute interview with Johnson alone in his study. Several days later, they all received calls from him, Wormald being told he was too old, Romeo that she was too young for it this time. For Romeo, Symonds' opposition was later revealed,[5] but her cause was hampered by others briefing against her, believing her too publicity-happy.

For a time, Whitehall farce, without the light relief. It seemed as if no suitable candidate could be found. So No. 10 approached outsiders, including Minouche Shafik, former International Development permanent secretary before going to the Bank of England and subsequently to the London School of Economics.

Johnson pushed to see more candidates, Case being one of them. They were told to write manifestos, as had happened when Gus O'Donnell was appointed in 2005. Case believed his pitch highlighted the need to rebuild the civil service, arguing in effect 'the war on Whitehall has to stop. Your relationship with it has truly broken down because of the "hard rain" attitude.' 'You are right. I have let them go too far. Alienating people has not been good. I need the machine on my side,' Johnson allegedly responded. Johnson had reservations, but thought that Case was the best of the pick.

Cummings was only interested in Case, though others in the civil service and outside also suggested him. 'I recommended him to Dom,' says Oliver Lewis, who had been very impressed when working with him on Covid shielding and volunteering.[6] Aged forty-one, Case had never been a permanent secretary or run a department or even held a director general posting. But he had been PPS at No. 10 between Martin and Hill, his intelligence and diplomacy highly regarded. He was a fresh skin too, having been out of the May melee after 2017 as private secretary to the Duke of Cambridge before his return to No. 10 on Covid in May 2020. Cummings may not have been wholly responsible for his appointment as the most important official in the country but Case was widely seen as his man. 'Simon was very clearly not the choice of Boris. Dom decided that we needed someone he could work with to bring about changes to the civil service. Simon indicated he was happy to sign up to it. He ticked a lot of boxes for Dom,' says an aide. Johnson was happy enough: he spoke to Cameron about the time Case had worked as his acting PPS and who thought highly of him. That was good enough for Johnson: 'He was really thinking only of a permanent secretary at No. 10 job,' says an official.

The question of whether Case should combine Cabinet Secretary with head of the civil service was raised. He was reasonably well qualified for the former, but not even remotely for the latter. Case took soundings and concluded he wouldn't have sufficient authority in the former unless he was also the latter. Being head of the civil service meant a leapfrog in seniority and having to chair meetings with experienced figures several years his senior. The appointment went down badly in Whitehall: 'A clear and extraordinary statement that the PM thought it more important to have a courtier by his side than someone to look after and lead 450,000 civil servants,' says an official, a view widely echoed.

Dougie Smith, the second maverick after Cummings, was becoming increasingly forceful throughout this first phase. His colourful life running sex parties was not a conventional stepping stone to No. 10,[7] though working his way up the Conservative ladder with a series of posts was. With libertarian beliefs, he attached himself to figures such as James Goldsmith, founder of the anti-EU Referendum Party. Brought into CCHQ by Party Chair Ben Elliot, his work included vetting candidates, finding out about their private lives. 'Dougie operated in the shadows. None of us and No. 10 knew what he actually did. But he gave the impression that he had something on everyone,' says an official. Dark secrets about people with influence in government, including presence at exotic events, was said to be one of the secrets to his influence with the powerful. 'He was just very frightening, very bad tempered, a ruthless leaker to the press, very motivated by staying in power and keeping in with whoever has power,' says an aide. Influential in his initial ministerial appointments, he rose in Johnson's trust as a fierce protector of Carrie Symonds in the first months in power. Johnson chose to listen to his advice to keep Cummings after the Barnard

Castle debacle rather than Crosby's: 'Simple. He was more afraid of Dougie than Lynton,' says an aide. His main policy impact in No. 10 was as 'the king of the culture wars', pushing for anti-'woke' Robbie Gibb to join the BBC board one of his scores. Inch by inch, though, as the political tide turned, he edged towards Sunak.

This first period came to a crashing end at the close of 2020. Smith was incandescent with Johnson for letting it happen. Long before then, it had become evident that the system Johnson had been running since the election was utterly shambolic. Covid was the most obvious example of the dysfunctionality. More generally, it could be seen in spluttering policy initiatives, weak responses to external events and a failure to secure an optimal deal to make sense of Brexit.

Johnson's other big beasts in No. 10 were all caught in the crosshairs. Mirza was having a torrid time, with Johnson first talking about moving her on in the middle of the year: the plan was to make her a minister, 'to play to her strengths'. Her Policy Unit had lost its mojo. Reynolds continued in post, with Glassborow doing much of the heavy lifting, and the system worked, but not as it needed to. Gascoigne replaced Kruger as political secretary, and could have been a key figure for building bridges with the party, had Johnson's retention of Cummings not poisoned the well, a more assertive Chief Whip than Spencer been in situ and Johnson not been so apathetic about putting in the work to drag MPs with him. Lockdown didn't help, of course, but the idea that Johnson had to woo and charm his MPs to win them over never seemed to have occurred to him.

Johnson was bored by Cabinet, as was Cummings. While Johnson saw Cabinet meetings as a chore to be raced through, Cummings treated them as an inconvenience to be managed and ridden over. As a body, Cabinet had been docile from the start, becoming even more subdued after the general election victory, when Johnson's control over them became absolute. 'A weak and compliant Cabinet suited Johnson,' says an official. Sunak had begun testing the water during this period, and Raab, whom he had been forced to trust during his Covid bout, had his powers rapidly clipped back on Johnson's return. Even when Raab officially became Deputy Prime Minister later on, it was in name alone.

The *primi ordines* was running into the sand. Cummings and Cain were on their way out from the late summer after a tortured series of manoeuvres. The second wave of Covid was surging from September, sucking vitality out of the centre. Bedlam reigned in No. 10.

Secundi ordines: December 2020–January 2022

Johnson had squandered his moment of peak opportunity and power after the general election. He had lost an entire year since, lost his team and lost any sense of what he was PM to do (in as far as he was ever clear). His thoughts turned in the autumn to a new team. He was not ready yet to drop Mirza as policy chief, wouldn't ever move Reynolds and realized he was stuck with Case. He knew he couldn't be moved soon without grave damage, and as Cummings' person and prone to leak, he needed careful managing. But Case had his uses, even if he fell short of the dynamic make-things-happen person Johnson thought Jeremy Heywood must have been.

But Johnson did have a chief of staff slot to fill, someone he hoped would make all his worries go away. He had never spoken to or studied Jonathan Powell. But the idea took root that he needed 'his Jonathan', just as earlier he had said he needed 'his Jeremy', omnicompetent and loyal, to organize his life and premiership. Just as later he started saying 'I need an Anji', a reference to Anji Hunter, long-term gatekeeper to Blair. The harsh truth is that the time for him to have had his Jeremys, Jonathans and Anjis is when he set out on his voyage. His latter-day, if incomplete, understanding of how Prime Ministers need grown-ups came too late, far too late, to save his premiership.

Finding his Jonathan wasn't easy. If top people were reluctant to board Johnson's ship when he first set sail because they worried it might soon sink, they were now reluctant to join a vessel so haplessly captained. Indeed, those who didn't want to join him in July 2019, knowing what a nightmare he could be to work for, now had screeds of evidence that the *ephialtes* was no different in Downing Street. His best hope was finding careerists who thought their CV would be embellished by working a spell at No. 10, a 'yes-man or -woman', or those who were blissfully unaware what he was like.

All was not lost, he confided in friends, boosting his own confidence as he talked up the prospect of future glory. The right officers on the bridge would help steer his premiership to great things, Global Britain and a regenerated country and government after Brexit.

So finding a new chief of staff to replace Cummings was his top priority. But the farcical efforts to do so foreshadowed future divisions. Lister said he wasn't interested in a full-time post. In October, Mirza and Smith, anxious to find a figure who could bind Johnson's fractious team together, alighted on Nikki da Costa, the director of Legislative Affairs who was back in No. 10 after maternity leave. 'Boris never finds his own people, but relies on others to do so,' they told her. 'Would you be interested in becoming chief of staff?' Indeed she was. Cummings was an obstacle, torn over whether he was coming or going, so they arranged an inconclusive meeting in the Terracotta Room upstairs in No. 10 to try to win him round. The weeks dragged on with no resolution. Michael Gove suggested Rupert Harrison, who had been chief of staff to Osborne. Endless other names were dangled in front of Johnson including Ben Elliot, who was not interested. Johnson had a conversation with Andrew Feldman, Cameron's party chair, who said thank you but no thanks. It threatened to be a repeat of the appointment of Case, with no one wanting to do it. A fly was cast over Javid, who said emphatically, 'This is not a job for an MP.' Which was precisely what Johnson did a year later.

By early November, with Johnson becoming desperate, a new name emerged: Lee Cain, who had stepped up to the job to general acclaim when everyone had been ill with Covid in April. Johnson had been surreptitiously speaking to him about it since the summer. When early on he raised the possibility with Sedwill and MacNamara, they thought it could work: 'Officials had a high opinion of Lee,' one says. The main question in Johnson's mind was 'Will Lee be able to transfer his loyalty from Dom to me?'

Cain, no sycophant, produced instead of a letter of application, a devastating analysis for Johnson on how he had made a mess of his premiership to date, and how the centre should work in the future. His critique cut to the heart of the Johnson problem: no agreed and firmly communicated PM agenda, leading to duplication, confusion and poor policy development across Whitehall, compounded by a lack of internal discipline at No. 10 with no one believing any decision by the PM would stick, and too many with access to him driving their own agendas. On 9 November, Case sidled up to Cain in No. 10. 'The Prime Minister wants you to be chief of staff,' he whispered. The next day, Cain saw Johnson in his office. 'You are my guide. I agree with all you wrote in your note, you are my person, we have been together through thick and thin,' the PM told him. Cain asked for time to think it through, not certain whether to believe Johnson. But that evening, before he committed himself, news of the appointment was leaked to *The Times*. He concluded that Symonds was behind it in an attempt to torpedo the whole plan. She had seen Cummings and Cain all but destroy her partner in the previous months: she had her own ideas about the staff needed to make sense of his premiership.

What followed on 11 November gives a mesmerizing portrait of how deranged Johnson's life as PM could be. When early in the day Cain confronted him about the leak he became very bothered. 'Hose it down, hose it down – this is a disaster,' Johnson said, telling him, 'Say it's not true about the appointment.' 'But it *is* true, you offered me the job, and we can't escape it,' Cain replied. When Alex Wickham at Politico, Carrie's friend and godfather to baby Wilfred,[8] put out that the offer was a fabrication,[9] Cain saw red, now certain beyond any doubt it could only have been briefed by Johnson himself or Carrie. He stormed in to see him and vented his anger. 'I've worked with you for four years, I am not f**king happy and I am going to quit.'

'Please stay with me, you can have it. I'll offer you any job.'

'You have actively briefed against me, and I have no intention of taking the job.'

With them still at standoff, Johnson had to rush out for a visit so they agreed to reconvene later that afternoon. Johnson returned via a Covid meeting at 5 p.m. and they sat down again. 'I'm really sorry, Lee. You have to do the job. It wouldn't work any other way,' Johnson told him. Cain was persistent that he couldn't work with him any more. 'Look, I'm really sorry,' he replied. 'I've had Carrie all over me. I'm very sorry. I can only trust you.'

'I don't believe you.'

'This whole thing is driving me crazy. You have to do the job. It wouldn't work any other way. I don't care about what Carrie thinks, you are the only person who protects me.'

At that point, Reynolds interrupted them to say the weekly call with the Queen was imminent. They agreed to meet again as soon as it was over. Cain waited and waited, the Palace call long over, but saw no sign of him. He was about to give up when the PM suddenly reappeared dishevelled and distraught. 'I'm so sorry, Commissar. Carrie has been onto me. She says that you and Dom are totally against me. Oh my God, Lee, it's a disaster. What am I going to do?'

'Hang on, an hour ago you told me that she would no longer have any influence. Now you're telling me that you have to do what she says. I'm going to resign tonight. I've had enough. This whole building is so toxic, I'll resign.'

'Please don't.'

'I'll talk to James Slack, and you can appoint him director of communications in my place.'

Cain stormed out leaving Johnson alone; he sought out Cummings and told him about the bizarre day. 'If you're off, it's a total madhouse and I will quit as well,' Cummings said. For Cummings, the parting of the ways was much more cerebral – he had long ago lost any respect for Johnson and been toying with quitting for many weeks; for Cain, the bond was personal and emotional, and the parting far more painful.

After the initially cordial departure that day, it looked as if relations had calmed. Any hope of a rapprochement was soon dashed as the opening salvo of briefings began on 13 November. Cain and Cummings both squarely blamed Symonds for poisoning Johnson against them, and believed she had vindictively leaked after their departure – 'Not content with killing us off, she wanted a public burning of our bodies,' one was heard to say. It prompted a fresh escalation of counter-briefings by the two men. The headlines that weekend were lurid. 'It's time to clean up toxic boys' club, Boris,' splashed the *Evening Standard*. 'Downing St slams "vicious and cowardly" attacks on Symonds,' read the *Sunday Telegraph*. And most mordant of them all, Tim Shipman's *Sunday Times* exposé was topped with a tag invoking Princess Diana: 'There were three in this marriage: Boris, Carrie and Dominic Cummings'. Johnson was at first hurt, then puzzled, then became intensely angry as the briefings went on and on.

The reign of *primi ordines* was well and truly over.

Johnson was beside himself. He had lost Cain, and he knew what ammunition he and Cummings both had against him. He had no chief of staff, and his efforts since the summer to find one had become a humiliation. He was panicking about finding anyone, when out of the blue Comrade Coleman from City Hall days texted him. He produced a name of someone first suggested when Johnson was standing for the leadership.[10] Dan Rosenfield had been a long-serving and feisty PPS to Alistair Darling and Osborne as Chancellors before becoming an MD at the Bank of America. He had had an exploratory conversation about joining with Lister in the summer of 2019, but nothing had come of it.

Rosenfield was out shopping in North London on Saturday 14 November when his phone rang: 'Can you come in and talk to me?' a voice said. Rosenfield murmured he would indeed. The next morning, he spent two hours in No. 10 talking to Johnson. It appeared to be a meeting of minds. Rosenfield told him he admired his authenticity and leadership, which he thought outstanding in his generation. Johnson was impressed and asked him to run the machine. In a text exchange that evening, Johnson asked if he could take up a reference from Paul Deighton, Rosenfield's chair at Hakluyt, the strategic advisory firm where he now worked. Deighton responded very positively. To Johnson, it was the answer to a prayer. Here was somebody who was neither a Cummings/Cain person nor in the Carrie camp, and someone who might at last become *his* person. For the next two weeks, they spoke every evening about plans and he talked over plans with Johnson's two most trusted advisers, Lister and Mirza.

Indicatively, though, Johnson never specified the task of chief of staff he wanted him to do. In the absence of a job description, clarity at the start matters. The impression Rosenfield was left with was that he was working to Johnson alone, would be totally his person and that the PM would back him all the way. But here we hit a problem that went to the heart of why the *secundi ordines* broke down. The bitter experience of Cummings meant that, deep down, Johnson would never trust any one person again, as he had done at City Hall. His close friends attest that he chose Rosenfield in part because he thought he'd be pliable. 'He thought that Dan wouldn't question him: the appointment was an illusion. The truth was that Boris wanted to be his own chief of staff,' says a senior party official. As ever with Johnson, there were multiple layers.

Rosenfield started work on 7 December, spending three weeks shadowing the PM and meeting every Cabinet minister, senior party officers and No. 10 staff, against a background of frantic pressure to finalize a Brexit deal by 24 December and responding to the Kent variant of Covid.

It began promisingly. At last, Johnson had a chief of staff who knew the Treasury and Whitehall: 'I'm more excited than I've ever been as Prime Minister,' he told an aide after two months. James

Slack stepped up effortlessly to director of communications with his steady hand. Case promised the machine would work for the Prime Minister as never before. A significant strategy day was set up by Glassborow in No. 10's Pillared Room, akin to the Chequers summit in January 2020, to focus on Johnson's priorities post-Covid. The conclusion? No. 10 needed to narrow the grand ambitions down considerably to focus on backlogs in the NHS and education, with a fresh focus on skills and the criminal justice system. Not *grands projets* whizzy infrastructure or levelling-up transformations maybe, but sound stuff nevertheless: it seemed as if the launch of the *secundi ordines* was going really rather well.

But the more Rosenfield probed, the more disturbed he became at quite how amateur No. 10 was. The lack of proper paper trails was one big surprise, which came to light over the Wallpapergate renovations saga in the Downing Street flat. On 23 April, Cummings had published a statement on his blog alleging that the plans for donors to pay for the work were 'unethical, foolish, possibly illegal' and 'almost certainly broke the rules on proper disclosure of political donations if conducted in the way he intended'. Rosenfield suddenly found himself having to clear up the mess.

Johnson should have picked up that Cummings' whole critique of his style of governing was devastatingly similar to Cain's analysis two months before: no clarity over structure or processes nor over jobs and roles, inadequate data, an underpowered Private Office with insufficient grip of No. 10 and connections across Whitehall. He compared the bloated-yet-underpowered Cabinet Office and leadership of the civil service unfavourably to the outfit he had left nearly a decade before. He worried No. 10 was not doing the basic job it was there to do, to serve the interests of the Prime Minister and deliver his agenda. Too many discordant voices, too little process, and a Prime Minister insufficiently sure of his agenda. Johnson now had two separate reports about how he should be improving No. 10. He cannot claim he didn't know.

'Things have to change, and quickly,' Rosenfield bluntly announced to Johnson and the senior team. The status quo and team leaders, he said, were not good enough to deliver his political strategy over the coming four years leading up to the next general election. 'Heavy lifting needs to take place now.' Some moves were relatively straightforward, such as insisting that Lister must go as Rosenfield didn't want him in the way, least of all still carrying the residual title 'chief of staff'. Lister was on his way out regardless, having promised his wife he would take a backseat, and had only agreed to stay on for the transition under sufferance. He departed amicably at the start of 2021, the gentleman that he is. While initially Rosenfield thought he could work out a *modus operandi* with Reynolds, who retained Johnson's unswerving support, he ran headlong into problems with Mirza, who didn't. He didn't like the way she talked about 'her priorities' rather than the Prime Minister's, and she didn't like him telling her so. Nor did she welcome his plans for a smaller Policy Unit better aligned as he saw it to the priorities of the PM. He wanted the unit out of day-to-day churn and instead focused on the medium to long term – especially considering they were only two years out from starting work on the manifesto for 2024. Nor did she appreciate being told her Policy Unit was interfering in areas outside its remit. From the spring, there was a tense standoff between them.

The arrival of Rosenfield after many months of chaos in No. 10 was bound to run headlong into a sense of entitlement, creating resentment and resistance. He certainly needed to crack the whip when he joined, but the way he did it left many feeling excluded and bruised, especially women (Mirza included). He told an early meeting for senior officials and advisers that they would have to get used to it – slim down, be efficient and stop 'running towards the boar' (i.e. the PM). When staff expressed concern at being left off meeting lists (smaller, more focused sessions with the PM were one of his aims) or receiving no response to their messages to him, he shrugged his shoulders.

'No chief of staff, however brilliant, will have any traction if the centre knows that they don't enjoy the total backing of the Prime Minister,' says an official. Every chief of staff since Powell had enjoyed it. But early on, staff started noticing that, in meetings, the body language between Johnson and Rosenfield was not good: 'He would rarely look at him,' says an aide. Those who disliked what Rosenfield was doing began to believe they were safe.

After his first weeks, Rosenfield told Johnson, 'I need a deputy, a very good organizer,' producing a list of names including Sam Cohen, a protégé of Lynton Crosby. She had worked at Buckingham Palace for eighteen years, and most recently for Meghan Markle, and came highly recommended. But Johnson said he wanted Simone Finn, a former special adviser, former partner of Gove after university and close friend of Symonds: 'She knows the Conservative Party very well,' he said. Johnson prevailed and she joined on 1 March, at the head of 'the three musketeers', as Johnson called them: Meg Powell-Chandler to oversee messaging and strategy, Henry Newman the Home Office, and Henry Cook on Covid. All friends of Symonds and Gove. All very capable people, but it was a total disaster for Johnson to put a competing team into No. 10 with allegiance to his partner. 'The adults in the room' they were immediately dubbed in friendly briefings.[11]

Johnson was right that Rosenfield needed a colleague with deep roots into the party to compensate for his own lack, as Jonathan

Powell had in Sally Morgan, or Cameron's Ed Llewellyn (to whom Rosenfield spoke) had with Deputy Chief of Staff Kate Fall. It needed the chief and the party specialist to work in close concert and total trust, as happened in these earlier models. But Rosenfield's relationship with Finn went wrong almost from the outset. They sat opposite each other in the office just outside Johnson's door, but proximity didn't produce harmony. He found her factional, disloyal and insufficiently knowledgeable of the party. She found him secretive and evasive, and questioned his judgements. Finn's new team found him sexist and cliquey too, taking decisions with Simon Case and Jack Doyle, Slack's successor as director of communications from March. Slack's judgement and experience, extending deep back into the May premiership, was a far bigger loss than was realized at the time. He quit for personal reasons, but was savvy enough to read the runes.

Finn soon felt Rosenfield was deliberately excluding her and Henry Newman, making a nonsense of his claims to be making No. 10 a more unified working community. 'I regularly had conversations with her only to find that Dan hadn't kept them in the loop,' says one adviser. Cummings' daily 'pre-meeting' to keep Johnson on track ahead of his own morning meeting was replaced by Rosenfield's brief 'stand-up' session which some felt no longer identified the urgent issues. Rosenfield worked well with Henry Cook, not least on the Covid roadmap and in keeping Johnson on message. But noise rather than harmony was the leitmotif of the regime, and by May 2021, just six months after they quit, No. 10 was back in a civil war every bit as damaging as when Cummings and Cain had been in office.

One fruit of Rosenfield's relationship with Case was their bringing in Michael Barber, creator of the Delivery Unit under Blair, to imagine a similar structure for Johnson. The idea originated with Cummings and Tom Shinner, who wrote a paper in mid-2020, with the aim to drive policy and enhance Cabinet minister accountability to No. 10. When Barber wrote to Case to congratulate him on his appointment, he texted back, 'It would be great if you talked to the PM about delivery.' Barber was chuffed to be told that Johnson had read his book *How to Run a Government*. (Johnson was a voracious reader, but this title sounds incongruous: a more implausible title for him to read would be hard to conceive.) Barber had come to a meeting in Johnson's office with the PM and Cummings on 24 September 2020. 'Would you be willing to set up for me what you did for Tony?' Johnson asked. The appointment revealed Johnson at his best: non-tribal in welcoming Barber despite his association with Labour, and willingness to innovate. Barber helped establish the new unit's credibility by getting ministers and their permanent secretaries on board. 'I'd brief Johnson in his office before the "stocktakes" with ministers so he knew what was coming up: he was good at it,' says Barber.[12]

The Delivery Unit's impact was significantly boosted by Emily Lawson arriving in July 2021 as full-time head. She focused work on five missions agreed with Johnson: energy, education/jobs/skills, criminal justice, health and levelling up. To keep him fully in the loop, which she quickly realized was an uphill task, she wrote a monthly note to him and Mirza called the 'Top 35 Report' with updates on the key thirty-five areas of his interest that they had identified. In August, she produced a report on delivery of the PM's core objectives, with dashboards on each for him and others to follow. Like Barber, she found Johnson could tune in before the ministerial stocktakes, read the papers and ask searching questions, albeit reluctant to confront people or to hold them personally to account. Johnson expressed pleasure at the innovation: 'You're like Dom. You are going to be my Queen of Data. You're doing what Dom did, but you are nicer to people,' he told her. The unit became the principal innovation in domestic machinery of government under Johnson, with some solid progress on skills, health and energy to its credit. But like so much in Johnson's premiership, promising initiatives floundered because of his variable attention, and the distraction of events often of his own making.

Over the months, it became evident that Rosenfield's strengths were as a bureaucrat, and those of the PPS, juggling several balls at the same time. Policy and process were his metiers, not politics, people or presentation. He had little interest in the pastoral role of the chief of staff, looking after and encouraging staff in No. 10. Conservative MPs and special advisers he found no more congenial than Cummings, preferring to spend time with people he understood best, senior officials, and to look for solutions directly with them. He found the incessant negative briefing and hostility from staff difficult: 'I'm a professional guy, I spent ten years working in the corporate sector, I'm neither a dick nor a bully,' he confided in a colleague. His critics countered that he had worked in investment banking, which is far sharper-elbowed, and he was out of tune with the civil service ten years on. Could he have been subtler in the way he went about his mission? Almost certainly. But he was on a hiding to nothing from the start, doing a job no one wanted, working for an impossible man and up against a team seeking to destroy him. Finn took over the weekly meetings with special advisers, moved from Cummings' punishing evening slot on Friday to the morning. But her attempts to instil order with weekly diary sessions were shunned by Rosenfield, and by the summer, as the crises were piled on top of each other – Wallpapergate, ethics investigations and the withdrawal from Afghanistan – the relationships fractured still further. Briefing wars reached new levels with details of confidential conversations within the building appearing in the papers, and stories about Rosenfield watching sport rather than dealing with the Afghanistan evacuation crisis.[13]

No. 10 cannot operate, nor serve the Prime Minister, if it is at war with itself. Nor can the headquarters of any organization operate effectively if there's no trust between the key players. Yet after six months of the new regime, the atmosphere was as toxic as in the worst days of Gordon Brown. Thatcher, Blair and Cameron would never have tolerated such infighting; in contrast Johnson seemed to relish the chaos. 'A regime with different sources of power was what the PM was looking for. I used to think Dom was messy, but it had nothing on what was going on between Dan and people like Finn and Newman,' says a No. 10 official.

The full force of Johnson's mistake in appointing a courtier rather than an experienced leader as Cabinet Secretary came home to roost. Case liked to sit at a desk outside the Prime Minister's office, as he had done when he had been PPS to Cameron. Like Rosenfield, he was reverting to type. It meant in effect that Johnson had three PPSs, Reynolds, Rosenfield and Case – but no one sufficiently looking after Whitehall. Disillusion spread across the civil service at not having a champion to defend them against attacks and leaks from ministers. No one was ensuring that the system was working properly, with clear lines of responsibility at the centre. It was an accident waiting to happen.

In early July 2021, with the summer recess looming, feelings exploded into the open at a strategic meeting that Rosenfield called for the political team. Nikki da Costa had complained to Johnson about Rosenfield's excluding staff, especially women, from meetings.

'Why does Dan do this?' he asked her. 'Does he have a problem with women?'[14] To Rosenfield, she was yet another member of staff who was straying outside her remit, in her case legislation in Parliament, rather than sticking to her lane. If he was to bring order to No. 10, it had to end, however much the individuals concerned might not like it. But she took a very different view, relaying to Rosenfield at the strategy meeting the resentment within the building that staff felt at being shut out, not listened to or valued, and that he was underplaying politics in the way he did his job. Da Costa decided to quit. But after she left, the divisions further magnified.

No. 10, where proximity and access to a single individual in the Prime Minister determine influence and the effectiveness of your work, is trickier to run than most organizations. Revoking and limiting exposure to the boss is a surefire way to make enemies, and it needed someone to bang heads together or the *secundi ordines* would founder. The three figures who could have done it, Johnson, Case and Reynolds, didn't. Rosenfield had not given up hope in Case, but he told Johnson that Reynolds would have to go if the operation was to work properly.

The loss of the by-election at Chesham and Amersham with a 25 per cent swing to the Lib Dems in June, opinion polls going south and Conservative MPs increasingly rebellious were all causing alarm by the summer recess. In a crucial House of Commons vote on social care in the autumn, the government's majority was slashed from seventy-nine to twenty-six: 'the first major turbulence we've experienced', said an ally.[15]

Johnson realized he was isolated and alone. So he reached out to someone who always made him feel safe, his bag-carrier *par excellence*. 'I need you back, Gazza,' he said to Ben Gascoigne who had quit as political secretary that May, and who came back as a deputy chief of staff alongside Finn in November. Widely liked, Gascoigne personified a decency that people found attractive, but he was too amiable to be a big-hitter or trouble-shooter. The political world he found himself in was very different to the one he left. Team Vote Leave might have departed, but he was nowhere near being able to bring order to a No. 10 so riven by tribes. Team Gove/Carrie, headed by Finn and the three musketeers, were joined by Declan Lyons, Gascoigne's successor as political secretary. Team Rosenfield had Doyle and Case in support. Then Team City Hall with Mirza, Smith and Gascoigne. The first two factions were 'understandably jealous' that Johnson had asked Gascoigne to come back to be his enforcer across Whitehall, with a mission, wildly improbable, of 'bang[ing] on department doors and telling Cabinet ministers what the PM wants to be done'.[16]

The party conference in early October with the Tories twelve points ahead in the polls and successful vaccine rollout were the bright spots in the autumn. Mirza, though, was struggling and increasingly disillusioned. She was one of the very few people in the building who would tell Johnson the truth. But her deep bond with Johnson was long over, initially fractured by Covid, when she barely figured. He had pulled back from moving her not only because of his fondness for her: he was afraid of her husband. His rift with Mirza was not just personal; she was too ideological and obsessive about culture wars, he thought, she hadn't gathered the best people around her and she didn't know how to drive policy across Whitehall. 'What do you stand for?' was a question Johnson hated being asked by his MPs, as he was with increasing regularity; unfairly, he blamed her for not making his policy agenda more evident. On her side, she felt he made her job impossible because he had no sense of policy priority, kept changing his mind and hadn't built a team to help her structure policy. Her relations with Rosenfield never recovered after he told her 'to keep in her lane', and that it was 'his job alone to be across every single aspect of No. 10', as aides recall. They hit rock bottom when Rosenfield told Smith he wanted to sack her, apparently not realizing Mirza was married to him. All hell broke loose. An unhealthy standoff ensued, with Smith proving a tricky adversary for Rosenfield, and Mirza's unhappiness widely known in the building. Tension between both men reached sky high, with flaming rows, and Smith squaring up to Rosenfield at the end of one disagreement. Rosenfield had had enough and wanted to oust Smith, but Johnson didn't back him in the fight, and never would ('Boris would never sack Dougie because he was afraid of him,' confirms an aide). Rosenfield had made sworn enemies of Mirza, the most loved person in the building, and Smith, the most lethal.

As winter 2021 approached, it became clear that the Panglossian dream Johnson had fondly outlined at the start of the year was never going to materialize. Mirza was edging closer to the departure lounge as briefing against her intensified. Smith was furious with Johnson for excluding him, and for not listening to his advocacy of an ultra-strong line on small boats crossing the Channel. Reynolds and Doyle were caught up in the Partygate scandal, and Rosenfield in the botched response. All were considering their futures. With the Owen Paterson scandal bleeding into the Partygate scandal (both discussed in the next chapter), the mood in the building became very dark. 'The skates were under the operation from December 2021. We were drifting, with morale very bad,' says an official.

Johnson worked down the contact list on his phone of trusted allies over the Christmas holiday, including Elliot and Crosby. 'Why is No. 10 not working? How could I restructure it?' he asked them. Then news dropped that the Metropolitan Police would be investigating twelve gatherings at No. 10 and Whitehall, suspected of being in breach of Covid regulations. A still deeper gloom, if that was possible, descended across the building. Johnson knew that Rosenfield and Doyle would soon be going, and perhaps Reynolds. But he had no idea that Mirza was at the end of her tether. The final straw was the comments made by Johnson on 31 January 2022 to Keir Starmer in a debate on Partygate, accusing him when Director of Public Prosecutions of not prosecuting serial sex offender Jimmy Savile. He subsequently refused to apologize. 'But frankly, it could've been anything else. She was just waiting for something. She felt she was just no longer in the room. She was in a very unhappy frame of mind,' says an aide. On the morning of 3 February, believing Johnson had given her assurances that he would apologize, she quit. Her resignation letter spoke of 'an inappropriate and partisan reference to a horrendous case of child sex abuse'.[17]

Johnson called Crosby in a state of high agitation, as an ally recounts, telling him he was suspicious because it sounded 'as if she was reading from a script'. Something didn't feel right because she hadn't expressed concerns earlier, he said. 'Absolute crap about this Savile excuse: I don't believe a word of it,' said Johnson. Then he had a call from Smith. 'We will back you if you stand down now, and if you do so, there is a chance that you will come back,' Smith said, Johnson making a careful note of the pronoun 'we'. 'But if you don't go now, we will destroy you. It will be death by a thousand cuts.' Mirza's departure is 'an unmistakeable signal the bunker is collapsing and this PM is finished', Cummings gleefully said.[18] Simon Clarke, Sunak's Chief Secretary to the Treasury, did not try to hide the dire situation on the evening newsround, admitting to Channel 4, 'I think the last days of Rome were more fun.'[19]

Johnson was in a state of shock. He had lost his closest woman on his staff, and he now believed she had turned on him with her husband and was threatening to destroy him. Crosby wasted no time in reminding Johnson that Smith would be allying with Cummings, who had been out to destroy him from the day he left. 'Smith and Cummings were now on Team Sunak,' says an insider. As if to confirm his worst suspicions, 'I wouldn't have said it,' Sunak pointedly and brazenly said of his Savile remark.[20]

Mirza's departure caused widespread upset and tears across No. 10. 'Everyone admired Munira – civil servants, special advisers and women in particular,' says an aide. Dismay was compounded when Rosenfield then spoke to staff about her departure: 'I know this is very hard for you, a great loss and great friend of yours, and a friend of mine.' 'Everyone knew that was not true. It was incredibly gauche,' says an aide.

Johnson was in a cold sweat. He knew he needed to plug the gap at once. His options were limited. Andrew Griffith, in whose Westminster house Johnson's leadership team had planned the transition into No. 10 in the halcyon days of July 2019, was in his car when his phone vibrated. 'I need you, I need you back. I want you to head my policy team,' Johnson jabbered wildly down the phone.

'You want me to do what?'

'To be my policy chief.'

'What about Munira?'

'No no no, Munira has gone.'

'What! Can we get her back?'

'There's no way to get her back.' Johnson was very animated, Griffith says. 'Come across now,' he instructed him. 'Jack [Doyle] will put it out in the next hour.'[21]

For all his frustrations with Mirza, he mourned being abandoned by his moral compass. Far more, he realized how it would look. 'Her departure was what really shook him up, he was totally thrown by that,' says Dowden, who Johnson suspected was in cahoots with her, Sunak and Smith (Dowden is adamant that he was unaware Mirza would resign). Johnson, rather than reflect on the morality of what he had done, doubled down on his position. 'He called me up and said, "Just to be totally clear with you. They will have to bring in a Panzer division to get me out of this building."'[22]

Mirza's departure put huge pressure on Johnson's team. Tory MPs were demanding a clearout of senior staff at No. 10 as a condition of not ousting Johnson in a confidence vote. As part of his apology for Partygate, he promised to reshape an office who were independently falling on their swords. Doyle was very cut up about Mirza: it was the last straw. He had been named in the Partygate scandal for handing out awards at a 2020 Christmas event in No. 10, and left, saying the scandal had taken 'a terrible toll' on his family life.

Reynolds reasoned that it was either him or Case who would have to go. He wanted to defend the man he had served at No. 10 faithfully to a fault for the last two and a half years. 'Martin left to protect the Prime Minister and the Cabinet Secretary,' says an official. Deep inside, he knew too that the moment in January when his infamous email telling staff to 'bring your own booze' was leaked, his continuation was untenable.

The departure of Rosenfield was an even bigger moment for the premiership. While Mirza's departure was significant for what it portended, she had long since ceased to drive the premiership. But Rosenfield was Johnson's top man, his personal pick whose arrival he had widely serenaded after a long time looking.

Rosenfield's handling of staff aside, he had been doing the right job by bringing an order and direction to the premiership it had lacked since the general election. But by the summer of 2021, it was clear to everybody in the building that Johnson was not sticking by his man, and neither Rosenfield nor Case were capable of showing him how to improve. Johnson's loss of confidence in Rosenfield was shared by many staff in No. 10, by Sunak's team in the Treasury, and by Conservative backbenchers who blamed him for the poor handling of Paterson and Partygate. Once Johnson returned after Christmas, Rosenfield realized when he was getting no traction with him and that the game was up: 'I can't do the job if people just come to you and complain about what I'm doing,' he told Johnson.

Was Johnson learning from his errors? Apparently not.

He was about to repeat the three mistakes he had made in the *primi* and *secundi ordines*: personal not institutional appointments with recognized job descriptions; failing to stick by his decisions and support those he appointed; and his total addiction to court politics. The last led to his failing to impose his will on warring parties, preferring that they spend their time vying for his attention rather than enabling him to govern. Johnson's own credibility was bound up in the fate of Rosenfield. The Prime Minister had chosen his man then publicly failed to back him. How could he convince any successor they would not suffer the same fate?

Tertii ordines: February–July 2022

'Be my chief of staff,' a frantic Johnson bellowed down the line to Lynton Crosby in Australia at four o'clock in the morning. Johnson felt the ground falling away beneath his feet. His old team – Reynolds, Mirza, Smith – had all gone. He worried he might be stabbed in the back anytime. He had nowhere to turn but to Crosby. 'He realized that things were very wrong. Cummings and Sunak were on manoeuvres and he had problems in the office and upstairs,' an aide says.

When Johnson was in a deep hole, he turned to Crosby, the man he credits with bringing him to national prominence by masterminding his mayoral victories in 2008 and 2012. Here was a man who could get the premiership back on track, Johnson believed, who he could bring in 'to calm the 1922 Committee and throw them some red meat', as one party source puts it. The others whose opinion he respected were lost to him: Lister was there as always for him, but 'he hardly ever spoke to me after I left', he says.[23] Marina Wheeler had left him forever as a result of his infidelity. Mirza abandoned him. Cummings and Smith had become his mortal enemies. Levido, who had masterminded the 2019 victory, was tacking towards Sunak. He had no soulmates in Cabinet. There was no one else but Crosby.

Bar one. Carrie. Here was the ultimate source of torture for Johnson. To whom should he listen? His wife, whom he loved, but whose views especially on people he often found uncongenial. Or his stalwart Crosby, whom he loved, but whose views he often found unpalatable. He feared Crosby's disapproval. But he feared Carrie's wrath.

'Why can't the two just get on together?' he often wondered. It caused his head to boil over at times. But Carrie, ever since she deserted Johnson in 2016 to join Team Gove after he pulled out of the leadership contest, was *persona non grata* to Crosby. As was Gove, Johnson's nemesis. 'Lynton could never understand why Boris listened to Michael. He thought his influence on him and on politics was utterly pernicious,' says an aide. Crosby had often caused Johnson to doubt Carrie and Gove. Now he was forcing him to choose…

'I'm not going to be your chief of staff,' Crosby told Johnson after his *nth* time of asking. 'But I will come back to help put a team together for you.' Johnson heaved a sigh of relief. 'But you need to make changes. I've got strong views on the people you need,' he said. Crosby knew that Johnson wouldn't be allowed by Carrie to clear out all her people, though some left, such as Henry Newman. But he couldn't prise out Finn and Lyons, to Crosby's horror. Options for helping Johnson had narrowed severely. Crosby told him he'd spoken to Will Lewis, well known to Johnson from when he had edited the *Telegraph*, who would help sort a team. They'd seriously considered Lewis for the chief of staff, but decided against it because of the need for someone who had worked in the system to drive through change. They looked at bringing in a Cabinet minister. Dowden was approached, and the moment he declined, Johnson became suspicious. Shapps was considered, as was Williamson.

Rosenfield himself came up with the idea of Steve Barclay, the Minister for the Cabinet Office, considered loyal and capable. Rosenfield had worked closely with him and rated him. More precisely, he was available and willing to take on what most considered career suicide. His appointment was announced on 5 February. Rosenfield was also responsible for the appointment of Sam Jones as permanent secretary at No. 10.

The team was still far from complete, and was guided more by balancing the Carrie faction and stuffing the building with people considered loyal to Johnson. Any thought of a rational structure to No. 10 was out of the window. 'Boris was in a bad state, realizing he would have to move fast if he was to stop the rot and reassert control,' says an aide. Crosby suggested Sam Cohen for the third time, who joined as chief of operations, 'to fill the job that Anji Hunter had done serving as gatekeeper to Tony Blair', says an aide. She was one of the better performers of the *tertii ordines*, yet still disempowered by a Prime Minister unwilling to let others organize him or quell inter-factional No. 10 conflicts.

Had Johnson been willing to read up about the history of past premierships during his long lifetime yearning for the post, he could have appointed his Jeremys, Jonathans and Anjis to his heart's content. Now, the moment had long gone. His other appointments contained rum characters, but also good and capable people who, because of the utter chaos Johnson presided over and inability to provide any leadership, were soon at each other's throats, disagreeing about access and power, but also politics and presentation. William Golding's *Lord of the Flies* had been transported to Downing Street.

The worst No. 10 operation since the modern office was created in December 1916 was the inevitable result. Positive activity in this period, like Johnson's leadership on Ukraine, or energy security policy, occurred outside the maelstrom of his bickering political staff. The return of Emily Lawson in March from the vaccine programme to run the Delivery Unit brought back a welcome focus on policy, with five stocktakes chaired by Johnson in the final months. But she found No. 10 a much less effective place without Rosenfield and Mirza, with traction visibly slipping away.

Why did it all go wrong? Simple. Johnson repeated, though it's hard to believe, exactly the same three mistakes made in the *primi* and *secundi ordines*. He continued to appoint safe rather than suitable people to top positions. The most egregious example was Reynolds' successor as his PPS. Rather than appointing a commanding figure versed in Whitehall and economic policy, he went for a diplomat whose skills, like Reynolds', were not attuned to running the Private Office of a Prime Minister with such a large personality and so hard to manage. Peter Wilson had to be yanked back prematurely from his ambassadorship in Brazil, just like Reynolds from Libya. As with Reynolds, Johnson felt comfortable with Wilson, a friend of his brother Leo. Appointing mates, though, however talented, is rarely good in any office including No. 10. 'Frankly, we were very surprised at the appointment,' says a diplomat. So was the rest of the political world. Wilson, lacking independent authority from the start, never stood a chance. When Glassborow, who had been holding the Private Office together, quit in May the system was in trouble.

Johnson neither stuck by his man, Chief of Staff Barclay, nor by his domestic policies – Ukraine was the exception, his most consistent commitment to a policy since the general election. Barclay without Johnson's full-blooded support, like Rosenfield, never stood a chance. Johnson's fast-declining political stock, long before the confidence vote in June and the Chris Pincher scandal (covered in the next chapter), didn't help either. As a result, he was incapable of enforcing order either inside or outside No. 10. 'Within a week or two of Barclay's appointment, Cabinet ministers were totally disregarding what he said,' says one. The words that should instil terror in Whitehall and Westminster, 'the Prime Minister wants', were diminished currency.

Finally, Johnson's addiction to court politics and playing factions off against each other remained until the bitter end. He never confronted those who were in his favour, or held them to account. Crosby's presence at the daily 8.45 a.m. meetings upstairs in the Thatcher Study steadied the ship, but his deliberate closing the door on 'Carrie and Gove's crew', Finn, Gascoigne and Lyons, didn't keep the peace. Incessant criticism and leaks suggested that their exclusion was responsible for a whole series of mishaps culminating in the Pincher debacle. For political journalists, it was a golden era.

Prime Ministers need to learn on the job, not least because it takes them so far beyond anything they have ever experienced before. But Johnson seems to have learned little over his three successive regimes in No. 10. There is no reason to believe that, were there ever to be a fourth regime, he would not make exactly the same mistakes.

The Degrading of the Civil Service

'The civil service wants to destroy me,' Johnson told Lister on the eve of becoming Prime Minister. Cummings held the agents of annihilation at bay for the first six months but the general election was the spur to act. 'Top civil servants on Tories' "hit list"', was the headline in the *Sunday Telegraph* on 22 February 2020. 'Boris Johnson wants to replace a series of mandarins as part of a move to change dramatically the approach in some of Whitehall's most influential departments', the article claimed.[24]

Prime Ministers and Cabinet ministers at large have to work through Whitehall. Establishing a *modus operandi* early on is a hallmark of all successful leaders. A deep hostility to the civil service, though, had been brewing for many years. Thatcher was often frustrated with it, but she channelled it into a series of modernizing reforms including an 'Efficiency Unit' and her 'Next Steps' reforms in 1987.[25] Blair and Brown removed Terry Burns as permanent secretary at the Treasury in 1998 who had been brought in by Thatcher as a political appointee in 1980, but they developed a successful way of working with the civil service. From the 2010s, a new element was added to the traditional Conservative suspicion of the public service for being inefficient, bloated and with its own cautious agenda. Britain's progress was being held back not just by membership of the EU, but by its antiquated and anti-enterprise state bureaucracy.

The Treasury was seen as the very heart of Mordor. Osborne's threatened 'punishment budget' five weeks before the referendum which claimed that a vote to leave would result in a £30 billion black hole caused great bitterness, as did the Treasury's studies on the impact of Brexit, with its short-term report in particular seen as alarmist and wrong. Further damage was caused by Chancellor Philip Hammond's strident resistance to a hard Brexit under May, for which the Treasury took some blame. Better preparations for a hard Brexit could indeed have been made: Vote Leave blamed the Treasury, though it was Hammond not officials who resisted work being done. Despite scant evidence that neither Treasury nor the wider civil service were impeding Brexit, the overwhelming majority being pro-Remain notwithstanding, cynicism from some ministers only intensified. 'They weren't actively resisting Brexit. Some definitely thought it an error, but they made it work', is the verdict of Gove who drove Brexit through Whitehall in 2019.[26]

Tom Scholar, Treasury permanent secretary since 2016, was the principal target on what became known by aides as the 's**t list'. While No. 10 was silent in defence of the permanent secretaries, newly appointed Chancellor Sunak took Scholar on one side and assured him that he would be safe with him. The 's**t list' proved a bonding experience for them both, the opposite of No. 10's intentions. Simon McDonald at the FCO and Philip Rutnam had no such cover from their Secretaries of State. The latter, in dispute with Home Secretary Patel over her bullying of staff in which he received a settlement, departed from government, as did McDonald later in the year along with some seven others of permanent secretary rank, the biggest cull of top officials in the entire history of the civil service, which dates back to 1870. Attempts were made to justify the blood spilling by reference to Thatcher; but unlike Johnson, her spilling of blood was tiny, and she improved the civil service while not degrading it. With silence from Johnson himself, it was left to a Brexiteer to deliver the obvious truth: 'You don't solve a piece of managerial reform with a firing squad,' said David Davis on BBC television the morning the *Sunday Telegraph* story broke.[27]

The unforced switch of Britain's top official did nothing to enhance the quality of government, least of all during such a grave health crisis. 'The firing of Mark Sedwill sent out a painful message – that the Cabinet Secretary was no longer guardian of the constitution, but a personal appointment by the Prime Minister of the moment,' says an official. Within very little time, Johnson was disappointed in the man he had appointed to the job he had never comprehended. Nor did the switch enhance the effectiveness of Britain's national security with imminent challenges in Afghanistan and Russian aggression.

Nor did the cull of permanent secretaries lead to the promised greater quality in performance in the delivery of the government's agenda. The deficiencies of the civil service had been clearly identified by countless figures: too little initiative, isolation from the private sector, lack of focus on delivery, too siloed and lacking in specialists. Rather than implementing reforms, Johnson's regime encouraged a culture throughout Whitehall where civil servants told ministers what they wanted to hear. 'Officials became hesitant about raising genuine concerns and speaking truth to power, on the Northern Ireland Protocol and every other issue,' says an official. The dismissal of Jonathan Slater from Education in August 2020 for errors the department made over exams was seen by some 'as a deliberate message that officials were taking the rap for mistakes by ministers', an inversion of the convention of individual ministerial responsibility – that a Cabinet minister bears the ultimate responsibility for the actions of their department.

Case, uniquely for a Cabinet Secretary, began his tenure without the confidence of the permanent secretaries he had to lead, and for the remaining twenty-two months of the premiership, their confidence in him remained problematic. As one of his allies admits, 'It was a surprising appointment. The civil service had had to deal with Covid and Brexit and it was going to be very tough to have a young and inexperienced Cabinet Secretary running the whole show, and trying to run and motivate permanent secretaries who didn't want to be led by him or to embrace collective accountability under him.'

Case was aware from the moment he began in September 2020 that he was on the back foot, with trust between ministers and Whitehall totally shot. Behind the scenes, he tried, while retaining the confidence of the PM and Cabinet, to restore trust with officials. His first priority was 'to get civil servants back in the room because they'd been excluded', helping ensure ministers listened to officials on everything from Covid to Ukraine. He made securing Tom Scholar's long-term position a condition of his appointment, with his contract later renewed indefinitely, and preventing further sackings of permanent secretaries till Johnson left (Scholar was sacked as soon as Truss took over). Case insisted Sedwill's successor as NSA was a civil servant. Bit by bit, he tried to change the culture among ministers towards the civil service. Gove and Sunak he found particularly helpful, with others such as Hancock and Wallace supportive, while getting nowhere with the ultra-sceptics Patel, Raab, Rees-Mogg and Truss.

In public, with Gove he oversaw the launch in July 2021 of 'The Declaration on Government Reform' to open up the civil service to fresh skills, talent and ideas, embrace digital technology and data-based decision-making, and move away from Whitehall.[28] To signal the new culture of trust, the first joint meeting of many planned between the Cabinet and permanent secretaries took place.

Case's actions, however, did not succeed in getting the civil service to work as a unit behind Johnson's agenda. The joint Cabinet/ permanent secretary meeting was never repeated. Case's low standing among permanent secretaries remained despite his best efforts. 'He came in saying he would improve the male, stale and toxic culture, but little changed,' says an official. Johnson either couldn't or wouldn't listen to him: No. 10 and the Cabinet Office, Case's area of expertise, continued chaotically. The first few months of a new Cabinet Secretary, as for a Prime Minister, define their tenure. Incomers are nigh-on untouchable, particularly when, like Sunak after Javid, Johnson could not supplant the new incumbent. But at his moment of maximum power, Case made a string of errors in the eyes of his colleagues.

He was criticized for his response to the allegations against Patel's treatment of Home Office staff. Alex Allan, the PM's independent adviser on ministerial standards, concluded that her approach 'amounted to behaviour that can be described as bullying'.[29] Johnson backed her, his immediate response to tell everybody to 'rally round the Prittster'. Case did not or could not dissuade him, and it was Allan not Patel who resigned. It sent shockwaves throughout Whitehall: 'It meant we knew that if we stood up and challenged our Secretary of State on their behaviour, we would have no guarantee of support from the centre,' says a top official. 'Johnson's immediate response was to back Priti Patel, not look at her conduct. Case not challenging that meant other [permanent secretaries] such as Philip Barton had no leg to stand on when trying to push back against Raab's behaviour at the FCDO,' adds another. Case was criticized for not standing up for the welfare of officials against Johnson when the second Covid wave struck, under heavy pressure from the press for them to return to work: 'In the face of no personal evidence that it was safe to return, Johnson pushed for it, and Case didn't overturn him,' says an insider. Then in September, swipe to the resignation of Jonathan Jones, the government's most senior lawyer over the UK Internal Markets Bill; Case was believed to have waved the bill through with little pushback against the measures which broke international law. These were perceptions which may not have been fully justified, but they contributed to disillusion and a dysfunctional top of the civil service. One senior official concludes, 'Simon was perfectly nice but he was not qualified for the job. It was a personal appointment and everyone knew it. He wasn't able or willing to stand up and defend those he was supposed to lead.' Another is even stronger in their denouncing of his work: 'Sedwill was incomparably better. He was the leader, and Simon wasn't.' Permanent secretaries disliked Case's own leaking, and his reluctance to stand up for them when ministers leaked against them.

Case, as did everyone working under Johnson, found himself isolated. He needed strong support behind him. MacNamara had been promoted to deputy Cabinet Secretary by Sedwill in April. But she had a difficult relationship with Cummings and No. 10 over allegations of their bullying staff and ethics misconduct. Trying to uphold standards of the ministerial code, she ran foursquare into a Prime Minister and Cummings who had little respect for it. Her efforts to try to bring order to Cabinet government, and to improve the culture at the centre, were constantly thwarted. Attempts to mediate the toxic relationship between Sedwill and Cummings damaged her too, as she was seen as too close to Sedwill. Cummings and Johnson started gunning for her ('They didn't want her asking difficult questions,' says an official), offering her permanent secretary of any department just to be free of her – an offer she refused. Despite her refusal, in July 2020 news of her imminent departure was leaked, believed to have been by Cummings. She weathered the storm, deciding that she would go after settling in Case; her departure was so delayed by the winter crises that she outlasted him, officially leaving the civil service in February 2021. 'They made her life impossible. Another good person spat out by the system,' says a fellow civil servant. With her departure, Case lost a strong independent force, and the most senior female leader at the centre.

Over the following months, a succession of senior officials leaving and looking for jobs outside, and repeated failures to protect the civil service, saw morale sink even lower. The announcement of 91,000 job cuts, the ending of the fast stream recruitment programme for those seeking to join the civil service and the continued war on working from home contributed to low morale. The weak leadership by Case gave the civil service a let-out – blaming ministers, as they in turn were being blamed by ministers. It was all an unnecessary distraction from what needed to happen: systemic modernization of Whitehall.

Nothing did Case more damage, though, than Partygate: not doing more to challenge the culture that allowed the events to happen, nor ensuring a fairer response once they came to light, while escaping fines himself. Case confided in an associate his angst over the parties.

'I don't know what more I can do to stand up to a Prime Minister who lies.'

'You have to tell him.'

'I have. He doesn't listen to me.'

'You could resign?'

'I can't do that so soon after Mark has left.'

'It would make a very strong point.'

'But what's the guarantee that he won't bring in someone in my place even less able to stand up to him?'

Johnson came into office saying the civil service would destroy him. On his final full day as Prime Minister, Johnson had lunch with Case. 'I made a mistake alienating Whitehall so badly,' he told him. To the end Johnson would say what he thought people wanted to hear. But experience nevertheless, not least in Covid and Ukraine, had taught him that officials served him often much better than his aides. His last day. Too late. Too late.

The Degrading of Cabinet Government

The top Prime Ministers have all appointed and used their Cabinets to the full, knowing that they themselves possess no executive authority, and they have to govern through Cabinet government. Clement Attlee would have achieved nothing without Ernest Bevin, Nye Bevan, Herbert Morrison, Hugh Dalton and Stafford Cripps. Churchill and Thatcher equally governed through Cabinet and were great respecters of it.

'Cabinet are hardly great,' Johnson was prone to admit to his close circle throughout his premiership. He arrived in No. 10 with a jaundiced view of the institution, hating Cabinet meetings in his two years under May. 'He thought they dragged on forever. He felt frustrated and marginalized under her,' says Lister.[30] So he arrived determined to be different. During the first six months with Brexit decisions to the fore, he would meet beforehand with Cummings, Frost and Lewis to be briefed on exactly what he would say. A weak

Cabinet suited Cummings, who found such meetings with second-rate politicians beneath him. 'They were over very quickly, about thirty minutes often. The Cabinet understood what they had signed up for, so no one was challenging him,' says an official.

In the following two years until his authority began to wane from late 2021, the pattern scarcely changed. Observers are unanimous. 'Cabinet government never worked. Boris gave the impression to everyone that our meetings were an annoyance to him, and he wanted them over as quickly as possible. You could see it in his eyes. He hated it when we spoke beyond our brief. He preferred us to say nothing,' says a Cabinet minister. 'Hungry sheep' was his name for his colleagues. 'He continued to think they were pointless,' says an aide. Johnson's impatience with pomposity was to the fore: 'He thought ministers often just read the scripts like a church service, or doing performative speaking so they could brief it out later. He loathed all that,' says Gove.[31] Hancock, Truss and Javid would speak the most. But of all his Cabinet ministers, he would be most inclined to ask the ever-polite Gove to talk. The other colleague he most rated, Sunak, tried to disguise his impatience with Johnson for not keeping to business or building consensus. 'It was obvious to us that Rishi had a problem with the Prime Minister from early on. You could see it in his body language. Rather than leaning into him, he inclined himself at an angle away,' says a minister.

Officials challenged Johnson, pointing out that Cabinet was the only occasion in the week when his government came together, and it was his opportunity 'to point them all in the same direction'. They tried to dissuade him from starting meetings with 'let's set a world record for getting through an agenda'.

'You do know you have to stop saying that, please.'

'Why?' he asked.

'Because it's tantamount to telling your Cabinet colleagues that you don't want to spend your time with them.'

'Oh, I see.'

He still didn't see it, though, so they reminded him of the historic symbolism and romance of meeting in the Cabinet Room where so many world-changing decisions had been taken. 'But he never felt that sense of history.'

In the morning pre-meetings, officials would talk him through the agenda and ask him how he would like to play the issues. 'Time and again, he would say he would do one thing, then say something completely different to the Cabinet, and then have a different recollection of what was said. It made Cabinet government very difficult,' says an aide. Ministers often felt steamrollered. 'He would get his own way even though he didn't follow the agenda,' says Shapps.[32] 'Boris would say something like "right, I think we've all agreed on this" when it wasn't at all clear that everyone *had* agreed,' says another. 'The joke among us was that his team had already decided what the minutes were going to say before the meeting.'

Johnson would open meetings at 9.30 a.m. on Tuesdays typically with a joke or anecdote. The general election victory had made him not more accommodating, but more impatient. Then Covid struck, and for the first time in history Cabinet meetings took place remotely, from March until 15 September 2020 when face-to-face meetings resumed in the grandeur of the Locarno Suite in the Foreign Office on the other side of Downing Street: 'the Foreign Office's idea of a modest seminar room… nothing propinks like propinquity', were his opening remarks.[33]

The euphoria of the first fifteen months slowly drained away over the course of 2021, principally over lockdown. The Cabinet meeting on 20 December 2021, lasting an unprecedented two hours to debate the response to the Omicron variant of Covid, stands out in his premiership as the one major occasion when Cabinet decided something, in this case not to have another lockdown. 2022 too saw genuine discussions in the Cabinet on the cost of living crisis and at stages in the Ukraine War. Johnson had not become a late convert to the doctrine of 'collective responsibility' and to Cabinet government; rather, it was a symptom of his dwindling authority and to present a common voice to Parliament. Necessity dressed up as principle.

Leaking was another symptom of his declining stock. Gove, Truss and Wallace were among the leakiest, other ministers believed, but most were at the game. 'The Prime Minister knew that within ten or fifteen minutes of Cabinet ending, it would be briefed out, usually hostile. It made him wary and incline him towards just "show and tell" Cabinets,' says an official. There were no safe spaces. 'Leaking was a major problem for the premiership, even from the small ministerial discussions before full Cabinet,' says another.

Lack of trust and mutual respect was another serious issue for Johnson. When his poll ratings began to dip after the first eighteen months, there was no support bank of good relationships for him to fall back on. Unlike many incoming Conservative Prime Ministers, including Major, Cameron and May, he hadn't had the opportunity to build up a network of deep friendships over many years. He was friendly with several such as Hancock, Alister Jack and Javid, but they were not actual friends. Most, he hardly knew: the shallowness of the roots were just waiting to be exposed. 'He never came to respect most of them, continuing to call them the "stooges",' says an aide. Ministers began to suspect his sincerity: 'He smiled, praised, made us feel we were the only people in the room,' says one. 'Then as soon as we were out of the door he would say "what's that f**ker doing?" I can't think of a single Cabinet minister he wasn't rude about behind their back – Patel ("why can't she get a grip?"), Sunak ("that little f**ker"), Truss (endless sneers), Raab ("what's all his crap about the Bill of Rights?").' To the end, he never appreciated that badmouthing colleagues in front of others would be speedily passed on, detracting from his own stature.

Johnson's near-total neglect of Cabinet as a tool begs the question: where were the major decisions in his premiership taken? In private with ministerial colleagues, especially Sunak, or in small meetings is the answer. The latter included Cabinet committee meetings, EU Exit Operations and Exit Strategy during Brexit, and Covid Operations during the pandemic, the first and last chaired by Gove, which would take decisions that would then be merely referred up to full Cabinet. But committees bored Johnson every bit as much as full Cabinet, as seen in his irregular and unenthusiastic chairing of the National Security Council. The shame as always with Johnson is that, when he wanted to be, he could be an outstanding chair. Like Thatcher, he would love to interrogate and challenge forensically: 'His manner of thinking was to test arguments and play devil's advocate. He liked people to come in, speak their view clearly, even if he disagreed,' says a Cabinet minister. He relished talking to individuals who knew their stuff. All too rarely did Cabinet ministers get a vision of how exceptional he could be. Ever optimistic, Johnson approached Cabinet reshuffles as the opportunities for reconfiguring his entire premiership, despite his sparse knowledge of the talent or the skills they would need in post proving a handicap. 'I always advised him to keep them to a minimum, that every reshuffle creates more enemies, that May had made such a mess of reshuffles and we should learn from that,' counsels Lister.[34]

The first of his three was at the start of the premiership in July 2019, motivated entirely by a desire to hold the divided party together and push through Brexit. It was only ever a temporary fix. All eyes were set on the reshuffle if he won the general election. The size of his victory boosted expectations that he would use his political capital for a defining new face to his government for the next five years. The intervention of Christmas and the Chequers strategy day in January delayed it till February. Cummings and Cain were now the influencers, with minor inputs from Lister, Gascoigne, Mirza and Smith. Sedwill wrote him notes, as Cabinet Secretaries do at reshuffles assessing ministerial strengths, with MacNamara working alongside Gascoigne to find possible skill matches between prospective ministers and departments. They were largely ignored.

'We had to pin his diary down, then build in time for him to think about it and to change his mind,' says Chief Whip Spencer.[35] 'Imagine the most capable and effective Cabinet you can for the next five years', was the homework Johnson's team gave him. He ruffled his hair and came up with Gove at the Home Office and Sunak at the Treasury. 'But I can't pick them because of the politics,' he sighed. Javid was now the target. Pressure from Cummings for him to go intensified in the final days before it, and his departure shaped the entire reshuffle. Johnson's dislike of confrontation and causing upset prevented more spaces opening for a dramatic refresh. Patel remained at the Home Office because he liked her and she provided balance. Truss (termed 'the human hand grenade' by Cummings ten years before[36]) was similarly retained at Trade, 'where we thought she would do little damage, wave flags, and her officials would do all the work', says an aide. Johnson had no illusions about Raab or Wallace, but didn't want to risk the turbulence of moving them from the Foreign Office and Defence. So no room there either. The Eye of Sauron then descended on Thérèse Coffey at Work and Pensions. 'How can we be expected to do our job when we have briefings undermining us from your advisers?' she complained to Johnson. 'That can't be true. They would never do that,' Johnson replied.

She remained, not least for gender balance with Nicky Morgan, Andrea Leadsom, Theresa Villiers and Esther McVey all departing Team Boris. But Geoffrey Cox was sacked as Attorney General and Julian Smith as Northern Ireland Secretary 'because they wouldn't toe the line and weren't going in the direction he wanted', says an aide. 'I gather you're about to sack me. I know the ropes,' Smith said when summoned to see Johnson.[37] 'Not at all, you've done a great job, blah blah blah,' Johnson replied. Cox, meanwhile, recalls, 'Given the signs, I had no doubt my services would be dispensed with at the first opportunity. I suspect my card was marked even before the landslide was won. What was apparently wanted was an AG willing to countenance what I would not and advise in a way I could not.'[38] Their departure sent a very clear message to Cabinet about what happens to people who challenge Johnson. His team thought Brandon Lewis would provide balance, and had to work hard on Johnson because of Carrie's opposition to him dating back to his time as party chair. Suella Braverman was selected as Attorney General to replace Cox. She ticked every conceivable box.

Supposing Johnson had been brave, and partnered Sunak at the Treasury with Gove at the Home Office, Hunt as Foreign Secretary, and talent like Amber Rudd, Rory Stewart and Damian Green to run the delivery departments. It's hard not to imagine that he would have achieved more; but he would still have been without a clear plan for his government.

The last roll of the dice came eighteen months later, with options narrowing as the skies darkened. 'Supposing you were to have your dream Cabinet. What would it look like?' 'Really?' 'Yes. Capability would be the key consideration?' Rosenfield first posed these questions to Johnson at Chequers one Sunday morning in April 2021. Finding the best possible Secretaries of State was the target. Johnson was shown a list of Ministers of State, the second rung, who might be promoted, 'but he didn't know most of them', says an aide.

They were aiming for a July reshuffle. With No. 10 so prone to leak, they had no wish to repeat the prolonged and damaging speculation around the earlier reshuffle. Communications director Doyle joined the discussions but not Case ('not very involved') nor Chief Whip Spencer, not because of a leak risk, but because he was a target for the chop. Johnson thought Spencer had done well in the difficult first six months and beyond but could readily see a more forceful and astute Chief Whip was now needed. They considered Shapps, Brandon Lewis and Chris Heaton-Harris (who succeeded Spencer in February 2022). After a long debate, Johnson's reliable loyalty prevailed.

So too did his caution. Jeremy Hunt was back on the active consideration list, but Johnson got cold feet and never approached him. Too risky. Nor did he move Sunak. They asked themselves if they had the right Chancellor, thinking hard about moving him to the Foreign Office or to a major delivery department. A swap at Health with Hancock was considered, but they judged it too early to move him, for all Johnson's reservations. Wallace in these pre-Ukraine days was considered lacklustre and 'a bit grumpy', but Johnson felt too insecure to move him. Raab was another dour performer who he did decide to move long before his handling of the Afghan evacuation in August became an issue. Truss in contrast was considered just the kind of 'can-do' operator he wanted, optimistically pushing his agenda. So she became Foreign Secretary, the check to Sunak's leadership ambitions entirely deliberate. Sunak made his displeasure known to Johnson, another staging post in their downward spiral.

At the final moment the reshuffle had to be postponed to September. The lockdown in July would have meant ministers being sacked by Zoom, which was considered dangerous. 'Boris was mightily pissed off by the delay,' says an aide. But it provided more time for some last-minute tuning before the day itself. The search was on for 'bright optimists' to exemplify the famously inchoate Johnsonism. Nadhim Zahawi, thought to have done well on vaccines, fitted the bill. He was asked to be Education Secretary, rather than Dowden who expected it, who was dispatched to CCHQ as party chair. '"I need you to be party chair," Johnson said. "Why?" I asked him. "Because you're great on the media." It was all flannel. But there was no point in arguing,' says Dowden.[39] Nadine Dorries was selected as his successor as Culture Secretary, less to bait the 'luvvy' arts establishment, though that was certainly not unappealing to No. 10, but because she was 'a northern working-class woman who had worked her way up the system', argues a supportive No. 10 aide. Dorries was the personification of the 'optimist, can-do' leitmotif of the reshuffle.

Gove was moved to the Levelling Up portfolio to drive Johnson's flagship but flagging domestic policy. His portfolio included housing, communities and local government, as well as the Union and elections. 'It was an easy decision. Way back, we had concluded that Michael made no sense at the centre. He needed to be in a department delivering things,' says an aide. Gove never achieved his ambition of becoming Foreign or Home Secretary. His chairing the key Cabinet committees and leadership of departments made him easily the most effective of all Johnson's ministers. But he never changed his mind that Johnson was fundamentally unfit to be PM.

'He just thought him frivolous and shallow, endlessly changing his mind,' says a senior Conservative. Johnson's phobia about sacking people was kept to a minimum, with Williamson and Jenrick shown the door after perceived policy failures, and Robert Buckland as Justice Secretary for being vanilla and sackable *sans risque*.

Raab was given the additional title of Deputy Prime Minister as a face-saver for his downward move. But it was only ever titular: 'The office never figured in Johnson's mind. It's not the way he operates,' says a senior adviser. If ever a Prime Minister needed an omnicompetent DPM to oversee domestic policy and bang heads together, it was Johnson. But to be effective, they required power, and to cede that to them required the commodity Johnson found hardest to give, trust. Long before the DPM post was formalized by Churchill in 1942, Prime Ministers had senior colleagues who acted as their deputies.[40] Major invested wide-ranging powers in Michael Heseltine, as did Cameron in Hague. Neither deputy had still harboured ambitions for the top post, but Raab did, another reason why he was marginalized (far more than any concerns over his odd behaviour). 'Boris always worried more about Raab than anyone else in Cabinet until the end,' says a minister who worked with Raab when Johnson was incapacitated by Covid. 'Every PM finds it difficult to let go. It's hard for any PM to delegate because they want to keep their hands on the tiller, but I like to think Boris was learning to trust me more, particularly after he'd been unwell,' says Raab.[41]

Johnson never used or understood Cabinet well enough, and he diminished his premiership's impact as a result. His neglect of Cabinet was but a continuation of the theme. Where were the grown-ups, those who approached the task of governing the United Kingdom with the seriousness it deserved? Ultimately, he could not behave as a grown-up, nor trust other people to do so. Johnson's failure to appoint and trust grown-ups, as had underpinned every other successful premiership in British history, though, was only one reason for his disappointing performance and fall.

Johnson delivers his resignation speech outside No. 10 on 7 July 2022

10

DOWNFALL

'This is not a programme for one year or one Parliament; it is a blueprint for the future of Britain. Just imagine where this country could be in 10 years' time,' a gushing Johnson told the House of Commons the week after the general election.[1] It was a vision he intended to drive all the way, carving out his place in the pantheon of great Prime Ministers by transforming the nation and its standing in the world, and securing the Conservative Party an unprecedented fifth consecutive term.

In September 2021, bloodied but unbowed, Johnson set out his aims for the duration of his premiership and its central project, levelling up. 'It's going to take a while, it's going to take ten years,' he told journalist Sebastian Payne.[2] Many believed that Johnson, with his sheer force of personality and ideas spanning the political spectrum, would last the course – perhaps even the full decade. Covid was in retreat. The fall in polling since May 2021 was just a mid-term blip as the vaccine bounce wore off, not yet the start of a fatal decline in the appeal of the party and the Prime Minister. The Wallpapergate controversy over the funding of the No. 10 flat renovation merely an isolated question mark on Johnson's conduct in office, not yet an indication of chronic rule-breaking.

In June 2022, as all came crashing down around him, he was asked once again about his longevity as Prime Minister, and whether he would like to serve a full second term. 'At the moment I'm thinking actively about the third term and what could happen then, but I will review that when I get to it,' he responded.[3] Everyone but he and some ultra-loyalists knew this was ludicrous. The hope for a decade of Johnson had been replaced by derision even from his own benches.[4] Just nine days after his comments, following the highest number of ministerial resignations in history, he announced he would be stepping down.

It was a uniquely precipitous fall for a fresh leader who had won a commanding majority less than three years before. Lloyd George fell within four years of the December 1918 election victory for the Coalition government; but he was the head of the Liberals, the minority party, and the Conservatives were soon straining to break free of him. Clement Attlee finally fell six years after Labour's mighty 1945 victory, and Harold Wilson four years after his 1966 landslide. But they were both victims of general election defeats, not regicide by colleagues. The closest parallel to Johnson's fall in the hundred years prior is Margaret Thatcher, who was ejected from power in November 1990, three and a half years after her famous landslide victory in June 1987. But she had been in power for over eleven years, and the forces that brought her down had built up during that time.

Johnson's downfall requires some explaining.

All Prime Ministers are unusual people, exceptionally talented and individualistic. They see the world differently to the rest of us. But even among recent Prime Ministers, there was nothing remotely normal about the rise, the summit or the downfall of Boris Johnson.

Johnson himself and his Praetorian Guard of loyalists who remained with him to the end look to factors beyond their control to explain the inexplicable, the downfall of their Claudius.[5] With the Conservatives trailing Labour by just 6 per cent in the polls in mid-June before the scandal to come, a perfectly respectable deficit mid-term, the anger was all the greater.[6] 'When he first fell, he went through all stages of grief, and came up with this explanation,' says an aide. First, 'the big institutions who always hated him', namely the civil service, business, the City, the press and the BBC. Second, 'the establishment', he said, ensured his fall because they could never forgive him for Brexit, including his two ethics advisers Alex Allan and Christopher Geidt, as well as former editor of the *Daily Mail* Geordie Greig. Third, the 'disloyal lieutenants, Sunak, Gove and Cummings', the last of whom he came to believe 'I should have let go the moment I got Brexit done'.

There are several lesser omissions from his diagnosis, and one glaring one. We will come on to that later. Many of the forces that his team chose to blame, which we now examine, did turn against him; but they didn't bring him down.

Big Institutions: Whitehall, Business, the City, the Press and the BBC

Johnson genuinely convinced himself early on that the civil service would destroy him if he let it. True believers continue to assert that failures of the civil service had been responsible for much of Britain's malaise, including the delayed departure from the EU, and personally let Johnson down. But those inside No. 10, the Prime Minister included, came to form a very different view. Eddie Lister reflects that 'there is no evidence that the civil service impeded the delivery of Brexit'.[7] Rather than a hindrance, Johnson found officials his most effective colleagues, including Stuart Glassborow on economic and fiscal policy, Will Gelling and John Bew on foreign policy, Emily Lawson on delivery, James Bowler and Simon Ridley on Covid, and a whole series of diplomats such as Philip Barton and Karen Pierce on international relations. In contrast to his advisers and Cabinet, he did not have to fret over that greatest fear of his, an eventual betrayal. In the effective civil servants by his side he saw individuals who could deliver without the risk of them later working to unseat him. For all his late conversion, he did nothing to stand up for the civil service against his Cabinet colleagues and elements in the press who continued to regard it as the enemy, a convenient scapegoat for poor ministerial performance and the failure to achieve the benefits of Brexit. In his final months blow after blow landed on civil service morale: 91,000 planned job cuts, a briefing war against working from home, attacks on 'a Remain bias'.[8] He consistently refused to defend it from hostile briefings by his team and ministers, and didn't stand up against bullying or motivate the civil service in a way that suggested he had any understanding of how leaders of large organizations operate. It is difficult to find another Prime Minister in the modern era who has been such a poor leader of the nation's executive. The civil service would undoubtedly have performed better if he had known how to lead and improve it. But there is no evidence that, through omission or commission, it ended his premiership.

Nor did business or the City bring him down, though his handling of the former might have inclined them. He never owned his 'f**k business' throwaway line in 2018, dismissing it as of no consequence which continued to be given currency only by his critics. But it was significant to the business community. Johnson found it hard to stomach polls regularly indicating that 85 per cent of members of the Confederation of British Industry (CBI), which represents 190,000 businesses and trade associations, disagreed with Brexit. 'Business people were just not his cup of tea,' says a No. 10 adviser. 'Eccentric entrepreneurs and oddballs, now they were much more Boris's type of person, not the polished suits of the CBI, he just couldn't get interested in them.' His animosity was not softened when his speech received a lukewarm response at the annual CBI conference in November 2019, when the chair had to wind him up because he was running into the time allotted for Jeremy Corbyn, and he left feeling he had been disrespectfully treated by his hosts.

Karan Bilimoria, upon becoming the CBI's president in June 2020, arrived determined to rebuild bridges. He went to No. 10, but unable to see Johnson himself, listened to aides explain why he was upset with business and the CBI. A meeting with Lister promised better relations in future. That autumn, Johnson provoked further upset when he pulled out of the CBI conference at the last minute: 'Never in the history of the CBI has the Prime Minister not spoken at our conference,' says Bilimoria.[9] Cancellation of May's industrial strategy without any clear successor plan also went down like a lead balloon: 'Not good: business leaders were all beginning to engage with it, and were then rudely rebuffed. If anyone thought the PM could replace it by invitations to receptions at No. 10, they were absurd,' says John Manzoni, former chief executive of the civil service.[10]

Some lost ground was made up when Tony Danker succeeded Carolyn Fairbairn as director general of the CBI, determined to inject new positivity into the relationship and move the discussion beyond Brexit. At a virtual meeting with Johnson in March 2021, he explored how business could help levelling up and the ten-point plan: 'Prime Minister, we're on your side, what can we do to help you?' Johnson's speech to the conference in the autumn of 2021 was billed as the opportunity for the public big reset. The venue in the North-East was chosen in part to chime with Johnson's levelling-up agenda. But things went south when he lost his place in his speech, and broke off to ask mystified delegates, 'Hands up anybody who's been to Peppa Pig World.' He continued to fumble among his unnumbered pages, making strange noises and ad-libbing embarrassingly. 'Business leaders are very smart people who got there by being on top of their brief and by being very well organized. Here was a Prime Minister being hopelessly ill-organized,' says one present. 'The speech designed to build bridges between the Prime Minister and the business community saw the very opposite happen,' says a No. 10 adviser. 'After the disastrous 2021 speech, it was downhill all the way, no recovery possible,' says Bilimoria. 'Prime Ministers have to take business people seriously, to treat them with respect, and he hadn't.'[11]

At his best, as when he spoke at the Global Investment Summit at the Science Museum in London in October 2021, Johnson won widespread admiration. The 180 international leaders present were ecstatic about his inspiring words about 'green is good', celebrating the moral virtues of private enterprise. But he couldn't maintain the momentum. On the rare occasions when chief executives were invited in to see him, and he didn't cancel, they were baffled that he was not offering them his vision, but sat there like a journalist with a notepad writing down their answers to his questions. Even some of his favoured entrepreneurs lost patience: for James Dyson, it was the government's message to work from home which exasperated him, resulting in screeds of insistent messages flooding No. 10.

Few business people when asked respond that Johnson would have risen far up their own organizations, so idiosyncratic was he. To the end, the incomprehension was mutual. Johnson, to the exasperation of his minders and Tory Party treasurers, did not have a clue what business leaders expected from a Prime Minister. But neither did they bring him down. Andrew Bailey served Johnson relatively well as Governor of the Bank of England, and he could have few complaints himself about the City, which did play a role in bringing down his successor. But that's another story.

Johnson was obsessed by the press, but was far less strategic and adept at handling them than most of his predecessors, despite having been a journalist, veering between disengagement and overfamiliarity. Prime Ministers are famously reactive to what they read in the press. Churchill, during his last government from 1951 to 1955, would regularly phone up his ministers at any hour of the night to demand an explanation for a story he had read in the first editions.[12] But Johnson took reactivity to new levels, never developed an overall rationale for his government, nor tried to communicate a gravitas to editors in a way that might have secured their respect if not agreement.

The *Sun*, the *Daily Mail* and the *Telegraph* were the daily and Sunday papers he cared about. The only publications he would read regularly were the *Telegraph*, *Financial Times* and the *Spectator*. The *Express* and the *Sun* were supportive of him to the end. Johnson priced in their loyalty and did little to nothing to keep them sweet: he barely knew or took time out to engage with their editors Gary Jones and Victoria Newton.

His relationship with Rupert Murdoch, owner of News Corporation, had deepened when he was Mayor. In 2012, Johnson invited Murdoch and his then wife Wendi Deng to watch Rebecca Adlington defend her 800 metre swimming gold medal at the Olympic Games.[13] At the 2016 leadership election, Murdoch backed Johnson over his former journalist at *The Times*, Gove: 'Michael is a good politician, but he is unelectable. Boris is electable,' he told a former employee. While in No. 10 Johnson and Murdoch spoke regularly. It didn't translate, to Johnson's frustration, into favourable headlines. Martin Ivens, a Brexit supporter, had a good relationship with Johnson as editor of *The Sunday Times* but it became distant when Emma Tucker succeeded him in January 2020. Tim Shipman of *The Sunday Times* had a spat with Cummings at the start of Covid when he ran a story about the government going for herd immunity which resulted in him being put on the naughty step, 'but after a couple of months, he was brought back in from the cold', says a No. 10 aide. No. 10 might have thought they needed Shipman, but his forensic weekly articles were often far from what they expected or hoped. Johnson's deep distrust of Gove led him to suspect that he and his aides were leaking stories to the paper for which he worked, *The Times*. For Steve Swinford, its influential political editor, confidence in Johnson was lost over the alleged lies and continuously changing story from No. 10 around Partygate.

The *Sun* was favourable till near the end. Here Murdoch's influence was felt more than in the two *Times* titles. But then its veteran journalist Trevor Kavanagh called time on Johnson in July 2022, writing, 'I think… Boris is basically finished, he's done, he's a dead man walking. It is very difficult to continue supporting a Prime Minister who has basically bought [*sic*] this entirely upon his own head, not just because of the recent days and weeks.'[14] A distraught Johnson spoke to Murdoch about it, who, for all his continuing indulgence of him, pulled no punches in his response, telling him that there is 'no great plan or direction, taxes need to be cut, you need to get a grip', according to those to whom Murdoch later recounted the conversation. All Murdoch's titles had turned against the PM, and it was Johnson who had alienated them.

He and Carrie Symonds were much closer personally to Claudia and Jonathan Rothermere who owned the *Mail* than to Murdoch. Geordie Greig was appointed editor of the group's flagship title, the *Daily Mail*, in September 2018 in succession to long-serving Paul Dacre, and in June 2020 it overtook the *Sun* as the UK's bestselling daily paper. Fired by Greig's crusading mission to 'detoxify the brand', the *Mail* regularly ran disobliging stories about Symonds and on a series of Johnsonian embarrassments including the refurbishment of the Downing Street flat and the Owen Paterson affair (on which more later). It stung, and Johnson would agonize over why Greig was so hostile: 'Was it Brexit, rivalry of an Eton contemporary, jealousy?' he would ask himself. He never found out. But in November 2021, Greig was suddenly dismissed, and overnight, under the editorship of Ted Verity, critical stories about the Johnsons disappeared into thin air. The atmosphere was thick with suggestions, if unprovable, that the Rothermeres had intervened at the Johnsons' behest, or Dacre's, who disliked the anti-Brexit direction of the paper under Greig. The irony was that, at the very moment in late 2021 that the editor changed from a sworn critic to an unashamed loyalist, Johnson's fortunes dived catastrophically for the worse.

The title he was most obsessed with, the one for which he had worked, was the *Telegraph*. It drove Cummings to distraction: 'All you care about is the *Telegraph*,' he would regularly lament. When the paper published a favourable profile of Starmer after his election as Labour leader in April 2020,[15] Johnson 'threw a fit' and went around the building saying, 'We are not giving them enough of what they want,' recalls an aide. Will Lewis, editor until 2014, was a periodic conversant, and came in to bolster Johnson's last leadership team in early 2022. But it was his successor, Chris Evans, with whom he had most constant conversations. 'As regular as two times a week, all very covert. You would walk in on him and he would say, "I've just been talking to Chris. We need to do XYZ,"' says an aide. While more influential throughout his premiership than any other single editor, or indeed proprietor, Evans' impact was uneven, never more impactful than on resisting lockdown, though Tory MPs equally were pressuring the PM in the same direction. Steadily, the *Telegraph* became more critical of other decisions, not least of the U-turns, tax increases and failure to produce a growth strategy. Chris Evans would say, 'We love Boris. He's one of ours. But is he the Tory PM that we thought we had?' While some *Telegraph* journalists wanted the paper to abandon him, the view that prevailed was that they should remain a 'critical friend' to Johnson, not calling in the editorials for him to go, but to be more conservative, to stop blaming others, and to start being a dynamic leader seizing the benefits of Brexit and leading the country to a high-growth future.

Associate editor Camilla Tominey relayed her thinking on Johnson over lunch with his comms director Guto Harri on 21 April. At the party conference in 2017, she had fired up Johnson with the notion of a full-on 'balls out Brexit'. She was back on the same theme now. She told Harri that if Johnson really wanted to emulate Churchill or Thatcher, people needed to see more courage, a 'balls out Boris', to step on the nitro, to strap on his 'Thatcher cojones'. 'I accept the challenge to make you love ballsy Boris again,' Harri wrote to her afterwards, before relaying to Johnson what she had said. The Prime Minister, not happy that the potency of such a treasured part of his anatomy was again in question, thrashed around for solutions in the ever smaller political landing-space left to him. Sunak was the new figure to blame. 'I want him to make things happen, reduce tax, produce a growth plan, unleash the power of business,' he said. 'But all I get is blancmange.' At a disastrous dinner on 3 July, Johnson pushed Sunak for tax cuts and an immediate slash to VAT. Had Sunak not jumped ship two days later, Johnson was planning to fire or move him. He wanted the constantly loyal Rees-Mogg to 'kick arse and persuade the Treasury to free up pension funds for investment'.

Fraser Nelson, editor of Johnson's other outlet, the *Spectator*, had grown sceptical too. He would call in irregularly to see Johnson at No. 10, on one occasion near the end saying, 'I keep wondering what Boris the editor would make of Boris the Prime Minister.' This 'gentle torturing' of Johnson, as one No. 10 aide puts it, placed the Prime Minister on the back foot, and meant he ignored the script his team had agreed with him in advance in favour of promising Fraser what Johnson thought he wanted to hear. 'You wait and see what happens on tax!' Johnson told him. Fraser was not impressed and chose not to write up the meeting.

Pippa Crerar of the *Daily Mirror* who broke the Partygate story is the newspaper journalist who inflicted more harm on Johnson than any other. 'People often say to me "You brought Boris Johnson down", and I'm like – no! He brought himself down!' she said.[16] She had broken the Barnard Castle story in April 2020, and started receiving reports in 2021, believed to have come from a disaffected figure in the Cabinet Office, of parties during lockdown in Downing Street. The first report appeared in the *Daily Mirror* on 30 November, and resulted in Starmer, at Prime Minister's Questions (PMQs) in Parliament the next day, eliciting from Johnson the answer: 'All the guidance was followed completely by No. 10.'[17] The continuing furore resulted in Johnson announcing he was setting up the inquiry which came to be chaired by Sue

Gray, the Cabinet Office second permanent secretary. 'Knowing Boris Johnson, as I did, what happened, and the denials, were just so true to his character,' says Crerar, who had known him well since he was Mayor. Details of further events flooded into her, and she continued to reveal stories over the following months.[18] Not to be outdone, Cummings, who had chosen not to reveal details about the events earlier, now fanned the flames with his own disclosures.

Shortly after the 2019 general election, Johnson hosted a reception for the press in No. 10, using the opportunity less to set out his agenda than to rail against the BBC (and against the left-wing papers, a select club consisting of the *Daily Mirror* and the *Guardian/Observer*). The BBC continued to infuriate him, as it did many of his pro-Brexit ministers, the impression in their minds that it had been dishonest about its bias in favour of the EU remaining even after the deed was done. 'Johnson was not as rabid as some Tories, but he still basically thought the BBC was full of lefty Remainers,' says an aide. Cummings himself saw the BBC as the 'mortal enemy' of the Conservative Party.[19] While recognizing its unique position was vital in reaching the country, he worked with Cain to restrict access of ministers to it, including a boycott of BBC Radio 4's flagship *Today* programme.[20]

Johnson had high hopes of a more favourable reception when appointing his friend Richard Sharp to chair the BBC in February 2021. But he 'soon became frustrated that he didn't do more to rein in the BBC against the government and against Brexit', says an aide. 'I was surprised by just how negative Johnson was about BBC journalists, notably Nick Robinson and Laura Kuenssberg,' says an aide who arrived mid-premiership. The appointment to the BBC board of Robbie Gibb, the former director of communications at No. 10, and well known for his pro-Brexit and anti-'woke' views, had been designed to keep an eye on Tim Davie who succeeded Tony Hall as BBC director-general in September 2020, another figure to disappoint Johnson. Had Dacre been appointed chair of Ofcom, Johnson would have had another handle over the BBC. The coverage of Partygate caused further explosions in No. 10: 'The PM thought that the coverage from the BBC news lacked all perspective, and was trying to pin all the blame on him personally,' says an aide.

An olive branch was extended to the BBC in early 2022. Presenter Sophie Raworth broke the stand-off on interviews with the BBC on 20 February, and was less gentle with the Prime Minister than No. 10 had hoped for. Conversation reopened between Johnson and Kuenssberg, whom he continued to think was overly critical and close to Cummings, and a sigh of relief went round No. 10 when she was replaced as BBC political editor by Chris Mason in May. Johnson wrote him a handwritten letter of congratulations and offered him an interview. Even Nadine Dorries, among Johnson's close supporters, thought he was an improvement.

Even if the BBC did have an anti-Brexit and anti-Johnson culture, as many still believe, it is hard to see that it brought him down. Without Johnson acting like he did, the BBC would not have reported as it did. No, if we are to find the cause of Johnson's fall, we will have to look elsewhere than the BBC and the other institutions.

The Establishment

Johnson, though deeply forged by his privileged upbringing at Eton and Oxford, with his finishing school the *Spectator*, liked to see himself as apart from the establishment. He had no time for its conventions and mores, which sought to restrain and criticize his free spirit to act entirely as he willed. People in uniforms who were conventional and spoke to their script bored and antagonized him. Until the war in Ukraine, he had little of the admiration most Prime Ministers have for the Army, Royal Navy and RAF, nor for the intelligence services. For whole swathes of the establishment, universities, the professions, the Conservative Party, Parliament and the judiciary, alongside business, Whitehall and the BBC, he had an airy disregard. This he shared with Cummings. Johnson bounced between treating them as a bit of a joke, seeing them as his enemy and yet seeking their approval.

Johnson's relationship with religion was as irregular as any. Baptized as Catholic thanks to the influence of his mother, he was then confirmed in the Church of England while at Eton. Johnson was the first baptized Catholic Prime Minister to inhabit No. 10. The premiership thus boasted a former Catholic (Johnson) and a future Catholic (Blair), but never a practising Catholic.

He and Carrie Symonds married at the Catholic Westminster Cathedral on 29 May 2021 on account of her tradition, and their children were baptized as Catholics. But there is no evidence that he took the vows he spoke, nor the Christian message, seriously. While respectful of those in the faith, he had no time for it himself: he didn't want to hear any moral commentary on his three marriages, multiple affairs, numerous children and the rest. Johnson was happy to borrow from the canon of religious creeds, as from political ones, but loath to take preachers seriously. Johnson didn't want to belong to any tribe. He belonged to no gang and had few friends in politics. To his wedding came just thirty guests, the maximum allowed under Covid restrictions in England at that time: beyond close family, they were mostly Carrie's friends.

The one part of the establishment he did take seriously was the monarchy. He revered the institution, seeing it as integral to his notion of British history despite previous comments intended to provoke (he once wrote in his *Telegraph* column, 'It is said that the Queen has come to love the Commonwealth, partly because it supplies her with regular cheering crowds of flag-waving piccaninnies').[21] Not often mortified, he was when, after his first audience with the Queen, he blurted out within earshot of a journalist that she had told him, 'I don't know why anyone would want your job.'[22] He listened contritely while he was told firmly that he must never discuss his private conversations with Her Majesty again. The Queen inspired another rare moment of genuine contrition when he realized how close he had been to giving her Covid, had his audience on 25 March 2020 not been switched at the last moment to a phone call. The audiences remained an anchor to him throughout his premiership: indeed, Queen Elizabeth, alert and fully engaged to the end, came the closest to being the consistent anchor of his premiership.

The Queen aside, the establishment was as ambivalent to Johnson as he was to it. To gain power, it had been advantageous to position himself on the side of the masses against the largely Remain establishment. Once in No. 10, he never built bridges to it. When needed, he was content to listen to its Etonian scions such as Ben Elliot, Charles Moore or Jacob Rees-Mogg. But only the first came close to being a 'friend', and he was equally comfortable with those brought up in more prosaic circumstances, such as Cain (till the break), Dorries and Gascoigne. Old Etonian/Oxfordian Cameron had 'chums' in and out of No 10. Johnson, neither. Prominent figures certainly stood up to him, including his two ethics advisers Alex Allan and Christopher Geidt, who were impeccably members of the establishment: the former, an ex-PPS to the Prime Minister, the latter to the Queen. So too were others, such as the academic

Peter Hennessy, co-author of the November 2021 polemic on Johnson's conduct *The Bonfire of the Decencies*,[23] and former Prime Minister John Major, who accused Johnson in February 2022 of breaking the law, eroding trust and harming Britain's standing in the world.[24]

Hennessy and Major epitomized the growing disgust that many in the establishment had for Johnson. But it is fanciful to argue that the establishment brought him down. We must again look elsewhere for the answer.

Loyal Lieutenants: Cummings, Symonds, Gove and Sunak?

Johnson never knew what he thought about Cummings. Johnson indeed never knew what he thought about most people. But particularly, not about Cummings.

Cummings and he were each other's alter egos. Johnson couldn't live with Cummings, and he couldn't live without him. They were incomplete people alone and thus became mutually dependent. Before Johnson came into his life, Cummings was best known as Gove's firebrand: too dangerous, too controversial to climb the Conservative Party's hierarchy on his own. Johnson made him for a brief time the most famous and influential political figure in the country and the realizer of his dreams, if only in part. After Johnson, Cummings shrunk, becoming again a mere commentator, To Johnson, Cummings drove his government for the first six months, its most politically successful period, and kept his premiership alive. The question for Johnson was: could he be the Colossus he had been in 2019 without Cummings? Johnson's need for Cummings had been made inevitable by his absence of a coterie or knowledge of people in the world of national politics, as well as by his own indecisiveness. So he needed Cummings, or thought he did, to make it to the top. That Faustian pact the terror memorandum had been a necessary evil. After the general election he wanted to be his own man. The Barnard Castle visit which broke in May 2020, in which he defended Cummings, was the first serious reputational black mark of the premiership. Cummings showed him no gratitude; rather destruction. 'He was backing up his intelligence and poison. We didn't realize that he'd gone rogue till late,' says an aide. Johnson's preternatural intuition made him wary of living without his lieutenant, until Carrie Symonds brought it to crisis point.

'I will spend every waking hour of my life working to bring him down,' Cummings texted one of Johnson's team in the days following his exit from No. 10 in November 2020, incensed by the briefing he believed to be coming from Symonds and then Johnson after his departure. Johnson could not have found a more poisonous adversary. Cummings had kept copious WhatsApps, emails and documents from his time at No. 10 and had a critique of the premiership that many found compelling, even if some disagreed with its self-aggrandizing and framing of his role. Cummings was a master too at playing the media, honed when he oversaw communications for Gove at Education. He knew exactly who in the press and broadcasting to approach with any particular story. They lapped it up – and who can blame them? Never had an adviser to a Prime Minister gone so off-message like this. After the initial briefings back and forth upon Cummings' resignation, six months after there was a second major exchange, his 1,000-word blog post in April 2021 responding to No. 10's accusations of leaking.[25] Johnson's attempt to counter it provoked concern among aides that Cummings had enough 'kompromat' to go on and 'destroy'

Johnson.[26] The Joint Parliamentary Committee inquiry into the pandemic a month later, into Partygate in 2022 and into Covid in 2023 were manna from heaven, the perfect opportunities to keep himself, and Johnson's failings, centre-stage.

Did Cummings, then, bring down Johnson? The City Hall team – Lister, Walden and Harri – believe he did by bringing in a group of radicals led by him and Cain who were not in tune with Johnson personally nor with his ambitions. 'They were polar opposites to Boris, and they brought out the worst in him,' says one. Carrie and her friends think Cummings was responsible and cannot forgive him for the personal and repeated attacks on her. Some officials within No. 10 believe he was: 'His systematic hand grenades were incredibly effective and made the Prime Minister's job much more difficult. They were fundamentally the catalyst for the fall,' says one. The Barclay team in 2022 did too, not least for estranging Tory MPs. 'The problems dated back to Cummings for forbidding Boris to talk to his MPs. It really killed him,' says Andrew Griffith.[27]

Cummings certainly contributed to the informal and lawless culture that permitted the lockdown gatherings to happen, and to the habit that became ingrained of automatically denying the truth when anything uncomfortable came up. The message given to the building by the handling of Barnard Castle and Cummings' own refusal to resign for a patent breach of restrictions was clear: No. 10 staff were somehow in their own category, one the rules did not apply to. The message to Johnson, who felt utterly betrayed by Cummings' attacks, was just as devastating: never place too much trust in one person. From then on the Prime Minister would never allow any single adviser to get to the level of power from which they could effectively direct No. 10; court politics were dialled up to 11, with each faction played off against another to keep them in thrall to the self-described 'f**king king around here'.

But Cummings cannot be held responsible for the poor conduct and judgement of others. Stories about the lockdown events had come out without him, as had accounts of Johnson's inadequate leadership, his inability to win over MPs, his undermining of aides. Cummings might have wanted to kill off Johnson, but he merely accelerated the end of the premiership, nothing more. The direction of travel was locked in.

Did Carrie hasten his fall, as his City Hall team believe? Johnson needed her, or thought he did, to make it to the summit. Her arrival on the scene in 2018 provided him with the confidence to crank up for the top job, which he had the wit to realize in his mind (if not heart) was an almighty step up. In the same way, he needed Cummings to give him the intellectual confidence to perform once at the top. He then needed Carrie to provide him cover against Cummings, and Cummings to provide him cover against Carrie. They were a strange trio, bound together by love and hate. Symonds came to hate Cummings, Cummings to hate Johnson, and Johnson to hate having to choose between them. Cummings' vitriol against her was quite unlike any previous relationship between a Prime Minister's spouse and their chief adviser.

Carrie is a highly intelligent and accomplished woman. She brought much to Johnson besides greater confidence to do the job. She connected him to the aspirations of younger voters, and to causes and debates with which he was unfamiliar. She brought him happiness and joy in their partnership and two children, Wilfred, born in 2020, and Romy, born in 2021, and provided him with a home life and love which he sought. But she was not an unmitigated joy for Johnson. Her distrust of Cummings and Cain caused massive instability within the system, even if it was best for Johnson that they left. She made an avowed enemy of one of Johnson's few political rocks, Lynton Crosby, a frequent source of anguish to him. Her favoured causes, including LGBTQ issues, animal welfare and the environment, were not those of Johnson's right-wing MPs, the *Telegraph* or indeed of several in the building, including Mirza. Her periodic brusqueness and desire to exert influence on appointments upset Johnson's party, managers and figures in No. 10: ultimately, it was her backing of Allegra Stratton that precipitated the big walkout. Her friendship and patronage of a bevy of young aides contributed significantly to the heavily dysfunctional relationship with the chiefs of staff Johnson had appointed to run his second and third teams, Rosenfield and Barclay. Other actions she took too were not from the usual playbook of spouses to the Prime Minister, including regular leaking and hosting social events in the upstairs flat with her own clique.[28] In the final weeks of the premiership before his resignation, Johnson implored *The Times* to take down a story about an embryonic plan to hire her as his chief of staff when Foreign Secretary, and that the two had been caught in his office in a compromising position.[29] They both knew it was true.

One of the prices of being a spouse to the Prime Minister is that the relationship for the duration is not, and perhaps never can be, equal. Had Johnson understood the job and responsibilities of being Prime Minister better, he would have known this. For a young, determined, politically charged individual such as Symonds there would always be issues of interest where she sought to influence her partner. But if she made mistakes in her advice to Johnson, the blame must fall on the Prime Minister for acting upon them. Throughout the premiership he confided to close associates that he was reluctant to challenge her: 'My mental health will not stand it,' he confessed to an aide, ever desperate to avoid confrontation and reprimands from those around him. He was not so innocent; his wife was as much a shield for Johnson as a thorn, and he would not hesitate to deflect blame upon her for decisions he knew to be unpopular with others. Playing upstairs off against downstairs was how he prevented either from wielding too much influence. To any extent that Carrie was more liability than asset, Johnson alone was to blame. But he didn't blame her for the downfall, unlike those who knew him of old like Crosby, and his right-wing supporters repelled by her progressive views. But not him, and he was right not to do so.

Johnson's second wife Marina Wheeler was a much-vaunted 'what if' among those who knew Johnson well. A formidable intellect, she became a respected barrister, specializing in public law. Composed and circumspect, she had her own views, but was reticent about advancing them. She was politically savvy too, unsurprisingly perhaps being the daughter of veteran BBC journalist Charles Wheeler. Johnson's affair with Carrie Symonds was the final straw for her, and he was unable to persuade her to return to him. They issued a joint statement in September 2018, saying that after twenty-five years of marriage, they were to separate. Johnson agonized about his decision, not least after she announced the following year that she had been diagnosed with cancer, and with their four children very obviously unhappy with their father.

She had provided in their marriage precisely the judgement and wisdom for which he was often so wanting in No. 10. 'She would have made all the difference. He still would have gone around chasing other women, but she'd have grounded him,' says a friend. She provided a steady income too from her work as a barrister: ever after, he was in dire need of money, to the anxiety of his minders and interest of the intelligence services. Her absence can be compared to the effect of the loss of another formidable woman on would-be Tory leader R.A. Butler, also given to self-indulgence. When his wife Sydney Courtauld died in December 1954, he lost a critical friend who stood up to him.[30] After Johnson parted from Marina, he was always searching for that voice.

What, then, of Gove, the final figure of the four *bestiae magnae* to strut through the long 2010s decade? Crosby was one of many voices in Johnson's ear telling him that Gove was no good and was just looking for the moment to bring him down, that he had thwarted him in 2016, was angry to have been beaten by him in 2019, and waiting. 'I could never understand what the hold was that Michael had over Boris,' says a close confidant. It contributed to another agonizing split in Johnson's head: he knew Gove was the best he had in the Cabinet and he had to use him, but could he ever trust him? He knew too how closely Gove had worked with Cummings at Education and during the referendum campaign: were they still operating in league to do him down? Had they indeed been working against him all along, content to use him to get Brexit done, then *finito*?

Gove certainly had no illusions about Johnson, and never truly changed his mind from his damning 2016 verdict that he 'cannot provide the leadership or build the team for the task ahead'.[31] But he believed in Brexit, beating Covid and in levelling up, the causes he championed. He loved being an influential minister, and he would have deplored being on the backbenches again as he had been under May from 2016 to 2017, which is where he would have returned to if he didn't serve under Johnson. He saw himself as Cyrano to Johnson's Christian in Edmond Rostand's play, writing the words to be mouthed by a figurehead. 'Michael knew that he never had it in him to achieve his dream of becoming Prime Minister, so contented himself with being the power behind the throne to a show-and-tell puppet,' says an insider. When Cummings, who shared Gove's opinion of Johnson, held sway in the first fifteen months, Gove had an ally at the heart of the machine. When Cummings stormed off, his acolytes, who were equally close to Symonds, glided seamlessly into central positions in the second (Finn, Newman, Cook) and third (Finn) leadership teams.

Gove was wary too, as he told us when we were writing *May at 10*, of doing anything to be seen as bringing down another Prime Minister, as he had with Cameron. Hence his ultra-loyalty to May; hence too his loyalty to his new boss. 'I made it a point of principle not to talk to Dom while Boris was Prime Minister to avoid anyone misconstruing those encounters,' he says.[32] Johnson himself felt under no such compunction about beating him in the competition to be the most regicidal. He had helped bring down Cameron, had helped bring down May, and was inadvertently about to bring down a third Prime Minister. His ministerial colleagues respected but did not warm to Gove: they saw him using levelling up as a device to extend his tentacles across the departments, and they didn't appreciate it. Given the fondness of Johnson for drawing comparisons between his team and that of Blair, Gove was the Peter Mandelson of his premiership.

The underlying tension between both men exploded in their heated conversations as Johnson's power was crumbling on 6 July, as discussed later.[33] Our verdict is that Gove had both underpinned and undermined Johnson's premiership. His tacit encouragement of the second and third rival teams at No. 10 made the jobs of the successive chiefs of staff, Rosenfield and Barclay, far more difficult. But Gove ultimately was not the reason Johnson fell.

Which brings us to the final figure blamed for the downfall, and here we get closer. In his last days before his resignation and in his first weeks out of office, Johnson convinced himself that he had been brought down by Sunak. It became almost an obsession, enhanced by Johnson's bitterness that his Chancellor gave him no warning of his resignation on 5 July.

Sunak had been on a journey over his two and a half years as Chancellor. His late support for Johnson in the July 2019 leadership election was not without reservation, but he knew he owed him a great debt for his appointment to Chief Secretary that month, and to Chancellor the following February. The first cracks in their relationship appeared in the summer of 2020, with Sunak's Treasury team concerned about negative stories in the press. 'Small bits started appearing chipping away at Rishi. Boris we assumed didn't like him being so popular over furlough. He was jealous,' says a Sunak aide. Sunak, though, remained meticulously polite to Johnson all the way through, unlike Hammond (Chancellor from 2016 to 2019) who did not conceal his frustration at May's uncertain grasp of numbers. Lockdown sparked further tension once Johnson became a keen advocate. Cummings' departure in November 2020 destabilized the No. 10–Treasury axis further. 'All close to Dom – and that included Rishi – became targets once the war started,' says the aide.

Rosenfield's arrival in December 2020 was the chance for a reset. On his first day, Rosenfield told Sunak, 'When I was PPS to the Chancellor, I saw two very different relationships: Osborne with Cameron, and Darling with Brown. The fallout from the latter was the most corrosive I've seen.' The goal, he said, was the former. In an effort to resolve the increasingly glaring misalignment between Prime Minister and Chancellor over policy and politics, they endeavoured to meet over breakfast each month. It was a brave effort to keep the relationship on the rails, but the chemistry between Rosenfield and Sunak was never right: 'It was weird to hear him speaking down to the Chancellor,' says a No. 10 aide.

Tensions mounted over 2021. According to one of Sunak's team, 'The Prime Minister was pitting Cabinet ministers deliberately against the Treasury, egging them on and asking them "what's your biggest idea?" And then telling them "get on with it", regardless of how we would finance them.' Nothing did more damage to their relationship than Sunak's perception of Johnson's financial incontinence and flip-flopping of decisions. 'Watch Sunak carefully,' Johnson was warned throughout 2021 by his advisers. He brushed such cautions aside. 'Of course Rishi wants my job! Every top-ranked Chancellor wants to be Prime Minister. That's what they do,' he told staff.

Johnson's team were taking no chances, even if their principal was turning a blind eye. 'You know Rishi is on manoeuvres,' Wallace periodically whispered in Johnson's ear. He discounted the notion. 'You have one fatal weakness, your judgement of people,' Wallace retorted. Chief Whip Mark Spencer was giving Johnson the same warnings. June and July 2021, he says, just eighteen months after the landslide, was when Johnson's team woke up to would-be challengers testing the water. 'Lots of rumours started coming in that Rishi was talking to people, and Liz was holding court at her club at 5 Hertford Street,' says Spencer.[34] As the year went on they were watching Jeremy Hunt too, who 'was being pleasant with people and asking them in for chats', and Penny Mordaunt 'doing a lot of drinks, events and schmoozing'. Concerns reached a high point at the party conference in October, the Johnson and Sunak camps in a virtual standoff. Truss's and Sunak's teams were eyeing each other's moves warily too. Kwasi Kwarteng was promoting Truss, who had a new spring in her step now she was Foreign Secretary, while anti-lockdown hardliner Mark Harper was building support in a subtler way for Sunak.

Having ducked the opportunity to reshuffle him out of the Treasury in September, Johnson realized he had no other recourse but to hug his Chancellor close, with regular confidential meetings that autumn on Sunday mornings in No. 10. Cordiality ruled on the surface, but beneath it lurked Sunak's continuing unhappiness at Johnson's 'spend, spend, spend' approach and total disregard for any inflationary consequences, while 'Boris felt Rishi was trying to bamboozle him with data, and find ways to get around him', according to an aide. Peak irritation came over Johnson's plans for a new national yacht, with a £250 million price tag, and his hope to see a bridge or tunnel to Northern Ireland. To Sunak, with the economy struggling to regain momentum after Covid, both schemes were madness.

Even though the relationship dived in the autumn over paying for education, recovery, social care, Net Zero and the NIC increase, culminating in the Spending Review confrontation, it was still salvageable until the New Year. The press was briefed that 'the Prime Minister and Chancellor are speaking every day' (always a sign there are problems), and that any disagreements were nothing compared to the bad blood of Brown's, Darling's or Hammond's relationships with their respective PMs (not reassuring comparisons).[35] At the 'away day' at No. 10 on levelling up on 11 November, a series of ministers thanked Sunak for his help with funding in their constituencies. Reports soon after filtered into No. 10 of Sunak having breakfast with Cabinet ministers, sounding them out for a possible bid.

To Sunak, it was Johnson's handling of Partygate which offended his sense of propriety and took him to the brink. From here to the end, the relationship was toxic. No. 10 had no doubt where the leaks were coming from: 'A lot of the Partygate leaks came from Rishi and his team. We regularly read stories in the press fed by their side,' says a No. 10 aide. Sunak's statement in February after Johnson's comments to Keir Starmer about Jimmy Savile, that 'I wouldn't have said it', raised eyebrows in No. 10. Then came the leaking in early April of Akshata Murty (Sunak's wife) claiming non-dom status, which caused days of bad headlines. 'We had a strong suspicion that No. 10 had leaked it. But Rishi said, "It doesn't matter. We can't prove No. 10 did it, and even if we could, it won't fix the problem,"' according to a Treasury aide.

Johnson's eye turned to Cummings' relationship with Sunak. Crosby was among the first warning him that his senior adviser had 'changed sides, mate, the moment he walked out of No. 10'. Sunak was then a suspicious omission from Cummings' critique presented to the Coronavirus: Lessons Learned inquiry in May 2021, despite his lead role in delaying the second lockdown and pursuing a poor policy which he would ordinarily rail against. 'I didn't pay huge attention to eat out to help out,' he said, placing the blame instead on the Prime Minister's 'general strategy' rather than the poor judgement of the Chancellor.[36] The committee appearance set rumours abuzz that Cummings was supporting Sunak against the Prime Minister and angling for a job. Worse still to No. 10 was the news that 'Levido is working with Cummings behind the scenes on the Sunak cause', recalls another aide. His former economics adviser Liam Booth-Smith was working with Cummings and Levido too, he was told. Treasury aides deny that Sunak, like Gove, had any contact with Cummings: 'Dom thought a bunch of people would be a better PM, not just Rishi. They genuinely haven't seen each other since the day he left,' one said shortly before Sunak became Prime Minister.

But it was Dougie Smith operating in the building under his very nose who Johnson didn't spot. 'He has more capability than Dom who's just working at a distance banging away at his social media. But Dougie is right at the heart. He's not on your side,' an old friend warned him. Johnson was reminded that Smith had helped Sunak get selected as candidate for the safe seat of Richmond, previously held by William Hague in October 2014, and a position at the Policy Exchange think tank the same year. That his voice had been decisive in bringing in Cummings in July 2019. Johnson was starting to question where Smith's loyalties lay. Still, he was reluctant to believe it. Not until Smith's verbal assault on him in February 2022 after Mirza's resignation did Johnson fully realize what was happening. 'I'm going to rescind his No. 10 pass and stop him coming into the building ever again,' Johnson declared, following news of Dowden's resignation which he blamed on Smith. But, hours later, he changed his mind completely. '*What* does this man have on Boris?' some close to him asked.

By spring 2022, 'Sunak had concluded, "This guy next door is an absolute joke",' as a senior Conservative put it. He had totally given up on him. 'Sunak realized that if he didn't go for Boris mid-premiership, after twelve years of Conservative government, he would leave it too late, and he'd never be Prime Minister,' says a Johnson loyalist. Sunak's problem was this – when to jump? Gavin Williamson, earmarked as a possible Chief Whip in a Sunak administration, was one of those he consulted after the non-dom crisis blew up. 'You are damaged,' Williamson told him, 'so your best hope is for Johnson to last another few months so you can repair it. At present, you will make it to the final two, but you will lose in the country. Every bit of your personal interest involves Johnson lasting longer.'[37] Williamson's form in helping make May and Johnson Prime Minister made him a go-to man among leadership contenders. When he was summoned to Truss's room in the House of Commons to talk about Somaliland, claiming she knew little about it, he found a bottle of wine and two glasses awaiting a discussion on whether he would help her become Prime Minister.

Both Truss and Sunak wanted Johnson gone, and to succeed themselves. Sunak took the hit from Johnson's team. He did more to bring about the downfall than her; but he was not ultimately the assassin.

The World Starts Collapsing: Covid, Economy, Ukraine

Covid, strangely, is not a factor mentioned much by Johnson or his acolytes to explain the downfall. Yet it caused him great harm coming before his victory honeymoon was even over. It divided an already fractured Conservative Party even further: *any* course of action Johnson decided would have alienated large numbers of his MPs. Parliament working from home during lockdown was, to Eddie Lister, 'the biggest mistake that Boris made'.[38] Initially between thirty and forty MPs were unhappy about it, but in November 2020, the Covid Recovery Group (CRG) was formed with seventy MPs in support, with the Remain-voting former Chief Whip Mark Harper in the chair, and Steve Baker, veteran pro-Brexit campaigner and scourge of Theresa May, as deputy chair. It pressed for alternative advice to government scientists on SAGE, and for the publication of a full analysis of the economic and health costs of lockdown. Worse news still for Johnson was that, prominent among lockdown sceptics, was the one man no PM wants to cross, clerk to the jury which pronounces on your life or death, 1922 Committee Chair Graham Brady. Whips grew very bitter about him: 'He clearly didn't like lockdown, but his ego was bruised because he wasn't offered a Cabinet post. He wasn't good news at all for us,' says a whip. Brady was a formidable adversary: 'Everyone would have understood if elderly and ill MPs had been advised to stay away,' he says. 'But it felt like an attempt to make the whole of Parliament disappear, at exactly the time when the government was imposing the most extreme restrictions on the liberty of British citizens – precisely the time when the House of Commons was needed most.'[39]

Lockdown proved a nightmare for the whips. 'I couldn't get my team patrolling the tearooms and bars, hoovering up worries, I couldn't get wobbly MPs in front of ministers face-to-face, we couldn't really know what was being said on the WhatsApp groups or Twitter DMs,' says Spencer.[40] The damage was felt particularly on the large 2019 intake of 107 MPs, nearly all new to Parliament with more than the usual number of mavericks, who were never properly inducted in its ways.[41] Though he had never been one to frequent the tearooms, a closed Parliament denied Johnson deployment of his greatest asset, his personal charm. He couldn't explain to his MPs in person why he was having to lock down the country. Anger focused on Johnson and No. 10, not helped in Brady's opinion by Cummings' 'total disdain' towards MPs. To Brady, as to many members of the CRG, the scientists were 'manipulating the evidence to scare people to continue lockdown by raising public anxiety'.[42]

CRG MPs were of the same mind as the *Telegraph*, which month after month ran a relentless and damaging campaign against lockdown. Any sympathy towards Johnson for being so ill with Covid in April was then rapidly eroded by his retaining Cummings after the Barnard Castle visit in May. Anger peaked again after the Christmas 2020 lockdown and U-turn. Covid cleaved Cabinet down the middle too: it is indicative that the most serious Cabinet debate in the premiership, in December 2021, was on whether to have another lockdown. Ministers were also divided over how to respond to the direct costs of Covid, estimated to be £400 billion, which wrenched money away from what they sought to do in their departments. 'If he had been allowed to spend the £400 billion blown on Covid building bridges, roads, rails, nuclear power stations, schools and hospitals he'd have been viewed more as Roosevelt,' writes Guto Harri.[43]

Covid cost Johnson the first year of his premiership too when his political capital was at its highest. Covid, and Johnson's response to it, certainly didn't help his premiership. But it didn't bring him down. The problems that brought him down were all present before Covid arrived on British shores. The factionalization and ill-discipline within the party had already been exposed and deepened by Brexit before Covid, not least by Johnson stoking the fires of rebellion. New MPs may not have been house trained, but the independently minded, pro-Brexit, anti-'woke' candidates selected in newly won battlegrounds were never likely to be.

Prime ministerial success is defined by their response to external shocks. Thatcher's standing was boosted by her response to the Falklands invasion and the collapse of communism, as Brown's was by his actions during the financial crisis; Blair's standing was damaged by the Iraq War, and Major by the run on the pound after 'Black Wednesday'. Johnson falls in the latter camp in his response to the deteriorating economic position of Britain, to which Brexit was a contributory factor. The UK's rate of inflation jumped to 10.1 per cent in July 2022, the month he resigned, a forty-year high, and the UK's recovery after Covid was the slowest in the G7.[44] Frustration that Johnson was not doing more to drive growth after Covid damaged him badly, and contributed to the decline in the polls from June 2021. Johnson was increasingly aware of the problem, tried to address it himself, and in his final weeks before resignation tried to give economic growth a major shove. The war in Ukraine contributed to the cost of living crisis which overshadowed his final months. In contrast to his other external crises, he turned it in his favour by providing the strongest and most confident example of personal leadership of his entire premiership. For all the plaudits he received, and the rallying of his MPs and the Conservative press around him, the public had grown tired of his flaws and it did little to arrest the decline in the polls. Ukraine gave a glimpse of what the premiership might have been, rather than the lifeline to save it.

The Mission Starts Collapsing: Agenda, Scandals, MPs

A Prime Minister can survive any shock, policy failure, scandal and reversal, as long as their MPs want them to remain and Cabinet continues to have confidence in them. Prime Ministers only continue in office on their sufferance. Savvy PMs know this and hug their MPs and Cabinets close. Churchill had been evicted in 1945 at a general election; if Johnson had to fall, he reasoned, that would be his fate. He would have done better to reflect on Lloyd George's fall instead. Even three-time election winners Thatcher and Blair were eased out after losing the support of their MPs and Cabinet.

We are now moving to the heart of why Johnson fell.

Prime Ministers need a rallying cry around which to unite their party. Before the general election, it was Brexit and Corbyn. The Conservative manifesto, conceived with the electorate in mind and shaped by the electorate, had the sole goal of winning the general election. 'This will be interesting,' Sedwill mused the day after the victory. The aide to whom he said it recalls, 'The realization slowly dawned on us that it was an undeliverable manifesto – promising high spending and low tax, appealing to traditional Tory seats and the Red Wall. It wouldn't work.' 'The manifesto was absolute bollocks,' another insider puts it more bluntly. No leader can set off on a journey with their team if they have no clear destination. Even his team couldn't agree what it was about. 'If it had one uniting theme, it was using Brexit to transform the country, but it was full of classic Johnsonisms based on who he has just been talking to,' says David Canzini, deputy chief of staff under Barclay.[45] This was a far cry from the vision set out by Rachel Wolf described in Chapter 3. From the very genesis of the new government, lacking an agreed roadmap for the five years ahead, it gave a green light to different individuals and factions to shout out what the destination was. Mayhem followed as everyone tried grabbing the steering wheel to yank the Johnson battle bus in one direction, then another, then another.

Not since Macmillan was Prime Minister (1957–63) was there so much confusion over what the party stood for. It was both Johnson's luck and misfortune to be the leader at a time when the Conservatives were in transition – though to where, they knew not. Did it favour low tax and pared-back spending, as Truss and Kwarteng wanted, or larger spending and state, as Johnson himself favoured? Being libertarian and sceptical about the state's role in

Covid, as Sunak, Shapps and Rees-Mogg were, or interventionist as were Gove and Hancock? Socially conservative, as Patel, Braverman and Badenoch among Cabinet, and Mirza and Smith in No. 10 favoured, or progressive as Carrie and her set wanted? A hard Brexit as Raab and Frost demanded, or more alignment with the EU, as Javid and departed ministers Morgan, Rudd and Smith advocated? The absence of Conservative scripture had helped Johnson, with his own contradictory and messy ideas, ascend to the top. It was somewhat less helpful when attempting to govern.

With no clarity on the route, when the problems that afflict all premierships – policy reversals, scandals, resignations, economic turbulence – appeared like forest fires through the windscreen, they forced the Johnson bus to deviate or double back till eventually it veered totally out of control off the cliff, with Johnson at the wheel screaming wildly as it dived headlong into the sea, 'What the hell is going on?'

The 2019 victory was where many of Johnson's problems started. While it would be going too far to say that the landslide itself was 'absolute bollocks', it created a dangerous impression in the minds of Johnson and others that he himself had won the victory, and that it put enough credit in the bank to see him through for the next five years at least. Johnson never fully accepted that he was only one factor in the victory, alongside Brexit and Corbyn, and the least important of the three at that. It was foundational to his beliefs and winning brand that it was a personal mandate. But the 365 Conservative MPs were never remotely a coherent force, and certainly not united behind him after the sheen of the win wore off. On top of ideological divisions came personal factions and egos. At least three groups never liked Johnson: those who blamed him for the fall of May and thought him unsuitable for office, Remainers who couldn't forgive him for Brexit, and the ultras, many in the ERG who claimed that he was never a true Conservative in belief or act. One senior Tory put the number at just shy of a hundred 'who were appalled to have Johnson as leader, and who went underground after the election victory, biding their time'. To them can be added a group of some twenty-five former ministers and those he was never going to appoint to a job. Johnson never accepted that the party had not voted for him as a leader in July 2019 because they loved him, but because, in the wake of the May 2019 European elections with a 9 per cent vote nationally, MPs were desperate for someone who could win. It was a contractual relationship, in which his side of the bargain was to keep the party ahead in the opinion polls. Was it entitlement or ignorance on his part? Both. The price of Johnson maintaining his supreme self-confidence was to buy into his own myth, and disregard any evidence to the contrary.

Eurosceptics were disappointed that Johnson wasn't delivering the Brexit dream, and expected more spoils from Johnson now they were in the promised land. Iain Duncan Smith, the former party leader, was upset that no proper use was found for him, as were his supporters who blamed Cummings and Gove for blocking him. Bernard Jenkin had never liked Johnson. His rival for the backing of the faction in 2016–18, David Davis, was left out in the cold. John Redwood had jobs constantly dangled in front of him, only to disappear. He knew better than most the difficulties of holding long-serving governments together: it was he who challenged John Major for the leadership in 1995.

Early harbingers of trouble came in the opposition to Huawei from the China Research Group, set up by Tory MPs, and NIMBY MPs resisting his planning reforms. Long before the Covid Recovery Group began to ply its wares, 'The factions, the briefing, the leaking, the rebellious attitude from so many MPs was evident,' says a No. 10 aide. The message many MPs felt they received from No. 10 was: 'well done, chums, now bugger off', as a party apparatchik puts it.

Corbyn's replacement by Starmer in April 2020 gave the opportunity for Johnson to rally the party around a new threat. Johnson had known Starmer from Mayor days and considered him far more left-wing than popularly portrayed. In his view, 'Starmer was Corbyn without the Jew-hating bit, who did little more than purge Momentum from Labour HQ and party committees and nothing radical like Blair and Brown had done after 1994,' says Canzini.[46] But Johnson never managed to portray him as a figure to fear, least of all as they agreed broadly on how to respond to Covid, that Britain would not be going back into the EU and that levelling up disadvantaged areas was a priority.

Johnson had lost ground with his MPs since the Barnard Castle debacle. But 'it was the Owen Paterson affair in late 2021 that was the start of serious discontent among colleagues', says Brady. 'MPs disliked what they saw as a lack of clarity and lack of candour from No. 10. Many thought they had been whipped to vote against their instincts.'[47] Brady, the barometer keeper of discontent, was the one person who knew how many letters from MPs demanding a confidence vote in the Prime Minister had been submitted: fifty-four MPs were required before a vote could be triggered. Brady kept a careful tally in his head, with the letters in a safe in his office. He revelled in the mystery.

In this, the first full-on scandal since the general election, Johnson sought to defend Paterson, an MP who was receiving strong support from the right-wing of the party and press after being found in breach of advocacy rules by the Parliamentary Commissioner for Standards in October 2021. Paterson resolutely refused to apologize. The Standards Committee called for him to be suspended for thirty days, which could have triggered a recall petition in his North Shropshire constituency. Johnson's attempt to find a way though by replacing the existing disciplinary system for MPs by a new, Tory-majority committee was whipped through the House to the resentment of many Conservative MPs, only to U-turn a day later when Labour said they'd boycott the new system. Johnson claimed he had been motivated by sympathy for Paterson who had recently lost his wife Rose to suicide, which was undoubtedly true; but a desire to placate the right had been the more powerful motive. He had again rushed headlong to defend, without examining the evidence properly. Did his own dubious financial affairs mean he was reluctant to condemn Paterson, people asked? The details of the affair have been exhaustively written up.[48] Our concern is rather the impact on Johnson and his handling of it, which sparked two weeks of intense focus on paid lobbying and other secondary employment by MPs, and accusations of sleaze and incompetence. 'We were completely trapped because of Paterson's refusal to apologize,' says Spencer, though he adds, 'The skates were already under the premiership. The problems went back to 2019.'[49] 'Incredibly damaging and very badly handled. It was so blatant that Boris was pandering to the right', was the verdict of Spencer's predecessor bar one as Chief Whip, Williamson.[50] 'The Paterson affair was the moment it all went wrong, because it became impossible after it for No. 10 to claim any moral high ground again,' says an official in the building. Within No. 10, it brought to the fore divisions between opponents and defenders of Dan Rosenfield. 'It raised concerns, rumbling under the surface since I joined, about why this non-political guy was running No. 10,' he says. MPs, many of whom Johnson had never met and who didn't know the patrician Paterson from Adam, blamed him and Mark Spencer. Further turbulence and accusations of Tory sleaze came from the focus the affair put on Tory MPs' second jobs, with former Attorney General Geoffrey Cox in the spotlight. The episode taught Johnson nothing about the need for candour and evidence when handling scandals. Over Paterson, he again clung to his 'brazen it out: no surrender to the media' mantra.

With Starmer's Labour set to overtake the Conservatives in the polls in November, Johnson needed to ensure there were no more scandals. But three weeks later, on 30 November, Pippa Crerar published her first Partygate story and ten days afterwards a video was leaked showing Press Secretary Allegra Stratton making light of concerns about lockdown parties. On 17 December, Simon Case recused himself from investigating them after a story broke that he attended one in his own office, and the following day, Sue Gray was named to lead the investigation. The story did not go away after Christmas, as No. 10 hoped, and on 25 January, the Metropolitan Police launched 'Operation Hillman' to investigate. Fixed penalty notices were handed out in March and April, including for Johnson, Carrie and Sunak. Investigations finally came to an end with the Met concluding its operation on 19 May with fixed penalty notices handed out to eighty-three individuals, and, a week later, with the final Sue Gray report.

The impact on opinion polls was very clear. Labour moved ahead of the Conservatives in December 2021, with the gulf growing throughout January, and remaining wide till Johnson's resignation in July. News stories following week after week about parties had a major effect, the whole affair showing Johnson at his worst. No attempt to establish the truth himself, no leadership from the front, and blaming others for the events themselves and for No. 10's public response to the crisis. 'Get your chief of staff immediately to get every diary, every meeting, every event, every CCTV, and collate exactly what happened. Only when you're totally clear will you be able to fix it,' Crosby said down the phone to him from Australia as the story was first breaking.[51] Johnson didn't listen. A better leader would have gone straight to the House of Commons and made a statement to say he was gripping the issue himself. He might have said that, while he didn't attend most of the events himself, his staff who did were working throughout Covid under uniquely testing conditions in the building and at the very limit of their endurance, that he understood the public's concerns, and he would put all the facts once he'd established them out in the open, with a paper in the House of Commons library providing all the details.

But that wasn't the leader Johnson was.

The Prime Minister sets the culture and tone for the government, never more so than within No. 10 itself. An instinctive rule-breaker, and indeed rule-denier himself, those around him naturally picked up his style. '"F**k off, establishment. We don't play by the rules", was the dominant atmosphere from Dom,' says an aide. But it was Johnson who licensed Cummings and set the tone himself. Because he had banished rule-minded figures from No. 10 and appointed those who found it difficult to stand up to him, there was no one to say 'we have to be the absolute model of what we're enforcing on others'. Nor did he insist on the rules being strictly enforced in the No. 10 flat. Once the first post-lockdown gatherings had been tolerated in the summer of 2020, the precedent had been set. 'No leader was standing up to draw a line,' says an aide. The response was bungled, with the weak shouldering the blame rather than the two leaders, himself and Case. Longer-serving staff look back to the Ed Llewellyn and Gavin Barwell regimes as chiefs of staff in the 2010s, or to Gus O'Donnell and Jeremy Heywood as Cabinet Secretaries, and say that they would have handled it properly, and that is no doubt true. So would Theresa May as PM.

Why did Johnson act as he did? Because, in the words of a friend, 'he didn't think it was such a big deal. I don't think he wanted to realize how bad it was till the end.' A scandal had erupted in 1922 when it became known that Lloyd George had awarded honours and titles to rich businessmen in return for cash via intermediary Maundy Gregory. Like Lloyd George exactly a hundred years before, his instinct was deny and dodge. Like Lloyd George too, he left a host of very angry and disillusioned people in his wake. If a mark of an admirable leader is to take responsibility, Johnson massively failed.

The MPs speak: May to 6 June

Disapproval was felt strongly in the May 2022 local elections, in which the Conservatives lost 487 seats across the country. Had it been a general election, Labour would have won with 35 per cent of the vote to the Conservatives with 30 per cent. The number of no-confidence letters had been quite low up to Partygate in fact, but stories about events in No. 10 caused a huge surge of unhappy colleagues, says Brady.[52] Johnson's contractual relationship with the Conservative Party was being probed. 'Johnson's dishonesty and mishandling upset people so badly,' says a senior Tory. 'The sheer volume of letters from readers complaining about his conduct was what persuaded the *Telegraph* to move away from Johnson,' says one of its senior staff.

A poll found that party support had dropped to 2005 levels in the wake of the scandal, its projections showing that in a general election, fifty-five of the sixty-five Red Wall constituencies would be lost, and seventy of the 107 Conservative seats won in 2019.[53] Reports were circulating in January that the number of letters handed in had reached thirty,[54] but Brady advises caution, pointing out cryptically that 'you have to be careful with MPs saying sometimes they were submitting letters when they hadn't'.[55]

The outbreak of war in Ukraine gave Johnson a period of grace. Veteran MP Roger Gale was seen as the bellwether. On 17 December, he was the first MP to confirm in public that he had submitted a letter of no confidence to Brady. But on 17 March, to the absolute delight of No. 10, he tweeted that, in the light of the Ukraine invasion, 'Is now the time to change our leader? No it isn't.' Gale pointedly refused, though, to say whether he had actually withdrawn his letter.[56] 'We had come through Paterson, through Partygate, the Gray report, we thought we might be in the clear,' says a Johnson aide.

By May, however, Brady was noticing that the mood among MPs was changing again. 'MPs started to say that the war had come down the agenda, there was no third world war, no nuclear war, no British troops involved, that the crisis was serious but not acute, and a critical spotlight was back again on Johnson.'[57] A U-turn on a windfall tax on oil and gas companies that month provoked an explosion of anger at yet another climb-down. The *Evening Standard* totted up forty-eight government U-turns since May 2020.[58] The number of letters started to rise again in late May.

The critical figure of fifty-four was reached during the Queen's Platinum Jubilee ten days later. Brady waited till the final day, Sunday 5 June, before calling Johnson at noon to say, 'Prime Minister, the numbers have been reached.' Johnson left Downing Street soon after for the Platinum Jubilee concert. 'Haven't told a soul, but Brady's just told me he's got the numbers,' he whispered to an aide before he left. Johnson then had to spend two and a half hours at the rock concert outside Buckingham Palace on his own with television cameras periodically probing him pretending all was well, listening to Duran Duran, Rod Stewart and Queen. 'I don't think he enjoyed the concert much: Keith Richards is more his thing,' says an aide.

When he eventually returned to Downing Street, he assembled his team in the flat to strategize how to handle the vote the following day. He threw out various lines, including 'Stick with me, and we will win the next general election. Ditch me, and it will be a whole world of hell.' Not Cicero exactly. His political team were reconciled to a big vote against. 'Two hundred for you will be OK,' one of them said. 'I tell you, a majority of one will be enough for me,' Johnson replied defiantly.

To the surprise of many across Westminster, No. 10 didn't leap into action with a tightly monitored rota of loyalists to lobby MPs. There was none of the urgency that a predecessor team had shown when May faced a confidence vote in December 2018. Seasoned MPs read the absence of fervour as significant. Both warring teams in No. 10 blamed each other: 'They refused to share their information with us,' says one group; 'They were f**king useless and didn't know what they were doing,' responds the other. Not even in his hour of greatest need could the No. 10 team Johnson selected rally together in concerted effort. He was incapable of instilling that harmony.

Monday 6 June was the day of reckoning. Two hours before voting opened, Johnson addressed the 1922 Committee, pleading for his future. 'We have to stop talking about ourselves and start addressing people in the country – we need to deliver and unite. You all know how incredible we can be when we are united. You are the people in this room who won the biggest election victory for forty years under my leadership.' It was not his finest performance. When asked about attending farewell events during lockdown, incomprehension was evident when he said he would 'do it again'. MPs then went off to vote on the simple question on the ballot paper: 'I have confidence in Boris Johnson as leader of the Conservative Party.'

Brady texted the results to Johnson shortly before they were declared in public: 'My executive thought it was a courtesy to let the Prime Minister know, but not to give him too much time for his team to spin it before it was announced officially to colleagues,' he says.[59] The result was far from conclusive: 211 MPs (58.8 per cent) for, 148 (41.2 per cent) against. Johnson's supporters crowded the front row of the committee room for the announcement, cheering uproariously at the result. Johnson claimed it was 'a new mandate from my party'. It wasn't. Theresa May had secured support from 63 per cent of MPs in 2018, and John Major in a comparable contest in 1995, 64 per cent. Harri had advised him to say that it was a 'convincing and decisive' two-thirds majority, but in the press pool he added 'extremely' and billed it as a great victory, which struck most as hubris.

That evening, his two brothers Leo and Jo and sister Rachel spontaneously decided to descend on Downing Street as a display of filial support and affection. While having drinks in No. 10 garden before dinner in the flat, they were conscious of being watched by faces staring down at them from a party at No. 11.

But for now, Johnson was the victor, and he had the chance to show he had listened and to refresh his team. Voices in the Barclay camp recommended now was the time to bring in figures such as Jeremy Hunt and Tom Tugendhat to broaden his appeal. But the political team including Nigel Adams and Declan Lyons told him that he wasn't strong enough to do it, and it would produce too many headaches – that he would have to wait till the summer. Johnson chose to heed the advice of tribalists who saw breadth as a sign of weakness. If not already too late, it might have been the last chance to save himself.

Cabinet Starts Collapsing: June to July

MPs had now shot their bolt. The letters of no confidence were destroyed. Something more would be needed to unseat him. As long as the 1922 Committee didn't change the rules, Johnson was safe for another year. Even if fresh letters reached the threshold again, a new confidence vote could not be triggered before June 2023.

The jury deciding on Johnson's future now switched from his MPs to his Cabinet. 'The Prime Minister was quite calm about it. His attitude was "we're through it now, it's back to work, time to rebuild and restore",' says Finn.[60] What he had to do was to retain his colleagues' confidence and avoid any more scandals. No compelling successor was parading themselves in front of MPs and the party in the country. Hunt, the front runner, was a credible and respected figure, but one who had campaigned for Remain and lacked Johnson's charisma and appeal across the country. Johnson felt confident. Too confident. After Cabinet the next day, 7 June, Javid caught him to say, 'Unless you change very quickly, it will be over.'

'It was a convincing win, Saj.'

'That's not true.'

'I got more support than I had in the leadership election.'

'Look, 40 per cent of your colleagues said they have no confidence in you.'

The conversation finished inconclusively with Johnson assuring him, 'Saj, I get it.'[61]

Johnson remembered his instructions: 'Be nice to Cabinet and don't screw up.' 'In meetings following the vote, he made deliberate attempts to get ministers on board, keep them engaged, to make certain everyone had their say,' says an official. Barclay tried to revive Cabinet government with much more authority devolved to ministers, and respect for their autonomy. His team tried to institute a proper Conservative agenda: Rwanda as the destination for illegal immigrants to send a clear message about control over borders, Rees-Mogg appointed Minister for Brexit Opportunities, a timetable to get out of the European Court of Justice and resolve the Northern Ireland Protocol impasse. But infighting within No. 10 continued to be tolerated by Johnson, leaking was totally out of control, and jockeying between ministers showed Johnson again unwilling or incapable of stamping it out. Attempts to bind the government behind a collective sense of direction were doomed. Cabinet ministers found themselves caught in the bitter and apparently insoluble disagreement between a Chancellor concerned about inflation and spending, and a Prime Minister pushing for growth and tax cuts. The atmosphere had subtly changed in the final weeks: 'Authority had gone. Something was in the air. People sniffed blood,' says an official.

Shocking Conservative defeats followed on 23 June. Tiverton and Honiton saw the largest majority ever overturned in a by-election, while Wakefield saw the first Labour gain in a by-election since 2012. No. 10 was in denial: 'Mid-term governments lose by-elections: get over it,' was the attitude, an aide recalls. Johnson had feared the results would be bad, but he had not anticipated what was to happen next. On the 23rd, Johnson flew to Kigali in Rwanda to attend the Commonwealth Heads of Government Meeting. The following morning, a jovial Johnson was just back in the hotel after an early swim. At 7.30 a.m., he received a call at the meeting, later recounted to advisers on both sides. 'I'm very sorry, Prime Minister, but I'm going to have to resign,' Party Chair Oliver Dowden told him down the line.

'Don't be so ridiculous.'

'I'm serious. It isn't credible to remain as party chair having lost two by-elections.'

'Look, it's just mid-term election blues.'

'I've got to do the right thing. We can't carry on with the pretence that by-election losses don't matter.'

'If you were doing the right thing, you would stay on in your job and defend me,' said a Prime Minister now dripping with more than just pool water. The conversation ended abruptly.

Dowden had already written his letter, and released it on Twitter, 'or he faced the risk that the next thing we would hear is that he had been sacked. We knew them,' says a Dowden ally. 'Someone has to take responsibility,' said Dowden pointedly in his public message.[62]

An exchange of texts followed, each man seeking to dial down. 'If I had wanted to bring you down, I would have resigned over the confidence vote,' Dowden wrote. 'There is no plot, Prime Minister: Rishi doesn't know that I am resigning.' Johnson wasn't convinced. 'There's a plot. Dougie is behind this,' he muttered to himself. From the Kigali hotel he and Harri rang round Cabinet to check that they were not having wobbles. Most messaged back quickly that they were fine. Two were harder to track down. After a while, Johnson got hold of the first: 'I just want to take you off suicide watch,' Johnson said to an assenting Health Secretary. It took time to get hold of Sunak, who gave the impression that 'he'd only recently woken up, hadn't heard the news, sounded breezy, but was convincing', says an aide. Johnson felt reassured and was soon back in upbeat mode revelling in his whirlwind week abroad, far removed from the incessant domestic noise and pleased with his performance at the G7 in Germany, the NATO summit in Brussels and in talks with President Zelenskyy before flying to Rwanda.

For Dowden, the resignation was the end of a long process. Rare for a figure who had been close to Cameron – he had been his deputy chief of staff at No. 10 – he rose high in the Johnson court, but 'had never bought into the Boris vision', says a Johnson aide. He was not trusted to have been included in the discussion on the confidence vote, 'which led me to question why I was there. I received a call from No. 10, only fifteen minutes before the news broke,' he says.[63] Briefing against him intensified afterwards. 'I became convinced it was all going to end badly,' he says. The response from No. 10 was predictable: 'Retaliation from a man bitter about being moved from DCMS. Never happy as party chair: jumped before he was pushed.'

Johnson was already weakened when the Chris Pincher scandal erupted a week later. To his detractors, it was appropriate that Johnson's premiership should have ended over such a sordid affair. Johnson had appointed ex-minister Pincher as Deputy Chief Whip in February 2022 on the advice, among others, of Nigel Adams, the ultra-tribal MP Johnson had brought into the heart of his team in the final months. Four months later, allegations that Pincher had groped two males at the Carlton Club became public. Pincher promptly resigned on 30 June, admitting he had 'drunk far too much'.[64] Further allegations then emerged about historic episodes, leading to questions about why he had been put back into the Whip's office. 'We just didn't see Pincher as a game changer,' says one of his close team. 'Boris didn't want to be forced into firing him unless the alleged victim made a complaint; we didn't see that whatever he did would not be enough,' says another.

Johnson indeed misread the mood of the public and his own parliamentary party, didn't respond quickly enough to the demand Pincher lose the whip, and allowed a response to be put out from No. 10 without it being fully checked. On the morning of Monday 4 July on Radio 4's *Today* programme, it was denied that Johnson had been aware of any specific complaints when appointing Pincher. No. 10 then admitted at 11.30 a.m. that he had been aware and the issues were 'either resolved or did not progress to a formal complaint'. The BBC contradicted this and reported that an official complaint and investigation into Pincher had taken place while he was a junior minister at the FCO, and that Johnson, now PM, had been told about it.

Simon McDonald, former permanent secretary at the FCO, now entered the fray. He had contacted Downing Street on 3 July privately to alert them to the mistruths, giving them the chance to retract. But nothing had happened, leading him to tweet at 7.30 a.m. on 5 July that he had written to the Parliamentary Commissioner for Standards to say the Prime Minister had been briefed: 'No. 10 keep changing their story, and it's still not telling the truth.'[65] No. 10's response that he was bitter not to have had his contract renewed at the FCO, one of the victims of the cull of the mandarins, cut little ice. McDonald had certainly had his fill of Johnson's behaviour: 'I was furious at the inability of No. 10 to get its facts straight, as usual going in hard before ascertaining what had actually happened, then belatedly shifting their ground. It had happened once too often,' he says.[66] 'Be careful what you wish for,' his wife had warned him before he fired off his letter, knowing it could help end Johnson's premiership and lead to yet more political turmoil.

To the ultras around Johnson, blame for the Pincher mess fell on the usual suspects – the BBC, the left-wing press and Whitehall – for conspiring together to bring him down. To the more thoughtful in the building, 'there was a sense across MPs that their constituents thought their leader was not being straight with them again. It was one time too many', says an aide. That view was echoed by others outside. 'MPs were fed up being taken for granted, as cannon fodder to do whatever No. 10 wanted,' says a senior MP. 'The lies. It proved his casual relationship to the truth. MPs hated being sent out to defend the Pincher appointment, and then being told that the Prime Minister did know,' says an MP. McDonald's intervention was significant because it opened the critique right out with the message, in the words of another MP: 'If you politicians can't sort it out, we must sort it out for you; we cannot continue with such a blithe disregard for the truth.'

Johnson was all but dead. It would take just one more swing of the axe to fell him.

It came late on 5 July with news of the all-but simultaneous resignations of the current and the former Chancellors, unprecedented in modern history. Javid had been toying with it for some time. On Sunday 3 July, he spoke about it with colleagues who counselled holding off for now. On 5 July, he says he had one of those mystical experiences in the morning, when he attended the annual National Parliamentary Prayer Breakfast in Westminster Hall, and the preacher, Reverend Les Isaac, was talking on the stage about integrity and the need for politicians to rise above self-interest 'for the common good'. Directly in front of Javid's sight-line sat Johnson: 'I started to think, "I have to go now."'[67] Then, as he got up to leave '95 per cent certain' he would be quitting, he received a message about the McDonald letter which clinched it for him.

A particularly fractious Cabinet followed which debated tax cuts and revealed again the deep dividing lines between Kwarteng and Truss on the one side, and Gove and Sunak on the other highlighting the risk of inflation. After it was over, Javid told his permanent secretary, Chris Wormald, that he was going to see Johnson to tell him the news face-to-face.

Nine minutes after Javid tweeted his resignation on Tuesday evening, Sunak followed suit with his own. 'Hundred per cent. He didn't coordinate with Saj on their resignations,' says a Sunak aide. The final straw for the Chancellor, his aides say, was less Pincher, 'who he didn't like', than Johnson's continuing financial profligacy, specifically the ambitious plans being pumped out by Andrew Griffith from the No. 10 Policy Unit. Sunak had been teetering in the resignation lounge for several weeks. Gove had spoken to both men, who had confided in him their deep unhappiness: 'Rishi was very concerned by the McDonald letter,' Gove says. 'I'm thinking of resigning,' Sunak said to Dowden on the evening of Sunday 3 July. They had spoken about it before, but, as he talked over his reasons, there was a new urgency. Sunak talked calmly through the reasons for his going. 'Let me sleep on it, so then I'll come back to you,' Dowden said.[68] The next day, they had an inkling that Javid was about to resign, 'So Rishi brought it forward,' says an aide. He released his resignation letter to Johnson, which antagonized him greatly for, in his eyes, distorting their relationship. 'Rishi didn't text or didn't call the PM. The first time we heard was that he tweeted that he'd gone. It went down *very* badly with Boris. He thought it very bad manners. He thought there was something cowardly about it,' says an aide.

Thus was hatched the great betrayal thesis, that Johnson, still doing well in the polls and with much left to offer the country, was hacked down. 'He was absolutely determined to fight on after the resignations,' says a No. 10 aide. 'They tried to compute to us some kind of Machiavellian or Mandelsonian deviousness,' says one of the Sunak team. 'It came from Dorries, Rees-Mogg, the *Daily Mail* editor Ted Verity and Johnson himself. The great betrayal thesis was pumped out every day. Liz Truss very clearly used it to help her.'

Johnson reached out to Crosby as always when under great pressure, who was on a plane just about to take off. 'We had a coded conversation because of people sitting around me,' he says.[69] Johnson then sent him several WhatsApp messages asking, 'When can we speak?' A worried Johnson assembled his team together again in No. 10 in the Thatcher Study on the first floor as if her magic would rub off. 'Is it all over?' 'Could we still form a government?' they asked. The loss of two such prominent figures was perilous, but a ring round by the team reassured them that most of the Cabinet were solid. 'Let's see if we can form a government,' Johnson declared. The linchpin would be, could they find a Chancellor? 'Let's go for Kit Malthouse or Liz Truss,' Johnson said. 'Why?' one asked incredulously. 'It would f**k off Rishi so much,' Johnson responded. Zahawi and Barclay were the two serious choices. The latter was asked to leave the room while they debated it, with the team deciding the best pairing would be Barclay in Health and Zahawi at the Treasury.

Zahawi was promptly invited in and told a relieved Johnson, 'I'd love to do it.' His excitement was infectious: 'Give me a week and I'll come up with a growth plan to give you. We need a post-Covid Growth manifesto. I will cut taxes and I don't want corporation tax to go up,' he said, which had been due to increase. After he left, Johnson said, 'Rishi was ankle chaining me.' His team agreed: 'This is an unlock,' Griffith said, expressing their frustration that Sunak had not come up with a growth strategy or tax cuts, nor had he agreed to stop the rise in corporation tax, as the *Telegraph* and his right-wing were demanding. 'No. 10 had moved very quickly. It all felt possible,' thought Griffith as he went home late that evening after multiple conversations with Zahawi about government relaunches.[70]

Wednesday 6 July was a very long day for Boris Johnson. The evening before, agonizing discussions had gone on late into the night between ministers, most concluding, with varying degrees of regret, that Johnson would have to go. Early on the Wednesday morning, Gove requested a meeting with Johnson alone: 'I was aware of a significant number of junior ministers, including those fond of him, who had decided that the time was up. I was acting alone,' he says.[71] The moment had come for the final two big beasts standing to confront each other – as in 2016 and 2019. Gove made ready to speak: 'You have an opportunity to take control of events by acting now and standing down,' he told a 'hurt but composed' Johnson, who responded with a story. 'I had a relative who was to be extricated after a planning dispute, but he hunkered down refusing to go, and that is what I will do,' he explained to a baffled Gove.

Gove insisted that no one should know of their conversation. Then, as if to underline their utterly bizarre relationship over the previous six years, having just told Johnson he should quit, he then calmly joined the team at 10.30 a.m. to prepare Johnson for the imminent PMQs to help justify his remaining in office, as if nothing had happened. As the day progressed, and junior ministerial resignations mounted, intelligence came into the building that Gove's telling him to go that morning had leaked. 'You have to sack Michael *at once*,' his team told him. Johnson was reluctant.

'Why?' he asked. 'Because it's out there: you will have no authority unless you do. You have to stamp it out now.'

The best lines at the gruelling PMQs encounter in the Commons chamber were not his but Starmer's. Having excoriated Johnson for a series of failures of integrity, the Labour leader turned to the growing list of ministerial resignations: 'Is this the first recorded case of the sinking ship fleeing the rat?' he asked, before dubbing those departing 'the charge of the lightweight brigade'. 'Boris just couldn't rouse the benches behind him. It was like the worst days under Theresa May,' says Canzini.[72] Worse was to follow at the two-hour Liaison Committee, in front of which the Prime Minister appears several times a year to be scrutinized. To Johnson, it was the ultimate test of his ability to remain optimistic as humiliating questions from members cascaded in on each other, to the mournful, steady drumbeat of resignation after resignation on television screens and mobile phones, marking out the slow death of his premiership.

He returned to No. 10, utterly exhausted but still determined to fight on. He hoped still that he had secured a new Cabinet. Brady had wanted to come in late afternoon to see him in the Cabinet Room. 'We can tell him he can f**k off,' said Johnson before he arrived. 'Even if he comes in with a flamethrower, I'm not leaving,' he told a member of his family. 'Boris wasn't going to be unseated by the men in grey suits telling him to go,' confirms an aide. 'We had worked out that Brady was going to be saying that there would be a new election for the 1922 executive to give it a new legitimacy, that they would then change the rules on timing, that there would be a new confidence vote, and that he would lose. Boris was going to tell him to "bugger off" and had no intention of caving in.'

'As I sat down opposite him over the Cabinet table, he immediately said, "So you've changed the rules?" He often tried to anticipate what his interlocutor was going to say,' Brady says. In fact, the 1922 Committee executive had decided not to change the rules but to hold fresh elections and leave it to a newly elected committee to decide, with the benefit of a fresh mandate. So Brady told him, 'No. We will have a new election on Monday for a fresh committee, but I should tell you that the mood of the party is that they want to change the rules to trigger a confidence vote. I think that you will lose that vote, Prime Minister.' 'If colleagues are foolish enough to get rid of the leader with an eighty-seat majority, they're welcome to try,' retorted Johnson tartly. The meeting lasted barely twenty minutes. Brady left, sensing that 'Johnson was determined to stay, he wanted to be forced out, and not go of his own volition'.[73] 'The feeling among us was that it was all nuts, just Westminster bubble stuff. We couldn't understand what all the concerns were about,' says an aide, exemplifying how cut off and abstracted Downing Street becomes at the end of premierships.

Johnson's mood swayed back and forth for the rest of the day, at one time thinking it was all over, at another, thinking that he'd make it through to the summer vacation and then all would be well. Did he think seriously about calling a snap general election and appealing directly to those he believed had voted him in? 'He definitely became a bit Trumpy in his final hours, but he was never remotely serious about calling a new election,' says a close friend. 'Categorically not true,' says Andrew Griffith.[74] As the Private Office struggled to keep abreast of official responses to ministers resigning, his political team in the Thatcher Study battled to put a new government together. 'What is the smallest number of ministers we need to form a government?' Case was asked. 'That was the point I hoped others realized it was not going to work,' says Canzini. 'It had become a farce.'[75]

A dining room farce was indeed unfolding in No. 10's elegant small dining room on the first floor. Sitting there around the polished wooden table were the big three, Deputy PM Raab, Chancellor Zahawi and Chief Whip Heaton-Harris. 'Where are you?' Zahawi had texted Raab an hour before. 'We need to meet in No. 10 and need to talk to the Chief [Whip].' Raab agreed. They had been watching news of the rising resignations with mounting horror. 'Where are you, Chief?' he then texted Heaton-Harris, who replied, 'I'm in No. 10. You must come in. Boris is not listening.' When they were alone, Zahawi said, 'This is just going to become horrific for Boris. I've known him for so long. We are very fond of him and we have to work together to help him transition out of this.' 'I agree with you,' said Heaton-Harris. He knew the game was up but was disturbed by those around the Prime Minister telling him that he could go on as usual. They were soon joined in the small room by others, including Priti Patel, Anne-Marie Trevelyan and Michelle Donelan. They all fulminated at the tight rump around the Prime Minister, including Adams, Gascoigne, Lyons and Griffith urging him to 'fight on'. The last joined them at this point to implore them to stick by Johnson. 'Let's look at the numbers. We have enough to make this work,' he told them. 'You may have enough numbers now, but in one hour the numbers will have fallen, and in five hours, they'll have fallen even more. It's the herd beginning to move,' Heaton-Harris and Zahawi replied. They told Griffith that they wanted to go and see Johnson 'as a group' to say that he must resign and that they were there to help him with the transition. Griffith replied, 'No, he will see you one by one.' As Chancellor, Zahawi was first in.

'How are you, boss?' he said.

'I'm fine. Look, Nadhim. I'm going to do all in my power to make this work. I need seven to ten days.'

'I have something to say.'

'I should have put you in the Treasury months ago. You'd have had the post-Covid economic growth that we needed.'

'Boris, I don't think this is going to work. The herd is moving.'

'Really? Let's give it one more go.'

'I can't see a way out. Your colleagues are genuinely panicking.'

'I still have a lot of support.'

'It's heartbreaking to tell you this. They are panicking because of Twitter. A genuine stampede is starting.'

'OK, go back to the Treasury and do more work on our plan,' Johnson replied, as if he wasn't fully grasping what was being said.

'I'm saying, I can't let it happen to you. They'll drag your carcass out of here.'

'I am not leaving', was the parting message he heard from Johnson. Conversations with other Cabinet ministers swung back and forth crazily.

At 5.45 p.m. Griffith texted Johnson: 'I am with Nadhim and he is solid.' But Grant Shapps then told Johnson's team, 'It's over, he hasn't got the numbers.' 'That isn't true, you have old numbers, and we haven't yet done a new set of numbers,' a team member replied bravely to the numbers maestro. Foreign Secretary Liz Truss was in Indonesia, 'doing a John Major', says a team member, a reference to Thatcher's successor lying low when the heat was on in November 1990, an analogy unfair to both Thatcher and Truss. Business Secretary Kwasi Kwarteng was contacted by phone in the North of England: 'I'm not going to say anything to the media. I'm not resigning, but I think there's too much bad stuff happening,' he said, citing the corporation tax rises, 'which will set us back two years in our relationship with business.'

But still, Johnson wanted to fight on. His head was full of new faces and new activist policies. That evening, he phoned Gove.

'I don't want to keep you long,' he said. 'I've been thinking of our conversation this morning.'

'Thank you, Prime Minister. Tell me more.'

'I'm going to do my best to deliver on the mandate I've been given. But in order to do that I've got to make some changes to Cabinet. And in view of your position on the whole thing, which I understand, I wondered if you would mind stepping back – at least for the time being?'

'You will not resign?' Gove shot back.

'That's not the issue.'

'It *is* the issue, Prime Minister. You have to go – if you carry on, you will do more damage to the party and the country.'

'Let's leave that aside. You may be right. But I need to make some changes.'

'You can't go on,' Gove insisted. 'I'm afraid you will do huge damage to yourself too.'

'That's my decision. Thank you for everything. I didn't want to get you to come to No. 10 in person.'

To Johnson's team, with memories going back to the 2016 'betrayal', this had become very personal. The news was promptly put out that Gove had been fired for disloyalty before he could put out his own story. An aide gleefully texted Crosby to say: 'He's *finally* gone, he has finally sacked Gove!'

A series of events then conspired to pull the carpet from under Johnson. Zahawi had gone back to the Treasury but at 7 p.m. was flabbergasted to read a story that he and Johnson were going to be giving a joint economic address in the morning. To Zahawi, whoever leaked the story was desperate. Now, seriously worried about whether he could possibly continue, he spoke to his old friend Brandon Lewis who had just landed at London City Airport from Belfast. Lewis was driven straight to No. 10 for a meeting with Heaton-Harris and Johnson around the Cabinet table at 8.30 p.m. 'It was surreal, Boris was very positive about the future in a way that made absolutely no sense given the gravity of the position,' Lewis says.[76] He recounts the meeting:

'I'm going to promote you, we're going to do this and I want you to be part of the solution. I want you to do Levelling Up,' Johnson told him.

'What about Michael?' Lewis replied.

'I'm sacking him, he needs a break.'

'Prime Minister, it's just not going to work out…'

Johnson, unsure where to go next, attempted to push Lewis towards other ministerial gaps. 'Will you at least do CDL [Chancellor of the Duchy of Lancaster]?'

'Prime Minister, I'm really not sure.'

For Lewis, Johnson's position was simply too far gone, with the 1922 Committee rule changes imminent and lethal. He offered Johnson a conciliatory gesture nevertheless, saying he'd 'think it over that evening'. Even as they were talking, yet more names fell from the reshuffle whiteboard, with long-standing junior Health Minister Ed Argar walking, and Education Secretary Michelle Donelan resigning (less than forty-eight hours after her appointment). At 10.30 that evening, Simon Hart, who had himself refused to take on the Gove portfolio of Levelling Up, resigned as Welsh Secretary, the only minister of Cabinet rank formally to do so (as opposed to being fired) that day.

To Johnson, the failure to find a decent minister willing to head his flagship levelling up policy was a very bitter blow. 'As in 2016, he saw Michael having betrayed him,' says a friend. The drama of 2016, never far from his mind, was indeed about to be re-enacted in these final hours with an amended cast list: Crosby, the constant, Carrie replacing Marina, and Harri, who had become one of his closest allies, taking the place of Will Walden. Late that night, Johnson at last got through to Crosby in Brisbane, the words tumbling out of him: 'I'm up in the flat. I don't want to destroy the Conservative Party. I think I should stand down. What do you think I should do?'

Crosby didn't know if he'd already spoken to Carrie but it was clear to him that he had decided to go. So he said, 'From everything I know, Boris, it sounds like going is the right decision.'[77]

Carrie's view was that it was up to him, a view Harri shared too. They agreed, though, that he should sleep on it. 'One of his greatest regrets about the Gove betrayal in 2016 was he walked away from it too quickly. He had to be the person taking the decision, which he would live with forever,' Harri says.[78] Had he made his mind up to go before going to sleep? 'I think he had,' says Ben Elliot. 'Not when I spoke to him at midnight, saying it was difficult, but he decided the corporation tax rise wasn't going ahead,' says Griffith. But when an old friend called him at 5.15 in the morning, he told him, 'I think it's all over, friend.' 'Good morning. It's looking very difficult now. What do you think?' Harri texted him at 6 a.m. 'I'm just writing something, I'll ping it over,' Johnson replied, his decision taken.

His senior ministers still didn't know about his *volte-face*. At 6 a.m., a fraught Zahawi called Barclay who said, 'What do we do? It's a disaster. It's over.' 'He wasn't listening to me,' Zahawi replied, who shortly after submitted a letter not of his own resignation, instead imploring the Prime Minister to go. Entering No. 10 supported by Hart, Donelan and Lewis, the last of whom had submitted his resignation that morning, he repeated his line Johnson would soon borrow: 'The herd have bolted, Prime Minister, and once it's started you can't stop it.' At 7.30 a.m., the No. 10 switchboard contacted Brady telling him to expect a call from the Prime Minister. 'I reflected on our conversation last night. I've changed my mind, I will be going,' Johnson told him at 8 a.m. 'I will be making a statement later in the day.' 'His mood seemed to me to be to blame his colleagues for throwing over a great leader, and he thought the criticisms and concerns were complete nonsense and trivia,' says Brady. 'The reality is that he had discovered overnight he could not populate a possible government.'[79]

The team had begun reassembling in the Thatcher Study from 7 a.m. All hope of life gone, the energy had left the building and attention focused on the departure. One of his team spoke to Simon Case on the staircase, to ask how official plans were going: 'The Palace are not early risers,' he replied. The team pored over his overnight draft speech. Several of the most distinctive Johnsonian flourishes were destined for the cutting-room floor. The expunged lines included: 'In the last forty-eight hours, a number of my MPs have been on to me to go with dignity, as though I was off to a Swiss euthanasia clinic. I think dignity is a grossly, overrated commodity, and I prefer to fight to the end.' Too edgy, it was thought. 'I can't ask good friends and colleagues to superglue Humpty together again, when they are frankly hesitant, or not supportive.' Too pointed. 'There is still part of me that thinks that if we had got the MPs to go off to the beach for twenty-four hours and turned off Twitter, then we would have gone on to thrash Labour at the next general election.' Too flippant.

Cabinet that morning was a sombre affair. Johnson told them, 'People want to be reassured that we have a government. We have to provide stability until the new Prime Minister takes over.' Then he said, more whimsically, 'The situation has developed not necessarily to our advantage,' as Emperor Hirohito said on Japan's surrender in the Second World War. Still with his mind on the Pacific, he said he had felt at times like the Japanese soldier Hiroo Onada who had hid in the jungle until 1974 refusing to accept the capitulation. Rees-Mogg saw enemies closer to home. Anticipating the divisiveness of the regime that followed, he said, 'Good riddance to the socialist Chancellor [Sunak].' Scotland Minister Alister Jack caught the mood better: 'There are three things about you, Boris. You are kind, perhaps too kind. You are loyal, perhaps too loyal. You are fearless. Each of these brought you down.'

Defiance, not resignation, was the tone of his final speech outside Downing Street, drowned out for those present by noisy protesters in Whitehall, which the microphones cut out altogether for the news broadcasts. It was, he said, 'eccentric' of his fellow MPs to want to change government 'when we're delivering so much and when we have such a vast mandate and when we're actually only a handful of points behind in the polls'. But 'as we have seen at Westminster, the herd instinct is powerful, and when the herd moves, it moves'.

Zahawi's herd analogy summed up for Johnson the aberrant behaviour of his colleagues. Like Lloyd George, a century before, he could not understand in his heart why he had been hung out to dry. He returned to the building and went round cheering up his staff, many of whom were in tears. 'He was determined to be strong for them, to keep up appearances,' says an aide. Inside, he was fuming and baffled to know what had happened. 'I'm afraid our enemies were just too many and too ubiquitous,' he said to a friend. 'And as we are now seeing, just too duplicitous.'

Making a call to the politician who inspired him more than any other was one of his first actions as 'caretaker' Prime Minister. 'I regret that political developments in the UK mean I will be standing down,' he told President Zelenskyy, 'but there will be strong support from the public, from me and from all political parties for Ukraine.'

'All of us are disappointed,' Zelenskyy said. 'I am personally disappointed.'

'You're a hero, Volodomyr. Everyone in this country loves you.'

'You're a hero, Boris. Everyone in this country loves *you*.'

Those were the sweetest words of Johnson's premiership.

The Third Prime Minister Johnson Brought Down

Johnson remained in power for another two months till 6 September, but his premiership was effectively over. Unlike Churchill's two-month 'caretaker government' in 1945 which was full of purpose, it achieved little beyond some announcements as on nuclear power, but with huge gaps on energy, cost of living, health and social care. Johnson was less eager than most departing Prime Ministers to consolidate his legacy, enjoying holidays in Slovenia and Greece before his time was up. One of his last announcements was to back ARIA. To the very end, the presence was felt of Cummings.

Johnson himself is the ultimate answer to the question of this chapter and indeed the entire book: why, given his landslide victory in December 2019, and his not inconsiderable talents, did he fall so quickly? He brought himself down.

An ability to *govern* is the most crucial of all the qualities Prime Ministers need to display: setting a clear course, taking firm decisions regardless of criticism, confronting people when necessary, appointing the very best and then backing them, creating an orderly and respectful culture in No. 10 and across government, understanding trade-offs and being consistent in word and deed. Johnson never understood how to be Prime Minister nor how to govern. He improved a little in some areas, where he could learn from repeated errors on matters which did not require an admission of his character weaknesses or fundamental change: Covid and foreign policy, particularly on Russia, being the standouts. But to Johnson so much of politics was the personal, and in the personal he could not escape his base self. After backing Cummings for too long and putting too much of his trust in a man he feared would eventually turn against him, he took the lesson to run a court divided, appointing people who he knew carried little authority and could not challenge him. He never wanted anyone near him who insisted on convention and set boundaries, or who would tell him when he was wrong or what he didn't want to hear. Optimism and comedy were no substitute for what all Prime Ministers need: dignity and gravitas. The PM is not a President with a direct mandate from the electorate as Johnson thought: they need to govern through Cabinet ministers, their party, Parliament and Whitehall. Johnson never understood any of this. Nor did he allow others to build a system around him that would have allowed his strengths to blossom, as President Reagan, one of his heroes, did. Premierships need stability, continuity and predictability, none of which remotely interested him. He was at his most effective when there was a clear course of action for which he could bang the drum and let others handle the details, as in getting Brexit 'done', rolling out the vaccine or supporting Zelenskyy in Ukraine. In his relations with foreign leaders, he was too inconsistent: brilliant in flashes, but incapable of building bridges and sustaining positive relations, notably and most significantly with the leaders of Germany and France, to Britain's loss. His weakest moments came when decisions were complex and contentious, as they all too often are for Prime Ministers, and Johnson felt unable and unwilling to make a decision which might make him unpopular. With a Shakespearean irony Johnson would appreciate, if only he could recognize it, his very desire to please his colleagues had the opposite effect. All but a small rump lost the necessary confidence in him to be a leader they respected. To govern is to choose, and Johnson could not choose.

His *political* weakness was his total inability to build a coherent mission for his government or for the Conservatives in the 2020s. He hadn't thought any more about *what* he wanted to do as Prime Minister than about how to do it. He wasn't very interested in what the Conservative Party wanted, but he was fired up by fanciful ideas of transforming the British state and its place in the world after Brexit, and by a 'new deal' in the manner of Franklin D. Roosevelt. Before the general election in 2019, the objective was clear; after it, it wasn't. Most of his parliamentary party wanted the mission to be galvanizing the country and economy to demonstrate the benefits of Brexit, for immigration to be controlled and public services to be improved. 'Brexit opportunity was the glue that won the landslide and brought in the new MPs and voters, but we just basically forgot about them,' as a loyalist puts it. But such a mission would always be incoherent; Johnson had campaigned for Brexit without any end state in mind, and his tendency towards cakeism had promised too much to too many. The two contradictory visions of a free-trading, low-tax, deregulated economy versus a protectionist, levelling-up, pro-environmental agenda would always be irreconcilable. The nature of turning Brexit into a reality necessarily involved disappointing one of these groups. In the end Johnson committed himself to the latter, against the majority of his party, but despite capturing the public mood he could not build alliances within Westminster to bring about change. His colleagues ultimately abandoned him because he failed to build a consensus around *any* vision for the future.

Above all else, it was his *personal* weaknesses which proved fatal in the end. He wasn't interested enough in the people a Prime Minister needs to be interested in, unless it was very clear that they could quickly give him something back. He wasn't interested in his MPs, in his ministers or in a host of others from public servants to business people. His individual mores and chequered life made him reluctant to set moral parameters on personal behaviour, or make ethical judgments, both on himself and on the private lives of others. He possessed a chronic aversion to the truth, lying 'morning, noon and night', as a No. 10 aide devastatingly puts it. He had survived previous questioning about his sex life and his finances by brazening it out, and that is exactly the strategy he deployed in handling the bullying claims against Priti Patel which led to the resignation of Alex Allan, the first of his two ethics advisers to quit. He adopted the same approach in a succession of scandals, from demeaning appointments to Wallpapergate, from Barnard Castle to Owen Paterson, from Partygate to Chris Pincher. Aides who have worked with him for years still question whether he even knew the difference between right and wrong. He never listened, never learned, never changed: he *never believed he had done anything wrong*.

Johnson fell because his second Chancellor, who had given up on him in January, eventually resigned, as did his first Chancellor. His third Chancellor had given up on him, so had his Chief Whip, so had his Levelling Up Secretary. So had his Parliamentary party.

No Prime Minister can continue with just a loyalist rump with the likes of Nadine Dorries and Nigel Adams in support.

Speaking to Radio 4's *Today* programme from Kigali following Dowden's resignation, Johnson summed up his inability to change from this assessment better than any. 'If you're saying you want me to undergo some sort of psychological transformation, I think that our listeners would know that is not going to happen.'[80] It was the most honest moment of his premiership.

Ultimately, it was his lack of personal responsibility for his actions and for those for whom he was responsible that resulted in his demise.

In his beginning was his end.

Rishi Sunak's growing differences with Johnson culminated in his resignation, later in the day of this Cabinet meeting on 5 July 2022

CONCLUSION

What will history make of Boris Johnson? It is facile and wrong to declare it is 'too early to say'. There is never the perfect moment for historical judgement: the reputation of Prime Ministers, as with all other leaders, will be constantly re-evaluated according to fad and perspective. Besides, at the end of every premiership we have studied in this series – Major, Blair, Brown, Cameron and May – we have broadly known where they will land up in the prime ministerial pantheon. We can make statements about Johnson's premiership right now which will last the test of time.

All his life he sought not just to be Prime Minister, but to be a *great* Prime Minister. So where does he rank among those who genuinely were? Did he have what it takes to be a Prime Minister who makes history, who changes the political weather? We believe there have been just nine such since the office was created in 1721: Robert Walpole, William Pitt the Younger, Robert Peel, Lord Palmerston, William Gladstone, David Lloyd George, Winston Churchill, Clement Attlee and Margaret Thatcher. They all rose to the historical challenges of their period in power, won notable general elections, changed the course of the country and with it the way the job of Prime Minister was seen. They raised the standing of the country internationally, or bolstered the Union, or both. Their influence was felt moreover for many years after they stood down, with their successors choosing to emulate them, or deliberately choosing to be unlike them – but none capable of escaping their long shadows.[1]

They were all remarkable people. Johnson possessed some of their traits and benefits. He was an exceptional communicator with an inimitable ability to reach out beyond his party, he possessed a strong constitution, an even temperament, an iron will and self-belief. Luck, that vital ingredient that all successful PMs need, was mostly on his side. But critically he did not possess other top tier traits: moral seriousness, an ability to work relentlessly hard when the pressure eased, decisiveness and resolution, mature and stable core relationships, the courage to appoint strong Cabinet and No. 10 teams, and a gift for managing Cabinet and the media proactively.

Johnson lacked other attributes too which the landmark Prime Ministers enjoyed. They all served in No. 10 for long periods: their average length was ten years, precisely the time that Johnson aspired to after the 2019 election victory. All bar William Pitt the Younger (aged twenty-four when appointed) had served lengthy apprenticeships in politics as an MP, averaging over twenty-five years, and had several ministerial posts under their belts. Johnson was a novice. All had robust and clear agendas for office, sometimes thrust upon them, most often in the case of war. Johnson did at least win a landslide, which all except Churchill among the historic Prime Ministers achieved.

One significant factor, though, that Johnson shared with the top nine is that they were all in office at moments of great historical importance, begging the question, do great leaders make history or are they instead made by it?

Johnson came to office in the midst of a political crisis threatening to blend into a constitutional one, in no small part due to his own agitation. Britain's eventual departure from the EU, a three-year struggle which had already toppled two Prime Ministers, was bitterly won as Johnson risked all. No tactic was deemed too radical as he expelled twenty-one MPs from the Conservative Party, advised the Queen of a prorogation later found unlawful and drove the nation towards a perilous no deal exit from the European Union.

The gambit was deemed politically successful: Parliament was deemed the illness, Johnson the remedy. Labour's own electoral flaws, notably having Corbyn at its head, combined with the Brexit dilemma to deliver a sizeable majority after nine years of Conservative government, comparable to Thatcher's victory of 1987. At Johnson's feet lay now the opportunity to enact his vision, to reimagine the country post-Brexit, to reverse the damage of austerity and deliver transformative change on levelling up and infrastructure as he had promised. But within two months of that glorious election victory, any hope of immediately focusing on realizing his dreams was dashed as he found himself facing the deadliest pandemic in a century.

What followed was a near-overnight transformation of society, a collective experience unlike anything the United Kingdom had seen since the Second World War. The level of national restrictions and economic aid necessary to combat the effects of the virus was far beyond any eventuality for which the state had prepared; so too were the over 200,000 deaths. Not content with two major events, Brexit and Covid, history then heaped a third upon Johnson's premiership. In 2022, the largest war in Europe since 1945 erupted as Russia invaded Ukraine, Johnson vocally pushing for both the UK and the international community to supply weapons and aid in greater measure.

Such moments are the forges on which great premierships are hammered out. They are necessary, but not sufficient for landmark premierships: the response from the Prime Minister is all. Lord North (1770–82) thus failed to rise to his test, the spread of protest in the American colonies, as did Neville Chamberlain (1937–40) to the challenge of Hitler. The opportunities for Johnson to be a great Prime Minister, for all his shortcomings, was there for him to milk. His place in history rested upon his response to his three crises. How did he fare?

On the first test, Johnson's ability to campaign relentlessly for Brexit injected an impetus utterly unlike any other alternative leader might have provided. He was at his most effective and focused in those early months at No. 10, where the sword of Damocles hung above him by a single hair and he had no choice but to place his trust in others to compensate for his weaknesses, keeping him driven and on the tracks, while he beat the drum for an end to the uncertainty. The landslide he delivered on 12 December 2019 offered the prospect that Johnson would write his name in the list of post-war Conservative greats, defeating a Labour leader detested like no other since 1945 and rescuing the party from its self-cannibalism over Brexit.

He may have won the Brexit war, but he lost the peace. The promised benefits of Brexit on which he campaigned did not materialize in his premiership. The nation remained unpersuaded. Since he announced his resignation in July 2022, the percentage of those believing Britain was wrong to leave the European Union has not dipped below 50 per cent.[2] As one of its principal architects, the success or failure of Brexit was always to be a key determinant in Johnson's legacy; it was not enough to get it done, but to show it the right decision too. Johnson's deal pushed the UK into constant and avoidable renegotiation over the issues of the Northern Ireland Protocol, with limited progress made through newfound freedoms. That the UK was outside the cultural orbit of the EU on vaccine procurement, and therefore would not have opted out if still inside the EU, is the only Brexit achievement Johnson could confidently articulate, and a contested one at that. Since the end of the transition period UK trade has slumped in comparison to G7 countries due to the increased regulatory burdens,[3] and though difficult to disentangle from inflationary pressures and the economic effects of the pandemic and the Ukraine War, Brexit has decreased growth and increased the UK's cost of living.[4] If the Brexit argument was that economics was always the trade-off for newly won regulatory freedom and much-vaunted sovereignty, little was done by Johnson smartly and specifically to use that freedom to diverge from the EU on points of comparative advantage for the UK. The opportunity for a post-Brexit cultural renaissance of the country was lost: rather than rising to the chance for an unparalleled fillip to British culture and history, Johnson allowed himself to be lost down the rabbit hole of the culture and history wars.

A top tier Prime Minister would, unlike him, have worked ferociously hard to drive through the benefits of Brexit and to show definitively that the decision had been the right one for the country. To those such as his comrade in arms Michael Gove who say it is 'too early' to assess the impact of Brexit, the response is: Ted Heath. Exactly fifty years before, the Prime Minister who was almost the mirror opposite of Johnson took Britain into the EU. There is no settled opinion on the benefits of Britain's entry, even after all this time, and in fifty years' time, the same will be true of Britain's departure. Yet we had a clear view of Heath's quality as Prime Minister when he stood down in 1974, whose three-plus years ended like Johnson's in 2022 in inflation, industrial unrest and economic woes. And it's not a favourable assessment.

What of Johnson's handling of Covid? A global pandemic would have stretched the limits of any Prime Minister. Most, though, would have handled it better. Hampered by his libertarian tendencies, it was his inability to be consistent in decision, disavow his equivocating nature and provide real leadership to No. 10 and government which handicapped the response of the nation to the virus. The flawed choices made during the second wave of the pandemic in late 2020, where Johnson was ultimately responsible for decision-making, cost far too many lives. It was only by 2021 that he had learned from his mistakes, with successes on the vaccine, reopening and the handling of the Omicron variant better suited to his optimistic ways, with the good fortune of the Conservative Party's anti-lockdown principles no longer being a hindrance but a help.

The UK's strengths in combating the virus, including its elite scientific research institutions which produced a vaccine saving 6.2 million lives globally over its first year,[5] puts the nation in the middle of the pack compared to its closest European countries in health terms, with roughly 315 excess deaths per 100,000 people since the outbreak of the pandemic – higher than France (220), on par with Germany (290) and Spain (340), and lower than Italy (470). In economic terms, however, the UK fared poorly – far surpassing all other G7 members bar Canada in its budgetary response to the virus relative to GDP,[6] yet when Johnson exited office the UK was the only G7 country to have not yet recovered to pre-Covid levels.[7]

The importance of individual leaders in responding to such events can be overstated: much of the determinant is institutional, the Prime Minister at the mercy of the advice they receive from specialists operating under extreme uncertainty and the government's ability to execute upon decisions. For those reasons the UK's poor response in the first wave was, by and large, not the fault of Johnson, rather the product of shortcomings in both health advice and the ability of institutions at the heart of government to coordinate in an admittedly unprecedented scenario. But landmark Prime Ministers see such shortcomings as an opportunity to enact new ways of government: out of the wars with France Pitt the Younger introduced income tax; out of the First World War Lloyd George formed the Cabinet Office; and out of the Second World War Attlee reinvented the role of the state in British life. Johnson, who struggled to conceptualize the machinery of government beyond the people immediate to him, did not seize Covid, any more than he did Brexit, as an opportunity to deliver transformative change. Even Gordon Brown, not in our top tier, had his finest moment in helping organize an international response to the global financial crisis of 2007–08, in contrast to the lack of a coordinated international response during Covid. The curse of the missed opportunity was not one Johnson feared, or even foresaw.

His handling of the third major event to occur in his time in office was his most successful performance, showing he could be capable of taking effective decisions and producing statesmanlike leadership in response to the invasion of Ukraine. It was no coincidence that his best moment was in an area where he had learned through experience, and he still felt keenly the sting of the Salisbury poisonings following his attempt to reset relations with Russia as Foreign Secretary. As with the late period of Covid, the crisis played into his hand both politically and personally: the Conservative Party and his Cabinet had arrived at a consensus on the supply of weapons and aid to Ukraine, and the crisis allowed him to utilize his strengths of communication and interpersonal relationships when all else was going south at home. Johnson deserves great credit for the government's efforts to drag both domestic and international partners to go further and faster in the effort to deliver military aid.

If Ukraine saw Johnson at his most impactful, it was also the least consequential of the three shocks of his premiership: the UK could be never be more than a minor player in the conflict. Where hardline military commitments to combat the Russian threat to Europe underlined Palmerston's claim to be one of the great Prime Ministers a century and a half before, Britain's role as a global power had diminished severely in the years between. Such opportunities for greatness were beyond Johnson's reach; he would have to settle for goodness.

What then of his three signature enthusiasms, his three 'broad impulses' which formed his personal credo? On infrastructure, he achieved nothing like the transformative impact on the country at large that he'd sought to deliver. HS2, which he may not have initiated but drove through in its crucial stages, is set to happen, but in a reduced form. Levelling up was barely acted upon and Britain is more regionally unequal now than it had been when he assumed power in July 2019.[8] He initiated a major change in energy and nuclear policy, and Britain's policy on Net Zero, but the exact value of his contribution is at the whim of his successors. His bold effort to solve the chronic social care problem has been scaled back. For all the progress and drive in areas such as skills, he did nothing enduring to solve education problems, shortages in the NHS or in housing. He found it difficult to meet need in any sustained way, and much preferred to rush in with pet projects, rather than thinking strategically about Britain, the state and its relationship to citizens post-Brexit.

Though successfully avoiding the question of Scottish independence during his premiership, his decision to establish a border in the Irish Sea to deliver Brexit meant the Union was weaker in 2022 compared to 2019. Britain's position in the world has not been transformed, for all the temporary uplift given by his strong stance on Ukraine, and his leadership of the G7 and COP26 in 2021. Had he been prepared to work harder and in a more systematic way, as affirmed by those working at his shoulder, he would have achieved more.

He had wanted to be a leader like Presidents Roosevelt and Reagan, remodelling the country and the state after Brexit. He didn't achieve either.

The Prime Minister must also be assessed as a party, a government and a national leader. Is there evidence here of worthiness to be included in the top tier? As leader of the Conservative Party, he failed to bind it together, unable to provide Conservative MPs with a clear strategy to unite behind. Johnson provided a much-needed shot of adrenaline into the heart of the Tory Party for the 2019 election, continuing the realignment of parties unleashed by Brexit, but it proved just a temporary reinvention. After nine years of Conservative government Johnson could mask the stench of decline, but he could not eliminate it entirely and refresh the party against the electoral cycle. He left a party in a poor state for Truss and Sunak to inherit.

As leader of government, he left the civil service in its weakest state since 1918. He legitimized Cummings to act in a way that was often counter-productive to good government, with little after the general election to show for the often brilliant ideas he had. Rarely in 300 years and never since 1916 has a Prime Minister been so poor at appointments, so incompetent at running Cabinet government, or so incapable of finding a stable team to run No. 10. The Prime

Minister is the chief executive, yet he belittled the executive and allowed his ministers to do the same, but without producing badly needed practical solutions for improvement. Nor did he act on ambitious plans to reform central government after Brexit. It is hard to find a Prime Minister who has done more to damage the fabric of government.

What then, finally, of Johnson as a *national* leader? He sought to lead the country in the same ebullient yet inclusive way that he had led London as its Mayor. He helped the country to move beyond the deep divisions that had characterized the premiership of his predecessor, aided by an emergent national purpose in the pandemic. He was at his best, perhaps, communicating with the nation, at times daily, during Covid, and he brought pride and purpose to the nation while avoiding jingoism over Ukraine. But he left the office of Prime Minister and public trust in government at its lowest ebb since before the Second World War. In his opportunism, dishonesty and willingness to violate the constitutional and ethical norms upon which politics relies, he can best be compared with Lloyd George, with whom we opened the book.

Lloyd George's steering of Britain to a successful conclusion in the First World War and oversight of the post-war settlement justifies his inclusion in the top league in a way that Johnson falls far short of.

Given Johnson's pre-premiership behaviour, his failings in office should come as no surprise. Lloyd George too carried a reputation as both a womanizer and rule-breaker in his ascent to No. 10, the most serious of allegations being the 1912–13 Marconi scandal, when as Chancellor he purchased shares in an American company whose British parallel was to receive a governmental contract. Johnson's reputation was even more transparent to the public: just 14 per cent of voters believed he was honest and of good moral character during the leadership election.[9] He imagined he could carry on as Prime Minister in the same cavalier way with disregard to rules and conventions as he had all his life.

Johnson departed from office believing that his time at the top was not yet over. His aborted tilt at the leadership after the fall of Liz Truss in October 2022 was the first, and he hints it may not be the last. His belief is that the herd shall calm, he can reassert his narrative as the Conservative Party's great winner, and, like Cincinnatus from the plough, be called back to lead them in their hour of need. Any shortcomings of his premiership are explained away as the failure of others: he was poorly advised, betrayed, let down by those he trusted. The fault lies with Cummings, Sunak – even his own wife – but never the chief.

The narrative he has embraced suggests that he left No. 10 largely unchanged by the experience of being Prime Minister, incapable of learning from personal failures and possessing a childlike belief in the notion that his actions could be consequence-free. It is all the more surprising that he appears unchanged given the upheaval in his private life in the years covered by this book: divorce, marriage, two children – not even a brush with death appears to have had a genuine lasting impact on his outlook.

But the Boris Johnson of today does not hold the same appeal as the one who walked into No. 10 in July 2019. The mistakes he repeated over Barnard Castle, Paterson, Partygate and Pincher have disillusioned the public, who are no longer willing to give him the benefit of the doubt, labelling him a liar above all else.[10] The charisma and humour which underpinned his persona are now held in suspicion. Over the course of his premiership a credibility gap widened to a chasm – he was a gambler chasing his losses.

The more he promised the more he disappointed, then the more he disappointed the more he promised, until people eventually stopped believing his promises and anticipated the disappointment.

The scandals that already follow in his wake will continue to dog his every attempt to return to the fore, making a liability out of the man who was once considered the party's greatest electoral asset. Johnson's message in the 2019 general election was that the people wanted a politics which work for them, not endless headlines and debates. His self-centredness, combined with his inclination for the scandalous, has made him the very subject of that message for all who campaign against him.

The stories and events which have emerged between the authors completing the text and the writing of this conclusion have only strengthened our confidence in the findings within. Johnson's brazen attempt to knight his father, the new material published by the Privileges Committee, and conversations revealed in the leaked WhatsApp messages of Hancock tell us little more than we already knew about the failings of the premiership.

Johnson had the potential, the aspirations and the opportunity to be one of Britain's great Prime Ministers. His unequivocal exclusion from that club can be laid at the feet of no one else, but himself.

Anthony Seldon and Raymond Newell, March 2023

ACKNOWLEDGEMENTS

This book would never have happened without the insights and kindness of very large numbers of people, most of whom are anonymous. But you know who you are, and we hope you know how grateful we are.

It was written with the smallest team of any of the seven books in the series on recently departed Prime Ministers. Our greatest thanks are due to Tom Egerton, who took a year out from the University of Warwick to act as our principal researcher. His high intelligence and ability to work relentlessly hard are quite remarkable. This young man will go very far, we are convinced. We were delighted that Rex Bodycombe joined in the latter stages, and was particularly helpful with fact checking.

We were blessed with Atlantic as our publisher. Writing and publishing books on contemporary history takes the craft to an altogether different level of complexity. We reached even higher levels in this book, given the uncertainty about Johnson's resignation and the timing of various inquiries, and thus the understandable reluctance of large numbers of people to speak to us until very late in the day. We were initially planning on publishing in the autumn of 2022, then shortly after Christmas. It was a testing time for all. Particular thanks are due to editor James Pulford, publicist Karen Duffy, publishing director Poppy Hampson and managing director Will Atkinson.

We share an agent in Martin Redfern of Northbank who was outstanding, and thanks too for the help and support from the boss, Diane Banks.

Thank you to our diligent readers Stuart Ball, John Taylor, Will Walden, Bob Newell and Alex Thomas for their fine work.

We would like to thank fellow academics for their guidance and support: Jeremy Black, Tim Bale, Andrew Blick, Meg Russell, Tony Travers and Matthew Goodwin. Stuart Ball, the distinguished historian of twentieth-century British history, was exceptionally generous with his help and advice on the introduction and the conclusion, and for classical advice we would like to thank John Claughton and John Taylor in particular.

We would like to thank Isaac Farnworth and John Paton, but cannot for the life of us remember what you did to help.

We are so grateful for the work of other writers. For early years, biographical works by Andrew Gimson and Sonia Purnell were hugely important in laying the groundwork. As always, credit to Tim Shipman for his outstanding insight in his two iconic Brexit works. Rob Ford, Tim Bale, Will Jennings and Paula Surridge were pivotal on the 2019 general election. Andrew Gimson's updated work on Johnson added vivid colour to his premiership, while Sebastian Payne's two books – firstly on the Red Wall and then on the downfall of Johnson – were both perceptive and rich.

These accounts were boosted by very fine reporting and commentary in the media. We also spoke to a number of people in political broadcasting. We do not think you would appreciate it if we thank you by name here, so instead we thank you silently.

To all the anonymous and meticulous writers for Wikipedia, thank you. We guess that more authors rely on your work than is acknowledged.

Anthony Seldon would like to thank his wife Sarah for her forbearance, and children Jessica, Susie and Adam.

Raymond Newell would like to thank his partner Jessie, whose patience and kindness have been nothing short of extraordinary, and his parents Bob and Elizabeth.

NOTES

INTRODUCTION

1 *Lord Riddell's War Diary*, p. 265.

1: RISE

1 School reports by Martin Hammond, written between April and July 1982, edited via email (15 November 2022).
2 For further reading on his pre-Prime Minister years, see Andrew Gimson and Sonia Purnell's works.
3 Anthony Seldon with Jonathan Meakin and Illias Thoms, *The Impossible Office?: The History of the British Prime Minister*, Cambridge, Cambridge University Press, 2021, pp. 174–8.
4 https://www.thetimes.co.uk/article/conradblackondonaldtrumpborisjohnsonandhisprisondaysbp8pcqj2w
5 Jacob Freedland, *Varsity*, 2022, https://www.varsity.co.uk/interviews/23675
6 Interview, Martin Vander Weyer.
7 https://www.thetimes.co.uk/article/charlotteedwardesonborisjohnsonswanderinghandshnxnqwbb8
8 https://twitter.com/bbclaurak/status/1178632915510538240
9 Peter Snowdon, *Back from the Brink: The Inside Story of the Tory Resurrection*, London, HarperCollins, 2010, p. 297.
10 https://www.independent.co.uk/news/uk/politics/aneraendsatthesextatorasjohnsonchoosespoliticsoverjournalism518864.html
11 Interview, Eddie Lister.
12 Interview, George Osborne.
13 The 'Festival of Brexit' (branded as 'UNBOXED') and COP26 would both prove inadequate replications of the grand stage of the Olympics for Johnson, though the latter was a success in its own right.
14 Interview, Neale Coleman.
15 Interview, George Osborne.
16 *Evening Standard*, 3 March 2016.
17 https://www.independent.co.uk/news/uk/politics/londonmayoralelections2016ananalysisofborisjohnsonsrecordaftereightyearsinofficea7013971.html
18 https://yougov.co.uk/topics/politics/articlesreports/2021/03/15/londonersthinktheywouldbebettermayor
19 Interview, Guto Harri.
20 Interview, Mark Fullbrook.
21 https://www.theguardian.com/politics/2015/mar/23/davidcameroniwouldnotservethirdtermaspm
22 Tim Shipman, *All Out War: The Full Story of How Brexit Sank Britain's Political Class*, London, William Collins, 2016, pp. 159–60.
23 https://www.thetimes.co.uk/article/bloodiedborisbagspound500000forlifeofbardsbz5hmcd2ln
24 David Cameron, 2015 Conference Speech.
25 Interview, George Osborne.
26 Interview, Oliver Lewis.
27 Correspondence, Will Walden, 29 November 2022.
28 Interview, Will Walden.
29 David Cameron, resignation speech outside No. 10.
30 Anthony Seldon and Raymond Newell, *May at 10*, London, Biteback, 2019, p. 30.
31 https://www.theguardian.com/politics/2016/mar/09/davidcameronrulesoutresigningeureferendumbrexit
32 Interview, Mark Fullbrook.
33 Interview, Paul Stephenson.
34 Seldon and Newell, *May at 10*, p. 74.
35 Interview, Eddie Lister.
36 Interview, Simon McDonald.
37 Seldon and Newell, *May at 10*, p. 155.
38 Interview, Simon McDonald.
39 Interview, David Frost.
40 Seldon and Newell, *May at 10*, p. 265.
41 https://www.economist.com/europe/2018/07/11/thankstoborisjohnsonafarcicalwestbalkansummitinlondon
42 Seldon and Newell, *May at 10*, p. 443.

43 Boris Johnson, Foreign Secretary resignation speech, 9 July 2022, https://www.bbc.co.uk/news/ukpolitics44772804
44 Seldon and Newell, *May at 10*, p. 443.
45 https://www.bbc.co.uk/news/ukpolitics44767848
46 https://www.telegraph.co.uk/politics/2018/06/23/eudiplomatsshockedboriss fourletterreplybusinessconcerns/
47 Interview, David Frost.
48 https://www.telegraph.co.uk/politics/2018/09/16/headingcarcrashbrexittheresa mayschequersplan/
49 https://twitter.com/Peston/status/1047452616584830976?ref_src=twsrc%5Etfw
50 https://yougov.co.uk/topics/politics/articlesreports/2018/10/16/borisjohnsons popularityhasplummetedamongcons
51 Tim Shipman, 'Boris Johnson sex dossier sparks Tory civil war', *Sunday Times*, 9 September 2018.
52 Interview, Gavin Williamson.
53 Interview, James Wharton.
54 https://www.theguardian.com/politics/2019/jun/21/policecalledtoloudaltercation atborisjohnsonshome
55 Interview, Eddie Lister.
56 Seldon et al., *The Impossible Office?*, pp. 136–7.
57 https://www.tortoisemedia.com/2021/06/03/theinvisiblefixer/
58 https://www.telegraph.co.uk/politics/0/muniramirzadougiesmithpowerfulcouple downingstreet/

2: BREXIT

1 Interview, Guto Harri.
2 See Chapter 8 for the repercussions of Brexit and the UK's ongoing relationship with the EU.
3 The Uccle school was also attended by European Commission President Ursula von der Leyen, and the two later reminisced about shared teachers during their meetings.
4 Andrew Gimson, *Boris: The Rise of Boris Johnson*, London, Simon & Schuster, 2006, p. 27.
5 Boris Johnson, *Lend Me* Your *Ears*, London, HarperCollins, 2003, Afterword.
6 Gimson, *Boris*, p. 104.
7 Boris Johnson, BBC Radio 4, *Desert Island Discs*, 2005, https://www.bbc.co.uk/programmes/p00935b6
8 Interview, David Frost.
9 A view largely borrowed from Sir Humphrey Appleby's explanation of British diplomatic objectives in Series 1, Episode 5 of *Yes Minister*; Boris Johnson, *Friends, Voters, Countrymen*, London, HarperCollins, 2001, p. 39.
10 The most indicative Johnson speech on the EU from this period is his intervention in the 2003 Commons debate on current and future EU expansion: 'I do not know whether any hon. Members are foolish enough to oppose eventual Turkish membership of the European Union. If so, I ask them where they think Europa was when she was raped by the bull?… I am not by any means an ultraEurosceptic. In some ways, I am a bit of a fan of the European Union. If we did not have one, we would invent something like it… My only contention is that, in order to reap the benefits [of EU membership], it is not necessary to build a single European polity, as we appear to be trying to do.' House of Commons Hansard, 21 May 2003, Column 1081–1082.
11 Interview, George Osborne.
12 https://www.spectator.co.uk/article/michaelgovewhyimbackingbrexit/
13 David Cameron, *For the Record*, London, William Collins, 2019, p. 651.
14 Ibid., p. 660.
15 Ibid., p. 665.
16 Kate Fall, *The Gatekeeper*, London, HarperCollins, 2020, p. 283.
17 https://www.theguardian.com/politics/2016/feb/20/eureferendumdavidcameron borisjohnsoneurope
18 Interview, Neale Coleman.
19 Interview, Will Walden.
20 Interview, David Frost.
21 Marina Wheeler, 'A court of injustice', *Spectator*, 13 February 2016.
22 Interview, David Frost.
23 Ibid.
24 Ibid.
25 Tim Shipman and Caroline Wheeler, *Sunday Times*, 18 November 2018.
26 *Telegraph*, 10 March 2019.
27 https://www.gov.uk/government/speeches/pmstatementonbrexit20march2019
28 Seldon and Newell, *May at 10*, p. 578.
29 Interview, David Frost.

30 Although it contained some of the prototypical strategy, the whiteboard was as much a marketing tool for the 'new look' serious Johnson as a genuine planning document. The bullet points as to the method by which he would deliver Brexit included the impossibly vague 'sort Northern Ireland' and a self-imposed decree of 'no holidays'.
31 Interview, Michael Gove.
32 Interview, David Frost.
33 https://www.theguardian.com/politics/2021/may/26/dominiccummingscovidchaosno10likeoutofcontrolmovieborisjohnson
34 Interview, Mark Fullbrook.
35 Interview, Nikki da Costa.
36 Ibid.
37 Interview, Eddie Lister.
38 See Chapter 6 for further details on Cummings and staffing structure (July–December 2019).
39 Interview, Oliver Lewis.
40 Interview, Nikki da Costa.
41 https://www.telegraph.co.uk/politics/2019/03/10/brusselshastreatedbritishgovernmentcondescensionbordering/
42 Michael Gove, 'We must leave the EU on time. We cannot let voters down again', *Sunday Times*, 22 September 2019.
43 Institute for Government, *The civil service after Brexit: lessons from the Article 50 period* (2020), p. 22.
44 Interview, Nikki da Costa.
45 Interview, Oliver Lewis.
46 Interview, Geoffrey Cox.
47 Exhibit JGJ/1, R (Miller) v The Prime Minister.
48 Interview, Geoffrey Cox.
49 https://news.sky.com/story/exclusivepmwasadvisedbyattorneygeneralsuspensionwaslawful11818599
50 Ministers Reflect, Dominic Grieve, Institute for Government, 20 July 2015.
51 Interview, Oliver Lewis.
52 https://www.thetimes.co.uk/article/thisisntanotherfinemessivegotyouintoborisitsacummingsplantocrushlabourinageneralelection0q3c0swhr
53 Interview, Amber Rudd.
54 Interview, Nikki da Costa.
55 For further details on the attempt to secure a general election, see Chapter 3.
56 Politico Playbook, Jack Blanchard, 26 September 2019.
57 Interview, Nikki da Costa.
58 Whether prorogation fell within the bounds of justiciability continues to be a highly controversial topic within the legal community, even as we publish.
59 https://www.supremecourt.uk/cases/docs/uksc20190192judgment.pdf
60 Tim Shipman, 'Cling on tight – Boris Johnson and co's whiteknuckle Brexit ride just got wilder', *Sunday Times*, 20 October 2019.
61 https://www.irishtimes.com/culture/books/2022/10/01/brexitbackstopbluesweweintheroomonourownforagoodwhilethatwasthelongesttimeweweretogetherjustthetwoofusoverteaandbiscuits/
62 Interview, David Frost.
63 https://www.thetimes.co.uk/article/brexitnoprimeministercouldagreetodividewithnorthernirelandmaysaysstt0fwhhw
64 https://www.newsletter.co.uk/news/politics/watchborisjohnsontelldup2018hewouldneverputborderirishseatodayheputborderirishsea816300
65 https://twitter.com/SkyNews/status/1203657804722135040
66 https://twitter.com/Dominic2306/status/1448059195807440902
67 https://www.itv.com/news/utv/20200813/irishseatradeborderovermydeadbodysaysjohnson
68 Interview, David Frost.
69 https://twitter.com/steve_hawkes/status/1170979456611233792?s=20&t=b4qnpdTAVpXIrOlww56Xqg
70 https://www.theguardian.com/politics/2019/sep/05/borisjohnsonratherbedeadinditchthanagreebrexitextension
71 Their demands were that: any monetary contributions were conditional on a deal, a sovereignty clause in the agreement; a joint committee rather than the European Court of Justice would be the arbiter of any future trade agreements; and the ECJ had no veto power in the future relationship.
72 Interview, Oliver Lewis.
73 https://www.thetimes.co.uk/article/clingontightborisjohnsonandcoswhiteknucklebrexitridejustgotwilder66g7mstqg

3: ELECTION

1 https://yougov.co.uk/topics/politics/trackers/governmentapproval

2 https://yougov.co.uk/topics/politics/articlesreports/2019/07/24/votingintentioncon25libdem23lab19brex17
3 https://www.telegraph.co.uk/politics/2019/08/05/brexitlatestnewsnodealborisjohnsonlive1/
4 Interview, Graham Brady.
5 Interview, Nikki da Costa.
6 Interview, Isaac Levido.
7 Ibid.
8 Ibid.
9 The public antipathy towards the 2017 general election was best summed up by Brenda, a woman from Bristol interviewed on the street by a BBC reporter, whose reaction upon hearing the news went viral: 'Not another one!'
10 Ironically, Theresa May had been instrumental in laying the foundation for this narrative, her 20 March 2019 speech in Downing Street lashing out at MPs for their indecision on the issue. https://www.gov.uk/government/speeches/pmstatementonbrexit20march2019
11 Sebastian Payne, *Broken Heartlands: A Journey through Labour's Lost England*, London, Macmillan, 2020, p. 25.
12 Interview, Michael Brooks.
13 For more on Johnson's approach to Brexit negotiations and no deal, see Chapter 2.
14 Interview, Michael Brooks.
15 For further detail on the 2019 Spending Review, see Chapter 7.
16 https://www.mirror.co.uk/news/politics/borisjohnsons40newhospitals20327320
17 Johnson would later entertain Conservative campaign staffers at pep talks by going on extensive tangents that touched on every possible linguistic alternative to the slogan he could conjure.
18 Tim Shipman and Caroline Wheeler, 'This isn't another fine mess I've got you into, Boris. It's a Cummings plan to crush Labour in a general election', *Sunday Times*, 8 September 2019.
19 https://d25d2506sfb94s.cloudfront.net/cumulus_uploads/document/unhyjkudnd/InternalResults_190829_VI_w.pdf
20 Interview, Michael Brooks.
21 Boris Johnson, Hansard, 25 September 2019, Column 777.
22 Interview, David Canzini.
23 Interview, Michael Brooks.
24 Payne, *Broken Heartlands*, pp. 19–20 – named the Red Wall by James Kanagasooriam after the Brian Jacques children's fantasy novels.
25 James Kanagasooriam and Elizabeth Simon, 'Red Wall: The Definitive Description', *Political Insight*, 12(3), 8–11, 2021, https://doi.org/10.1177/20419058211045127
26 https://www.britishelectionstudy.com/besresources/pressreleasemostvolatilebritishelectorateinmoderntimes/#.Y4PhTHbP2Ul
27 https://www.insider.com/brexitdonorarronbankstellsfaragetostanddowninlabourmarginalseats201911
28 Interview, Nigel Farage.
29 https://www.theguardian.com/politics/2021/nov/03/nigelfaragesbrexitpartysavedlabourseatsin2019electionanalysisfinds
30 Robert Ford et al., *The British General Election of 2019*, London, Palgrave Macmillan, Chapter 13.
31 https://ukandeu.ac.uk/arethenewconservativempsreallysodifferent/
32 https://news.sky.com/story/borisjohnsonspersonalappealwaslessimportantin2019victorythanmanythought12598727
33 https://yougov.co.uk/topics/politics/surveyresults/daily/2019/11/19/43ac2/1
34 https://www.politicshome.com/news/article/watchconservativeministerapologisesfordoctoredkeirstarmervideo
35 Interview, Rachel Wolf.
36 Ibid.
37 Ibid.
38 Although ostensibly popular and attracting significant media attention, Labour's manifesto would soon turn out to be less successful than CCHQ feared. Though most of the individual policies Labour presented were popular, the public feared the package as a whole was economically irresponsible. https://yougov.co.uk/topics/politics/articlesreports/2019/11/12/laboureconomicpoliciesarepopularsowhyarent
39 Interview, Michael Brooks.
40 Interview, Paul Stephenson.
41 Ford et al., *The British General Election of 2019*, p. 223.
42 Interview, Isaac Levido.
43 https://www.thetimes.co.uk/article/sedgefieldfellandtheyeruptedintosongthingscanonlygetbetter9cjfz9hj8
44 For more on Cummings' vision for government, see Chapter 6.
45 https://www.gov.uk/government/speeches/pmstatementindowningstreet13december2019

46 https://www.thenorthernecho.co.uk/news/18101982.borisjohnsonholdsvictoryrally sedgefield/
47 https://news.sky.com/story/borisjohnsons personalappealwaslessimportantin2019 victorythanmanythought12598727
48 Interview, Michael Brooks.

4: DREAMS

1 Seldon et al., *The Impossible Office?*, pp. 313–16.
2 https://renewal.org.uk/archive/vol302022/conservatismintheageofborisjohnson/
3 *The Prime Minister at 300*, BBC Radio 4, May 2021.
4 Benjamin Disraeli, *Vindication of the English Constitution in a Letter to a Noble and Learned Lord*, London, 1835.
5 Douglas Hurd and Edward Young, *Disraeli: or, The Two Lives*, London, Weidenfeld & Nicolson, 2013, Chapter 8.
6 Johnson kept a bust of the Athenian statesman on his desk in 10 Downing Street.
7 IQ2 debate, 29 June 2013, Chalke Valley History Festival. https://cvhf.org.uk/historyhub/iq2debateancientsvmoderns/
8 Interview, Guto Harri.
9 Ibid.
10 Tom Bower, *Boris Johnson: The Gambler*, London, W.H. Allen, p. 64.
11 https://hansard.parliament.uk/commons/20220720/debates/63F450D46D44 4D0B915A8D06DCDD7E4A/Engagements
12 Interview, Guto Harri.
13 Interview, Michael Gove.
14 Boris Johnson, Foreword to 2019 Conservative Manifesto.
15 Interview, David Frost.
16 https://www.theguardian.com/politics/2020/mar/29/20000nhsstaffreturnto servicejohnsonsaysfromcoronavirus isolation
17 Interview, Guto Harri.
18 Interview, Mark Spencer.
19 Interview, Ross Kempsell.
20 https://graziadaily.co.uk/life/inthenews/borisjohnsoninspiringwomen/
21 https://www.theguardian.com/commentisfree/2019/feb/17/absurdvanity projectforourageborisjohnsongardenbridge
22 For more on the differences between Cummings and Johnson in ideology, see Chapter 6.
23 Interview, Cleo Watson.
24 https://twitter.com/mragilligan/status/1592154352776798209?s=20&t=KSkeMZA4ueZLfdXG3deog
25 Interview, Grant Shapps.
26 Interview, Will Walden.
27 Ibid.
28 https://www.telegraph.co.uk/politics/2019/11/05/dealovenreadygetbrexitdone takecountryforward/
29 Interview, George Osborne.
30 Hansard, House of Commons, 22 May 1868, Second reading. https://api.parliament.uk/historichansard/commons/1868/may/22/secondreading
31 Interview, Andy Haldane.
32 Johnson and Windsor had first bonded when he was Mayor, Windsor his adviser for street parties.
33 Interview, David Frost.
34 Dominic Cummings Blog, Snippets 6, 16 July 2022.
35 Interview, Michael Gove.
36 https://www.telegraph.co.uk/news/earth/energy/10154424/Windfarmscouldntpull theskinoffaricepuddingsaysBorisJohnson.html
37 https://www.telegraph.co.uk/news/uknews/immigration/10404421/BorisIam theonlyBritishpoliticianwhowilladmitto beingproimmigration.html
38 http://www.voteleavetakecontrol.org/boris_johnson_the_only_way_to_take_back_control_of_immigration_is_to_vote_leave_on_23_june.html
39 https://www.reuters.com/article/britaineu johnsoncommentsidCNL8N19J1UK
40 https://www.bsa.natcen.ac.uk/latestreport/britishsocialattitudes38/immigration.aspx
41 Interview, Gavin Williamson.

5: COVID

1 Perhaps the notable exception being Gordon Brown, whose Downing Street equalled Johnson's in factionalized chaos. Combined with his inability to delegate and take big decisions without certainty and confidence, he would likely have struggled with the pace and intensity of choices presented by the pandemic.

2 Exercise Cygnus Report, published 13 July 2017. https://assets.publishing.service.gov.uk/government/uploads/system/uploads/attachment_data/file/927770/exercisecygnusreport.pdf
3 https://www.gov.uk/government/publications/coronavirusactionplan
4 https://journals.plos.org/plosone/article?id=10.1371/journal.pone.0257978
5 https://www.reuters.com/investigates/specialreport/healthcoronavirusbritaintracing/
6 Q1003, https://committees.parliament.uk/oralevidence/2249/html/
7 https://twitter.com/Dominic2306/status/1397452170249842691?s=20&t=Sj7axt30_ziDbGLwaUqN7w
8 https://www.imperial.ac.uk/mrcglobalinfectiousdiseaseanalysis/covid19/report9impactofnpisoncovid19/
9 https://www.gov.uk/government/speeches/pmstatementoncoronavirus16march2020
10 Interview, Eddie Lister.
11 https://www.gov.uk/government/speeches/chancelloroftheexchequerrishisunakoncovid19response
12 https://www.gov.uk/government/publications/hmrcissuebriefingtacklingerrorandfraudinthecovid19supportschemes/tacklingerrorandfraudinthecovid19supportschemes#errorandfraudestimates
13 https://royalsocietypublishing.org/doi/10.1098/rstb.2020.0264
14 Although the announcement was made on 23 March, the legislation underpinning it would not be introduced until 26 March.
15 https://www.gov.uk/government/speeches/pmaddresstothenationoncoronavirus23march2020
16 https://www.theguardian.com/tvandradio/2020/mar/24/borisjohnsonscovid19addressisoneofmostwatchedtvprogrammesever?CMP=gu_com
17 Sonia Purnell, *Just Boris: A Tale of Blond Ambition*, London, Aurum Press, 2011, p. 25.
18 Interview, David Halpern.
19 Interview, Isaac Levido.
20 https://www.reuters.com/world/uk/ukpmjohnsondismissedcovid19lockdownonlyelderlywoulddieexaidesays20210719/
21 https://liberalhistory.org.uk/2020/04/lloydgeorgeandspanishfluinsicknessandinhealth/
22 For more on Johnson and the Roman goddess of luck, see the conversation between Tom McTague and Tom Holland quoted in https://www.theatlantic.com/international/archive/2022/04/borisjohnsonukrainecovidlockdownparty/629576/
23 Matt Hancock, *Pandemic Diaries*, London, Biteback, 2022, pp. 173, 189.
24 https://www.bbc.co.uk/news/health52374513
25 Interview, Gavin Williamson.
26 https://assets.publishing.service.gov.uk/government/uploads/system/uploads/attachment_data/file/884760/Our_plan_to_rebuild_The_UK_Government_s_COVID19_recovery_strategy.pdf
27 https://www.thetimes.co.uk/article/coronavirusborisjohnsonandcivilservicechiefsirmarksedwillclashoveractionplang05tx5256
28 For more on the Cummings–Sedwill and Cummings–Case relationships, and the appointments process, see Chapter 6.
29 The extent to which attempts were successful at detoxifying the atmosphere is discussed in Chapter 9.
30 https://twitter.com/Dominic2306/status/1405112267729952770
31 https://academic.oup.com/ej/article/132/643/1200/6382847
32 Interview, Graham Brady.
33 https://twitter.com/Dominic2306/status/1524394482938093571?s=20&t=KgZRiHqWma79CcoA5GGQ
34 Interview, Michael Gove.
35 Both contemporaneous analysis observing patterns of per capita deaths in different countries (https://www.ncbi.nlm.nih.gov/pmc/articles/PMC7289569/) and subsequent antibody analysis (https://www.ons.gov.uk/peoplepopulationandcommunity/healthandsocialcare/conditionsanddiseases/articles/coronaviruscovid19latestinsights/antibodies) strongly opposed claims of widespread herd immunity. The antibody analysis showed less than 10 per cent of the population possessed a low level of antibodies by 7 December 2020.
36 https://www.thetimes.co.uk/article/48hoursinseptemberwhenministersandscientistssplitovercovidlockdownvg5xbpsfx
37 https://www.gov.uk/government/publications/summaryoftheeffectivenessandharmsofdifferentnonpharmaceuticalinterventions16september2020/summaryoftheeffectivenessandharmsofdifferentnonpharmaceuticalinterventions21september2020

38 See Chapter 6 for more on Covid and its effect on the Cummings–Johnson relationship.
39 https://www.gov.uk/government/publications/sage61minutescoronavirus covid19response8october2020
40 https://www.ons.gov.uk/peoplepopulationandcommunity/healthandsocialcare/conditions anddiseases/bulletins/coronavirus covid19infectionsurveypilot/30october2020
41 https://www.manchestereveningnews.co.uk/news/greatermanchesternews/andy burnhamlivepressconference19083297
42 https://www.dailymail.co.uk/news/article 9510133/BorisJohnsonsaidbodiespilehigh orderlockdownsourcesclaim.html
43 https://www.gov.uk/government/speeches/primeministersstatementoncoronavirus covid1931october2020
44 https://www.theguardian.com/politics/2020/oct/31/downingstreetlaunchescovid lockdownleakinquiry
45 https://www.gov.uk/government/speeches/primeministersstatementoncoronavirus covid1923november2020
46 Interview, Gavin Williamson.
47 Hancock, *Pandemic Diaries*, p. 442.
48 https://www.thetimes.co.uk/article/borisjohnsonsaidhewouldletcovidripin lockdownrowfs0ffz5mg
49 https://www.who.int/data/stories/global excessdeathsassociatedwithcovid19 january2020december2021. https://www.theguardian.com/business/2022/sep/30/ukisonlyg7countrywithsmallereconomy thanbeforecovid19
50 https://www.theguardian.com/politics/2022/jan/30/wegotthebigcallsrightsaid borisjohnsonbutdidhereally

6: CUMMINGS

1 For a structural overview of the role of chief adviser, see Dennis Kavanagh and Anthony Seldon, *The Powers Behind the Prime Minister: The Hidden Influence of Number Ten*, London, HarperCollins, 2020, and Andrew Blick and George Jones, *At Power's Elbow: Aides to the Prime Minister from Robert Walpole to David Cameron*, London, Biteback, 2013.
2 https://www.lrb.co.uk/thepaper/v05/n07/erichobsbawm/beforethefall
3 https://www.ft.com/content/0bf8a910 372e11eaa6d39a26f8c3cba4
4 Ibid.
5 Anthony Seldon with Peter Snowdon and Daniel Collings, *Blair Unbound*, London, Simon & Schuster, 2007, pp. 205–14.
6 https://conservativehome.com/2014/05/15/aprofileofdominiccummingsfriendof goveandenemyofclegg/
7 https://bylinetimes.com/2020/01/09/theodysseanprojectinsearchofdominic cummingspartone/
8 https://conservativehome.com/2014/05/15/aprofileofdominiccummingsfriendof goveandenemyofclegg/
9 Interview, Sam Freedman.
10 Interview, David Bell.
11 Interview, Alison Wolf.
12 https://www.theguardian.com/politics/2019/jul/26/dominiccummingsacareer psychopathindowningstreet
13 https://www.ft.com/content/e78f9402 ab6111e3aad900144feab7de
14 Anthony Seldon and Peter Snowdon, *Cameron at 10: The Verdict*, London, William Collins, 2016, p. 403.
15 https://dominiccummings.com/the odysseanproject2/
16 https://www.newstatesman.com/politics/2019/09/dominiccummingsthemachiavel indowningstreet
17 https://www.economist.com/bagehots notebook/2016/01/21/aninterviewwith dominiccummings
18 Interview, Sam Freedman.
19 https://dominiccummings.substack.com/p/howcouldlabourwinswapduddead
20 https://www.theguardian.com/politics/2019/jul/26/dominiccummingsacareer psychopathindowningstreet
21 Interview, James Wharton.
22 https://dominiccummings.substack.com/p/whyiwenttono10insummer2019
23 Interview, Ben Elliot.
24 Interview, David Bell.
25 Interview, Eddie Lister.
26 https://dominiccummings.com/2019/06/26/onthereferendum33highperformance governmentcognitivetechnologiesmichael nielsenbretvictorseeingrooms/
27 https://www.thetimes.co.uk/article/tantrumstearsthetruthaboutbullyingin westminstervc5c7qqfn
28 Interview, Sajid Javid.
29 https://www.theguardian.com/politics/2019/sep/05/borisjohnsonratherbedeadin ditchthanagreebrexitextension

30 https://www.thetimes.co.uk/article/this isntanotherfinemessivegotyouintoborisits acummingsplantocrushlabourinageneral election0q3c0swhr
31 Interview, David Frost.
32 Interview, Michael Gove.
33 Interview, Cleo Watson.
34 https://www.theguardian.com/uknews/ 2020/mar/07/parliamentarywatchdog investigatesjohnsoncaribbeanholiday
35 Interview, Will Walden.
36 Interview, Guto Harri.
37 Interview, Gavin Williamson.
38 Interview, Michael Gove.
39 For more on the Integrated Review, see Chapter 8.
40 Interview, Michael Gove.
41 Interview, David Frost.
42 Interview, George Osborne.
43 Interview, Sajid Javid.
44 Ibid.
45 Interview, Mark Spencer.
46 https://twitter.com/Dominic2306/status/ 1408866176323706891
47 The key difference between the two was the skillsets of the Chancellors, and as a result their lead aides Harrison and Booth -Smith, as mirror opposites. Sunak and Harrison handled the economics, Osborne and Booth-Smith the politics.
48 https://www.dailymail.co.uk/news/article 8101229/Herisenchallengeexchancellor SajidJavidleadsBudgetpraiseRishiSunak. html
49 https://dominiccummings.com/2020/ 01/02/twohandsarealotwerehiringdata scientistsprojectmanagerspolicyexperts assortedweirdos/
50 https://www.theguardian.com/politics/ 2020/feb/17/andrewsabiskyborisjohnsons exadviserinhisownwords
51 https://www.theguardian.com/politics/ 2020/feb/03/politicaljournalistsboycottno 10briefingafterreporterban
52 https://dominiccummings.substack.com/ p/peopleideasmachinesinoteson
53 For further explanation of Sedwill's departure and replacement, see Chapter 9.
54 Interview, Graham Brady.
55 https://www.independent.co.uk/news/ uk/politics/dominiccummingsstatement speechtranscriptdurhamfulltextread lockdowna9531856.html
56 Interview, Will Walden.
57 Interview, Ben Elliot.
58 Interview, Sajid Javid.
59 Interview, Mark Spencer.
60 https://www.theguardian.com/tvandradio/ 2020/dec/23/tvnews2020covidratings dominiccummings
61 Interview, Mark Spencer.
62 Interview, Graham Brady.
63 https://www.dailymail.co.uk/news/article 8950507/CruelPrincessNutNutnickname Carrieusedmonths.html
64 Interview, Oliver Lewis.
65 Interview, Eddie Lister.
66 https://www.thetimes.co.uk/article/ therewerethreeoftheminthismarriage 33xpxgmn7
67 https://dominiccummings.substack.com/ p/partiesphotostrolleysvariants
68 It's no surprise Friedrich Nietzsche's *Beyond Good and Evil* remains outwardly Cummings' favourite book for explaining the world of UK politics.

7: DOMESTIC

1 Interview, Kate Bingham.
2 https://www.independent.co.uk/news/uk/ politics/matthancockvaccinekatebingham prb1720247.html
3 https://www.telegraph.co.uk/politics/ 2022/08/31/liztrussrishisunaktory leadershipfinalhustingslondon/
4 https://www.gov.uk/government/speeches/ pmstatementtothehouseofcommonson roadmapforeasinglockdownrestrictionsin england22february2021
5 https://yougov.co.uk/topics/politics/ articlesreports/2021/05/22/voting intentioncon46lab281920may
6 https://www.politico.eu/newsletter/ londonplaybook/politicolondonplaybook lizandlyntonatthelodgefreedoomedbojoin brussels/
7 For more on the delivery unit, see Chapter 9.
8 Interview, Michael Barber.
9 A fifth was added later, covering crime and immigration.
10 https://twitter.com/BorisJohnson/status/ 1198340442451935232?s=20&t=pDNA vuwGtCbVPrCOKa315w
11 https://www.ukonward.com/reports/ measuringupforlevellingup/
12 https://www.gov.uk/government/speeches/ theprimeministerslevellingupspeech15july 2021
13 Interview, Andy Haldane.
14 Ibid.

15 For more, see UKICE's Levelling Up: What England Thinks. https://ukandeu.ac.uk/wpcontent/uploads/2022/09/UKICELevellingUpReport.pdf
16 https://www.gov.uk/government/speeches/pmstatementontransportinfrastructure11february2020
17 Interview, Michael Gove.
18 https://www.gov.uk/government/speeches/pmsskillsspeech29september2020
19 Interview, Alison Wolf.
20 Ibid.
21 Interview, Dan Rosenfield.
22 Interview, Andrew Dilnot.
23 Original quoted from Churchill's 'Four Years Plan' speech delivered on 21 March 1943 – which Dilnot found in Martin Gilbert's *Churchill: A Life*.
24 https://www.instituteforgovernment.org.uk/explainer/healthandsocialcarelevy
25 Interview, Meg Powell-Chandler.
26 https://hansard.parliament.uk/commons/20221117/debates/97DB3122006846CDB026F757C8DF39AF/AutumnStatement
27 https://www.bma.org.uk/adviceandsupport/nhsdeliveryandworkforce/pressures/nhsbacklogdataanalysis
28 https://committees.parliament.uk/publications/23246/documents/171671/default/
29 https://www.bmj.com/content/377/bmj.o1068
30 Anthony Seldon, 'A vision for culture under Johnson: "Build a team, then let Boris be Boris", *Evening Standard*, 22 July 2019.
31 Interview, Damon Buffini.
32 Interview, Oliver Dowden.
33 https://www.theguardian.com/education/2020/nov/08/marcusrashfordforcesborisjohnsonintoseconduturnonchildfoodpoverty
34 https://www.telegraph.co.uk/politics/2020/06/18/takingkneesymbolsubjugationsubordinationdominicraabsays/
35 https://twitter.com/TyroneMings/status/1414655312074784785?lang=es
36 https://www.theguardian.com/football/2021/apr/20/ukgovernmentmaylegislatetostopeuropeansuperleaguesaysminister
37 https://www.telegraph.co.uk/politics/2020/06/14/rathertearpeopleshouldbuildothers/
38 Interview, Jack Doyle.
39 https://longreads.politicshome.com/truthliesandracismthestorybehindthesewellreport
40 https://ukandeu.ac.uk/partnerreports/peoplesstatedreasonsforvotingleaveorremain/
41 https://twitter.com/RidgeOnSunday/status/1203604209993682945
42 https://www.bbc.co.uk/news/uk63743259
43 https://www.politicshome.com/news/article/cabinettaskforcemigrantsmallboatcrossingsnickthomassymondspritipatel
44 https://yougov.co.uk/topics/travel/surveyresults/daily/2022/04/14/8bb29/1
45 https://www.carbonbrief.org/revealedthe11slidesthatfinallyconvincedborisjohnsonaboutglobalwarming/
46 https://www.bbc.co.uk/news/scienceenvironment54285497
47 https://www.gov.uk/government/publications/thetenpointplanforagreenindustrialrevolution
48 https://www.dailymail.co.uk/news/article2510936/CutgreencpCameronsprivateviewenergytaxationhorrifyenvironmentalcampaigners.html
49 https://www.newstatesman.com/chartoftheday/2022/12/austeritydevastatedukhomeinsulationclimatechange
50 https://www.thetimes.co.uk/article/rishisunakitsavoltfarceasenergyfirmtaxisfinallyagreedgwt02ndj9
51 https://www.ft.com/content/6f584312d76049789be04897cbc8b172
52 https://www.gov.uk/government/publications/britishenergysecuritystrategy/britishenergysecuritystrategy
53 Interview, Rory Gribbell.
54 https://schoolsweek.co.uk/dfes14bneducationrecoveryplanwhatyouneedtoknow/
55 https://www.cypnow.co.uk/news/article/collinscallsfor10yeareducationcatchupplanfundedthroughpupilpremium
56 The meeting was organized by Anthony Seldon.
57 Interview, Alison Wolf.
58 https://www.gov.uk/government/news/pmbuildbuildbuild
59 https://hansard.parliament.uk/Commons/20211214/division/4E14706680234651A796E71754052043/publichealth
60 https://www.gov.uk/government/speeches/primeministersaddresstothenationonboosterjabs12december2021
61 https://www.ft.com/content/2b309e14046e4dbd976f1bffb66188ab
62 https://committees.parliament.uk/event/6214/formalmeetingoralevidencesession/
63 Interview, Michael Gove.

64 https://www.gov.uk/government/speeches/cabinetsecretarylecturewednesday13october20212
65 https://www.telegraph.co.uk/politics/2023/01/10/borisjohnsontellsconservativesfightlowtaxbritainchallenge/
66 https://twitter.com/ShippersUnbound/status/1445711840378511360?s=20&t=Mcjgcq139kU5o4he7xeR7g

8: GLOBAL

1 Interview, Michael Gove.
2 https://www.gov.uk/government/speeches/pmspeechingreenwich3february2020
3 Interview, David Frost.
4 https://www.theguardian.com/politics/2020/jun/30/theresamaysaysdavidfrostuksnewnationalsecurityadviserhasnoprovenexpertise
5 Anthony Seldon, 'The prime minister's private office from John Martin to Chris Martin', in Andrew Holt and Warren Dockter (eds), *Private Secretaries to the Prime Minister: Foreign Affairs from Churchill to Thatcher*, London, Routledge, 2017.
6 Anthony Seldon and Dennis Kavanaugh (eds), *The Thatcher Effect: A Decade of Change*, Oxford, Oxford University Press, 1989.
7 https://www.ft.com/content/a9ce4564930f439aac42d9b055712ee6
8 Before joining Johnson in the Foreign Office, Frost was chief executive of the Scotch Whisky Association.
9 Interview, Simon McDonald.
10 https://www.telegraph.co.uk/news/politics/borisjohnson/12039931/BorisJohnsonTheonlyreasonIwouldntvisitsomepartsofNewYorkistherealriskofmeetingDonaldTrump.html
11 https://www.theguardian.com/politics/2016/nov/11/borisjohnsondoomandgloomdonaldtrumpnigelfaragetheresamay
12 Interview, Kim Darroch.
13 https://www.theguardian.com/politics/2017/jan/09/borisjohnsonholdswarmandfranktalkswithtrumpaides
14 https://www.politico.com/news/2019/12/12/trumpborisjohnsonrelationship083732
15 Interview, Kim Darroch.
16 Interview, Gerard Lyons.
17 https://www.theguardian.com/politics/2016/apr/22/barackobamabrexitukbackofqueuefortradetalks
18 https://www.bbc.co.uk/news/uk49325620
19 https://twitter.com/realDonaldTrump/status/1205368801438707713
20 https://www.newstatesman.com/world/americas/northamerica/2022/06/sarahchurchwellborisjohnsondislikedbidenracisttreatmentobama
21 Anthony Seldon, *Churchill's Indian Summer: The Conservative Government, 1951–55*, London, Hodder & Stoughton, 1981, p. 212.
22 Interview, David Frost.
23 Ibid.
24 https://www.ft.com/content/cc6b0d9ad8cc4ddb8c57726df018c10e
25 Interview, David Frost.
26 Ibid.
27 https://dominiccummings.substack.com/p/riskaggressionbrexitandarticle
28 Ibid.
29 Interview, Julian Smith.
30 Interview, Geoffrey Cox.
31 Interview, Julian Smith.
32 Interview, David Frost.
33 Interview, Oliver Lewis.
34 https://www.reuters.com/article/usbritaineulewislawidINKBN25Z1ZS
35 https://www.bbc.co.uk/news/ukpolitics54073836
36 https://www.mirror.co.uk/news/politics/brexitjohnmajorblastsgovernment22656613
37 https://www.mirror.co.uk/news/politics/brexitextoryleadermichael22661092
38 https://www.gov.uk/government/publications/governmentstatementonnotwithstandingclauses/governmentstatementonnotwithstandingclauses
39 https://www.ft.com/content/cc6b0d9ad8cc4ddb8c57726df018c10e
40 Interview, David Frost.
41 https://www.ft.com/content/cc6b0d9ad8cc4ddb8c57726df018c10e
42 https://hansard.parliament.uk/commons/20201230/debates/9E132CEF83CA40BAB8B4A7127A968B68/EuropeanUnion(FutureRelationship)Bill
43 https://www.bbc.co.uk/news/ukpolitics55486081
44 https://www.ft.com/content/cc6b0d9ad8cc4ddb8c57726df018c10e
45 https://www.france24.com/en/livenews/20210129macronastrazenecavaccinequasiineffectiveforover65s

46 https://twitter.com/BorisJohnson/status/1463973204456878080
47 https://www.theguardian.com/world/2021/nov/26/macrontellsjohnsontogetseriousonchannelcrisisaftertweetedletter
48 Interview, David Frost.
49 Interview, Andrew Griffith.
50 https://www.spectator.co.uk/article/indefenceofbrexit/
51 Interview, Michael Gove.
52 https://www.telegraph.co.uk/politics/2019/08/07/momentcomesborisshouldnotafraidenlistqueenshelpfoiling/
53 https://bfpg.co.uk/2021/03/integratedreview10things/
54 Interview, John Holmes.
55 Interview, Michael Gove.
56 https://dominiccummings.substack.com/p/whyiwenttono10insummer2019
57 Interview, Anouka Dhadda.
58 Interview, Cleo Watson.
59 https://www.gov.uk/government/speeches/pmaddressatcop26worldleaderssummitopeningceremony
60 https://www.gov.uk/government/speeches/pmsstatementtothehouseoncop2615november2021
61 https://www.gov.uk/government/speeches/pmspeechatthemunichsecurityconference19february2022
62 https://www.nytimes.com/2022/03/06/opinion/borisjohnsonrussiaputinukrainewar.html
63 https://www.thetimes.co.uk/article/iwasafooltothinkwecouldresetrelationswithrussiasaysjohnsonvpm2wgr9k
64 Interview, Ben Wallace.
65 https://www.gov.uk/government/speeches/pmstatementtothehouseofcommonsonukraine24february2022
66 Ibid.
67 https://www.gov.uk/government/speeches/pmremarksatthesirwinstonchurchillleadershipawardceremony26july2022
68 BBC Two, *Putin vs the West*, episode 3, 30 January 2023.

9: GROWNUPS

1 https://www.standard.co.uk/eveningstandard/comment/comment/buildateamtodothehardgraftthenletborisbeborisandwatchthefunatno10a4195396.html
2 Anthony Seldon diary, 14 October 2021.
3 https://www.mirror.co.uk/news/politics/newspindoctornumberten18796857
4 https://www.ft.com/content/ba389c9cba0a11eaa05defc604854c3f
5 https://www.dailymail.co.uk/news/article9408161/SIMONWALTERSsisterhoodCarrie.html
6 Interview, Oliver Lewis.
7 https://www.thetimes.co.uk/article/toptoryaideiskingoftheurbanswingersh9w5bbm9dk6
8 https://www.spectator.co.uk/article/insidethecourtofcarriesymondsprincessofwhales/
9 https://www.politico.eu/newsletter/londonplaybook/politicolondonplaybookspadshockwavesbattleforno10staggeringhome/
10 Neale Coleman email, 11 January 2023.
11 https://www.spectator.co.uk/article/howthegoveitestookchargeofno10/
12 Interview, Michael Barber.
13 https://www.telegraph.co.uk/politics/2022/01/29/borisjohnsonssenioraidewatchedcricketkabulfell/
14 Interview, Nikki da Costa.
15 https://www.ft.com/content/48eaa0838bba40a18087bd07a66b2f1a
16 https://www.telegraph.co.uk/news/2021/11/12/no10snewenforcersparkspaniccourtkingboris/
17 https://www.theguardian.com/uknews/2022/feb/03/whatmuniramirzasaidinherletterresigningasborisjohnsonspolicychief
18 https://www.independent.co.uk/news/uk/politics/borisjohnsondoylemirzapartiesb2007175.html
19 https://www.channel4.com/news/taxincreaseregrettablebutresponsiblesaystreasurysecretary
20 https://www.independent.co.uk/tv/news/iwouldnthavesaiditrishisunakdistanceshimselffrompmsjimmysavilesmearatkeirstarmerb2193328.html
21 Interview, Andrew Griffith.
22 Interview, Oliver Dowden.
23 Interview, Eddie Lister.
24 https://www.telegraph.co.uk/politics/2020/02/22/topcivilservantstorieshitlist/
25 Catherine Haddon, *Reforming the Civil Service: The Efficiency Unit in the Early 1980s and the 1987 Next Steps Report*, Institute for Government, 2012.
26 Interview, Michael Gove.
27 *The Andrew Marr Show*, BBC One, 23 February 2020.
28 https://www.gov.uk/government/publications/declarationongovernmentreform

29 https://assets.publishing.service.gov.uk/government/uploads/system/uploads/attachment_data/file/937010/Findings_of_the_Independent_Adviser.pdf
30 Interview, Eddie Lister.
31 Interview, Michael Gove.
32 Interview, Grant Shapps.
33 https://www.itv.com/news/20200721/johnsonandcabinetministersgetonwithworkinsociallydistancedmeeting
34 Interview, Eddie Lister.
35 Interview, Mark Spencer.
36 https://www.spectator.co.uk/article/thehumanhandgrenade/
37 Interview, Julian Smith.
38 Interview, Geoffrey Cox.
39 Interview, Oliver Dowden.
40 Seldon, *The Impossible Office?*, pp. 170–2.
41 Interview, Dominic Raab.

10: DOWNFALL

1 https://hansard.parliament.uk/commons/2019-12-19/debates/66EEE94D-F200-4889-90AC-5EE34753AC3E/DebateOnTheAddress
2 https://www.thetimes.co.uk/article/boris-johnson-eyes-another-decade-in-power-jp0chz9xl
3 https://www.bbc.co.uk/news/uk-politics-61939938
4 https://twitter.com/LOS_Fisher/status/1541008924782088192
5 https://www.telegraph.co.uk/politics/2022/01/22/boris-johnson-attempts-quell-backbench-tory-revolt-help-praetorian/
6 https://docs.cdn.yougov.com/csigp10a5l/YG%20trackers%20-%20Voting%20Intention%20since%20GE%202019_W.pdf
7 Interview, Eddie Lister.
8 https://www.telegraph.co.uk/news/2022/07/02/suella-braverman-remainer-civil-servants-thwarting-reforms/
9 Interview, Karan Bilimoria.
10 Interview, John Manzoni.
11 Interview, Karan Bilimoria.
12 Seldon, *Churchill's Indian Summer*.
13 https://www.theguardian.com/media/2012/jul/31/boris-johnson-rupert-murdoch-olympics
14 https://www.thesun.co.uk/news/politics/19104256/boris-johnson-trevor-kavanagh-talktv-peter-bone/
15 https://www.telegraph.co.uk/politics/2020/04/03/keir-starmer-profile/
16 https://pressgazette.co.uk/publishers/nationals/pippa-crerar-on-partygate-scoops/
17 https://hansard.parliament.uk/commons/2021-12-01/debates/A0E282CF-039D-4F26-8F16-946B8C6E2ABC/Engagements
18 Interview, Pippa Crerar.
19 https://www.theguardian.com/politics/2020/jan/21/mortal-enemy-what-cummings-thinktank-said-about-bbc
20 https://www.telegraph.co.uk/politics/2019/12/15/no-10-boycotts-today-programme-citing-failure-senior-management/
21 https://www.telegraph.co.uk/comment/personal-view/3571742/If-Blairs-so-good-at-running-the-Congo-let-him-stay-there.html
22 https://www.telegraph.co.uk/politics/2019/07/25/boris-johnson-breaches-royal-protocol-meeting-queen/
23 https://www.hauspublishing.com/product/bonfire-of-the-decencies/
24 https://www.theguardian.com/politics/2022/feb/10/john-major-scathing-attack-boris-johnson-key-charges
25 https://dominiccummings.com/2021/04/23/statement-regarding-no10-claims-today/
26 https://www.thetimes.co.uk/article/guerrilla-warfare-johnson-steels-himself-for-final-assault-from-cummings-hf6vkwt2x
27 Interview, Andrew Griffith.
28 https://www.spectator.co.uk/article/inside-the-court-of-carrie-symonds-princess-of-whales/
29 https://www.newstatesman.com/politics/media/2022/06/did-no-10-really-think-blocking-the-carrie-johnson-story-would-help
30 Seldon, *Churchill's Indian Summer.*
31 https://www.theguardian.com/politics/2016/jun/30/goves-leadership-bid-statement-in-full
32 Interview, Michael Gove.
33 Sebastian Payne, *The Fall of Boris Johnson: The Inside Story*, London, Macmillan, 2022, p. 217.
34 Interview, Mark Spencer.
35 *The Times*, 6 August 2021.

36 https://committees.parliament.uk/oralevidence/2249/pdf/
37 Interview, Gavin Williamson.
38 Interview, Eddie Lister.
39 Interview, Graham Brady.
40 Interview, Mark Spencer.
41 https://conservativehome.com/2019/12/13/2019-general-election-newly-elected-conservative-mps/
42 Interview, Graham Brady.
43 Email to authors, 31 January 2023.
44 https://www.ft.com/content/2fb6f361-a7bb-4b98-8100-6847b5df79b4
45 Interview, David Canzini.
46 Ibid.
47 Interview, Graham Brady.
48 Payne, *The Fall of Boris Johnson*, pp. 4–20, and Andrew Gimson, *Boris Johnson: The Rise and Fall of a Troublemaker at Number 10*, London, Simon & Schuster, 2022, pp. 377–9.
49 Interview, Mark Spencer.
50 Interview, Gavin Williamson.
51 Interview, Lynton Crosby.
52 Interview, Graham Brady.
53 https://www.thetimes.co.uk/article/half-the-cabinets-seats-now-at-risk-reveals-new-poll-gtktx2r0w
54 https://www.telegraph.co.uk/politics/2022/01/13/brexiteer-becomes-fifth-tory-mp-week-submit-boris-johnson-no/
55 Interview, Graham Brady.
56 https://twitter.com/SirRogerGale/status/1513898118504493060?s=20&t=kKWOGbLW2W9nuO3BRPLhXQ
57 Interview, Graham Brady.
58 *Evening Standard*, 1 April 2022.
59 Interview, Graham Brady.
60 Interview, Simone Finn.
61 Interview, Sajid Javid.
62 https://twitter.com/OliverDowden/status/1540191893258207232
63 Interview, Oliver Dowden.
64 https://www.independent.co.uk/news/uk/politics/chris-pincher-resignation-letter-sleaze-b2113552.html
65 https://twitter.com/SimonMcDonaldUK/status/1544206976820854784
66 Interview, Simon McDonald.
67 Interview, Sajid Javid.
68 Interview, Oliver Dowden.
69 Interview, Lynton Crosby.
70 Interview, Andrew Griffith.
71 Interview, Michael Gove.
72 Interview, David Canzini.
73 Interview, Graham Brady.
74 Interview, Andrew Griffith.
75 Interview, David Canzini.
76 Interview, Brandon Lewis.
77 Interview, Lynton Crosby.
78 Interview, Guto Harri.
79 Interview, Graham Brady.
80 https://www.theguardian.com/politics/2022/jun/25/boris-johnson-not-undergo-psychological-transformation-byelections

CONCLUSION

1 Seldon et al., *The Impossible Office?*, p. 135.
2 https://www.statista.com/statistics/987347/brexitopinionpoll/
3 https://www.ons.gov.uk/businessindustryandtrade/internationaltrade/articles/recenttrendsintheinternationaltradeflowsofg7economies/20221010#:~:text=Trade%20openness%20is%20measured%20as,and%20imports%20for%20these%20countries.
4 https://economy2030.resolutionfoundation.org/reports/thebigbrexit/
5 https://www.bloomberg.com/news/articles/20220713/astrascovidvaccinesavedoversixmillionlivesinfirstyear
6 https://www.ft.com/content/1f52fd2b7daf418ebe8bacc38f819b8d
7 https://www.theguardian.com/business/2022/sep/30/ukisonlyg7countrywithsmallereconomythanbeforecovid19
8 https://www.bloomberg.com/graphics/uklevellingup/borisjohnsonlevelupplanintrouble.html
9 https://yougov.co.uk/topics/politics/articlesreports/2019/06/28/jeremyhuntnowleadsborisjohnsonpublicsprefer
10 https://www.thetimes.co.uk/article/defiantborisjohnsoninsistshedidntbreakcovidrules8k5m6d73r

ILLUSTRATION CREDITS

Dramatis Personae: *Johnson and Liz Truss* (WPA Pool/Pool/Getty)

Introduction: *Johnson leaves No. 10 for the House of Commons* (SOPA Images Limited/Alamy)

1. Rise: *Johnson and Theresa May* (WPA Pool/Pool/Getty)
2. Brexit: *Johnson and David Frost* (Leon Neal/Staff/Getty)
3. Election: *Johnson speaking to supporters* (Leon Neal/Staff/Getty)
4. Dreams: *Johnson in Dorset* (WPA Pool/Pool/Getty)
5. Covid: *Johnson at Covid-19 press conference* (WPA Pool/Pool/Getty)
6. Cummings: *Dominic Cummings departs No. 10* (Bloomberg/Contributor/Getty)
7. Domestic: *Johnson at the 2021 Party Conference* (Ian Forsyth/Stringer/Getty)
8. Global: *Johnson and Volodymir Zelenskyy* (Geopix/Alamy)
9. Grown-ups: *Johnson and Simon Case, Dan Rosenfield and Stuart Glassborow* (Leon Neal/Staff/Getty)
10. Downfall: *Johnson outside No. 10* (Dan Kitwood/Staff/Getty)

Conclusion: *Johnson and Rishi Sunak* (Pool/Getty)

INDEX

ALSO BY ANTHONY SELDON

Churchill's Indian Summer: The Conservative Government 1951–55
By Word of Mouth: Elite Oral History
Ruling Performance: Governments since 1945 (ed. with Peter Hennessy)
Political Parties Since 1945 (ed.)
The Thatcher Effect (ed. with Dennis Kavanagh)
Politics UK (joint author)
Conservative Century (ed. with Stuart Ball)
The Major Effect (ed. with Dennis Kavanagh)
The Heath Government 1970–1974 (ed. with Stuart Ball)
The Contemporary History Handbook (ed. with Brian Brivati et al.)
The Ideas That Shaped PostWar Britain (ed. with David Marquand)
How Tory Governments Fall (ed.)
Major: A Political Life
10 Downing Street: An Illustrated History
The Powers Behind the Prime Minister (with Dennis Kavanagh)
Britain under Thatcher (with Daniel Collings)
The Foreign Office: An Illustrated History
A New Conservative Century (with Peter Snowdon)
The Blair Effect 1997–2001 (ed.)
Public and Private Education: The Divide Must End
Partnership not Paternalism
Brave New City: Brighton & Hove, Past, Present, Future
The Conservative Party: An Illustrated History (with Peter Snowdon)
New Labour, Old Labour: The Wilson and Callaghan Governments, 1974–79
Blair
The Blair Effect 2001–5 (ed. with Dennis Kavanagh)
Recovering Power: The Conservatives in Opposition since 1867 (ed. with Stuart Ball)
Blair Unbound (with Peter Snowdon and Daniel Collings)
Blair's Britain 1997–2007 (ed.)
Trust: How We Lost it and How to Get It Back
An End to Factory Schools
Why Schools, Why Universities?
Brown at 10 (with Guy Lodge)
Public Schools and the Great War (with David Walsh)
Schools United
The Architecture of Diplomacy (with Daniel Collings)
Beyond Happiness: The Trap of Happiness and How to Find Deeper Meaning and Joy
The Coalition Effect, 2010–2015 (ed. with Mike Finn)
Cameron at 10 (with Peter Snowdon)
Teaching and Learning at British Universities
The Cabinet Office 1916–2016 – The Birth of Modern British Government (with Jonathan Meakin)
The Positive and Mindful University (with Alan Martin)
The Fourth Education Revolution (with Oladimeji Abidoye)
May at 10 (with Raymond Newell)
Public Schools and the Second World War (with David Walsh)
Fourth Education Revolution Reconsidered (with Oladimeji Abidoye and Timothy Metcalf)
The Impossible Office?: The History of the British Prime Minister (with Jonathan Meakin and Illias Thoms)
The Path of Peace: Walking the Western Front Way